Envision in Depth

READING, WRITING, AND RESEARCHING ARGUMENTS

FOURTH EDITION

Christine L. Alfano and Alyssa J. O'Brien
Stanford University

PEARSON

Boston Columbus Indianapolis New York City San
Amsterdam Cape Town Dubai London Madrid Milan Munich
Delhi Mexico City São Paulo Sydney Hong Kong Seoul Sing

…or Acquisition Editor: Brad Potthoff
Development Editor: David Kear
Marketing Manager: Allison Arnold
Content Producer: Laura Olson
Media Editor: Kelsey Loveday
Media Producer: Elizabeth Bravo
Team Lead/Program Management: Lauren Finn
Project Manager: Denise Phillip Grant
Project Coordination, Text Design, and Electronic Page Makeup: Lumina Datamatics, Inc.
Program Design Lead/Designer: Barbara Atkinson
Cover Photos: WIN-Initiative/Getty Images.
Top (left to right): Zhang Bo/Getty Images; ChandrashekarReddy/iStock/Getty Images; Abed Omar Qusini AOQ/GOT/Reuters; Anges Costes/AP Images
Senior Manufacturing Buyer: Roy L. Pickering, Jr.
Printer/Binder: R.R. Donnelley/Crawfordsville
Cover Printer: Phoenix Color/Hagerstown

Acknowledgments of third-party content appear on pages 543–547, which constitute an extension of this copyright page.

Library of Congress Cataloging-in-Publication Data

Names: Alfano, Christine L., author. | O'Brien, Alyssa J., author.
Title: Envision in Depth : Reading, Writing, and Researching Arguments/Christine L. Alfano and Alyssa J. O'Brien.
Description: Fourth edition. | Boston : Pearson, 2016.| Includes bibliographical references and index.
Identifiers: LCCN 2015039727 | ISBN 9780134093987
Subjects: LCSH: English language—Rhetoric. | Persuasion (Rhetoric) | College readers. | Report writing. | Visual communication. | Visual perception.
Classification: LCC PE1431 .E56 2016 | DDC 808/.0427--dc23
LC record available at http://lccn.loc.gov/ 2015039727

… 7 6 5 4 3 2 1—DOC—19 18 17 16

www.pearsonhighered.com

Student Edition ISBN 10: 0-13-409398-4
Student Edition ISBN 13: 978-0-13-409398-7
A la Carte ISBN 10: 0-13-406353-8
A la Carte ISBN 13: 978-0-13-406353-9

CONTENTS

PART II: PLANNING AND CONDUCTING RESEARCH 135

Chapter 7 Documenting Sources and Avoiding Plagiarism 265

Chapter 8 Designing Arguments 296

FOOD, INC.

PREFACE

The Story of This Book

Several years ago, we (the authors) met as colleagues in the Program in Writing and Rhetoric at Stanford University. Our shared focus on teaching writing through attention to both written and multimedia texts led us to look for materials we could use in the classroom that would provide both excellence in pedagogical instruction—attending to such essentials as thesis statements, style, integrating sources, and avoiding plagiarism—along with cutting edge and even *fun* examples that offer sound rhetorical models for analysis and research. While we were able to gather materials from a variety of sources, our students wanted more than a collection of handouts: they wanted a textbook that they could use to guide and inspire their development as writers.

The result was *Envision*, an argument and research guide designed from the ground up to serve the needs of real student writers. In fact, throughout the many editions, students remain an indispensable part of the process, reading our drafts in progress, offering suggestions, and submitting their own writing as examples. Now in its fifth edition, *Envision* has expanded and changed over time, but remains true to its original vision: guiding students through the processes of analysis, argument, source evaluation, and research-based essay writing while keeping the examples fresh and relevant to student lives. Students learn to analyze written texts and a range of visual texts, from cartoons and ads to websites and film, while working through the nuts of bolts of writing thesis statements, titles, introductions, conclusions, in-text citations, and MLA-style bibliographies. Additional writing lessons focus on diverse modes of argument, plagiarism, academic document design, and multimodal production.

After the release of *Envision*, we received positive feedback from many instructors but also learned of the additional challenge that many faced: they needed to pair the rhetorical lessons of a textbook like *Envision* with a collection of substantive, timely, and interesting readings on a range of subjects that would interest students. In response, we created *Envision in Depth*, which contains the same material as the original *Envision* but also includes Part IV, a section that offers students the opportunity to build on the lessons from the earlier parts, inviting them to respond in writing to key controversies and develop research projects from source materials.

Each of these later chapters opens with an overview, asking pressing questions and presenting diverse perspectives to consider. We then provide a range of readings, visual texts, interviews, competing articles, and media excerpts on the topic, along with thorough pedagogical guidelines to help students engage critically with the material. Headnotes frame each piece and offer essential context. Reflect & Write questions follow each text to provide opportunities for class discussion, written assignments, and even research projects on related materials. The prompts for collaborative writing enable in-class group work or simply ideas for additional assignments. Finally, each chapter concludes with a robust series of questions: both Analyzing Perspectives on the Issue and From Reading to Research Assignments prompt students to put readings in conversation, consider multiple interpretations at once, or conduct independent research and writing to advance their skills and expertise in meeting key composition outcomes.

As we now finalize the fifth edition of *Envision* and the fourth edition of *Envision in Depth*, our continued hope is that these textbooks might help students develop the skills, confidence, and enthusiasm for writing, researching, and communicating effectively about issues that matter to them.

What's New in This Edition

Feedback from our insightful reviewers as well as suggestions from the many students and instructors who have used *Envision* and *Envision in Depth* in the classroom have been indispensable in guiding our most recent revisions. In this new edition, you'll find the same commitment to supporting our readers in developing critical competencies in analysis, argumentation, and research as in prior editions. However, you'll also find increased attention to helping students accomplish the following learning outcomes:

- **Learn from Model Writing:** New and updated annotated articles and student writing show readers exactly how to move from invention to argument, whether they are analyzing a written text, a visual text, or developing a research-based argument.
- **Experiment with Different Modes of Argumentation**: The refreshed section in Chapter 3 on classical argumentation, Toulmin logic, and Rogerian argument offers students guidance in exploring different strategies of arrangement to construct effective arguments.

- **Explore Contemporary Issues:** New readings and examples have been integrated into the first eight chapters of *Envision in Depth*, focusing on relevant and timely cultural issues: the BlackLivesMatter movement, the Charlie Hebdo shootings, the "cult" of Apple products, fast food marketing, the influence of online social networks, photo manipulation in teen fashion magazines, women in computer science, the addictive properties of sugar, vegetarianism, and texting and driving.
- **Understand Advanced Concepts in Rhetoric:** In addition to the focus on rhetorical appeals and the canons of rhetoric found in prior editions, this new edition features expanded coverage of *ethos* and *logos*, as well as more detailed examination of persona and rhetorical stance.
- **Focus on the Writing Process:** Expanded sections on invention in Chapters 3, 4, and 6—complete with additional student samples—encourage students to find modes of prewriting that best suit their learning style, writing habits, and the parameters of their writing tasks. In addition, a new section on developing a writer's portfolio in Chapter 8 encourages readers to develop reflective practices to help them identify their strengths and growth as writers.
- **Develop Strategies for Analyzing Arguments in Diverse Media:** Student writing in the chapters showcases ways to analyze a variety of types of argument, from written to visual arguments. In addition to guided instruction in the body of each chapter, the Spotlighted Analysis feature offers students the opportunity to apply strategies of rhetorical analysis to a diverse range of texts, from traditional written arguments, to political cartoons, advertisements, photographs, posters, websites, and even film trailers.
- **Engage Deeply with the Research Process:** A refreshed section on search methodologies includes discussion of adapting search methodology to different search engines (i.e., Google vs. academic databases) and how to effectively conduct Boolean searches. In addition, the streamlined discussion of evaluating sources is designed to provide students with a useful process for assessing materials for their own research once they find them. Lastly, a brief introduction to Joseph Bizzup's BEAM approach to research encourages students to move beyond categorizing sources in terms of primary and secondary materials to considering how to use those sources to produce effective research-based arguments.

With regard to the changes in **Part IV**—where students can explore topics in rich complexity through engaging with a range of interrelated texts—we have continued to focus on providing a robust set of readings designed to work in conjunction with the first three parts of *Envision* to help students develop critical literacy skills that they can use in their own writing and research. Supported by careful pedagogical scaffolding, this refreshed set of readings has been updated to speak to students about issues that matter in their lives today.

The Substance at a Glance

From the very beginning, our philosophy in *Envision in Depth* has been to teach students about writing, rhetoric, and research by considering the different modes of argument that operate in our culture every day. Each chapter uses interactive and engaging lessons, and focuses both on analyzing and producing words (print materials, articles, blog posts, and even tweets) as well as on writing *about* images and other contemporary media (cartoons, ads, photographs, films, video games, and websites, to name a few). In this way, the book teaches *critical literacy* about all kinds of texts. Moreover, we provide numerous student writing examples and professional, published readings—both with annotations—in order to reinforce the writing lessons in each chapter and to demonstrate how students might successfully implement such strategies in their own texts. Our aim is to help students accomplish specific writing tasks for your courses as they encounter, analyze, research, and produce a range of compositions.

We have designed *Envision in Depth* to be flexible enough to adjust to different curricula or teaching styles. You can either follow the chronological sequence of chapters—moving from analysis to argument, bringing in research, and then considering design and presentations—or you can consult the chapters and assignments in any order that meets the needs of your course and curriculum. More specifically, we have organized *Envision in Depth* into four parts:

Part I: Analysis and Argument

Chapters 1 through 3 encourage students to become proficient, careful readers of rhetorical texts and to learn practical strategies for crafting thesis statements, rhetorical analysis essays, and position papers incorporating various perspectives. Students learn how to analyze the forms of persuasion in verbal and visual texts—from short articles and essays to political cartoons, ads, and photos—with an emphasis on rhetorical conventions. At the same time, we teach students key rhetorical concepts for effective communication, such as attending to audience, understanding rhetorical appeals and fallacies, and attending to exigency and motive.

Part II: Planning and Conducting Research

Chapters 4 and 5 focus on strategies of research argument for sustained writing projects. The lessons in this section of the book take students through key writing practices: writing a research proposal, keeping a research log, locating sources, and understanding the complexities of evaluating and documenting sources. Students have sample proposals, outlines, and annotations to consult as well as articles, propaganda posters, and Websites to analyze.

Part III: Drafting and Designing Arguments

Chapters 6, 7, and 8 teach students how to write and deliver an effective research-based argument, with a focus on the process of drafting and revising. Students learn how to identify, assess, and incorporate research into their own arguments, while avoiding plagiarism and accomplishing successful documentation of sources. They learn to present their writing effectively through a discussion of document design—both for academic papers and for visual and multimodal arguments. They also gain important skills in practicing the canons of rhetoric and differentiating among levels of decorum.

Part IV: Readings

The last five chapters expand the scope of the book through readings, writing activities, and research prompts on clusters of topics. Our revised selections for the fourth edition focus on today's most engaging topics, which we hope will interest both students and teachers. These topics include debates over the food industry, explorations of new writing and social media technologies, challenges to contemporary sports culture, issues related to representations of crisis and resilience, and current controversies regarding citizenship.

Meeting WPA Outcomes for Writers

Each chapter in Parts I, II, and III offers specific activities and assignments designed to help students meet the WPA Outcomes for First-Year Composition. The following table indicates the chapter's specific learning goals as they are aligned with the WPA outcomes statement, the major assignments offered in each chapter, and the media focus.

MAJOR ASSIGNMENTS AND LEARNING OBJECTIVES

CHAPTER TITLE	WPA OBJECTIVES MET BY THIS CHAPTER	MAJOR ASSIGNMENTS	MEDIA FOCUS
1: Analyzing Texts and Writing Thesis Statements	■ Understanding the rhetorical situation ■ Considering relationships among audience, text, and purpose ■ Textual analysis ■ Developing thesis statements	■ Personal narrative essay ■ Rhetorical analysis essay	■ Cartoons, comic strips, and editorial articles
2: Understanding Strategies of Persuasion	■ Strategies of argumentation ■ Understanding rhetorical appeals: *logos, pathos,* and *ethos* ■ Fallacies or exaggerated uses of rhetorical appeals ■ Importance of *kairos* and *doxa*	■ Contextual analysis essay ■ Analysis of rhetorical appeals and fallacies ■ Comparison/contrast essay	■ Advertisements and written analysis of ads
3: Composing Arguments	■ Introductions and conclusions ■ Arrangement and structure of argument ■ Considering various modes of argument: Toulmin, Rogerian ■ Developing persona and rhetorical stance ■ Addressing opposing opinion in an argument ■ Writing with style	■ Position paper ■ Classical argument assignment ■ Toulmin and Rogerian argument analysis ■ Synthesis essay	■ Photographs, newspaper articles and images, opinion pieces, visual analysis essays
4: Planning and Proposing Research Arguments	■ Generating and narrowing research topics ■ Prewriting strategies ■ Developing a research plan ■ Drafting a formal proposal	■ Visual brainstorm ■ Research log ■ Informal research plan ■ Research proposal	■ Propaganda posters, historical images, rhetorical analysis essay

CHAPTER TITLE	WPA OBJECTIVES MET BY THIS CHAPTER	MAJOR ASSIGNMENTS	MEDIA FOCUS
5: Finding and Evaluating Research Sources	■ Research strategies ■ Evaluating sources ■ Distinguishing between primary and secondary sources ■ Locating sources ■ Conducting field research, interviews, and surveys ■ Best practices for note taking	■ Critical evaluation of sources ■ Annotated bibliography ■ Field research ■ Dialogue of sources	■ Magazine and journal covers, Websites, and annotated bibliographies
6: Organizing and Writing Research Arguments	■ Organizing and outlining arguments ■ Multiple drafts and revision ■ Integrating research sources: summary, paraphrase, and quotations ■ Writing and peer review	■ Formal outline ■ Peer review and response ■ Integrating sources ■ Writing the research argument	■ Film and movie trailers, film review and critique, drafts and revisions
7: Documenting Sources and Avoiding Plagiarism	■ Understanding intellectual property ■ Best practices in documenting sources: in-text citation and notes ■ MLA-style rules and examples	■ Working with multimedia sources ■ Ethical note-taking ■ Citation practice ■ Producing a Works Cited list	■ Documentation examples, MLA-style essay
8: Designing Arguments	■ Understanding the conventions of academic writing ■ Writing an abstract and bio ■ Decorum: appropriate voice and tone ■ Relationship between rhetorical situation and types of argument ■ Formatting and genre considerations ■ Transforming written arguments into visual or spoken texts	■ Writing an abstract ■ Constructing a bio ■ Integrating images in academic writing ■ Creating electronic arguments using multimedia (audio and visual) ■ Considering different delivery techniques	■ Academic design examples, abstracts, bios, op-ads, photo essays, Websites, posters, slidedecks, and multiple media

Online Resources

The Instructor's Manual

The Instructor's Manual for *Envision in Depth* provides teachers with pedagogical advice for each chapter, including conceptual overviews, teaching tips for working with the main concepts and reading selections in the chapter, and suggestions for classroom exercises and writing assignments. The Instructor's Manual also offers ideas for organizing the reading and exercises according to days of the week. For access to the Instructor's Manual, please contact your Pearson representative.

MyWritingLab for Composition

MyWritingLab is an online practice, tutorial, and assessment program that provides engaging experiences for teaching and learning.

MyWritingLab includes most of the writing assignments from your accompanying textbook. Now, students can complete and submit assignments, and teachers can then track and respond to submissions easily-right in MyWritingLab-making the response process easier for the instructor and more engaging for the student.

In the Writing Assignments, students can use instructor-created peer review rubrics to evaluate and comment on other students' writing. When giving feedback on student writing, instructors can add links to activities that address issues and strategies needed for review. Instructors may link to multimedia resources in Pearson Writer, which include curated content from Purdue OWL. Paper review by specialized tutors through Smart-Thinking is available, as is plagiarism detection through TurnItIn.

Respond to Student Writing with Targeted Feedback and Remediation

MyWritingLab unites instructor comments and feedback with targeted remediation via rich multimedia activities, allowing students to learn from and through their own writing.

Writing Help for Varying Skill Levels

For students who enter the course at widely varying skill levels, MyWritingLab provides unique, targeted remediation through personalized and adaptive instruction. Starting with a preassessment known as the Path Builder, MyWritingLab diagnoses students' strengths and weaknesses on prerequisite writing skills. The results of the preassessment inform each student's Learning Path, a personalized pathway for students to work on requisite skills through multimodal activities. In doing so, students feel supported and ready to succeed in class.

Learning Tools for Student Engagement

Learning Catalytics Generate class discussion, guide lectures, and promote peer-to-peer learning with real-time analytics. MyLab and Mastering with eText now provides Learning Catalytics—an interactive student response tool that uses students' smartphones, tablets, or laptops to engage them in more sophisticated tasks and thinking.

MediaShare MediaShare allows students to post multimodal assignments easily—whether they are audio, video, or visual compositions—for peer review and instructor feedback. In both face-to-face and online course settings, MediaShare saves instructors valuable time and enriches the student learning experience by enabling contextual feedback to be provided quickly and easily.

Direct Access to MyLab Users can link from any Learning Management System (LMS) to Pearson's MyWritingLab. Access MyLab assignments, rosters, and resources, and synchronize MyLab grades with the LMS gradebook. New direct, single sign-on provides access to all the personalized learning MyLab resources that make studying more efficient and effective.

Visit www.mywritinglab.com for more information.

Acknowledgments

Our work with *Envision* and *Envision in Depth* has spanned many years, students, writing classes, and colleagues. However, one element remains constant: this project started out inherently collaborative and remains so. The revisions we have made in this edition and our ongoing work in this field could only have been accomplished through the ongoing support and guidance from others. For that reason, we'd like to offer our deepest thanks to all those who helped us with the book over the years, and in the revision of this edition in particular.

We've been fortunate to have a particularly helpful group of reviewers provide us guidance for this revision: John Aramini, Erie Community College; Diana Bell, University of Alabama–Huntsville; Shannon Griffin Blair, Central Piedmont Community College; Ronald Brooks, Oklahoma State University; Linsey Cuti, Kankakee Community College; Trevor Dodge, Clackamas Community College; Susanna Kelly Engbers, Kendall College of Art and Design; Rachel McKenny, Iowa State University; Patrick T. Niner, Florida Gulf Coast University; Jenny Rice, University of Kentucky; Elizabeth Rollins, Pima Community College; Matthew Schmeer, Johnson County Community College; Andrew Scott, Ball State University; and Kay Siebler, Missouri Western State University.

In addition, we are grateful to our other "reviewers"—our students who use our textbook in the classroom and who are always happy to share praise—or suggestions—about *Envision*. In particular, we are grateful for the students who played a concrete role into shaping this new revision by contributing their own writing to serve as models to inspire our readers: Oishi Banerjee, Ali Batouli, Tucker Burnett, Vincent Chen, Clare Conratto, Molly Fehr, Will Hang, Savi Hawkins, Samantha Kargilis, Lucas Lin, Catherine Mullings, Emmanuel Omvenga, Ryan O'Rourke, Wanjin Park, Stephanie Parker, Trevor Rex, Claire Shu, Miranda Alfano-Smith, Jared Sun, Ada Throckmorton, Michael Vela, and Thomas Zhao.

We'd also like to express our gratitude to our colleagues at Stanford who have supported our revisions to *Envision* and *Envision in Depth* and whose commitment to pedagogy and to their students inspires our own. In particular, we'd like to thank Julia Bleakney, Karli Cerankowski, Erica Cirillo-McCarthy, Annelise Heinz, Donna Hunter, Kiersten Jakobsen, Raechel Lee, Kimberly Moekle, John Peterson, Emily Polk, Carolyn Ross, Felicia Smith, and Trisha Stan, whose advice, scholarship, and inspiring pedagogy helped enrich our work in this text. In addition, we'd especially like to recognize those colleagues who graciously allowed us to include versions of their exemplary class-tested activities in this new edition: Mary Stroud, who contributed the Twitter dialogue of sources activity in Chapter 5; Marvin Diogenes and Ethan Plaut, who permitted us to use a version of their Accordion prewrite activity in Chapter 4; Russ Carpenter and Sohui Lee, whose scholarship on poster design informed our section on that topic in Chapter 8; Sarah Pittock, whose activity on titles inspired our own expanded section; and Jennifer Stonaker, who provided insight and guidance on the rhetoric of podcasting. So much of what we've accomplished over our years of work on the *Envision* series has been possible by the supportive atmosphere found in our academic home in Stanford's Program in Writing and Rhetoric; the people and the program continually remind us of the importance of providing the best resources and instruction to students and of fostering a culture of intellectual curiosity, sharing, and collegiality among our teaching faculty.

We'd also like to extend out thanks to our expert team at Pearson, the dedicated drivers of the *Envision* series: Joe Opiela, and Brad Potthoff; our development editor David Kear; Katy Gabel and her staff at Lumina Datamatics; our contract support Jim Miller; and Michael Greer, who went from guiding the drafting of the first edition of Envision to now helping us refresh and reinvigorate the reader section of the most recent edition of *Envision in Depth*.

Of course, there's another expert team to thank as well: our friends and family who keep life running smoothly even amid the creative chaos of writing and revision. Without their love, support, and expansive understanding, this revision would never have been transformed from a marked-up manuscript to the bound copy that now sits before you.

Lastly, thank you, our readers, for your interest in *Envision*; we hope you find the book as useful to your teaching as it has been rewarding for us to work on and use with our own students over the years.

Christine L. Alfano and Alyssa J. O'Brien

Part I

ANALYSIS AND ARGUMENT

CHAPTER 1

Analyzing Texts and Writing Thesis Statements

Chapter Preview Questions

1.1 How do we read and analyze texts rhetorically?
1.2 How do we define the rhetorical situation?
1.3 How do exigence and purpose affect persuasion?
1.4 What are effective strategies for analyzing rhetorical texts?
1.5 How should I brainstorm parts of an essay, including the thesis statement?

Everywhere around us, words and images try to persuade us to think about the world in certain ways. We can see this persuasive power at every turn: from newspaper articles to television broadcasts, blog posts, advertisements, political campaign posters, Facebook status posts, tweets, and even video footage circulated online. In each case, such texts—whether verbal, visual, or a combination of the two—try to move us, convince us to buy something, shape our opinions, or make us laugh.

Consider the text in Figure 1.1 by Mike Luckovich, a Pulitzer Prize–winning cartoonist who publishes in the *Atlanta Journal Constitution*. Luckovich created this cartoon after the 2011 assassination attempt on Gabrielle Giffords, a member of the U.S. House of Representatives, outside a Safeway store in Tucson, Arizona. Six people were killed, including a 9-year-old girl. Giffords herself was critically injured, along with 12 other people. The incident raised concerns over political speeches and Website images that had used gun metaphors to target Democrats such as Giffords in upcoming elections. Some feared that such language and imagery might have contributed to the attack. In response to the controversy, Luckovich composed a cartoon as a persuasive text indicating his view. How does his text use both words and images to persuade audiences to think a certain way about the top term: "Violent Rhetoric"? Look at the hierarchy of values, beginning with "happy talk" at the bottom, moving through "warm conversation" and "friendly debate" to a more vigorous "spirited discussion." Notice how the words then become more negative, including "angry discourse" and "hateful speech." While we usually consider "hateful speech" to be the worst form of communication, Luckovich places "violent rhetoric" above it, as the very apex of dangerous discourse. The cartoon is ironic since when most people think of *rhetoric*, they often think of political rhetoric, which they perceive as either empty and meaningless (all talk, no action) or worse, as negative: harmful to the reputation of others, fear-mongering, and even hateful. The cartoon emphasizes this common view placing the words "violent rhetoric" at the top.

FIGURE 1.1 Mike Luckovich's political cartoon demonstrates through words and images how people commonly view "rhetoric" as a negative and dangerous form of communication.

But understanding this cartoon depends not just on analyzing the words. The location of words in particular places within the visual—and the visual elements themselves—also contribute in crucial ways to the meaning of the text. The lowered flag, for instance, might indicate that Giffords nearly died from her critical injuries, and indeed six people did die. The purposeful lowering of the flag to half-mast is itself a form of visual communication, well understood across America; it represents the nation's act of honoring a deceased person. The dome of the Capitol Building in the background suggests that the government has lowered the flag and wants people to move from "violent rhetoric" to "spirited discussion." In this way, the cartoon combines words and visual details to suggest both a tribute to Giffords and the need for calmer, gentler political communication. That is our understanding of the cartoon's argument when we **analyze the text rhetorically**. As you develop your skills of critical thinking and rhetorical analysis, you will also learn how to interpret and write your own arguments about such texts.

At the same time, you will learn how to apply your skills of analysis across a range of media, including printed or spoken words. With regard to the assassination attempt, many writers commented on the event through newspaper articles, on blogs, via email, and on social media. In a post on the political blog *Daily Kos*, for example, Barbara Morrill used the term *rhetoric* right in her title: "Violent Rhetoric and the Attempted Assassination of Gabrielle Giffords." While the title seems objective in tone, the writer draws on very strong language in the opening paragraph in order to connect the two parts of the title:

> In the two days since the attempted assassination of Rep. Gabrielle Giffords, the debate has been raging over the culpability of the violent rhetoric that is so commonplace in today's political climate. Which of course has led to the rapid-fire peddling of false equivalencies by the right, where now, saying a congressional district is being targeted is the same as actually putting cross-hairs on a district and saying it's time to "RELOAD."

By accusing the right of "rapid-fire peddling," the author frames words through a gun metaphor in a way that creates a vivid image in the reader's mind. She also refers to the metaphoric language that politicians had used—targeting a district, crosshairs, and "reload"—as evidence for her claim. The details of her written text parallel the elements of the cartoon (Figure 1.1). As you develop your skills of analysis about texts, keep in mind that you can understand them better if you look closely at all the specific elements, whether verbal or visual. Once you recognize how texts function *rhetorically*—that is, how texts try to persuade you and shape your opinion about the world around you—then you can decide whether or not to agree with the many messages you encounter every day. To grasp this concept, let's follow one hypothetical student—we'll call her Alex—as she walks across campus and note the rhetorical texts she sees along the way.

1.1 How do we read and analyze texts rhetorically?

UNDERSTANDING TEXTS RHETORICALLY

By shadowing Alex and noticing what she notices, you can construct her **personal narrative**, or written account of her journey, about the rhetorical texts she sees along the way.

Let's begin in her dorm room, which Alex and her roommate have decorated with a concert tour poster, an artsy map of New York City, a poster for the women's basketball team, and a photo collage of pictures from their spring break cross-country trip. As she prepares to leave, she smiles as she glances at a meme she's printed and taped over her desk: the black-turtleneck-wearing Hipster Barista, with the caption, "$120,000 Art Degree ... Draws faces in latte foam."

As Alex walks down the hall, she pauses when a friend calls her into the lounge to watch a brief clip from a rerun of *Last Week Tonight with John Oliver* on his laptop. Oliver is in top form, providing a satirical critique of the militarization of American police forces, and Alex and her friend laugh for a few minutes about the sketch before she heads out. Walking down the stairwell, she glances briefly at the flyers that decorate the walls—for a charity dance for the victims of a recent earthquake, a dorm meeting about a ski trip, and a rally against immigration laws. She does a double-take to look at the clever design of a flyer for the Zen club (see Figure 1.2), making a mental note about the meeting time, and then walks into the cool autumn air.

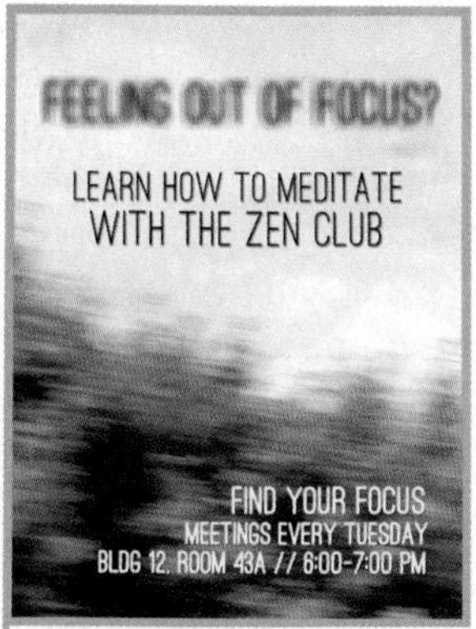

FIGURE 1.2 A flyer that Alex notices on her way to class.

Outside, Alex looks down at her smartphone, scrolling through recent Instagram posts as she walks along. She sees one friend's updated profile photo, another's pictures from a recent trip to New Orleans, and a third's reposting of a link to a parody video of a Taylor Swift song. She stops at the outdoor café and checks her Twitter feed while waiting for her coffee, amused by her favorite celebrity's posting about the Academy Awards. As her coffee arrives, her phone buzzes, and she opens a funny Snapchat photo from her younger sister, pausing for a moment to send a selfie of her own, which she captions with the phrase, "Must have coffee." Looking at the time, she realizes she's running late and hurries off to class.

FIGURE 1.3 A snapchat from Alex's younger sister.

Now Alex has only 2 minutes before class starts, so she takes the shortcut through the student union, past a sign advertising the latest Apple laptop, and then heads outside and crosses in front of an administration building where a group of student protestors are chanting and waving signs demanding that the university divest from fossil fuels. She weaves alongside a cluster of gleaming steel buildings that constitute the engineering quad and passes the thin metal sculpture called *Knowledge* that guards the entrance to the library.

Finally she reaches her destination: the Communications department. Walking into the building, she stops to glance at the front page of the school newspaper, stacked by the door; intrigued by the headline, "Greek Life Claims University Targets Them," she grabs a copy to read later. She slips into the classroom for her Com 101 class on Media and Society and realizes that the class has already started. Ducking into the back row, Alex watches the professor advance his PowerPoint slides to one containing key questions for that day's class (see Figure 1.4). As she sits down, the TA passes her a handout, and she opens her laptop to take notes. She's immediately distracted by posts on the social media sites that pop up, calling for her attention: targeted advertisements, viral videos, even Buzzfeed quizzes. Ignoring them, she opens a blank document instead and then turns to examine the handout, which includes an editorial about a tragic shooting at the offices of a French satirical magazine.

With Alex safely at her seat, think about how many texts you noticed along her journey. Flyers, ads, posters, videos, Websites, newspapers, television shows, photographs, memes, sculpture, signs, PowerPoint slides, even architectural design: each is an example of rhetoric. Why? Because each text offers a specific message to a particular audience. Each one is a persuasive act. Once you begin to look at the world rhetorically, you'll see that just about everywhere you are being persuaded to agree, act, buy, attend, or accept an argument: rhetoric permeates our cultural landscape. Just as we did above, you might pay attention to the rhetorical texts that you find on your way to class and then construct your own personal narrative consisting of words and images. Learning to recognize the persuasive power of texts and read them rhetorically is the first step in thinking critically about the world.

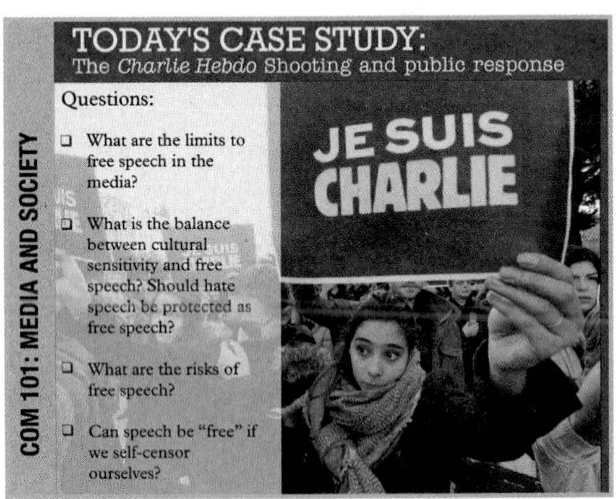

FIGURE 1.4 PowerPoint slide from Alex's class.

WRITER'S PRACTICE

MyWritingLab

Look back at the texts that Alex encountered in Figures 1.2, 1.3, and 1.4. How do they attempt to persuade their audience? For each one, jot down some notes about each text's message and the different ways the texts try to make their arguments. Consider how they use words and images, alone and in combination, to convey their message.

UNDERSTANDING THE RHETORICAL SITUATION

1.2 How do we define the rhetorical situation?

In one of the earliest definitions, the ancient Greek philosopher Aristotle characterized **rhetoric** as *the ability to see the available means of persuasion in any given situation*. While Aristotle's lessons in rhetoric emerged in the fourth century BCE as a form of instruction for oral communication—specifically, to help free men represent themselves in court—today, the term *rhetoric* has expanded to include any verbal, visual, or multimedia text that aims to persuade a specific audience in a certain place and time. More generally, you can understand rhetoric as the strategies people use to convey ideas; in the words of scholar and rhetorician Andrea Lunsford, "Rhetoric is the art, practice, and study of human communication."

To understand how a rhetorical text works, you need to analyze how it targets a specific **audience**, how it has been composed by a specific **author**, and how it conveys a particular **argument**. This dynamic relationship is called the **rhetorical situation**, and we have represented it with a triangle in Figure 1.5.

As a writer, when you compose persuasive texts, you need to determine which strategies will work to convince your audience in a particular situation. There are many different choices to consider, and that is why rhetoric is both a dynamic and a practical art. Imagine, for instance, that you are involved in the following rhetorical situations and have to decide which strategies would be most persuasive for each case.

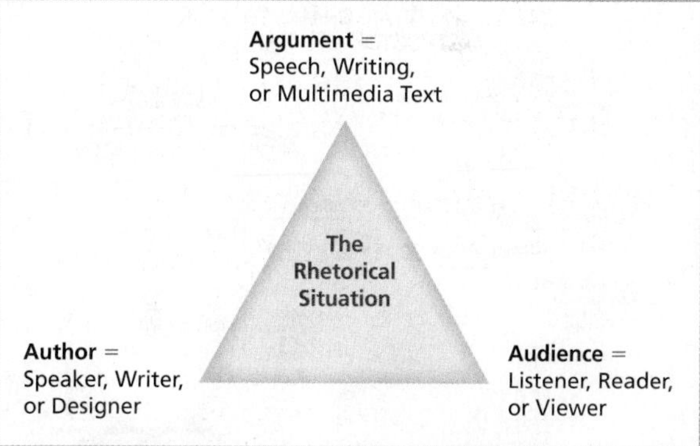

FIGURE 1.5 The rhetorical situation is dynamic and governs all communication, whether oral, written, or multimedia.

- **Attend to *audience*.** If you were a politician writing an editorial for a newspaper or speaking at an interview on CNN about your definition of marriage, you would use strikingly different metaphors and statistics depending on which constituency (or *audience*) you are addressing.
- **Attend to *author*.** If you wanted to publicize a

message against drug use to local middle school students, you might compose pamphlets, emails, presentations, or posters with information graphics, and each one would be designed based on your position as *author*—teacher or police officer? student or parent?—while trying to reach that teenage audience.

- **Attend to *argument*.** If you were fashion industry intern updating the company's social media marketing campaign, you would revise the message (or *argument*) of the advertisements to fit the media, whether Facebook posts, tweets, or even Internet videos.

Cartoonist Jorge Cham offers us an example in Figure 1.6 of how the rhetorical situation affects persuasion in relation to a communicative act that might be even more familiar to you: a students' email to the instructor. In a panel for his series *PhD comics*, he shows how a misunderstanding of the rhetorical situation can sabotage successful communication.

What the comic illustrates is the instructor's analysis of the student's communication and his implicit criticism that the student misreads his *audience* and therefore composes an ineffective *argument.* The agitated arrows point us to evidence for this interpretation: misspellings, punctuation mistakes, jargon, and an uninformed message (the answers to the email apparently are all in the syllabus). However, the comic also invites us to critique the instructor's assessment of the rhetorical situation. On the one hand, the fictional instructor has treated the email communication like an essay, scoring it with red-inked annotations; on the other, he uses an angry voice that seems inappropriate to the instructor–student relationship ("OMG, what are you, 14?"; "we are not friends"). In both cases, he fails in the same way as his student to create a moment of effective communication.

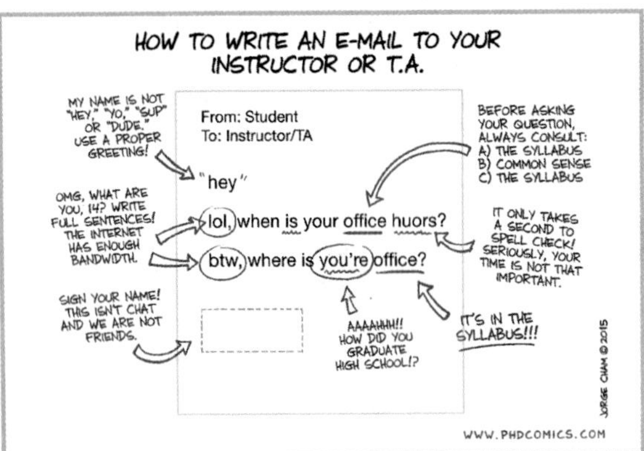

FIGURE 1.6 This comic from *PhD comics* offers a pointed analysis of a hypothetical student's misjudging of the rhetorical situation in emailing his instructor.

In fact, there are two layers to this cartoon, two rhetorical situations that we can explore (see Figure 1.7): the fictional situation of the email, where the relationship is between student (writer), instructor (audience), and

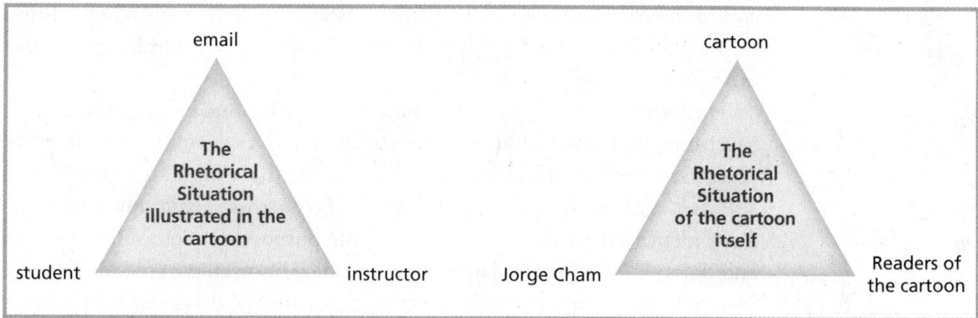

FIGURE 1.7 The cartoon's two rhetorical situations.

email (argument), and then the rhetorical situation of the editorial cartoon itself, which triangulates the relationship between Jorge Cham (writer), the cartoon's readers (audience), and cartoon (argument). Cham encourages us to engage with both levels explicitly by including the asterisk and footnote. In his qualifier, "No offense to those actually called 'Hey,' 'Yo,' 'Sup,' or 'Dude,'" he differentiates his own voice from that of the fictional instructor, helping us remember there are dual levels at work in the cartoon.

UNDERSTANDING EXIGENCE AND PURPOSE

1.3 How do exigence and purpose affect persuasion?

As you move toward better understanding rhetoric, another important concept to consider is **exigence**—the *urgent demand* that writers feel to respond to a situation, his or her motive for writing. Have you ever seen a news article or heard about an event on campus that prompted you to respond strongly? When this happens, in rhetoric, we call this the **exigencies of a situation**, or the demands put on a writer to respond immediately and urgently in the attempt to take action or raise a concern about a specific problem or issue.

Think about tweets sent out in response to a sports team winning a championship, a flash of celebrity gossip, a political debate, or a crisis on campus. These are all contemporary instances of exigency. The scholar who gave us the rhetorical situation shown in Figure 1.5, Lloyd Bitzer, emphasized that *rhetorical exigency* happens when change is possible: "An exigence is rhetorical when it is capable of positive modification and when positive modification *requires* discourse or can be *assisted* by discourse." That is, rhetorical exigency exists when there is the possibility that **discourse** (i.e., forms of communication) can effect change. For instance, policies regulating parking on campus can potentially be modified through discourse or language, but drought and death cannot.

Understanding exigence can help us likewise understand an author's **purpose**. Whether that purpose be internal and emotional or more objective—for instance, seeking to affirm or reaffirm the status quo—*motive* and *purpose* shape the way authors write texts across media. Many rhetoricians identify three broad types of possible purposes for communication: to entertain, to inform or explain, or to persuade. However, purpose can be more nuanced. An author's purpose might be to describe, to define, to influence, or to call to action, for instance; in fact, an author might have complementary purposes in crafting a text. By examining an author's *motive* or *purpose*—what he wanted to accomplish with the text—we can get a better understanding of the rhetorical choices he made in communicating with his audience.

Let's look at a contemporary example to see how rhetorical exigency combines with purpose to create persuasive texts. When Disney announced its acquisition of the Star Wars enterprise from George Lucas in 2012, people were shocked and even outraged. Many felt the need to respond through discourse—by tweeting, writing blog posts, composing articles in popular online magazines, and even drawing cartoons. In each case, the author felt prompted to respond urgently and immediately to what was widely viewed as a problem situation.

FIGURE 1.8 Nate Beeler's cartoon uses humor in response to Disney's purchase of Star Wars.

Consider, for instance, the cartoon in Figure 1.8 by Nate Beeler, an award-winning editorial cartoonist for the *Columbus Dispatch*, which he created in response to the merger. Entitled, "Disney Acquires 'Star Wars,'" the cartoon demonstrates the exigency that caused so many Americans to speak out or write about this surprising amalgamation between two enormous entertainment companies.

The giant head of Mickey Mouse, floating in space toward the galactic fleet, has an ominous look to it, creating a sense of foreboding. It suggests the *motive* of the cartoonist might have been to criticize this acquisition. In fact, this critique is further amplified by the way Mickey's head has been transformed into a version of the iconic Death Star, threatening to supplant the original space station/super weapon, which seems small and less imposing by comparison. Beeler is clearly presenting Mickey (and, by association, Disney) as the new "bad guy" of the Star Wars universe.

Moreover, the words emerging from the space station, "I sense a great disturbance in the force," echo Obi-Wan Kenobi's classic line from *Star Wars Episode IV*, "I felt a great disturbance in the force, as if millions of voices suddenly cried out in terror and were suddenly silenced." In the original context, Obi-Wan refers to the destruction of an entire planet and the death of its inhabitants; here the fleet makes a similarly ominous pronouncement about the impact of the Disney acquisition on the Star Wars franchise. Putting the visual and the verbal together, we perceive that Beeler exploits the imagery and lexicon of Star Wars fans themselves for a specific *purpose*: to persuade his audience of the negative implications of Disney's acquisition of Star Wars. It is a comic argument, to be sure, but it is an important position that arises from the exigencies of the situation.

Some writers opted for a different mode of editorial commentary, turning to Twitter to offer their perspective on the acquisition. As urgent responses to the deal, the tweets demonstrate how authors react in an attempt to use discourse to voice a personal position or in the hopes of modifying the situation. For instance, writer Andrés de Rojas, who goes by the Twitter handle @aderojas, tweeted the following:

> May the Force be with … Mickey Mouse?

He plays on the iconic phrase, "May the Force be with you," using ellipses and substituting Mickey Mouse for "you" to create a humorous tone. The final question mark, too, functions rhetorically, to convey his uncertainty over the implications of the acquisition. Raymond Kemp (@RaymondKemp) similarly responded to the exigence of the situation, composing a tweet that, like Nate Beeler's cartoon, adapts Obi-Wan's famous line:

> There was a disturbance in the force like the voices of a million nerds were silenced.

His tweet would have greatest resonance with readers familiar with the Star Wars series, but his critique would be evident even to a broader audience. By stating that "the voices of a million nerds were silenced," he demonstrates his motive or purpose: joining the outcry against the way in which the "nerdy" series of Star Wars might change under the ownership of the more pop culture-oriented vision of Disney.

Clearly, although tweets are brief, they still function as rhetorical acts. Authors who recognize the unique rhetorical situation of the tweet can turn these concise epithets into powerful editorial commentaries. Even the hashtags that writers append to their tweets add a layer of argument. Consider how a tweet about the Disney-Star Wars acquisition becomes more powerful when tagged with a hashtag such as #Depresseddarth, #Darthgoofy, #Don'tpanic, or #awholenewworld. In addition, some authors take advantage of the viral nature of Twitter to punctuate their tweets by attaching pictures, often mash-ups of popular images. For instance, over the first week after the acquisition announcement, scores of images spread through Twitter: photoshopped pictures of Mickey Mouse in Darth Vader's robes, saying, "Luke, I am now your father"; visual remixes of a Disney poster with the caption, "When you wish upon a Deathstar"; a photo of R2D2 wearing mouse ears; a still from *A New Hope* showing the three suns of Luke Skywalker's planet aligned to resemble Mickey Mouse's head. One of the most widely re-tweeted images was originally posted by Eric Alper (@ThatEricAlper): a photoshopped version of a popular image of the Disney princesses with a cartoon version of Princess Leia from Star Wars, wielding her blaster rifle, inserted in the middle. Re-tweeted over 200 times to an ever-broader circle of audiences, the image makes a pointed argument about how it might be the Disney world—not the Star Wars universe—that would change most because of the merger. In each of these examples, the author was responding to the exigence of the situation, using the best available means of persuasion to make his argument to a broad audience.

Considering the concepts of rhetorical exigence and purpose reinforces the fact that rhetoric, since Aristotle, has been linked to *action*. It is far from "empty" but rather can motivate audiences to produce particular outcomes. As Bitzer has argued: "Rhetoric is a mode of altering reality [. . .] by the creation of discourse which *changes reality* through the mediation of thought and action."

STRATEGIES FOR ANALYZING RHETORICAL TEXTS

1.4 What are effective strategies for analyzing rhetorical texts?

As we turn to discussing practical strategies for analyzing texts, it's important to understand how these can contribute to helping you develop **critical literacy**—a life skill that entails knowing how to read, analyze, understand, and even create texts that function as powerful arguments about culture and the world around us. In fact, some have argued that writing itself no longer refers just to words on a page, but that writing, redefined for the twenty-first century, invites us to express ourselves and make arguments across media and genres—whether in a book chapter, a podcast, a blog post, a video, or comic. In fact, in many cases, the most powerful arguments are those that combine word and image, the verbal and the visual; such multimedia texts often have greater persuasiveness and reach a broader audience than words alone.

This is the argument made by Scott McCloud in his groundbreaking book, *Understanding Comics*, one of the first texts to use graphic novel form to help readers understand visual rhetoric:

> When pictures are more abstracted from "reality," they require greater levels of perception, more like words. When words are bolder, more direct, they require lower levels of perception and are received faster, more like pictures.

McCloud tells us we need to develop "greater levels of perception," or *critical literacy*, in order to read with greater levels of perception. In fact, we can look to the brief passage quoted here as an example of persuasive written rhetoric, in which McCloud makes very deliberate choices to strengthen his point. Notice how his words use comparison–contrast (pictures versus words), qualified language ("reality"), and parallel structure (both sentences move from "When" to a final phrase beginning with "more like") in order to convince his audience that images and words operate in similar ways. Such attention to detail is the first step in *rhetorical analysis*—looking at the way the writer chooses the most effective means of persuasion to make a point.

What is interesting about McCloud's piece is the way in which he uses both words and images to make his point. To fully appreciate McCloud's rhetorical decisions, we need to consider the passage in its original context. As you can see in Figure 1.9, McCloud amplifies his argument about comics by using the form of the graphic novel itself.

FIGURE 1.9 Scott McCloud writes in the medium of cartoons to explain comics.

Source: Courtesy of Scott McCloud

This complex diagram relies on the visual–verbal relationship to map out the complicated nature of how we understand both written text and images. The repetition and echoes that we found in the quoted passage are graphically represented in Figure 1.9; in fact, translated into comic book form, the division between word and image becomes a visual continuum that strongly suggests McCloud's vision of the interrelationship between these rhetorical elements. The power of this argument comes from McCloud's strategic assessment of the rhetorical situation: he, the *author*, recognizes that his *audience* (people interested in visual media) would find an *argument* that relies on both visual and verbal elements to be highly persuasive.

McCloud's example is also instructive for demonstrating the way in which authors can strategically adapt their argument to different media. More than ever, rhetoric operates not just through word choice but also through choice of multimedia elements—images in a commercial, the audio of a viral ad on the Internet, the design choices of a website or flyer, even the layout strategies of your textbook. Therefore, we need to develop skills of analysis for all rhetorical texts. We need to understand argument *as writing across diverse media* and we need, therefore, to develop *critical literacy*, or a careful way of reading, analyzing, and understanding media (visual, verbal, and other rhetorical texts).

Understanding how rhetoric works across different media will give you the ability and confidence to analyze and produce texts of your own. That is, these skills of analysis will help you approach other kinds of texts rhetorically: scholarly articles, books, editorials, letters to the editor, political speeches, and—as writing continues to evolve into new forms—blog posts, memes, mash-ups, and more.

Analyzing Visual Rhetoric

When persuasion—discourse or communication intended to change—happens through visual means, we often look to investigate its *visual rhetoric*. As we saw earlier in the chapter, such visual arguments surround us constantly in our everyday lives. We can use them as a starting point for developing strategies for analysis that we can then transfer to how we approach analysis of written rhetoric.

Editorial cartoons offer a rich resource for this sort of work since, as cultural critic Matthew Diamond asserts, they "provide alternative perspectives at a glance because they are visual and vivid and often seem to communicate a clear or obvious message." Those messages might be powerful, but they sometimes might offend, as Pulitzer Prize–winning cartoonists Doug Marlette has suggested: "[T]he objective of political cartooning 'is not to soothe and tend sensitive psyches, but to jab and poke in an attempt to get at deeper truths, popular or otherwise.'" Marlette's words confirm what you probably already know—that cartoons are not just humorous texts but rather, as we have seen, they are rhetorical—they intend to persuade, and sometimes even to provoke.

Let's begin with the editorial cartoon in Figure 1.10 by Bill Bramhall. Originally published in the *Daily News* on December 4, 2014, the cartoon represents a pointed response to the news that a grand jury declined to bring charges against a New York police officer for the death of Eric Garner, a 43-year-old black man, who died after being put in a chokehold during his arrest. In Bramhall's cartoon, "I can't breathe"—Garner's last words—take on greater resonance when uttered by Lady Justice, shown sprawled on the sidewalk.

FIGURE 1.10 Bill Bramhall composed this powerful cartoon to comment on the 2014 death of Eric Garner.

By replacing Garner with the symbol of Justice, Bramhall is making a much stronger argument than just that Garner's death was tragic: his cartoon suggests that justice itself has been laid low by the grand jury decision and that the American people can no longer look to the justice system to defend their rights (with its sword and balancing scales).

Keeping this analysis in mind, consider the different rhetorical effect the cartoon would have had if it had been drawn differently. What if the central figure speaking the words "I can't breathe" were the Statue of Liberty? What if she were represented as African American? What if instead of being laid out on the sidewalk, she was shown crushed to her pedestal under three police officers, actively trying to restrain her? How would these changes alter the way you understood the cartoon's argument? This is, in fact, the composition of a different cartoon created by editorial cartoonist Steve Benson. In both Bramhall's and Benson's cases, the text was generated out of the same exigence—the grand jury decision—but made different claims about the implications of the event.

Let's look at another example of how a cartoonist uses visual rhetoric to make a powerful cultural critique on a similar theme.

Appearing days after the Bramhall cartoon we examined above, this cartoon by Adam Zyglis (Figure 1.11) moves beyond the specifics of the Garner case to address the tense U.S. conversations over race prompted by the deaths of Michael Brown (which catalyzed riots in Ferguson, Missouri,

FIGURE 1.11 Adam Zyglis's 2014 cartoon addresses larger issues of race relations in America.

in late summer 2014) and Eric Garner. Notice the ways in which Zyglis uses seemingly simple rhetorical elements to convey a multilayered message:

- He heads the cartoon with a powerful title that plays on the word "color" both to refer to how we "fill in" or "shade" our conversations on race (the way a child would color in a picture in a coloring book) and also to allude to the issue of "color" that in itself underlies many discussions of race relations.
- He features an iconic image of a crayon box, replacing the trademark Crayola symbol with an American flag to make the symbolic force of his argument clearer to the audience.
- Instead of filling the box with a multitude of crayon colors, he simply draws one black and one white crayon, underscoring how all other variations, shades, and hues (i.e., racial and cultural identities) are absent from the "conversation."

Looking at these elements, we can see his message: that conversations about race in America seem limited to a Caucasian-versus-African-American perspective. However, we can push this analysis even further. In choosing a crayon box, Zyglis seems to be indicating that we take a somewhat childish approach to these conversations. Additionally, if we consider the crayon colors to represent argumentative stances rather than symbols of racial identity, he also seems to be arguing against a "black versus white" approach to the issue, that is, an approach to an argument that relies on extreme oppositional stances rather than looking at the complexities or nuances of the issue.

As a final example, let's turn to a visual argument that responds directly to an event very appropriate to the focus of this chapter: the *Charlie Hebdo* shootings. On January 7, 2015, two Al-Qaeda gunmen entered the offices of the French weekly newspaper, Charlie Hebdo, known around the world for its provocative and satirical articles, jokes, and political cartoons. By the time the shooting spree was over, 12 people were dead and 11 injured. Charlie Hebdo had long been a target of criticism from many groups, offended by their risqué portrayal of different cultural icons and customs; Muslim readers in particular often expressed displeasure at its irreverent caricatures of the Prophet Mohammed. However, despite the newspaper's notoriety, the actions of the terrorist extremists were completely unanticipated and sent shock waves across the world.

As might be expected, the editorial cartoonist community in particular responded immediately to this assault on their French colleagues, and

FIGURE 1.12 Clay Bennet's cartoon response to the Charlie Hebdo shootings centers on the pen as a symbol for Free Expression.

newspaper columns and Internet websites were flooded with editorials—in words and images— reacting to this tragedy. Many of them relied on a central symbol to catalyze their argument: the pen or pencil as a symbol for free speech. One example can be found in Figure 1.12. This image by cartoonist Clay Bennett makes a powerful argument of resilience echoed by many of the other editorial cartoonists who responded to the incident. Notice the way that even with an extremely simplistic design, it articulates a powerful position: the pen, labeled "free expression," takes center stage on the white background; broken in half and yet mended hastily with string, it suggests that free speech might have been damaged by tragic events, but it has not been destroyed and is ready to be wielded again by the next author who picks up the pen.

Bennett's cartoon was one of many such visual responses to the tragedy. Graphic designer Lucille Cleric circulated a similar image on social media. Her cartoon featured three pencils stacked on top one another: on top, a sharpened pencil (labeled "yesterday), in the middle, a broken pencil (labeled "today"), and, on the bottom, the broken pencil, resharpened to form two smaller pencils (labeled "tomorrow"). In its original version, Cleric reinforced her visual message with the caption, "Break one, thousand will rise." She further punctuated her point by circulating it with the hashtag #raiseyourpencilforfreedom.

Her graphic accumulated over 100,000 "likes" almost immediately after its release, demonstrating its resonance with the "Je Suis Charlie" (I am Charlie) movement that swept the world within hours after the attack, as cartoonists, journalists, and citizens offered a hydra-headed expression of solidarity with those who had died in the service of free expression of ideas. In an interview with the website Mashable, Cleric made her motive for creating the cartoon clear, saying, "I can only hope [the cartoon] will inspire people to use their pencils too and that there will be thousands of drawings like this very soon." This purpose—to inspire, to move others to action— speaks once again to the power of rhetoric, visual and verbal, not only influence people's ideas but, in some cases, to call them to action.

WRITER'S PRACTICE MyWritingLab

Look at this editorial cartoon created by Adam Zyglis (Figure 1.13). Practice your own skills of rhetorical and critical analysis by analyzing the editorial cartoon, taking into account color, composition, characters, and action. Then, try to answer the following questions:

- Who is the audience for the cartoon? How can you tell?
- What is the argument? What elements of cartoon contribute to this message?
- What is the exigency of the cartoon?
- What was the author's motive or purpose for creating the cartoon?

Consider carefully how the artist uses words, images, and elements of composition to convey his message.

FIGURE 1.13 by Adam Zyglis

Analyzing Written Rhetoric

As we turn to developing your own analytical skills with regard to written rhetoric, you might find encouragement in Scott McCloud's point from *Understanding Comics* that "Writing is perceived information. It takes time and specialized knowledge to decode the abstract symbols of language." The purpose of this book is to help you develop the tools and acquire the knowledge to understand—or decode—the symbols we use to communicate with each other, including visual images but also written rhetoric in all its complexity. The strategies of rhetorical analysis that we discussed above—considering the rhetorical situation, exigence, and the motive and purpose behind a text—will serve you well as you examine communication in its many different forms. However, while with visual rhetoric we layered in more detailed examination of image, layout, color, and composition, as we move to more conventional written forms, you'll correspondingly need to take into account additional rhetorical elements: word choice, word usage, structure, rhetorical devices (such as symbolism, metaphor, and allusion), and tone, to name just a few.

Let's look at an article that derives from the same exigency as the cartoon in Figure 1.1: the assassination of Gabrielle Gifford. If we return to the blog post by Barbara Morrill that we looked at earlier in the chapter, we can see how the genre of the blog affords her different rhetorical opportunities than those presented to editorial cartoonists. In her piece, Morrill writes:

> And while there are many examples of the violent language employed by the right: "Second Amendment remedies," "resorting to the bullet box," calls to be "armed and dangerous," to name just a few, it's more than that. [...]
>
> Because since the election of Barack Obama, the right, both elected Republicans and their minions in the media, have pounded the non-stop drumbeat that Obama/Democrats/liberals want to destroy the country, they want to kill your grandmother, they're shredding the Constitution, they're terrorist sympathizers, they're going to take away your guns, that they're enemies of humanity, that the government is the enemy ...
>
> And that, as much as the obvious examples of violent rhetoric, can appeal to the extremist, the mentally unstable, or the "lone nut," to act. And last Saturday, one of them did.

The same way an editorial cartoonist sketches his argument with different shades, shapes, and strokes, so Morrill as an author powerfully draws her points through language. Consider some of the rhetorical techniques she uses:

- Morrill includes direct quotations of phrases used during the congressional election, listing them in a way that generates intensity and a sense of escalation (similar to the how the hierarchy of words on the flagpole operated in Figure 1.1).
- In the second paragraph, she switches to a set of images that attack the character of elected Republicans through criticizing their "minions in the media" and asserting that they have "pounded the nonstop drumbeat" as if at war with Democrats. This condemning language produces a strong animosity in the writing that might also sway a reader toward condemning the Republicans.

- Morrill uses a strategy called *anaphora*—deliberate repetition for rhetorical effect—by repeating "they're" at the end of the second paragraph to create a powerful rhythm and build emotional energy.
- The list itself relies on hyperbole and exaggeration ("destroy the country," "kill your grandmother," "shredding the Constitution," and so on) to present Morrill's version of what Republicans tend to suggest in their media statements.
- She concludes by reminding the reader of the exigence of the situation—how the "violent rhetoric" she has critiqued produced tragic action: the shooting of Giffords.

As you can see, such details can deeply move an audience. What we learn from reading this blog post rhetorically is that when you analyze written texts, you can apply similar strategies to those you use when reading visual texts: look for the vivid details, which in the case of language might include repetition, concrete metaphors, emotional phrases, and characterization of others that together act as what Aristotle would call "available means of persuasion" in writing. In this way, such written rhetoric, even while it disparages "violent language," is actually also forceful, even violent in its emphasis. It, too, is a form of communication that has as its purpose the goal of persuading audiences.

Let's consider a longer passage of writing. Remember Alex and her walk across campus? When she arrived at her Communication 101 class on "Media and Society," her TA gave her a handout containing an editorial about the *Charlie Hebdo* attack from the news site *Humanosphere*. Back in her dorm room, Alex sits down to read the article, writing **annotations** in the margins that indicate brief points of analysis or observation about the strategies of persuasion at work in each part of the article. As you read the article and Alex's accompanying commentary, add your own marks on points that you find provocative or interesting. Use the strategies of *critical literacy* that we've been developing throughout this chapter and ask yourself:

- Who is the main *audience*?
- How does David Horsey position himself as *author*?
- What is his *purpose* or *motive* in response to the *exigency* of the situation?
- Where and what is his *argument*?
- What rhetorical strategies does Horsey use to persuade the audience?
- What is your response to the text?

The title captures my attention—what does he mean by *obnoxious freedom*?

Interesting to read an article by an author who usually expresses his opinions in cartoons.

Sets up context right away. Also, the *Charlie Hebdo* shooting clearly is the exigence for this article.

His emphasis here indicates that this is the driving point of his essay. It echoes his title somewhat, too.

"My career of giving offense" and the story at the end of the paragraph seem both blunt and cynical—sounds like the voice of an editorial cartoonist!

Repetition here ("sometimes") is very powerful.

Makes an assumption about his audience here.

OBNOXIOUS FREEDOM

David Horsey

I have received many messages of solidarity from friends and readers in the couple of days since Islamic terrorists stormed into the Paris office of the satirical magazine *Charlie Hebdo* and murdered 12 people, including several cartoonists.

One friend—a prominent officeholder who, despite getting his share of barbs from reporters, nevertheless understands the absolute necessity of maintaining an unfettered news media—wrote in an email, "I am thinking of you following the France assault on journalists. It follows the loss of something like 40 journalists in the Mideast. Freedom cannot exist without people willing to ferret out the truth."

I appreciated his words, but I responded with a crucial caveat:

"Not only can freedom not exist without truth tellers, freedom cannot exist without obnoxious expressions of opinion, no matter who is offended."

Throughout my career of giving offense, I have received an unending stream of comments from people who disagree with what I draw or write. Sometimes they are rude. Sometimes they are insulting. Sometimes they are seriously angry. And sometimes they are just having fun sparring with me. Only once have I gotten anything like a death threat, which was unsettling, but quickly forgotten. One guy offered to fight me, but he lived 3000 miles away, so the bout never happened.

Love or hate the way I think, though, just about everyone would agree my right to free speech is unassailable. That's what makes America great, of course, and why there is near unanimous shock about the attack on the cartoonists in Paris. But, as people get a closer look at the kinds of images those French satirists were publishing, some are having second thoughts about all this freedom.

Editorial cartoonists in the United States are an essentially tame species. Traditionally part of the establishment media,

American cartoonists mostly poke fun at obvious targets. Even when the cartoons my ink-spewing compatriots and I produce are sharply barbed and a little bold, they stay within fairly tight boundaries of social responsibility and good taste. I do not think that's a terrible thing—even though it encourages too many bland cartoons with elephants and donkeys and labels galore—but it does mean we very seldom really test the limits of what our readers will tolerate.

Great word choice here!

Paragraph topic: state of U.S. editorial cartooning. Interesting that it ends in a critique of American editorial cartoons. Is he asking if these cartoons achieve their rhetorical purpose?

The martyred cartoonists at *Charlie Hebdo* were different. Unrestrained mockery, not reasoned commentary, was their raison d'etre. Page after page, week after week, they turned out scatological, simplistic images attacking not only the political figures everyone picks on, but the cherished images and idols of organized religions. There were cartoons of Christ partaking of three-way sex with God and the Holy Spirit; nasty cartoons of the pope that got the magazine sued numerous times by Catholics; images of Orthodox Jews reminiscent of the anti-Semitic art of Nazi Germany; and, of course, caricatures of Mohammed doing all manner of disgusting things, sometimes with his genitals exposed.

Now he moves to French cartooning practice. Effective comparison/contrast move.

These examples are really important given that many websites and newspapers refused to publish these cartoons.

It is those images that outraged the Parisian Muslim community and brought the cartoonists into the extremists' line of fire. The magazine office was firebombed in 2011 and the publication's editor, Stephane Charbonnier, received enough death threats to justify hiring a bodyguard. The editor and the bodyguard are now among the dead.

Sets up background for the attack. So this wasn't the first time that Charlie Hebdo suffered for its "unrestrained" cartoons.

Even with all our proud proclamations in favor of free speech, would a wildly iconoclastic magazine like *Charlie Hebdo* be tolerated in the United States? Conservative religious people would be deeply offended, of course, but neither would such a publication fare well on liberally minded university campuses. Given the social sensitivities in the academic world, a student cartoonist who drew even one cartoon of the type regularly produced by the *Charlie Hebdo* crew would be pilloried and run off campus.

Great question. I think he must assume his audience is predominantly American readers.

I'm thinking that this essay is getting at a comparative between U.S. editorial practices and French ones ...

My take? Most of the *Charlie Hebdo* cartoons I have seen are crudely drawn, crass, and juvenile. Giving offense simply for its

Nice move here—says they're crude, but then praises the principle behind them.

Powerful way to show multiple perspectives.

"Terror" is a charged word. Great ending line; echoes "Je Suis Charlie." He is Charlie, though he says he wouldn't cartoon that way.

own sake has never been my style. Yet, I appreciate the principle on which Charbonnier took a stand. He kept publishing outrageous depictions of Mohammed mostly because people kept insisting he had no right to do it.

Religious fundamentalists may believe limits to free expression are what the Deity demands. College administrators may think it is the politically correct thing to do. Politicians may believe it will keep their constituents calm. But, without the freedom to offend—even in the most outrageous way—freedom is circumscribed and tepid. The French cartoonists were constant offenders and most people would not like their work, but they believed in freedom with a dedication few of us can match. And they died for it.

As Parisians are now saying in response to the terror, "Je suis Charlie."

By annotating the essay, Alex acts as an *active reader* and begins to identify which aspects of the article's written rhetoric interest her most. Her analysis evokes the *rhetorical situation* (see Figure 1.5): she analyzes the way the writer (or *author*) uses language (or *argument*) to persuade the reader (or *audience*) of the article (or *text*). She also noted the rhetorical moves of the author: word choice, structure, style tone, voice. She could then use those points in order to formulate her own argument about Horsey's article.

As you develop your own skills of analyzing written rhetoric, you can also use annotations to help you identify and track your observations on how rhetoric works; these notes, gathered together, will enable you to generate your own interpretation and, ultimately, a persuasive argument. In fact, Sir Francis Bacon, the great philosopher, politician, and scientist from the Age of Enlightenment, developed a system of logical "inductive" reasoning based on the very practice of gathering observations and using them to construct knowledge, a new conclusion, or an argument. Echoing the position of Aristotle, he also saw rhetoric as that which moves others. Bacon asserted: "The duty and office of rhetoric is to apply reason to imagination for the better moving of the will."

The varied ways that you and your classmates might read and respond to this editorial depend on both *audience* and *context,* bringing to light again the importance of the *rhetorical situation*. Differences in your interpretation also reveal the importance of learning effective means of persuading others to see the text through a certain lens or way of reading and analyzing the text. That is, your task as a reader and a writer is both to study a text carefully and to learn how to persuade others to see the text as you see it. In order to learn how to do so, we will turn next to the key elements in writing an argumentative essay about your interpretation of a text, so you, too, can "apply reason to imagination" to persuade others.

WRITER'S PRACTICE

MyWritingLab

Practice your skills of rhetorical analysis on this 2014 editorial by Chris Baker, also known as "Angry Nerd," who critiques Disney's decision to "destroy" what Star Wars fans call the "Expanded Universe canon"—including comic books, video games, and hundreds of pieces of fan fiction and unauthorized Star Wars–derivative texts—as part of creating continuity in the new Disney version of the Star Wars saga. Annotate like Alex did in the example above, looking for elements of the piece that make it particularly persuasive. Consider how Baker takes into account the rhetorical situation as well as exigency and purpose through style and composition. For added challenge, consider analyzing the video version of this editorial, available through YouTube.

"IS DARTH DISNEY DESTROYING STAR WARS' EXPANDED UNIVERSE?"

By Chris Baker

Help me, George Lucas, you're my only hope. Darth Disney is destroying the Expanded Universe. Please come back, George Lucas; this is our most desperate hour.

I felt a great disturbance in the force as if thousands of storylines cried out and were suddenly silenced. The Star Wars franchise is committing "canon-icide." The fate of an entire universe is at stake. You've understand: the Star Wars movies are the barest fraction of star war stories out there.

The so-called "Expanded Universe" has existed in comic books and novels and games for decades, and Lucas film is now air-locking it all. The Thrawn trilogy novels; *Shadow of the Empire* for Nintendo 64; the Tattoine manhunt module for the Star Wars RPG; the holiday special: erased from existence. Only a Sith Lord would decree that everything except the Star Wars films and the Clone Wars series did not happen. All future tie-in cartoons and novels—everything—will be forced to march in lockstep with the JJ Abrams sequel films. You know who else marched in lockstep? [The storm troopers.] And a new story group inside Lucasfilm will make sure that all elements in the Star Wars continuity fit together.

Normally I approve of an orderly and cohesive continuity, but this crisis on infinite Endoors is deleting incidents that are more interesting than almost anything that happened in the movies. No Expanded Universe means Boba Fett never escaped from the Sarlacc Pit, Luke Skywalker never flirted with the dark side, and Han Solo never befriended … Jackson Starhopper… .

Oh, Darth Disney, only you could be so bold! To think that I was cautiously optimistic about your stewardship of Star Wars. I was far too trusting.

The survival of the Expanded Universe is now in the hands of Star Wars fans. Fan fiction kept Star Trek alive through the lean years. We can do with the same for Star Wars. The more you tighten your grip, Darth Disney, the more Expanded Universe stories will slip through your fingers. You may control the canon, but you will never control the Fan-on. Your tightly controlled continuity can't handle the pulse-pounding exploits of Pedanticus Nitpickser, a bald bespectacled jedi, who lectures the entire galaxy about how lightsabers are scientifically impossible and how you couldn't actually hear explosions in the vacuum of space.

Strong he is in the force … of logic.

WRITING A RHETORICAL ANALYSIS

1.5 How should I brainstorm parts of the essay, including the thesis statement?

We've seen that rhetoric works as a means of persuading an audience to accept the argument of the author. This is also true for the argument you make about a text. When you write an analysis essay for class, you are crafting a rhetorical text in order to persuade your readers (the instructor and your peers) to accept your interpretation. In some cases, your instructor might ask you to select your own text for analysis; in others, you may be assigned a particular text. In either case, ask yourself the following questions:

- What elements stand out that you might analyze in your essay?
- What do you know about the author or the intended audience?
- What do you know about the timing or context of this text?
- What is your interpretation of the meaning or message of this text?

As you work through the questions above, you can see that your task as a writer is to argue convincingly for your audience to see the text the way you yourself see it. In the case of Figure 1.14, what is the cartoon's argument about the NFL's response to recent allegations of domestic violence among the players? What details could you discuss in order to support your interpretation?

FIGURE 1.14 Gary Markstein's comic humorously tackles the sensitive issue of domestic violence in the NFL.

Your challenge as a student of writing and rhetoric is not only to identify the argument contained by a text but also to *craft your own interpretation of that text*. This involves careful assessment of the ways in which the elements of the rhetorical situation work together to produce meaning in a text.

In looking at Markstein's comic, you may notice many details—the uniforms, the hand gestures, the captions, the facial expressions, the shading on the referee's pants, the use of black shadows, and the fact that the lettering on the hats is yellow. However, when crafting your own argument, it's valuable to remember that a successful rhetorical analysis does not need to discuss every component in the source text, only those relevant to supporting your interpretation. In fact, it's also important to tailor your analysis itself to prioritize a particular approach. You might decide to focus on any one of these elements as you shape your overall interpretation:

- **Argument:** What is the text's argument, and is it persuasive? How does the author use evidence to support his interpretation?
- **Audience:** How did the author compose the text to persuade a particular audience? How did he take into account their context and predispositions to try to create a convincing argument?
- **Genre:** How did the author either trade on or depart from the conventions of a particular genre (such as the conventional essay, blogging, twitter, even email as we saw in Figure 1.6)? How did that decision influence the persuasiveness of the argument?
- **Style:** How did the author use style as a persuasive tool? How did he use symbol, metaphor, word choice, voice, and other stylistic devices?
- **Exigence and Purpose:** How does the cartoon respond to a pressing need? What is the author's purpose, and to what extent does he accomplish it?

AT A GLANCE

Selecting and Evaluating a Text for Rhetorical Analysis

When choosing a text for analysis, ask yourself the following questions:

- What is the text's purpose? To entertain? Educate? Persuade?
- Are there sufficient elements in the text to analyze?
- What do you know about the author, the intended audience, and the context?
- What's your interpretation of this image? Can you develop a strong claim that you can support with evidence from the text?

Ultimately, your analysis might touch on aspects of the different approaches; however, it is important to try to achieve a unified interpretation, so you probably will need to focus on one more than the others. To help you through this process, we recommend writing out your answers to the questions above. Many times it is through writing itself that we can access—and create—our best ideas.

Developing a Thesis Statement

In brainstorming your essay, you need to determine your interpretation of the meaning or message of a specific text (whether written, visual, or a combination of the two). In writing studies, we call this interpretation your **thesis**, or *the concise statement of your claim or interpretation about a particular text, issue, or event*. A thesis should be more than a statement of observation or a fact. It should also be more than merely your opinion. It needs to combine **observation + evidence** (based on the elements of the text).

To understand how to generate a *thesis statement* using your skills of critical analysis, let's work through an example. Imagine that you want to write an argument about the cartoon in Figure 1.15, a commentary on recent debates about immigration policy. How might you develop a thesis statement that persuasively conveys your interpretation of how this cartoon contributes to the debate surrounding the status of undocumented immigrants?

FIGURE 1.15 This cartoon by Daryl Cagle uses engaging visuals and well-chosen words to make an argument.

Source: Daryl Cagle, Cagle Cartoons, Inc.

Start by jotting down what you see; make *close observations* about the text. Then use questions to bring your argument into focus and to make a specific claim. The end product will be a *working thesis.* The process of developing your thesis might look like this:

1. **Write down your observations.**

   Close observations: The cartoon focuses on the border between the United

States and Mexico and on the way that we set up fences to keep illegal immigrants out. A key element is the gap in the fence that people are crawling through to get into the United States. The contradictory messages are interesting, too. The big sign says "Keep out," while the smaller signs are designed to draw people in.

2. **Work with your observations to construct a preliminary thesis statement.**

   First statement: The cartoon focuses on the contradiction in American border policy.

3. **Refine your argument by asking questions that make your statement less general.**

   Ask yourself: How? What contradiction? To what effect? How do I know this?

4. **Revise your preliminary thesis statement to be more specific; perhaps include specific evidence that drives your claim.**

   Revised statement: The cartoon in Figure 1.15 focuses on the contradictions in American border policy by showing that, on the one hand, the American government wants to keep illegal immigrants out, but, on the other hand, economic forces encourage them to enter the United States illegally.

5. **Further polish your thesis by refining your language and asking questions about the implications of your working thesis statement.**

   Ask yourself: What do you find interesting about this observation? How does it tap into larger social or cultural issues?

6. **Revise your working thesis to include the implications or significance of your claim. Sometimes we call this the "So what?" point.**

   Working Thesis: The political cartoon in Figure 1.15 offers a sharp commentary on the recent immigration debate, suggesting that official government policies against illegal immigration are undermined by economic forces that tolerate, if not welcome, the entry of undocumented workers into the United States. Yet the added detail of the hole in the fence suggests that such entry comes at great cost to immigrants who enter illegally.

In the working thesis, the significance appears as the final point about "great cost"—that is, the cartoon indicates that current immigration policies have serious consequences for undocumented laborers entering the United States. From this example, you can tell that a strong argumentative thesis does more than state a topic: it makes a claim about that topic that you will develop in the rest of your paper.

Let's look at one more example to further consider ways to produce sharp, clear, and persuasive thesis statements. For her rhetorical analysis assignment, Alex decided to write about David Horsey's editorial from earlier in the chapter. As we saw in her annotations, she had already noted several elements that struck her about the text: the comparison between the United States and France, the word choice, and Horsey's unique position as an editorial cartoonist/author. While drafting her essay, she experimented with a variety of different thesis statements before arriving at a strong claim:

Thesis 1: David Horsey's article offers a powerful perspective on the *Charlie Hebdo* shooting and free speech.

Assessment: This thesis statement relies too heavily on subjective opinion: the author offers no criteria for evaluating the cartoon. What does it mean to be "powerful"? Moreover, the author does not include any elements of analysis or use evidence.

Thesis 2: David Horsey's article makes an argument about free speech.

Assessment: This thesis statement is too much of a broad generalization and offers no critical interpretation of the meaning of the text. It does not make a claim as to what Horsey's opinion is, and it relies too heavily on vague language.

Thesis 3: According to my analysis, David Horsey, a well-known editorial cartoonist, discusses both American and French approaches to editorial cartoons in this article.

Assessment: While this thesis is promising in that it offers some more detail, it nevertheless only describes the content of the essay rather than offering a focused interpretation, despite the writer's claim to be making an argument.

Thesis 4: In the article, Horsey, a well-known editorial cartoonist, uses an underlying compare-and-contrast strategy bolstered by strong word choice to make the argument for solidarity with *Charlie Hebdo* in defense of all levels of free speech.

Assessment: While a bit long, this working thesis statement does combine observation and significance. Of the four examples, it provides the most specific and argumentative articulation of Alex's interpretation of Horsey's editorial.

As the examples above demonstrate, a strong thesis is characterized by a specific and contestable claim. This central claim in turn functions as the heart and driver of a successful rhetorical analysis essay.

AT A GLANCE

Testing Your Thesis

- Does your thesis present an interesting angle on your topic?
- Does it avoid being overly obvious or a commonplace statement? Is it nuanced?
- Does it present a debatable point? That is, could someone argue against it?
- Is it too dense (trying to compact the entire paper into a single sentence)? Conversely, is it overly simplistic or general (neglecting to adequately develop your claim)?
- Does it use concrete and vivid language?
- Does it suggest the significance of your topic?

Analyzing Student Writing

Let's look at how Alex combines effective strategies of analysis with her carefully crafted thesis statement to compose her rhetorical analysis of the David Horsey article that she read for class. As you read through this selection, consider how she analyzes "Obnoxious Freedom" as well as the ways in which she herself uses rhetorical strategies to make her own argument persuasive.

Ramirez 1

Alexandra Ramirez
Rhetorical Analysis Essay
Comm 101

Alex crafts a title that refers to the article but also hints at her own thesis.

"Obnoxious Freedom":

A Cartoonist's Defense of the Freedom to Be Crass

On the morning of January 7, 2015, two brothers entered the Paris office of *Charlie Hebdo*, a weekly satirical newspaper. Armed with assault rifles and other weapons, the pair of brothers

Ramirez 2

killed 12 people in the office that day: cartoonists, writers, maintenance workers, editors, and a bodyguard. The brothers, who identified as members of the Yemeni branch of Al Qaeda, took issue with cartoons published in *Charlie Hebdo* that they considered disrespectful to Mohammed and to Islam as a whole (Smith-Spark, Ford, and Mullen).

She designs her opening paragraph to set up context for her essay, drawing on a source that she found through a quick Google search. Note how she makes sure to cite the source from which she got her information, even though she doesn't use a direct quotation here.

Following the attack, there was both great mourning for the victims and outrage at a terrorist strike against the freedom of press. In days following the attack, the *Charlie Hebdo* shooting caught the international media by firestorm and sparked a new conversation (and controversy) on freedom of speech. One article contributing to the conversation is David Horsey's "Obnoxious Freedom." In this article, Horsey, a well-known editorial cartoonist, uses an underlying compare-and-contrast strategy bolstered by strong word choice to make the argument for solidarity with *Charlie Hebdo* in defense of all levels of free speech. As he does so, however, Horsey also makes a subtle criticism of the status of American free speech as well, adding another dimension to the debate surrounding the *Charlie Hebdo* tragedy.

Alex places her thesis statement near the end of the introductory section.

In writing her essay, Alex adds a layer of complexity to her preliminary thesis statement (which we saw on p. 31).

At a basic level, Horsey made a very significant choice in choosing to publish an article expressing his opinion about the *Charlie Hebdo* tragedy. Indeed, as a two-time Pulitzer Prize–winning cartoonist speaking about a retaliation to cartoons, it might be expected that Horsey would choose to express himself via a cartoon ("David Horsey"). Yet in this case, Horsey

Her thesis implies levels of interpretation, so Alex begins her main body by referring to the most basic level, implying that she will engage with the more complex aspects of Horsey's argument later in her essay.

Even from the beginning of her essay, she grounds her analysis in terms of the rhetorical situation—the relation of the audience and author to the argument.

Her transition here demonstrates that she's moving from the "basic" to more nuanced elements of Horsey's essay.

Alex cites specific examples from the text to support her points and also explains their significance.

Ramirez 3

chose prose. To some extent, this choice alone sets a tone of seriousness; it is as though the jokester has finally learned to be serious. The effect of this is ultimately that the audience is forced to take the article—and the argument within—more seriously.

Beyond just setting the serious tone for the argument, however, the prose format also allows for Horsey to demonstrate both more nuance and voice, and even include his own credentials as an author. For example, the extensive discussion of both Horsey's own cartoon style and that of the works published in *Charlie Hebdo* allows Horsey to make multilevel arguments such as the idea that although more tame cartoons can sometimes be more effective, the crass ones must be allowed to exist as well in order to not give in to a sliding scale of censorship. Along with this substance, however, Horsey expresses a strong, humorous voice using asides such as a story about a guy that "offered to fight [Horsey], but he lived 3000 miles away, so the bout never happened." Ultimately, the serious arguments in tandem with witty humor are an effective method of capturing the audience's attention while capitalizing on the author's strengths. It is also significant to note that the longer form also allows Horsey to introduce himself more to the reader. In some ways, Horsey relates himself to the cartoonists at *Charlie Hebdo* by, for example, referencing his "career of giving offense." At other points in the article, Horsey chooses to distance himself more, stating that "giving offense simply for its own sake" isn't his

Ramirez 4

style. This creates a sense of impartiality on the part of the author, which makes him appear more trustworthy to the reader.

Alex continues her emphasis on how Horsey constructs himself as an *author* in his article and how that relates to the strength of his argument.

And yet, at the same time that Horsey works to appear impartial in some ways such as his relation to the *Charlie Hebdo* cartoonists, he also actively plays upon almost nationalistic, patriotic writing he presumes to resonate with his audience. This strategy is first capitalized on by a comparison of French and American culture and cartoons. For example, when describing American cartoons, Horsey paints the pictures of "tame species" that only criticize targets that are well-accepted as targets and can become "bland."

In this paragraph, Alex shows her powers of critical thinking and analysis in the way she interprets specific elements of the text.

By comparison, Horsey describes the *Charlie Hebdo* cartoons as "unrestrained mockery" that go after widely idolized figures. While this might seem to equally criticize both cartoon cultures for their shortcomings, when paired with the rest of the article, Horsey's feelings about both cultures become more clear. First, the buildup to this portion of the article features rather dramatic and even patriotic word choice such as "unassailable" free speech as well as cartoonists that are both "compatriots" and martyrs (Horsey). Evoking these images prime the audience, reminding them how great the foundation of American society (freedom) really is. But through the comparison to French cartoons, Horsey implicitly asks the reader a new question: how free *are* American cartoons?

As he more directly begins his conclusion by asking the rhetorical question ("My take?"), Horsey clearly delineates the

Alex pauses here to clarify her interpretation of Horsey's argument.

argument that he builds up to throughout the rest of the piece: Americans need to be supporting *Charlie Hebdo*, and American free speech might not represent pure freedom any more. Indeed, as Horsey lists what he considers to be opposing groups to free speech in America—religious fundamentalists, college administrations, and politicians—he attaches them with somewhat stigmatized or less-than-altruistic goals such as political correctness or just trying to assuage constituents. Further capitalizing on American readers raised hearing the "give me liberty or give me death" battle cry, Horsey praises the *Charlie Hebdo* cartoonists as having the utmost dedication to freedom, ultimately making the victims into martyrs. As just another subtle touch of preference for the French culture of freedom, Horsey ends his argument with a resounding phrase of solidarity with the French, "Je suis Charlie," or *I am Charlie*.

Alex draws attention to how Horsey devises his argument to appeal to his specifically American audience.

Note how Alex includes a translation of the French phrase here for clarity.

Could this support and solidarity with the French be felt without a sense of the author's giving a warning about American culture? Perhaps, but throughout the piece Horsey leaves subtle indicators that in the very system he publishes in everything isn't perfect, such as hinting that the fear of offending is creating "bland" cartoons or that politicians pressure media to produce cartoons that will keep people "calm." These insinuations, in combination with the overall comparison to the French, allow for Horsey to not only stand in solidarity with *Charlie Hebdo* but also make a commentary on the true meaning of free speech. Perhaps Horsey meant his signatory "Je suis Charlie" merely as solidarity with fellow cartoonists. However, perhaps he felt his cautionary piece alerts Americans to guard their

Alex uses a question here to transition into her own conclusion, mirroring the question-asking strategy that Horsey used in the original essay.

Alex concedes here that not all might agree, but then reaffirms her own claim.

Ramirez 6

freedoms just as the cartoonists of *Charlie Hebdo* remind the people of France to do so with each of their "obnoxious" cartoons.

Alex designs a conclusion that again plays off of Horsey's, leaving her audience to interpret as they will.

Ramirez 7

Works Cited

"David Horsey." *Los Angeles Times*. Los Angeles Times, Jan. 2015. Web. 28 May 2015.

Horsey, David. "Obnoxious Freedom: Editorial Cartoonist David Horsey on the Charlie Hebdo Murders." *Humanosphere*. Tom Paulson's Humanosphere, 9 Jan. 2015. Web. 28 May 2015.

Smith-Spark, Laura, Dana Ford, and Jethro Mullen. "Charlie Hebdo Attack: What We Know and Don't Know." CNN.com. Cable News Network, 21 Jan. 2015. Web. 26 May 2015.

Alex includes a Works Cited that lists not only the original article that she was analyzing but also the two texts she used for background on the *Charlie Hebdo* shooting.

THE WRITER'S PROCESS

As you turn now to write your own rhetorical analysis of a text, you'll be putting into practice all the skills you've learned in this chapter. You'll need to write down your observations of the text, spend time analyzing them in detail, and use these points of analysis as *evidence* to make an argument that will persuade others to see the text the way you see it. In other words, when composing your own rhetorical analysis, you need to use the same process we have worked through when analyzing different texts in this chapter:

- First, look carefully at all the elements in the text. Create a list of your observations to help you analyze the text more closely.

- Then, consider the argument of each element. How does it contribute to the text as a whole?
- Next, complete the rhetorical triangle (see Figure 1.5) for the text, identifying the author, the intended audience, and the argument, based on your observations of the details. In addition, identify the rhetorical exigence and the author's purpose or motive in creating the argument.
- Finally, put all these elements together and develop your thesis statement about the argument and significance of the text.

It's crucial to remember that when you write a rhetorical analysis, you perform a rhetorical act of persuasion yourself. Accordingly, you need to include the key elements of analytical writing: (1) have a point of interpretation to share with your readers, (2) take time to walk readers through concrete details to prove your point, and (3) lead your readers through the essay in an engaging and convincing way. But of all these, the most important is your thesis, your interpretation of or position on the text—your *argument*.

Spend some time working on your thesis before composing the entire draft. Make sure your angle is sharp and your interpretation takes into

AT A GLANCE

Composing Rhetorical Analysis Essays

- Do you have a sharp point of interpretation, or *thesis*, to make about the text?
- Have you selected key elements or details to analyze in support of your thesis?
- Do you lead readers through your interpretation of the text by discussing important aspects in sequence? These might include:
  - Verbal elements in the text (words, font, quotes, dates)
  - Visual composition, layout, and images
  - Framing words for the text (article title, cartoon caption)
  - Color, arrangement, and meaning of items
- Can you include information about the author, intended audience, or context?
- Have you drafted a title for your own essay?
- Does your introduction name the author, date, and rhetorical situation for your text?
- Do your paragraphs build and progress through the essay using transitions?
- Have you offered a summary and a larger point or implication in the conclusion?
- Can you insert the image right into the essay and label it?

account audience, author, and argument as well as concrete points of visual and verbal composition.

Moreover, keep in mind the need to begin with observations, but avoid simply describing the elements you notice. Instead, zoom in on specific details and think hard about their meaning. Make a persuasive argument by using *specific* evidence to support your analysis of how the text succeeds at convincing an audience to perceive an issue in a particular way. These writing strategies will enable you to craft a persuasive and effective rhetorical analysis essay.

Seeing Connections
See Chapter 7 for more instructions on integrating images in your writing and referring to them correctly.

SPOTLIGHTED ANALYSIS: EDITORIAL CARTOONS

MyWritingLab

Pick a cartoon to analyze from a news magazine such as *Time*, a newspaper, a Web comic collection such as *xkcd* or *Penny Arcade*, or an online archive such as Daryl Cagle's political cartoon Website. Using the skills of analysis you have learned in this chapter, work through the questions below to guide your analysis.

- **Audience:** Who is the audience for this comic? How does it address this audience? In what country and in what historical moment was the cartoon produced? In what type of text did it first appear? A journal? A newspaper? Online? Is this text conservative? liberal? How does it speak to this audience?
- **Author:** What do you know about the artist? What kinds of cartoons (or other types of texts) does he or she regularly produce? Where does he or she live and publish?
- **Argument:** What issue does the cartoon address, and what is the cartoon's argument about it? Is there irony involved (does the cartoon advocate one point of view, but the cartoonist wants you to take the opposite view)?
- **Composition:** Is this political cartoon a single frame or a series of sequential frames? If the latter, how does the argument evolve over the series? How do elements like color choices, layout, and style shape its impact on the audience?
- **Imagery:** What choices of imagery and content does the artist make? Are the drawings realistic? Do they rely on caricatures? How are character and setting portrayed? Does the artist include allusions or references to past or present events or ideas? How do images and words work together in the cartoon?
- **Tone:** Is the cartoon primarily comic or serious in tone? How does this choice of tone create a powerful rhetorical impact on readers?
- **Cultural resonance:** Does the cartoon implicitly or explicitly refer to any actual people, events, or pop culture icons? What sort of symbolism is used in the cartoon? Would the symbols speak to a broad or narrow audience? How does the cultural resonance function as a rhetorical strategy in making the argument?

WRITING ASSIGNMENTS

MyWritingLab

1. **Rhetoric Practice:** Experiment with the scenarios below in order to understand the power of rhetoric as a persuasive act. In each case, first write down your ideas. Then, following the directions, write, speak, design, or present your own rhetorical text. Keep in mind that the success of your argument will depend on your choice of media (verbal plea, written email, cover letter, visual poster, etc.) in relation to the specific audience you are addressing (coach, professor, potential employer, or peers).
   - Scenario 1: When you realize that you will never finish an essay on time because of your heavy work schedule, you decide to ask for an extension on the paper's deadline. Craft an argument asking for extra time on the assignment that would appeal to the personality of your teacher; compose it in a way appropriate for an email communication.
   - Scenario 2: Imagine that you have a conflict with your practice schedule for your sport—a midterm, interview, or visit from your parents. Compose an oral argument that persuades your coach to let practice out early. After you write out your ideas, make your case face-to-face through in-class role-playing.
   - Scenario 3: When applying for a summer internship, you are asked to submit a formal résumé in order to indicate your qualifications for the position. As you design your résumé think about how to most persuasively present yourself: What content will you include? How will you describe yourself, your goals, and your duties in past positions? How will you organize it and lay it out? What font will you use? Consider taking your résumé to your Writing Center or Career Center for expert feedback.
   - Scenario 4: As Social Chair for your Greek House, you need to advertise an upcoming charity event: create an effective flyer and also a brief paragraph for email and social media distribution. Consider how you'll need to adapt your rhetorical techniques to adjust to the different media.

2. **Personal Narrative Essay:** Recall Alex's observations of rhetoric on her way to class; conduct a similar study of the rhetoric in your world. Write your reflections into a *personal narrative essay.* Discuss which types of visual, verbal, bodily, or architectural rhetoric were most evident, which were most subtle, and which you found the most persuasive. Conclude with a statement or argument about these texts—what do they collectively say about your community or culture? How do these texts try to shape the views of audiences through specific messages or arguments?

3. **Rhetorical Analysis:** Using the At a Glance box on p. 28 as a starting point, develop your analysis of a text of your choice into a full *rhetorical analysis*, complete with a persuasive thesis statement. Make sure that your writing supports a thesis about elements and messages of all the texts you are analyzing.

4. **Comparative Rhetorical Analysis:** Refer back to the article by David Horsey included in this chapter. Now search online for his editorial cartoon on the same subject, entitled "The Death Cult." Write a comparative rhetorical analysis of these texts that examines the similarities and differences in their arguments and composition. (If you prefer, choose two texts of your own—whether two visual texts, two verbal texts, or a visual and a verbal text—that address the same issue to analyze instead.) What rhetorical strategies does each one use to make an argument? How do their arguments about the issue in question differ, and how is each composed to convey that argument? Include a persuasive thesis statement and specific supporting details about each text. Don't forget to take into account your own rhetorical situation (the relationship between your audience, your argument, and your own identity as a writer) in composing your essay.

MyWritingLab Visit Ch. 1 Analyzing Texts and Writing Thesis Statements in MyWritingLab to complete the Writer's Practices, Spotlighted Analyses, and Writing Assignments, and to test your understanding of the chapter objectives.

CHAPTER 2

Understanding Strategies of Persuasion

Chapter Preview Questions

2.1 What specific strategies of argumentation can I use to write persuasively?

2.2 What role do the rhetorical appeals of *pathos*, *logos*, and *ethos* play in persuasion?

2.3 How can I shape my argument based on time, place, and shared values?

What convinced you to buy that new smartphone, to try that new sports drink—or even to decide which college to attend? Chances are that your decision was influenced by a moment of persuasive communication—whether that was a pitch from a college recruiter, a brochure, a printed ad, commercial, product review, or even a billboard. Any time someone tries to market or sell us something, he or she is acting as a rhetorician, carefully assessing the *rhetorical situation* and crafting arguments designed to persuade the target audience. In this chapter, we'll turn our attention to analyzing advertisements as a way to help us discern specific strategies of argumentation that you can use to convince others in your own persuasive writing.

For instance, while walking down a city street, you might cross under billboards such as the one for a clothing store in Figure 2.1, positioned strategically alongside the busy Manhattan sidewalks. Look carefully at its design: what strategies of persuasion does it use to engage the passersby? Does it make a logical argument about its clothing line? Does it appeal to the audience's emotions? How much does it rely on the product's reputation to market its products? How might this ad be revised to provide an even more persuasive argument that would convince a consumer not only to stop and enter the store but also to purchase a piece of clothing? As you can see,

FIGURE 2.1 This New York City street scene presents a typical example of how the rhetoric of advertising looms over our every day lives.

even a seemingly simple advertisement like this one is a carefully composed text, constructed to make a particular argument about a product.

Think of how other ads you've seen make you pause and pay attention. Much like the billboard in Figure 2.1, ads in fashion or sports magazines often feature a photo of a celebrity or an attractive person to try to get their readers to connect emotionally with their products. Commercials often use compelling stories or memorable examples to hook their audiences. Brochures tend to incorporate impressive statistics or factual evidence to support their claims. Targeted ads on social media sites draw on information from your personal profile and search history to connect to you through customized product suggestions. Often, in fact, it is not one but a combination of factors that we find persuasive—and many times these factors are so subtle that we hardly recognize them. Such techniques that are used to move and convince an audience are called **rhetorical strategies**.

While such strategies are a vital part of any successful persuasion, advertisements offer us a particularly productive means of analyzing them because they represent arguments in compact forms. An ad has to be quite efficient; it has to convey its message persuasively before its audience flips the page, fast forwards, hits mute, or scrolls further down the page. Ads also provide us with a particularly effective example of contemporary argument through their sheer ubiquity. Consider all the places ads appear nowadays: not just in magazines or on the television or radio, but also (as we saw in Figure 2.1) on billboards, the sides of buses, trains, and buildings; in sports stadiums and movie theaters; on T-shirts and baseball hats; as banners on Webpages and sidebars on social media sites; even spray-painted on sidewalks or integrated into video games.

By analyzing advertisements, we can detect the rhetorical strategies writers select to make their points and convince their audiences. More importantly, by using advertising as a way to understand persuasion, we can take away lessons that apply to the composition of all sorts of texts, including those that you will produce in academic situations. In this way, you'll gain a working vocabulary and learn specific principles that you can use both to become a savvy reader of advertisements and also to produce your own persuasive written texts.

2.1 What specific strategies of argumentation can I use to write persuasively?

IDENTIFYING STRATEGIES OF ARGUMENTATION

Like more traditional writing, advertising often deploys **strategies of argumentation to persuade**. These can be used effectively to structure either a small unit (in an essay, a paragraph or section of the argument; in an ad, a small subset of the text) or a larger one (the argument as a whole). Let's look at how such strategies might operate in both advertising and academic texts:

- **Narration:** Using a story to draw in the audience.

  The Budweiser, commercial, "Brotherhood," for example (see Figure 2.2), tells the story of a man who raises a foal, sells it so it can become one of the Budweiser Clydesdales, and then is unexpectedly reunited with it after a city parade.

  Similarly, a writer might use narration to hook her reader by telling a story that illustrates a key point of her argument or predisposes them to her line of thinking. For instance, in writing about the ethical implications of marketing fast-food to children, you might open your essay with the story of how a young child watches a McDonalds commercial, is drawn in by its cheerful music, appealing colors, and product information, and then begs his mother for a Happy Meal for lunch.

FIGURE 2.2 The Budweiser "Brotherhood" commercial relies on narration to hook its audience, using the reunion of the man and his horse as the emotional climax of the story.

- **Comparison-Contrast:** Making a point through showing the similarities or differences between two or more items.

  For instance, soap manufacturer Olay ran a comparison-contrast ad campaign arguing the superiority of its product due to how much moisturizer it contained; it juxtaposed a picture of Dove soap next to a measuring cup marked "1/4 moisture" with a picture of Olay soap next to a measuring cup "1/3 moisture" to support this claim.

  In an essay, relatedly, a writer might contrast two different texts as a way that gives the reader a better understanding of a larger claim. For instance, if you were writing an essay that argued that a famous *New York Times* columnist's approach to an issue had become more conservative over time, you might compare one of her articles from the 1990s with one that she wrote within the last five years.

- **Example/Illustration:** Focusing on a specific, representative example to persuade your reader.

  We can see this strategy at work in the Lego ad in Figure 2.3, which spotlights a smiling girl, holding her Lego creation, as an example of who might use the new Lego Friends products and what she might build.

  In a similar way, writers often help readers understand a larger issue by exploring one or more example. In an essay on nationalism in advertising, for example, you might examine the commercials with a patriotic theme

FIGURE 2.3 This Lego ad speaks to the target audience for the Friends line by showing the types of creations that can be made with that product.

that were broadcast during the 2002 Superbowl, shortly after the 9/11 terrorist attacks.

- **Cause and Effect:** Structuring an argument around the causal relationship between two elements, considering why something occurred or happened.

  Acne face wash companies and weight loss programs such as Jenny Craig are famous for cause-and-effect arguments, organizing their commercials around the idea that using their facial scrub or following their diet (cause) helps their customers achieve a clear complexion or lose weight (effect).

  Many writers find cause and effect a powerful way to argue for the logical consequences of an action, event, or phenomenon. For instance, a cause-and-effect essay might argue how the rise of DVR and online subscription services for television shows (cause) has changed the marketing strategies and design of commercials (effect).

- **Definition:** Defining a term, concept, or theoretical premise for your reader.

  Advertisers for the search engine Bing used definition to drive their 2009 marketing campaign through a series of commercials that defined "search overload syndrome," which they claimed was the tendency of Google users to succumb to spontaneous verbal outbursts of unrelated information as a result of their unfocused Internet searches.

  Often in assessing their audience's understanding of concepts fundamental to their argument, writers will take time to define an important term or idea to make their claims more persuasive. For instance, if you were writing an essay on emergent forms of online advertising, you might devote a paragraph to defining the term "advergaming" before moving on to examine examples of this new genre of interactive games designed to promote a product or company.

- **Analogy:** Using a simpler or more familiar concept or metaphor to help an audience understand a complicated idea.

Consider how analogy works in an ad series from the pharmaceutical company, Elter Drugs. In 2007, it created several magazine ads, sponsored by its "Gastric and Antibacterial Therapy Divisions," with the slogan "An Unwashed Vegetable Can Become a Deadly Weapon" and the tagline "Always wash your vegetables to win the battle against foodborne illnesses such as amoebiasis, dysentery, and cholera." What made the ads so powerful was the way the imagery built on the slogan's metaphor. One ad featured a close up of a tomato, against a red background, with a lit fuse on its top stem, turning it into a bomb; another transformed an artichoke into a grenade by replacing its stalk with a fuse and safety pin; a third ad stood a mushroom on a base of billowing smoke, turning it into a visual equivalent of a mushroom cloud. In each case, the ad used analogy to drive home its argument about the potential dangers of eating unwashed vegetables.

Analogies found in essays are often not as heavy-handed as those found in this ad series, but they can be very persuasive in establishing a rich correlative that helps the reader better understand the argument. In an essay analyzing social media marketing, for instance, you might find it useful to employ a Cinderella analogy throughout the essay to persuade your reader that the seemingly insignificant strategy of Twitter advertising actually just needs the right "fairy godmother" to usher it into prominence and power in the marketing scene.

- **Description:** Describing an element, event, or idea in detail so as to set up background or create an impression on your reader.

Advertisements for resorts and tropical getaways generally paint a picture of the destination they are promoting, using vivid, descriptive language and beautiful images to motivate audiences to choose that locale for their next vacation.

When analyzing texts, writers often use descriptive language to paint a picture for their readers to make a stronger point. For instance, if you were to write a rhetorical analysis about a commercial, you probably would include a detailed description of the commercial—which your readers might not have seen; alternately, if you were writing an essay about a place that had had a profound impact on you, you would describe the location in vivid detail. In both cases, you would be helping your reader "see" something in a way that would incline them be more persuaded by your claim.

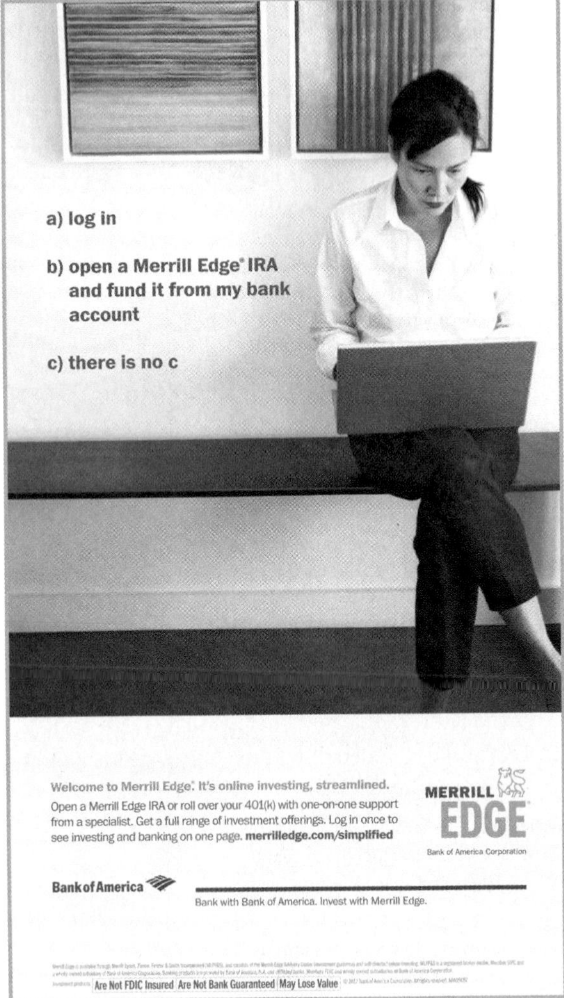

a) log in
b) open a Merrill Edge® IRA and fund it from my bank account
c) there is no c
Welcome to Merrill Edge®. It's online investing, streamlined.
Open a Merrill Edge IRA or roll over your 401(k) with one-on-one support from a specialist. Get a full range of investment offerings. Log in once to see investing and banking on one page. merrilledge.com/simplified
MERRILL EDGE
Bank of America Corporation
Bank of America
Bank with Bank of America. Invest with Merrill Edge.
Are Not FDIC Insured | Are Not Bank Guaranteed | May Lose Value

FIGURE 2.4 This ad for Merrill Edge shows the simplicity of the investment process to persuade readers to try out its services.

- **Process:** Persuading through showing a series of sequential steps.

  The ad in Figure 2.4 relies on a process-based argument; it argues that Merrill's IRA is easy to use by showing the simple a-b-c steps the woman follows to invest her money.

  Process can be extremely effective in a written text to advocate for a certain course of action. If you decided to write an article presenting what you thought was the best way to navigate the college admissions process, you could use this strategy to move your readers step-by-step from campus visits, to standardized test-taking, interviewing, composing a strong application essay, and finally to deciding which school to attend.

- **Classification and Division:** Helping the reader understand either how individual elements fit into a larger category or set of ideas or how a larger category breaks down into component parts.

  We can see classification and division at work in many car ads; automobile manufacturers like Honda and Toyota often run ads that promote their entire product line—from SUVs to compact cars—to show the variety of models they produce and invite their audience to select the one that best suits their needs.

  In an essay, classification and division can help your reader understand the complexities of what you're discussing and better understand the differences between a set of items. Think how useful this strategy might be in an essay about celebrity endorsements. Rather than discussing all types of spokespersons, you might formulate categories to help your reader understand the different ways such advertising is structured: for instance, expert ads (ads based on the expertise of the celebrity); reputation ads (ads that draw on the celebrity's overall public status, not necessarily related to the product); and parody ads (ads that mock the celebrity's character or actions as a selling point). Using this technique could help you produce more sophisticated and nuanced analysis.

Let's now turn to a more extended analysis of a text to see the way in which you can combine multiple strategies of argumentation to make your own writing more persuasive. Consider this excerpt from Ian Bogost's discussion of advertising in his book *Persuasive Games*, in which he sets up a theoretical foundation that he will later use in his discussion of "persuasion games" (short interactive games designed to advertise a product). As you read this selection, look carefully for the strategies Bogost uses to support his analysis.

PERSUASIVE GAMES

Ian Bogost

There are three important types of advertising that can participate in such persuasion games: *demonstrative, illustrative,* and *associative* advertising.

Demonstrative advertising provides direct information. These ads communicate tangibles about the nature of a product. This type of advertising is closely related to the product as commodity; demonstrative ads focus on the functional utility of products and services. Among this category of advertisements, one might think of the "sponsor messages" of the golden age of television, ads that featured live demonstrations of detergent or "miracle" appliances. Also among this category are the copy-heavy print ads of the 1960s–1980s (examples abound in back issues of magazines like *National Geographic*), as well as modern-day television infomercials.

Ads like these focus on communicating the features and function of products or services. Consider [a] magazine ad for

Here Bogost uses **classification/division** to taxonomize different types of advertising: he takes a larger category (advertising) and breaks it into component parts.

Having established the different parts, he now moves to **definition**.

To clarify his definition of demonstrative advertising, Bogost gives a brief list of **examples.**

He follows up with a more detailed **example** that relies on more detailed **description** to help the reader understand his point.

As he moves to the second category of advertising that he has identified above, he once again leads with **definition** and follows up with **example** and **description.**

Notice the use of **comparison-contrast** here to promote dialogue between the different terms and help his reader better understand how each of these types of advertising works.

In the paragraph that follows in the original chapter, Bogost proceeds to use the same structure to explore the concept of associative advertising.

a Datsun hatchback [from the 1970s]. In the aftermath of the oil crisis of the 1970s, the ad foregrounds the car's focus on fuel economy, a tangible benefit, with the large headline "Nifty Fifty." Additional copy at the bottom of the ad further rationalizes and defends this position, citing a five-speed transmission with overdrive as a contributor to the car's increased fuel economy.

Illustrative advertising communicates indirect information. Illustrative ads can communicate both tangibles and intangibles about a product, with a focus on the marginal utility, or the incremental benefit of buying this product over another, or over not buying at all. These ads often contextualize a product or service differently than demonstrative ads, focusing more on social and cultural context. Consider another automobile ad, this one for a Saab sedan [...]. Unlike the Datsun ad, which depicts the vehicle in an empty space, the Saab ad places the car on a road and uses photographic panning to telegraph motion. No additional copy accompanies the ad, but the vehicle in motion serves to illustrate speed. The ad makes a case for the liveliness of the vehicle despite its "practical" four-door sedan frame, which is clearly visible in the center of the image.

2.2 What role do the rhetorical appeals of *pathos*, *logos*, and *ethos* play in persuasion?

UNDERSTANDING THE RHETORICAL APPEALS

The rhetorical strategies we've examined so far can be filtered through the lens of classical modes of persuasion dating back to 500 BCE. In writing about persuasion, Aristotle differentiated between **inartistic** and **artistic proofs.** He defined *inartistic proofs* as elements available to the writer but not created by the writer. Statistics, laws, quotations from others, facts: these all fall under the category of inartistic proofs. *Artistic proofs*, conversely, comprise arguments that the speaker constructs through rhetorical strategies. The strategies and structures of argumentation analyzed above are examples of artistic proofs; they might leverage facts or external evidence, but the arguments themselves are designed by the author. For the rest of this chapter, we'll continue to focus on artistic proofs and how you can learn to wield such strategies of argument effectively in composing your own persuasive texts.

From Aristotle's perspective, artistic proofs were derived from one of three rhetorical appeals: the formal terms are ***pathos***, ***logos***, and ***ethos***. You might recognize them more readily by how they work: *pathos* operates through developing an emotional connection with the audience; *logos* persuades through facts and reasoning; and *ethos* functions as an appeal to the authority or credibility of a person's character.

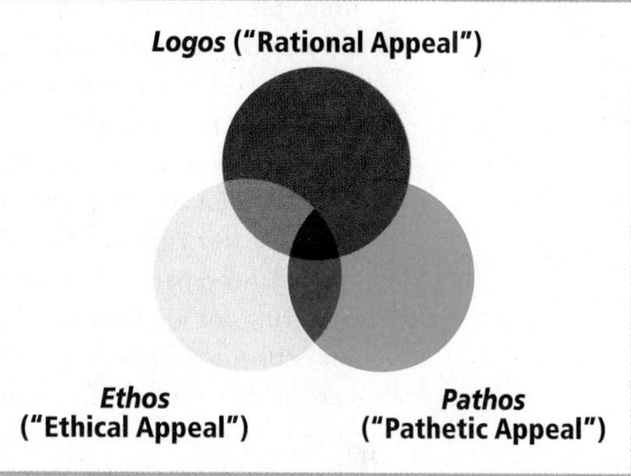

FIGURE 2.5 Rhetorical appeals as intersecting strategies of persuasion.

Since, as we discussed in Chapter 1, rhetoric involves careful and strategic assessment of the rhetorical situation in constructing persuasive arguments, let's look carefully at each of the appeals in turn to help you understand how you might use them in your own writing.

AT A GLANCE

Rhetorical Appeals

- ***Pathos***, or "the pathetic appeal," refers to an appeal to the emotions: the speaker attempts to put the audience into a particular emotional state so that they will be more receptive to the speaker's message. Inflammatory language, sad stories, appeals to nationalist sentiments, and jokes are all examples of *pathos*.
- ***Logos*** entails rational argument: it appeals to reason and persuades the audience through clear reasoning and evidence. Statistics, facts, definitions, and formal proofs, as well as interpretations such as syllogisms or deductively reasoned arguments, are all examples of "the logical appeal."
- ***Ethos*** is an appeal to authority or character; according to Aristotle, *ethos* means the character or goodwill of the speaker. Today we also consider the speaker's reliance on authority, credibility, or benevolence when discussing strategies of *ethos*. Although we call this third mode of persuasion the "ethical appeal," it does not strictly mean the use of ethics or ethical reasoning. Rather, *ethos* is the deliberate use of the speaker's character as a mode of persuasion.

Appeals to Emotion: *Pathos*

Roughly defined as "suffering" or "feeling" in its original Greek, the term *pathos* actually means to put the audience in a particular mood or frame of mind. Modern derivations of the word *pathos* include *pathology* and *pathetic,* and indeed we speak of *pathos* as "the pathetic appeal." But *pathos* is more a technique than a state: writers use it as a tool of persuasion to establish an intimate connection with the audience by soliciting powerful emotions.

We encounter ads that rely on *pathos* all the time, and, indeed, the composition of an ad often taps our emotions in ways that we barely recognize. Many use description or an analogy to set the mood, such as displaying an idyllic landscape scene to serve as the backdrop for a commercial for engagement rings or retirement funds or choosing a color scheme (bright primary colors or muted pastels) to create a specific effect. The music in the commercials, whether on television or radio, also produces a *pathos* effect on the audience, from the catchy, up-beat jingles that create a positive association with a product to well-known songs that are repurposed to appeal to a particular generation, demographic, or type of consumer. For instance, when Hyundai filmed a commercial for its Sonata model car using Mozart's playful Piano Sonata #11 as the score, their message was clear: this car is sophisticated, classic, and yet still embodies a sense of lively fun.

Even more blatant examples of *pathos* in advertising abound: from an Iams dog food commercial showing an Irish Wolfhound exuberantly greeting his owner just home from a military tour abroad; to a Subaru commercial where a mother looks into her car and sees not her teenager, but a 5-year-old version of her, getting ready to drive off in the car by herself for the first time; to the previously mentioned Budweiser "Brotherhood" example (Figure 2.2), where a man is reunited with a horse he had sold. In each case, the advertisement relies on creating an emotionally laden narrative to sell its product. The power of such stories is perhaps no better used than in commercials that sell life insurance or property insurance. The formulaic, yet powerful template for these types of *pathos*-infused ads are no doubt familiar to you: show images of devastated homes and families, especially small children; lead the audience step by step through the story of destruction or death; offer up the product (insurance) as a way to mitigate the depicted tragedy.

However, *pathos* does not only operate through triggering the highs and lows of sentiment in audiences. Sometimes the *pathos* appeal is more subtle, operating by evoking deep feelings such as patriotism, indignation, even hope or fantasy. Consider the Porsche commercial showing a sleek red car speeding along a windy mountain road, the Jeep "beautiful lands" commercial that shows the Renegade crisscrossing breath-taking landscapes in the United States and abroad, or the Fiat ad playing on the car's unique, quirky design. Each of these ads uses *pathos* to produce a specific feeling in viewers: I want to drive fast, wind in my hair; I want to explore and see the world; I want to stand out in a crowd and have fun.

You are probably even more familiar with another type of *pathos* appeal—the appeal to sexuality. Clearly, sex sells. Look at Victoria's Secret models who posed in near nudity or at Abercrombie & Fitch or Hollister poster displays featuring models more likely to show off their toned abs than a pair of jeans, and you can see how advertisers tend to appeal more to nonrational impulses than to our powers of reasoning. Perfume and cologne advertisers in particular often use the rhetoric of sexuality to sell their products, whether it be Calvin Klein's Eternity Aqua, Ralph Lauren's Polo Black, or even Axe's cologne commercials, which demonstrate the "Axe effect" by showing cologne-wearers being mobbed by bikini-clad women. Such ads work cleverly to sell fragrance, not on the merits of the scent or on its chemical composition, but through the visual rhetoric of sexuality and our emotional responses to it.

Yet there is an even more powerful *pathos* appeal: what some students refer to as *humos*. Humor remains one of the most effective forms of persuasion; against our more rational impulses, the ads that make us laugh are usually the ones we remember. To prove this point, you need only think back to last year's Superbowl ads: Which ads do you remember? Which ads did you talk over with your friends during and after the game? Probably most of the ones you recall relied on humor. In fact, some of the most memorable—and at times controversial ads—combine a *pathos* appeal to sexuality with humor. Case and point? Carl's Juniors long-lasting ad campaign showing a scantily clad woman messily eating a burger. The arguments such ads make may not always be the most logically sound, but the way they foster a connection with the audience makes them persuasive nonetheless.

Many of these same *pathos*-based strategies can be used in academic writing to foster a connection with your audience. You might use the **first-person perspective** to invite your readers into your point of view or, in some cases, use **second-person direct address** to speak to them directly. You might include vivid **description, narration,** or **example** to draw them in, supplemented with careful attention to powerful **word choice** and **figurative language** (such as using metaphor, analogy, or personification). Depending on your rhetorical situation and purpose, you might even experiment with **tone** and **humor** as a way to get your readers to engage with your argument.

Consider, for instance, the way in which pop culture critic Doug Barry increases the persuasiveness of his analysis by using *pathos* to connect with his audience in his analysis of a Tide laundry detergent commercial below:

> Ah, the American father—that beer-guzzling, football-watching, hamburger-grilling lump of a human who so often prostrates himself on the family couch before his stupefied children like a sedated gorilla has been soundly mocked as a hapless oaf since, well, General Yepanchin in *The Idiot*. Then, of course, there's *every sitcom father ever,* even lumpy dinosaur Earl Sinclair, whose mere presence in the sitcom-dad pantheon suggests that working and middle class fathers have been supreme idiots since human fathers even existed.
>
> It's refreshing, then, to see a dad not play the dumb-dad clown every now and then. When Stereotypical American Clown Father appears in a commercial for some housekeeping chemical, it's usually to demonstrate his utter incompetence (dads don't clean, silly! they spill rib juice all over the couch as they slip into a meat stupor over the course of a lazy Sunday afternoon) and promptly exit stage right, a freshly chastised goon. A (relatively) new Tide commercial, however, doesn't rely on goon-father to hawk its detergent—Tide Dad is just a normal parent having a blast playing-pretend with his daughter. And what do they play in this blissful domestic imaginarium? Everything from fairy tale princess to wild west sheriff (hint: dad has to stay in a jail made of chairs until his power-drunk daughter decides to free him).

Many authors use narrative as a *pathos* device since readers tend to react powerfully to storytelling; however, here we see Barry relying on alternative methods to produce a similar effect. He uses rich imagery and word choice to paint an engaging description of the American father's typical pop culture incarnation: notice how he employs unusual and catchy modifiers ("beer-guzzling," "football-watching," "hamburger-grilling"); how he integrates striking imagery ("sedated gorilla," "hapless oaf," "dumb-dad clown"); how his allusions anchor his description in other cultural texts (General Yepanchin, Earl Sinclair). Even his strategies of emphasis—from italics for highlighting a point to rhetorical questions and his comical parenthetical asides—foster his connection with the reader by capturing his voice vividly. In its original online version, Barry's analysis was accompanied by a link to the commercial itself, which offered yet another mode of engaging the audience on an emotional level. In your own writing, you might similarly use *pathos*-driven language and images to solidify your argument and persuade your reader.

Exaggerated Uses of Pathos. Although writers often use pathos to move their audiences, sometimes they exaggerate the appeal to emotion for dramatic effect. While the intention might be to enhance persuasion, this misuse of pathos can significantly undermine an argument's effectiveness. Let's look at some of the most typical emotional fallacies:

- **Scare tactic:** In this case, *pathos* capitalizes on the audience's fears, sometimes unreasonably, to make a point. For instance, Allstate Insurance's recent Mayhem commercials—with actor Dean Winter personifying different types of "mayhem" (from heavy snow that collapses your garage roof, to a screaming toddler in the backseat, to a raccoon in your attic)—employ this sort of tactic to prompt viewers to update their insurance coverage.
- **Slippery slope:** This variation of the *scare tactic* suggests that one act will lead to a chain of events that results in an unforeseen, inevitable, and (usually) undesirable conclusion, without providing any evidence to support the claim. An AT&T smartphone commercial put a positive spin on this fallacy, demonstrating how the simple act of being able to check a train schedule on his smartphone led a man to meet his future wife, and then experience a series of positive life events that culminated in his son becoming the president of the United States.

- **Oversentimentalization:** The overabundant use of *pathos* can outweigh a focus on relevant issues. Occasionally, for instance, organizations like PETA overreach in their emotional appeals, showing the results of animal abuse in such graphic detail that audiences actually tune out in horror rather than take action.
- **Bandwagon appeal:** Sometimes called the *ad populum* argument, this emotional fallacy hinges on the premise that since everyone else is doing something, you should too. Pepsi's campaign "The Choice of a New Generation" used the bandwagon appeal to argue that if you wanted to be identified with part of the new, hip generation, you needed to drink Pepsi.
- **False need:** In this fallacy, the author amplifies a perceived need or creates a completely new one. Companies market their products based on false needs all the time: think of the commercials you've seen advertising men's or women's razors, transparent Band-Aids, cinch-tie garbage bags, "smart" water, or lash-curling mascara. How many of those products reflect actual *needs*, and how many rely on a false need that has been constructed by the company or advertiser?

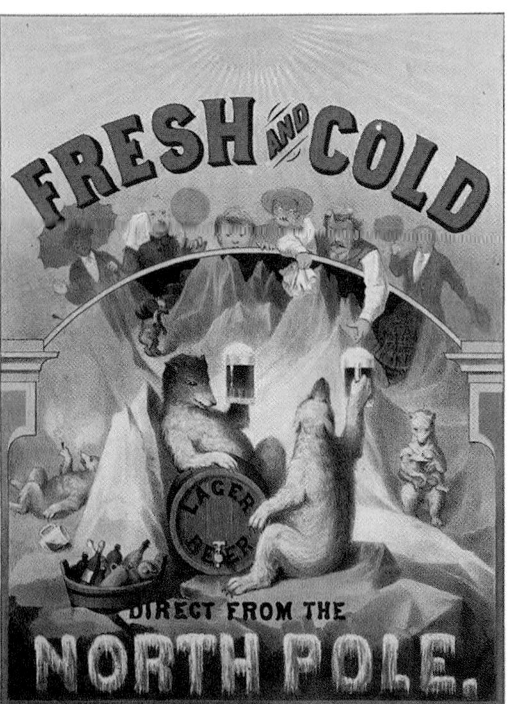

WRITER'S PRACTICE MyWritingLab

Consider how the nineteenth-century advertisement in the figure uses *pathos* to make its argument. What is its main pitch about why the consumer should buy Lager Beer, and how does it back that up with visually and textually? What other strategies of argumentation do you see it at work in the ad? Write down some notes and compare your analysis with a partner's. For added challenge, compare this marketing strategy to that currently used by twenty-first beer and soft drink companies to sell their products. What similarities and differences do you see?

Appeals to Reason: *Logos*

Although some call *logos* the "logical appeal," it pertains to more than just formal logic. While *pathos* moves an audience on a nonrational level, *logos* engages our critical reasoning faculties to make a point. As a writer, you use *logos* when you construct an essay around facts and reason. That is, you provide both a solid line of reasoning as well as evidence to support it.

A *logos*-based argument can take many forms. You might use:

- **Inductive reasoning,** a line of argument that moves from specific examples to a generalized conclusion. For instance, if you reflect on all the times that you pulled all-nighters and ended up falling asleep in your afternoon classes, you might inductively reason that pulling all-nighters have a negative effect on your grade (generalized conclusion). In an inductive essay, you might open with a question or general statement, then move through specific examples to arrive at a statement of your argument in your conclusion; alternately, you might closely examine a particular case study and specific example and then draw a broader, more general conclusion from it.
- **Deductive reasoning,** a form of logic that bases argument on how premises (often unstated assumptions) work together to prove the argument. The idea behind deductive reasoning is that if the premises are accepted as true, then the argument must be true. For instance:

  Premise 1: A college degree helps students find a fulfilling career.

  Premise 2: Everyone wants a fulfilling career.

  Argument from premises: University students, by virtue of being enrolled in college, do so to position themselves to have a fulfilling career.

  In essays, this form of argument often means you lead with a strong thesis statement, which you then support with examples to arrive at a conclusion.
- **A cause-and-effect strategy of development** that demonstrates logically how one idea, event, or element caused another. As we've discussed earlier in this chapter, the logic of causality can be a strong support for an argument.
- **A reliance on example** to support claims. By providing evidence—whether in the form of statistical evidence, empirical

data, proven facts, testimony, or quotations from authorities or experts—you can demonstrate that abstract concepts and generalizations have a grounding in concrete example. For instance, while the statement "Companies rely too heavily on ethnic stereotype in their marketing campaigns" might seem an interesting claim, it becomes much more persuasive when supported by examples from recent commercials that illustrate this point.

Let's build on this last example and get look more carefully at how *logos* works by turning our attention once again to advertising. In that medium, the mode of persuasion we call *logos* often operates through the written text; significantly, the Greek word *logos* can be translated as "word," indicating the way in which we, culturally, often look to words as repositories of fact and reason. However, in advertising, just as in academic writing, *logos* also emerges through the use of quantifiable data, statistics, and facts. The type of *logos*-based reasoning found in the Chevrolet Volt marketing display in Figure 2.6 appears in many ads that you may also be familiar with: think, for instance, of a computer ad that juxtaposes a striking photo of a laptop

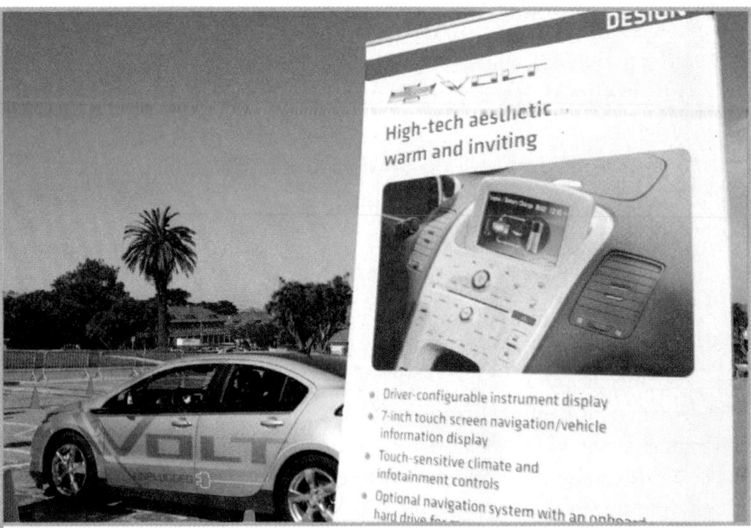

FIGURE 2.6 This Chevrolet Volt promotional display is designed to persuade its reader through *logos* by listing the car's various features.

with a chart detailing its processor type, memory capacity, screen size, and graphics features; a commercial for a bank that features a smiling agent listing the reasons to open a checking account at that branch; the smartphone commercial that rattles off facts about its data plan, wireless coverage, and contracts terms. In each case, the advertisement drives its point through facts, evidence, and reason.

Some might even argue that *logos* as an appeal underlies almost all advertising, specifically because most advertising uses an implicit *causal argument:* if you buy this product, then you or your life will be like the one featured in the ad. Often the associations are explicit: if you use Pantene shampoo, then your hair will be shinier; if you buy Tide detergent, then your clothes will be cleaner; if you buy a Subaru, then your family will be safer driving on the road. Sometimes the *cause-and-effect* argument is more subtle: buying Sure deodorant will make you more confident; drinking Coke will make you happier; wearing Nikes will make you perform better on the court. In each case, *logos*, or the use of logical reasoning, is the tool of persuasion responsible for the ad's argumentative force.

In academic situations, writers often privilege a *logos*-based approach to persuasion because many scholarly claims draw on evidence from research to substantiate assertions. Consider the way Laurence Bowen and Jill Schmid use *logos* as a strategy of argumentation in this passage from "Minority Presence and Portrayal in Mainstream Magazine Advertising: An Update":

> Some might argue that the small number of minorities featured in mainstream magazine advertising may be due to a very deliberate media strategy that successfully targets minorities in specialized and minority media. However, each of the magazines analyzed does have a minority readership and, in some cases, that readership is quite substantial. For example, according to *Simmons 1993 Study of Media and Markets*, the Hispanic readership of *Life* is 9.9%, yet the inclusion of Hispanics in *Life's* advertisements was only .8%. *Cosmopolitan* has a 11.3% Black readership, yet only 4.3% of the advertisements included Blacks; 13.3% of the magazines' readership is Hispanic and only .5% of the advertisements use Hispanics.

Notice how the authors drive their point home through reference to their research with mainstream magazines as well as to statistical data that they have both uncovered and analyzed. Their use of such concrete information and examples makes their argument much more convincing than had they provided a more general rebuttal to the statement that begins their paragraph. In this way, appeals to logic can take on many forms, including interpretations of "hard evidence," such as found in syllogisms (formal, structured arguments), reasoned arguments, closing statements in law, inferences in the form of statistical models, and appeals to "common sense" or cultural assumptions.

Logical Fallacies. As with *pathos, logos* can be susceptible to misuse. Such mistaken or misleading uses of *logos*, commonly called **logical fallacies,** often involve faulty reasoning that undermines the validity of an argument.

- **Post hoc ergo propter hoc fallacy:** This fallacy confuses *cause* and *effect*, namely, the idea that because something happened first (showering with an aloe-enhanced body gel), it causes something that happened afterward (getting a person you like to ask you out on a date).
- **Cum hoc ergo propter hoc fallacy:** A variation of the *post hoc fallacy*, this type of argument is often called a *correlation-causation fallacy* because it suggests that since two unrelated events happen at the same time (are correlated), they should thus be interpreted as *cause* and *effect*. For instance, the following syllogism is an example of a *cum hoc fallacy*: (1) a teenager plays his varsity basketball game wearing his new Air Jordans; (2) the teenager makes many key rebounds and jump shots while playing the game; (3) the Air Jordans caused his success in the game.
- **The hasty generalization:** Writers who use *hasty generalizations* draw conclusions too quickly without providing enough supporting evidence or considering all the nuances of the issue. A comic example of this type of argument can be found in a commercial for the Taco Bell bacon club chalupa taco: a young woman confides to her friend that she's carrying a chalupa tucked in her purse because "guys love bacon," a generalization the ad attempts to substantiate by showing her, moments later, surrounded by men who had been drawn to the woman by the "intoxicating" smell.
- **The either-or argument:** This fallacy involves the oversimplification of a complicated issue, reducing it to a choice between two diametrically opposed choices that ignore other possible scenarios. We see this fallacy often in commercials that compare a pair of competing products (iPhone versus Android, McDonalds versus Burger King, Verizon versus AT&T) without taking into consideration the other alternatives available to the consumer.

- **Stacking the evidence:** An argument that *stacks the evidence* presents only one side of an issue. Political candidates frequently use this strategy in their campaign ads by stating facts and data that support only their policy platform, without presenting an issue in its full complexity.
- **Begging the question:** This form of circular logic uses an argument as evidence for itself, thereby evading the issue at hand. For instance, consider the conversation between a mother and her six year old daughter in a commercial for the Wannabee-Mommy doll:

  Mother: So I guess it's that time again – time to start your birthday list. What do you want for your birthday?

  Daughter: The Wannabee-Mommy doll, of course! I don't need anything else.

  Woman: Really? That's it? That's all you want?

  Daughter: Yup. Everyone wants the Wannabee-Mommy doll. Jessica want it. Kirsten wants it. Maria wants it …

  Woman: [interrupting] Really? Why does everyone want the doll so badly?

  Daughter: Mommy, don't you know anything? Because it's the most popular doll of the year!

  In this quick exchange, the daughter "begs the question" by using the fact that the doll was popular (i.e. many children want it) to argue for why so many children want it. The commercial could have avoided this fallacy simply by changing its line of reasoning, linking the toy's popularity to its design, quality, marketing or even its price.
- **The red herring or non sequitor:** Some arguments employ unrelated information or a *non sequitor* (in Latin, literally meaning "does not follow") in order to distract the audience's attention from the issue at hand. A sudden shift of topic or focus in an ad can function as a *red herring*. Dow Chemical's ad "The Human Element" shows a plethora of artistic and ecofriendly scenes that make the logical argument that the company relates to human connection and nature, but in fact serve as a red herring to distract the viewer from Dow's massive industrial production of oil, gas, and electronic products.
- **Straw man argument:** The visual metaphor of the *straw man* effectively represents this fallacy; the writer sets up a fake or distorted representation of a counterargument so as to have something to easily argue against and to present the writer's own position in a more favorable light. Here's one example: during the 2012 presidential

campaign, vice presidential candidate Paul Ryan accused President Obama of using *straw man* tactics, citing the way the president characterized Republicans as anti-government and pessimistic about the country in his speeches. According to Ryan, in doing so, Obama was misrepresenting the opposing party's stance so as to ingratiate himself with the American people.

- **Equivocation:** Arguments that fall prey to this fallacy use ambiguous terminology that misleads the audience or confuses the issue. For instance, a 2008 commercial for California's Proposition 8 undermined its argument for marriage equality by using the term "rights" indiscriminately to refer to both legal rights and moral rights.
- **False analogy:** While an *analogy* can be a powerful strategy of argumentation, a *false analogy* claims that two things resemble each other when they actually do not. For instance, one Mercedes-Benz commercial suggested that refraining from eating ice cream is like refraining from buying one of their cars, when in fact there is very little connection between the two actions.

WRITER'S PRACTICE

MyWritingLab

Look carefully at the hypothetical advertising pitches below, each one of which represents a flawed use of *logos* as a marketing strategy. For each one, identify which type of logical fallacy it contains: *post hoc ergo propter hoc, cum hoc ergo propter hoc*, hasty generalization, either/or, stacking the evidence, begging the question, red herring, straw man, equivocation, or false analogy. Then, consider ways in which the pitch might be revised so as to make a more solid *logos*-based argument.

- Buy American because our products are made right here in the United States!
- In these increasingly complex financial times, if you try to manage your finances without a trained professional advisor, you could well find your life savings wiped out. Protect your savings: contact your local GoodCents agent today for a full portfolio review.
- Corey uses Sparkle Fresh mouthwash every morning and recently received a promotion at work. If you start using Sparkle Fresh, your career will take off too!
- Other paper towel companies don't care about global warming or climate change. Use Greener World paper towels: there's always 100% recycled paper on every roll.

- Buying the right car is like choosing the right spouse: you need to find one perfect for you. So choose a What-a-Catch-Car: it's dependable, affordable, and built to last.

For added challenge: find your own examples of writing that display logical fallacies; identify the fallacy and consider how to revise it in a way that eliminates the problematic use of *logos*.

Appeals to Character and Authority: *Ethos*

The last of the three classical appeals that we'll learn in this chapter is *ethos*—literally, "character." Perhaps you have used *ethos* in other disciplines to mean an argument based on ethical principles. But the *rhetorical* meaning of the term is slightly different: according to Aristotle, *ethos* works as a rhetorical strategy by establishing the goodwill or credibility of the writer or speaker. Based on the Aristotelian model, we can distinguish between three different operations of *ethos*:

1. *Ethos* based on practical skills and wisdom
2. *Ethos* based on virtue and goodness
3. *Ethos* based on goodwill toward the audience

When conceived in this way, the *ethos* appeal clearly functions as a very powerful persuasive tool by establishing a bond of trust with the audience. In fact, almost more than with any other appeal, *ethos* involves a critical awareness of audience. It is the audience who evaluates your "good character" or credibility as a writer and, therefore, the persuasiveness of your argument.

Another way to understand *ethos* is to think about it in terms of two different types: *situated ethos* and *invented ethos*. The first form refers to the credibility you possess because of your expertise (i.e., how you are *situated*) in a field; it is an authority you bring to your argument because of your own experience. For instance, when Nike signed Michael Jordan as a spokesperson for their basketball shoes, they were counting on his fame as an NBA player to sell their product; likewise, Gatorade traded on Jordan's career as an athlete to argue that he knew a good sports drink when he drank one.

Invented ethos, conversely, refers to the authority you create for yourself through rhetorical strategies rather than through situated expertise.

Namely, it is the way that an author or speaker persuades the audience of his trustworthiness on a subject that seems unrelated to his area of expertise. Advertising occasionally trades on the *invented ethos* of a spokesperson rather than expertise: when we are persuaded by the Geico's talking gecko lizard to consider buying insurance from the company, for instance, it is not because we recognize the lizard as an authority on car insurance; it is because his monologue in the commercial develops his likeability, his sincerity, and clear goodwill toward the audience.

As a writer, you rely on the *ethos* appeal at the most basic level every time you pick up a pen, open a blank document on your laptop, or proofread your essay—that is, you construct your *ethos* through your word choice, your tone, your grammar, your punctuation, and the way your present your argument. However, as our discussion above suggests, you can establish *ethos* in other ways as well. By establishing your authority in relation to the topic—whether because of your depth of knowledge or your close engagement with the subject—you help your readers trust your claims. By constructing a sense of **common ground** with your audience, you can invoke shared values to draw more of a connection with your audience. By using **credible sources** in your research, you attest to the quality of your argument and analytic methodology. Likewise, by respectfully acknowledging **other arguments**, you establish yourself as fair-minded and well-informed on your topic; whether you ultimately concede a point or refute the counterargument, your willingness to entertain alternative positions increases your *ethos*. Consider one more characteristic of *ethos*: while your *situated ethos* rarely changes, your *invented ethos* can fluctuate and shift depending on how effectively you construct your sense of credibility in your text.

The example that follows demonstrates how one writer uses *ethos* to set up the foundations for a complex argument. In this excerpt from her famous piece, "Sex, Lies, and Advertising," Gloria Steinem, founding editor of the feminist magazine *Ms.*, deliberately builds her *ethos* through an opening narrative. Her decision is strategic: she anticipates that the issue itself—the constraints that advertisers put on the content of women's magazines—might produce a skeptical reaction from her readers. Accordingly, she devotes her opening paragraphs to establishing both the validity of the problem and her own qualifications in terms of addressing it.

About three years ago, as *glasnost* was beginning and *Ms.* seemed to be ending, I was invited to a press lunch for a Soviet official. He entertained us with anecdotes about new problems of democracy in his country. Local Communist leaders were being criticized in their media for the first time, he explained, and they were angry.

To build her *ethos*, Steinem first mentions that she was invited to a lunch with a political figure, indicating her importance in journalistic circles.

"So I'll have to ask my American friends," he finished pointedly, "how more subtly to control the press." In the silence that followed, I said, "Advertising."

The reporters laughed, but later, one of them took me aside: How dare I suggest that freedom of the press was limited? How dare I imply that his newsweekly could be influenced by ads?

Next, after humorously introducing her main argument (that freedom of the press is curtailed by advertising), she demonstrates how she gracefully addresses counterarguments.

I explained that I was thinking of advertising's media-wide influence on most of what we read. Even newsmagazines use "soft" cover stories to sell ads, confuse readers with "advertorials," and occasionally self-censor on subjects known to be a problem with big advertisers.

But I also explained, I was thinking especially of women's magazines. There, it isn't just a little content that's devoted to attracting ads, it's almost all of it. That's why advertisers—not readers—have always been the problem for *Ms.* As the only women's magazine that didn't supply what the ad world euphemistically describes as "supportive editorial atmosphere" or "complementary copy" (for instance, articles that praise food/fashion/beauty subjects to "support" and "complement" food/fashion/beauty ads), *Ms.* could never attract enough advertising to break even.

Then, she utilizes the discourse of magazine publishing ("supportive editorial atmosphere" and "complementary copy") to remind her audience of her insider status in the industry.

"Oh, *women's* magazines," the journalist said with contempt. "Everybody knows they're catalogs—but who cares? They have nothing to do with journalism."

I can't tell you how many times I've had this argument in 25 years of working for many kinds of publications. Except as moneymaking machines—"cash cows" as they are so elegantly called in the trade—women's magazines are rarely taken seriously. Though changes being made by women have been called more far-reaching than the industrial revolution—and though many editors try hard to reflect some of them in the few pages left

Lastly, she informs the reader directly about her long professional history working in media ("... in 25 years of working for many kinds of publications"). In this move, she situates her *ethos* not only in the current moment of her opening narrative but also in her continued involvement in the publishing field.

to them after all the ad-related subjects have been covered—the magazines serving the female half of the country are still far below the journalistic and ethical strands of news and general interest publications. Most depressing of all, this doesn't even rate an exposé.

Having established her *ethos* in this opening section, Steinem can then move forward with her argument, which is driven largely by an accumulation of examples designed to further underscore her expertise and authority. Thus, *ethos* is a driving force in the persuasiveness of her writing.

To continue our exploration of the complexities of *ethos*, let's look to advertising once again and see how companies have long recognized the persuasive power of *ethos*. In fact, a brand logo is in essence *ethos* distilled into a single symbol: it transmits in a single icon the entire reputation of a company, organization, or brand identity. From the Nike swoosh to McDonald's golden arches or the Apple computer apple, symbols serve to mark (or brand) products with *ethos*. When Apple began construction on a new store in Madrid, for example, the iconic Apple logo itself was all the marketing it needed to publicize its new store (see Figure 2.7).

FIGURE 2.7 Apple used its logo on a billboard surrounding its construction site to advertise a new store in Madrid.

Yet the power of the brand logo as a seat of *ethos* relies on the company's overall reputation with the consumer—a reputation that the company carefully cultivates through advertising campaigns. Many companies, for instance, trade on *ethos* by using spokespeople in their advertising campaigns. You've probably seen ads that invoke the practical skills or knowledge (*situated ethos*) of the celebrity to sell a product: basketball superstar LeBron James selling basketball shoes or Martha Stewart selling linens, towels, and dishware. Sometimes companies even rely on this strategy when using a less famous spokesperson; for instance, we trust Flo from the Progressive commercials because of her clear, empathetic personality (*invented ethos)* and the expertise and information she shares during their commercials (*situated ethos*).

However, many campaigns rely not only on the spokesperson's expertise, but also on the person's star appeal, character, and virtue. Consider the power of the billboard shown in Figure 2.8. On display during the summer of 2012, this billboard used gold-medalist Cullen Jones's fame to vouch for Citibank's reputation and quality of services. We might not believe that

FIGURE 2.8 A Citibank billboard in New York City leverages Olympian Cullen Jones's *ethos* to draw in new customers.

Jones knows much about banking, but we trust him as a recognizable and admirable public figure. We find his argument persuasive because of our "knowledge" of his character and his willingness to put his reputation on the line to promote a product. Of course, ad campaigns based on celebrity endorsements—specifically those based on Aristotle's categories of virtue and goodness—can backfire. Lance Armstrong's 2012 confession about his steroid use left advertisers from Nike to Giro and Radioshack scrambling to distance themselves from their endorsement deals with the world-class cyclist.

Clearly, *ethos* matters to companies because so much of their business relies on their reputation. For this reason, we often come across ads that market not a product but a corporate *ethos* intended to establish that company's credibility. One recurrent example of this appears in various oil company ads that have emerged over the last few years. Battling the perception that Big Oil, heedless of its role in global warming, is motivated only by ever-increasing profits, these ads inform us endlessly of each company's "green" policies and efforts to give back to the earth. In addition, *ethos* can be used as a tool in attack ads. Often, companies deliberately attempt to undermine the *ethos* of their competition as a way of promoting their own products. You probably have seen ads of this sort, perhaps a DIRECTV ad that criticized cable providers or a Pepsi commercial that suggested their beverage was more refreshing than Coke. You might have even seen one of the Samsung smartphone commercials that targeted Apple—whether spots that mocked iPhone users standing in endless lines for the newest product release or commercials that demonstrated how the Samsung features easily trumped the capabilities of its Apple-brand competitor. In each case, the deliberate *comparison-contrast* builds up one company's *ethos* at another's expense.

Misuses of Ethos. Since *ethos* derives from credibility or trustworthiness, misuses of *ethos* tend to involve a breach of trust between the author and the audience. For this reason, you should take special care as a writer not to abuse this ethical contract with your reader. What follows are some of the most common misuses of *ethos*:

- ***Ad hominem***: This strategy attempts to persuade by reducing the credibility of opposing positions through attacks on a person's character. Rather than focus on the argument itself, *ad hominem* criticizes the speaker or writer who makes the argument. We see *ad hominem* at work most often in political campaign advertisements, where candidates focus less on the issues at hand and instead emphasize their opponents' weaknesses. This misuse of *ethos* also happens in commercials where companies attack each other for the way they run their businesses rather than the quality of their products.

- ***Argument from authority***: This type of argument involves a misrepresentation of skills and wisdom; the writer contends to be an authority—or holds another up to be an authority—based on an overinflated or fallacious suggestion of expertise. For instance, Oprah Winfrey came under fire in 2012 for tweeting an endorsement for the Windows Surface from her iPad; her credibility as a Surface user was immediately called into question.
- ***Association fallacies***: This fallacy often takes the form of "guilt by association," where an argument is dismissed because it is associated with an undesirable person or position. Conversely, this fallacy can also unfairly promote or advocate an argument based on unrelated positive associations. We can find prominent examples of this technique at work in the political advertising during the 2008 presidential campaign: both Barack Obama and John McCain released commercials that used *guilt by association* to denigrate each other's characters.
- ***Appeal to anonymous authority***: This type of argument references broad, unspecified groups as its authority. For instance, while the taglines "Four out of five dentists surveyed ..." or "Studies indicate ..." lend some credibility to advertising campaigns, unless the ads provide tangible references to *which* dentists, *which* studies, and *what* context, the argument is ultimately empty and unsupported.
- ***Authority over evidence***: This mode of argument involves the practice of overemphasizing authority or *ethos* rather than focusing on the merits of the evidence itself. Celebrity endorsements based on goodwill can verge on this fallacy.

WRITER'S PRACTICE MyWritingLab

Review the different fallacies and misuses of appeals and then, alone or with a group, draft your own advertisement or commercial that clearly hinges on a particular fallacy of argument. Look ahead to Chapter 6 and Chapter 8 for strategies for developing your visual argument, whether as a storyboard for a commercial (Chapter 6) or a mock-up of an ad (Chapter 8). Write a cover memo for your draft in which you define the fallacy that you're illustrating and provide a brief analysis to underscore your point for your readers.

Combining the Rhetorical Appeals

As we've seen, the rhetorical appeals provide writers with powerful modes of persuading their audience. However, while each appeal functions as an effective mode of persuasion alone, in most cases, successful writers and communicators use them in combination, depending on their understanding of the rhetorical situation. As you might imagine, a text may employ a combined mode of persuasion, such as "passionate logic" (a rational argument written with highly charged prose), "good-willed *pathos*" (an emotional statement that relies on the character of the speaker to be believed), or "logical *ethos*" (a strong line of reasoning employed by a speaker to build authority). Since they appear so frequently in combination, you might find that conceptualizing *pathos*, *logos*, and *ethos* through a visual representation helps you to conceptualize how they relate to one another (see Figure 2.5).

To better understand how this works, let's look at Derek Thompson's analysis of brand advertising, originally published in *The Atlantic*. As you read, consider not only how he examines the *ethos* of branding, but the way in which he draws on the rhetorical appeals and various strategies of development in his own writing.

TURNING CUSTOMERS INTO CULTISTS

Why many companies now take their cues from cults.

Derek Thompson

The very first sentence relies on a *pathos* appeal by using **description** to capture the reader's interest.

In the third week of September, thousands of people organized themselves into neat lines that snaked along the city blocks of New York, Seattle, London, and dozens of other cities around the world. Sleeping in cardboard boxes, or keeping wakeful vigil through the night, they were participants in a biennial ritual: waiting in line to buy the new iPhone. Like most quasi-religious ceremonies, this one made little sense to outside observers. But the iPhone isn't just another phone, and Apple isn't just another phone manufacturer. It's a brand with a cult following, whose new products inspire sane people to squat for hours outside the nearest Apple store like Wiccans worshipping before Stonehenge.

Thompson continues to build on *pathos* as he gently develops the **analogy** suggested by his title with words like "ritual," "quasi-religious" and "ceremonies" and by describing Apple customers as "Wiccans worshipping before Stonehenge."

What is a brand, anyway? The word seems gaseous in its ability to expand or contract to fill any space. Is it a promise, a lie, a reputation, or just a TED Talk buzzword? To companies and consumers, it can be any of those things, but to economists, the definition is simple: a brand is a signal, good or bad, that influences a consumer's decision to buy a product. And according to some economists, this signal is now in danger of being drowned out by the sheer amount of competing information on the Internet.

Thompson devotes his second paragraph to **definition** to lay a foundation for his analysis of contemporary brand marketing.

Research shows that typically, the more information consumers have, the better they are at ignoring corporate iconography. One 2014 study, for instance, found that pharmacists and physicians are three times less likely than the typical customer to buy national brands of headache medicine when cheaper store brands are available. If all consumers became as informed as medical experts, the study concluded, national headache-remedy brands would see their sales cut in half.

He now amplifies the *ethos* of his argument by including an **example** from a 2014 study and, in the next paragraph, a reference to the work of a Stanford professor.

An economy filled with product experts would wreck certain brands, according to Itamar Simonson, a marketing professor at Stanford. Advertising thrives in markets where consumers are essentially clueless, often because quality is hard to assess before you buy the product (medicine, mattresses, wine). But on sites like Amazon or eBay, and across social media, information from other sources—ratings, reviews, comments from friends—is abundant. We're more likely to trust these signals precisely because they aren't beamed from corporate headquarters.

By **contrasting** sites like eBay and Amazon to "markets where consumers are essentially clueless," Thompson strengthens his point.

The market for high-definition TVs shows how too much access to information can destroy the brand premium. A TV's two most salient features—its screen size and resolution—are easy to look up, which makes it difficult for companies to charge extra for

In the this paragraph, he uses *logos*, presenting evidence to support the claim from the previous paragraph through a specific **example**, facts and statistics.

a logo. Making televisions is a notoriously low-margin business, and the price of TVs has declined 95 percent since 1994. Sony's TV unit had been in the red for 10 years when the company spun it of in July.

Once again, Thompson uses vivid word choice ("Homo economicus super-shoppers") as part of a *pathos* appeal. He also, again, grounds his general statements ("Sites … provide an exhaustive array of choices") in a specific **example** ("like Amazon") to make a connection with the reader's own experience—a technique he uses continuously through his essay.

And yet Apple, among many other brands, still means a great deal to a great many people. There are at least two reasons to question the notion that we're evolving into a race of Homo economicus super-shoppers, or ever will. First, even with perfect information, consumers often make imperfect decisions. Sites like Amazon provide an exhaustive array of choices, but having too many options can make us feel both overwhelmed as we shop (the "paradox of choice") and less satisfied with the choices we make (buyer's remorse). Returning to an old brand is a mental shortcut that is not only simple but also, in its own way, blissful.

Here again, Thompson incorporates the voice of an authority to boost the *ethos* of his argument.

More important, in categories like cars or clothes, brands aren't just signals of quality; they also help us communicate our identities. When somebody totes a Fendi bag or drives a Harley-Davidson chopper, she is sending a message (particularly when doing both at the same time). "People are meaning-seeking creatures," says Susan Fournier, a professor of management at Boston University. "The brands we buy and wear and use are symbols to express our identities. I don't think any of that is diluted by the Internet."

At this point, he finally returns to the central analogy that informs his argument: the connection between modern branding and religious cults.

As branding loses some of its influence as a marker of quality, savvy companies are shifting their marketing efforts ever more strongly to this other source of brand advantage—identity and community. Recently, many of the most successful new brands have been looking to an unusual but powerful source of inspiration: religious cults.

He turns again to **example**, focusing on a 1984 academic study to lend authority to his developing argument. In this paragraph and the ones that follow, he continues to build *ethos* by showcasing the research he has done on the cult phenomenon, sometimes incorporating direct quotations.

In 1984, the British sociologist Eileen Barker published *The Making of a Moonie,* a seven-year investigation of the Unification Church, based on interviews with members of one of America's most popular cults. While many cults are portrayed as preying on the poor and uneducated, and particularly people from broken homes, Barker discovered that Moonies tended to be middle-class, with college degrees and stable families. The cult inculcated new members through simple techniques: weekend retreats, deep conversations, shared meals, and, most seductive, an environment of love and support.

Cults like the Moonies are built on the paradox that we feel most like ourselves when we're part of a group, says Douglas Atkin, the global head of community at the room-sharing company Airbnb, and the author of the 2004 book *The Culting of Brands*. "The common belief is that people join cults to conform," Atkin wrote. "Actually, the very opposite is true. They join to become more individual."

Notice the way he uses first person plural here (we) to help the reader connect more personally with Douglas Atkin's theory.

A number of Bay Area companies have come to incorporate this insight into their marketing strategies. In 2004, shortly after launching the restaurant-review site Yelp, the founders were struggling to grow the company. They decided to convene a gathering of about 100 power-users. The get-together "was a big success," Ligaya Tichy, who later served as Yelp's senior community manager, told me. "Bringing users together to share what they loved about the site led to a huge spike in activity. What we realized is that people aren't really motivated by companies. They're motivated by other people. We needed to get the message across: you are what makes this product cool." The number of reviewers on the site grew from 12,000 in 2005 to 100,000 in 2006.

Thompson builds his point through a moment of **narration** that underscores the **cause–effect** relationship between developing the interpersonal connections between users and increasing the popularity of the product.

Even today, Yelp still holds exclusive events for its most prolific reviewers, the Yelp Elite Squad, which a 2011 *Bloomberg Businessweek* article noted for its "cult influence." "People have been thinking about the similarities between cults and brands for years," Tichy says. "Only now you're really seeing people start to codify these practices with evangelists and groups like Yelp Elite."

In 2009, the founders of Airbnb were facing a similar challenge. They had a product that wasn't growing and a customer base that wasn't talking. "I call this period the Midwest of analytics," says co-founder Joe Gebbia. "It was the fattest growth you've ever seen."

Encouraged by an early investor to "meet your customers," Gebbia and his team flew to New York to visit with users, take pictures of their living rooms, and gather feedback. The team quickly realized that it needed to bring users together to share

He follows the Yelp example with a moment of **narration**, once again both providing evidence while also helping readers connect more with his points, using examples from companies they probably would be familiar with.

their experiences and enthusiasm. They organized the first Airbnb meet-up, which has since been replicated more than 1,000 times around the world. "I don't think of it as a cult," Gebbia says. "We're a community- driven brand, but at the same time, we want every host in every home to recognize that they're all individuals, and to use Airbnb as an expression of their individuality."

Thompson now returns to the cult comparison, reminding his reader of his **definition** of how a cult operates. This is an important paragraph for solidifying his argument, and transitioning back to Apple, the example he used in his introduction.

One of the hallmarks of a cult is that members unite to oppose what they see as an oppressive or illegitimate mainstream culture. Collaborative-economy companies—from Airbnb to the ride-sharing service Uber—have proved particularly savvy at exploiting this sense, and in so doing converting both merchants and consumers (the line between which sometimes blurs). But companies like Apple show that the creation of a cult mentality can be just as powerful with customers of regular goods—even products that have grown so popular, they would seem to be poor markers of individuality or special identity.

He strategically inserts a direct quotation here from a source that explicitly connects a brand (Apple) with the cult phenomenon.

"Apple was more of a cult in the 1980s, when it was the converted few supporting the company against Microsoft and IBM," says Jennifer Edson Escalas, an associate professor of marketing at Vanderbilt University. From its famous hammer-smashing "1984" ad against IBM to its 1998 commercial "Crazy Ones," Apple has been deliberate in reinforcing an us-against-the-world ethos. The fact that it has preserved its devoted following while becoming larger than its opponents "shows that culting is useful, even when it's misleading," Escalas says.

In his conclusion, he once again uses word choice ("creepy"; the use of first person) to solidify his *pathos* connection with the reader, while also addressing a possible counter argument. Notice also how the first sentence of his conclusion functions as a statement of his argument, showing his use of an inductive line of reasoning (many examples, leading to a specific conclusion). He ends with a provocative question from one of his sources that asks the reader to consider the interplay between *logos, ethos* and *pathos* in brand marketing.

It might seem creepy that some successful marketers are taking their cues from cult theory. But all advertising is manipulation. This new wrinkle takes advantage of a particular vulnerability—our need to be unique and belong to a group at the same time. Even experts like Susan Fournier, who doubts that cults offer a relevant model for marketing, think that brands play an important role beyond the simple provision of economic information. "I'm more frightened by a world that assumes we are rational actors optimizing all the time, without a sense of emotional connection, comfort, stability, or belonging," she said. "Who would want that?"

CONSIDERING CONTEXT AND VALUES: *KAIROS* AND *DOXA*

2.3 How can I shape my argument based on time, place, and shared values?

As you can tell from the examples we've examined so far, a successful argument must take into account not only the *rhetorical situation* but also the context—or right time and place—as well as the values of an audience. That is why the Citibank billboard of Cullen Jones shown in Figure 2.8 had tremendous resonance when first displayed right after the London Olympics in 2012, but was passed over in favor of a more timely ad once "Olympics fever" had died down. In ancient Greece rhetoricians called this aspect of the rhetorical situation ***kairos***—namely, attention to the right time and place for an argument.

In your own writing, you should consider *kairos* along with the other aspects of the rhetorical situation: audience, text, and writer. It is important to recognize the *kairos*—the opportune historical, ideological, or cultural moment—of a text when analyzing its rhetorical force. You undoubtedly already consider the context for persuasive communication in your everyday life. For instance, whether you are asking a friend to dinner or a professor for a recommendation, your assessment of the timeliness and the appropriate strategies for that time probably determine the shape your argument takes. In essence, by picking the right moment and place to make your case, you are in fact paying attention to the *kairos* of your argument.

FIGURE 2.9 This Coca-Cola ad used *kairos* to create a powerful argument for its World War II audience.

Consider Coca-Cola's ad campaigns. Coke has exerted a powerful presence in the beverage industry for many years, in part because of its strategic advertising. During World War II, Coke ran a series of ads featuring servicemen and showing inspiring slices of Americana that built its campaign around the nationalistic sentiment of a specific cultural moment. Look at Figure 2.9, an advertisement for Coke from the 1940s. This picture uses *pathos* to appeal to the audience's sense of patriotism by featuring a row of seemingly carefree servicemen, leaning from the windows of a military bus, the refreshing Cokes in their hands producing smiles even far away from home. The picture draws in the audience by reassuring them on two fronts:

- It builds on the nationalistic pride in the young, handsome servicemen who so happily serve their country.
- It is designed to appease fears about the hostile climate abroad: as both the picture and the accompanying text assure us, Coca-Cola (and the servicemen) "goes along" and "gets a hearty welcome."

The power of this message relates directly to *kairos*. An ad such as this one, premised on patriotism and pride in military service, would be most persuasive during wartime when many more people tend to support the spirit of nationalism and therefore would be moved by the image of the young serviceman shipping off to war. It is through understanding the *kairos* of this advertisement that you can appreciate the strength of the ad's rhetorical appeal.

An awareness of *kairos* likewise helps us see how even more in a contemporary setting, companies can develop a marketing campaign whose success relies on its timeliness. For instance, in 2015, Lane Bryant launched its "I'm No Angel" campaign, which featured lingerie models staring provocatively from the pages of magazines, TV screens, and billboards (Figure 2.10).

On the surface, the campaign relies on a *pathos* appeal to sexuality, both in terms of the image and the provocative tagline. However, our analysis of the argument becomes sharper when we consider how *kairos* comes into play. Both the text and image implicitly are in dialogue with a *different* advertisement: Victoria's Secret's advertising for its "Angel" line. Often under fire for presenting a waif-like version of ideal feminine beauty, Victoria's Secret here suffers a pointed critique from Lane Bryant's campaign, as more realistically proportioned models set themselves up in direct opposition to the Victoria's Secret Angel image. While the power of the Lane Bryant marketing does not lie solely in its conversation with its competitor, the dialogue between the two campaigns undoubtedly makes it more resonant at that particular moment in time.

Our examples also call attention to the way in which ads appeal to an audience's values, or ***doxa***. A crucial concept to the ancient Greeks, *doxa*

FIGURE 2.10 The Lane Bryant store supercharges its argument by implicitly criticizing the Victoria's Secret "Angels" campaign.

means "popular opinion" or "belief"—a learned value system—since it refers to those values or beliefs that are deeply held by a particular community at a particular place and moment in time. The term is related to a concept you may know, *dogma*—or unchanging doctrine—but importantly, *doxa* can and does change over time. When an author considers *doxa* while crafting a persuasive text, she constructs an argument based on her understanding of the values held in common by a group of people. The Victoria's Secret and Lane Bryant campaigns provide us with an interesting example of conflicting doxa. Both move beyond simple *pathos*-laden sex appeal to tap into cultural ideas about beauty. While Victoria's Secret's marketing trades on cultural assumptions that value extreme slenderness, the Lane Bryant campaign appeals to a rising contemporary sentiment that values more realistically proportioned ideals of beauty.

Likewise, in its recent campaign for its new beverage "Coke Life," Coca-Cola used *doxa* when tapping into the audience's commitment to healthy living. The selling point of the ads for this re-vamped beverage is that Coke Life uses only sugar and stevia extract as sweeteners, so the ads promise lower calorie "sweetness from natural sources." Replacing its signature red background with vivid green, the Coke ads reach out to a health-conscious populous who might be persuaded to indulge in a soft drink that uses only natural sweeteners. However, some critics have dismissed this campaign as an empty marketing gesture toward health rather than a concerted effort to promote healthier dietary habits, accusing the soft drink giant of "green-washing"—that is, using the rhetoric of environmental consciousness to distract from a less commendable agenda. Moreover, while the appeal to national health works for an ad in the United States today, a contemporary Coca-Cola ad in Lebanon, by contrast, appeals to the culture's celebration of voluptuous singing divas, such as Nancy Ajram, and therefore presents a video focused on romance among adults rather than nutrition and children. By invoking the cultural values of each location, Coca-Cola deliberately uses *doxa* as a rhetorical strategy. You can probably think of many other examples of how attention to *doxa* works in arguments aimed at a specific demographic, even within the United States (for instance, Diet Mountain Dew ads that target Nascar lovers versus Honest Tea ads targeting bicycling enthusiasts). Consider also how political ads appeal to popular opinion or deeply held values of a specific community (such as a depressed region needing manufacturing jobs or a rural constituency opposed to gun control).

Attending to *kairos* and *doxa* in these ways enables us to understand differences in context and values, to see how persuasion makes powerful use of the present place and moment, and finally, to learn how we can implement these rhetorical strategies when composing our own arguments.

READING AN AD ANALYSIS

Now that we've seen how strategies of argumentation and the rhetorical appeals operate in advertising, let's look at how they come together in a written analysis. As you read student Clare Conrotto's rhetorical analysis of a McDonald's commercial, consider not only whether you find her analysis persuasive, but also how she leverages different rhetorical strategies to make a compelling argument to her audience.

Conrotto 1

Clare Conrotto
Writing & Rhetoric 1

I'll Have the Lies on the Side, Please

Tranquil pastoral fields, waving peacefully in the breeze. Contented cattle, grazing freely under a delicate sunrise. A family tending happily to their beloved animals, smiling as they stroll alongside the cattle. These scenes from a recent McDonald's commercial is made all the more perfect by the viewer's desire to believe that such is the reality of our foodstuff before it is slaughtered, processed, packaged, and sold. But one must look beyond the polished images and ask the question, *Could this possibly be true?*

Clare begins her essay with descriptive language that sketches some scenes from the McDonald's commercial to hook her audience and help them visualize the text she will be analyzing.

Current national sentiment in America yearns to answer this question with a resounding *yes*, but as public opinion scrutinizes the ever more attentively glossed-over and brushed-under culture in which advertising companies flourish, it soon becomes clear that many companies have merely exploited viewers' expectations. Indeed, McDonald's, keenly aware of modern Americans' hypersensitivity to issues regarding the food industry, seizes the opportunity to revitalize its reputation tarnished by decades of horrifying revelations; in one of McDonald's most recent advertising campaigns, the company attempts to assure viewers that the corporative giant has become both socially and ethically responsible, going so far as to paint a utopian portrait of the traditional American family farm in its video "Raising Cattle and a Family." However, McDonald's is largely unsuccessful in

Clare uses a question-answer format to transition between her first and second paragraph.

Although Clare doesn't use the term *ethos*, her analysis focuses on the way in which the commercial fails to persuade the audience of McDonalds's credibility and integrity.

As she moves toward her thesis statement, Clare suggests how she will push beyond a surface reading of the commercial to more in-depth analysis.

The use of a charged word like "pandering" underscores Clare's critical stance in relation to the McDonald's advertising campaign.

While *ethos* (McDonald's credibility) is a foundation for her argument, in her thesis she indicates that she also will examine *pathos* (connection with audience) in her essay.

In her first main body paragraph, Clare begins with an examination of *ethos*, relying on strategies of description and example to make her point.

Conrotto 2

this endeavor, despite its intuitive awareness of the American social mindset. Although it may convince a passive audience that trusts the products it already consumes, for many more critical viewers, the company's rhetorical persuasive strategies fall short when the countless implicit and explicit assertions of the advertisement are compared with reality. Thus, despite evidence of McDonald's keen awareness of its audience's priorities and careful execution of a video pandering to these ideals, the company fails to establish a meaningful connection with the viewer and therefore fails to effectively convince its audience.

This disconnect between author and viewer is due largely to McDonald's inability to persuade the audience of its transparency and integrity. Although the entire advertisement indirectly boasts of McDonald's fine moral standing, the disparity between concrete reality and the impossible construction of reality as it is presented in the video is too large a gap to be ignored. That is, in "Raising Cattle and a Family," McDonald's effort to relate to the modern American public manifests itself most obviously in the deceivingly simplistic cinematographic techniques of the video. Indeed, at the very beginning of the advertisement, the viewer is immediately greeted by an idealized version of an American farm when the screen fades from black to the image of a lush field at dawn, the unbroken view of sky and grass only enhanced by cows standing happily within nature: all appears open, peaceful, and idyllic. Although this reveals McDonald's

Conrotto 3

intimate understanding of modern Americans' growing desire to return to honesty and simplicity regarding the food industry, and most certainly an appeal to *kairos*, the subtle techniques which McDonald's employs focus primarily on the audience's unconscious inclinations. In other words, McDonald's appeals to *pathos*, to the emotional impulses of the audience. It is true that humans respond to such quiet beauty and peacefulness strongly, especially in an era overwrought by a constant influx of errands that must be accomplished, emails which must be answered, and tasks that must be finished by a looming deadline. Nonetheless, the argument that McDonald's asserts with this technique is effective for a very short time, if at all. As the video progresses, with continually intensifying images of what appears to be a ranching utopia filled with peaceful cattle and striking views of nature, analytical viewers will soon begin to question the validity of this indirect claim. Could it be true that McDonald's sources its beef only from local U.S. farms that focus on sustainable and humane practices, allowing the cattle to graze as happily as they do in the video?

The short answer is, quite simply, no. With a few simple clicks of the mouse, the audience finds that, according to McDonald's own answer section on its website, all of the meat it purchases "comes from cattle *corn-fed* [italics added] in the U.S." and that "in order to keep up with demand, a small percentage of grass-fed beef is imported from Australia and New Zealand" (McDonald's). Thus are the viewers' misgivings proven true in an instant: not

Clare examines the interchange between the rhetorical appeals; while she uses rhetorical terminology here (*pathos*, *kairos*), she could have used less discipline-specific terminology if she wanted to present her argument to a more general audience.

Again, Clare considers the *kairos* of the commercial as a way of analyzing its influence on the audience.

She concludes this paragraph with a rhetorical question that she then answers as her transition into her next paragraph, indicating a shift to a more skeptical perspective.

Clare considers the commercial's impact on varying audiences—as she continues to scrutinize its *ethos*. She recognizes here the multiple, interrelated audiences for this text.

Again, she weaves an understanding of audience and *kairos* into her analysis.

Clare turns her attention at this point to the *situated ethos* of the spokesperson.

Conrotto 4

once does the audience see even one kernel of corn or the metal cages which inevitably accompany such fodder when it replaces the natural act of grazing. McDonald's idyllic American farm setting is therefore already established as a web of lies, immeasurably weakening any future arguments. As a result, actively thinking viewers will remain skeptical, and passive viewers will remain unaffected in their loyalty to the products they already consume at McDonald's; the ultimate purpose of the advertisement—to persuade its audience of its new reputation—will have failed.

This lack of credibility continues to plague the video, even as McDonald's works desperately to seem more convincing. Already burdened by the weight of a tarnished status in the minds of millions of Americans, owed partially to such documentaries as the 2004 hit *Super Size Me* and celebrity chef Jamie Oliver's recent uncovering of the fast food industry's horrifying chemical-treated "pink slime" meat product (Reilly), McDonald's embarked on a new advertising style, determined to develop a similarly new reputation: the company well understood that the timing for its next move was ripe. Turning to the human instinct to trust familiar faces, the primary spokesperson in the advertisement is Steve Foglesong, former president of the National Cattlemen's Beef Association (Goodman), a fact that, one fancies, ought to lend immediate weight to any statement made during the video. Unfortunately, not even this appeal to *ethos* can persuade viewers—of any level of passivity, or, conversely, activeness in thought—that there is any

Conrotto 5

credibility to be found in this advertisement. McDonald's flails; seeking to promote any fact about the Foglesongs that might help its case, the company highlights the authority of Foglesong as a father and grandfather whose family has owned a cattle ranch for three generations (and who apparently enjoys McDonald's burgers himself, as manifested by a scene in which he and his sons smilingly eat McDonald's on a short lunch break) by indirectly likening time spent on a project to quality. A failed attempt to appeal to *logos* thus surfaces, one of many flaws in logic offered by McDonald's largely emotion-driven video. Although there might be a correlation between the implication that a man with the knowledge and authority of decades of ranching ought to understand the farming process and thus produce high-quality products, the claim that this is of course the end result, and that McDonald's should be trusted because of this conclusion, remains unproven.

Clare moves to pointing to flaws in logic and reasoning to underscore the shortcomings of the commercial.

Here Clare points to what she sees as a correlation-causation fallacy.

Finally, to continue the evaluation of such logical fallacies, it is vital to understand that most viewers will be aware of the fact that since this video is an advertisement, Foglesong may be former president of the NCBA, a third-generation rancher, and seemingly a strong voice to be trusted, but he is a *hired actor* and is thus self-promoting. This consequently undermines any seemingly rational argument offered by the spokesperson or his experience with raising cattle. Even his manner of delivery—endearing and informal—does little to move the viewer when she acknowledges the fact that Foglesong is *paid* to speak in such a way. This might have

Once again, Clare points to fallacies in the argument, this time questioning the *ethos* of the spokesperson.

In her penultimate paragraph, Clare concedes that some of the commercial's techniques foster a connection with the audience, but then — at the end of the paragraph — reasserts her argument that more critical viewers will see past *pathos* appeals in a way that compromises McDonald's *ethos*.

Clare's use of vivid, descriptive language ("serene harmony," "endearingly folksy", "evocative stimuli") adds increased *pathos* appeal to her own writing

Conrotto 6

been persuasive had the interview-like situation been genuinely spontaneous, due to its ability to transport the viewer to what feels like an intimate acquaintance with Foglesong and, by extension, McDonald's. Unfortunately, like most of McDonald's rhetorical appeals, this, too, fails to convince even the most inactive viewer due to the contrived nature of Foglesong's participation.

Conversely, it must be noted that one of the more simplistic techniques in "Raising Cattle and a Family" proves to be one of the most effective in this largely insufficient attempt to revitalize McDonald's reputation. The audio of the advertisement, which serves chiefly the same purpose as the technical photographic angles and focuses, begins with the serene harmony of chirping birds and gently mooing cows. The suave vocals of Foglesong slide over the sounds of nature before an endearingly folksy guitar is heard strumming in the background of Foglesong's narration. Immediately the audience responds to these emotionally evocative stimuli—the audio is simple and peaceful, emphasizing the apparent tranquility to be found on McDonald's farms. To a certain extent, logic does take over to render even this attempt at persuasion somewhat irrelevant. The viewer grasps that, just as with the utopian visual scenes, the music is simply a ploy to force audiences to reassess their current view of McDonald's and connect the chain with the ever sought-after small business dream. However, most viewers will remain passive in this analysis of audio strategies and thus the unconscious appeal to *pathos* will have been more or less successful. Nevertheless, this small

Conrotto 7

victory in persuasion does little to improve the overall success of the advertisement and McDonald's aim of rebuilding its reputation in order to better relate to potential consumers. The other faulty attempts at persuasion outweigh the minor victory of the audio's appeal, and the advertisement remains, ultimately, ineffective.

Claire moves into her conclusion paragraph by reasserting her argument in the opening sentence.

Encumbered with the insurmountable task of reworking its reputation, McDonald's simply cannot connect with its viewers on a level that encourages mutual respect and confidence. Despite the modestly successful audio and visual techniques utilized by the company, the advertisement still falls short of convincing: active viewers remains capable of examining such emotive appeals as defined by their allure, and passive viewers who do accept the advertisement's premise are typically already loyal to a company from which they have been purchasing for years. Ultimately, the seeds for a new reputation may have been planted, but most Americans are currently too suspicious of large corporations to uncritically accept concepts established in an advertisement overrun by sweeping generalizations and vague half-truths. By failing to foster trust between Americans and its company, McDonald's ultimately fails to win over its audience.

Her own argument rests on the idea of *doxa* — that current, shared skepticism about Big Business influences how susceptible the audience is to the commercial's message.

Her final sentence is a succinct and powerful reiteration of her main claim.

Conrotto 8

Works Cited

Goodman, Ryan. "McDonald's Launches Farmer Ad Campaign." *Agriculture Proud*, 10 Jan. 2012. Web. 1 Oct. 2012.

McDonald's Corporation. "Meats." McDonald's, n.d. Web. 1 Oct. 2012.

Reilly, Jill. "Victory for Jamie Oliver in the U.S. as McDonald's Is Forced to Stop Using 'Pink Slime' in Its Burger Recipe." *Mail Online*. Daily Mail, 7 Oct. 2012. Web. 1 Oct. 2012.

THE WRITER'S PROCESS

As you turn to write up your analysis of advertisements in the way that Clare did above, consider the ways in which your own writing can "sell" your argument to the reader. What is the rhetorical situation of your writing assignment? What *strategies of argumentation* and *rhetorical appeals* would be most effective in reaching your target audience? Do you want to use narration, a humorous analogy, or a stirring example to forge a connection with your readers based on *pathos*? Or is your written analysis better suited to *logos*, following the step-by-step process of reading an ad, drawing on empirical evidence, or looking at cause and effect? Perhaps you will decide to enrich your discussion through cultivating your *ethos* as a writer, establishing your own authority on a subject or citing reputable work done by other scholars. Finally, how can you make use of *kairos* and *doxa* as persuasive tools by evoking something from today's culture in your writing or appealing to the beliefs of your reader? In your essay, you certainly will use many of these strategies and a combination of rhetorical appeals; as we saw in the examples from this chapter, a successful argument uses various techniques to persuade its audience.

SPOTLIGHTED ANALYSIS: ADVERTISEMENTS

MyWritingLab

Use the following prompts to guide your analysis of the advertisement of your choice, focusing on how the ad relies on particular strategies of development and rhetorical appeals to persuade its audience.

- **Content:** What exactly is the ad selling? An object? An experience? An idea?
- **Argument:** How is the ad selling the product? What message is the ad sending to the audience?
- **Character and setting:** What is featured by the ad? An object? A scene? A person? How are these elements portrayed? How do these choices relate to the ad's intended audience and reflect deliberate rhetorical choices?
- **Rhetorical appeals:** Which rhetorical appeals does the ad rely on to persuade its audience? *Pathos*? *Logos*? *Ethos*? *Kairos*? *Doxa*? How do these appeals operate both through language and through imagery?
- **Strategies of development:** Which strategies of argumentation does the ad use? Narration? Definition? Comparison–contrast? Example or illustration? Classification? Process? Analogy? Cause and effect? How do these strategies contribute to the ad's persuasive appeal?
- **Word & image:** What is the relationship between the word (written or spoken) and the imagery in the ad? How does this relationship affect the persuasiveness of the advertisement?
- **Layout & design:** How are the elements of the ad arranged—on a page (for a print ad) or in sequence (for a television or Internet commercial)? What is the purpose behind this arrangement? How does the ad's organization facilitate its argument? How do elements like choice or coloring of typeface, filtering or cropping of photographs, or the overall tone of the advertisement (informal, personal, authoritative, technical, comic, serious) affect its persuasiveness?
- **Design:** What typeface is used? What size? What color? What tone do these choices create for the advertisement? How do these decisions reflect attention to the ad's rhetorical situation or use of rhetorical appeals?
- **Medium and context:** How was the ad distributed (i.e., television, Internet, radio, magazine, billboard)? In what country and at what historical moment was the advertisement produced? How does the ad reflect, comment on, challenge, or reinforce contemporary political, economic, or gender ideology?
- **Cultural resonance:** Does the ad use famous events or places or recognizable symbols to increase its persuasiveness? If so, how does that establish audience or a relationship to a cultural moment?

WRITING ASSIGNMENTS

MyWritingLab

1. **Rhetorical Analysis Brainstorm:** Review David Horsey's article "Obnoxious Freedom" from Chapter 1. Take notes on how he uses strategies of development and rhetorical appeals in constructing his argument. Then look at Alex's essay at the end of that chapter. Where is she addressing his use of these techniques during her analysis? Jot some notes down about what you would suggest that she add to her argument if she were to revise it to better feature how Horsey uses rhetorical strategies (such as rhetorical appeals and strategies of argumentation) in his essay.

2. **Rhetorical Analysis Essay:** Building from your own reading of Derek Thompson's article and the accompanying annotations, develop your thoughts into a cohesive rhetorical analysis essay, driven by a strong thesis statement and drawing on evidence from the article to support your claim. If you prefer, write instead on the article of your choice.

3. **Rhetorical Analysis of an Advertisement:** Using the analysis you started for the Spotlighted Analysis above as a starting point, write a rhetorical analysis of an advertisement, using a strong claim to guide your argument. Be sure to draw on evidence to support your claim, but be selective in which details you include in your essay: your goal is not to produce a list of all your observations but to produce a focused analysis that argues for how the advertiser used specific rhetorical appeals or strategies to produce a persuasive argument.

4. **Rhetorical Analysis—Fallacies:** Working alone or with a group, select an article, editorial, op-ed, essay, or even an advertisement that includes a misuse of either *pathos*, *logos*, or *ethos* as a persuasive strategy. Compose an essay (or a PowerPoint or Prezi) in which you define the fallacy and then analyze how it functions in the text. In your conclusion, suggest how the text itself could be altered to avoid this line of argument.

5. **Rhetorical Analysis—*Kairos*:** Working in groups, look at several ads from different time periods produced by the same company, such as ads for cigarettes, cars, hygiene products, or personal computers. Each member of your group should choose a single ad and prepare a rhetorical analysis of its persuasive appeals. Share your analyses to explore how this company has modified its rhetorical approach over time. Collaborate on a paper in which you chart the evolution of the company's persuasive strategies and how that evolution was informed by *kairos*.

6. **Reflection and Revision:** Select an essay that you have written, whether for one of the assignments above or that you have written for a class previously. Perform a rhetorical analysis on *your own essay*, taking notes in the margins to guide your thinking. When do you use *pathos*, *logos*, or *ethos* in your writing? Do you take into account *kairos* or *doxa*? Refer back to the strategies of development: to what extent do you use the strategies listed on pages 44–49? How do you take into account the concepts of rhetorical situation, exigence and purpose that we discussed in Chapter 1? Having completed this analysis, revise your essay in a way that more deliberately leverages the powers of rhetoric to persuade your reader. Remember that you don't need to use *all* the appeals or every strategy in your essay: the key is to use a strategic combination that will produce the most powerful effect. Finish the revision by drafting a memo in which you reflect on the process of rhetorical analysis and revision that you put into practice.

MyWritingLab Visit Ch. 2 Understanding Strategies of Persuasion in MyWritingLab to complete the Writer's Practices, Spotlighted Analyses, and Writing Assignments, and to test your understanding of the chapter objectives.

CHAPTER 3

Composing Arguments

Chapter Preview Questions

3.1 How do the Canons of Rhetoric determine the content, shape, and style of arguments?

3.2 What is the role of invention in creating persuasive arguments?

3.3 How does the canon of arrangement influence a reader's response to a text?

3.4 How can style be used to compose a powerful argument?

3.5 How can I write a persuasive position paper?

When you skim news stories online or watch media coverage of dramatic events, you are in fact reading about an issue through a filter: the newscaster's selection of images and quotations as well as the reporter's choice of words in composing a story about that event. Such writing aims to persuade you to read further—to stay on the Website, share the link with friends, or post a comment with your response—and in that way even the news functions as argument. Let's consider an example. Imagine that it is September 2005 and the United States is still reeling from the aftermath of Hurricane Katrina. As you click through several news sites, you pause to look at the images they display. One features a striking photo of a military helicopter dropping supplies to the citizens of New Orleans (see Figure 3.1). Another shows a mother clutching two small children and wading through waist-deep water. Yet another displays the image of a mob of angry people, packed together and arguing as they try to evacuate the city. A final site uses the picture of a child's dirt-smeared doll, swept

FIGURE 3.1 A photograph of supplies being dropped to survivors of a hurricane in New Orleans.

into a pile of debris on the road, as its poignant commentary on natural disaster.

Based on these images, which site would you visit? How does each image make a different argument about what happened? How might the words that accompany the photo shape your interpretation of the visual texts? How does the choice of a particular visual–verbal combination present a specific point of view or argument about an event in the news?

Photographs and their accompanying text on news sites or in newspapers rely on the same tools of persuasion that we examined in earlier chapters. In this chapter, we'll continue to explore how rhetoric shapes our reality. We'll become acquainted with the *Canons of Rhetoric*—five classifications of argument established by Aristotle—and we'll work through the process of composing an argument: coming up with ideas, structuring those ideas, and developing a style for your position, or stance, on an issue. We'll also explore how you can apply these lessons about arrangement and style through specific strategies for how you can write compelling titles, introductions, and conclusions for your own essays. Finally, we'll build on these lessons to consider how to craft a powerful position paper that takes into account counterarguments while persuasively articulating your stance on an issue.

3.1 How do the Canons of Rhetoric determine the content, shape, and style of arguments?

UNDERSTANDING THE CANONS OF RHETORIC

In ancient Greece, all communicative acts were classified into five categories, or what Aristotle called the **Canons of Rhetoric**:

- **Invention:** creating and constructing ideas and identifying the best modes of persuasion
- **Arrangement:** ordering and laying out ideas through effective organization
- **Style:** developing the appropriate expression for those ideas
- **Memory:** retaining invented ideas, recalling additional supporting ideas, and facilitating memory in the audience
- **Delivery:** presenting or performing ideas with the aim of persuading

Each one of these canons is necessary for persuasive communication, whether that be through spoken word, written discourse, or, more recently, multimedia texts. For our discussion of composing arguments in this chapter, we'll focus on the first three canons.

INVENTION IN ARGUMENT

3.2 What is the role of invention in creating persuasive arguments?

Aristotle defined *invention* as methods for "finding all available arguments." When you craft language with the purpose of persuading your audience, you are **inventing** an argument. That is, you are generating ideas about a topic and the ways to best persuade your audience. Classical rhetoricians recommended two systems for invention: *stasis*, a series of question that speakers could use to identify a point or topic for debate, and *topoi*, a set of categories or topics that help a speaker discern the relationships between ideas. In your own writing, you can draw from their central premise of categories and directed questioning to help you familiarize yourself with your topic and the options for argument available to you:

- **Fact:** What are you talking about, exactly? Is it a person, a text, an idea, an event? Is it in the real world or speculative?
- **Definition:** What does it *mean*? What are other examples?
- **Division:** What are its *parts*? What are its different features?
- **Comparison:** How does it *compare* to other topics or texts? Does it mean something new now versus years ago?
- **Purpose:** What is its *purpose*? To inform? Teach? Entertain? Persuade? Promote action? How does that purpose influence its structure?
- **Quality:** Is it possible to *evaluate* what you're talking about? Where does it fall into the categories of right/wrong, moral/immoral, important/insignificant? Does it resist such a binary interpretation?
- **Causes and Consequences:** What *causes* the issue or text? What are the *results* or consequences of it?
- **Testimony:** What do *others* say about it?

Some of these lines of questioning might be more applicable to your topic than others; however, taken in combination, they offer you a variety of strategies to help you generate the foundation for a persuasive argument.

To further develop ideas as you continue to "invent" your argument during the drafting stage, you can use a range of **rhetorical strategies**, including those you learned in the previous chapter: you might invoke *pathos*, use *ethos* or appeals to character, or employ *logos* to reason with your readers or listeners. Your task as a writer is to forge a powerful text that argues your point—the focus of your *invention*—and to convince others to agree with you. In composing arguments, you can look for examples in texts all around you and learn from them how *invention*—or the way the author chooses the most effective mode of persuasion—generates particular perspectives that the author wishes to convey to the audience.

Invention is the "discovery of valid or seemingly valid arguments to render one's cause probable."

—*Cicero*, De Inventione, I.vii

Consider pictures. We might think that a photograph provides a window on another person's reality. But in fact photographs, like written works, are texts of *rhetorical invention*. The "reality" that photographs display is actually a version of reality created by a photographer's rhetorical and artistic decisions: whether to use color or black-and-white film; what sort of lighting to use; how to position the subject of the photograph; whether to opt for a panorama or close-up shot; what backdrop to use; how to crop, or trim, the image once it is printed. In effect, when we see photographs in a newspaper or art gallery, we are looking at the product of deliberate *strategies of invention.* In photography, these strategies include key elements of composition, such as selection, placement, perspective, and framing. So when we look carefully at the image shown in Figure 3.2, we can see that the photograph is more powerful because of its composition. The photographer deliberately maximized the power of both foreground (the doves in flight) and background (the advancing tank) to transform a photograph of a middle-eastern street scene into a commentary on peace and war. In written texts, the same elements—selection, placement, perspective, and framing—are critical to making an argument.

FIGURE 3.2 The powerful image of doves in front of a tank in the Middle East suggests the photographer's view on the tensions between foreign aid and military occupation.

Let's consider another example, the photograph in Figure 3.3, an image captured by photojournalist Margaret Bourke-White, which shows a line of homeless African Americans, displaced by the 1937 Louisville flood, waiting in line to

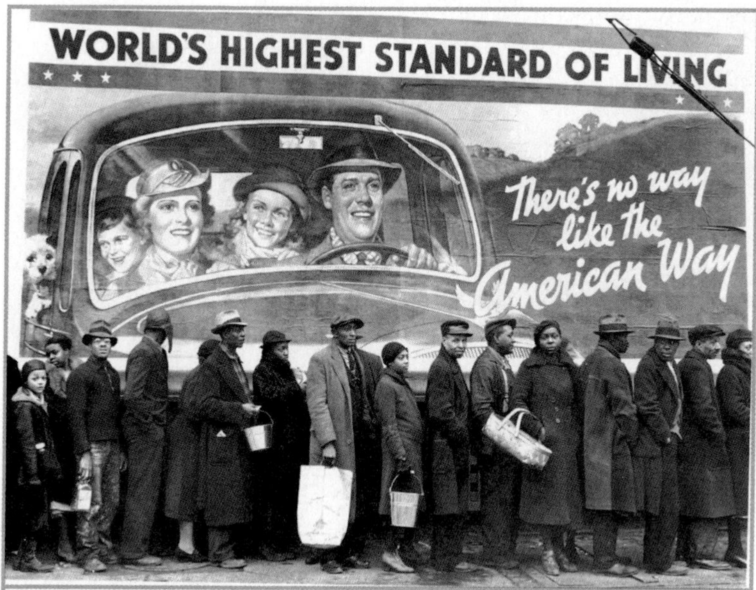

FIGURE 3.3 Margaret Bourke "At the Time of the Louisville Flood," 1937.

receive food and clothing from a local Red Cross center. Does the photo merely document a moment in the history of Kentucky? Or have the choice of subject, the cropping, the angle, the background, and the elements within the frame been selected by the photographer to make a specific argument about race and American culture during the first half of the twentieth century?

In your own writing, you could use this photograph as a springboard for inventing an argument. Perhaps you would write a historically focused argument that examines the catastrophic 1937 Louisville flood and its impact on the local community. Or you could refer to this photograph as visual evidence in a paper that examines the link between social status, race, and disaster relief. Either argument could draw on the power of the photograph, which reveals the invention strategies of the artist.

Let's look more closely at how invention factors into the way photographers and writers compose arguments. Consider two famous photographs by Dorothea Lange (see Figures 3.4 and 3.5), which offer very different

FIGURE 3.4 Dorothea Lange's wide shot gives a stark sense of the experience of migrant farmers.

FIGURE 3.5 The close-up focuses on the struggles of the migrant mother.

representations of migrant workers during the Great Depression. In each case, we see a migrant family huddled inside a tent. The subjects seem to be poor, hungry, and struggling to make a living. Their material conditions are bleak.

But notice the effects of the different perspectives. In Figure 3.5, we get an intimate look inside this woman's eyes, where we can see her concern. The lines on her face, visible in this close-up, are evidence of her hard life and worries. The photograph in Figure 3.4 has a wider frame that encompasses the tent and the barren ground. This perspective makes a different kind of argument, one that addresses the condition of the soil, the landscape, and the living quarters. We can hardly make out the woman huddled in the darkness of the tent. When we look for visual evidence of the living conditions of migrant workers in the American West during the 1930s, each photograph offers different angles on our argument. Which one would we use to support a thesis about the labor conditions of migrant workers? Which one would we use to argue that the human body is scarred by hardship? Depending on our purpose, we would choose one photograph over the other to serve as evidence for our claims about the Great Depression. Each photograph demonstrates a particular strategy of invention, creating and constructing ideas in visual form about the "reality" of life for migrant workers. We, in turn, can invent different arguments based on our starting point: which photo do we use as evidence for our thesis?

Similarly, in written documents, divergent perspectives on the same topic can yield different arguments. Commentary on Lange's *Migrant Mother* photographs exposes the variety of perspectives not only on the photographs' status as "documentary" evidence from the Great Depression but also on the way our historical understanding of that period itself is constructed by the invention or arguments of others. For instance, the following excerpt from historian James Curtis's article "Dorothea Lange, Migrant Mother, and the Culture of the Great Depression" demonstrates the way in which Lange's photos are often interpreted as windows into that period:

> In addition to being a timeless work of art, *Migrant Mother* is a vital reflection of the times. Examined in its original context, the series reveals powerful cultural forces of the 1930s: the impact of the increasing centralization and bureaucratization of American life; the anxiety about the status and solidarity of the family in an era of urbanization and modernization; a need to atone for the guilt induced by the destruction of cherished ideals, and a craving for reassurance that democratic traditions would stand the test of modern times.

For Curtis, the images function both as what elsewhere in the article he calls "a timeless and universal symbol of suffering in the face of adversity" as well as the key to understanding Lange's relationship to the evolving genre of documentary photography. For journalist Geoffrey Dunn, however, Lange's series prompts a different response:

> The photographs taken by Lange and her colleagues at the Resettlement Administration (later to become better known as the Farm Security Administration) have been widely heralded as the epitome of documentary photography. The eminent photographer and curator Edward Steichen called them "the most remarkable human documents ever rendered in pictures."
>
> In recent years, however, the FSA photographs have come under a growing criticism. Many view them as manipulative and condescending, to the point of assuming a "colonialistic" attitude toward their subjects. Still others have argued that they are misleading and disingenuous, and in some instances, fabricated.
>
> In a compelling essay entitled "The Historian and the Icon," University of California at Berkeley professor Lawrence Levine has argued that the FSA

> photographers focused their lenses on "perfect victims," and in so doing, rendered a caricatured portrait of the era.
>
> "Americans suffered, materially and physically, during the years of the Great Depression to an extent which we still do not fully fathom," Levine asserted. "But they also continued, as people always must, the business of living. They ate and they laughed, they loved and they fought, they worried and they hoped ... they filled their days, as we fill ours, with the essentials of everyday living."
>
> With the notable exception of FSA photographer Russell Lee, and later, Marion Post Wolcott, whose largely overlooked bodies of work actually capture the dimensions of "everyday living," Lange and her colleagues focused almost exclusively on human suffering. That is most certainly the reason that people like Florence Owens Thompson [the mother in these photographs]—and many others who appeared in FSA images—resented their photographic portrayal.
>
> "Mother was a woman who loved to enjoy life, who loved her children," says Thompson's youngest daughter, Norma Rydlewski, who appears as a young child in Lange's classic photograph. "She loved music and she loved to dance. When I look at that photo of mother, it saddens me. That's not how I like to remember her."

Like Curtis, Dunn uses the photographs as the basis for an argument about Lange's practice of documentary photography; however, Dunn considers first-person accounts from other witnesses of that historical moment and arrives at a different argument. He concludes that the series exemplifies not reflection but misrepresentation.

All texts—whether written accounts or photographs—are actually shaped by individual perspective and point of view. Texts are "invented" for a specific audience. Your own writing is a text informed by your invention strategies, your purpose, your point of view, and the rhetorical situation of your argument. In your writing, you are like a photographer, making important compositional decisions: What will be the subject of your text: an individual, a group, an institution? How will you pose that subject to best convey your own perspective? Should you zoom in, focusing on one particular example as a way of addressing a larger concern? Or should you take a step back, situating your argument in relation to the broader context that surrounds the issue? The choices you make will determine the ultimate impact of your argument: like photographs, effective writing persuades the viewer to look at a topic through the lens of the author's interpretation.

WRITER'S PRACTICE MyWritingLab

Examine the picture in Figure 3.6, taken by photographer Todd Heisler, of a soldier's coffin returning home on a civilian flight into Reno, Nevada, being draped with the American flag prior to being unloaded from the plane. What argument is Heisler making about Americans' response to the war and casualties? Now consider this image as the basis for inventing your own position: What types of arguments might you construct that would use this image as visual evidence? What other sorts of images or evidence would you use to develop your argument?

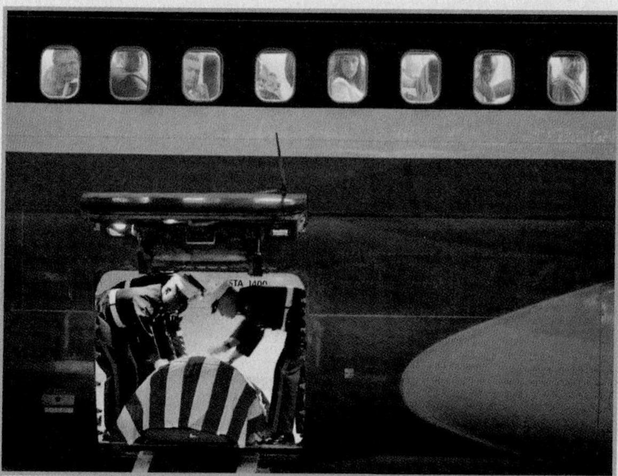

FIGURE 3.6 Photograph of the arrival of a soldier's coffin in Reno.

ARRANGEMENT IN ARGUMENT

3.3 How does the canon of arrangement influence a reader's response to a text?

After invention, the second canon of rhetoric, **arrangement**, becomes your key consideration because the way in which you present material on the page will shape a reader's response to your ideas. In many cases, attention to *arrangement* takes the form of the way you order elements in your argument—whether that be the layout of images and text on a newspaper front page or the way you structure a written argument in an academic paper. It is the arrangement of an argument that separates a spontaneous reaction or stream-of-consciousness freewrite from a carefully developed and argued essay on a specific issue or topic.

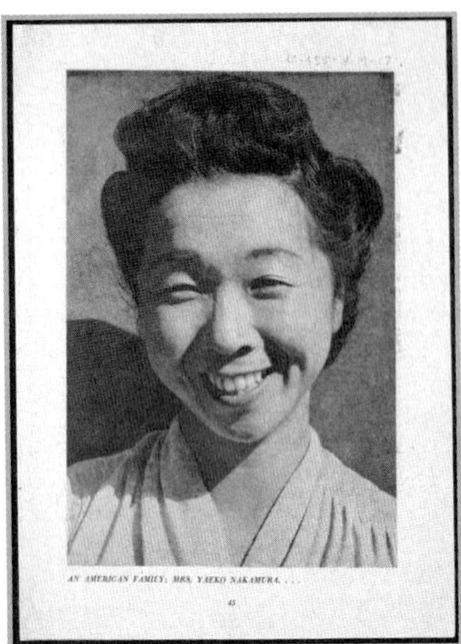

FIGURE 3.7

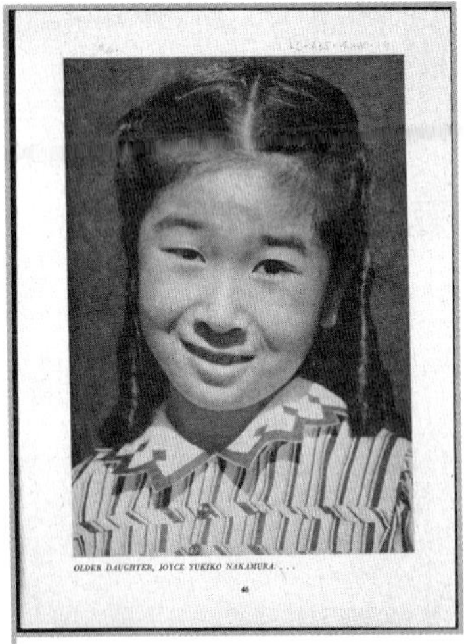

FIGURE 3.8

To return once again to our photography example, let's look at how award-winning photographer Ansel Adams approached the issue of arrangement in his 1944 photo essay, *Born Free and Equal*, which captures his impressions of the Japanese-American residents of the Manzanar internment camp during World War II. Adams explained his purpose for writing the book most clearly to his friend, Nancy Newhall: "Through the pictures the reader will be introduced to about twenty individuals . . . loyal American citizens who are anxious to get back into the stream of life and contribute to our victory." The work as a whole follows a *thematic structure*, moving the reader from "The Land" to "The Place," "The History," "The People," and finally "The Problem." On the surface, Adams seems to have arranged the sections to move from broader context, to the individuals, to the articulation of the social and political realities of the internment process. However, closer analysis shows that his strategy is much more complicated; he interweaves portraiture with his more panoramic, contextualizing photographs so as to constantly remind his audience of the fact that the people who have been imprisoned in this way are Americans—everyday people with everyday lives.

The selections gathered here are from the "People" chapter; note how the strategic arrangement amplifies many of the concepts that Adams stresses in his summary to Newhall. Figure 3.7 and Figure 3.8 first create an emotional connection with the reader by focusing on individual example.

By showing close-ups of mother and daughter, with the caption strategically emphasizing the fact that these are "An American Family," Adams suggests the unfairness of the relocation process. Subsequently, he widens his frame to show "A Manzanar Household" (Figure 3.9), portraying a quotidian family scene, little girl at her desk doing homework, family clustered around in a typical domestic setting. From here, we can see Adams' next move in strategic arrangement in Figure 3.10: the pair of adorable young boys eating at a mess hall. Having engaged the reader once more, Adams broadens his scope yet again to give us context for this scene. We are no longer inside the faux middle class home; we see the barracks, the food lines, and the unforgiving landscape. As we saw with Dorothea Lange's *Migrant Mother series*, Adams uses shifting perspectives rhetorically, and in tandem, in order to emphasize his argument about in the injustices of the internment process.

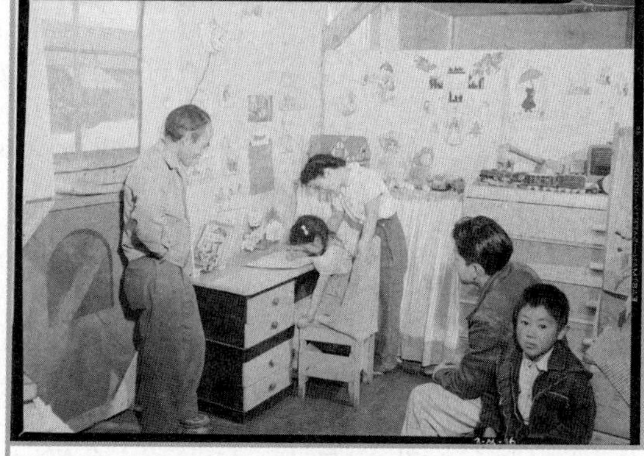

FIGURE 3.9

From this example we can see how, as a photographer, Adams made deliberate rhetorical choices in moving from capturing individual images to arranging them into powerful sequences and arguments on the page. Contemporary photojournalists have an even more expansive range of possibilities available to them through online publication, where modes of arrangement are designed to be versatile, flexible, and hyperlinked, often allowing the audience to customize their reading experience.

FIGURE 3.10

As a writer, you, too, need to assess the possibilities and limitations of the genre in which you're writing. In practical terms, this means that the way you organize your essay should be dictated by the conventions of the discipline or genre: a history term paper, for instance, will have a different structure from a lab report or a public policy white paper. In deciding which mode of arrangement might work best for your argument, you might decide to draw on one of these common structures that authors often use to organize their ideas into a convincing and well-organized written argument:

- **Chronological Structure:** Demonstrates change over time. Chronology relies on examples arranged in a temporal sequence, so it would be an effective structure, for instance, for an analysis of the changes in the rhetoric of the Black Panthers between their founding in 1966 and their peak influence in 1970.
- **Process or Narrative:** Arranges information sequentially, moving from beginning to end. If you were writing an essay proposing how activists could best leverage social media for their cause, you

might organize it to move from starting with the basics (setting up a Facebook page) to the more complex strategies such as customized messaging or integrating offline and online communications.

- **Cause–effect:** Shows how one event causes another. An essay confronting the issue of sexist language in rap music might start by exploring the words and allusions used to refer to women in popular rap music (*cause*) and then conclude by discussing the impact of this representation on the self-esteem of young girls (*effect*).
- **Problem–solution:** Defines the problem and then offers a solution. A paper about violence and video games might devote the first half of the paper to exploring the *problem* of desensitization and then focus in the second half of the paper on proposing a possible *solution*.
- **Block Structure:** Works systematically through a series of examples or case studies. For instance, in an essay about the underlying social and political themes in young adult fantasy literature, you might structure your essay to analyze first *The Lightning Thief*, then *The City of Bones*, and lastly *The Hunger Games*.
- **Thematic or Topical Structure:** Organizes by themes or subtopics. An essay on reality TV might include sections on voyeurism, capitalism, and Darwinism (*the themes*), integrating examples from *Survivor*, *American Idol*, and *So You Think You Can Dance* as evidence in each section.
- **Inductive Reasoning:** Begins with a guiding question and defers your thesis to your conclusion. For instance, an essay on media coverage of national disasters might contain a thesis question at the end of the introduction, such as "How do images featured in the news define our understanding of the impact of natural disasters on specific communities?", then synthesizing its evidence and building toward its claim at the end.

As you can see, you have many methods at your disposal to help you approach the question of arrangement strategically and deliberately. In the next sections, we'll examine a few organizational approaches you might emulate in your own writing and then suggest ways in which you can further customize your arrangement to best suit your individual assignment, purpose, and academic discipline.

Using Classical Strategies of Arrangement

In his *Rhetoric*, Aristotle proposed a relatively streamlined approach to arrangement, suggesting that an argument should be composed of two components: the statement of the case and the proof or support for that case. However, other rhetoricians, including Cicero and Quintilian, espoused a more complex approach. They maintained that persuasive speeches relied on a six-part structure:

I. Introduction (or *exordium*). In this section, the orator states the topic and develops his *ethos* as well as a connection with the audience.
II. Statement of facts or background (or *narratio*). This section provides the audience with context and any key information.
III. Division (or *partitio*). The orator uses this section to summarize the different lines of argument he will present, providing an overview or road map of the *parts* of the argument to follow. Often what we would consider the "thesis" occurs in this section.
IV. Proof (or *confirmatio*). This section contains the heart of the argument; it is where the orator presents his central claims, supported by evidence, facts, and reasons. This section would comprise what we might consider the "main body" of the argument.
V. Refutation (or *refutatio*). Once he has shared the argument, the orator then anticipates any objections to his claims and evaluates those counterarguments.
VI. Conclusion (or *peroratio*). In closing, the orator summarizes the strongest points of his claim and makes a final appeal to the audience.

Each of the parts could be comprised of a single paragraph or of several paragraphs. Notice how this structure moves from a firm grounding in the claim (I–IV) to a consideration of counterarguments (V) before reemphasizing the orator's position at the end (VI). The inclusion of step V might surprise you. Too often, when we present an argument, we're tempted to focus only on our own position, concerned that allowing other voices in the conversation might undermine our authority. However, classical rhetoricians recognized that this is not the case, that we build credibility as a writer or speaker by demonstrating that we have thought through alternate arguments and anticipated objections before arriving at our own claim.

It is worth noting that even in developing these models, classical scholars recognized that a formulaic approach to argument was limiting. They considered the orator's understanding of his rhetorical situation and the *kairos* of his argument to be of primary importance in determining the rhetorical arrangement of argument. In more modern times, contemporary rhetoricians have built on this principle to develop alternate models for argumentation that they considered best suited to the types of topics, situations, and audiences that writers and speakers address today.

Using the Toulmin Model to Analyze or Arrange an Argument

The Toulmin model of argumentation was developed by British philosopher Stephen Toulmin in 1969 as a way to define a system of persuasive reasoning. Toulmin found formal logic limited in its ability to apply to everyday, nonacademic issues and so decided to develop a structure that could have relevance to more common instances of argumentation and persuasion. At the most basic level, Toulmin identified three common features of argument: claims, warrants, and grounding.

The **claim** represents the writer's argument. It often manifests itself in the thesis statement, although many essays contain a series of linked smaller claims, or subclaims, which build together to the central thesis. One characteristic of a claim is that it is debatable, and so the burden is on the author to persuade his or her audience of its merit and validity.

That's where the **grounds** come in, which are comprised of the reasons and the evidence that support the claim. When an author doesn't back his claim with sufficient grounds, the claim can come off as unsupported opinion and be dismissed by his audience. In presenting their grounds, authors tend to draw on the *logos* appeal that we discussed in Chapter 2, supporting strong reasons with hard data, facts, testimonials, and even relevant personal experience.

The last feature, **warrants**, is an often unspoken element of the argument; it represents the unspoken assumptions that connect the claim to the grounds. Persuasion can easily be short-circuited if an author's audience doesn't agree with the warrants or the underlying ideas that support the argument.

Figure 3.11 lays out how these different elements work together to produce an argument, using the argument in favor of government-subsidized college education as an example. This model demonstrates the intricate relationship between the different elements of the argument: the claim itself is only as strong as the grounds (reasons and evidence) that support it and the degree to which the audience concurs with the warrant (assumptions or premises) that underlies it.

However, while the relationship between *claim*, *grounding*, and *warrant* provides the foundation for the Toulmin approach to argumentation, Toulmin himself expanded his model to account for the additional complexities

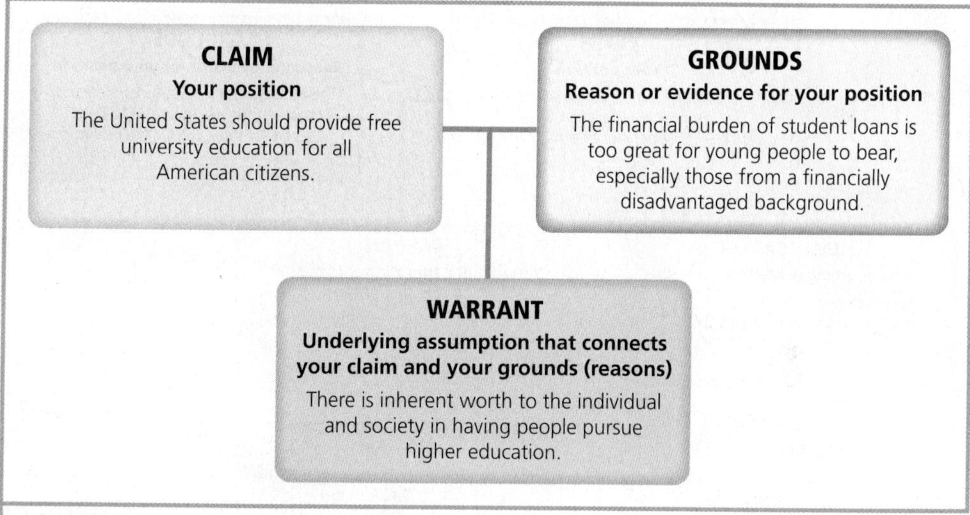

FIGURE 3.11 Toulmin Model

that often accompany everyday argument. The complete Toulmin model includes three additional elements:

- **Backing**: reasons, examples, or evidence that support the warrant. These may or may not also support the central claim.
- **Rebuttal**: a description and refutation of anticipated counterpoints and opposing claims. Keep in mind, it is important in this section to not only identify alternate perspectives and respond to them but also to do so in a fair, unbiased, and respectful way that enhances your *ethos*.
- **Qualification**: words or statements that adjust your claim to take into account counterarguments. These might be as subtle as hedging language that makes your claim more conditional (words like *perhaps*, *probably*, *in most cases*), or they might involve a separate sentence or point that softens or revises your original stance. Taking the time to adjust your claim based on alternate opinions demonstrates your willingness to consider the limitations to your position.

These additional features help us remember that arguments operate not in a vacuum but in dialogue with larger conversations, and that the most persuasive claims take into account other perspectives.

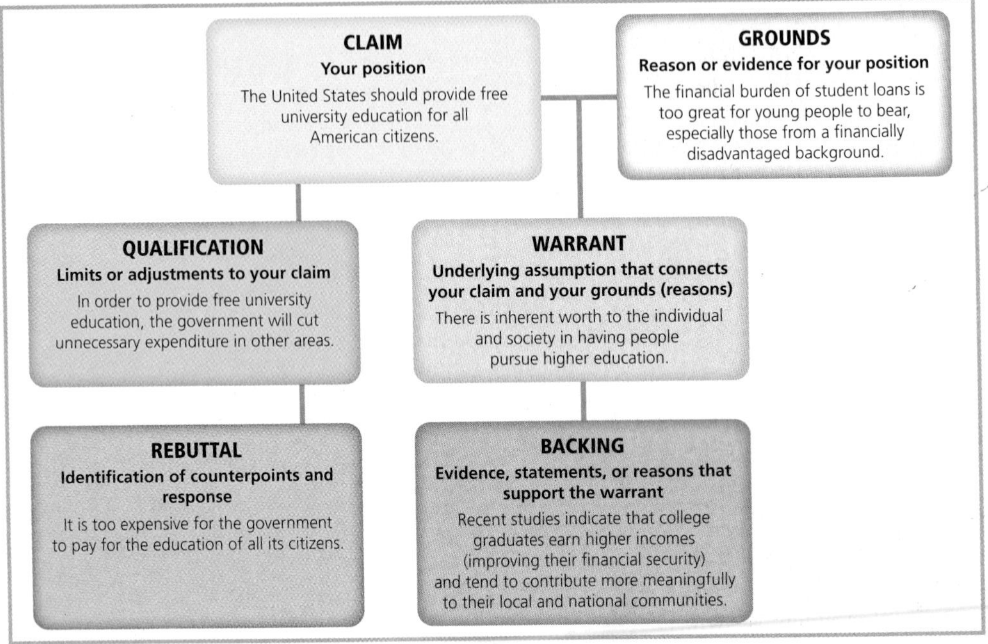

FIGURE 3.12 Complete Toulmin Model

In Figure 3.12, we can see the addition of *backing*, *rebuttal*, and *qualification* yield a more rigorous and persuasive treatment of the issue.

Developed as a paragraph, a draft of this argument would look something like this:

> The financial burden of student loans is too great for young people to bear, especially those from a financially disadvantaged background. [grounds] Consequently, the United States should provide free university education for all Americans. [claim] This financial investment would be a worthwhile one for the government, since a higher education degree is valuable to both the individual and society. [warrant] As recent studies have shown, college graduates earn higher incomes and tend to contribute more meaningfully to their local and national communities. [backing] However, in order to afford such a program, the government would need to take a hard look at its other expenditures and streamline its budget for other programs. [qualifier] Without such careful auditing and reassignment of resources, the costs of universal education would be prohibitive, even for the government. [rebuttal]

In reading this paragraph, you can see how the Toulmin approach generates a reasoned and logical argumentative structure. However, you probably also can identify areas for expansion or elaboration: additional specific details needed to make the grounds and backing more persuasive; further counterpoints or opposing perspectives that need to be addressed; added adjustments to the claim or the qualification. You might even want to fine-tune the warrant further to make the underlying premise of the claim more persuasive. Expanding on the basic structure in this way would allow you to develop this idea into a more robust argument, one that could serve the foundation for a well-reasoned and persuasive essay. The At a Glance box offers a model for how you could use the Toulmin method for a full-length essay.

AT A GLANCE

Following the Toulmin Model

Rely on this structure to strengthen a claim by looking at unstated assumptions (warrants) and alternate viewpoints:

1. Introduction of topic
2. Thesis claim
3. Grounds (reasons and evidence to support the claim)
4. Warrants (connections between the grounds and the claim)
5. Backing (support for the warrants)
6. Rebuttals (including qualification)
7. Conclusion

As you can see, the Toulmin model provides a framework that helps you think through the complexities of your claim and produce a more nuanced argument. You can rely on the Toulmin method to compose a claim of your own, support it with appropriate evidence, and explain clearly how and why that evidence does in fact prove, or support, your claim; you can use it on a small scale to build a well-reasoned paragraph or on a larger scale for an entire essay. In addition, keep in mind that Toulmin himself developed this structure as an analytic tool, so you can draw on it to help you further develop the way you critically engage with and assess the arguments made by others.

WRITER'S PRACTICE MyWritingLab

Select one of the topics below (or one of your own choosing) and use invention techniques to identify your stand on the issue:

- High school uniforms or dress codes
- General education requirements at colleges and universities
- Standardized tests and college admissions

Next, using the chart in Figure 3.12 as a model, diagram your argument to identify your *claim*, *grounding*, *warrant*, *backing*, *rebuttal*, and *qualification*. Afterward, follow the process showcased above and transform your diagram into a cohesive paragraph.

Considering Rogerian Arguments

An alternative mode of argumentation was developed by rhetoricians Richard Young, Kenneth Pike, and Alton Becker in 1970. Drawing from the communication practices of Carl Rogers—an influential psychologist—Young, Pike, and Becker modeled a process of persuasion based on a deep understanding and appreciation of an opponent's perspective. Their model of argumentation was empathic and conciliatory rather than adversarial, putting into practice Rogers's suggestion from 1951 that communication based on finding common ground can help resolve emotionally intense situations such as found in negotiations or diplomacy.

As a writer, you might wonder how the Rogerian approach differs from other types of argument. Consider this example from an argument about Instagram posts:

> Some media watchdog groups argue that parents should be able to arbitrarily override their teenagers' Instagram account settings so that the parents can remove any photos they deem objectionable, which is a clear violation of the right to free speech.

On the one hand, in this statement, the author clearly articulates her opinion. On the other hand, however, she offers only a dismissive and cursory glimpse of the opposing viewpoint, closing down any possibility of dialogue or negotiation. Notice how an exchange using a Rogerian approach fosters a greater possibility for a productive conversation on this issue:

> Some media watchdog groups worry that teenagers post pictures on Instagram without considering the future implications of the images. They believe that provocative photos (featuring teenagers in sexualized poses or engaged in reckless activities) might produce unforeseen results, such as limiting the Instagram user's college or employment prospects later in life, or even attracting sexual predators. For this reason, they argue, Instagram should put into place parental overrides to allow a parent to monitor and safeguard their children's well-being. This raises an important question: would this mechanism impinge on the teenager's right to free speech?

The revision does more than simply removing inflammatory or biased language; it offers acknowledgment and fair assessment of the counterposition. For this reason, a Rogerian argument hinges on establishing a sense of **common ground** between diverse opinions, and, as Douglas Brent has argued, necessitates "imagining [the counter-position] with empathy." By fostering more open and nonjudgmental dialogue, a Rogerian approach can help transform volatile exchanges into opportunities for productive consensus. To adopt this strategy in your own writing, incorporate the following steps into your writing process:

1. When you introduce the issue, be sure to restate your opponent's position in a respectful way that shows a rich knowledge and understanding of that stance.
2. In discussing the opposing opinion, elaborate on the contexts in which such a stance might be valid.
3. In stating your own position, likewise be sure to suggest the contexts in which your stance might be valid.
4. As the closing moment in your argument, move toward compromise or conciliation, suggesting how your opponent's stance might benefit from incorporating components of your own position. Ideally, you would demonstrate how the positions can complement each other, rather than showing which one "wins."

Keep in mind that while you can use a Rogerian method to shape your entire essay, you can also employ it in certain sections of your argument, such as when you are restating counterarguments to show your own nuanced understanding of your topic.

AT A GLANCE

Arguing from Common Ground with the Rogerian Approach

Center your argument on mutual understanding and common ground to make your audience more open to your position:

1. Introduction
2. Summary of opposing viewpoint
3. Statement of common ground or understanding
4. Statement of your claim and position
5. Statement of contexts
6. Conclusion (appealing to self-interests of the audience)

WRITER'S PRACTICE

MyWritingLab

Return to the chart and paragraph you composed for the Writer's Practice on page 105. Addressing the same topic, now draft a paragraph about it using a Rogerian structure (arguing from common ground). Compare your Toulmin paragraph to your Rogerian paragraph on the topic. Which seems to be the most effective way to make your particular argument? What type of audience would each resonate best with? Why?

Exploring Effective Modes of Arrangement

Whether you are working with the classical model of arrangement, the Toulmin method, or the Rogerian approach, each asks you to reflect on one key question: how can you best articulate your argument when taking into account your audience and alternate arguments on the topic? While you may choose to adopt one of these frameworks to organize your own writing or presentations, in most cases you need to do more than simply follow a rigidly defined structural paradigm. As we discussed above, even classical rhetoricians recognized that following a certain formula for structure was less important than reflecting on what would be most persuasive to a particular audience.

Consider the strategies represented in the Strategies of Arrangement table, which represent variations on the classical, Toulmin, and Rogerian structures discussed above. Notice the way these alternative modes of arrangement balance making your own argument with taking into account diverse perspectives on the issue.

Strategies of Arrangement

Leading with Your Claim

Use when you want to ground the reader in your argument before bringing up opposing perspectives:

1. Introduction, identification of rhetorical stance
2. Thesis
3. Statement of background, definition, or context
4. Evidence and development of argument
5. Opposing opinion, concession, qualification, refutation
6. Conclusion

Leading with Counterarguments

Establish opposing opinion up front so that the entire piece functions as an extended rebuttal or refutation of that line of argument:

1. Introduction and opposing viewpoint
2. Thesis and identification of rhetorical stance
3. Evidence and development of argument
4. Conclusion

Integrating Claims and Counterclaims

Treat diverse viewpoints as appropriate during the development of your argument and presentation of your evidence:

1. Introduction, identification of rhetorical stance
2. Thesis
3. Statement of background, definition, or context
4. Evidence, opposing opinion, concession, qualification, refutation
5. Conclusion

These models of arrangement are not designed to function as rigid templates for organization. Instead, they suggest possibilities and potentially effective strategies of arrangement. In your own writing, you will have to select the most productive way to lay out your argument, depending in part on your claim, your understanding of your audience, and your approach to alternate perspectives on your issue.

In considering these various modes of arrangement, first consider your audience:

- How much do they know about the issue? *Their level of familiarity with the topic will influence how much background information you incorporate into your essay and where you introduce it.*
- What is their rhetorical stance toward the issue? *If addressing a hostile or resistant audience, you might begin your essay by trying to forge a connection with your readers or trying to soften their stance.*
- What is their stance toward you as a writer or speaker? *If they already consider you credible, you do not need to do too much ethos-building in your essay; however, if you have not yet established your trustworthiness or expertise, you will need to organize your argument in such a way as to assert your authority on the issue.*

Second, take into account how you want to integrate diverse viewpoints, asking yourself:

- Do the alternate perspectives corroborate your argument? *If so, you could include them as supporting evidence.*
- Do they offer points of view that you can disprove? *If they do, you might present the opinion and provide a rebuttal, or refutation of the points, demonstrating why they are not valid.*
- Do they offer points of view that are irrelevant to your argument? *If so, you demonstrate that these perspectives, while perhaps salient in some situations, are not directly relevant to the issue as you define it.*
- Do they offer points of view that you can't disprove? *In this case, you might concede the validity of some parts of their argument but go on to qualify their points by showing why your own argument is nonetheless persuasive.*

The key is to treat these other voices with respect; always represent their points of view fairly and without bias, even if you disagree with them.

3.4 How can style be used to compose a powerful argument?

STYLE IN ARGUMENT

Inventing a thesis or main idea and *arranging* the elements of your writing are two steps in completing your task of written persuasion. You also need to spend some time considering what tone, word choice, and voice you will use in your writing. This is where **style**—the third canon of rhetoric—enters the scene. While "style" often suggests basic grammar or mechanical correctness, from the vantage point of classical rhetoric, style—according to the Roman rhetorician Cicero—concerns choosing the appropriate expression for the ideas of your argument; these choices relate to language, tone, syntax, rhetorical appeals, metaphors, imagery, quotations, level of emphasis, and nuance.

We often translate *style* into *voice* to indicate how a writer's perspective is manifested in word choice, syntax, pacing, and tone. To construct a successful argument, you need to be able to employ the voice or style that best meets the needs of your rhetorical situation. As Cicero famously stated: "I don't always adopt the same style. What similarity is there between a letter and an oration in court or at a public meeting?"

Now consider two contemporary examples of style, both focused on President Obama. The first is an excerpt from a *Sports Illustrated* piece:

> Obama's erect carriage and lefthandedness led me to think of Lionel "Train" Hollins, who commanded the Portland Trail Blazers' backcourt when the kid then known as "Barry O'Bomber" was making his way through high school.

Using basketball lingo ("backcourt") and casual vocabulary ("the kid" and "making his way"), the writer Alexander Wolff describes Obama as someone who speaks the language of popular readers—what Cicero would have called "plain style." Moreover, the naming of famous players gives credibility or *ethos* to Wolff himself as someone who knows the players and even their nicknames. In this way, his style or writing contributes to building his authority as an author.

In contrast, a writer from the academic journal *Rhetoric & Public Affairs* uses what Cicero called *high style*, or elevated diction, in making a critique of President Obama:

> While Obama's rhetoric of *consilience* approximates dialogic coherence, it nonetheless falls short of the discursive demands of racial reconciliation.

By using sophisticated concepts—such as "dialogic coherence" and "discursive demands"—familiar only to a highly educated academic audience, writer Mark McPhail uses the style of an erudite member of the intellectual class. His "backcourt buddies" can be understood as the colleagues who understand that "dialogic coherence" and "discursive demands" refer to ways of speaking and writing. While McPhail's style is radically different from Wolff's, it has a parallel function in that it builds his authority as a writer for those familiar with the journal's conventions.

Let's consider another case, this time examining how an author adjusts his rhetorical style when presenting the same material to two different audiences, in two different forms and contexts. Yale Professor Nicholas Christakis is well known in his field for his work on how social networks influence the behaviors of individuals; more specifically, he looks at how networks create behavior "clusters," that is, groups of people connected through social networks who exhibit similar inclinations, habits, or behavior patterns. As part of his exploration of this topic, Christakis examined how people's likelihood of becoming obese statistically increased in relation to the presence of other obese people in their social network, even at a remove (i.e., their friends, their friends' friends, and even their friends' friends' friends). When giving a TED talk on the topic in 2010, he adopted plain style, focusing on translating his scientific findings into a format that would be both engaging and clear for a public audience. Here he describes his three initial hypotheses for why he found obesity clusters in his research into social networks; Figure 3.13 shows the slide he used to accompany his description:

> Well, what might be causing this clustering? There are at least three possibilities: One possibility is that, as I gain weight, it causes you to gain weight. A kind of induction, a kind of spread from person to person. Another possibility, very obvious, is homophily, or, birds of a feather flock together; here, I form my tie to you because you and I share a similar body size. And the last possibility is what is known as confounding, because it confounds our ability to figure out what's going on. And here, the idea is not that my weight gain is causing your weight gain, nor that I preferentially form a tie with you because you and I share the same body size, but rather that we share a common exposure to something, like a health club that makes us both lose weight at the same time.

Notice his stylistic choices: his reliance on first and second person to personalize the three hypotheses, connecting them to ideas or experiences that

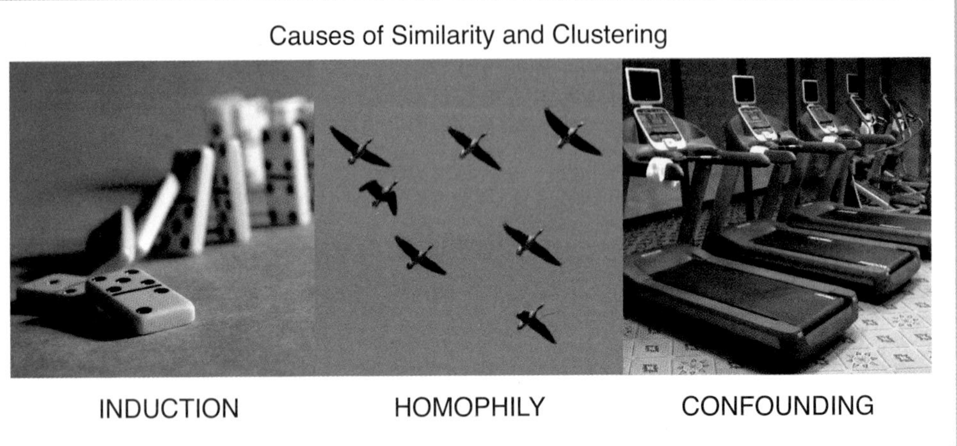

FIGURE 3.13 Nicholas Christakis's slide designed to provide visual analogies for his three hypotheses about the reasons for obesity clusters on social networks.

would be familiar to his audience; his integration of a common expression ("birds of a feather flock together") that translates the idea of "homophily" into more commonplace terms; his use of an analogy ("like a health club") to help his audience better understand his point; and his use of more informal sentence structures, contractions, and word choice ("to figure out what's going on"). Even the slide itself follows the same method, providing visual correlatives for the technical concepts that he's been describing to speak to an audience unfamiliar with network theory.

When addressing his academic peers, however, Christakis had to convey the same information, but in a way that would take into account their expertise and advanced understanding. Consider the way he shifted to a more elevated level of style in his article from *The New England Journal of Medicine* to describe the same three hypotheses:

> We considered three explanations for the clustering of obese people. First, egos might choose to associate with like alters ("homophily").[21,23,24] Second, egos and alters might share attributes or jointly experience unobserved contemporaneous events that cause their weight to vary at the same time (confounding). Third, alters might exert social influence or peer effects on egos ("induction"). Distinguishing the interpersonal induction of obesity from homophily requires dynamic, longitudinal network information about the

> emergence of ties between people ("nodes") in a network and also about the attributes of nodes (i.e., repeated measures of the body-mass index).[25]

In reading the two paragraphs, you might think that they were written by two separate people because the style varies so greatly; in reality, what they showcase is the ability of a single author to accommodate different rhetorical situations through his stylistic choices. In the journal article, Christakis does not need define all his terms; he can use words like *egos* and *alters* without additional definition because he knows they would be familiar to the readers of *NEJM*. In addition, because this article is meant to be read silently (instead of listened to, as the TED talk was), he could use a different technique when he did decide to offer definitions, providing the definition first ("egos might choose to associate with like alters") and then glossing it with the term in parenthesis ("homophily"). That strategy would be hard to follow if you were listening to the paragraph, but is much easier to comprehend when reading. Even Christakis's use of footnotes presents a stylistic choice, one that indicates that he prioritized building his *ethos* with his colleagues through referencing his knowledge of other work in the field, a move he did not feel as necessary in his TED presentation. While the information in the *NEJM* paragraph is essentially identical to that found in the TED paragraph, it has been styled to better suit the discourse of Christakis's professional community.

Similarly, in your own writing, your choice of style should address a specific audience and can thus build your *ethos* with those readers. If you are wondering how to move from invention and arrangement to developing your own style, then it is time to learn about constructing a *persona* and developing a *rhetorical stance* in your writing.

Constructing Your Persona

The term *persona* has its roots in Latin word for "mask," referring to the theatrical masks worn by actors in ancient Greece. In more contemporary terms, we use persona to refer to *a deliberately crafted version of yourself* that you construct and project in response to a specific audience or context.

You probably are already practiced at the art of tailoring your persona for specific rhetorical situations. Think about how you represent yourself on different social media platforms. The persona you project—both in your profile picture and the written information you share online—on a platform like Facebook, Instagram, or Tumblr, is probably different than the one you would craft for a site like LinkedIn or a university department Webpage. Even the fleeting images you share on Snapchat might represent a different "you," one that you anticipate will last only a few seconds before disappearing into the ether. In each case, while attending to the type of *ethos* you want to cultivate, you make a series of strategic choices about what type of "mask" you want to show to the world.

We see the power of persona at play in the public sphere every day. Candidates for a presidential election might book appearances on late night TV to show their lighter side; Hollywood celebrities might appear at high profile charity events to overlay their glamorous image with one that shows they care deeply about important social issues. President Barack Obama might choose to give a speech about war flanked by a group of military men and women or a speech about health care surrounded by doctors, as we see in Figure 3.14. In each case, persona functions as a rhetorical construction of self-designed to present a certain argument about the individual that directly influences his *ethos*.

The same principle governs the writing process. When you compose a text (whether verbal, visual, or multimedia), you decide how to use language to shape your particular *persona* as a writer and rhetorician. That is, you create a portrait of yourself as the author of your argument through a number of stylistic choices:

- Tone (formal or informal, humorous or serious)
- Word choice and diction (academic, colloquial, technical, or clichéd)

FIGURE 3.14 When President Barack Obama talks about health care surrounded by white-coated medical personnel, he creates a persona for himself as a friend and supporter of physicians.

- Imagery (allusions, metaphor, vivid descriptions)
- Sentence structure (complex or simple and direct)
- Use of rhetorical appeals (*pathos*, *logos*, *ethos*, *kairos*, *doxa*)
- Strategies of persuasion (narration, example, cause and effect, analogy, process, description, classification, or definition)

Creating a persona requires care. A well-designed one can facilitate a strong connection with your readers and therefore make your argument more persuasive. However, a *poorly constructed persona*—one that is, for instance, biased, inconsistent, or underdeveloped—can have the opposite effect, alienating readers and undercutting your text's overall effectiveness. An additional challenge in constructing your persona lies in retaining a sense of authenticity—in your voice, your perspective, and your argument—despite the fact that you're speaking through a rhetorical mask. What's key here is to realize that an effective persona represents a version of yourself, not a completely new character, and you should support it in your writing with other elements that contribute to your trustworthiness as an author: unbiased language, reasoned claims, respect for alternate viewpoints, ethical use of sources, and supporting evidence for your points.

Choosing a Rhetorical Stance

To be persuasive, you must not only create a persona that responds appropriately to your specific rhetorical situation and engages both audience and text, but you must also convey a *position* that Wayne Booth, one of the most important revivalists of classical rhetoric, defined as the **rhetorical stance**. In essence, a writer's rhetorical stance refers to the position the author assumes in relation to subject, audience, and context; it is a careful and deliberate navigation of the rhetorical situation and appeals with an intent to persuade an audience. In this sense, we can understand rhetorical stance not just as the "stand" that you take in relation to an issue, but as a more dynamic position we assume to accommodate to our understanding of the rhetorical situation.

Booth argued that communication failed between people (or a text failed to persuade a reader) if the writer takes on a stance that ignored the balance of the rhetorical situation. We see examples of inappropriate rhetorical stances constantly: the TV evangelist who moves his congregation with a polished sermon that completely distracts them from flaws in his moral character; the used-car salesman who pads his sales pitch with offers of free gifts, rebate specials, and low percentage rates; the actor who uses her celebrity status to drive a product endorsement, rather than clearly articulating the merits of that product itself. In each case, the *rhetorical situation*—the relationship between author, audience, and text—is out of balance, and the argument itself, ultimately, is less persuasive.

In your own writing, therefore, you need to pay special attention not only to the *persona* you create but also to the *rhetorical stance* you assume in relation to your specific situation. Before you even begin writing, take some time to identify your stance and consider how explicitly you want to convey it to your audience. Are they likely to align themselves with your position? Resist it? What sort of tone, style, and approach should you adopt to most persuasively present your position to your readers? These choices will shape your reader's understanding of your argument.

AT A GLANCE

Three Poorly Constructed Rhetorical Stances

The famous rhetoric scholar Wayne Booth identified three ways in which communication can break down, resulting in a failure that indicates a lack of balance among author, audience, and text. Booth emphasized that a poorly constructed persona leads to this demise, so you should avoid these situations in your own writing:

- **The pedant or preacher:** the text is paramount and both the audience's needs and the speaker's character are ignored.
- **The advertiser:** the effect on the audience is valued above all, ignoring the quality of the text and the credibility of the speaker.
- **The entertainer:** the character of the speaker is elevated above the text and the audience.

3.5 How can I write a persuasive position paper?

CRAFTING A POSITION PAPER

One way to put into practice the canons of rhetoric—*invention*, *arrangement*, and *style*—and to explore constructing a persuasive persona and assuming an effective rhetorical stance—is to write a position paper. By definition, a **position paper** offers you the opportunity to write about your opinion on an issue. This can take many forms: a letter to the editor of a newspaper, an op-ed (opinion editorial), a brief short, oral position statement, or even a white paper in politics or a memory aid in law. In each case, the writer focuses in on an issue and presents opinion backed by evidence. Many times, a position paper contains a very strong tone, taking one side of a controversial issue, much as you would find in a debate, and actively arguing in direct opposition to alternative positions on the issue. A successful position paper incorporates the following elements:

An introduction that provides an overview of the topic, providing background and a sense of its relevance. The introduction also establishes the author's rhetorical stance and claim, usually culminating in a strong thesis statement.

A strong assertion of the author's position. The main force of the argument in a position paper lies in this section, where the author persuades the reader that his position on the issue is the stronger one, supporting his points through evidence and logical reasoning.

A fair treatment of counterarguments. For each counterclaim, the author objectively describes the position and then either refutes it, concedes the point, or qualifies the argument.

A conclusion that reemphasizes the author's claim and once again reasserts the larger relevance of the issue.

While all strong position papers contain these components, the arrangement of the different parts might vary depending on your style, rhetorical situation, and topic. As we saw in the Strategies of Arrangement table on page 108, you have many options available to you. You might choose a block structure where you separate your treatment of the opposition's claims from the section where you focus on your own position. Alternately, you might adopt a more point-by-point model, where you present a series of counterarguments, debunking each in turn before developing your own position. Sometimes, a position paper might be less adversarial, relying on the Rogerian technique of understanding the issue from another's point of view in order to communicate that material to a third party, such as found in policy statement papers delivered to the United Nations, or law briefs, or statements of original research. Because of such variance, when you write a position paper, you should select your strategy of arrangement as carefully as you craft your style for the essay. Moreover, both organization and style should relate to your purpose and audience, in support of the main point of invention.

Before we look at how style and arrangement come together in a full-length position paper, let's zoom in on three key features that help frame your audience's understanding of your argument in this sort of paper—and in other types of essays as well: title, introduction, and conclusion.

Composing a Title

Your reader's first encounter with your topic and position comes through your **title**; in this way, the title itself operates as a rhetorical act that provides a frame and sets up the argument. To better understand this, consider how headlines perform a similar function. On September 2, 2005, many newspapers featured the photograph shown in Figure 3.1 on their front pages—but accompanied by different headlines. Figures 3.15 and 3.16 offer two examples. Notice how each newspaper indicates its rhetorical stance through the combination of words and images contained on its front page.

How does the headline "Mayor Sends 'Desperate SOS'" (see Figure 3.15) suggest a different argument than "New Orleans Roiled by Chaos" paired with the same photo? The difference in tone, perspective, and rhetorical stance apparent from these contrasting examples underscores the role a headline—or title—plays in forming a reader's expectations for the argument that follows. In effect, a *title* is the first step in writing an interpretation or making an argument.

In writing your own essays, you should spend some time brainstorming your titles. Some writers find constructing a powerful title to be a useful *invention* activity to start their composition process; others construct the title only after completing the first draft of their paper, as a way of synthesizing the argument and bringing it into sharper focus. In either case, developing a strong title can help you both clarify your central claim and rhetorical stance and also set up clear expectations for your audience.

As you work with a title, think about its role in setting up your stance on your topic, indicating to your readers not only the scope of your analysis but also your angle on it. A strong title should accomplish at least two goals: first, it should clearly identify the essay's topic and (occasionally) the claim; second, it should capture the reader's attention. Keeping these goals in mind, experiment with the following strategies when writing titles for your essays:

- *Link the title to your main point or claim*. Sometimes the most direct and transparent titles can be the most powerful. Example: "Why We Need to Re-think the Common Core Initiative."

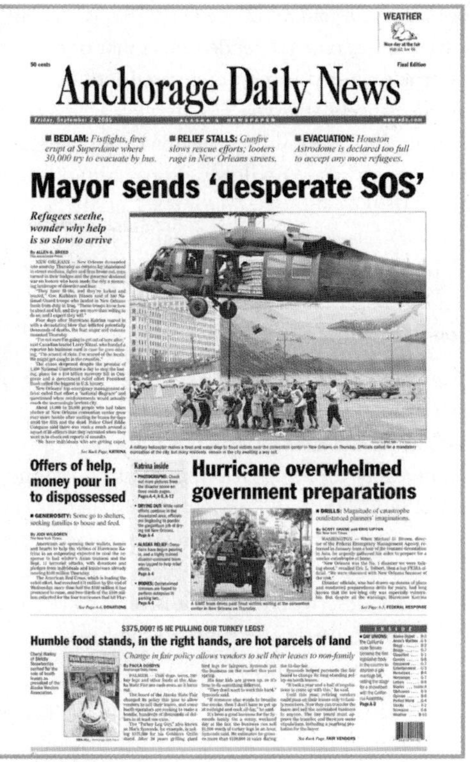

WEATHER

50 cents

Final Edition

Anchorage Daily News

Friday, September 2, 2005 ALASKA'S NEWSPAPER www.adn.com

■ BEDLAM: *Fistfights, fires erupt at Superdome where 30,000 try to evacuate by bus.*

■ RELIEF STALLS: *Gunfire slows rescue efforts; looters rage in New Orleans streets.*

■ EVACUATION: *Houston Astrodome is declared too full to accept any more refugees.*

Mayor sends 'desperate SOS'

Refugees seethe, wonder why help is so slow to arrive

Offers of help, money pour in to dispossessed

■ GENEROSITY: Some go to shelters, seeking families to house and feed.

Katrina inside

Hurricane overwhelmed government preparations

$375,000? IS HE PULLING OUR TURKEY LEGS?

Humble food stands, in the right hands, are hot parcels of land

Change in fair policy allows vendors to sell their leases to non-family

OPENING WIN: Washington State kicks off season by defeating Idaho /B1

The Columbian

Weekend

Taste of Vancouver is a culinary and musical treat this weekend

your Guide:

New Orleans roiled by chaos

Anger, tension, violence mount as thousands try to escape ravaged city

'I'm not sure I'm going to get out of here alive.'

Katrina unleashes storm surge on U.S. economy

Waterfront district with 10,000 residents envisioned

Development council listens to professor's ideas for Vancouver

FIGURE 3.15 Front page of the *Anchorage Daily News*.

FIGURE 3.16 Front page of the *Columbian*, a newspaper from Clark County, Washington.

- *Pose a question raised by your argument.* A variation of the first strategy, this approach invites the reader to consider an issue rather than explicitly focusing on your stance. Example: "Should We Re-think the Common Core in Elementary and Secondary Education?"
- *Play with language.* As an alternative, you may want to use techniques such as alliteration (using two or more words with the same initial sound) or a play on words to make a title more engaging. Examples: "The Trouble with Teens and Twitter" and "Great Expectorations: Behind the Culture of Chewing Tobacco."

- *Connect to a key image, underlying metaphor, or guiding concept*. When composing an essay that relies on an extended metaphor or central idea, you can use the title as your first opportunity to introduce your readers to the concept that you will develop at length in your argument. Examples: "Rebuilding the Tower of Babel through Bilingual Education" and "Endlessly Propagating Networks without End … or Purpose; Reevaluating Social Media."
- *Use a quote from one of your sources*. This strategy allows you to use a key quotation to establish *ethos* and set the stage for your argument. Example: "'Make It So'; Redesigning *Star Trek* for the Next Generation."

How you develop your title depends in part on your understanding of audience and your rhetorical situation. The title for a narrative essay might be more whimsical and creative, while the title for an expository essay might prioritize clearly articulating the essay topic. A title for an essay designed to be shared online might deliberately incorporate key words that would make it more searchable through Google or a database search. In academic essays and research papers, we often see authors using a two-part title, pairing a catchy initial title with a more descriptive subtitle after a colon. For instance, one student chose the following title and subtitle combination for her essay on the portrayal of women in videogames:

> "Sexualized Sabotage. Representations of Female Protagonists in Video Games"

The two halves of the title work well together. The first part is catchy, implying the author's critical stance about the topic; however, on its own, it does not clearly convey the topic of the essay. The second half of the title much more directly communicates the focus of the essay, but it lacks flare and stops short of sharing the author's claim. Joined together, the two parts provide an engaging combination designed to pique the reader's interest while conveying relevant information.

Use some caution with two-part titles, however. While this style can be quite effective in certain situations, at times they also can seem overly complicated. Avoid sacrificing clarity for the sake of what some call "academese"—a style of writing intended to sound erudite, but which often instead obfuscates meaning or sounds pretentious due to relying on unnecessarily complex sentence structures, passive voice, or obscure vocabulary. As you devise your title, keep in mind your audience's knowledge, expectations, and the conventions of your disciplinary field and writing assignment. The style of a title for a lab report for a Biology class will differ from the style for a title for a paper you write for a Biomedical Ethics class. It's a matter of rhetoric: understanding the logistics of your rhetorical situation so as to determine how to create a title that most effectively engages your audience.

WRITER'S PRACTICE MyWritingLab

Complete the steps below (many based on Richard Leahy's "Twenty Titles for the Writer") to experiment with creating different titles for an essay you've already written. Alternately, use the steps to develop alternate titles for the sample student essays in Chapter 1 or Chapter 2. The goal is not necessarily to develop a single perfect title but to explore a process of *invention.* As you work through this Writer's Practice, reflect on how the steps—individually or as a process—help you reflect more purposefully different strategies for composing an effective title. When you're done, discuss your alternate titles and your observations with a partner.

1. Combine key terms or concepts into a title.
2. Transform the drafted title from step 1 into one that clearly demonstrates your claim or rhetorical stance.
3. Select a phrase or sentence from your essay or from one of the sources you quote in your essay for your title (be sure to use quotation marks if it's a direct quote from a source!).
4. Use a gerund (an -ing verb) or the preposition "On" as the first word of your title.
5. Experiment with an alliterative title.
6. Develop a title that asks a question (one that starts either with Who/What/When/Where/How/Why or Do/Does/Is/Are/Will).
7. Create a one-word title, then a two-word title, then a three-word title, then a four-word title, and then, finally, a five-word title.
8. Develop a title that alludes to or makes a pun about a common phrase or the title of a movie, book, or song.
9. Write a two-part title; feel free to combine two of the titles you've created above.

Composing Your Introduction

Like your title, your introduction offers your readers insight into the persona and rhetorical stance that will characterize your essay as a whole. An introduction may be a single paragraph or a section composed of two or more paragraphs; in it, you establish your voice (informal? formal?), your tone (measured? firm? angry? cautious?), your persona, and your stance on your topic through careful attention to word choice, sentence structure, and strategies of development. Most introductions also provide some background information and the first articulation of your argument as well, moving from a general statement of topic to a more focused statement of your *thesis*.

However, perhaps just as importantly, the introduction is the place where you capture the attention of your reader, often through a stylistic device that we call a "hook." For instance, let's return to Ansel Adams's photo essay, *Born Free and Equal*. He hooks his audience through a combination of word and image from the very first pages of the book. On one page, he reproduces the Fourteenth Amendment to the U.S. Constitution, which states, "No state shall make or enforce any law which shall abridge the privileges or immunities of citizens of the United States …"; he then juxtaposes that line with the smiling face of the "American School Girl" shown in Figure 3.17. Here *logos* and *pathos* work side by side to prompt readers to wonder about this apparent contradiction. This is the hook that gets readers interested—and compels them to keep reading.

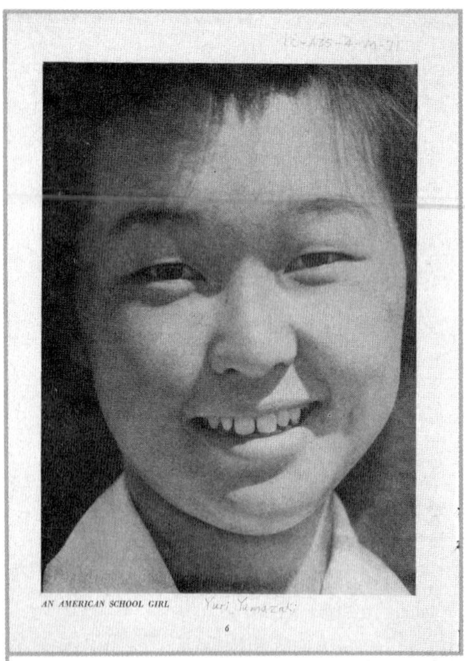

FIGURE 3.17

In written texts, you can use your introduction to hook your readers through one of several methods. You might use one or a combination of the following techniques:

- Define your terms (especially if you're writing on a subject that may not be familiar to your audience).
- Include a significant quotation, thought-provoking question, or a startling statistic or fact.
- Present an overview of the issue you're discussing.
- Provide some background on the topic.
- Use an anecdote or narration.
- Incorporate a vivid example.
- Draw on a relevant analogy or metaphor.
- Use the second-person pronoun (*you*) to connect with your readers.
- Use the first-person pronoun (*I*/*we*) to demonstrate your personal investment in the topic.

Your decision about how to craft your introduction will depend to a large extent on your broader stylistic choices about your essay and the way in which you want to develop your argument. For instance, for assignments that require a more formal, academic style, using "you" or "I" might not be an appropriate choice; alternately, that same sort of direct address might prove an extremely effective choice in an essay modeled after an op-ed or a call to action. The key to making the best stylistic choices lies in understanding the expectations of your assignment, your audience, and the genre that you're writing.

Let's look at how one student took style into consideration while composing her introduction to a position paper about the use of photo-retouching in teen fashion magazines:

> *I love my fashion magazines. I love flipping through the pages and seeing the cool fashions, the colorful ads, and all the beautiful celebs and models. But every time I read them, I can't help but feel a little worse about myself. Why can't I look like that? What do I have to do to be that beautiful, that perfect?* (Interview)
>
> This conflicted sentiment, expressed here by a 15 year old *Teen Vogue* reader, is not unusual. Even in this age of digital media, teen magazines such as *Teen Vogue* and *Seventeen* continue to have a strong following among teenage girls. However, these publications, which are meant to provide entertainment and "style inspiration" (Astley qtd. in Haughney), have a dark side effect: they promote an unhealthy culture of perfectionism that is detrimental to their readers. They do so not only by showcasing the Beautiful People of the fashion and entertainment industry, but also by making them even more beautiful through techniques like retouching, airbrushing, and photoshopping images. When considering that nearly 70% of middle school and high school aged girls report that their idea of the ideal body shape is influenced by magazines and, even more significantly, 50% say they want to lose weight because of it (Levin), the seriousness of this issue becomes clear. These unrealistic representations of beauty are putting teenage girls at risk, at best serving as sources for "thinspiration" and at worst inciting self-loathing in their readership. Teen fashion magazines need show a greater sense of responsibility to their readers; they need to listen to the many voices that are criticizing these photo altering practices and start making real changes to promote more realistic images of beauty in both the covers and contents of their magazines.

What hooks the reader first is the quotation that heads the introduction from a reader of teen fashion magazines. This quote announces the essay's topic at the same time that it provides a sharp contrast for the writing style of the main body of the introduction that follows. By comparison, the author's voice or writing style seems crisp, focused, and academic, establishing a *persona* that shows she is both informed on her subject and knowledgeable about the larger context. Note how she connects the hook to the rest of the introduction, fashioning her first sentence to serve as a bridge. From the rest of the introduction, we can tell that she will ground her argument in research and has developed a strong position on the topic. Notice the stylistic detail in the paragraph: the use of statistics to provide a *logos* appeal; judicious use of direct quotes, enough to provide *ethos*, but not enough to overwhelm her own voice; the strategic use of strong, specific words and phrases; the movement toward articulating her own stance and position on the topic. She ends the introduction with her thesis statement, pointing implicitly to how she will develop her argument (by discussing the strategies proposed by the "many voices" and advocating for change).

Writing Your Conclusion

If the introduction offers the writer the opportunity to hook the audience while providing a rhetorical stance on a subject, the **conclusion** is the final opportunity to reinforce an essay's argument while making a lasting impact on readers. For this reason, although a conclusion by its nature should include some gesture toward the materials covered in the essay and may synthesize the key points from the essay, it should also have a rhetorical power of its own. Let's look at how the author above concluded her essay:

> The collective momentum of the critiques and suggestions from these many anti-photoshop voices—from grassroots activists like Julia Bluhm, to media movements like "Keep it Real," and forward-thinking magazines like *Verily*—have promoted a climate that seems inclined toward change. In fact, to many, the cover of the April 2014 *Teen Vogue* seemed like a testament to how far the industry has come. Right on the cover, it featured an empowering quote from singer Lorde, announcing that "prescribed ideals of how girls should look are over" (Cover). However, even here a troubling ambiguity is still at work. The cover photo of Lorde that accompanies the quote, is, ironically, photoshopped, a fact that the artist herself pointed out, tweeting, "apart from the fact that i'm pretty sure this magazine gave me a new nose (:|), i really like this photo" (Lorde). When magazines continue to gesture toward compliance with a more natural standard of female beauty while simultaneously still reinforcing these negative ideals of female beauty, the conversation clearly is not over. If these magazines are finally to act responsibly toward their teenage readers, they need to not only talk the talk but also really *listen* and then make

> substantive changes to their photoshopping policies. Only then will teen fashion magazines become what they should be: not a place that tears young women down, but instead a place that builds them up, helping them create a positive sense of self and affirm their own inherent strength and beauty.

While gesturing toward the different activist organizations she discussed in her position paper (the "anti-photoshop voices"), the author takes care to make her conclusion as stylistically sophisticated as her introduction. Notice her careful word choice ("forward-thinking," "conversation") that works in tandem with the idea of talking and listening that she integrated into her introduction. In addition, consider the effect of sharing a final concrete example that synthesizes her main takeaway. If we build on the metaphor of the "hook" as a way to draw readers into the introduction, then perhaps this element in the conclusion is the "sinker"—a compact, weighty element designed to make a final, lasting impression on the reader. Some writers save a representative statistic, quotation, or—as in this case—example to create this effect. The key is that is not to introduce a new point, but instead to use the "sinker" to draw together key elements discussed in the essay as a whole and to allow the author to rearticulate her argument one last time. Lastly, note how the author carefully structures her final sentence to end on an affirmative statement. Even though her position paper addresses a real problem and offers a pointed critique, it ends with a positive hope for the future.

In composing your own conclusion, you need to balance several priorities. First, you need to signal to your reader that you are moving to the end of your argument. Avoid relying exclusively on a phrase like "In conclusion" to signpost this for your reader; consider more elegant gestures—such as a more subtle transition or arranging your argument in a clear arc from beginning to middle to end. A second priority for your conclusion should be reiterating your main point or argument. This step is crucial for all types of argument, not just those that follow inductive reasoning; this is your last opportunity to make your case to your reader. Lastly, you should employ one or more of the following strategies to move your final section beyond simple summary toward a more robust, engaging, and well-designed close to your argument:

- Use a key quotation, example, or reference that either epitomizes or synthesizes your points (the "sinker").
- Return to an example, anecdote, allusion, or analogy from your introduction, offering a slightly different, perhaps more informed

perspective on it to connect to your opening paragraphs and provide a sense of a "frame" for your argument.

- Use a chronological structure to move from the past to recent times, perhaps ending with a projection into the future.
- Use your conclusion to suggest broader implications that could increase the reader's sense of the importance of the topic, whether it be its significance to you (the writer), to the reader, or to the larger community. As appropriate, consider including a call to action to motivate future change.

No matter which strategy you choose, remember to maximize the persuasive potential of your conclusion as a means of reaffirming the strength of your argument with your readers.

WRITER'S PRACTICE MyWritingLab

Look back at either the student essay in Chapter 1 (p. 32) or the student essay in Chapter 2 (p. 79). Read the introduction of the essay aloud; then flip to the end and read the conclusion aloud. Note which strategies the author used to craft an effective opening and closing to her argument; use the bullet lists of strategies above to help you identify the author's rhetorical choices. Having done so, now experiment with rewriting either the introduction or the conclusion for that essay, relying on a different strategy or strategies that you feel would support or enhance the author's claim. Share your alternate version with a partner. Discuss:

- Why did you choose the strategies you used in revision?
- How did your revisions change the reader's experience with the essay or the way the claim was presented?
- To what extent did they produce a change in the author's persona or rhetorical stance?
- How would you need to change the other framing section (the conclusion, if you revised the introduction, or the introduction, if you revised the conclusion) to accommodate your revision?

Analyzing a Position Paper

Having carefully considered the components that contribute to framing a strong argument, let's look at how one published position paper puts into practice many of the strategies of invention, style, and arrangement that we've discussed above. In this opinion piece, Tufts Professor Bill Martel takes a strong stand on an issue we've already touched on earlier in this chapter: the right of the media at Dover Airforce Base to photograph the coffins of soldiers killed abroad. In the article, Martel is reacting to a change in policy that lifted the blanket ban on that practice, allowing the grieving families instead to make that decision about whether the caskets could be photographed. As you read through his article, consider the ways in which he uses invention, arrangement, and style to convey a strong position on this issue. In addition, notice how he carefully constructs a rhetorical stance that balances his own personal position with opposing viewpoints in order to craft a fully developed, persuasive argument.

BAN ON PHOTOGRAPHING MILITARY COFFINS PROTECTED GRIEVING FAMILIES FROM MEDIA

William C. Martel

While not overly catchy, the **title** clearly establishes Martel's **claim** that the article will later support.

The ban on photographing soldiers' coffins as they return to Dover Air Force Base in Delaware was not simply about images but also about shielding grief-stricken military families from a media maelstrom. It was not an issue of freedom of the press but one of respect and one of fairness.

Martel begins his essay with a statement of position in relation to the prior ban on photographing military coffins at Dover Air Force Base.

Nevertheless, pressure built in Washington to change the old policy, which dated to 1991. On Jan. 7, 2009, Rep. Walter Jones, a Republican from North Carolina, introduced House Resolution 269, the "Fallen Hero Commemoration Act." This bill called for "the Department of Defense to grant access to accredited members of the media when the remains of members of the Armed Forces arrive at military installations in the United States."

He then provides an overview of the issue, situating it in a particular historical moment (*kairos*) and introducing the context for the conversation about the ban.

President Obama and Secretary of Defense Robert Gates ordered a review of the issue, and an announcement of the Pentagon's conclusions came Thursday when Gates announced that media coverage would be allowed in cases where families give permission.

Again, Martel invokes *kairos*, reminding his audience of the timeliness and relevance of this issue.

Critics of the ban argued that there are several benefits to be gained by allowing the media to photograph the coffins. For example, they argued that lifting the ban would affirm the public's right

At this point, Martel shares the first **counterargument**. Notice his fair and balanced tone, building his own *ethos* as a writer.

In the next paragraph, Martel includes a second and then a third **counterargument** to his position. At this point, it is clear he is using a **block structure** for his argument and that he has decided to frontload the opposing arguments before moving on to his own position.

In this key paragraph, Martel **concedes** that the opposing arguments have some merit before indicating the turn in the essay toward arguing his own position.

Here he begins making a series of subclaims (smaller claims in support of his overriding position) supported by evidence and reasons.

He trades on the rhetoric surrounding the issue ("dignified transfer of remains") to make his point about the dangers of sensationalization.

Notice how he uses clear **signposting** (first, second, third) to help his reader clearly navigate the structure of his argument.

to know, a right that Americans deeply value. In addition, such photographs would show the American people the human cost of war.

Some also argued that it would prevent the Department of Defense from manipulating public opinion by suppressing images of the human cost of war. Finally, the ban was such a deeply polarizing and emotionally charged issue in American society that lifting it might start to heal the rift between those who legitimately differ over this policy.

These are all perfectly sensible arguments, made by reasonable people. But despite growing momentum that culminated in the lifting of the ban, there were several reasons to oppose such a reverse in policy.

First, the solemn act of bringing home our military dead will become sensationalized. We inevitably will see private family moments turned into public events.

The act of returning those who have died in war is known in U.S. military parlance as the "dignified transfer of remains." However, the very act of photographing the coffins of our fallen will be part and parcel of a classic public spectacle—featuring grieving military families who will be overwhelmed by media coverage.

Second, each family's right to privacy in this moment will be immediately and irrevocably sacrificed. We are obligated to honor those who have fallen in war in a way that preserves each military family's right to privacy. Otherwise, we risk exploiting their loss.

Military families deserve privacy, including the right to decide whether to allow the public to intrude, so including the family-permission clause helps some. Simply lifting the ban outright would have hurt families who are caught in the middle of searing pain and grief.

Furthermore, our obligation to put families first in protecting their privacy must trump the public's right to see the coffins of our war dead. Compassion for military families must outweigh well-intentioned arguments that defend the public's right to know.

The challenge for policymakers is to artfully balance what is in the best interests of democratic governance with compassion for those whose loved ones made the ultimate sacrifice in war. In such moments, we must err on the side of protecting those who bear the greatest burden.

Third, some argue that one reason for lifting the ban is to make political statements about the costs of war. The public's right to see photographs of soldiers' coffins—so that, as one reporter said to President Obama, they can "see the full human cost of war"—seems hollow in the face of private grief. If people want to understand the costs of war, they can visit Arlington National Cemetery, where 300,000 are buried—or read newspapers that routinely list names of the dead.

Images of grief-stricken military families will make powerful statements about war's human toll. Many were rightly offended when activists exploited military funerals for political purposes. Many members of the military have objected to having their images used for antiwar messages. How will this be any different?

What should the Pentagon have done? It is reasonable to give families the right to veto media coverage of the "dignified transfer of remains" at Dover Air Force Base. But what military family wants to make such a decision in its moment of grief?

Still, with this veto power, quite soon we will know how many military families are in favor of media coverage. My instinct is that fewer rather than more will want this private moment opened to cameras. According to polls of families who have lost a loved one in war, the vast majority oppose lifting the ban.

In the end, it is all the rage to talk about the sacrifices of military families. Many, in fact, have cited these sacrifices as reasons to withdraw U.S. troops from Iraq.

In fairness, by revoking the ban on media coverage of returning fallen heroes, allowing military families to be photographed when they are most vulnerable in their grief, we are not listening to military families or looking out for their best interests.

Put simply, lifting the ban on photographing coffins was not the right thing to do for military families who have lost loved ones in war.

He uses strong language like "must" to reinforce his position.

In his third subclaim, Martel once again shares an opposing viewpoint before refuting it. Notice the use of direct quotations that allows the reader to directly encounter the counterargument before Martel rebuts it.

Martel draws on a parallel example here (photographing grieving families at military funerals) to support his point and then turns to rhetorical questions to prod at the additional complexity of this issue.

As he moves toward his final comments, he gestures toward the uncertainty of the public reaction to the lifting of the ban, pointing to both his "instinct" (personal opinion) and polls (more objective evidence) in speculating about the outcome.

He concludes by moving to a forceful articulation of his claim.

Bill Martel's article demonstrates interesting possibilities for developing your own persuasive writing. Sometimes when we write from our own point of view, we get so locked into our individual perspective that we fail to take into account diverse views on our topics. Such limited vision can weaken our persuasiveness; if we fail to consider or acknowledge alternative positions on our topics, we produce one-sided arguments that lack complexity or credibility with our readers. Recall our earlier discussion of photographs: each photograph suggests a different angle, a unique "version" of an event, and the perspective of a particular persona. When we bring these different sides to light, we find that suddenly an incident or issue that seems polarized—or "black and white"—is actually much more complex. The same holds true for the issues we confront every day as writers and rhetoricians: it is only through exploring multiple perspectives on an argument that we can engage it persuasively and effectively.

WRITER'S PRACTICE MyWritingLab

Bill Martel originally published his piece in the opinion section of *US News & World Report* and so wrote it in a minimalist, journalistic style appropriate to his rhetorical situation. If you were writing a position paper on this topic for your class, how would you adjust the style and arrangement? Experiment by revising the title and either the introduction or the conclusion to be more appropriate for—and persuasive in—an academic context. Refer back to the criteria on titles, introductions, and conclusions above to aid you in your revision. In addition, feel free to draw some of his points or allusions from his main body into your expanded introduction or conclusion as needed.

THE WRITER'S PROCESS

In this chapter, you've learned to harness the canons of rhetoric—*invention*, *arrangement*, and *style*—to compose effective arguments of your own. You've developed strategies for crafting *titles*, *introductions*, and *conclusions*; you've explored the importance of *persona* and *rhetorical stance* in argument. You've learned the differences between three models of argumentation—classical, Toulmin, and Rogerian—and how they relate to your purpose and your audience. Now it's time to implement these skills. Practice inventing a position on an issue, arranging claims and evidence for your argument (including working with images as evidence for your points), developing a rhetorical stance, and working on persona through style by crafting your prose with care. Experiment with inventing diverse perspectives to achieve a thorough understanding of the complexity of the situation. Although you may be tempted to think of these various perspectives in oppositional terms—as the "pro" or "con" of an issue—such an approach closes off a richer understanding of the issue. In general, try to think of arguments not in terms of right or wrong but rather as a spectrum of differing perspectives. As you turn now to write your own position paper, recall the many options available to you and select the ones that best meet the needs of your rhetorical situation.

SPOTLIGHTED ANALYSIS: PHOTOGRAPHS

MyWritingLab

Select a photograph to analyze: you might select the work by a well-known photographer such as Ansel Adams, Dorothea Lange, Carrie Mae Weems, W. Eugene Smith, or Cindy Sherman; one from the Library of Congress "American Memory" archives online; or even a photograph from a newspaper, news magazine, or *Life* magazine's photographer Website. Sharpen your skills at analysis by writing out answers to the questions on the checklist below:

- **Content:** What does the photograph depict? Is it meant to represent reality, or is it deliberately abstract?
- **Argument:** What argument is the photographer conveying through the image? For instance, while the photo might show a group of people standing together, its argument might be about love, family unity across generations, or a promise for the future.
- **Photographer:** Who took this photograph? What is her or his reputation? What style of photography or famous photos is she or he known for?
- **Audience:** Who was the photographer's intended audience?
- **Context:** What was the historical and cultural context of the photograph? Where was it reproduced or displayed (an art gallery, the cover of a magazine, or the front page of a newspaper)?
- **Purpose:** What is the photograph's purpose or motive for capturing this image? Is it intended to be overtly argumentative and to move its audience to action? Or is the argument more subtle, even to the point of seeming objective or representational?
- **Rhetorical stance:** How does the composition of the photo convey a sense of the rhetorical stance of the photographer? Pay attention to issues of focus, cropping, color, setting, perspective, and editing or photo manipulation.
- **Word and image:** Does the photo have a caption or does it accompany written text? How does the image function in dialogue with this verbal text? As visual evidence? As a counterargument?

WRITING ASSIGNMENTS

MyWritingLab

1. **Argument Analysis.** Read a news article or watch a recorded debate (such as on a news station) about a current controversial issue. Take notes on the elements of the argument. When does the speaker state her claim? her grounds or reasons? What are the unspoken assumptions or warrants that underlie her argument? To what extent does she take into account alternative positions? Does she rebut them, concede the point, or qualify her argument? What type of persona does she embody? What rhetorical stance does she assume in relation to her topic and her audience? Try to draft a persuasive, cohesive claim, referring back on the lessons from Chapter 1, about how the writer or speaker deliberately crafted her text to be persuasive.

2. **Draft Alternate Introductions.** Draft two alternate introductions for the analysis you brainstormed for Assignment #1. First review the section on introductions earlier in this chapter. Next identify your claim or thesis statement for your rhetorical analysis, using the techniques you practiced in Chapter 1. Then develop two possible introductions for the essay, utilizing different strategies for each one. As you craft the introductions, ask yourself:

    - Do you want to prioritize facts (*logos*), an emotional connection with the reader (*pathos*), or your own authority on the subject (*ethos*)?
    - Do you want to use comparison–contrast? Definition of terms? Process? Classification? Description? Narration? Definition? Cause–effect? Example?
    - Do you want to include a startling statistic? A relevant quotation or question? A vivid statement of the problem? An intriguing anecdote? A representative example or examples?
    - What type of persona will you construct? How will you use word choice, syntax, and tone to establish style?

    Keep in mind that you may employ several techniques or strategies in each introduction. Your goal is to imagine two alternate possibilities for how to introduce your topic and argument to your reader. When you have drafted the two introductions, share them with a partner in class and assess which offers the strongest foundation for your argument.

3. **Compose a Position Paper:** Develop the paragraph you wrote for the Writer's Practice on page 107 into a full position paper; alternately, write on a controversial topic about an issue that moves you and about which you can take a strong stance. Be sure to anticipate counterclaims and to address them through rebuttal, concession, or qualification. In addition, frame your essay with a powerful introduction and conclusion. When you complete your essay, preface it with a reflective memo in which you discuss your choices in relation to the arrangement and style of your argument.

4. **Consider Multiple Perspectives:** Identify different positions on an issue and then assign various members of your group each to write a position paper on one of those stances. You might, for instance, write about the conflict between your college campus and the surrounding town: one student could write a position paper that represents the staff perspective, another one on the administrator's perspective, another the city council's perspective, and a fourth person could represent the study body's perspective. Collaboratively write an introduction and conclusion for this series of papers that provide an overview of the topic and the conversation between the multiple perspectives.

MyWritingLab Visit Ch. 3 Composing Arguments in MyWritingLab to complete the Writer's Practices, Spotlighted Analyses, and Writing Assignments, and to test your understanding of the chapter objectives.

Part II

PLANNING AND CONDUCTING RESEARCH

CHAPTER 4
Planning and Proposing Research Arguments

CHAPTER 5
Finding and Evaluating Research Sources

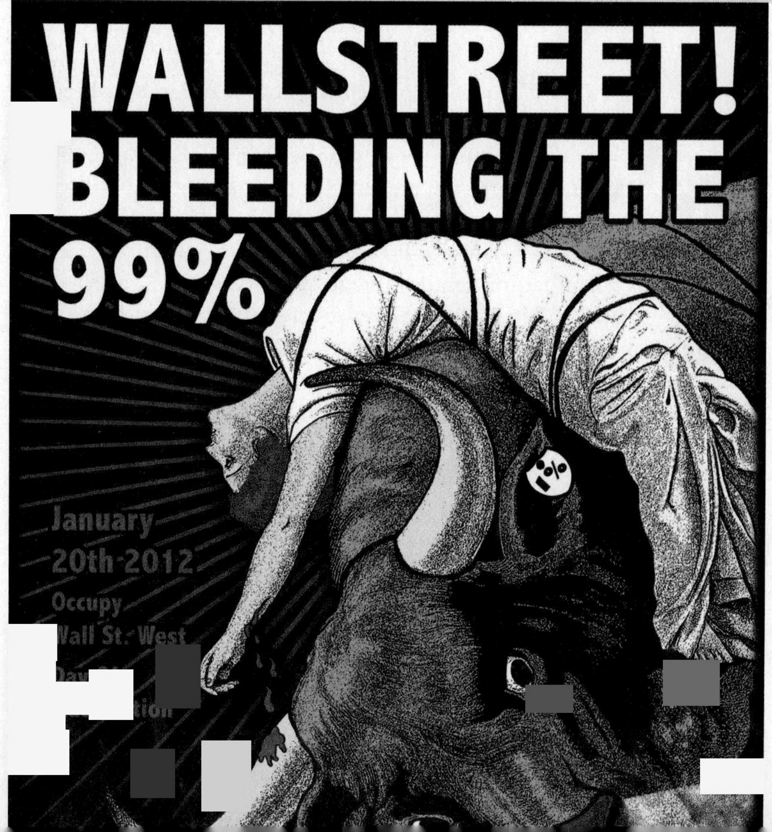

CHAPTER 4

Planning and Proposing Research Arguments

Chapter Preview Questions

4.1 How do I use questions to get started on finding a research topic?

4.2 How do I generate a productive topic?

4.3 What prewriting techniques can I use to narrow my topic?

4.4 What are the steps for developing a strong research plan?

4.5 How do I write a formal research proposal?

When we approach the task of research, it becomes clear that we can use many of the skills of analysis that we've practiced in previous chapters to help us interpret the meaning of texts and provide us with a starting point for our own line of inquiry. For instance, look at the poster shown in Figure 4.1. What you probably see first is a familiar image: the vintage 1943 Rosie the Riveter poster. With her hair tied up in a red kerchief, her direct, forceful gaze, and her bicep flexed as she rolls up her sleeve, she operates as a recognizable symbol for resilience, hard work, and motivation. However a closer look complicates this initial impression. How does realizing that Rosie's face has been redrawn in the fashion of a Guy Fawkes mask (a symbol used by the Anonymous movement) change your understanding of whom she represents? How do other alterations to the iconic image – a tattoo, a revision of her catch phrase, the reference to "99%" — sharpen your sense of the poster's context? As you begin to assess these different elements, you realize that the image has been repurposed into a call to action for the recent Occupy Movement. More specifically, by reading the additional information on the

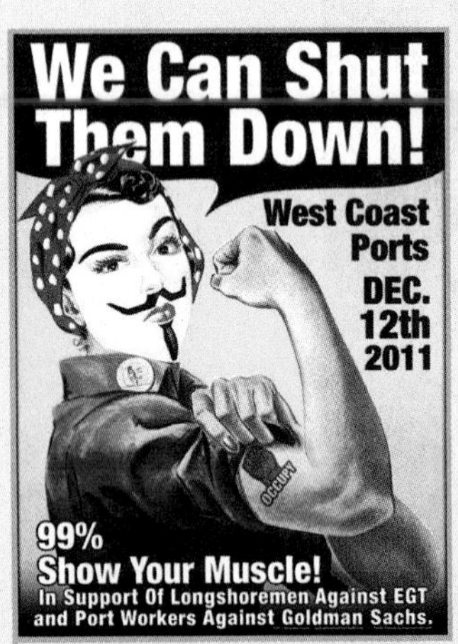

We Can Shut Them Down!
West Coast Ports
DEC. 12th 2011
OCCUPY
99%
Show Your Muscle!
In Support Of Longshoremen Against EGT
and Port Workers Against Goldman Sachs.

FIGURE 4.1 How does this poster use visual elements and an iconic American image to motivate members of the Occupy Movement?

poster, you see that she has been appropriated to address longshoremen on the West Coast. Such careful observations will help you begin to develop an argument about the poster, but in order to back up or substantiate your claims, you need to do some research. That is, you need to place the rhetorical elements of the poster in their historical and critical contexts, including propaganda posters from the World War II era and the events related to the 2011–2012 Occupy Movement.

Research can be conducted in any number of ways, including interviews, fieldwork, and the exploration of sources both online and in print. However, the starting point of any research effort is to determine what questions to ask and what inquiries to pursue. In this chapter, you will learn how to become an active participant in a research community and begin to develop the skills for narrowing your research question and creating an effective research plan and a solid research proposal.

ASKING RESEARCH QUESTIONS

4.1 How do I use questions to get started on finding a research topic?

The discussion in this chapter focuses on the subset of persuasion—propaganda—because such texts make very powerful public statements and because, for many of us, we have to perform a certain amount of research in order to understand the motives and purpose behind them. Often this research involves seeking answers to questions we have formulated about the text. In fact, most research begins with the act of asking questions.

One way you can get started on your research is to pick a text that moves you and start brainstorming questions about it. Let's say that you came across the 1917 American enlistment poster shown in Figure 4.2 in an exhibit on campus or as part of a class discussion about World War I posters. Approaching it for the first time, you probably will start to analyze the visual rhetoric, much as we did in the earlier chapters of this book.

What are your eyes drawn to first, the words or the image? Maybe you look first at the simian figure in the middle, roaring menacingly at you, and then at the swooning, semi-naked woman in his arms. In contrast, maybe the person next to you is attracted first to the bold yellow text at the top and then to the bottom, where the words "U.S. Army" in black are superimposed on the imperative "Enlist." In synthesizing various responses to the text, you most likely would find yourself with more questions than answers—a good thing, for those questions can be the beginning of your research inquiry.

FIGURE 4.2 This World War I propaganda poster (originally published in 1917) offers a wealth of detail for historical analysis.

You might ask: Is that gorilla King Kong? Your research would allow you to confidently answer, No, since you would discover that the poster was made decades before the movie was released. That same research might lead you to discover several books that discuss the wartime practice of casting enemies as subhuman creatures, offering a possible explanation for why the enemy nation is portrayed as a threatening gorilla in this poster. Adding to that your observation that "culture" is spelled "Kultur" (on the club the gorilla is holding), you probably would realize that the enemy symbolized here is in fact Germany.

Then you might ask: What is the significance of that bloody club? Why is the woman unconscious and partly naked? More research might provide insight on how bestiality emerged as a wartime theme in World War I enlistment posters. If a nation's women were threatened with potential attack by such "monsters," these posters implied, then the men would surely step up to save and protect their wives, daughters, sisters, and mothers.

By asking questions about your text, you can move beyond an initial response and into the realm of intellectual discovery. In fact, your first questions about a text will lead you to ask more pointed questions about the context, political environment, key players, and social trends informing your text. For the propaganda poster in Figure 4.2, such questions might include:

- What conflict was America involved in at the time that this poster was made?
- What was the meaning of the word on the gorilla's hat, "Militarism," at that time?

- How would an appeal to enlist factor into that historical situation?
- Who was the poster's audience?
- Did other posters of the time use similar rhetorical strategies?

Many of these questions have fact-based answers that invite you to start to better understand the rhetorical situation of the text. By putting a rhetorical spin on traditional journalistic questions (who, what, where, when, how, why), you can sharpen your approach to the text and open up the possibility for it to serve as the foundation for a more rigorous line of inquiry:

- Who is the author?
- What is the claim?
- What strategies are used?
- Who is the audience?
- When was it made?
- What is the purpose and exigency of the argument?

Working with the poster from Figure 4.2, you might chart these questions in a way that both provides you with an enriched understanding of the text and also positions it as the starting point for additional research:

Who: Author	U.S. Army or the U.S. government
What: Claim	Americans (men) need to enlist in the Army to rescue Liberty from the grasp of German militarism.
How: Strategies	*Pathos* appeal: uses emotionally charged symbolism (Germany as the "mad brute"; Liberty as the female victim)
For Whom: Audience	The American public
When: Context	World War I (specifically 1917)
Why: Purpose and Exigency	With the United States joining the war in 1917, this poster seems a timely effort to persuade Americans to back the war effort, both ideologically (by identifying Germany as a threat) and practically (by enlisting).

Possible research topic: American enlistment posters and war propaganda in World War I

Using such questions to arrive at a possible research topic, you can then take the next step, moving from the individual text to consider it as part of a larger issue, event, or system of meaning. You could develop a line of questions that encourage you to make connections and explore the larger significance:

- To what extent did other World War I enlistment posters use similar imagery and rhetorical strategies? How did they differ in their strategies?
- How do the techniques used in early twentieth-century posters differ from those used during World War II?
- How are the rhetorical strategies used in this poster similar to or different from enlistment posters or advertisements you might encounter today?
- In what ways have enlistment propaganda changed over time?

Seeing Connections
Look at the invention questions in Chapter 3 for further ways to use questions to develop a topic.

Each of these questions could lead to a more focused *research topic* and, ultimately, a written essay that draws on and contributes to the arguments that others have made about such texts. Generating a range of interesting and productive **research questions** is the first step in any research project; they will guide your work and lead you to your final argument. You can generate these questions by responding to the rhetorical situation provided by a text and by considering what interests *you* most about either the text or the topic. This process of inquiry itself helps you to define a project and make it your own.

WRITER'S PRACTICE

MyWritingLab

I'm Proud... my husband wants me to do my part
SEE YOUR U. S. EMPLOYMENT SERVICE
WAR MANPOWER COMMISSION

Using the poster in Figure 4.3 as a starting point, create your own analysis table like the one above, answering the questions:

- Who? (Author)
- What? (Claim)
- How? (Strategies)
- For whom? (Audience)
- When? (Context)
- Why? (Exigency and purpose)

Use this process of critical thinking and rhetorical analysis to lead you toward a topic that you might explore for a research topic.

FIGURE 4.3 This 1944 poster was produced by the Office of War Information and the War Manpower Commission.

GENERATING TOPICS

4.2 How do I generate a productive topic?

At the beginning of this chapter, we suggested that you might use an individual text as the starting point for developing a research topic. However, while sometimes you might find the inspiration for a research project in a text that you encounter inside or outside the classroom, other times you find yourself searching for other modes of inspiration to help you discover that perfect research topic.

If you think back to our discussion of *invention* in Chapter 3, you'll understand that one of the most crucial aspects of starting a research project is selecting a viable and engaging topic. The word *topic*, in fact, comes from the ancient Greek word *topos*, translated literally as "place." The earliest students of rhetoric used the physical space of the papyrus page—given to them by their teachers—to locate their topics for writing. Similarly, your teacher may suggest certain guidelines or parameters for you to follow when it comes to your topic; for instance, you may be given a specific topic (such as representations of race in Dr. Seuss cartoons) or you may be limited to a theme (the rhetoric of political advertisements on television, radio, and the Internet).

In some cases, you may not have any restrictions at all. Sometimes that might feel overwhelming, but consider ways to make the task of finding a topic more manageable. Review your class notes or readings to see what topics intrigued or even provoked you; do some additional background reading to spark ideas, talk with a friend about possible ideas, and consult with your instructor about topics that might match your interests.

As you consider possible research topics, keep this key principle in mind: successful topics need to interest you, inspire you, or even provoke you. Even with assigned topics, you should be able to find some aspect of the assignment that speaks to you. That is, there needs to be a *connection* between you and your topic to motivate you to follow through and transform it into a successful argument.

Regardless of the degree to which your topic has been mapped out for you, you still can—and should—make it your own. You do this partly by generating your own **research questions** about an issue, an event, a controversy, or—as we did above—a specific text. These questions can guide your work, help you identify a productive topic to explore, and lead you to your final argument. You can generate these questions by responding to the

AT A GLANCE

Looking for the "Perfect" Topic

1. ***Look inward.*** What issues, events, or ideas interest you? Are there any hot-button topics you find yourself drawn to again and again? What topic is compelling enough that you would watch a news program, television special, YouTube video, film, or relevant lecture on it?
2. ***Look outward.*** What are the central issues of student life on campus? Do you walk by a classroom and see the students inside busy writing on laptops or using interactive whiteboards? Topic: technology and education. Do you see a fraternity's poster about a "dry" party? Topic: alcohol on campus. Do you see workers outside the food service building on strike? Topic: labor relations at the college.
3. ***Use creative visualization.*** Imagine that you are chatting casually with a friend when you overhear someone talking. Suddenly, you feel so interested—or so angry—that you go over and participate in the conversation. What would move you so strongly?
4. ***Use the materials of the moment.*** Perhaps the *topos* might be closer to the classical Greek model; although not a roll of papyrus, your class reading list or a single issue of a newspaper can house many topics. Scan the front page and opinion section of your school or community newspaper to see what issues people are talking about. What issues are gripping the community at large?

rhetorical situation provided by your assignment and by considering what interests *you* most about the topic. Even if your whole class is writing on the same topic, each person will present a different argument or approach to the issue. Some will use a different stance or persona, some will rely on different sources, some will use different rhetorical appeals, and all will argue different positions about the topic.

In addition, while selecting your topic, you might consider the type of research you'll need to do to pursue it; in fact, you might select your topic based mostly on the sorts of research it allows you to do. For instance, a student writing on propaganda of the Prohibition era will draw extensively on paper sources, which might involve archival work with original letters, pamphlets, or government documents from that time period. A student writing on visual advertising for ethnic-theme dorms on campus will be more likely to complement paper sources with interviews with the university housing staff, student surveys, and first-person observations. A student writing on sexualized rhetoric in student campaign materials might take a poll, gather concrete examples, and research both print and online coverage of past and present elections. Think broadly and creatively about what kinds of research you might use and what types of research—archival work versus fieldwork involving interviews and survey taking—appeal most to you. Finally, consider whether you can actually get your hands on the source material you need to construct a persuasive argument.

WRITER'S PRACTICE MyWritingLab

Select a preliminary topic for a research paper, whether from a list provided for you by your instructor or from your own interests. Put it to the test to assess its viability as the foundation for a successful project by answering the following questions:

1. **What is interesting about this topic?** We write best about ideas, events, and issues that we connect with through curiosity, passion, or intellectual interest.
2. **Can I make a claim or argue a position about this topic?** At this stage, you may not have developed a position on the topic, but you should see promise for advancing a new perspective or for taking a stand.
3. **Will I be able to find enough research material on this topic?** Brainstorm some possible sources you might use to write this paper.
4. **Does this sort of research appeal to me?** Since you will be working with this topic for an extended period, it is best to have a genuine interest in the type of research that it will require (for instance, doing archival work, reading scholarly sources, conducting original research, or engaging in fieldwork).

Constructing a Research Log

From the very beginning of your research process—as you move from asking questions about a text to identifying a productive topic, to gathering information and taking notes—keep track of your ideas in a *research log*. This log will help you organize your ideas, collect your materials, chart your progress, and assemble the different pieces of your research.

Your research log can take many forms, from a handwritten journal, to a series of word processing documents, a personal blog, a Google doc, or a collection of bookmarked Webpages. It can contain primarily written text, or it can include images, video, or audio files as well. The key lies not in what your research log looks like, but in the way you use it to help you develop an interesting and provocative research project that keeps careful track of the sources you encounter along the way.

In the early stages of a project, you can use your log to help you record and track your ideas; it provides you with an open, creative platform to begin your research journey. You might use your research log in a variety of ways:

- To list possible topic ideas
- To annotate excerpts from newspaper articles, magazine sources, blog posts, or even email or forum threads that offer interesting potential topics
- To respond to provocative images related to potential topics
- To write a reaction to ideas brought up during class discussion
- To list questions about your potential topics: What do you know? What do you need to find out? Note down answers as well.
- To track your preliminary Internet searches
- To explore some of the challenges of the topic and also note what excites you about it as well

This page from Oishi Banerjee's research log (Figure 4.4) shows how she used this space as a way to brainstorm ideas for a research paper on the suffrage movement. She moved from close analysis of a primary source—a variety of anti-suffragette postcards—to broader questions that help her situate the postcards in context, consider their cultural impact, and develop several powerful research questions that she could use as the foundation for her ongoing inquiry into this topic.

4.3 What prewriting techniques can I use to narrow my topic?

NARROWING YOUR TOPIC

Once you have selected a topic and generated some research questions, the next step in the research project involves *narrowing* your topic to make your research project feasible and focused. A productive way to do this is through **prewriting**, or writing that precedes the official drafting of the paper, but, practically speaking, can take many forms. Lists, scribbled notes, informal outlines, drawings—all different types of *prewriting* can help you move from a broad topic to a much more focused one.

Using Prewriting Techniques to Focus Your Topic

For many writers, **freewriting** is a very productive strategy to help focus and sharpen ideas. In its most pure form, freewriting involves writing without stopping for a set period of time; the idea is to simply keep writing out

Research Topic: Pro- and anti-suffrage propaganda in America, at the beginning of the 1900s
Primary Sources: Postcards from the Palczewski Suffrage Postcard Archive, at the University Northern Iowa (http://www.uni.edu/palczews/NEW postcard webpage/BSseries.html)

Anti-suffragette themes in the postcards:

- fear of a reversal of gender roles:
  - makes fun of men tending children
  - mockery of men attempting other domestic tasks (cooking and so on)
- vilification of suffragettes:
  - images of women using violence against men
  - wordplay with "suffragette" and men's "suffering"
  - images of crying children, implying suffragettes were bad mothers
  - misspelling "women" as "wimmen" on suffragettes' sashes (both implies that suffragettes were unfeminine and wanted to be men, and that suffragettes weren't well-educated)
  - reducing suffragettes to sex objects ("I'd rather kiss her than hear her talk")

Broader questions:

- Are there any other anti-suffragette themes in the postcards that I haven't yet noticed?
- How powerful were these postcards? To what extent could they influence political discourse in the early 1900s? Did they change public opinion, or simply reflect it?
- What made postcard propaganda different from propaganda in other media?
- Besides postcards, what other works so explicitly attacked suffragettes?
- Who made these postcards? Political groups? Commercial postcard businesses? Independent artists?
- Who bought these postcards? How were these postcards used? Were they kept as private mementos, or were they actually used and sent to other people?
- How do these anti-suffrage postcards compare to pro-suffrage postcards?

FIGURE 4.4 In her research log, Oishi recorded her analysis of her primary source as a first step to formulating broader questions.

your ideas, without worrying about grammar, punctuation, or even structure so that you can follow your thoughts fluidly and freely. The key is to not hesitate, edit, or even read the freewrite over before the time for writing is up. We've known some writers who even freewrite with their eyes closed or with their computer screen dimmed to prevent themselves from interrupting the flow of ideas.

Such stream-of-consciousness writing on a topic can yield useful insights into what interests you most, what questions you have, and how you might develop your ideas. In fact, many people see the act of writing itself as a way to make meaning and discover ideas. In that sense, freewriting doesn't just allow you to write out what you already know; it leads you to make new connections and create new knowledge.

When you're trying to narrow your topic, you might try a variation of this technique: **funneled freewriting**. Funneled freewriting asks you to do just what it suggests: progressively narrow your ideas into a more concentrated stream. You start by freewriting about your topic for a set amount of time, usually 5 or 10 minutes. When that's done, you stop and read over what you wrote, identifying one key idea or subtopic. Then you freewrite again for the same set amount of time, this time using that subtopic as your starting point. You continue this process for several iterations, each time reading what you've written, identifying a more focused key point, and using that for the next freewriting segment. At the end, you will arrive at a more narrowed topic, one that has been focused by your questions, interests, and ideas.

Occasionally, however, you'll have trouble anticipating when a research topic might be *too* narrow. An alternative prewriting method you might try is the **accordion prewrite**, a technique that asks you to slide between extremely broad and extremely narrow research questions as a way of finding one scaled most effectively for your particular assignment. Let's look at how one student used an accordion prewrite to brainstorm a possible topic about the use of propaganda related to same-sex marriage.

She began by drawing a horizontal line in her research log (Figure 4.5). On one end, she wrote a couple of overly broad questions (To what extent does advertising function as propaganda? How does propaganda affect civil rights?), on the other, she wrote an overly narrow question (Exactly how many Californians voted "Yes" on Proposition 8 because of Frank Schubert's ad campaign?). Having established the extremes, she then filled in a variety of different questions in the center of her "accordion," positioning them in relation to the broad or narrowed points as appropriate. When she was done, she had a spectrum of

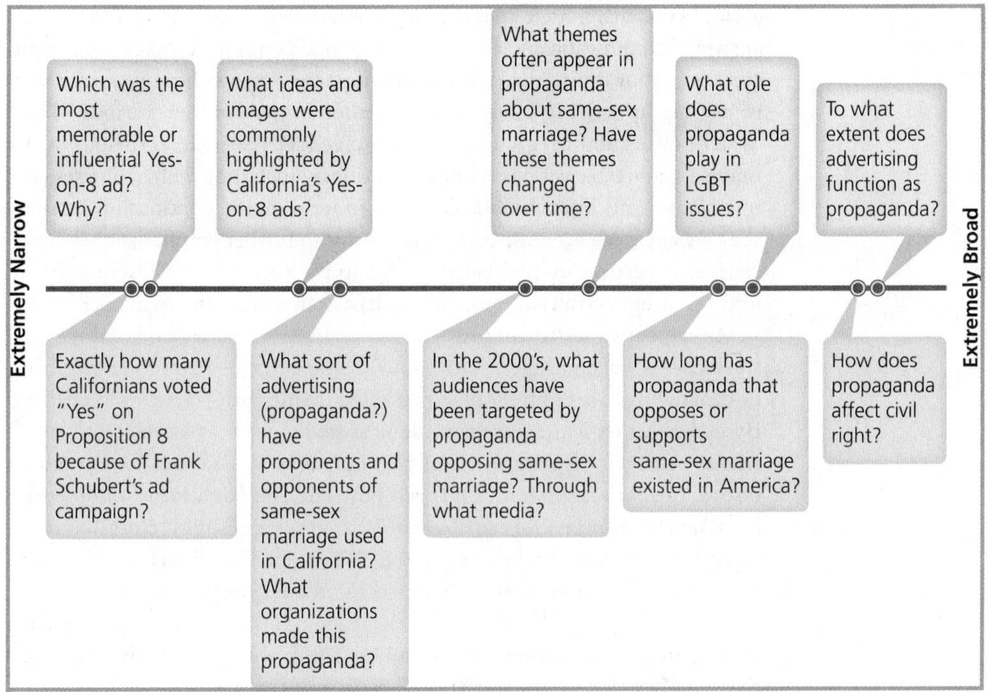

FIGURE 4.5 This student used an accordion prewrite to help her define the scope of her research.

possibilities that helped her conceptualize how she might scale her topic to a manageable size. After brainstorming in this way, she chose to focus on the questions clustered to the left side—about California's "Yes on [Proposition] 8" campaign—allowing her to narrow her focus in a way that suited both her research interests and the requirements of her assignment.

One benefit of the accordion model is that it allows writers to experiment with more visual means of experimenting with the scope of a topic. The practice of **graphic brainstorming** offers another effective way to visualize different ways to narrow a topic. This technique transforms traditional **brainstorming**—jotting down a series of related words and phrases on a topic—into a more visible process. Also called *webbing*, *clustering*, or *mapping*, the goal of *graphic brainstorming* is to help you develop your topic by exploring relationships among ideas. Begin by writing a topic in a circle, and then come up with ideas and questions about that topic. Next, arrange them in groups around your main circle to indicate the relationships between them. As you answer each question and pose more developed ones in response, you begin to narrow your topic. You'll notice that Figure 4.6 shows how we might start to do this by writing questions that differentiate between various World War I posters and by grouping them by gender issues. In addition, in our brainstorm, we use various types of notations—including words, phrases, and questions—and insert lines and arrows to indicate the relationship between the concepts. We even use images and color to further emphasize these associations. These techniques help us develop the argument and eventually can lead to a more narrowed topic and perhaps even a preliminary thesis.

As we continue to brainstorm—whether for an hour or over several sessions—it becomes clear why some people call this technique **webbing** or **clustering**. As Figure 4.6 shows, our graphic turns into a web of ideas. By using this technique, we have done more than simply develop our topic; we have made it visually apparent that our topic is too broad for a standard research paper assignment. Our web now offers enough ideas for an entire book on the subject. But our diagram also provides us with clues about the direction in which to take our project. We can pick a subsection of ideas to focus on in our writing. If we zoomed in on one part of the diagram—the part, color-coded yellow, that asks key questions about the representations of women in military posters, for instance—we could set the foundation for a focused essay that examines the implications of the way women are depicted in these texts. We could explore how cross-dressing is used as a deliberate appeal to the audience, or how military posters evoke the image of wife and mother to mobilize troops.

A final mode you might use to narrow a topic is **heuristic questioning**. In this method, you begin with a general topic and then sharpen it with a series of increasingly focused questions. For instance, if you were to take the topic of gender roles in World War I, you might follow this heuristic process to distill key issues that might help make the topic more manageable:

1. Write down your topic.

   Topic formulation: gender roles in World War I.

2. Work with that topic by asking a pointed question based on close analysis of the text at hand.

   First question: Is there a sexual undertone to the posters?

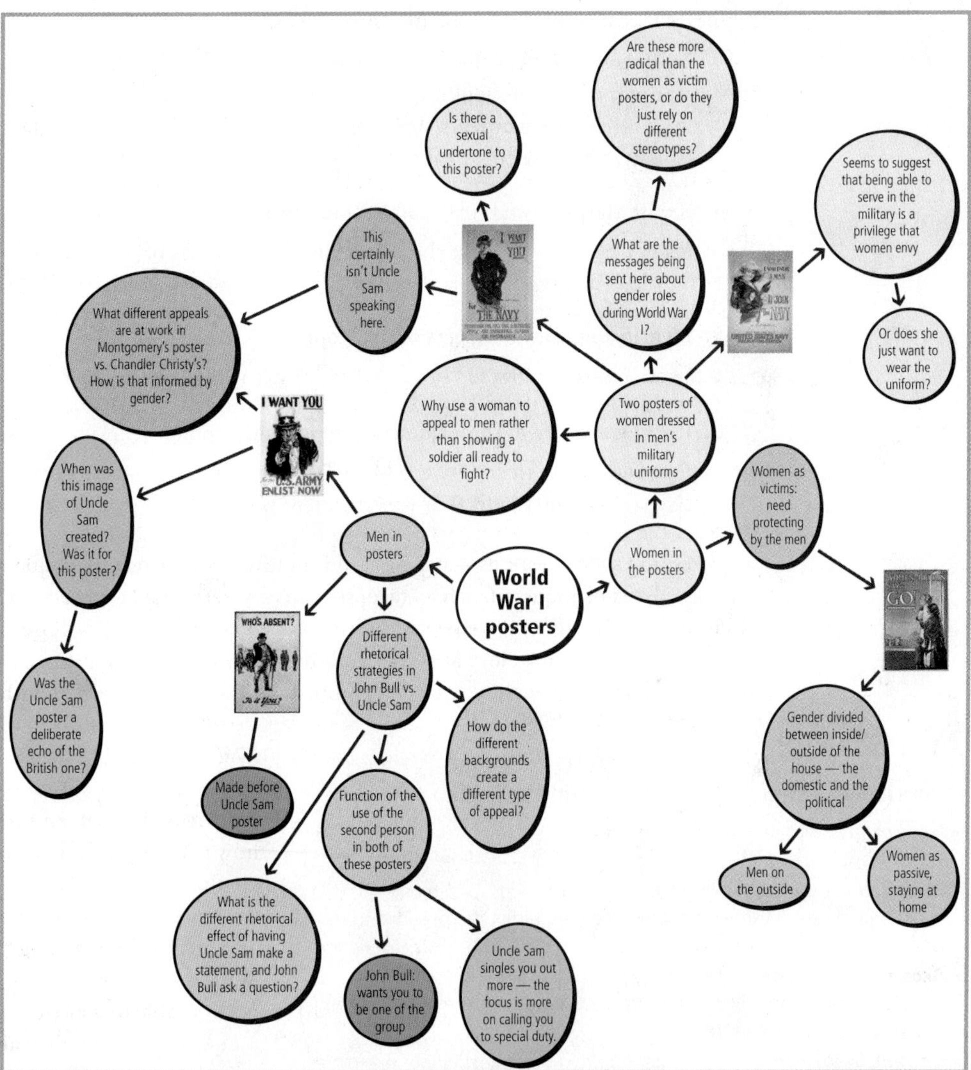

FIGURE 4.6 In this graphic brainstorm of the broad topic "World War I posters" (center white circle), the author identifies several more specific ways she might focus or narrow her research.

3. Refine the topic by answering that question.

   Topic narrowing: Yes, in one of the posters, the woman is standing in a provocative pose, looking at the audience in a sexual manner, but in another, the women seem more identified with family (mother, daughter) than with sexuality.

4. Revise the narrowed topic to be more specific.

   Revised topic formulation: the different constructions of femininity in World War I propaganda posters.

5. Identify significant aspects of that topic to explore.

   Second question: How so? In what way? What is the significance?

6. Use the answers to these questions to focus the topic.

   Final topic focus: the use of the Madonna–whore stereotype as a persuasive strategy in World War I recruitment posters.

By asking such questions—and we could come up with many others along different lines of inquiry (such as race, sexuality, international representations, and nationalism)—we begin to develop a *focused* topic that will offer us the opportunity for close analysis, rigorous research, and a sharp argumentative stance. That is, we can move from a topic loosely concerned with gender roles in World War I to one that focuses specifically on a subset of recruitment posters and how they deploy a particular sexist stereotype (the virgin–whore trope) as a persuasive strategy. With this narrowed topic, we'll be able to contribute a new opinion about war posters and write an essay that adds to the ongoing dialogue that we find in our research sources.

AT A GLANCE

Prewriting Techniques for Narrowing a Topic

- ***Freewriting:*** Write about your topic without stopping for a specific amount of time.
- ***Funneled freewriting:*** Complete a set of freewrites, each one focusing in a single specific question or idea generated in the previous freewrite.
- ***Accordion prewrite:*** Brainstorm research question on a scale from ridiculously broad to ridiculously narrow as a way of developing more appropriate questions in the middle.
- ***Graphic brainstorm:*** Use a clustering or webbing technique to explore questions, topics, and subtopics in a nonlinear fashion.
- ***Heuristic questions:*** Sharpen your topic through a series of progressively narrowed questions.

WRITER'S PRACTICE MyWritingLab

Working in a group or on your own, try out this practice of *narrowing a topic* with a selection of posters from the 2011 Occupy Movement. Look back at Figure 4.1 and consider it along with Figures 4.7 and 4.8 below; then use one of the methods described above (freewrite, funneled freewrite, graphic brainstorm, heuristic questions) to develop a feasible topic for a research paper. Be sure that you narrow your topic from "Occupy Posters" to a more focused one that you might pursue in a research paper. You might decide during your narrowing exercise to focus your topic by identifying which images you'd like to write about or by generating key questions to ask about particular texts: How do the words and images work together in these posters? How do they work against each other? How does symbolism operate in these posters? The more specific the questions you ask, the more focused your topic will be.

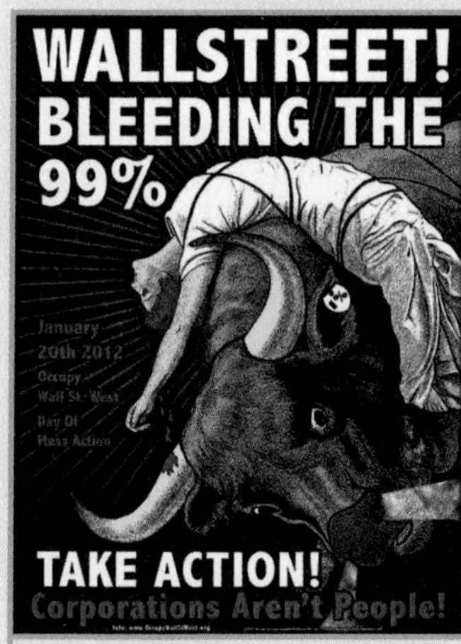

FIGURE 4.7

FIGURE 4.8

WRITING ABOUT YOUR RESEARCH PLANS

4.4 What are the steps for developing a strong research plan?

After you have narrowed your topic, you need to develop a plan for your research process. If you find yourself concerned that you don't have the knowledge necessary to write this essay or are worried that the gaps in your own knowledge will prevent you from answering those questions in a satisfactory way, then realize that you are in good company. All researchers and scholars fear the limitations of their knowledge. The key is to develop a concrete plan to guide you as you move forward with your project.

AT A GLANCE

The Research Freewrite

- Write your ideas in full sentences.
- Use a three-paragraph model to focus your answers:
  - Paragraph 1: State your topic and your guiding research question.
  - Paragraph 2: Identify key sources.
  - Paragraph 3: Anticipate challenges.

The Research Freewrite

One way to start planning your research process is complete a focused freewrite about your ideas in your research log—it's called a *focused* freewrite because while you still adhere to the principle of informal writing, you do so within the constraints of a concrete structure. In completing your research freewrite, follow a **three-paragraph model**: in the *first paragraph*, announce your topic and state a preliminary thesis so that you can begin the project with a critical and focused perspective; in the *second paragraph*, identify the sources you plan to use to investigate this topic; and in the *third paragraph*, speculate on obstacles or problems you might encounter in your research and how you might avoid or solve these problems. This freewrite will help you concretize your topic and assess your next steps in research.

Let's look at a freewrite from student Rafe Salinas, who shaped his research inquiry to explore the relationship between U.S. propaganda and the destabilization of Salvador Allende's government in Chile in the 1970s.

This first paragraph introduces the research topic and describes what Rafe thinks the main focus of his paper might be. At the end of the paragraph, he includes a preliminary research question to help him focus his interest and argument as he begins researching this topic.

Research Freewrite

The destruction of the government that Salvador Allende instituted in Chile in the early 1970s was as a result of several key factors, including direct and indirect intervention by the United States of America. I want to examine the extent to which the United States was responsible for the downfall of Allende's government by investigating the role of propaganda created and distributed by the U.S. government in Chile before and during Allende's term as president. I'm hoping to analyze specific examples of propaganda to get a closer look at the United States' rhetorical strategies, what the primary appeals and methods were, including how they used *ethos*, *pathos*, *kairos*, and *logos*. By analyzing sources that indicate the political atmosphere following the use of this propaganda, I hope to get a deeper understanding about the destabilization of his government as well. *Guiding research question:* How, why, and to what extent did the propaganda produced by the United States lead to Allende's downfall?

In terms of key sources, I hope to examine the U.S. propaganda itself to understand the persuasive strategies behind the various types of propaganda. This includes press, radio, films, pamphlets, posters, leaflets, direct mailings, paper streamers, street activities, wall painting, etc. By examining intelligence from the U.S. government—I'm thinking specifically of analyzing a congressional report examining the years 1963–1973 (*The Church Committee and Report and the Hinchey Report as Presented to the U.S. Congress*, 2008)—I will gain insight into how the U.S. intervened, and what the intentions behind intervention were. Finally, I'm sure it will be important to read secondary sources on intervention, particularly those with emphasis on U.S. propaganda and the resultant political climate. Currently, I plan to use *The Nixon Administration and the Death of Allende's Chile: A Case of Assisted Suicide* by Jonathan Haslam and *The Black Book of American Intervention in Chile* by Armando Uribe for this part of the research.

In the second paragraph, Rafe discusses the sources he intends to use. Notice the broad range of possibilities he considers: flyers, television commercials, radio broadcasts, and both American and international sources.

In the third paragraph Rafe anticipates the difficulties he might face and how he can solve them.

> I have a feeling that I will encounter some difficulties in both the sources and the broadness of the topic (i.e., the reasons behind the destruction of Allende's government). Although I possess a working knowledge of Spanish, I know it's fairly limited, and given that propaganda targets a very specific audience in a very specific time period, I probably won't totally get the slang and popular references. I also realize that propaganda isn't the whole picture, and I will need to balance the analysis of the role of propaganda with an honest recognition of the impact of other elements (like military intervention) on Allende's downfall.

Drafting a Guiding Research Question and Research Hypothesis

In reading Rafe's freewrite, you might have noticed that as he developed this topic, he was simultaneously starting to experiment with how to formulate his own argument. That is, in his first paragraph, he moves from the open-ended language of a proposal ("I want to examine," "I'm hoping to analyze") to a restatement of his subject in terms of a guiding research question at the end of the paragraph. You might be tempted in your own freewrite to include a tentative thesis statement along with your research question. While an early hypothesis can be useful, be careful about forming your own argument about a topic too early. How can you responsibly make a claim about a topic that you have not yet researched completely? How can you know what to argue about an issue before you listen to what your sources have to say? These are often frustrating questions for many writers. If you decide on your claim too early, you may set in motion a research process that tempts you to cherry-pick your sources and dismiss

Seeing Connections
See Chapter 1 to review how to develop a strong preliminary thesis statement.

or ignore voices that do not concur with your hypothesis. For this reason, many scholars suggest that writers should focus on identifying a **guiding research question**, as Rafe does, at early stages of the research process, rather than formulating a tentative hypothesis.

There are many benefits to developing a question of this sort. A well-crafted research question can keep you focused as you delve into the research process. In addition, by posing your project as one grounded in inquiry, you can focus on finding sources that help you answer your question rather than prove your point, leading ultimately to a stronger, more persuasive argument. Your question may in fact undergo revision as you learn more about your topic; that is a natural step in the process of exploration and discovery that is at the heart of any research process. To begin, however, you can generate your guiding question by synthesizing some of the more pointed questions about your topic, similar to those we discussed at the beginning of this chapter. Alternately, you could use a prewriting activity like the accordion prewrite to help you identify a strong question to focus your research. In general, a strong research question:

- opens up a line of inquiry (rather than inviting a yes/no response)
- has a sharp focus, appropriate to the scope of the assignment (rather than being overly broad or overly narrow)
- avoids bias or preconceptions (rather than posing a "leading" question)
- offers a solid foundation for further research (rather than posing a question that you might not be able to answer, due to lack of sources or methods for exploring it)

Once you have your guiding research question and have begun to explore your topic, you can start to rework it into a hypothesis, or a working thesis that makes an argumentative claim that you'll attempt to prove. You may move to this step once you start researching, or you may wait until you begin drafting—or even revising—your research paper. Keep in mind that you will probably revise your hypothesis—and maybe your entire approach to the subject—several times over the course of your research. Indeed, this revision process is a natural part of what happens when you actually begin to read your sources, take notes in your research log, and read what your sources have to say about your topic.

4.5 How do I write a formal research proposal?

DRAFTING A RESEARCH PROPOSAL

In many academic contexts, you will be asked to formalize your research plan through composing a **research proposal**. This type of text—common in many disciplines and professions—is used by writers to develop agendas for research communities, secure funding for a study, publicize plans for inquiry and field research, and test the interest of potential audiences for a given project. In the writing classroom, the research proposal provides a similar formal structure for developing a project, but it also serves another purpose: it is a more structured means of organizing your thoughts to help you solidify your topic and move into the next stages of the research process. For these reasons, the *genre*, *organization*, and *content* of the research proposal differ in important ways from other kinds of popular and academic writing that you might do. To write your proposal, include the following elements:

- **Background:** What do I already know about my topic? What do I need to find out more about?
- **Methods:** How am I going to research this topic? What research questions are driving my inquiry?
- **Sources:** What specific texts will I analyze? What additional scholarly or popular sources can I research to help build my knowledge and my argument?
- **Timeline:** What are my goals for the different stages of research, and how can I schedule my work to most effectively meet these milestones?
- **Significance:** What do I hope to accomplish in my research? What are the broader issues or implications of my research? Why do these matter to me and to my readers?

As this list suggests, your proposal should explain your interest in your chosen subject and establish a set of questions to guide your inquiry. The proposal should delineate the timeline for your research and writing process—a crucial time management strategy.

Your proposal serves to clarify your research intentions, but it should also *persuade* an audience of the feasibility and significance of your project. In fact, perhaps the most important step in launching your research inquiry is to address the issue of your project's larger relevance or, as some writing instructors call it, the "So what?" part of the project. It is the

"So what?"—an awareness of the *significance* of the topic you're addressing and the questions you're asking—that moves the proposal from being a routine academic exercise to a powerful piece of persuasive writing. When addressing the "So what?" question, consider why anyone else would care enough to read a paper on your topic. Ask yourself:

- What is at stake in your topic?
- Why does it matter?
- What contribution will your project make to a wider community?

Let's look at an example: a research proposal Molly Fehr developed on Hitler's use of rhetoric.

Fehr 1

Molly Fehr
Dr. Alyssa O'Brien
PWR 2: Rhetoric and Global Leadership
Final Research Proposal
8 May 2016

Inspiring Nazi Germany:

How Hitler Rose to Power through the Use of Propaganda and Rousing Rhetoric

World War II involved all of the major world powers and was the deadliest conflict in human history. The men who led these powers into battle were extraordinary historical figures ranging from Winston Churchill to Franklin D. Roosevelt to Joseph Stalin. Perhaps the most infamous historical leader of all time, Adolf Hitler, was a major component of World War II. For this research project I will examine how Hitler used powerful rhetoric to inspire his followers. The speeches that Hitler gave to the German public were effective enough to convince an entire country to go to war to fight for his beliefs. His powerful

Molly's research proposal begins with a title that reflects her focused research question. In this way, she is sure to offer a more narrowed approach to her topic than the research freewrite.

The proposal opens with background, based on common knowledge.

In the last three sentences of the paragraph, Molly articulates her increasingly narrowed focus: from speeches to powerful rhetoric, to violent propaganda. This narrowed focus will help prevent her project from being too broad.

Fehr 2

rhetoric influenced a generation of German citizens to adopt his ideology and practice his principles. In addition to persuading countless people to embrace his ideas, he used a widespread and violent propaganda campaign to effectively silence his opposition.

As she generates specific research questions, Molly keeps her focus on "violence" as her main line of inquiry.

There are many different facets of World War II leadership and Hitler's power that one could explore. I will be focusing on Hitler specifically and how his use of violent rhetoric influenced both his supporters and his opposition. Some questions I will attempt to answer are: what part of his campaign was the most convincing? My focus will be on his overt use of violence and how that impacted his rise to power. So, what part did violence play in Hitler's rise to power? How did Hitler use fear as a rhetorical strategy? Is violent or emotional imagery the most powerful type of rhetoric? Then, more generally, how did Hitler's leadership affect Germany's role in the war? And finally, how does our understanding of his use of violence impact our view of Hitler as a leader?

Turning to research methods, Molly names and describes the texts she plans to analyze. This makes her proposal seem quite feasible and builds her *ethos* as a scholar.

Hitler's extremely lengthy and provocative speeches will be the cornerstone of my research as they are excellent examples of both *ethos* and *pathos*. I will examine several of Hitler's most famous speeches, focusing on those given each year on the anniversary of his rise to power. In each of these speeches he spoke of the superiority of the German race and his future plans for the great nation. My discussion of Hitler's leadership

Fehr 3

and rhetorical style will also include with an analysis of his book, *Mein Kampf*, which outlines his core beliefs. There have been several scholarly books and articles written about *Mein Kampf* that I will use as secondary sources in my analysis. One book in particular that I will devote time to is Felicity Rash's *The Language of Violence* in which she discusses how the linguistic style of *Mein Kampf* created powerful imagery and elicited strong emotions. Other secondary sources that I will explore include John Angus's article "Evil As the Allure of Protection," and Monika Zagar's *Knut Hamsun*. These sources and others investigate the violent imagery of Nazism and how its effects were far-reaching and dramatic. A possible field resource that I could interview might be a Stanford professor specializing in World War II. I could also interview one of the Stanford research librarians, specifically, either Nathalie Auerbach who specializes in German history or Patricia Harrington who is a general reference librarian.

She refers to several books that have made important contributions to her topic.

She also includes field research as part of her plan, identifying scholars she might interview to learn more about the field.

This project has significant implications for the manner in which historical and contemporary leaders inspire their followers into controversial actions. Understanding how Adolf Hitler employed violent rhetoric to convince people that genocide was not only acceptable but desirable is crucial to unraveling the power of other infamous leaders. Additionally, it is interesting to explore why Hitler was so successful. If certain types of

Molly ends the formal writing of the proposal with a strong statement of significance. Suggesting the "So what?" will help her focus on the importance of her work as a writer and researcher. This section on implications is often the most crucial to readers who evaluate proposals for merit and funding.

Fehr 4

rhetoric such as emotional imagery or evocation of pride are so profoundly effective, how can they be used for good? This brings me to my final point: practical application. There are relatively few historical examples of people who succeeded in amassing so many followers to support a cause that is inherently wrong.

A closer look at how Hitler managed to propagandize and affect a nation could reveal important lessons about how contemporary leaders can mobilize their supporters. Conversely, it could give important wisdom about how to prevent or combat such an influential leader in the future.

In her timeline, Molly lists not only deadlines assigned by her instructor but also key steps in the research process: finding books, evaluating sources, reading and taking notes, constructing a thesis, peer review, a second round of research, drafting, and revising.

Fehr 5

Timeline

1/20: Research Proposal due

1/21–1/23: In-depth research of speeches; write up notes

1/22–1/27: Read secondary sources and write up notes; search for more articles using online databases

1/27–2/1: Review notes and write a preliminary thesis; talk with peers and instructors for advice on thesis as well as for guidance on argument. Evaluate sources in research log and continue to read sources.

Fehr 6

2/2–2/7: Outline due: decide on major argument. Use subheads to indicate sections of the essay.
2/8–2/10: Conduct field research interviews, using my argument and questions.
2/12–2/17: Write first draft of argument. Compose topic sentences for each section. Include evidence for my claims in drafting the argument.
2/18–2/21: Peer review feedback and instructor conference (get feedback).
2/22–3/2: Additional research and revision, as necessary.
3/5: Submit second full draft for feedback.
3/8–3/12: Final revisions, proofreading, works cited list, format paper, include images where appropriate.
3/15: Submit final revision. Done!

With this detailed timeline, Molly shows her careful time management and builds her *ethos* by demonstrating her understanding of the research process.

Fehr 7

Preliminary Bibliography

Auerbach, Nathalie [Bibliographer for Germanic collections, Stanford Library]. Personal Interview. Feb. 2013 [to be scheduled].

Campbell, John Angus. "Evil as the Allure of Protection." *Rhetoric & Public Affairs* 6.3 (2003): 523–30. *Academic Search Premier*. Web. 22 Jan. 2013.

Fehr 8

Harrington, Patricia R. [Coordinator of Content Delivery, General Reference, Stanford Library]. Personal Interview. Feb. 2013 [to be scheduled].

Hitler, Adolf, and Ralph Manheim. *Mein Kampf*. Boston: Houghton, 1943. Print.

Hitler, Adolf. "Germany's Declaration of War against the United States. Reichstag Speech of December 11, 1941." *Institute for Historical Review*. N.d. Web. 19 Jan. 2013. http://www.ihr.org/jhr/v08/v08p389_Hitler.html

———. "Speech before the Reichstag." 30 Jan. 1937. *World Future Fund*. N.d. Web. 17 Jan. 2013.

———. "Speech at the Berlin Sportspalast." 30 Jan. 1940. *World Future Fund*. N.d. Web. 17 Jan. 2013.

———. "Speech at the Berlin Sportspalast." 30 Jan. 1942. *World Future Fund*. N.d. Web. 18 Jan. 2013.

Jowett, Garth S., Victoria O'Donnell, and Garth Jowett. *Readings in Propaganda and Persuasion: New and Classic Essays*. Thousand Oaks: SAGE, 2006. Print.

Maser, Werner. *Hitler's* Mein Kampf*: An Analysis*. London: Faber, 1970. Print.

Rash, Felicity J. *The Language of Violence: Adolf Hitler's* Mein Kampf. New York: Peter Lang, 2006. Print.

Žagar, Monika. *Knut Hamsun: The Dark Side of Literary Brilliance*. Seattle: U of Washington P, 2009. Print.

THE WRITER'S PROCESS

Now that you've learned about the process of generating research questions, narrowing your topic, developing a hypothesis, and then writing up your plans for research in a three-paragraph freewrite or a formal proposal, what might you argue about the first poster of this chapter (Figure 4.1) if you were asked to use it as a starting point for a research project?

In answering this question, you might start to work through the writing activities related to the research process that we've discussed. You might develop a research focus that begins with questions and ends with a "So what?" or statement of significance. You might speculate about which sources that you could use to answer your questions and on opportunities and obstacles you might encounter when pursuing this project. You might try to develop a proposal that concludes with a clear statement of your future authority on this topic as a researcher. Along the way, you might use a research log to keep track of your ideas and work in progress, setting a strong foundation for the next steps of research—gathering and evaluating sources—that we'll be exploring in the next chapter. Now it's time to get started on the research process for writing a persuasive argument about an issue that matters to you.

SPOTLIGHTED ANALYSIS: PROPAGANDA POSTERS

MyWritingLab

Use the following prewriting prompts to follow the example from the beginning of the chapter and analyze the propaganda poster of your choice (for instance, from the Library of Congress online archive):

- What is the poster's underlying message?
- What rhetorical situation informs this text? Who produced the poster? Who was its intended audience? How was it distributed or shared?
- What is its historical context? What was the contemporary social and political situation of the country that produced it?
- What types of rhetorical appeals (*logos*, *pathos*, *ethos*, *kairos*, or *doxa*) does the poster feature and how do they operate in the poster?
- Recalling Chapter 2's discussion of exaggerated use of appeals, does the poster rely on any logical fallacies? Any exaggerated use of *pathos*? Any fallacies of authority? If so, how do these work to persuade the audience?

- How do design elements such as color, font, layout, image selection, and the relationship between word and image operate as persuasive elements?
- How does the poster use stereotypes or symbols to convey its message? What is their cultural significance?
- What research questions can you develop about this poster?

WRITING ASSIGNMENTS

MyWritingLab

1. **Brainstorming Topics:** Early in this chapter, we used propaganda posters as a starting point for generating research topic ideas. Choose a written text—an essay you read for class, a newspaper article, a government report, a transcript of a speech—and create an analysis table such as the one on page 139 for it in which you answer questions about its author, claim, strategies, audience, context, and purpose. For added challenge, fill out the table on your own, but then circulate a blank version—accompanied by your text—among a small group of classmates. Have them answer the questions about your text in the table, each one filling in one or more of the columns and adding a potential research topic at the bottom. When they have done, compare the collaboratively authored table to the one you filled out yourself to get a deeper understanding of the text and how it might lend itself to additional research.

2. **Narrowing Topics:** Follow the instructions for the Writer's Practice on page 151, but instead of focusing on the Occupy posters, use your own research topic as the foundation for the narrowing exercises. Record your prewriting in your research log.

3. **Research Freewrite:** Develop your ideas for your research project by composing a three-paragraph freewrite. In the first paragraph, introduce your research paper topic and describe what you think the main focus of the paper might be. Include a guiding research question or a preliminary thesis in this paragraph. In the second paragraph, discuss the sources that you intend to use. In the third paragraph, speculate about what obstacles you foresee in this project and/or what you anticipate to be the most difficult part of the assignment. If appropriate, use an image to complement your written text. Share your three-paragraph freewrite to your instructor or your peers for feedback.

4. **Research Proposal:** Write a detailed research proposal that discusses your topic, planned method, and purpose in depth. Be sure to cover your topic, your hypothesis, your potential sources and problems, your method, timeline, and, most importantly, the significance of the proposed project. When you are done, present your proposal at a roundtable of research with other members of your class. Answer questions from your classmates to help you fine-tune your topic and troubleshoot your future research.

5. **Peer Review:** Collaboratively peer review your research proposals with a small group of classmates. Assume that you are on the review board granting approval and funding to the best two proposals of your group. Read through each proposal, and then draft proposal review letters for the members of your group that evaluates each proposal's strengths, weaknesses, and your assessment of whether it deserves funding. When you are done, discuss your letters with your group and what changes you can recommend to strengthen the proposal. Then revise your proposals to make them stronger, better written, and more persuasive. See Chapter 6 for more discussion of effective peer feedback sessions.

MyWritingLab Visit Ch. 4 Planning and Proposing Research Arguments in MyWritingLab to complete the Writer's Practices, Spotlighted Analyses, and Writing Assignments, and to test your understanding of the chapter objectives.

CHAPTER 5

Finding and Evaluating Research Sources

Chapter Preview Questions

5.1 What does the research process look like?
5.2 How do I develop effective search terms for my research?
5.3 What is the difference between a primary and a secondary source?
5.4 How do I critically evaluate both print and online sources?
5.5 How do I pursue field research for my project?
5.6 How can I understand the conversation my sources are having about my topic?
5.7 What is an annotated bibliography, and how can it help me develop my argument?

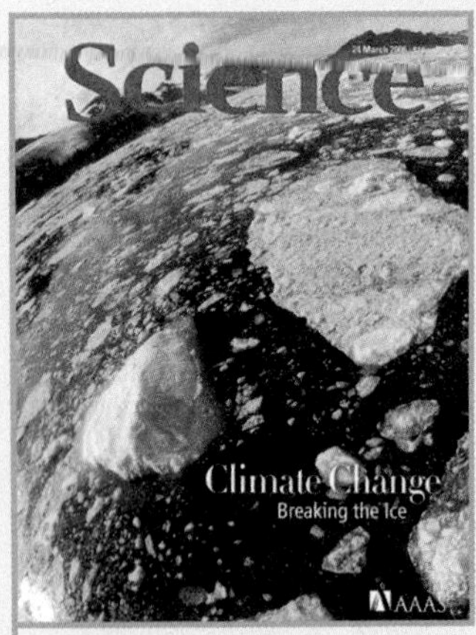

FIGURE 5.1 Cover of *Science*, March 24, 2006.

As you move from planning to conducting research, you'll need to investigate resources and evaluate them for your project. You can use your analytical skills to make important distinctions when locating, evaluating, and using research sources for your research project. Look, for instance, at the covers in Figures 5.1 and 5.2. Although they focus on the same topic—climate change—the visual rhetoric suggests that the content of each journal will be quite different. The audience for *Science* magazine differs from that of *The Economist*, and, consequently, the writing styles within the articles will be different as well. The cover of each magazine previews the content inside. As a researcher, studying the covers could help you understand the different ways that climate change has been understood over time. In this way, you are finding and evaluating research sources for your project.

Specifically, the cover of *Science* in Figure 5.1 conveys how the editors chose to represent global warming to their audience in 2006. It features a photograph of an ice-covered lake that appears to have been taken with a "fish-eye" lens, bringing several ice fragments into prominence in the foreground. Ask yourself: What is the argument conveyed by the visual rhetoric of the cover? What is the significance of the choice to use the lake as the "main character" in the image? How is color used strategically? What kind of stance toward the dangers of global warming does the cover suggest?

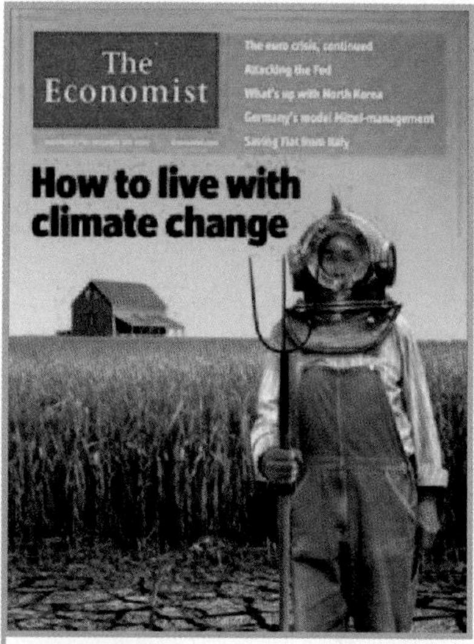

FIGURE 5.2 Cover of *The Economist*, 2010.

In contrast, *The Economist* cover from a few years later (see Figure 5.2) provides a very different perspective on the topic. While the *Science* cover focuses on the environmental effects of climate change, *The Economist* cover draws the reader in with its comic re-rendering of Grant Wood's famous *American Gothic* painting. It shows the impact of global warming not just on the landscape (dried up crops and cracked earth) but also on the individual (the farmer, his startled face hidden behind a diver's helmet). Consider the way that this rhetorical move humanizes the issue of global warning, framing it in a way that is designed specifically to resonate with readers of *The Economist*: the central figure is not just a person, but a farmer, a symbol of American agriculture; the setting is not just a natural landscape, but a farm, representative of U.S. agriculture more broadly. Notice that the language also suggests the magazine's stance. "How to live with climate change" is not a call to action, but a statement about the inevitability of a fact of life.

Clearly, in each case, the editors deliberately located, evaluated, and used materials for the covers that would reflect their magazine's contents. As a researcher, you can use your skills in rhetorical analysis to help you evaluate sources for your own research project, looking to the different elements of a text—from the cover design, to the table of contents, the index, and the writing itself—to better understand the text's perspective on your topic and its usefulness for your project.

Your task as a researcher is quite similar to that of the editors of *Science* and *The Economist*. As you begin gathering and evaluating sources for your own research argument, keep in mind that you will need to shape the argument into a paper addressed to a particular audience: your writing class, a group of scientists, a lobbying organization, an advertising firm, or browsers on the Web. To take part in any of these conversations, a researcher needs to learn:

- what is being talked about (the *topic*)
- how it is being discussed (the *conversation*)
- what the different positions are (*research context*).

5.1 What does the research process look like?

VISUALIZING RESEARCH

To grasp the specifics of the topic, the conversation, and the research context, it is helpful to take a moment to visualize the research process. When you think of the act of research, what comes to mind? Surfing the Web? Looking through a library? Interviewing experts in the field? All these images represent different research scenarios. The material you gather in each situation will compose the foundation for your research; it will inform your essay, but not all of it will find its way into your final paper. Nevertheless, you need to research widely and thoroughly to be fully informed about your topic and write a compelling research-based argument. One helpful way of visualizing the relationship between the *process* and the *product* of research is through the metaphor of the iceberg of research (see Figure 5.3). In essence, your final argument will be a synthesis of your research; beneath the surface lie the many different sources you will explore: books, journal articles, websites, field surveys, historical materials, interviews, multimedia, and more. All these constitute the research material. Your task as a researcher is to move beyond a surface knowledge of your topic; you need to gather, assess, keep, throw out, and ultimately use a variety of sources.

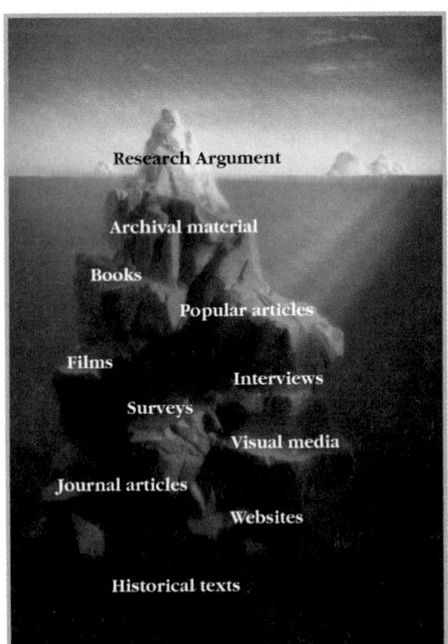

FIGURE 5.3 The iceberg of research demonstrates the many sources you might consult in building your argument.

By exploring such a wide range of material, you will encounter a rich array of scholarly and popular perspectives on your topic. In many ways, your research argument will be, in fact, a discussion with those research sources themselves. You add your voice to theirs. But your final paper may appear as only the tip of the iceberg or a result of your careful study of the work of others.

Sometimes, this process of building on others can be intimidating; we fear that we will have nothing new to add to the conversation. Yet if we think of research sources as texts written by people who were once, like us, struggling to figure out what they were trying to say, then we can see the process of gathering and assessing sources as a very social one, a process in which you *respect* and *acknowledge* the ideas of others and then seek to add your own voice to an ongoing conversation. One way to begin that conversation is to discover what others before you have said, thought, written, and published—and to keep track of that process in your research log, as explained in Chapter 4.

In this chapter, we'll use the metaphor of the *conversation* to accentuate the point that the research process is an act of composing a response to an ongoing dialogue about a topic. By gathering, synthesizing, and sorting the perspectives of others, you begin to shape your own stance on a research topic. By adding your voice as a writer, you are responding to others. Research is a *relationship* that you develop with the source material and the writers you encounter along the way.

DEVELOPING SEARCH TERMS

5.2 How do I develop effective search terms for my research?

The first step in the research process lies in locating relevant and interesting sources to draw into your conversation. This involves finding the best **search terms**—usually a noun or short phrase—to use when looking for sources on your topic. While online search engines like Google and Bing often can complete complex searches based on a colloquial phrase (i.e., "how eating broccoli prevents cancer"), most rigorous research projects rely on more academic search mechanisms, such as scholarly databases, online library catalogues, or reference materials (like encyclopedias or bibliographies). To use these tools effectively, you need to learn to speak their language; instead of using everyday terminology, you need to use **keywords** and **strategic search syntax** to set the parameters for your search.

A good starting point for developing your search terms is to look carefully at your research topic. If you write out your topic or your research question, what key concepts or words can you identify? For instance, if your preliminary topic is "the effect of fracking on groundwater," logical keywords might be "fracking" and "groundwater." To expand your search, you might consider ways to multiply your terms, through first identifying *synonyms* (e.g., drinking water, hydraulic fracturing, drilling), then *related concepts* (e.g., natural gas extraction, contamination), and then *specific examples or stakeholders* (e.g., Pennsylvania water contamination, Chevron). Adding these keywords and phrases to your initial search terminology will help diversify your search results so you can start to explore the different aspects of your topic.

While developing **search** terms is an important starting point for research, using specialized **syntax strategies** can help you conduct more productive searches in academic databases. Boolean searches combine keywords such as AND, NOT, and OR to help you refine your searches; similarly, techniques of truncation and quotation can likewise help you tailor your search results. Let's see how these techniques sharpen a search for a research project on the relationship between vaccines and autism.

AND: When you connect two keywords with "AND," you'll receive all results that include both terms, helping you narrow your search results.

Example: A search for vaccines AND autism *will find articles, books, and other texts that include both terms.* (Note: In Google searches and many database searches, the "AND" is automatically implied, so many search engines automatically would understand a search for *vaccines autism* as *vaccines* AND *autism*.)

OR: When you connect two keywords with "OR," you'll receive all results that contain either of those keywords, helping you expand your search results.

Example: A search for vaccines OR autism *will return a long list of texts that might be just tagged with the keyword* vaccine, *just tagged with the keyword* autism, *or is tagged with both words.*

NOT: When you connect two keywords with "NOT" or "EXCEPT" you'll receive all the results for the first keyword that do not also contain the second keyword, helping you better focus your search results.

Example: A search for vaccines NOT autism *will return texts about vaccines that do not mention autism.*

QUOTATION MARKS: When you enclose a keyword phrase in quotation marks, most search engines search for that specific phrase, helping you get more specific search results.

WRITER'S PRACTICE MyWritingLab

Develop search terms for your research project by filling in this chart in your research log. Focus on expanding your search by moving from keywords to *synonyms* (that allow you to explore similar ideas) to *related concepts* (that allow you to broaden your scope) to *specific examples* (that show you ways to narrow your search).

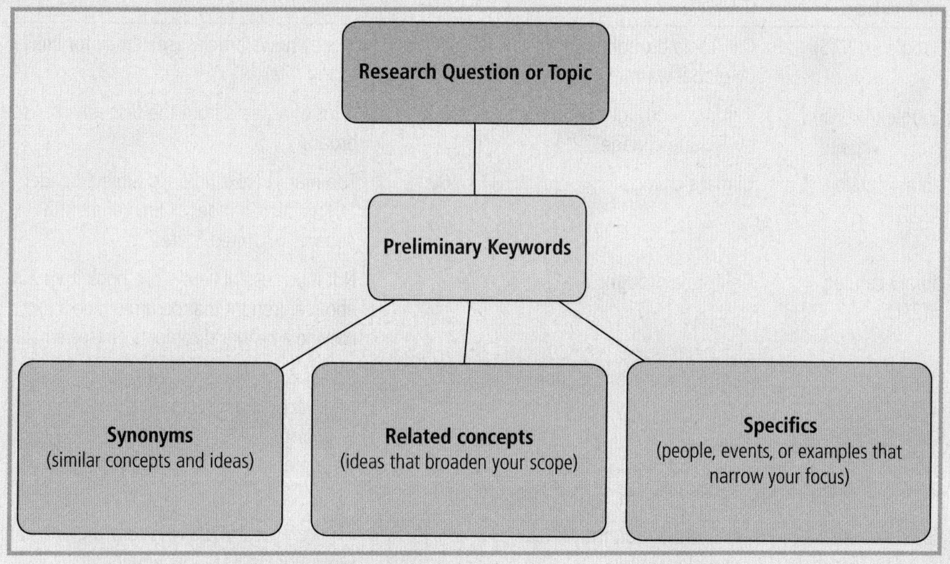

Example: If you searched "autism spectrum disorder," *you would get only results that include that exact phrase.*

TRUNCATION*: In some databases, you can search for different versions of a word by shortening it and appending an * to the end.

Example: Searching autis* *would produce results that include the terms autism or autistic.*

COMBINE TERMS: When you combine terms, you can customize your search even more powerfully.

Example: Searching (vaccines AND autism) NOT "Jenny McCarthy" *will yield results on autism and vaccines that don't mention actress Jenny McCarthy.*

Let's look at how one student adapted her search strategies to accommodate the different types of resources she was using on her project on the recent California drought (see Figure 5.4). Like many students, Ellie started

FINAL RESEARCH PROJECT
Topic: California drought and global warming
Preliminary search term chart and thoughts …

What I searched and when	Search terms	Results	Notes
Google (4/2/15)	California drought caused by global warming	472,000(!!!)	Mostly news articles (see email for links to top hits)
Google (4/2/15)	California drought caused by climate change	976,000 (!!!)	A lot of repeats from the first search – too broad.
Library catalog (4/2/15)	Climate change	13,760	Too many! Next time try subject header "Climactic Changes > Environmental Aspects > United States"
Library catalog (4/2/15)	California drought	170	Not much useful here – one book from 2008 about a drought that occurred then might provide a historical comparison (see email!)
Library catalog (4/2/15)	California drought global warming	11	Really nothing helpful except one reference book – *Encyclopedia of Global Warming and Climate Change.* ***Go to reference section at library to look at it ***
EBSCO database (4/4/15)	"California drought" AND "global warming"	2	*Nature* article (1/2014) really the only one worth looking at– see email
EBSCO database (4/4/15)	"California drought" AND "climate change"	21	Great articles! See email – esp. look at Tsiang et al (2014 – full text!!) and Mann (2015)

*****For next time:**

- Try limiting searches to "video" in the library to see if there's a documentary in one of the searches – might be interesting to watch if recent enough
- Try subject searches in EBSCO database – "CLIMATIC changes"; "droughts"; "RAIN & rainfall"; "California"; "Global warming – Environmental aspects"; "Global environmental change"
- Look up some of the studies mentioned in the news articles (i.e. Diffenbaugh, 2015) to get to the studies themselves (articles are good, but studies themselves would be great!)
- Climate change seems a better term for databases than global warming for this topic!
- Need to find a way to narrow my searches more. Read some articles – find more names of people, places, researchers etc. that I can use in my next searches
- Librarian suggested looking at some other databases: Web of Knowledge; Web of Science; BioOne; LexisNexis (only if you need more articles!); Environment index; GreenFile

FIGURE 5.4 This page from a student's research log shows how she tracked her initial searches.

with an Internet search based on her research question, What's the relationship between the California drought and climate change? Her phrasing—"California drought caused by global warming"—mirrored her everyday language and was designed to target the controversy surrounding this issue. As you might expect, her initial Google search yielded more results than she could use, leaving her to speculate about ways to include more specific keywords in future searches. Moving to her library catalog, she shifted from vernacular phrasing to keywords: "Climate change" and "California drought." The first provided too many results, leading her to identify a subject heading she found listed in one of the source records ("climatic change > environmental aspects > United States") that she could use in the future to narrow her search. Her second library search offered a more manageable range of materials; however, she recognized they would primarily serve as background material and reference sources for her topic. In her quest for more timely sources, she moved to the academic database, EBSCO. Here she used the Boolean operator "AND" to connect her key terms. Through trial and error, she determined that the phrase "climate change" yielded much better results than "global warming," and she was able to find over 20 current and relevant articles about her topic.

As you can see from Ellie's example, often the list of potential sources returned to you by your initial searches will be much larger than you can efficiently process. Your main task, then, will be to find ways to narrow your

AT A GLANCE

Tips for Choosing Search Terms

- ***Colloquial terminology and phrases*:** Use popular or colloquial terminology and phrases in your Internet searches because search engines pick up actual terms from the webpages they index.
- ***Keywords and strategic syntax*:** Use keywords for library catalogues and database searches. Since databases can house a wide range of materials, from academic publications to popular articles, experiment with different search terms to find the ones that work best for each database. In addition, use strategic search syntax (AND, OR, NOT, quotation marks, truncation) for more powerful Boolean searches.
- ***Subject headings or tags*:** Many times, the individual article or book citations that you find in your library catalog or scholarly database will include subject tags or headings that librarians use to catalog information and cross-reference related materials; most are based on the Library of Congress Subject Headings (LCSHs). Use these tags to expand your search. You can find the official LCSH terms online through the Library of Congress website. Subject tags also usually appear under the summary in a source record in your library catalog.

search and to adapt your strategies and terminology based on your search engine. Experimenting with a range of terms—particularly more limited ones—can help you with this task by finding materials specific to your topic; keeping track of your search terms, perhaps in a research log, can also be an invaluable way to organize your ideas and develop best practices for search protocols on your topic.

5.3 What is the difference between a primary and a secondary source?

UNDERSTANDING PRIMARY AND SECONDARY SOURCES

Your initial searches will yield a range of sources—from magazine articles to books, video recordings, and perhaps even manuscripts or a photograph collection. Each of these sources can play a vital role in your research. Scholars divide research into primary and secondary research, and sources, likewise, into **primary sources** (original texts you analyze in your research) and **secondary sources** (sources that provide commentary on your primary material or on your topic in general).

Consider, for instance, Molly Fehr's project, examined in Chapter 4. Hitler's speeches and his book, *Mein Kampf*, were her *primary sources*, and the articles, books, and transcribed interviews providing analysis of Hitler's propaganda were her *secondary sources*. Her own essay, when completed, became *another* secondary source, one that contributes to an ongoing intellectual discussion about the power of Nazi propaganda.

As you search for your research materials, keep in mind that no sources are *inherently* primary or secondary; those terms refer to *how you use them* in your paper. For instance, if you were working with the topic of Internet advertising, you might use actual Facebook ads and Flash animations as your primary sources, as well as press releases and advertising websites. For secondary sources you might turn to articles that discuss innovations in social media marketing, a Website on the history of digital advertising, and perhaps even a book by a famous economist about the impact of technology on corporate marketing strategies. However, imagine that you shift your topic slightly, making your new focus the economist's theories about the corruption of traditional advertising by multimedia technology. Now, that same book you looked at before as a *secondary* source becomes a *primary* source for this new topic.

As you can see, your inquiry will determine which sources will be primary and which will be secondary for your argument. In most cases, you will need to use a combination of primary and secondary materials to make a persuasive argument. The primary sources allow you to perform your own analysis, whereas the secondary sources offer you critical viewpoints that you need to take into account in your analysis and integrate into your argument to build up your *ethos*. How you respond to and combine your primary and secondary sources is a matter of choice, careful design, and rhetorical strategy.

Finding Primary Sources

The term *primary source* refers to any material that you will analyze for your paper, including speech scripts, advertisements, photographs, historical documents, film, artwork, audio files, and writing on Websites. Primary sources also can include testimonies by people with firsthand knowledge, direct quotations from a text, or, in some cases, interviews. Whatever is under the lens of your own analysis constitutes a *primary source.*

Searching for **primary sources**—original texts you analyze in your research paper—can be challenging, but they can be found in many places: in your library (whether in the general stacks, archives, or multimedia collections); at community centers such as library exhibits, museums, and city hall; or even in online digital archives such as the one maintained by the Library of Congress. These materials can be some of the most exciting sources to work within your research process and might include:

- original documents (examples: a handwritten letter by Mahatma Gandhi or Charles Lindbergh's journals)
- rare books and manuscripts (examples: a first edition of a Charlotte Brontë novel or Roger Manvell's manuscripts on the history of the Third Reich)
- portfolios of photographs (examples: photos of Japanese American internment camps or of Black Panther demonstrations from the 1960s)
- government documents (examples: U.S. censuses and surveys, reports from the Department of Agriculture or congressional papers)

- other one-of-a-kind texts (examples: AIDS prevention posters from South Africa, a noted artist's sketchbook, or a series of leaflets produced by the U.S. Psychological Warfare Department)

In many cases, you can work directly with these materials so you can perform your own firsthand analysis of that piece of cultural history.

Consider the sources that student Cam Russell used in her project on the history of computer programming. As she started her research, she came upon information about ENIAC, a World War II Army–run project involving the first programmable, electronic computer. Intrigued by the idea of a 1940s computer, she decided to look at some primary sources—photographs taken by the U.S. Army of the project. While searching the archives, she noticed something surprising: the programmers featured in the images were mostly women (see Figure 5.5). Intrigued by this discovery, Cam decided to narrow her research topic to focus on early women programmers. Image searches of online and university archives led her to another discovery—a cover of *Radio & Television News* featuring a woman working at a sprawling computer console, confirming the fact that as late as 1957, women occupied a public presence as computer programmers.

Seeing the *Radio & Television News* cover online prompted Cam to form questions about the magazine itself. Were female programmers just "cover girls" for this issue or were they discussed in the article itself? How did the magazine in general represent gender and its relation to technology? She also found herself thinking more expansively about how much the stereotype had changed over the past several decades. In this way, through her initial analysis of these primary sources, Cam was able to refine her research question to ask, If some of the earliest computer programmers were women, what caused the shift toward the "bro-grammer" stereotype that dominates today's Silicon Valley culture? This question provided a strong foundation for her further research that involved using secondary sources to provide key background information and critical perspectives on her topic.

FIGURE 5.5 One of Cam's first discoveries was this U.S. army photograph of Ester Gerston and Gloria Ruth Gorden programming the ENIAC computer.

Searching for Secondary Sources

As Cam's example suggests, while primary materials play an important role in your research, just as important are your **secondary sources**—texts that analyze or provide a perspective on a primary source. These include scholarly articles, popular commentaries, background materials (in print, video, or interview format), and survey data reinforcing your analysis. Whatever sources you can use as a lens to look at or understand the subject of your analysis constitutes a *secondary source.* The writers of such texts offer the voices with which you will engage in scholarly conversation as you develop the substance of your argument.

Although your instinct may send you directly to the Internet, your first stop in your search for secondary sources should actually be your library's reference area, the home of reference librarians—people trained to help you find what you need—as well as a treasure trove of encyclopedias, bibliographies, and other resource materials. These storehouses of information can be invaluable in providing you with the *foundational sources* for your project, including basic definitions, historical background, and bibliographies. Yet, while such "background" materials are necessary to help you construct a framework for your research argument, they represent only one part of your iceberg of research. For more rigorous analysis, you should turn to books and articles that provide critical analysis and arguments about your specific research subject.

AT A GLANCE

Finding Secondary Sources

- ***Dictionaries, guides, and encyclopedias*** provide helpful background information for your topic.
- ***Library catalogs*** allow you to search the library holdings for relevant books, newspapers, journals, documentaries, or other materials.
- ***CD-ROM indexes and bibliographies*** contain vast amounts of bibliographic information.
- ***Academic databases and indexes*** provide access to full-text versions of articles from a range of sources. Most are available by subscription only; many universities subscribe to multiple databases for student research.
- ***Electronic journals and ebooks*** offer access to the full digital versions of books and academic journals from a wide range of disciplines.
- ***Google scholar and Google books*** can be helpful resources, especially when used in conjunction with academic databases and library catalogs.

To locate these more specific secondary sources, you might search your library catalog for relevant books and films and other published materials.

You can also consult databases and indexes, indispensable research guides that will provide you with bibliographic citations for academic articles on your topic. Databases can come in many forms: collections of electronic journals, searchable Internet resources, or even CD-ROMs. Although some databases provide bibliographic citations that you can use to locate the source in your library catalog, many include a detailed abstract summarizing a source's argument, and others link you to full-text electronic copies of articles. Consider using a citation management program such as Zotero or RefWorks to help collect your citations or carefully record your search results in your research log; organizing your citations now will streamline both your research and writing processes moving forward.

Finally, although databases, catalogs, and search engines provide indispensable tools for conducting your research, remember also that your classmates can serve as secondary sources you might consult or even interview. Ask others who are working on similar topics to share resources, and help each other along the route of your research. This is particularly true for the stage in your research when you produce a **preliminary bibliography**—a working list of the sources for your iceberg of research.

AT A GLANCE

Recording Searches in Your Research Log

Use your research log to keep careful track of the dates, details, and key terms of your searches and to organize your sources and your notes:

- Date each entry in your log to keep track of your progress and show the evolution of your ideas.
- Track keywords, search terms, and the search engines and academic databases you've used.
- Keep a running list of your sources by call number, author, and title.
- Write down complete identifying information for any source you consult, including online images or articles, print copies of journals or magazines from the library, articles from library databases, and book chapters. Be sure to keep track of URLs for online sources and download them if possible.
- Double-check transcribed quotations for accuracy while you still have the source before you, and include page numbers (or paragraph numbers for Website articles). Be sure to include quotation marks around each direct quote you transcribe, even in your research log.
- Include printouts (or digital copies, if your log is electronic) of relevant articles or database entries, and especially of online articles, images, or Websites that might disappear when their site is updated.
- Annotate the entry by including an evaluation of the source and an indication of how you might use it as part of your final paper.

EVALUATING YOUR SOURCES

5.4 How do I critically evaluate both print and online sources?

Implementing these research strategies will provide you with access to many interesting sources, but how do you discriminate among them to find those that are credible, reliable, and authoritative? How do you know which ones will be the most useful for your argument? The key rests in understanding the argumentative perspective, or *rhetorical stance*, of each source. At times, the source's stance may be self-evident: you may automatically gravitate toward experts in the field, well known for their opinions and affiliations. It is just as likely, however, that you may not be familiar with the names or ideas of your sources. Therefore, it is essential to develop a method for evaluating the sources you encounter.

Seeing Connections
See Chapter 3 for a more complete discussion of rhetorical stance.

Questions for Evaluating Sources

As you begin to work with your sources, you'll need to repurpose the skills of critical thinking and rhetorical analysis that we discussed in earlier chapters to work through the following questions:

Authorship. Who is the author? Is he or she an expert on the topic? What institution or organization is he or she affiliated with? What else has he or she written on this subject? Have other sources that you've read referenced him or her, or his or her work? To answer this question, you might look the author up online or in a bibliography index to assess his or her *ethos*.

Publication information. Who published the source? Is it a university press or online academic journal (suggesting peer-reviewed scholarship) or a trade press or commercial website (suggesting a commercial venture)? Is it published by a foundation or organization (suggesting a political agenda) or self-published (suggesting the author's struggle to have his or her views accepted for publication)? If it's an online source, does the site include a gesture of accountability for the information it publishes, such as a "contact us" link?

- *Tip: For online sources, look at the URL to see if it's a ".gov" (government-affiliated site), ".com" (commercial site), ".org" (an organization's site), ".mil" (a military website), or ".edu" (educational or university site). Caution: If a site contains a tilde (~), that indicates it's a personal website rather than one sponsored by the organization or institution.*

Publication date. When was it published? Is it a recent contribution or an older study? If it's an electronic source, does it have a "last updated" notation? If not, do embedded links still work?

- *Tip: Don't dismiss older materials too quickly; sometimes an older source can provide historical context or provide a foundational perspective on your issue. However, usually you should use the more recent sources to engage the most timely perspectives on your topic.*

Purpose, occasion, and exigency. What was the occasion for the source? Was it written in reaction to a specific text or event or in response to a particular research question? Was it designed to inform? To instruct? To provide a call to action?

- *Tip: Sometimes the purpose or occasion might be explicit; other times it is less obvious. A quick online search (of author or the name of a key event or cited publication) can help you understand cultural or historical context if it not readily apparent; understanding the purpose behind the source can help you better assess the source's argument and motives.*

Audience. Who is its intended audience? Scholars? Experts in the field? A popular audience? A particular demographic, such as college students, parents, teens, or senior citizens? How is the argument and language shaped to address this audience? Does the author use rhetorical strategies—such as definition or community-specific terms (like jargon) to speak to his or her audience? Are you a member of the intended audience? If not, how does that affect the persuasiveness of the argument?

- *Tip: Keep in mind that there sometimes is a difference between the audience that an author intended to address and the audience who actually reads the argument. Is the argument flexible enough to speak to both types of readers?*

Argument. What is the source's argument? Does the author have a clear argument? Are there any implicit or unstated assumptions underlying the argument? Check the opening paragraphs, preface, or introduction to the text: does the author lay out his or her theoretical framework or a roadmap of how he or she will structure his argument?

- *Tip: As you work with a source, always write a paraphrase of its main claim in your research log for easy reference. To see others's critical assessments of a source's argument, consider looking at book reviews or literature reviews that discuss the text; for more popular reactions to electronic texts, check the "comments" section, if available, beneath blog posts or online articles.*

Evidence. What types of evidence does the author use to support his claim? Does he use primary research, such as analysis of primary texts or his own surveys or interviews? Does he use secondary sources as evidence? Does he use a combination of the two? Does he include a variety of sources or perspectives, or does he seem to cherry-pick his examples? Does he address counterarguments? Does he treat them respectfully? Does he cite his sources ethically and appropriately? Does he provide a works cited or list of references at the end? If it's an online source, does the author provide links to any Internet sources he cites?

- *Tip: Use your source's citations as the starting point for further research; if you find a cited quotation or piece of evidence from your source's argument particularly striking, use the associated link or the citation in the works cited to track down that additional source and read it to see how it might contribute to your own project.*

Tone. What is the tone of the source? Does it use objective language? Is its tone comic? Serious? Scholarly? Casual? Does it seem to represent a particular political, cultural, or ideological position or world view (i.e., feminist, conservative, fundamentalist, American)?

- *Tip: Just because a source is associated with a particular ideological position doesn't mean that you need to disqualify it from your research; however, you'll need to take into account how any bias might influence the strength of its argument and the evidence it provides for your research.*

As this evaluation criteria suggest, you probably won't use every source that you discover through your research. Sometimes you might need to set aside sources even though they have extremely strong *ethos* or arguments because they are outdated or represent a focus or stance that is not useful for your purposes. Be sure to keep a record of such sources, however, in your research log in case you have cause to return to them later in your research.

Let's look at how you might put this evaluation method into practice with the different types of sources that Cam discovered as she moved forward with her research project on women and computer programming. Consider, for instance, the online article "Researcher reveals how 'Computer Geeks' replaced 'Computer Girls,'" one of Cam's top hits on her Google search for "women and computer programming." Cam began the process of evaluating the source by looking at the URL: http://gender.stanford.edu/news/2011/researcher-reveals-how-computer-geeks-replaced-computergirls. In this case, she noted that the address of the host site (gender.stanford.edu) ends with .edu, indicating that this website is affiliated with an accredited educational institution and is not a commercial (.com), government (.gov), or personal site. She confirmed this affiliation by looking at the homepage itself, which features "Stanford University" and "The Clayman Institute for Gender Research" prominently in its header, granting it a strong *ethos* appeal. Cam identified other aspects of the page that enhanced its credibility: a clean and engaging design; a clearly identified author, Brenda Frink, who (Cam discovered through a quick Google search) is a social and cultural historian with a PhD from Stanford; a recent publication date; and a prominent "About" button in the top left and the "Contact Us" link at the bottom that speak to the site's accountability for the material it puts online.

Yet, evaluating a website involves more than simply assessing the *ethos* of its design. Cam recognized that she needed to look at the content of the article itself to assess its viability as a source for her project. As she began to read the article, she found it confirmed her initial impression from reading the title, namely that the subject matter spoke directly to her research question about how and why male computer culture displaced female programmers. However, she took her analysis further and looked carefully at other elements as she assessed the text:

- **Structure:** Cam noted that the article has a clear structure, scaffolded with subheads, and concludes with a paragraph that reasserts the author's main point.
- **Tone:** Cam was impressed by Frink's even, unbiased tone, which avoided jargon and used inclusive pronouns like "us" and "we" to connect with her readers.
- **Audience:** Cam found evidence that the author was making certain assumptions about her audience with lines like "It may be surprising

to learn ..." and "The world described in the Cosmopolitan article seems foreign to us today." In assessing these choices, Cam recognized that Frink is speaking specifically to an early twenty-first-century audience, one who is familiar with the contemporary male computer nerd stereotype.

- **Argument and evidence:** As Cam moved further through the text, she confirmed that Frink made a clear and solid argument, supporting her points with direct quotations and evidence (historical and statistical) from historian Nathan Ensmenger's work.
- **Scholarly conversation.** Lastly, Cam saw further evidence that the author situated her argument in terms of a larger, ongoing conversation on this issue by the way that Frink populates her paragraphs with links designed to point the reader toward reference sources, additional articles, and even secondary websites.

After evaluating the online article in this way, Cam found it to be persuasive, relevant, and credible—a solid source for her project. However, the open comment section underneath the article gave her pause. While the reader comments provided some interesting perspectives on the topic, Cam noted that the website had tagged each commenter with the label "unverified." In some rare contexts, online comments—whether on a blog, discussion forum, or online article—can be useful sources. However, unless the comments are moderated or approved by the website, they should be approached – as in this case—as "unverified," both in terms of the credibility of the author and the accuracy of the information. In most instances, the problematic nature of online comments is self-evident; you only have to look at the inflammatory comments posted under most YouTube videos to see how often biased and empty claims dominate these spaces. However, even more even-handed comments should be approached with care unless there is a way to verify either the identity of the writer or the validity of the information. Many researchers warn against using comments at all, and this is probably the best practice in most cases. Cam, for instance, decided against using the reader comments as part of her research, opting instead to focus on more credible online sources, scholarly books, and peer-reviewed articles.

Let's look now at another of her sources—a scholarly article by Jennifer S. Light, "When Computers Were Women." Cam found this source by searching "women AND Eniac" in an academic database, encountering it first as

◂ Result List | Refine Search ◂ **5** of **14** ▸

When Computers Were Women.

Authors:	Light, Jennifer S.
Source:	Technology & Culture. Jul99, Vol. 40 Issue 3, p455. 29p. 2 Black and White Photographs.
Document Type:	Article
Subject Terms:	*COMPUTERS *COMPUTER technicians ***WOMEN** in computer science
NAICS/Industry Codes:	334111 Electronic Computer Manufacturing 443144 Computer and software stores 443142 Electronics Stores 334110 Computer and peripheral equipment manufacturing 417310 Computer, computer peripheral and pre-packaged software merchant wholesalers 423430 Computer and Computer Peripheral Equipment and Software Merchant Wholesalers
Abstract:	Relates the history of Electronic Numerical Integrator and Calculator (**ENIAC**), the first electronic computer in the United States. Invention of **ENIAC**; Female technicians whom existing computer histories have rendered invisible; How the job of programmer originated as feminized clerical labor; **Women** in wartime; **Women's** entry into computing; Female computers and **ENIAC** girls.
ISSN:	0040-165X

FIGURE 5.6 One of Cam's search results for her search for "women AND Eniac" through a scholarly database.

a search result that she needed to assess to determine if she should read the source (Figure 5.6). Although brief, the record offered her much information:

- Clicking on the **author** link took her to a page listing many of Jennifer Light's other articles, helping her assess her *ethos* and expertise on the topic.
- Clicking on the **publication** link (*Technology & Culture*) brought her to a description of the journal, which confirmed that it was an academic, peer-reviewed journal.
- Looking at the **date** of the article, Cam realized that it was over 15 years old but decided the content might still be relevant given it was detailing a historical phenomenon.
- Scanning the page, she noticed the helpful linked **subject terms**, which she recorded in her research log for her future searches.
- Reading the abstract provided her with a brief summary of the **argument**, confirming the article's usefulness for her research.

Seeing Connections
See Chapter 8 for a full discussion of academic abstracts.

In this case, Cam conducted what we might call a "**cover**" **evaluation**—an initial evaluation process that helps a researcher determine whether a text might be a useful source. With popular magazines, we might look at the actual cover for such a preliminary assessment, as we did with Figures 5.1 and 5.2 at the beginning of the chapter. Web materials provide much of this information as part of their design, integrating the *cover evaluation* with the process of reading the text. We might be most familiar with this process for books—a savvy researcher flips between the title page, the table of contents, and the index to assess authorship, publication information, Library of Congress subject headers (back of title page), argument, and relevance to topic. However, academic journal articles require a different approach; many times, we don't see the cover of an academic journal at all because we use library copies that have been rebound for permanent shelving or we access issues online. In that case, search records such as the one in Figure 5.6 provide us with a virtual "cover" to assess.

To responsibly evaluate a text, however, we need to move past the cover to look at the argument itself. Let's look, as Cam did, at the first section of Light's article (Figure 5.7) and consider which characteristics suggest its suitability as a source for her project.

As you skim the first page of the article, notice the following elements:

- Light utilizes an objective, academic style of writing that suggests that this source will provide an authoritative and unbiased perspective on the topic.
- Her attention to style (for instance, the deliberate repetition of "While ..." phrases at the top of the second page) shows she deliberately crafted her piece to engage her readers.
- She carefully documents her sources through footnotes, demonstrating her ethics as a researcher and the fact that her argument is founded in a knowledge of the scholarship on the topic.
- Even further, she clearly indicates her unique contribution to the conversation and the methodology she will use.
- Finally, the author's biography at the bottom of the first page further contributes to her *ethos*, both by providing her institutional credentials and showing that the article derived from peer review—not just at the level of the publication but also in the drafting stages through feedback from her colleagues.

Such deeper evaluation makes clear that this is a useful source that you could trust for a research project on shifting gender stereotypes related to computer programming. As you can see, it is not enough simply to locate your sources: you need to use your skills of analysis to assess their viability for your individual project.

When Computers Were Women

JENNIFER S. LIGHT

J. Presper Eckert and John W. Mauchly, household names in the history of computing, developed America's first electronic computer, ENIAC, to automate ballistics computations during World War II. These two talented engineers dominate the story as it is usually told, but they hardly worked alone. Nearly two hundred young women, both civilian and military, worked on the project as human "computers," performing ballistics computations during the war. Six of them were selected to program a machine that, ironically, would take their name and replace them, a machine whose technical expertise would become vastly more celebrated than their own.[1]

The omission of women from the history of computer science perpetuates misconceptions of women as uninterested or incapable in the field. This article retells the history of ENIAC's "invention" with special focus on the female technicians whom existing computer histories have rendered invisible. In particular, it examines how the job of programmer, perceived in recent years as masculine work, originated as feminized clerical labor. The story presents an apparent paradox. It suggests that women were somehow hidden during this stage of computer history while the wartime popular press trumpeted just the opposite—that women were breaking into traditionally male occupations within science, technology, and engineering.

Dr. Light recently completed her Ph.D. in the history of science at Harvard University; beginning in the fall of 1999 she will be assistant professor of communication studies at Northwestern University. She thanks Peter Buck, Herman Goldstine, Rachel Prentice, Sherry Turkle, John Staudenmaier, and four anonymous reviewers for their contributions to this article. An early version of the article was presented at "Gender, 'Race,' and Science," a conference at Queen's University, Kingston, Ontario, 12–15 October, 1995.

0040-165X/99/4003-0001$8.00

1. History has valued hardware over programming to such an extent that even the *IEEE Annals of the History of Computing* issue devoted to ENIAC's fiftieth anniversary barely mentioned these women's roles. See *IEEE Annals of the History of Computing* 18, no. 1 (1996). Instead, they were featured two issues later in a special issue on women in computing.

TECHNOLOGY AND CULTURE

JULY
1999
VOL. 40

A closer look at this literature explicates the paradox by revealing widespread ambivalence about women's work. While celebrating women's presence, wartime writing minimized the complexities of their actual work. While describing the difficulty of their tasks, it classified their occupations as subprofessional. While showcasing them in formerly male occupations, it celebrated their work for its femininity. Despite the complexities—and often pathbreaking aspects—of the work women performed, they rarely received credit for innovation or invention.

The story of ENIAC's female computers supports Ruth Milkman's thesis of an "idiom of sex-typing" during World War II—that the rationale explaining why women performed certain jobs contradicted the actual sexual division of labor.[2] Following her lead, I will compare the actual contributions of these women with their media image. Prewar labor patterns in scientific and clerical occupations significantly influenced the way women with mathematical training were assigned to jobs, what kinds of work they did, and how contemporary media regarded (or failed to regard) this work. This article suggests why previous accounts of computer history did not portray women as significant and argues for a reappraisal of their contributions.[3]

2. Ruth Milkman, *Gender at Work: The Dynamics of Job Segregation by Sex During World War II* (Chicago, 1987).

3. Two books currently offer some information on the participation of women in computer history: see Autumn Stanley, *Mothers and Daughters of Invention: Notes for a Revised History of Technology* (Metuchen, N.J., 1993), and Herman Goldstine, *The Computer from Pascal to Von Neumann* (Princeton, 1972). For recollections from women who worked on the ENIAC, see W. Barkley Fritz, "The Women of ENIAC," *IEEE Annals of the History of Computing* 18, no. 3 (1996): 13–28. Other histories tend to make passing references to the women and to show photographs of them without identifying them by name.

FIGURE 5.7

USING FIELD RESEARCH

5.5 How do I pursue field research for my project?

In addition to the primary and secondary sources you will consult as you develop your research project, you may also have the chance to go out across campus, into the community, or into the virtual world to engage with people's opinions and use that information in your essay. That is, your project might provide you with the opportunity to enrich your argument by carrying out your own **field research**—conducting *interviews*, developing *surveys*, and engaging in *fieldwork*. Consider the possibilities: for an essay on YouTube mash-ups and copyright infringement, you could interview a faculty member who has written extensively on the Digital Millennium Copyright Act; for a project investigating cyberbullying, you could use your own survey of 50 college students to bring the voices of cyberbullying victims—and perhaps even bullies—into your paper; for an essay about urban murals, you could visit several local murals, take photographs, and even talk with local artists. In each case, you would be using *field research* to complement your text-based research and to strengthen your research-based claim.

Conducting Interviews

One of the most common forms of *field research*, an interview provides you with the opportunity to receive in-depth information from an expert on your topic. The information you gather from these interviews can supplement the material you've found in published sources, providing you with the opportunity to make an original research claim or unique contribution to the scholarly conversation on your topic. Keep in mind, however, that conducting interviews involves much more than simply having a chat with someone; it involves a careful process of planning and preparation before the meeting even takes place. If you decide to conduct an interview as part of your field research, you might incorporate these steps into your research process:

1. *Identify your purpose*: Even before setting up an interview, you need to clarify your research goals. What information would an interview provide that other types of research would not? What do you hope to get out of the interview?
2. *Decide on your interview subject*: Who would provide you with the most insight into your topic? Is the best source for your field research a professor at your college who is an expert in this area? A professional from the community? Peers in your class, dorm, athletic team, or town?
3. *Determine your preferred interview format*: Interviews can be conducted in many ways: face to face, over the phone, through videochat or text-chat, or by email. You'll need to choose the method that best suits your needs and your interviewee's preferred mode of communication.
4. *Prepare*: Know your interviewee: read an online biography or browse an online résumé or curriculum vita; familiarize yourself with what he or she has written and read any articles related to your topic; and understand your interviewee's position on your research issue. This information will

help you both construct useful questions and also cultivate your own *ethos* during the interview by showing you've taken the time to prepare.

5. *Develop questions*: Your questions will provide the framework for your discussion, so craft them with care. A successful range of questions can yield not only a wealth of in-depth information about a subject but also some useful "quotable moments" that can be featured as direct quotations and evidence in your essay. In designing your questions, therefore, keep these strategies in mind:
   - **Use specific language, be concise and clear:** If your interview subject has a hard time following your question, it's likely that he or she'll have trouble giving you a helpful answer. Be focused and eliminate wordiness.
   - **Avoid Yes/No questions:** Questions that lend themselves to yes or no answers can limit explanation and elaboration. Opt for open-ended questions instead. So, instead of asking, "Do you agree with the recent Faculty Senate vote?," you might ask, "What is your opinion on the recent Faculty Senate vote?"
   - **Watch out for leading questions:** Even if you have developed a tentative claim, you should avoid influencing your interview subject's answer. In other words, if you ask, "Don't you agree that there need to be more female faculty members in the Computer Science Department?", you are sending signals about your own opinions that might affect how your interviewee answers. Try to use neutral terms and to design unbiased questions.
   - **Frame your questions:** While drafting your questions, also take some time to develop ways to contextualize them in reference to your knowledge about your subject and your interviewee's areas of expertise. By showing that you've done some preliminary research, you enhance your own *ethos* and lay the groundwork for a richer conversation.
6. *Make contact*: In contacting your potential interviewee, clearly explain who you are, the topic of your research, and your goal for the field research. If you are planning a face-to-face interview or a video or text-based chat, suggest two or three possible times for the session; for all types of interviews, include your timeline in your request. In addition, provide a summary of the types of questions you might ask so that your interviewee can think them through before meeting

with you. Follow up unanswered requests with polite emails or phone calls. Don't hesitate to persist, but do so respectfully. Once you've set up the interview, be sure to confirm time and place the day before for a face-to-face interview or chat session.

7. *Maintain your ethos*: Your *persona* as an interviewer can be key to a successful session. Dress nicely, maintain a professional tone throughout the meeting, and have your materials organized before you start. Respect your interviewee's time: arrive on time for the interview, and keep it within the agreed on time span. Use your interview questions as a guide, but don't follow them too rigidly; listen to your interviewee's answers and follow up on key points even if it means asking a question that's not on your list. Conversely, be careful not to digress. Keep the conversation focused on the research topic.
8. *Record and document*: In your notes, be sure to write down the full name of the person, his or her title, and the time, date, and location of the interview; you will need this information to properly cite the interview in your essay. While you'll want to take some notes during the interview, recording the session can help you resist the impulse to transcribe the conversation word for word. However, be sure to ask your interviewee's permission before recording the meeting. At the end of the interview, get written permission from your interview subject to use direct quotations from the conversation in your essay. It is possible that she or he might ask be quoted anonymously, in which case you'll need to respect that request when incorporating material from the interview into your paper.

Seeing Connections
See Chapter 7 for instructions on how to cite an interview in a research paper.

9. *Analyze the conversation*: If you record an interview, create a transcript as soon as possible after the meeting. Take some time to process the information you received, highlighting key quotes or ideas in your notes or on the transcript, listing ideas or readings for further research, and reflecting on connections to your other sources. If you conducted a face-to-face or videochat interview, analyze the conversation or transcript shortly after it happens, while your impressions are still fresh.
10. *Follow-up*: Send a thank-you note to the person you interviewed and offer a copy of your completed paper.

Developing a Survey

In your research, you may come across published surveys that can provide important statistical data for your project, whether in scientific journals, newsmagazines like *Time*, or research organizations such as the Pew Research Center. Alternately, you might consider developing your own survey in order to retrieve information tailored to your particular research question or line of inquiry. The benefit of a survey is that it enables you to accumulate data from a broad range of participants; it works particularly well for gathering quantitative data but can also yield deeper insightful perspectives on your topic through short answer questions.

As you compose your survey, remember that it is like any other writing project in that it benefits a careful drafting process, one that takes into account the rhetorical situation and purpose of your project. The following steps can help you develop an effective survey:

1. *Identify your purpose*: The first step in developing any survey is clarify your goals. What research question are you trying to answer? What type of results would be most useful to your research? Do you want to gather statistical data? Do you want to solicit reflective or detailed responses that can use for qualitative analysis? The answers to these questions will help determine the shape of your survey.
2. *Determine your survey population*: In order to receive useful answers, you need to carefully target your survey population. You might select your survey subjects by age (i.e., teenagers, college students, parents, senior citizens); by occupation (i.e., students, instructors, administrators, athletes, artists); by location (i.e., residents of your town, your college campus); or by other characteristics, such as gender, political or religious affiliation, or even nationality.
3. *Aim for a representative sample*: To insure the most reliable results, don't skew your sample out of convenience (for instance, only distributing your survey to your fraternity brothers when the research question requires both a male and female perspective). In addition, consider how sample size influences the viability of your results: the results from a survey of ten students are less likely to yield persuasive findings than a survey of 40 students.
4. *Develop your questions*: In many ways, your purpose will determine the format of your survey. You have many options available to you:

   - Close-ended questions tend to generate quantitative data and offer no little or no opportunity for elaboration. Two typical formats for these questions include multiple choice (where the subject chooses one or more of a variety of options) and ranked questions (where the subject ranks a series of items according to a clear scale).

- Open-ended questions invite reflection and nuanced responses, whether they be as short as a single sentence or as long as a paragraph.

In general, it is best to design surveys that balance short, multiple choice questions, which yield primarily statistical data, with short answer questions that will produce more complex responses. Keep your survey short; the longer your form, the fewer completed surveys will probably be returned to you.

5. *Draft your survey*: As with any rhetorical text, you should craft your survey carefully:

   - Assess the best delivery method for your survey given your target population: Paper survey? Email? Electronic form? Your choice of medium might influence your survey design.
   - Consider the canon of arrangement. Put your questions in a logical order, use subcategories to help organize information, consider giving your survey subjects a sense of the scope of the survey (i.e., including an introduction that states, "This survey contains 10 questions ...") or markers that indicate their progress through it (e.g., if your survey is divided into pages, include a header with a notation such as "Page 3 of 4").
   - Focus on style. Use clear, concise language, and avoid creating Yes–No questions ("Was your freshman orientation session effective?") when you want to generate more nuanced responses ("Please comment on the most effective and least effective aspects of your freshman orientation session"). Avoid biased language or leading questions.
   - Construct an expository frame for the survey: a very brief introduction of a sentence or two that indicates the purpose and relevance of the survey; a concluding sentence that appears after the last question, thanking the participant for completing the survey.

6. *Test and revise your drafted survey*: As with any rhetorical text, it is important to take into account *audience* as you construct your argument. Test your draft by having a friend complete your survey and give you feedback on its clarity, organization, length, and the relevance of its questions to your purpose. Use that feedback to revise.

7. *Distribute your survey*: State your deadline clearly, and make sure the respondents know where and how to return the form.
8. *Analyze the results*: As you read through the completed surveys, look for patterns or trends in the responses and categorize them in a table or "code" the survey responses using a highlighter or jotting key terms in the margin; start to think about how to best organize and showcase data (through percentages? charts? graphs?); highlight key comments in the open responses to include as direct quotations in your research paper. Most of all, *listen* to your respondents, even if the data do not necessarily confirm your hypothesis: your developing research claim should be informed by your research findings.
9. *Follow-up*: Consider sharing your findings with survey participants, if possible, through an article in a local newspaper or college publication.

Seeing Connections
See Chapter 7 for instructions on how to cite a survey in your research paper.

WRITER'S PRACTICE MyWritingLab

What types of technology can be used most effectively in the college classroom? Please explain your answer.

Which types of technology are the most effective in the classroom as learning tools? Select as many apply.

- ☐ Overhead projectors
- ☐ Smartboards
- ☐ Laptops
- ☐ Desktop computers
- ☐ iPads or Tablets
- ☐ Cellphones

How effective are the following types of technology in the college classroom as learning tools?

	Very Ineffective	Ineffective	Somewhat Ineffective	Neither Effective nor Ineffective	Somewhat Effective	Effective	Very Effective
Overhead projectors	O	O	O	O	O	O	O
Smartboards	O	O	O	O	O	O	O
Laptops	O	O	O	O	O	O	O
Desktop computers	O	O	O	O	O	O	O
iPads or Tablets	O	O	O	O	O	O	O
Cellphones	O	O	O	O	O	O	O

For a research project on the use of technology in the college classroom, one writer decided to construct a survey to collect student perspectives on this issue. During the drafting process, she experimented with different variations of the same question to consider how format influenced the answers she might receive. Look over each variation carefully.

What is the implied purpose behind each question? Is it the same for each one? How might the questions elicit different responses? What would the author need to do to make sure she received useful responses from this survey? What revisions might you suggest?

Other Models of Fieldwork

While interviews and surveys represent two modes of fieldwork available to you, you might take your research even more actively into the field. Let's look at a more ambitious approach to this type of research. Student Vincent Chen used field research quite prominently in his research project about the rhetoric of climate change. As part of his research, Vincent attended the Copenhagen Conference on Climate Change in December of 2009. Included in this conference was a special session on the "15th Conference of the Parties to the UNFCCC (United Nations Framework Convention on Climate Change)," commonly known as "COP15." At the COP15, Vincent conducted extensive field research, such as talking to conference participants, taking photographs of people milling through the halls, attending talks, and listening to speakers present position statements about the environment. One of the most powerful products of Vincent's field research was a photo he took, showing the crowds of attendees stopping mid-motion to hear the speech of Mohamed Nasheed, then-president of the Republic of Maldives. The photo became central to making his argument that President Nasheed strongly differentiated himself from other climate leaders at the conference through his inflammatory rhetoric about the danger of rising seas as well as the *logos* argument of his country's small size and limited economic power. To argue this position, Vincent used his photo as visual evidence documenting the conference-stopping power of President Nasheed's speech (see Figure 5.9). He also supported his argument through additional field research in the form of interviews with other students who attended at the conference and an interview with Professor Stephen Schneider of the Interdisciplinary Environmental Studies Program at his university.

This field research added depth and power to Vincent's argument by allowing him to include his own evidence as strategic argumentative support for his argument. With regard to the photo in Figure 5.8, rather than just asserting his claim to be true, Vincent could allow his readers to *see* the evidence that would support his point that President Nasheed, out of all leaders at the climate conference, made people stop and listen to an argument for action.

Of course, not all fieldwork involves trips around the world. Sometimes you can gather your own evidence for your research project by using resources available within your local community. Consider these scenarios: if you were studying the impact of a new park in your community, you might meet with a city planner or the landscape architect responsible for the project and look at blueprints or concept art for the project; if you were writing about a city water reservoir, you might visit the site, take photographs, and meet with the site manager; and, if you were writing on the marketing strategies of a local baseball team, you might even write a letter to that team's marketing coordinator to set up an interview or gather information. Fieldwork such as this allows you to take your research to the next level and make a truly original contribution of your own.

FIGURE 5.8 Vincent Chen's field research includes this photo of Mohamed Nasheed, president of the Republic of Maldives, making a powerful speech to a riveted audience at the 2009 Copenhagen Climate Conference. © Vincent Chen 2009.

Evaluating Field Research Sources

When you conduct interviews and surveys, you are looking for materials to use in your paper as secondary sources. But keep in mind the need to evaluate your field research sources as carefully as you assess your other sources. If you interview a professor, a marketing executive, a witness, or a roommate, consider the rhetorical stance of that person. What kind of bias does the person have concerning the topic of your project? If you conduct a survey of your peers in your dorm, assess the value and credibility of your results as rigorously as you would evaluate the data of a published study. Don't fall into the trap of misusing statistics when making claims if you haven't taken into account the need for **statistical significance**, or to paraphrase the social psychologist Philip Zimbardo, the measure by which a number obtains meaning in scientific fields. To reach this number, you need to design the survey carefully, conduct what's called a *random sample*, interview a *large enough* number of people, and ask a *range of different people*. These are complex parameters to follow, but you will need to learn about them to conduct survey research that has reliable and credible results.

"Statistics are the backbone of research. They are used to understand observations and to determine whether findings are, in fact, correct and significant . . . But statistics can also be used poorly or deceptively, misleading those who do not understand them."

—*Philip Zimbardo* (595)

As Professor Zimbardo points out, statistics—though we often think of them as Truth—actually function rhetorically. Like words and images, numbers are a mode of persuasion that can mislead readers. You need to be especially vigilant when using a survey or statistics as a supposedly "objective" part of your iceberg of research, particularly if you plan to depend on such materials in your argument.

Take as much care with how you convey information visually as you do with how you convey it in writing. Consider Ryan O'Rourke's project about the student perceptions of the political environment on his college campus. Having uncovered some general statistics about politics on campus from secondary sources, Ryan decided to sharpen his argument—and make his own unique contribution to the conversation—by measuring student sentiment on this issue at his own university. Consequently, he designed and distributed a survey on the topic, which was filled out by over 71 students. In addition to including the data in the body of his essay, he created a series of bar graphs (see examples in Figure 5.9) to represent his findings. His argument was more powerful not just because of his impressive research but also because of how he represented it visually through responsible use of

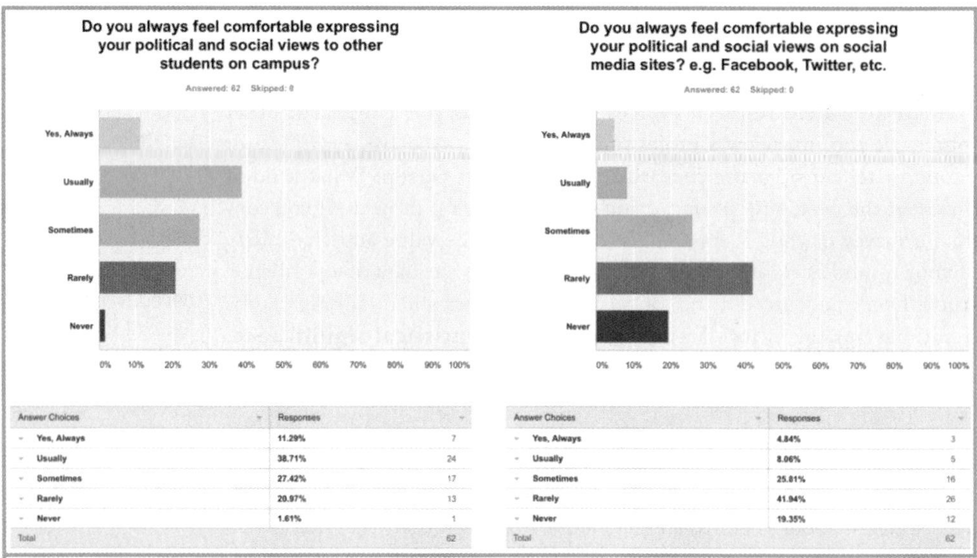

Answer Choices	Responses	
Yes, Always	11.29%	7
Usually	38.71%	24
Sometimes	27.42%	17
Rarely	20.97%	13
Never	1.61%	1
Total		62

Answer Choices	Responses	
Yes, Always	4.84%	3
Usually	8.06%	5
Sometimes	25.81%	16
Rarely	41.94%	26
Never	19.35%	12
Total		62

FIGURE 5.9 Ryan O'Rourke created these information graphics to help show the difference in students' attitudes about sharing their political views in person versus on social media.

statistics. The ability to create such powerful visualizations of information is within reach of many researchers these days as numerous software programs (from PowerPoint, to Excel, to Qualtrics) contain built-in shortcuts to help you display your original data as pie charts, bar graphs, and scatterplots.

Evaluating Sources by Use

The terms *primary source*, *secondary source*, and *field work* that we've been using so far in this chapter are familiar to most researchers and form a typical understanding of how texts operate in relation to the research process. However, scholar Joseph Bizzup has formulated an alternative way to conceptualize source materials—through how the materials are *used* rather than what they *are* (i.e., primary or secondary sources). Bizzup calls this approach "BEAM," and we find it useful specifically in how it asks writers to evaluate texts. BEAM stands for Background, Exhibit, Argument, and Methods and can be understood as follows:

- A **background** source provides foundational or general information for the topic.
- An **exhibit** source operates as an example or case study that the writer analyzes.
- An **argument** source is one that contributes an analytic perspective.
- A **method** source offers either a theoretical framework, overarching concept, or methodology that the writer incorporates into his or her own writing.

For many writers, the first three classifications are relatively easy to understand: exhibits often are what we might consider primary sources, texts to be analyzed; background and argument texts often fall under the category of secondary sources, texts that feature another author's analysis. Understanding the method source can be more challenging, for many researchers might not be in the practice of distinguishing between whether a source provides an argumentative perspective or contributes a critical framework. To help understand how this works, let's return to Jennifer Light's excerpt, which we considered above. In that case, the sources she refers to in footnotes 1 and 3 provide *background*; the media images that she says she'll analyze on the second page will function as *exhibits* in her article; Ruth Milkman's article serves as both an *argument* text (with its "idiom of sex-typing" thesis) and *method* (providing Light with a theoretical/methodological approach that she will "follow" in her own work).

By adjusting focus in this way from what a source *is* to how it can be *used*, you can approach the task of composing a research essay from a more rhetorical perspective, considering your collection of sources as another strategy designed to help you make best use of the available means of persuasion. The BEAM approach shifts your understanding so that your research-based writing becomes less a collection of source texts that support your argument and more a set of resources that you deploy meaningfully and deliberately to persuade your audience.

For this reason, as you evaluate your sources, you should ask one final set of questions:

> How might you use this source in your own research? Does the approach (popular, scientific, scholarly, informational) seem appropriate to your project's focus and goals? Does it offer a counterargument or a different disciplinary perspective? What will it contribute to your argument? Background? Exhibit material? Another person's analytic perspective? A guiding methodology, concept, or theory?

5.6 How can I understand the conversation my sources are having about my topic?

CREATING A DIALOGUE WITH YOUR SOURCES

Throughout this chapter, we have emphasized that research is social, a conversation with the people whose ideas and writing came before yours. As you gather, assess, and use sources, you are contributing to this conversation, building on the work of others, and adding a new perspective. Indeed, this notion of writing as communal is the reason why you need to use the author's name when citing a quotation or an idea; remember that all your sources are authored sources; each source mentioned in this chapter was composed by a person or a group of people. If you think of these texts as written *by people like you*, you will have an easier time remembering to acknowledge their ideas and integrate their quotations into your essay. In the process, you will go a long way toward avoiding unintentional plagiarism. You can begin this process through an exercise we call a **dialogue of**

sources—a fictional conversation among the primary and secondary sources of your research paper designed to help you identify each one's central argument and main idea.

Seeing Connections
See Chapter 7 for a more complete discussion of plagiarism and intellectual property.

For instance, to prepare for her research paper on the dangers of America's dietary dependence on sugar, Kim Felser wrote a dialogue between several sources she had found: John Yudkin, author of *Pure, White and Deadly*, a book on the dangers of sugar; Dr. Robert Lustig, professor of pediatrics at University of California, San Francisco, and author of *Fat Chance: The Bitter Truth about Sugar*; Nicole M. Avena, Pedro Rada, and Bartley G. Hoebel, co-authors of the scholarly article, "Evidence for sugar addiction"; and, Michael Moss, a *NY Times* award-winning journalist and author of *Salt, Sugar, Fat. Smoking?*. She read each text first, taking notes and analyzing their stance, and then put them in dialogue so as to better assess the nuances of her topic and distinguish between the sources' differing perspectives.

AT A GLANCE

Creating a Dialogue of Sources

- ***Identify the key players*** from your research log and your notes. Which ones have the most influential or important arguments?
- ***Create a cast of characters list*** with a short bio for each speaker, perhaps even including yourself. Describe each person's credentials and rhetorical stance—his or her *ethos* and argument. (You may even want to create identifying icons or pictures to give "faces" to the participants.)
- ***Draft the script.*** Write the key questions you want to ask your sources about your topic. Use quotes from your sources to respond where possible, and include page numbers or footnotes.
- ***Consider what your sources would say to each other.*** Write their fictional conversation by using quotes from your sources.
- ***Create a "moderator" to guide and catalyze the conversation.*** This can be either a character based on yourself or on one of the sources. Don't let the moderator be neutral; allow the moderator to develop a stance, respond to the sources, and use this process to develop an argument about the topic.
- ***Conclude with a synthesis statement.*** Use the closing paragraph to tie together the various views presented in your "dialogue of sources" and then indicate how you will build on that collection of knowledge. In this way, you offer both a summary and a synthesis, by bringing together and then adding to the conversation of research.

Kim's complete dialogue began with a list of speakers and their bios. Then she introduced the topic of her research project. She reproduced the argument of each source through paraphrase.

By allowing debate to evolve, Kim begins to see how she might use information from these sources in her paper.

Dialogue of Sources [excerpt]

John Yudkin: Sugar is poisoning our society. It's addictive, it's everywhere. It's inescapable. In short, it's sweet and dangerous. I'll make it easy on you: you've *got* to read my book, *Pure, White, and Deadly*. It's got some pretty revelatory information packed in those pages, if I do say so myself. And I was a trailblazer! *P,W&D* came out way back in the 1970s.

Robert Lustig: John, you're on the right track, though I'm not sure I'd brag about publishing a work that long ago. My recent research suggests that *fructose* is the incredibly toxic one, not just "sugar." A calorie isn't just a calorie, as I like to say; a bottle of high-fructose corn syrup and a jar of brown rice syrup are digested entirely differently in the body. Your poor liver takes a beating with HFCS. My lecture at UCSF back in 2013, "Sugar: The Bitter Truth" does a neat job of explaining the scientific processes. You can find it on YouTube; I recommend taking a look.

John: Maybe you have a point. But the real issue is that we can't just pick and choose sugars for the ultimate health. We need to remove all of them. We need some grade-A restriction on every type of sweetener.

Avena, Rada, Hoebel: Look, guys, maybe we should examine the mind-body factors, too. You seem to be neglecting the brain entirely, and that plays a key role in the sugar-dependency epidemic. We've been researching how rats respond to consuming sugar-water solutions, from both behavioral and neuroscientific perspectives, and, honestly, the evidence that sugar might be a substance of abuse is compelling.

Avena, Rada, Hoebel (continued): And, John, you said it yourself: sugar is addictive. It releases endorphins and we become hooked. That's where the real danger lies; the impact on the body is secondary when we examine the causal effects.

Michael Moss: Whoa, whoa, whoa—calm down there. I think you're forgetting a key element. If you're trying to understand why we're so addicted to the stuff, I think you need to look more closely at the way our food system is structured. Hello capitalism! CEOs for Coca-Cola and other big industries will stop at nothing to reshape our taste buds and drive us back to the convenience stores again and again—all for profit! Addiction is certainly a part of it, but maybe we need to look at why and how we got into this mess in the first place.

Robert: Michael, I can't tell you how right you are. As I began scouring the shelves of grocery stores in my quest to better understand the causes of childhood obesity, I realized that an astounding 80% of all food products in the typical American supermarket have been loaded with added sugar. *Eighty percent*! That's over two-thirds of the food products available to us as a nation!

Most importantly, through the dialogue she begins to understand the conversation between the sources so she can start formulating her own stance and contribution to this discussion.

Notice how Kim's work allowed her to write out the process of research *as a conversation*. This process helps her gain a more sophisticated understanding of her sources and topic, allowing her to evaluate their strengths, and encouraging her to move past a simple pro-con approach to the issue to better appreciate the different approaches (scientific, cultural, economic) that researchers have taken on the topic. In addition, by giving her sources *voices*, she is more likely to remember to attribute the ideas to her sources while writing her research paper, avoiding unintentional plagiarism. Moreover, she can conclude the dialogue with a summation of the arguments she has uncovered through her research and predict how she will build on them as she develops her thesis for her own research-based argument.

WRITER'S PRACTICE MyWritingLab

Put your own sources in dialogue by composing a social media version of the Dialogue of Sources activity. Select at least four sources, and identify each one's argument and rhetorical stance. Do a quick Google search on the author to understand his or her background and credentials. Then create a fake Twitter username for each one; be creative—even funny—but try to capture the *ethos* of the author in the Twitter handle. Make sure to create a Twitter identity for yourself as well. Next, imagine you were discussing your research topic with these authors on Twitter. What sort of conversation would you have? How would your sources communicate their positions? How would they react to each other? Write out the Twitter thread, creating hashtags as appropriate to underscore points and provide additional commentary on the conversation. Be sure to keep to the 140 character limit in creating each faux Tweet. At the end, take 5 minutes to free write about your Twitter Dialogue in your research log. What did you learn about the conversation about your topic from your dialogue? How do you better understand the relationship between your sources?

5.7 What is an annotated bibliography, and how can it help me develop my argument?

WRITING AN ANNOTATED BIBLIOGRAPHY

As you move further into your research, you might want to use your notes to create what researchers call an **annotated bibliography**—a list of research sources that provides informational notes about each source and how you might use it as you turn to drafting your paper. An annotated bibliography can work in conjunction with your research log and active note taking to encourage you to think critically, helping you to understand the larger research conversation on your topic and start to develop your own persuasive claim.

The format of an annotated bibliography follows a fairly standard pattern. For each source, you compose an entry containing:

- the **bibliographic citation**, correctly formatted to follow a particular citation form (such as MLA, APA, or Chicago Style)
- a **brief annotation** that concisely summarizes the content of the source and indicates its relevance to your project.

Seeing Connections
For a discussion of MLA style and guidelines, see Chapter 7.

Some researchers distinguish between two different types of annotation: the *descriptive annotation* and the *analytic annotation*. In writing the first type of annotation, you essentially create your own brief academic abstract for the source, providing an overview of its features and argument and suggesting its relevance to the larger conversation. In doing so, you would refer many of the elements we discussed above in relation to evaluating sources: author, place of publication, date of publication, purpose, audience, argument, evidence, tone, and relevance. For instance, consider this example of a *descriptive annotation* from a research project on teenagers and online privacy.

Ivester, Matt. *lol ... OMG! What Every Student Needs to Know About Online Reputation Management, Digital Citizenship, and Cyberbullying*. NV: Serra Knight Publishing, 2011. Print.

In *lol ... OMG!*, Matt Ivester provides an overview of the changing nature of digital citizenship; Ivester argues that in today's world we need to be conscious creators and curators of our online identities. A Duke University and Stanford Business School alumnus, Ivester was also creator of the infamous gossip website, JuicyCampus, providing him with an informed perspective on the more problematic elements of online culture. The book analyzes several powerful examples from the media of the dangers of digital citizenship, including the Duke Sexlist Powerpoint scandal, Alexandra Wallace's YouTube Rant, and the Tyler Clementi cyber-bullying tragedy. Of particular interest is Chapter 7, "Active Reputation Management," which provides seven steps readers can take to check their own online reputation. Aimed at a college audience and written in a direct and no-nonsense style, this book provides both valuable insight into the changing definitions of digital citizenship for the millennial generation and a concrete course of action that people can take to protect themselves online.

Notice that the annotation provides specific details about the source, including a summary of the argument; however, while the final sentence suggests the source's relevance, it refrains from critiquing the argument, producing an annotation that focuses more on summary than analysis. Some instructors also may request that you include at the end a note about which search engine or academic database you used and which keywords returned this result. This additional step would allow you to reflect on your own research methodology and what have been the most successful strategies that you've employed.

An *analytic annotation* follows the same model as the descriptive version, with one addition: it moves past simple summary to critique. For this reason, you'll find the *analytic annotation* an even more useful tool in your research process. Let's look at an example of this type of annotation for a research project on social activism and video games.

McGonigal, Jane. *Gaming Can Make a Better World*. TED Talks. Feb 2010. Web. 23 April 2013.

In this TED talk, video game designer Jane McGonigal passionately argues that we can use video games to solve larger cultural problems, such as the energy crisis and world hunger. Using examples from massive online games such as *World of Warcraft*, McGonigal insists that we embody the best qualities of ourselves when we play computer games: that we collaborate more readily, think more creatively, and have more self-confidence. In a provocative moment at the beginning of the talk, she suggests that we need to play video games more, not less—but that we need to play games designed to harness these qualities toward positive social good. While she offers some interesting examples of such games drawn from her work at the Institute of the Future (such as *World without Oil*), she discusses them only in the last four minutes of her 20-minute talk, so that key component of her argument (implementation) remains under-defined and under-developed. Overall, despite her compelling personality and her "exuberant" enthusiasm (11.43), her argument lacks in *logos* and evidentiary support; she provides some intriguing ideas for a future that unites gaming with social activism but does not convince her audience that it is actually possible.

This annotation has much in common with the *descriptive annotation* we looked at above: it addresses the credentials of the author, summarizes the argument, includes specific relevant detail, describes tone, and suggests its relevance. However, note the way the annotation's author integrates her own critique of McGonigal's claim throughout paragraph; she looks at this source through a critical lens, indicating that she will bring a similar approach to her treatment of this source material in her research paper. In some cases, you might even expand on the analytic model by including a final sentence that specifically indicates how you will use this source in relation to your

WRITER'S PRACTICE

MyWritingLab

Choose two sources from your preliminary research. Using the Questions for Evaluating Sources that start on p. 179 as a guide, evaluate the sources. Now write a *descriptive annotation* for one source and an *analytic annotation* for the other, drawing on the information from your evaluation. Be concrete and descriptive but also concise, writing no more than 150 words for each paragraph. Reflect on the two annotations when you have finished. How did each help you better understand your source material and how each text relates to your overall project and the development of your own thesis claim on the topic?

AT A GLANCE

Composing an Annotated Bibliography

1. Put your sources into alphabetical order; you can also categorize them by primary and secondary sources.
2. Provide complete identifying information for each source, including author's name, title, publication, date, page numbers, and database information for online sources.
3. Compose a concise annotation for each source:
   - Summarize the main argument or point of the source; use concrete language. Include quotations if you wish.
   - Take into account the writer's ethos and stance. How credible or biased is this source?
   - Consider the usefulness of this source to the conversation on this topic. Does the source provide background information? Does it offer a contrasting perspective to other sources you have found? Does it provide evidence that might back up your claims?

own research, perhaps even categorizing it according to Joseph Bizzup's BEAM taxonomy. In this way, you would provide your readers with more than a critical review of the text; you would offer them an understanding of how that source contributed to the way you were developing your own claim.

As the examples above demonstrate, writing an annotated bibliography involves more than merely recording information: it is a way for you to identify arguments and add your response to what the source has to say about your research topic.

THE WRITER'S PROCESS

As you begin to articulate your contribution to the research conversation about your topic, use the strategies that you've learned in this chapter. These include visualizing research as a conversation that you are joining and understanding the process of researching your argument as a movement from surface to depth. As you learn to search and locate your sources, you can engage in critical evaluation of these texts in your research log. You can also conduct innovative fieldwork of your own to generate original resource material to use in your argument. In writing your own annotated bibliography, remember that effective annotations and note-taking practices can help you develop the strategies of an academic writer and that these practices will move you toward finalizing your own argument about the topic.

AT A GLANCE

Note-Taking Strategies

As you read through your sources, take notes on materials that you could use in your paper:

- particularly memorable quotations
- background information
- a well-written passage providing context or a perspective useful to your argument

Be sure to double-check your notes for accuracy, use quotation marks for direct quotes, and include complete source details and page numbers.

Along the way, be sure to take careful notes. This is a crucial step in your writer's process. Many students make sense of the rich and diverse perspectives they encounter during their research through careful note taking. You can use the dialogue of sources method as a note-taking strategy while you work through your research sources. Or, you can take notes using a software program such as Endnote or Citelighter, bookmark pages and PDFs on your computer, or use the time-tested method of a spiral notebook or paper note cards. Whatever your method, be vigilant in your practice now so you won't have to retrace your steps and relocate your sources or quotations later. By putting into practice the techniques and lessons of this chapter, you will start to see connections among various research sources and begin to articulate your own research-based argument.

SPOTLIGHTED ANALYSIS: COVERS

MyWritingLab

Use the following prewriting prompts to follow the example from the beginning of the chapter and analyze the "cover" of your choice focused on a specific social, political, or cultural issue, whether that be a popular magazine cover (such as from *Time*, *The Economist*, or *Scientific American*) or a Website homepage (which serves as the "cover" for the larger site). Practice the techniques of rhetorical analysis that we used in relation to Figures 5.1 and 5.2, and brainstorm how the cover reflects its stance on the issue in question. Use the checklist below to guide your analysis:

- What images are featured on the cover? Are they photographs, hand-drawn sketches, cartoons, polished artwork? Are the images zoomed in (close-ups), portraits, or panoramic? What is the rhetorical effect of the style of the images?
- Does the cover feature people? Places? Symbols or abstract concepts? What do the cover images suggest about the contents of the larger text? How do they suggest a specific rhetorical stance or point of view?
- How do the words on the cover work in conjunction with the image suggest the entire text's rhetorical stance?
- To what extent does the cover appeal to the audience make an appeal based on facts, reason, or logic? Through emotion? Through an appeal to authority? To what extent does the cover trade on *kairos* in making its argument?
- Does the cover rely on any specific strategies of development to make its argument about its contents? Does it use narration? Comparison/contrast? Definition? Analogy? Example? Categorization? Process? How does its use of strategies make an argument about its contents?

- How does the layout function rhetorically? Does the cover use juxtaposition? Symmetry or asymmetry? To what extent does it draw the audience's eye through a pre-determined and strategic path?

WRITING ASSIGNMENTS

MyWritingLab

1. **Research Log Entries:** Keep a running commentary/assessment of potential research sources for your project. Realize that careful research notes are a crucial part of the process and will help you avoid unintentional plagiarism of material. Include a combination of notes, scanned articles, emails, sources from databases, scanned images, and other means of processing all the information you encounter. Be sure also to record your search terms and research methods so you can evaluate and fine-tune their effectiveness as you move forward.

2. **Source Analysis:** Using the criteria on page 179 as a starting point, write up a one- to two-page analysis of a source for your research project. Be sure to consider authorship, publication information, date, occasion, purpose, audience, and tone. Also evaluate its argument and how it uses evidence to support its points. Finally, identify how you might use it in your essay, drawing on BEAM terminology.

3. **Dialogue of Sources:** Using the instructions in the At a Glance box on page 200, create a *dialogue of sources* to showcase the conversation around your topic. Be sure to select sources that represent diverse views or perspectives to provide a well-rounded approach to your issue. Use your central research question as the starting point for the conversation and be sure to include your own voice in the dialogue.

4. **Annotated Bibliography and Reflection:** Expand on the Writer's Practice on page 207 and compose an analytic annotated bibliography to showcase the primary and secondary sources you intend to employ in your essay. After each citation, categorize it according to the BEAM taxonomy (background, exhibit, argument, method) and, if you wish, as a primary source, secondary source, or as field research. When you are done, review the bibliography as a whole and assess what types of additional sources you need to locate to construct a powerful argument. Write a reflection in your research log on this process, including a "wish list" at the end of the types of sources you still want to find.

5. **Collaborative Peer Review:** Present your annotated bibliographies to one another in groups. Pull the "greatest hits" from your research log, and tell the class about how your research is going. In other words, *present a discussion of your work in progress.* Identify obstacles and successes so far. You'll get feedback from the class about your developing research project.

6. **Analytic Note Taking:** Choose one of your research sources to focus on. Before you begin taking notes, divide your document into two columns, whether by folding your notebook sheet in half or applying a dual-column layout to your word-processing document. Use the left column to take summary notes on your source; be sure to enclose any direct quotations in quotation marks. For each note, also record the page number to indicate where you got it (if your source is not paginated, consider using paragraph numbers instead). Then read back through your summary comments. Use the right column to record your analysis of the text: What questions do you have? What connections can you make? How do you evaluate the source's claims? What responses do you have? Use the same technique for your other sources so that you can bring an analytic perspective to your research as a way of helping you move toward your own research claim.

MyWritingLab Visit Ch. 5 Finding and Evaluating Research Sources in MyWritingLab to complete the Writer's Practices, Spotlighted Analyses, and Writing Assignments, and to test your understanding of the chapter objectives.

Part III

DRAFTING AND DESIGNING ARGUMENTS

CHAPTER 6

Organizing and Writing Research Arguments

Chapter Preview Questions

6.1 What strategies of organization will work for my essay?

6.2 What strategies can I use to create an outline for my argument?

6.3 What are the best ways to get started writing a full draft and integrating research sources responsibly and rhetorically?

6.4 How do I analyze a draft of a research-based essay?

6.5 What strategies can I use to revise my draft?

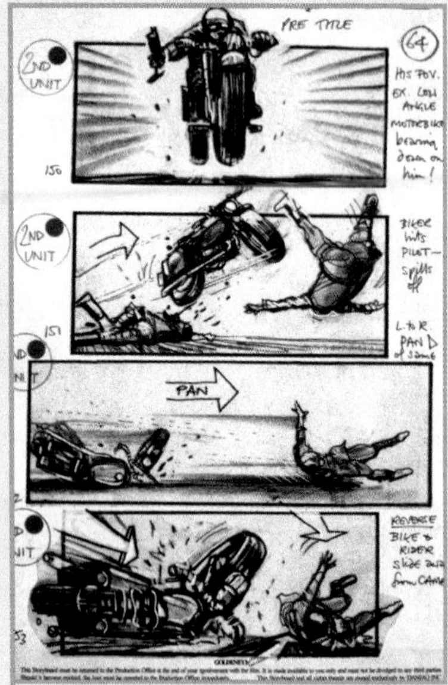

FIGURE 6.1 This storyboard for the James Bond film *Golden Eye* shows an initial draft for one of the film's action scenes.

Constructing a research argument is a complex and ongoing process. From selecting a topic to locating and evaluating sources and taking notes, it involves a series of interrelated steps. This is true of the drafting stage as well. In fact, organizing, drafting, and revising information is a prominent part of the process of creating any text—an academic essay, a research proposal, a podcast, a television commercial, or even a film.

Figure 6.1, for instance, lets us glimpse the drafting process behind the James Bond film *Golden Eye* (1995). This action scene from early in the film finds Bond fleeing from a Soviet chemical plant after the capture and execution of one of his colleagues. What you see in Figure 6.1 are a brief set of storyboards for part of this scene—an artist's draft that lays out the action in chronological increments, mapping out not only the movement of the characters but also the camera angles and thus the audience's experience of the events depicted. Notice how the storyboard shapes the narrative as it shifts between different angles on the chase: the first panel shows a close-up of the Soviet henchman who is pursuing Bond, establishing the threat; the second panel captures a sense of motion as the cyclist falls from his bike; the third panel gives camera direction ("pan") and follows the momentum of the biker's fall; the final panel zooms in further to focus on the fallen rider and the skidding bike – a bike that James Bond will then commandeer as the scene proceeds. Storyboards like this clearly operate as visual outlines, an organizational strategy that underlies almost all films. The polished final version seen in the theater is actually made possible by drafting steps like this one.

You probably recognize some implicit similarities between producing a research argument and producing a film:

- Both entail many small steps that support a grounding vision or main idea.
- Both have a carefully planned structure.
- Both involve rigorous editing.

Since they share such rich similarities, we can use the medium of film as a metaphor to help us understand the process of writing a research paper: from constructing a visual map and formal outline to integrating sources, key quotations, and evidence. We'll talk about incorporating sources responsibly in a way that sustains the conversation you began in the previous chapter, and we'll walk through the drafting and revision process. Just as filmmakers leave many scenes on the cutting room floor, you too will write, edit, cut, and rearrange much of the first draft of your research paper before it reaches its final form. You'll find that the process of completing your research argument is as collaborative as film production. Additionally, both film and writing require you to consider issues of length, cost, and time as you work to produce the best possible text. So let's get started moving from notes to writing the complete paper.

ORGANIZING YOUR DRAFT IN VISUAL FORM

6.1 What strategies of organization will work for my essay?

It can be quite challenging to turn on the computer and try to generate a complete draft of an essay without first taking the time to arrange your materials and ideas into some kind of order. Storyboards like those shown in

Figure 6.1 are just one example of the type of innovative, visual, or nonlinear technique you could use as part of your prewriting process. These methods of *invention*, similar to those that we discussed in Chapters 3 and 4, allow you to experiment with organizing your research notes and argumentative points in order to sort, arrange, and make connections between ideas.

You probably already instinctively organize your materials as you get ready to write. Perhaps you stack your research books, notes, and source printouts, either in the order you plan to use them or in groups by subject or relevance to your argument. Alternately, you might arrange and rearrange your notes on your desk or your computer, again spatially organizing them in a way that connects with how you plan to use them in your writing. If you've used notecards for taking notes, you probably shuffle and regroup them as you prepare to write. All these organizational strategies offer concrete ways to categorize the resources you have and figure out, visually, how they relate to one another.

Taking the practice of storyboarding as an inspiration, consider some additional strategies you might use to channel the canon of invention as part of your prewriting strategy.

- **Bubble web.** In Chapter 4, we explored using webbing or clustering as a technique for narrowing your topic. It can also provide a useful technique for experimenting with how to arrange your ideas by allowing you to explore relationships between them in a nonlinear fashion.
- **Graphic flowchart.** While a bubble web tends to focus on showing multiple connections between elements, a graphic flowchart foregrounds the more linear and hierarchical relationships between elements. In creating your flowchart, you list one idea and then draw an arrow to suggest connections between subsidiary points. Figure 6.2, for example, shows Thomas Zhao's preliminary flowchart for analysis of the changes in the process of adapting Japanese video games for U.S. audiences.
- **Idea roadmap.** You can push this technique further by "mapping" your argument on a large whiteboard space. Simply write out your thesis at one end of the board, and your conclusion (or your "destination") at the other, and then fill in the "sights" (ideas, arguments, evidence) that you'll see along the way. Visualizing your essay as a journey helps you keep your audience in mind and creates an underlying arc to your argument.
- **Post-it diagram.** Post-it notes offer you a very versatile medium for storyboarding. By writing your main ideas on post-its and

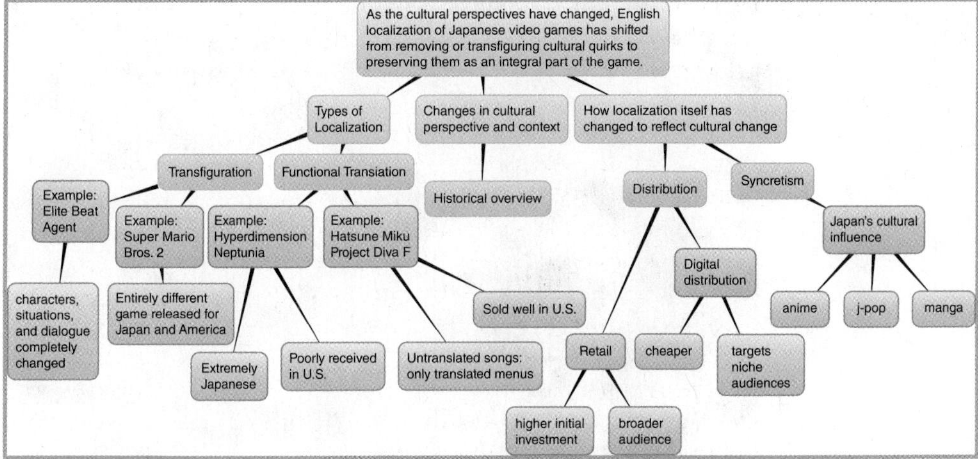

FIGURE 6.2 Thomas Zhao's graphic flowchart allowed him to visualize the sections of his essay and identify portions for which he needed to do additional research.

then arranging and rearranging them on a table or wall, you can easily experiment with different configurations for your argument. Figure 6.3 shows an example of how one writer used post-its to explore how she might organize her argument, using blue post-its for her main points, orange post-its for her supporting points, and smaller yellow post-its to indicate sources and notes.

Each of these strategies relies on some of the same principles that make storyboarding so powerful for filmmakers: they provide a flexible and dynamic mode of organizing the "story" of your essay; they allow you to zoom in on specific details, while also encouraging you to step back and assess the shape of the argument as a whole. When engaging in your own visualizations of your argument, be sure to use this prewriting process as an opportunity to ask yourself some key questions:

- Is each of my points developed thoroughly? What else do I need to make the points persuasive? *This will give you insight into whether you need to do more research or if you need to reformulate your argument or strengthen how you support your points.*
- Do I have a balance among the sections of my argument? *By answering this question, you will consider the relationship between the parts of your*

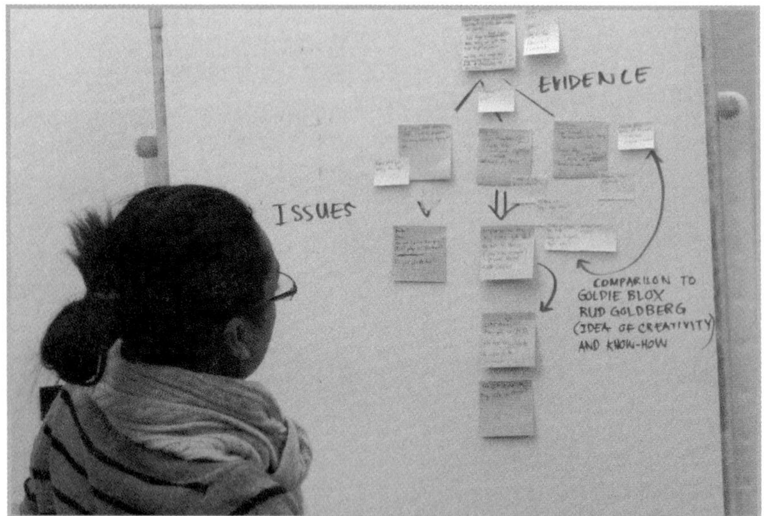

FIGURE 6.3 This student writer created her post-it note "outline" on a white board, so she could better experiment with arrangement and show connections between ideas through notes and arrows.

argument, identifying whether you've developed one section more than the others.

- Does the argument as a whole seem coherent? Are there outlier elements? *This big-picture question will help you discern whether your argument moves forward purposefully and clearly, or whether you stray into digressions along the way.*

WRITER'S PRACTICE

MyWritingLab

Explore different ways to organize an essay you're writing by experimenting with a post-it note diagram, such as the one in Figure 6.3.

- Write out your central claim on a post-it note. Place it on a flat blank space, such as a wall or table.
- Jot down some of your main ideas on other post-it notes, using one post-it for each idea.
- Arrange them next to your claim, positioning them according to their relationship to the claim and to each other.
- Write additional ideas on other post-its, grouping them near your first post-its according to how they support, develop, or even challenge those points. You might include here specific

examples or evidence, facts, counter arguments, unspoken assumptions (or warrants) that influence your argument, definitions, or background information.

- Select different color post-its and use them for notes about your sources, positioning these source notes adjacent to post-its representing points they'll support in your argument.
- Arrange and rearrange your post-its to consider the best flow possible between your ideas and to experiment with different structures of arrangement, referring to Chapter 3 for some ideas. For example, arrange them first in a block or thematic organization; then re-arrange them in a problem–solution or cause–effect structure; finally, experiment with a narrative or chronological structure. Which mode of arrangement best supports your argument?

When you've completed your diagram, write a 10-minute reflection on the process. What did you learn about the best ways to organize your argument? What challenges did you encounter? What insights do you have about further research you need to do or the best ways to support your claim?

LEARNING OUTLINING STRATEGIES

6.2 What strategies can I use to create an outline for my argument?

The visual organization strategies we discussed above can help you sort out your materials and prepare you for the next step: the detailed, written **outline**. For a longer, more complex paper, such as a research-based argument, an *outline* is an extremely useful method of arranging ideas and expediting the drafting process. Outlines offer a plan for your paper and should show the relationships among the various sections in your argument. If your outline simply consists of a list of topics, you won't be able to see the argument of the whole paper, nor will you be able to check for a strong progression between your individual points. In other words, the secret to producing a successful outline—and by extension a successful paper—is to pay special attention to the flow or development of ideas.

It's often hard to know for certain the best way to put together points in an outline: faced with so much information and so many ideas, even if you've created an effective visual brainstorm, you might have difficulty aligning your points sequentially so they effectively support your claim. Let's return to our focus on films to reflect on how an outline can work to draw different points together into a cohesive argument.

Looking at cinematic trailers can be instructive for thinking about organization. Although they generally are created after-the-fact (once the movie is through production), what trailers present to the audience is essentially a brief outline of the film, the elements arranged in a way designed to make a certain argument about the movie. In fact, many films have not one but several trailers, each one slightly different, designed with a particular context or audience in mind. For instance, one of the earliest trailers for the 2009 film *Avatar* organized its clips from the film to focus on the experience of taking on an alternate identity. By propelling the audience through a set of images—the wheelchair-bound protagonist, his first encounter with his avatar floating in a tank, the process of his coming to inhabit that body, and a series of rapid fire impressions of the adventure, war, and love that he experienced in that alternate form—the trailer argues that the film will be about a fantasy of identity and escape.

However, the official theatrical trailer arranged its film clips differently, promulgating a more provocative message. Although, like the previous version, it uses a narrative structure as its underlying strategy of arrangement, this longer trailer privileges plot over character. The images in Figure 6.4 illustrate this movement, taking the viewer from an introduction of the human characters in the corporate research facility, to scenes showing the protagonist's encounters with the native people (the Na'vi) and his gradual integration into their world, to scenes of the final explosive conflict between the soldiers and the indigenous inhabitants. In doing so, the trailer reproduces two of the central themes of *Avatar*: the dangers of imperialism and the clash between a spiritual worldview and one filtered through corporate greed.

In essence, then, the power of the trailer as an organizational tool or outline is that it allows filmmakers to experiment with order and, ultimately, meaning. Similarly, in your outline, you are deciding on the "story" you want to tell your readers about your research and your argument. The way you arrange the elements will influence how they understand the claims you make and how persuaded they will be by your argument.

Developing a Formal Outline

Like storyboards or movie trailers, a **formal outline** presents you with the opportunity to work step by step through the process of arguing your position. It asks you to organize your ideas hierarchically, arranging them in a detailed list that uses numbers and letters to indicate the main points of your argument and then the supporting points beneath.

FIGURE 6.4 These still shots from one of several trailers for the film *Avatar* transition the viewer from the human perspective into the world of Pandora, and then into the climactic conflict between the worlds.

While each finished outline differs, the basic template for a formal outline follows this logical pattern:

- I. Main point for the first section
  - A. First supporting point for section I.
    - 1. First supporting point, evidence, or detail for A.
    - 2. Second supporting point, evidence, or detail for A.
    - 3. Third supporting point, evidence, or detail for A.
  - B. Second supporting point for section I.
    - 1. First supporting point, evidence, or detail for B.
    - 2. Second supporting point, evidence, or detail for B.
      - a. First supporting point, evidence, or detail for 2.
      - b. Second supporting point, evidence, or detail for 2.
- II. Main point for the second section
  - A. First supporting point for section II.
    - 1. First supporting point, evidence, or detail for A.
    - 2. Second supporting point, evidence, or detail for A.
    - 3. Third supporting point, evidence, or detail for A.
  - B. Second supporting point for section II.
    - 1. First supporting point, evidence, or detail for B.
    - 2. Second supporting point, evidence, or detail for B.
      - a. First supporting point, evidence, or detail for 2.
      - b. Second supporting point, evidence, or detail for 2.
- III. Main point for section III. {etc.}

Your outline's shape should be like an accordion—the different sections will expand or contract depending on your material, research, and argument. In general, it's useful to think of the main sections (I, II, III, etc.) as just that—sections—not necessarily as paragraphs. If you start limiting the way you think about your argument to concrete units (paragraphs, number of pages, or amount of sources), you risk losing touch with the most important aspect of writing an essay: the conceptual development of your argument.

As you move toward outlining, approach it as a useful stage of your prewriting and drafting process. A strong, well-developed outline can help you in a number of ways. First and foremost, it allows you to work with the rhetorical canon of **arrangement**, experimenting with different organizational structures, such as those we discussed in Chapter 3: chronological, process, narrative, cause–effect, problem–solution, block structure, thematic or topical,

Seeing Connections
See Chapter 3 for more on the canon of arrangement.

or inductive. As you can see from the At a Glance box, it's useful to consider which mode of organization best suits the type of argument you intend to make and how you want to lead your reader through your information.

Furthermore, an outline—like the visual techniques we discussed above—provides you with a more panoramic perspective on your argument so that you better assess if you need to do supplement research or which areas of your argument are particularly troublesome or conceptually underdeveloped. In fact, if you write your outline with full sentences and include source notations, you can begin the process of generating content and language that you can draw on as you move toward your full written draft. At the same time, keep in mind that an outline is not a formal contract; it is a starting point. As you begin to write your essay, you may very well find it necessary to alter and reorganize your points, the same way you might have rearranged the post-its on the wall in the Writer's Practice above. However, a strong initial outline gives you a solid foundation to build from in constructing a well-conceived and well-developed argument.

Let's look at an outline generated by a student for a research project on the environmental impacts of vegetarianism. As you read through the outline, think about how the author used the formal outline form to organize her ideas in a way that developed her points and created a logical progression of ideas.

AT A GLANCE

Useful Organization Strategies for Writing

- ***Chronological:*** Works best with arguments tied to a progression of temporal events, so well-suited for historical discussions
- ***Process:*** Effective for leading readers from beginning to end through a series of steps
- ***Narrative:*** Employs personal experience or a story arc to move the reader through the argument
- ***Cause-effect:*** Works well for arguments that focus on consequences
- ***Problem-solution:*** Useful for papers where the writer proposes a particular solution for a problem, such as social issue papers
- ***Block structure:*** Effective structure for when you're working through a series of case studies or extended examples
- ***Comparison-contrast:*** Often arranged as a variant of block structure, this mode is most effective when you're discussing one element in relation to another
- ***Thematic or topical:*** Helpful for arguments that center on different conceptual categories or themes
- ***Inductive reasoning:*** Appropriate for essays where you want to move from general evidence to your specific conclusion

Notice how Ada includes a notation about her hook, right in the outline, showing how she prioritizes reaching her audience even in the early stages of writing her essay.

She includes a draft of her thesis claim, showing how she is using it to anchor how she develops and organizes her ideas.

She ends her outline of the introduction with questions designed to engage the reader and point to the larger "So what" of her topic.

For each section, she identifies the strategy of argumentation that would best support her subclaims, here choosing cause-effect as her mode of arrangement.

Ada Throckmorton

Research Paper—Outline

I. Introduction: Vegetarianism is Growing and Should Continue to Grow
   A. Hook: A brief anecdote about the fact that October is International Vegetarian Awareness Month and the fact that vegetarians are growing in number.
   B. Thesis: When it comes to many environmental concerns, skipping meat is an effective way to reduce our personal ecological footprints.
   C. Implications: How does vegetarianism compare to other ways that individuals can preserve the environment? In what way does eating meat harm the environment and contribute to climate change?

II. Direct Impact on Climate Change
   A. Cause: Energy input overall is greater to produce animal protein than plant protein due to the many steps required.
   B. Effect (and impact): Emissions of certain greenhouse gases are extremely high (Source: Kathy Freston's "Vegetarian Is the New Prius" in the Huffington Post on January 18, 2007).
      i. 9% of U.S. CO2
      ii. 37% of U.S. methane (23 times more powerful than CO2)
      iii. 67% of U.S. nitrous oxide emissions (296 times more powerful than CO2)

III. Other Environmental Impacts

A. Meat production requires huge inputs of water.

i. Context: 100× more water per gram of animal protein than plant protein (Source: David and Marcia Pimentel's "Sustainability of Meat-Based and Plant-Based Diets" from American Journal of Clinical Nutrition in January 2003).

ii. Context: Comparison of meat's water usage to showering, drinking shows it is a much larger water user (Source: Mike Sage's "Meat is the Huge Water Waster" in the Sierra Club April 2014).

iii. Suggested solution: Even skipping one hamburger can help as much as not showering for six months (Source: Lynn Hasselberger's "Veganism and the Environment: By the Numbers" in Elephant Journal on February 23, 2013).

B. Meat production pollutes water.

i. Context: Livestock waste (130× that of humans) is not treated and runs off into local water sources (Source: Worldwatch Institute's "Is Meat Sustainable?" in January 2013).

ii. Context: Nitrogen fertilizers and pesticides used to grow vast amounts of feed for livestock runs off into rivers (Source: Roddy Scheer and Doug Moss's "How Does Meat in the Diet Take an Environmental Toll?" in the Scientific American on December 28, 2011).

iii. Impact: Water pollution affects ecosystems but also hurts human health.

Note that she includes her sources right in her outline so she'll be sure to weave them into her essay.

In this early part of her outline, which is designed to present the environmental impact of meat-consumption, she uses a context-impact structure, first providing facts and then interpreting them for the reader.

C. Land dedicated to producing meat is large and displaces other activities.
    i. Context: 30% of ice-free land on earth is dedicated to feed-growing and grazing land for livestock (Source: Bryan Walsh's "The Triple Whopper Environmental Impact of Global Meat Production" in TIME Magazine on December 16, 2013).
    ii. Impact: This land is often cleared forests, which act as carbon sinks (removing CO2 from atmosphere).
    iii. Impact: Land use can cause habitat fragmentation that harms biodiversity.

IV. Approaching a Solution

As she moves to the solution portion of her essay, she identifies two claims that she will use as part of her argument. Even though she is still working on developing these ideas, she includes them as placeholders here.

A. Argument: Dietary choices are something that we all have personal control over so it has a greater impact.
    i. Supporting Claim: comparison to voting as civic duty
    ii. Supporting Claim: linear contributions make a difference

B. Argument: Polarized political climate necessitates that we act on our own.

C. Conclusion: We all can make a difference in whatever level we choose to cut our meat consumption.
    i. Context: Although vegetarianism is increasing as a percentage of the population, total meat consumption is increasing faster (Source: Kathy Freston's "Vegetarian Is the New Prius" in the Huffington Post on January 18, 2007).

Note how clearly Ada conceives of her conclusion as a place to clearly restate her claims, backed by clear evidence from sources. She resists simply summarizing and instead uses her closing section to reinforce her argument and implicitly call the reader to action.

ii. Supporting Claim: This makes it more important to cut meat now, and it means we can make more of a difference not less.

iii. Supporting Claim: If every American cut one serving of chicken, it would be equivalent to taking 500,000 cars off the road (Source: Lynn Hasselberger's "Veganism and the Environment: By the Numbers" in Elephant Journal on February 23, 2013).

iv. Final claim: Individual action is effective because it improves the situation regardless of what happens in any other sphere of action.

AT A GLANCE

Assessing Outlines

- ***Thesis:*** Is it complex, arguable, and interesting?
- ***Argument:*** Is there a logical and fluid progression of ideas? Does each one relate back to the thesis? Is there extraneous information that you can cut?
- ***Arrangement:*** Does your outline follow a consistent and clear model of arrangement?
- ***Development:*** Do any points need to more development? Do you see any areas that need further research? For instance, is there an "A" without a "B"? Is there one section that is much less developed than the others?
- ***Sources:*** Do you identify any primary sources that you'll analyze in the paper? Do you list your secondary sources at relevant points to provide support and authority for the argument? Are there sufficient sources listed for each point?
- ***Format:*** Is there a clear hierarchy of information, with main points associated with supporting points? Are the headings in corresponding sections (like the I, II, III headings or A, B, C headings) parallel in structure (i.e., all gerunds, all noun phrases, all questions)? Do they move the argument of the essay along?

As you can see from Ada's example, you can use your outline as an opportunity to combine argument and arrangement—developing your claims, starting to work through how to support those claims with evidence from your sources, and constructing an organizational framework (in her case, a problem-solution mode of arrangement) that can support a persuasive line of reasoning.

WRITER'S PRACTICE MyWritingLab

Evaluate the logical structure of an outline by disassembling and reassembling it. Print out a copy of the outline for your essay. Take scissors and cut up the outline so that each section is on a separate slip of paper, being sure to remove the Roman numeral or letter that labels each section. Then shuffle the different pieces of paper so that they are no longer in order. Having done so, reassemble your outline, trying to sequence them in a logical order to develop your argument. Alternately, have a partner try to reassemble your outline for you. When you are done, compare your new creation with the original version of your outline. How did the process help you reflect on the choices you made for organizing your argument?

6.3 What are the best ways to get started writing a full draft and integrating research sources responsibly and rhetorically?

DRAFTING YOUR RESEARCH ARGUMENT

As you continue to forge ahead with your research argument, turning it from an outline to a full draft, remember that there are many strategies for getting it done. The key is to start writing—and then just keep going. As the many methods in the At a Glance box indicate, there is no single right way to draft an essay; what's most important is to find the one that best supports your writing style. Whichever method you choose, you'll want to address several questions as you begin to flesh out your argument: how to retain a strong structure, facilitate clear connections between your ideas, spotlight your argument, integrate source material, and, most importantly, how to keep writing.

Structuring Your Argument with Subheads

One way to retain a clear structure while drafting is to borrow a practice from outlining and incorporate subheadings into your essay. You can use these as a temporary organizational aid in your draft (like the scaffolding surrounding a building under construction that eventually is dismantled and taken away) or you could incorporate them as permanent headings for your essay's sections (like the signposts that mark city streets and landmarks). In either case, such subheads help you transition from your outline to an essay while still allowing you to clearly map the progression of your argument. Subheads work particularly well for longer, research-based essays, especially ones that ask the reader to make sense of a complex argument.

Some disciplines, such as the social sciences, require subheadings like "Introduction," "Methods," "Results," and "Discussion," while others—such as those in the humanities—might even discourage the use of subheadings in academic essays. You'll need to assess your rhetorical situation and the parameters of your assignment to determine what part they might play in your essay. However, whether you use them as scaffolding (temporary) or signposts (permanent), consider the power of designing *rhetorical subheads* to help you sharpen your argument. A rhetorical subhead reinforces not just structure, but your claim; that is, rather than simply announcing a structural unit ("Case Study #1"), it situates the section in relation to the argument ("Case Study #1: Low Income and Low Status at an Elite University"). In addition, each subhead offers a mini-preview of the points to come in the section and can help keep your overall argument on track, for both your readers and for you as a writer.

AT A GLANCE

Strategies for Drafting

- ***Following the linear path:*** Start at the beginning, write the introduction, and then move sequentially through each point of argument.
- ***Fleshing out the outline:*** Gradually transform the outline into a full draft, moving from a keyword outline to a prose outline by systematically expanding each of the sections; as you add more detail, the keywords fall away, leaving behind drafted paragraphs.
- ***Writing from the middle:*** Start writing from a point of greatest strength or start with a section you can complete easily and then write around it and fill out sections as you go.
- ***Freewrite and then reverse outline:*** First, freewrite a few pages, then compose a **reverse outline** in which you record the point of each paragraph to assess the argument's flow and structure, and finally reorder and rewrite the paper until it begins to take the proper form for the argument.

When designing rhetorical subheads, you might link them thematically or use a single metaphor to add a rich layer of vivid words to your essay. This technique can provide consistency in language that can enhance the overall cohesiveness of the essay and make it more engaging to read. For instance, let's look at the subheads that one student, Ali Batouli, used in his essay on how the Internet enables online dissent in countries under authoritarian rule. Ali chose to thread a David-and-Goliath metaphor throughout his essay to heighten his analysis of the individual Internet user's confrontation with the authoritarian behemoth. Look at the way his subheads (listed below) help develop his argument:

- David's Slingshot of Freedom (*In this section, the first in the main body of his essay, Ali defined how individuals were using the Internet to circumvent censorship and oppression in their countries.*)
- Goliath's Defense (*In this section, he analyzed the government's response to such online dissent.*)
- Goliath's Intimidation (*In this section, he delved further into the government response, looking at the more aggressive actions.*)
- David's Size Disadvantage (*In this section, Ali assessed the reasons that the individual Internet user seemed unequal to the task of defeating government censorship.*)
- Goliath's Own Slingshot (*In this section, he examined some of the "weapons" that the authoritarian government used to squelch online dissent.*)
- Goliath's Unique Weapon: The Economy (*In this section, he focused his analysis more narrowly on how national economies contributed to these conflicts.*)
- A Revision: Goliath's Victory (*In this concluding section, Ali used the subhead to suggest his surprising claim: that in this version of David-and-Goliath, the giant wins.*)

These carefully developed subheads guide the reader through the argument much more powerfully than would more generic ones such as "Dissent Online" or "Government Response." While such creative subheads might not be appropriate for all contexts, the principle behind them—that subheads can be designed to reinforce the argument as much as to signpost structure—is worth considering no matter what writing situation.

Connecting Your Ideas with Transitions

Whether or not you use subheads, you can attend to the flow and development of your argument by careful attention to transitions. In fact, one myth associated with using subheads is that they obviate the need for transitions between paragraphs. This is not the case. With all the essays you write—especially longer, research-based arguments—you need to take care to provide clear connections and transitions between paragraphs and sections to help ensure that your arguments are both *coherent* (clear and easy to follow) and *cohesive* (unified).

In their simplest form, a transition gestures back at ideas you've already presented and then gestures forward to ideas you're about to present, providing a seamless, smooth connection between the two. In many cases, transitions might take the shape of a single word or phrase that provides links between paragraphs or sections in your essay. For instance, you might incorporate terms like that imply *addition* (e.g., furthermore, in addition, additionally), *sequential arrangement* (e.g., next, first, second, third, finally), *similarity* (e.g., likewise, similarly, in the same way), *contrast* (e.g., yet, however, conversely, on the one hand/on the other hand), *cause–effect* (e.g., therefore, consequently, as a result), or *elaboration* (e.g., for example, for instance, in other words). In each case, the word or phrase suggests a relationship between two elements: what you've already said and what you're about to say.

As our taxonomy of transitional words and phrases indicates, at their core, transitions represent relationships or connections between *ideas*. For this reason, you might decide to use more overtly *conceptual transitions* to streamline your writing. This sort of transition produces cohesion by using key terms from your argument or crafting more complex transitional sentences to connect your points. Consider, for instance, these three transitions from an essay critiquing the increased popularity of gluten-free diets:

> Version 1: Next, it is crucial to consider the role of the media in propagating an ill-informed, pseudo-scientific position that vilifies gluten-based foods.
>
> Version 2: Even more importantly, it is crucial to consider the role of the media in propagating an ill-informed, pseudo-scientific position that vilifies gluten-based foods.

> Version 3: Although such attention to contradictions in food labeling is important, it is even more crucial to consider the role of the media in propagating an ill-informed, pseudo-scientific position that vilifies gluten-based foods.

The first version provides a sequential transition. As a reader, you understand that you are reading the *next* in a series of points; however, there is no sense that this point is any more or less important than the others. The second version gives you a greater understanding of how this point relates to the one before it, suggesting that this section of the argument relies on an underlying structure of escalating importance. The final example takes the time to remind the reader of what he or she has just read (a discussion of contradictions in food labeling) before indicating the move to the next—and more important—topic (the role of the media). In many ways, it provides the most nuanced and clear transition between ideas, one that reinforces the essay's structure while facilitating the argument's forward momentum.

Whether you choose to rely primarily on transitional words/terms or to augment them with more expansive conceptual transitions, you'll need to go through the same process: in each case, think about how you can signal the next idea, build on the previous idea, or reiterate the key terms as you advance your argument. Many students like to think of the game of dominoes when composing transitions: each domino can only touch another domino with a matching number; two connects with two, three with three. Using this notion of progressive, connecting terms and ideas, you can incorporate transitions within sections of your outline to give it overall structure and flow.

Integrating Research Sources into Your Draft

A key moment in drafting your essay involves working with the sources you've uncovered in your research. However, before you begin this process, you must gain clarity about your own voice and rhetorical stance on the topic. The most important feature of your essay is in fact *your argument*, and—to continue our film metaphor—you need to decide how you will **spotlight your argument** so that it doesn't get lost in amid the many perspectives that inform your paper.

AT A GLANCE

Working with Sources Appropriately and Effectively

- ***Read.*** Read the source actively and carefully, underlining passages that suggest moments of deep meaning or that might contribute to your argument. If you are working with online texts, cut and paste the citation into a document and note the paragraph number (for websites) or page number. Always note the page number if you transcribe quotations as you read.

  You'll need this part in order to provide the citation in your own writing.
- ***Record.*** Keep a notebook or an annotated file of citations in which you record your reactions to a particular passage you've read. Does this passage strike you as important? Does it reveal the theme of the text, the climax of a scene, the point of the argument, the purpose of the passage?

  You'll need this part in order to provide your interpretation of the citation.
- ***Relate.*** While drafting, integrate the source material and your interpretation in an appropriate place in your essay. Think about where in the essay, and in which particular paragraph, the information should appear. Think about the context—what comes before and after the summary, paraphrase, or quotation? How does it related to the text around it?

  You'll need this part in order to integrate your source material effectively.

There is no single correct way to strike a balance between your position and your sources. At certain points in your essay, you might want to put your sources center stage and direct from behind the scenes, and sometimes you might want to step out of the shadows and articulate your argument more explicitly to the audience. The key is to choose the role that will produce the most effective argument on your topic, one that fits the needs of your rhetorical situation. After you decide on your approach to working with sources—as a strong explicit narrator or as the strategic synthesizer of information—you can turn to the task of evaluating how to most effectively utilize your source material to support your argument.

This is no simple task: you'll need to introduce and weave the voices of your sources into your written prose, integrating your sources appropriately (to avoid plagiarism), rhetorically (to decide on how much of a presence you will have in the paper), and also strategically (to provide a range of quotations and supporting evidence for your paper). This complex process of **integrating sources** occurs in three basic ways:

- **Summary:** synthesizing a great deal of information from a source
- **Paraphrase:** putting a source quotation into your own words
- **Direct quotation:** excerpting a specific passage from a source, enclosing it in quotation marks

You'll want to alternate among these methods while incorporating your sources for stylistic variety and to accommodate the different ways you'll be using your research as evidence for your argument. This means knowing your options as a writer and selecting the best method for each rhetorical situation within your research essay. Realize that you have many choices for how to integrate research sources and your decisions should be determined by the specific need of each part of your argument as well as the value of the research to build your *ethos*, provide background, offer an alternative perspective, or convey foundational knowledge.

Seeing Connections For an example of summary paragraph in an annotated bibliography, see Chapter 5, pages 204–205.

Selecting Summary A **summary** is a brief version—in your own words—of the content of a text. You might want to summarize the plot of a film or a book in a review, or you might want to summarize the basic argument presented by one of your sources in order to respond to it. Summaries are not analyses; you are not exploring your own ideas when you summarize but merely laying out the ideas explored by another writer in another text. In general, summaries do not use first person since it is the source material and not your interpretation of it that is most relevant. You need to make sure that you tell your readers exactly what you are summarizing and provide complete bibliographical information at the end of your paper. For example, a research paper about the Italian films produced after World War II might include a summary that begins:

> In their influential study *Italian Neorealism and Global Cinema*, cultural critics Laura Ruberto and Kristi Wilson provide a concise history of film innovations at the turn of the twentieth century and argue that Italian documentaries allowed international conflicts to seem real to viewers...

Your summary would follow, and your list of works cited at the end of your paper would include the following reference:

> Ruberto, Laura E. and Wilson, Kristi M. *Italian Neorealism and Global Cinema*. Detroit: Wayne State UP, 2007. Print.

If you wanted to include a brief quote within the body of your summary, then you would use quotation marks and a page number, as follows:

> In their influential study *Italian Neorealism and Global Cinema*, cultural critics Laura Ruberto and Kristi Wilson provide a concise history of film innovations

> at the turn of the twentieth century and argue that Italian documentaries "had a way of making the global seem local" (2).

Note that in this case, you are still writing a summary, but you include a direct quotation because it is rhetorically concise and powerful (with *pathos*-laden language) but also because citing the text gives you more *ethos* or authority as a writer.

Picking Paraphrase Unlike a summary, a **paraphrase** focuses in and restates one part of a text. While a summary is often shorter than the text it summarizes, a paraphrase may be longer or shorter than the text it paraphrases. You might want to paraphrase a text to help your readers understand it, particularly if the original text is dense or difficult. Or you might simply want to paraphrase to make sure that you understand the source yourself—to offer yourself an opportunity to think clearly about the words you are reading. For instance, you might select the following lines to paraphrase:

> "Film had a way of making the global seem local, and the effect of movement, and, later, sound created an immediacy that still photos and written narratives could not approach" (Ruberto and Wilson 2).

Your paraphrase might read as follows:

> Italian film brought world events home to viewers, especially through moving images and audio (Ruberto and Wilson 2).

Note that you replace all the words, not just some of them, for a paraphrase. You need to be careful that you are using your own words to create a new text, not simply cutting and pasting the words of your source together in a different order. For instance, the following sentence represents a failed and problematic paraphrasing:

> Film made the global seem local, and the effect of motion and audio tracks constructed a connection to the audience that photographs and books could not (Ruberto and Wilson 2).

Notice the strong echo of the original text: if you follow both the structure and the language of the source closely, substituting only an occasional synonym to avoid directly quoting, then you are actually plagiarizing—even if you do so accidentally and even if you provide an appropriate citation. You are plagiarizing because you are not informing your reader that the structure, ideas, and much of the language used in your paper were created by someone else.

Seeing Connections
See Chapter 7 for a more detailed discussion of plagiarism and intellectual property.

How to avoid this problem? As you paraphrase, try not to look at the original sentence; move beyond its specific wording to try to get at its meaning. Double-check after you've written your paraphrase to be sure that you don't too strongly replicate the original in phrasing or structure. In addition, be sure to provide your reader with the appropriate bibliographical information about your source by offering a lead-in phrase ("As Ruberto and Wilson argue in their book *Italian Neorealism and Global Cinema* ...") and then list the complete reference for this source at the end of your paper. Or you can provide a parenthetical citation after the summary or paraphrase including the author's name and, for a paraphrase, the page number where the passage you are paraphrasing appears in the original text. When in doubt, consider using a direct quotation instead of a paraphrase to bring your source's voice directly into your essay.

Using Direct Quotations Quoting directly from a source may seem much simpler than paraphrasing or summarizing, but quotations should be included to accomplish a specific rhetorical purpose, and they must be integrated responsibly so that you give the original writer credit. Consider how you might feel if someone took your writing and recycled it without acknowledging that it was your work. More importantly, realize that naming the author and background of a great passage can build your authority and *ethos* as a writer, so it is a wise move to name your sources in your paper. However, be careful not to swing to the opposite extreme and overfill your paper with quotations from others. If a quotation does not fit into any of the categories listed in the At a Glance box, consider paraphrasing or summarizing it. What you want to avoid is a paper dominated by unnecessary quotations; in such a case, your argument—what readers expect most in your paper—gets buried. It's similar to what happens in film when the filmmaker splices together too many different scenes; the audience becomes lost in the montage and can no longer follow the narrative.

AT A GLANCE

Reasons to Use Direct Quotations

- ***Evidence:*** the quotation provides tangible evidence for part of your argument.
- ***Ethos:*** the original author is a primary source or an expert on the subject, and including a direct quotation would increase the *ethos* of your argument.
- ***Language:*** the original author used memorable phrasing or has a particular voice that would be lost in paraphrase.

Working with Quotations in Your Writing But how, practically, do you go about *integrating* direct quotations appropriately and effectively? The key is to think carefully about how you are using the source material first and then choose an appropriate structure. Your temptation might be simply to "drop" a quote in between two of your sentences, as in the example below:

> More recently, *Hunger Games* protagonist Katniss has challenged the anti-feminist stereotype prominent in today's young adult fiction. "She's Jo March as coal miner's daughter in hunting boots, the opposite of Bella, the famously drippy, love-obsessed heroine of the *Twilight* books—and unlike clever and self-possessed Hermione of the *Harry Potter* series, she's the lead, not the sidekick" (Pollitt 10). Translated to the big screen in a blockbuster film, Katniss solidifies this image, providing a much-needed positive model for today's young women.

While Pollitt's sentence merits being quoted directly because of its language, the danger in this method is that you are using the quotation not as evidence, but as a substitute for your own writing. The original writer (Katha Pollitt) is given little credit for her work besides the parenthetical citation, making her more a ghostwriter than a source for your argument.

Rather than using a drop quote, integrate direct quotations strategically into your writing so as to leverage them more effectively as you develop your claim. One typical practice is to use a **signal phrase** to indicate the context of the quotation and to orient it in terms of your argument. A signal phrase can be located in many different positions in relation to the quotation, but most often it appears as an introductory phrase or clause that refers to the original author or title of the source, heightening the *ethos* of the source.

> In her 2012 article, Kate Pollitt argues, "She's Jo March as coal miner's daughter in hunting boots, the opposite of Bella, the famously drippy, love-obsessed heroine of the *Twilight* books—and unlike clever and self-possessed Hermione of the *Harry Potter* series, she's the lead, not the sidekick" (10).

An alternate method would be to limit the amount of text quoted and **integrate small sections into your own sentence**. This strategy works particularly well when you are trying to capture a unique turn of phrase or concept from the original text and tends to maintain the strength of your own voice as a writer. For example, consider how in this example, the author integrates a few words of direct quotation into her sentence so as to spotlight Pollitt's memorable characterization of Bella Swan's character:

> Pollitt argues that, unlike the "famously drippy, love-obsessed" Bella from the *Twilight* series, Katniss offers a smart, positive role model for today's young women (10).

In another variation, the author includes a slightly longer section of the original text that works in conjunction with paraphrase:

> Kate Pollitt offered a persuasive intertextual interpretation of Katniss's character when she suggested that Katniss is "Jo March as coal miner's daughter in hunting boots," directly opposing the model of femininity embodied by *Twilight*'s Bella (10).

This model can also be adapted to allow the writer to follow up the quotation with an end comment that advances the argument.

A third integration strategy involves **appending the quotation to one of your own sentences with a colon**. The syntactical function of the colon implies that what follows it (the quote) is directly related to what precedes the colon (your own observation). For this reason, this structure works well to suggest that the direct quotation operates as an elaboration of your point or as evidence.

> Pollitt argues that Katniss represents a new-and-improved model of female heroine: "She's Jo March as coal miner's daughter in hunting boots, the opposite of Bella, the famously drippy, love-obsessed heroine of the *Twilight* books—and unlike clever and self-possessed Hermione of the *Harry Potter* series, she's the lead, not the sidekick" (10).

At times, you may even decide to include a lengthier quotation in your essay, perhaps because of the strength of the author's argument or because you intend to analyze the passage. For direct quotations of four lines or longer, set the passage off from the rest of the text as a **block quote**. Here's an example using Pollitt once again.

> In discussing Katniss's role in revitalizing the female pop culture protagonist, Pollitt argues,
>
>> She's Jo March as coal miner's daughter in hunting boots, the opposite of Bella, the famously drippy, love-obsessed heroine of the *Twilight* books—and unlike clever and self-possessed Hermione of the *Harry Potter* series, she's the lead, not the sidekick. We're worlds away from the vicious-little-rich-girls of *Gossip Girl* and its knockoffs, where everything revolves around looks, clothes, consumerism, social status, and sexual competition (10).
>
> As Pollitt suggests, some of Katniss's appeal lies in how she embodies the intelligence and fortitude of previous female protagonists, qualities that have been increasingly obscured beneath superficiality and sentimentality in more recent years.

It's worth noting some technical details here: the quotation as a whole is indented one inch from the left margin; quotation marks are omitted in block quotes because the formatting itself marks it as a direct quotation; the final period precedes the parenthetical citation for a block quote; the author's analysis ("As Pollitt notes...") resumes flush with the left margin, indicating it is part of the same paragraph and same line of argument.

While including blocks of text might be tempting, especially when dealing with a particularly rich source, be judicious in your use of lengthy quotes. Including too many of them can fragment your argument, interrupt the flow of your essay, and drown out your own voice. Always follow up a block quote with analysis to clarify to your reader how it contributes to your argument and to return the spotlight onto your own research and claim.

As you work with direct quotations in your own writing, you might find these additional strategies helpful:

- To quote a source within a source, use (qtd. in ——) to indicate where *you* found the quotation, for instance:

  > Film critic Millicent Marcus argues that "neorealism is first and foremost a moral statement" (qtd. in Ruberto and Wilson 7).

  If you don't include the author's name in the signal phrase, insert in the parenthesis:

  > A different perspective might argue that "neorealism is first and foremost a moral statement" (Marcus qtd. in Ruberto and Wilson 7).

- To edit part of a quote, use square brackets, such as [ ]. This abridgement allows you to get concisely to the heart of the issue in your chosen quotation. For instance, you might edit the Pollitt quote above:

  > Kathy Pollitt argues in her 2012 article from *The Nation*, Katniss is "the opposite of Bella [...] and unlike clever and self-possessed Hermione [...], she's the lead, not the sidekick" (10).

Experiment with these strategies in your own writing to determine which best serves your rhetorical purpose. One key to remember is to avoid overusing any one type of integration strategy; in that case, your writing style might become

AT A GLANCE

Check for Integrating Sources

- Did you ***introduce*** the quotations that you used in various ways?
- Did you ***link*** the source material to your argument to show the relevance?
- Did you ***comment*** on them afterward to advance your argument?
- Did you ***cite*** them properly using the appropriate documentation style for your subject area?

monotonous, like a film that relies too heavily on the same types of shots. For instance, if you want to draw attention to the *author* of a quotation to add *ethos* to your argument, you might opt to provide attribution through an introductory clause; however, if you want to emphasize *information* rather than authorship, an incorporated structure might be more effective. Remember that the purpose of integrating sources is to demonstrate your work as a researcher and to show that you are building your argument on the work of others. Therefore, choose what types of integration strategies work best for each source and for each part of your paper.

Documentation During Integration

When integrating sources into your draft, be sure to include citations for each quotation or paraphrase. This would also be a good time to begin drafting your preliminary bibliography or Works Cited list, in order to save time later. The purpose of documentation is not only to provide a "list of credits" for your references but also to supply interested readers with the resources to continue learning about your topic. Just as you undoubtedly found certain articles inspiring while investigating your topic and used them as springboards for more focused research, so too might your paper serve as a means of leading your readers to intriguing ideas and articles. You can go back over the correct format for citations in your final edit, following the guidelines in Chapter 7 for documentation to do so.

WRITER'S PRACTICE MyWritingLab

In your efforts to integrate sources effectively, keep in mind that source material should *support* your argument, not supplant it. If you're worried that you have integrated too many sources (and lost your own voice), spend some time reviewing the draft and ask yourself:

- Am I still the moderator of this conversation?
- Is my voice clear, compelling, and original?
- Do I allow my own argument to emerge as foremost in this piece?

Keeping Your Passion to Keep Writing

As you move deeper into the writing process, working on the flow of your argument and integrating quotations, don't lose sight of your enthusiasm for your subject. Re-read your earliest freewrites and your entries in your research log. What goals prompted you to begin the project? What aspects of your topic excited you, angered you, or inspired you? What contribution did you imagine yourself making to this discussion? Remember, your audience will be reading your paper to learn *your* particular point of view on the subject.

Also realize that to write is to struggle with the process, as noted by Stanford University psychologist David Rasch: "Almost all writers are familiar with the experience of feeling stuck, blocked, overwhelmed, or behind schedule in their writing." What can help? Staying motivated and relying on others. A conversation with a classmate, your instructor, or even a writing tutor can help give you the inspiration and impetus to keep writing.

To keep yourself energized, you should also allow yourself well-needed breaks. Brief periods away from the writing process can often recharge and reinvigorate your approach to the paper and help you think through difficult points in the argument. Ironically, a pause in drafting can also help you avoid writer's block by allowing you to remember what interested you about this project in the first place.

Finally, if you are having trouble getting through the draft process, allow yourself to write what Anne Lamott, author of *Bird by Bird,* famously calls the "shitty first draft." In the words of Lamott, "All good writers write them. This is how they end up with good second drafts and terrific third drafts." That is, you should realize that the first version by no means has to be perfect or even close to what the final paper will look like. It is instead simply your first attempt at getting your ideas on paper. Freeing yourself to write something—anything—can help you escape from the weight of perfectionism or the fear of failure that often paralyzes writers. Allow yourself to experiment, play, arrange, rearrange, leave temporary placeholders, and jot notes to yourself. You will have plenty of opportunities to rework the material, show your draft to others, and move forward with the writing process. The key is to stop procrastinating, to get writing, and keep writing.

ANALYZING A STUDENT'S DRAFT OF A RESEARCH-BASED ESSAY

6.4 How do I analyze a draft of a research-based essay?

Let's examine now the draft of Stanford student Wanjin Park, who developed a research project comparing Gore's film *An Inconvenient Truth* (2006) to Gore's more recent PowerPoint slide show from his TED talk. Wanjin conducted a range of academic and field research, wrote a detailed outline, and then composed his draft. After feedback from his course instructor and his classroom peers, he revised his first partial draft and outline substantially, as demonstrated later in this chapter. But throughout, Wanjin kept his passion for his project and his respect for Gore as a leader trying to use rhetoric to persuade people of the importance of attending to climate change. We can study his first draft and conduct a rhetorical analysis of his writing strategies to see how you, too, can approach writing your research argument.

You'll see that the excerpt from Wanjin's draft integrates research sources in a variety of ways, begins to showcase Wanjin's own voice as a writer, and effectively relies on the outline as a prewriting tool.

Wanjin's working title is strong and raises an interesting issue—but in the revision, he will introduce his argument more forcefully.

His organizational strategy is to open with a counterargument, acknowledging that, today, even middle-schoolers know about global warming.

Then he introduces the film fully as well as his second primary source: Gore's 2008 TED talk.

Park 1

Wanjin Park
Working Draft + Outline

Environmental Leadership:
How Al Gore Illuminated an Overlooked Crisis

Rising levels of carbon dioxide emissions do not contribute to global warming. It has become silly and naïve to argue thus even before a group of middle school students. The awareness of the dangers of our carbon addicted lifestyle, however, would not be as widespread as it is today had it not been for the one man spearheading the global movement against climate change: Al Gore. Gore's rise to environmental influence is in large part due to Davis Guggenheim's documentary *An Inconvenient Truth*, which was then followed by a revised presentation at the TED Conference in March 2008. What strikes the audience, however, is not the revision of data and graphics in the slides, but rather, it is the change in Gore's rhetoric. In *An Inconvenient Truth*, Gore focuses on drawing in the audience and persuading them to join the environmental movement through the depiction of himself as a warm, dedicated, but lonely leader in the face of a global crisis; by contrast, at the TED presentation, Gore has garnered huge

Park 2

support, but senses a lack of change in the United States, and thus focuses on pushing the public toward increased initiative through his urgent and passionate rhetoric.

Even in his draft, Wanjin has strongly developed his thesis—this work will sustain him through the rest of the paper. He can use the key terms of the thesis to structure the remaining sections of the essay.

Gripping the Flames: Gore Leading the Environmental Movement

Wanjin's subheads show his gift for creative language; he uses *pathos* but also indicates this new part of his argument with the subhead.

At the forefront of the global environmental movement against climate change is Al Gore. In fact, the Nielsen Company, a leading global marketing and advertising research company, conducted a survey in conjunction with Oxford University which serves as a testament to Gore's environmental prominence. In a survey of 26,486 people across 47 countries, Gore has been voted as "the most influential spokesperson to champion the global warming debate," even "ahead of former United Nations" Secretary General Kofi Annan (Nielsen).

Already bringing in research, Wanjin starts with facts and statistics (*logos*) from survey and field research.

Gore has been active with the environmental movement since the beginning of his political career; however, his lasting, and perhaps most influential contribution did not come until the release of Davis Guggenheim's *An Inconvenient Truth* in May 2006. Although based on lectures "that Gore has been presenting in one form or another for nearly three decades," *An Inconvenient Truth* has achieved levels of popularity and influence unrivalled by those of any other medium employed in the environmental movement (Rosteck and Frentz). Earning over $49 million, it currently ranks as the fifth highest grossing documentary in the history of the United States. Further indicative of the documentary's influence are the results of another survey conducted by the

Next, he provides background and cites an article from his research (Rosteck and Frentz).

At this point, Wanjin offers a road map for the rest of his essay, referring back to his title and his thesis in a way that offers powerful coherence for the essay.

As Wanjin gets into the body of his essay, he takes his evidence one piece at a time, first providing a strong rhetorical analysis of the visual and audio elements of the film, then quoting directly from Gore's voice-over.

Park 3

Nielsen Company in April 2007. Of the viewers who have seen *An Inconvenient Truth*, eighty-nine percent reported to have become "more aware of the problem"; sixty-six percent "changed their mind about global warming"; and most importantly, seventy-four percent changed their habits as a result (Nielsen).

Considering the fact that *An Inconvenient Truth* is Gore's most influential rhetorical medium, an analysis of the documentary will thus illuminate the key characteristics that define the success of Gore's environmental leadership.

Contrasting Images: The Beautiful and the Doomed

An Inconvenient Truth begins with a beautiful depiction of nature. The camera focuses close-up on a branch full of small green tree leaves. The green hue is accentuated by the bright sunlight that is reflected off of the leaf blades. After a few seconds, the camera shifts to the right to reveal a sparkling river. The soft piano music in the background adds to the calm and peaceful mood. Al Gore then narrates in the background, purposefully emphasizing the sibilants as if to imitate the sounds of the river and the rustling leaves:

> You look at that river gently flowing by. You notice the leaves rustling with the wind. You hear the birds. You hear the tree frogs. In the distance, you hear a cow. You feel the grass. The mud gives a little bit on the riverbank. It's quiet; it's peaceful. (Inconvenient)

The first thirty seconds of the film is beautiful. However, Gore interjects and introduces human neglect of nature by

Park 4

stating, "all of a sudden, it's a gearshift inside you and it's like taking a deep breath and going 'Oh yeah, I forgot about this'" (Inconvenient). By using the word "gearshift," Gore metaphorically compares the audience to machines that are equipped with a gear; in essence, Gore argues that we have become the products of our industrial production, and have thus become so separate from our nature that we have completely forgot about it.

The consequences of our neglect are horrifying. After the establishment of our neglect, Gore's presentation shows images of the damages we made to nature. We see images of factories emitting thick black smog that obscures the sun. In one of the images, the hue of the sky is grayish purple; considering how the corpses of formerly sick bodies usually show this hue, this image is suggestive of the damage we have done to nature. Furthermore, as a demonstration of how global warming has aggravated natural disasters, we see footages of the aftermath of Hurricane Katrina. We see footage of crying babies without shelter and caretakers, a bloated dead body lying face down in the water, and a man stroking the forehead of his dead wife. Although Hurricane Katrina has been an American natural disaster, these scenes shock even the most foreign audience.

The presentation of these images after Gore's argument that we have forgotten about our nature compels the audience to feel guilt and responsibility. In effect, Gore induces the audience to

With the word, "However," Wanjin lets us know his view, introducing his argument.

The careful analysis of specific words such as "gearshift" makes this rhetorical argument persuasive.

Just as he analyzed the words in the film, Wanjin carefully analyzes the images, building his argument. His own voice as a writer here becomes adamant and urgent, evoking the mood of the film but also forcing us to take his argument seriously.

This section ends with a mini summary and strong statement of Wanjin's argument. In this way, he creates an effective organization for his larger paper, and from here can go about completing it one section at a time.

The next sections of the draft show in outline form the content Wanjin plans to cover, including his main arguments, his section of evidence, and his secondary source citations.

He provides an *ethos*-building introduction for his secondary source.

By working with more than two sources in this section—Inhofe and Olson—Wanjin shows potential to move from merely quoting sources (as we saw in Chapter 3) to synthesizing them in conversation with one another. He can then build on their combined ideas as he advances his own argument.

Park 5

personalize the issue of climate change, thereby making us more receptive to Gore's message of change.

The Dedicated Leader

- after fear, Gore portrays himself as a dedicated leader
- autobiographical threads in the documentary
- vulnerable moments in Gore's personal history
- Source: these stories "strengthen[ed] the hero's resolve"
- Secondary source: Kathryn Olson, Director of the Rhetorical Leadership Graduate Certificate Program at University of Wisconsin-Milwaukee, claims the autobiographical threads "persuasively documents Gore's single-mindedness in pursuing his public cause, often at his own expense, through a lifetime of disappointments and sacrificing a comfortable retirement to carry the message globally."
- Gore in a Beijing taxi on way to Tsing Hua University.

Lonely Leader

- personal footage depicts Gore as "emotional suffering"
- Senator James Inhofe attacks Gore's ideas
- Secondary source: Gore "inviting impression that encourages auditors to join him or her in social action" (Olson).

TED Presentation

- more passionate; more religious; his sense of urgency is raised
- his tone of voice, joking, moral issue

Park 6

- Quote: "The only two countries that didn't ratify—and now there's only one. Australia had an election. And there was a campaign in Australia that involved television and Internet and radio commercials to lift the **sense of urgency** for the people there. And we trained 250 people to give the slide show in every town and village and city in Australia."
- There has been progress: Gore contributed to the change through his environment
- "The cities supporting Kyoto in the US are up to 780"
- Returning to religious rhetoric, passion, urgency
- Evidence: He does not begin his presentation about how far we have come since 2006, when the documentary film *An Inconvenient Film* was released. Instead, he begins by quoting Karen Armstrong (I believe she is someone prominent in religious studies) who said "religion really properly understood is not about belief, but about behavior."
- In arguing this, he essentially says that what we lack with our response to climate change is a change in behavior.
- "But, as important as it is to change the light bulbs, it is more important to change the laws. And when we change our behavior in our daily lives, we sometimes leave out the citizenship part and the democracy part."

By selecting and arranging quotes in his draft, Wanjin can approach the writing with a keen sense of his argument and overall plan for persuading the reader. He has chosen his evidence and uses the draft to sort through it effectively.

Once more considering multiple sources, here Wanjin demonstrates careful *source evaluation*, a process that will in turn help him write a stronger argument. For more on evaluating sources, see Chapter 5.

As shown by Wanjin's paper, a working draft should have a strong and well-developed thesis. This will drive the entire argument. Then, you can begin to work through the sections of an outline, providing specific evidence and secondary source support in what in Chapter 5 we called "a conversation with your sources." As you continue, fill in parts of your draft and rely on your peers for support and feedback.

6.5 What strategies can I use to revise my draft?

REVISING YOUR DRAFT

As many professional writers can attest—and Wanjin would agree with this based on his drafting experience—a text goes through numerous drafts on its way to becoming a polished final product. Even filmmakers produce multiple drafts of their movies before they release their film, experimenting with different sequencing, camera shots, and pacing to create what they consider to be the fulfillment of their artistic vision. We've all seen the results of this process: deleted scenes or *outtakes* from popular films or television programs. What these segments represent are moments of work (writing, producing, and shooting) that, after review and editing, were removed to streamline the film.

As you might imagine, often it's difficult or even painful to reshape your work during revision; it's hard to leave some of your writing behind on the cutting room floor. However, as your project develops, its focus may change: sources or ideas that seemed important to you during the early stages of research may become less relevant, even tangential; a promising strategy of argumentation may turn out to be less suitable to your project; a key transition may no longer be necessary once you reorganize the argument. As you turn to your draft with a critical eye, what you should find is that in order to transform your paper into the best possible written product, you'll need to move beyond proofreading or editing and into the realm of macro changes, or **revision**.

Troubleshooting

Proofreading remains a critical part of the revision process. Careless grammatical and punctuation errors and spelling mistakes can damage your *ethos* as an author, and they need to be corrected. It is very probable that you've been doing such micro-revision throughout the drafting process—editing for style, grammar, punctuation, and spelling. However, sometimes it's difficult to do broader revisions until you have a substantial part of your paper written. It is only once your argument starts coming together that you can recognize the most productive ways to modify it in order to optimize its effectiveness. This is the key to successful revision: you have to be open to *both* micro-editing and large-scale, multiple revisions. Think of this process as **re-vision**, or seeing it again with new eyes, seeing it in a new light.

Let's look at decisions some students made during the revision process:

- **Content Overload.** Reading over her draft about the propagandistic elements in World War II films, Jennifer realized that she had gotten so caught up in presenting background information that her paper was top-heavy, with pages of background in the begnning and her own analysis and argument deferred too long to be effective.

  Revision: Jennifer sharpened her focus and adjusted her treatment of background information, eliminating some of the more extraneous material and also redistributing key foundation information throughout her essay so as to reprioritize developing her own argument.

- **Patchwork Paragraphs.** Similarly, in his essay about presidential rhetoric in the Health Care Debate, Ben let his sources take over. He focused so exclusively on including quotations from his primary and secondary sources that his paragraphs began to read like a patchwork quilt of other people's voices without sufficient analysis or exposition to situate them in terms of Ben's own argument.

  Revision: Ben reevaluated which direct quotations were necessary to his argument, eliminating some and transforming others into summary or paraphrase. In addition, he spent more time contextualizing and analyzing the source material, spotlighting his own argument first, and then using the source material as evidence.

- **Lack of Reliance on Sources.** Miranda had the opposite problem; in her draft she made a compelling argument about the literary status of graphic novels but did not really quote from or mention any of her sources, so she wasn't showcasing her work as a researcher.

Revision: She more prominently integrated her source material into her argument, both by referring to specific authors and articles she had read and by using additional direct quotations. In doing so, she greatly increased her *ethos* and the persuasiveness of her argument.

- **Overly Broad Thesis.** After drafting her paper on hip-hop and gender identity, Sharita realized that her thesis was too broad and that in trying to cover both male and female imagery, she wasn't able to be specific enough to craft a really persuasive argument.

  Revision: Realizing that her interest really lay in exploring the conflicted stereotype of powerful, sexualized women in hip-hop videos, Sharita cut large sections of her paper revolving around the male imagery. The result was a provocative argument based on concrete, persuasive examples.

- **Inconsistent Argument.** In reading over his drafted essay on the benefits of windfarms as an alternate energy source, Kyle discovered that in the process of writing the essay, he had actually changed his claim, so that the thesis statement in his introduction differed from what he actually argued in his essay and stated in his conclusion.

  Revision: Recognizing that his newer claim probably reflected the stronger argument, Kyle adjusted his thesis statement and the early sections of his draft to produce a strong, cohesive argument throughout the essay.

- **Tunnel-vision Argument.** The first version of Max's essay on the aesthetics of design in the Apple product line was visually stunning, detailed, and eloquently written. But it was so one-sided that it read more like a marketing brochure than an academic argument.

  Revision: Max's task in revision was to provide a more balanced perspective on the Apple computer phenomenon. After further research, he incorporated a greater diversity of perspectives in his paper and softened some of his language to be less biased in favor of Apple products.

As these examples indicate, you need to enter into the research process looking not just for mistakes to "fix" but also for larger issues that might relate to your structure, your thesis, your scope, or the development of your ideas.

AT A GLANCE

Revision Strategies

1. ***Read your essay out loud or have someone read it to you.*** This process will help you hear mistakes and inconsistencies that you unknowingly skipped over when reading silently.
2. ***Gain critical distance.*** Put your essay away for a few hours, or even a few days, and then come back to it fresh.
3. ***Don't be chained to your computer.*** For a change of pace, print out your draft, making revisions by hand. We conceptualize information differently on paper versus on a screen.
4. ***Look at your writing in different ways.*** Take a paragraph and divide it into distinct sentences, which you line up one under another. Look for patterns (for instance, is the repetition deliberate or accidental?), style issues (is sentence structure varied?), and fluidity of transitions between sentences.
5. ***Reevaluate your organization.*** Create a reverse outline for your essay by looking at your draft and listing out, in order, the main point of each paragraph in formal outline form. Looking at these points, assess whether their order is logical and clear, whether they refer back to the thesis, and whether there are any redundancies or omissions in the trajectory of development.
6. ***Answer peer review questions for your essay.*** Use materials provided by your instructor to guide your feedback on your classmates' work as a set of questions you can apply to your own revision process.
7. ***Share your draft with others.*** Whether you talk to your instructor, a classmate, or a writing tutor, consider getting some reader response to guide your revisions. Take their feedback into account, even if it initially doesn't seem significant. You might not decide to act on the advice, but at least consider it before dismissing it.
8. ***Revise out of order or in sections.*** Choose paragraphs at random and look at them individually, or begin at the end. Sometimes our conclusions are the weakest simply because we always get to them last, when we're tired; start revision by looking at your conclusion first.
9. ***Look at the revision as a whole.*** As you correct mistakes or prose problems, consider the impact that the revision makes on the rest of the essay. Sometimes it is possible just to add a missing comma or substitute a more precise verb, but often you need to revise more than just the isolated problem so that the sentence, paragraph, or essay as a whole continues to "fit" and flow together.

Collaboration Through Peer Feedback

In addition to your own assessment of your writing, you should take into account **peer evaluations** of your drafts; you might consider your peer feedback sessions to be "advance screenings" with your audience. In the film industry, such test screenings are standard practice, and through this process the audience becomes a collaborator with the director, producer, screenwriters, film editors, and actors in determining the final form of a film. Many films have been altered after audience feedback during test screenings, from their titles (*Licence to Kill*) to their narrative structures (*Blade Runner*), length (*Titanic*), and, most typically, their endings (*Pretty Woman*, *Fatal Attraction*, *28 Days Later*, *World War Z*). In each case, test audience feedback shaped the final edit and made evident the rhetorical relationship between audience, writer, and text. Similarly, writing needs to take into consideration the audience's expectations; we write to show our audience our thoughts, our research, and our claim, so we need to respond to audience needs when we write and revise our texts.

Peer feedback sessions provide you with an opportunity for a test screening of your argument. While a casual conversation about your draft with a peer can provide useful insights, taking a more structured approach can provide you with a stronger foundation for revision. To facilitate a productive peer review session:

- Write a cover memo that points your readers to specific questions you have about your draft. Your peer reviewers can customize their responses to address the particular issues that concern you as a writer
- Write down peer feedback; don't rely exclusively on oral comments. You can take notes during your peer review session, or each of your partners could bring written comments to the meeting. This will give you more tangible feedback to work with as you revise.
- Model good peer review behavior for your partners in how you work with their drafts: come prepared to the session, having read their essays and prepared written comments; praise the strengths of their work; offer constructive feedback in an even tone, pointing to specific points in the draft that need revision; balance attention to micro-editing (stylistics, punctuation, grammar, usage) with discussion of higher order thinking (argument, structure, use of evidence).

AT A GLANCE

Questions for Peer Review on the Draft

- ***Argument consistency:*** Do the introduction and conclusion argue the same points, or has the argument shifted by the end?
- ***Organization and progression:*** Does the paper flow logically, developing one idea seamlessly into the next? Does the author provide important theoretical foundations, definitions, or background at the beginning of the paper to guide the audience through the rest of the argument?
- ***The author's voice in relation to the sources:*** Does the essay foreground the author's argument, or does it focus primarily on the sources' arguments, locating the author's point of view primarily in the conclusion?
- ***Information:*** Are there any holes in the research? Does the author need to supplement his or her evidence with additional research, interviews, surveys, or other source materials?
- ***Opposition and concession:*** Does the author adequately address counterarguments? Does he or she integrate alternate perspectives into the argument (i.e., deal with them as they arise), or does he or she address them in a single paragraph?

- Listen to the feedback you receive. Don't become defensive about your writing. Take the suggestions in the spirit of collaboration, and ask questions to be sure that you understand your readers' comments.

Sometimes you'll find that your peer reviewers vocalize ideas that echo your own concerns about your draft; other times you may be surprised by their reactions. Keep in mind that their comments are informed *suggestions,* not mandates; your task, as the writer, is to assess the feedback you receive and implement those changes that seem to best address the needs of both your argument and your audience as you move forward with your revision process.

Analyzing a Student's Revision of a Research-Based Essay

Let's return now to Wanjin's draft paper and see how he used his own self-assessment and peer review suggestions to revise his paper and strengthen his argument.

Park 1

Wanjin Park

Research-Based Argument—Final

15 March, 2010

Wanjin's revised title actually conveys part of his argument—he has traded the general claim "Illuminates" to offer several new terms: soft, passionate, and dynamic rhetoric.

Balancing the Soft and the Passionate Rhetorician:
Gore's Dynamic Rhetoric in His Environmental Leadership

His introduction has a new sense of urgency, shown in short and long sentence variety, strong diction, and sign-posting (the two-part rhetoric).

Moreover, Wanjin spends a great deal of time advancing a more developed thesis, naming Gore as lonely leader with soft rhetoric and then as passionate leader with dynamic rhetoric. With this thesis, the paper will offer a more forceful argument.

Most importantly, Wanjin ends the opening with a "So what?" significance statement.

At the forefront of the global environmental movement is one man with the power to blur national boundaries, urge political leaders to adopt reforms, and motivate hundreds of thousands. That man is Al Gore. Gore has been a pivotal leader, attracting unprecedented levels of support for the once overlooked issue, especially through Davis Guggenheim's *An Inconvenient Truth*. The success of the documentary can be attributed to Gore's two-part rhetoric. He first induces fear and guilt in us, the audience, making us more receptive to his message. He then portrays himself as a warm, dedicated, but lonely leader, thereby arousing our desire to join him in social action. Despite the success of his soft rhetoric, Gore set it aside two years later at the TED2008 Conference and adopted a heightened sense of passion and urgency. The shift in rhetoric mirrors a change in Gore's agenda, and it is this dynamic rhetoric which Gore molds to fit specific goals that defines the success of his leadership. An understanding of Gore's rhetoric offers us invaluable insight on how to use dynamic rhetoric to bring overlooked social issues into the light.

Park 2

Before showing us a change in his rhetoric, Gore uses soft rhetoric in *An Inconvenient Truth*. Soft rhetoric, a newly coined term, refers to a rhetorical tool that draws in a guarded audience, not through impassioned words, but through the appeal to the audience's sense of guilt and the establishment of a warm and inviting *ethos.* Because the public was still guarded toward the issue of climate change before the release of the documentary, Gore shies away from passionate speech that is meant to inspire, and instead focuses on convincing his audience to join him through soft rhetoric.

He introduces his own term—one he made up.

Wanjin did not want to use "I" so he speaks in third person, but he clearly establishes his own argument in this revision.

His microedits to style and descriptive language make his writing even more vivid and memorable.

Contrasting Images: The Beautiful and the Doomed

Gore begins his soft rhetoric by inducing fear and guilt in us, the audience, through the juxtaposition of beauty and doom. He first offers us a beautiful depiction of nature. The camera focuses close-up on a branch full of green tree leaves. Bright sunlight reflects off of the leaf blades, accentuating the green hue. After a few seconds, the camera turns to the right to reveal a glistening river. The river is a mix of green and blue, both defining colors of nature. The soft piano music in the background adds to the calm and peaceful mood. Gore then narrates in the background, purposely emphasizing the sibilants as if to imitate the sounds of the river and the rustling leaves:

In the revision, Wanjin begins with a topic sentence that conveys his argument, rather than just launching into the rhetorical analysis of the film's details.

> You look at that river gently flowing by. You notice the leaves rustling with the wind. You hear the birds. You hear the tree frogs. In the distance, you hear a cow. You feel the grass. The mud gives a little bit on the riverbank. It's quiet; it's peaceful. (*An Inconvenient Truth*)

Since Wanjin quotes more than four lines in this passage, he formats the citation as a **block quote**.

Park 3

He has also incorporated more research, so he is not over-relying on only one source.

The sequence of images and narration encapsulates the beauty of nature so well that Professors Thomas Rosteck and Thomas Frentz write in "Myth and Multiple Readings in Environmental Rhetoric: The Case of *An Inconvenient Truth*" that "we experience, visually and through Gore's voiceover, the awe, sublime beauty, and wonder of Earth" (5).

Gore suddenly interrupts the experience and interjects that we have forgotten about nature in spite of its beauty: "all of a sudden, it's a gearshift inside you and it's like taking a deep breath and going 'Oh yeah, I forgot about this'" (*An Inconvenient Truth*). Through the use of the word "gearshift," Gore metaphorically compares us, the audience, to machines that are equipped with a gear; in essence, he argues that we have become so addicted to the industrial age that we have transformed into its products, becoming separate from and oblivious to our nature.

Here, Wanjin cites the article analyzed earlier in this chapter. He picks a strong quotation, sets it up by building the *ethos* of the source, and then, most importantly, comments on it in the next paragraph, emphasizing "frightening" and the building on Schulte's reading to develop his point about guilt.

* * *

The images arouse such horror that Bret Schulte, Assistant Professor of Journalism at University of Arkansas, writes that Gore shows us "the frightening future promised by global warming—an apocalyptic world of deadly hurricanes, rising oceans, disease, drought, and famine" (Schulte).

Notice here, he offers a strong conversation with many of his sources: Rosteck and Frentz, Olson, and looking back to Schulte.

By deliberately introducing the "frightening" images only after his "gearshift" metaphor, Gore compels us to feel not only frightened, but also responsible and guilty for the

Park 4

damages done to nature (Schulte; *An Inconvenient Truth*). The arousal of guilt is crucial in shaping *An Inconvenient Truth* into an effective environmental medium, as it "sets up the rhetorical tension with which Gore will leverage his message" (Rosteck and Frentz). Kathryn Olson, the author of "Rhetorical Leadership and Transferable Lessons for Successful Social Advocacy in *An Inconvenient Truth*," agrees and elaborates on what Gore's message is: "he asks [us] . . . to share the guilt of insufficient action with him and to redeem [our]selves . . . now that [we] grasp the gravity . . . of climate change" (11). The arousal of guilt, the first part of Gore's soft rhetoric, thus draws in a once guarded and reluctant public into the environmental movement.

Most powerfully, he ends with his own point, making sure the spotlight is on his argument.

Dedication Molded by Frustration and Failure

After rendering us more receptive through the appeal to our sense of fear and guilt, Gore portrays himself as a warm, vulnerable, and dedicated leader. Rosteck and Frentz also explore the second part of Gore's soft rhetoric and argue that Gore establishes such *ethos* through "personal images of frustration and failure" that are interspersed throughout the documentary (9). In fact, Gore expresses his frustration right from the beginning of *An Inconvenient Truth*, confessing that "I've been trying to tell this story for a long time, and I feel as if I've failed to get the message across" (*An Inconvenient Truth*). We then meet a naively optimistic Gore who fails to change the world through the first Congressional hearings on global warming; he

The revised subheads show his advanced thinking and reflect the suggestions of his classmates from peer review.

Park 5

almost loses his son to a car accident; he loses the presidential election in 2000; and his family, a group of tobacco farmers, loses Gore's sister, Nancy, to lung cancer (*An Inconvenient Truth*).

He has fleshed out the points from his working draft and outline. He strategically cites the words from his research sources (Rosteck and Frentz) to show how he views the text through the lens of those sources.

What these stories of failure and pain have in common are that they "strengthen[ed]" Gore's "resolve" and dedication to the environmental movement (Rosteck and Frentz 7). His son's near-death accident taught him how anything taken for granted, even our beautiful environment, can easily vanish. His sister's death taught him the importance of connecting the dots, of connecting our actions to future consequences. His presidential election campaign "brought into clear focus the mission that [he] had been pursuing all these years," convincing him to "[start] giving the slideshow again" (*An Inconvenient Truth*).

Here, Wanjin demonstrates writing as synthesis, in that he puts the many sources in conversation with one another and adds his own voice to that dialogue.

Because these stories "persuasively [document] Gore's single-mindedness in pursuing his public cause, often at his own expense, through a lifetime of disappointments," Olson also agrees with Rosteck and Frentz that the stories of personal failure and frustration are essential to Gore's portrayal as a human, vulnerable, but dedicated leader (Olson 99). This portrayal places us "in a position to hear demand for action in a more sympathetic light," and when coupled with our sense of guilt, it renders Gore's message irresistible (Rosteck and Frentz 10). And Gore's message is clear. He "shows his evolution from interested observer to committed activist" with the goal of "invit[ing] our own journey of transformation" through the environmental movement (5).

Park 6

Rosteck, Frentz, and Olson's arguments have merit. Gore's transformation into a dedicated leader as a result of his frustrations and failures does create an "inviting impression that encourages [us] to join him . . . in social action" (Olson 102). However, they leave unexplored a crucial aspect of Gore's rhetoric. What is more responsible for creating the warm and inviting *ethos* is the portrayal of Gore as a lonely leader.

At this point, Wanjin will credit the research that has come before him and then build on it.

Through effective synthesis, he acknowledges the opposing positions before him, but then adds to them, as if adding another brick on a foundation. His original contribution as a writer is to focus on the concept of *ethos*.

* * *

No Longer the Soft Leader

Despite the success of his soft rhetoric as a lonely leader in *An Inconvenient Truth*, Gore sets it aside and instead adopts a heightened level of passion and sense of urgency two years later in his follow-up presentation at the TED 2008 Conference. The change reflects a shift in Gore's primary agenda. Gore's primary goal is no longer attracting support for the environmental movement, as he has already achieved that goal. Gore even acknowledges in his TED presentation the extent of his success. He claims that "68 percent of Americans now believe that human activity is responsible for global warming, [and] 69 percent believe that the Earth is heating up in a significant way" (Gore 9.21). Furthermore . . .

After a significant amount of evidence (not represented here in this abridged version of his essay), Wanjin moves to the next point in his argument. His heading refers to terms in his title, using diction to offer coherence and force in the writing.

He sets up the argument about Gore's 2008 TED talk through citing Gore's own words and leading the reader through the *logos* from his rough draft.

* * *

Even his body language is imbued with the increased level of passion. As he delivers the line, "we need a worldwide, global mobilization for renewable energy, conservation, efficiency, and a global transition to a low carbon economy," he not only

In this revision, Wanjin took the suggestion of his peers: he analyzes not only the images and words but also the embodied rhetoric or body language of Gore's persona.

Park 7

stresses each word, but also moves his hands up and down as he speaks, visually emphasizing each word (Gore, 4.39). He also twists his upper body from left to right, with his arms extended, as he says, "the political will has to be mobilized," visually enacting the word "mobilized" (Gore, 4.57).

Introducing new concepts such as "honor" and "heroism," Wanjin increases the power of his words and the significance of his argument. He chooses then to use a direct quote as evidence.

The heightened passion in Gore's rhetoric becomes fully manifested near the end of the presentation when Gore appeals to honor and heroism, both qualities we have treasured throughout history, as he stresses the need for a hero generation:

> What we need is another hero generation. We have to . . . understand that history has presented us with a choice. And we have to find a way to create, in the generation of those alive today, a sense of generational mission. (Gore, 17.39)

Gore then alludes to the "hero generation that brought democracy to the planet . . . another that ended slavery . . . and that gave women the right to vote" in order to illustrate the level of passion and dedication that we need to emulate as we fight the climate crisis (Gore, 18.44). The climate crisis is no longer just a global issue, but is now the "opportunity to rise to a challenge that is worthy of our best efforts" (Gore, 20.12). In his last efforts to move the audience toward increased sense of urgency and initiative, Gore closes with the line:

Park 8

> We are the generation about which, a thousand years from now, philharmonic orchestras and poets and singers will celebrate by saying, they were the ones that found it within themselves to solve this crisis and lay the basis for a bright and optimistic human future. (Gore, 20.47)

The appeal to *pathos,* the appeal to honor, heroism, and love for our children and the ensuing desire to promise them a better future illustrates how Gore sets aside his soft rhetoric and transforms into an impassioned leader, urging his audience to become heroes of our generation.

He carefully chooses his lines and concludes with a strong interpretation of their meaning.

Seesaw: Balancing the Soft and the Passionate Rhetorician

Gore adopts different styles of rhetoric in *An Inconvenient Truth* and in his follow-up presentation for the TED2008 Conference. Gore uses a two-part soft rhetoric in *An Inconvenient Truth* in order to draw in a guarded audience. He first compels us to feel fear and guilt through the juxtaposition of images of the beautiful and the doomed, making us more receptive to his environmental message. He then builds his *ethos* as a warm, dedicated, but still lonely leader, creating the inviting impression that draws us in and encourages us to join him in social action. When Gore delivers his TED presentation, his primary goal changes to motivating increased initiative and political will; he thus sets aside his soft rhetoric and adopts a heightened level of passion and sense of urgency.

Moving to his conclusion, Wanjin explains the final term in his paper: dynamic rhetoric.

He also brings in contemporary events, appealing to *kairos* to make the reader receptive to his argument.

The impassioned tone in Wanjin's own writing suggests that he is moving toward the end of his paper, and indeed he closes with a compelling call to action.

Park 9

This dynamic rhetoric, which Gore molds to fit his specific agenda, is the key to Gore's successful environmental leadership. He can be the warm, authentic, and soft leader when he wants to disarm a guarded audience. He can be the energized leader when he needs to inspire increased initiative in those that look up to him. In light of the recent sufferings caused by earthquakes in Haiti and Chile, the understanding of Gore's rhetoric offers us invaluable insight. In order to bring the countless pertinent but overlooked issues into the light à la Gore, we need to learn how to mold our rhetoric and master the art of balancing the soft and the passionate rhetorician in us.

The Works Cited, on a separate page, provides proper MLA citation for all the research Wanjin quoted, paraphrased, or summarized in the paper.

MLA suggests that writers include URLs in their Works Cited only when absolutely necessary to find the original source, but this student's professor required that they be included as part of the assignment.

Wanjin shows a well-balanced "iceberg of research"—including scholarly journals, popular articles, videos, and surveys.

Park 10

Works Cited

An Inconvenient Truth. Dir. Davis Guggenheim. Perf. Al Gore. Paramount Classics, 2006. DVD.

Gore, Al. "Al Gore's New Thinking on the Climate Crisis." Lecture. *TED: Ideas Worth Spreading*. TED.com, Apr. 2008. Web. 15 Jan. 2010. <http://www.ted.com/talks/lang/eng/al_gore.html.>

---. "Al Gore on Averting Climate Crisis." Lecture. *TED: Ideas Worth Spreading*. TED.com, Feb. 2006. Web. 20 Jan. 2010. <http://www.ted.com/talks/lang/eng/al_gore.html.>

Nielsen Company. "Global Consumers Vote Al Gore, Oprah Winfreyand Kofi Annan Most Influential to Champion Global

Warming Cause: Nielsen Survey." *Nielsen: Trends & Insights*. 2 July 2007. Web. 18 Jan. 2010. <http://nz.nielsen.com.>

Olson, Kathryn M. "Rhetorical Leadership and Transferable Lessons for Successful Social Advocacy in Al Gore's *An Inconvenient Truth*." *Argumentation & Advocacy* 44.2 (2007): 90-109. *Communication & Mass Media Complete*. EBSCO. Web. 24 Feb. 2010.

Rosteck, Thomas, and Thomas S. Frentz. "Myth and Multiple Readings in Environmental Rhetoric: The Case of *An Inconvenient Truth*." *Quarterly Journal of Speech* 95.1 (2009): 1-19. *Communication & Mass Media Complete*. EBSCO. Web. 24 Feb. 2010.

Schulte, Bret. "Saying It in Cinema." *U.S. News*. 28 Mar. 2006. Web. 17 Jan. 2010. <http://www.usnews.com/usnews/news/5warming.b.htm.>

The strong ending of Wanjin's paper shows how careful revision can help you develop a compelling argument and use the last lines to leave your reader with your own memorable rhetoric. Consider, too, how the ending of Wanjin's essay expanded to encompass a broader frame and then addressed the reader directly, using "you." Finally, you might notice that his revised essay analyzed rhetoric in all the ways we have learned to understand it through the chapters in this book: that is, rhetoric as texts that are spoken, written, visual, multimedia, as well as embodied. As you turn to craft your own research-based argument, keep in mind the many approaches to rhetoric explored here, and offer your own original insights by building on the work of writers and scholars who have come before you.

WRITER'S PRACTICE

MyWritingLab

To assess the writing you have done on your research-based argument, exchange your essay with a peer in class. Then, create annotations using the comment feature of your word-processing program and indicate what strategies are at work in each section of the essay. You might compare the draft to the final revision in those comments.

Alternatively, you could comment on your own essay, adding marginal notes about what improvements you made from the draft to the final revision. Then, you can summarize your revisions in a concluding reflective paragraph. That will inform both you and your instructor about your progress as a writer, researcher, and rhetorician.

THE WRITER'S PROCESS

In this chapter, you have learned strategies for visual mapping, organizing, outlining, drafting, and revising your research paper. You have explored ways of casting your argument and acquired concrete methods for integrating both written sources and visual texts as evidence for your argument. Chances are you have written the first full draft of your paper. But don't forget revision. Revision shows us the way that all *writing is rewriting*.

Sometimes, when writing, we may continue to revise our papers even after we have "finished." While you may be satisfied with your final essay when you turn it in, it is possible that you have set the groundwork for a longer research project that you may return to later in your college career. Or you may decide to seek publication for your essay in a school newspaper, magazine, or a national journal. In such cases, you may need to modify or expand on your argument for this new rhetorical situation; you may produce your own "director's cut"—a paper identical in topic to the original but developed in a significantly different fashion. Keep in mind that revision is indeed "re-vision."

SPOTLIGHTED ANALYSIS: FILM TRAILERS

MyWritingLab

Put your strategies of rhetorical analysis into practice and analyze a film trailer. Use the prewriting checklist below to help guide your analysis.

- How does the genre of the film (comedy? horror? drama? documentary?) affect the audience's response to its content? Does the trailer combine elements of different genres? What is the rhetorical effect of this combination?

- What is the "plot" of the trailer? Alternately, what argument is it making about the longer film? What does it suggest the film is about?
- What is its organizational structure? Chronological? Thematic? Chronological? Reverse chronological? What is the rhetorical significance of arrangement?
- What types of shots does the filmmaker use in the trailer (e.g., zoom-ins, cuts between scenes, fade in/fade out, montage)? What is the rhetorical effect of these choices?
- Is there a narrator? Voice-over? What is the effect on the audience?
- Is there any framing—a way of setting the beginning and end in context?
- How are *pathos, ethos,* and *logos* produced by the different cinematic techniques? For instance, is *pathos* created through close-ups of characters? Is *ethos* created through allusions to famous films or filmmaking techniques? Is *logos* constructed through the insertion of a narrator's viewpoint?
- What is the audience's point of identification in the trailer? Is the audience supposed to identify with a single narrator or protagonist? Does the film negotiate or manipulate the audience's reaction in any specific ways? How?
- How is setting used to construct a specific mood that affects the impact of the message of the trailer?

WRITING ASSIGNMENTS

MyWritingLab

1. **Visual Outline:** Create a visual representation of your research argument: a bubble web, graphic flowchart, idea roadmap, or a post-it diagram. Write an annotation for each part of your drawing, model, or storyboard to help you move from mass of material to coherent research-based essay. Start by writing down your thesis statement, and then jot down the main points you want to make in your essay. Next, beneath each of them, include supporting material, asking yourself, "What details should I include? What evidence or material from my sources supports this point? What subclaim do I want to make? What order would make the most sense for my reader?" Continue expanding on your visual outline until you have developed your points, started integrating your sources, and have arrived at a structure that seems both logical and persuasive.

2. **Detailed Written Outline:** Working with your research materials and notes, or building from your work in Writing Assignment 1, create a written outline of your ideas, including your thesis statement and using numbers and letters to indicate subsections of your argument. As appropriate, layer into your outline definitions, examples, counterarguments, and additional details. For added challenge, experiment with crafting rhetorical subheadings for the different sections. After you've completed your outline, go back and insert your primary and secondary sources where you'll use them to inform your argument. Insert actual quotations (with page numbers) from your research where possible, and also don't forget to cite your sources for both paraphrase and summary. When you're done, use your outline to check the balance of sources, the progression of ideas, and the complexity of your argument.

3. **Research-Based Argument:** Write a 12- to 15-page argumentative research paper on a topic of your choice. Use the types of sources that best speak to your research topic: these may include articles, books, interviews, field research, surveys (either published or that you conduct yourself), documentaries, Internet texts, and other primary and secondary sources, including visuals. Be sure to balance primary and secondary materials as you construct your argument. Ultimately, your goal should be proving a thesis statement with apt evidence, using appropriate rhetorical and argumentative strategies.

4. **Reflection Essay:** After you have completed your essay, compose a one-page reflection letter that serves as a self-evaluation. Think back on the development of your argument through research and revision. Include comments on the strengths of the essay, the types of revisions you made throughout your writing process, and how the collaborative process of peer review improved your essay. Conclude by explaining how you might continue to write about this issue in future academic or professional situations.

MyWritingLab Visit Ch. 6 Organizing and Writing Research Arguments in MyWritingLab to complete the Writer's Practices, Spotlighted Analyses, and Writing Assignments, and to test your understanding of the chapter objectives.

CHAPTER 7

Documenting Sources and Avoiding Plagiarism

Chapter Preview Questions

7.1 What do the terms "intellectual property" and "plagiarism" mean?

7.2 What are the conventions of documentation style?

7.3 How do I produce a Works Cited list in MLA style?

"Creativity always builds on the past." For many writers, the debt to those who have written before them is carefully acknowledged—whether through direct references, parenthetical citations, or a list of sources. Even visual artists and multimedia writers name their sources explicitly to show that they belong to a larger community of writers and that they respect the work of others.

But Justin Cone, a designer and animator based in Austin, Texas, makes this point more emphatically through the multimedia montage shown in Figure 7.1, from a short film called *Building on the Past*, which recycles and modifies public-domain film footage to make an argument about the relationship between creativity and legislation. The visuals are accompanied by a musical score and a voice-over that repeats the same sentence intermittently throughout the film: "Creativity always builds on the past." In the scene shown here, which opens the film, Cone re-edits the public-domain footage to run

FIGURE 7.1 Justin Cone's film, *Building on the Past*, remixed visuals and sound to emphasize how all our ideas rely on the works of those before us.

in reverse, showing the children running backward uphill instead of forward downhill, offering a powerful argument about how we rely on others for our own creativity. Cone expresses that idea visually through his strategy of organization, word choice, and design.

Your research project, too, will undoubtedly draw its strength from previous work on the subject. It should be a merger of your argument and the already existing dialogue on the topic. So even as you re-edit it to suit the purpose of your paper—by selecting passages to quote, paraphrase, summarize, or even argue against—it is crucial that you let your readers know where the ideas originated by providing what we call complete and ethical **source attribution**, or the acknowledgment and identification of your sources.

In this chapter, you'll learn how the rhetorical art of imitation—the process by which we all learn to write, compose, speak, and produce texts—differs from the theft of others' ideas, which is called **plagiarism**. We'll discuss why it is important to respect the work of others—which in legal terms is now called *intellectual property*—and you'll acquire strategies for avoiding unintentional plagiarism. Finally, we'll provide a means of understanding the process of constructing in-text and end-of-paper citations, and we'll explain the logic of MLA, APA, CSE, and Chicago documentation styles. You'll discover that there is actually logic governing the arrangement of elements in documentation practices, much as there is logic shaping mathematical or chemical formulas, and that the specific order of a style addresses the values of a particular audience. Moreover, you'll find that correct source attribution actually builds your *ethos* as a writer and researcher by confirming your membership in that scholarly community.

7.1 What do the terms "intellectual property" and "plagiarism" mean?

UNDERSTANDING INTELLECTUAL PROPERTY AND PLAGIARISM

In ancient times, **rhetorical imitation**, or the practice of taking after others, was a celebrated form of instruction. Students carefully would copy a speech out word by word, studying the word choice, organization, rhythm, and art of the work. That is, students would compose a rhetorical analysis (as you have done in earlier chapters) to understand the speech's strategies of argumentation, use of rhetorical appeals, and organization. Finally, students would rearrange and reuse elements of the speeches they studied, including content (words) and form (arrangement), to create their own speeches. Through this process of imitation and reediting, the earliest students learned to become great rhetors.

This ancient process is actually very similar to your task as a modern writer. After analyzing articles and studying argumentative strategies from samples of student writing, at some point you need to move on to create your own text, inspired by what you learned and perhaps reediting parts, since "creativity builds on the past." But importantly, today, we don't just borrow and recycle the ideas of others without acknowledgement. We need to be aware that ideas, not just actual words but also the concepts developed by others, must be considered in terms of **intellectual property**, that is, words and ideas often legally belong to someone else as a form of property. In this increasingly litigious society, you need to understand when to stop imitation and when to start acknowledging your sources so that you preserve the rights of others and protect yourself as a developing writer.

Plagiarism—using another person's idea as your own—was not a crime in classical times, according to scholars Peter Morgan and Glenn Reynolds. But with the invention of printing technology, copyright law, and a cultural emphasis on the profitability of intellectual concepts came a concern about taking someone else's ideas—and therefore their earning potential—whether intentionally or unintentionally. Consequently, in colleges and universities today, plagiarism can lead to suspension or even expulsion because the perpetrator is charged with literally stealing someone else's *intellectual property*. In professional circles, charges of plagiarism can ruin a career and destroy the credibility of the writer.

But there is another reason for acknowledging sources and avoiding plagiarism: as we discussed in Chapter 5, research is always a conversation with those who came before. This reason is an ethical, not legal one. As you work with sources, realize that the claims you are able to make are in fact based on the foundation provided by others. Identifying your sources thus becomes an ethical writing strategy that you practice out of respect for those who have come before you. By acknowledging their names, ideas, and words, you contribute to a body of knowledge, graciously extending thanks to those who have paved the way. Therefore, while there are legal issues related to intellectual property, copyright law, and "fair use" that you need to know about, if you keep a principle of *respect* in mind, you will rarely fall into the trap of inadvertently "stealing" someone's work.

AT A GLANCE

When to Cite Sources

Remember that you must provide citations for your sources when you:

- Quote a source word for word
- Summarize or paraphrase information or ideas from another source in your own words
- Incorporate statistics, tables, figures, charts, graphs, or other visuals into your work from another source

You do not need to provide citations for the following:

- Your own observations, ideas, and opinions
- Factual information that is widely available in a number of sources ("common knowledge")
- Proverbs, sayings, or familiar quotations

Avoiding Unintentional Plagiarism

When you're working with many sources, it can be all too easy to fall into habits that lead you to assimilate the information you've read and then begin to think the ideas are your own. Indeed, unintentional plagiarism can happen for many reasons: fatigue, oversaturation of information, poor memory, or sloppy note taking. However, as we have discussed, plagiarism is a serious offense, even if it occurs unintentionally. To avoid accidentally taking someone else's ideas or words as your own, you might follow two practices:

- First, develop effective ways of taking notes while reading through your sources. If you come across a particularly relevant or striking quotation, don't just underline it or highlight it. Copy it directly into your notes or your research log and encase it in quotation marks; alternately, paraphrase it immediately, being careful to paraphrase in a way that distinguishes it clearly from the original phrasing. As you work with the material, jot down ideas how you might use the quotation, your own analysis, or how it connects to the topic you're exploring. Most importantly, write down the page number and source attribution right next to the quotation or paraphrase so that there's no confusion about where it came from.
- Second, review the guidelines for citation practices in the At a Glance box so that you make sure that you give attribution as needed when using direct quotations or specific ideas from your sources.

These practices might seem to add extra steps to your research process, but they help support you in developing a more persuasive—and ethical—argument. Keep in mind that, regardless of the circumstances, many colleges and universities have plagiarism policies that do not distinguish between intentional and unintentional plagiarism; the act will bring consequences ranging from a failure in the course to expulsion.

Working with Images and Multimedia as Sources

When you choose to include visuals or multimedia in your writing, keep in mind that it is not enough to include just the source and provide the citation for it. You also need to spend a few moments thinking about issues of **copyright** and **permissions**. Since oral culture gave way to print culture, copyright—or the *right* to *copy*—has been a pressing legal issue. However, with the advent of digital technologies, the problem has been exacerbated; with the prevalence of photo scanners, digital copy and paste tools, cell phone cameras, seemingly omniscient search engines, and the ever-expanding reach of the Internet, the possibilities for copying, sharing, and distributing materials are in more people's reach than ever before. As a writer yourself, it is important that you respect copyright restrictions and ethically attribute all your sources that you use in your own writing—including visual texts.

When you browse through catalogs of images, you need to record the source of each image you decide to use. If you have found a visual (such as a photograph, chart, ad) from a print source and scanned it into a computer, you need to list the print source in full as well as information about the original image (the name of the photographer, the image title, and the date). If you have copied an image from the Internet, you need to note as much of the full source information as you can find: the website's author, the title, the sponsoring organization, and the date. Listing Google as your source is not sufficient; be sure to find the original source and list it in full. Keep careful track as you locate images, give appropriate credit when you use them. If you plan to publish your work online or submit it to a campus publication, use public domain images (such as from the Library of Congress), select from images licensed appropriately through Creative Commons, or write the image's owner, asking for permission to use it.

UNDERSTANDING DOCUMENTATION STYLE

7.2 What are the conventions of documentation style?

So far in this chapter, we've emphasized the importance of *source attribution* as a means of avoiding plagiarism. But it might interest you to know that the method you use to provide information about your source corresponds to the values of a particular academic community. This is where **documentation** comes in—the responsible and correct acknowledgment of your sources and influences according to a specific *style*. Today, with software programs that can format your source attributions for you, it may seem confusing or even frustrating to worry about which documentation style to use. But realize that the guidelines for each style have a rhetorical purpose corresponding to the way that knowledge is constructed for that community (see the table below). Taking a moment to understand the logic behind the styles will help you practice proper citation without having to look up every instance of how to do it. In this chapter, we will focus on MLA style, but by familiarizing yourself with the rationale between the different citation styles, you can identify which ones might be most appropriate to your chosen discipline or your major and so build your *ethos* as a writer by showing that you understand how to speak the language of a particular academic community.

DOCUMENTATION STYLE	COMMUNITY OF WRITERS	DEFINING FEATURES	PURPOSE OF FEATURES	EXAMPLE
MLA	Modern Language Association (language, literature, writing, philosophy, and humanities scholars and teachers)	Citation begins with author's name (last name first, full first name), then publication information, date, medium of publication (then, if a Website, date you accessed it).	Knowledge advances based on individual author's contributions; thus, names are prioritized over dates; place of publication matters for building *ethos*.	McCloud, Scott. *Understanding Comics.* New York: Harper Perennial, 1994. Print.
APA	American Psychological Association (psychologists and social scientists)	Publication date immediately follows designation of author, multiple authors may be listed (last name and initials), titles are in sentence style (first word capitalized, rest lowercase).	Since knowledge advances based on dated contributions to the field, dates are prioritized; most writing is collaborative, so up to six authors are listed; titles, typically long and technical, are in lowercase.	Bruce, V., & Green, P. (1990). *Visual perception: Physiology, psychology, and ecology* (2nd ed.). London, England: Erlbaum.
CSE	Council of Science Editors (such as biology and physics)	References include last name and date; often superscript numbers are used.	Like APA style, emphasis is on knowledge advancing through studies and scientific research; a heavily cited style of writing.	[1]Goble, JL. Visual disorders in the handicapped child. New York (NY): M. Dekker; 1984. p. 265.
Chicago	University of Chicago (business writers, professional writers, and those in fine arts)	Sources are listed as footnotes or endnotes and include page numbers.	Knowledge is incremental, and readers like to check facts as they go along.	[2]Scott McCloud, *Understanding Comics* (New York: Harper Perennial, 1994), 33.

In-Text Citations: Documentation as Cross-Referencing

In addition to responsible source attribution, documentation also functions as a *road map* for your audience to locate the source—both in your bibliography and in the library or online. Accordingly, for sources appearing as **in-text citations**—or quoted right in the essay itself—the purpose of proper documentation is to point readers clearly to the list of sources at the end of the paper. The way this works is through **cross-referencing**, such that the reference in the text of the essay should correspond to the first word of the source listed in the bibliography.

Let's take a look at an *in-text citation* from Grady Thompson's paper on online activism and social media. As you can see, he follows typical MLA style that always places such references inside parentheses to set them off from the rest of the writing. Notice that the last name and page number in parentheses point the reader directly to the author's name in the "Works Cited" list.

. . . over 94% of contributors to the Facebook "Save Darfur Cause" donated only once, meaning that most of the financial contributions came from a very small number of "hyperactivists" (Lewis, Gray, and Meierhenrich 2).

* * *

Works Cited

Ayers, Michael. "Comparing Feminist Identity in Online and Offline Feminist Activists." *Cyberactivism: Online Theory and Practice.* Ed. Martha McCaughey. New York: Routledge, 2003. 145-64. Print.

Lewis, Kevin, Kurt Gray and Jens Meierhenrich. "The Structure of Online Activism." *Sociological Science 1* (2014): 1-9. *Academic Search Premier*. Web. 2 Feb. 2015.

Yang, Guobin. "Online Activism." *Journal of Democracy* 20.3 (2009): 33-36. *Project Muse.* Web. 2 Feb. 2015.

In his Works Cited (excerpted here), Grady has alphabetized the list by authors' last names, which corresponds to MLA documentation style and the logic of the humanities as an academic community. Readers need only scan down the page to look for the last name of the source cited earlier. This makes it very easy, and once you understand that this *cross-referencing logic* governs all MLA documentation, then you can begin to understand how to document sources—even new multimedia sources.

If there is no author to put in your parenthetical citation, begin with the first word of the source entry on the Works Cited page. Here is an example from Jamie Kesner's paper on the politics behind the World Cup, where she quotes an article from *The Economist.* Many of the articles in this magazine are collectively written, so no authors are named. In this case, Jamie uses the first words of the title. See how the cross-referencing logic of MLA style helps readers find the source in the Works Cited list:

> FIFA itself has reported that several exhibition matches before the 2010 World Cup were rigged ("Beautiful Game").
>
> * * *
>
> Works Cited
>
> "Beautiful Game, Dirty Business." *Economist* 7 June 2014: 55. Web. 12 Oct. 2014.

Notice also that Jamie does not list a page number since her online source does not include them. However, the attribution is still clear. Using this system, you can easily direct your readers to the correct source.

But there are two additional cases that can be tricky. First, occasionally you might come across a phrase or sentence that is one of your sources has quoted and decide that you, too, want to include that direct quotation in your own essay. Here's an example: when reading danah boyd's book, *It's*

Complicated: The Social Life of Networked Teens, you come across a line she quotes from cultural critic John Perry Barlow where he describes the Internet as a place that allowed for "identities [that] have no bodies." Given time, the best practice would be to flip to boyd's Works Cited, find the Barlow source citation, go online or to the library and find the Barlow text, and read it yourself to better understand his argument. However, in some cases, you might not have access to Barlow's original source and so decide to simply incorporate his quote into your own essay. To do that, you need to cite the quotation in a way that makes it clear that these are *Barlow's* words, not boyd's. Here are two options:

> As John Perry Barlow has suggested, the internet is a place that allows for "identities [that] have no bodies" (qtd. in boyd 37).
>
> The internet provides a space for people to fashion and re-fashion themselves; it is, in effect, inherently a home for "identities [that] have no bodies" (Barlow, qtd. in boyd 37).

Your Works Cited in each case would be identical, directing the reader toward boyd's text:

> boyd, danah. *It's Complicated: The Social Life of Networked Teens*. New Haven: Yale P, 2014.

Both versions of the in-text citation make it clear that you found the direct quotation in boyd's book but that Barlow is the quote's author.

Here's a second complicated citation issue: how would you handle creating an in-text citation for an author when you will be listing multiple sources by that author in your Works Cited? For instance, as we can see in this case, putting only the last name in parentheses would not suffice since the reader does not know which source by Clive Thompson the quotation is from.

> . . . a screenshot is "photography for life on the screen" (Thompson).
>
> Works Cited
>
> Thompson, Clive. *Smarter Than You Think: How Technology Is Changing Our Minds for the Better*. New York: Penguin, 2014. Print.
>
> ---. "The Invention of the Snapshot Changed the Way We Viewed the World." *Smithsonian*. Sept., 2014. Web. 12 June 2015.
>
> ---. "The Most Important Thing on the Internet is the Screenshot." *Wired,* 24 Mar. 2015. Web. 11 June 2015.

To resolve this issue, you need to list *both* the author's name and the first major keyword of the correct title in your in-text citation; following this practice, our example above becomes more clear:

> . . . a screenshot is "photography for life on the screen" (Thompson, "The Most Important").

Let's look at how Stephanie Parker mastered this situation. Here are two examples from her essay—an excerpt from which appears later in this chapter—where Stephanie cites from different works by Daniel Shim. Notice how the keyword following the author's last name functions as the *cross-reference* to the correct source:

Example 1: Here, since Stephanie mentioned the author in the sentence, she needs only include the keywords and the page number if there was one, but since this is an online text, there is no page number to cite.

> Daniel Shim relates his own experience: "I was born in Canada in white communities & I grew up to be like them. Soompi has given me knowledge about Asian culture that I would not get from my school or family" (Online interview).

Example 2: In this next case, Stephanie has not mentioned the author by name in the sentence, so she includes the author's last name as well as the first keyword of the source title in her MLA in-text citation. Moreover, since she is citing an article title, she includes the quotation marks; for a book title, she would italicize the keyword:

> . . . his YouTube videoblog, in which he comments on events in his daily life and makes fun of Asian stereotypes, has almost 30,000 subscribers and is the 4th most popular comedy blog in all of Canada (Shim, "Shimmycocopuffsss's").

Now let's look at the Works Cited list to locate those two sources. Note the color coding to see how the *cross-reference* system operates.

Works Cited

Shim, Daniel. Online interview. 12 Nov. 2008.

---. "Shimmycocopuffsss's Profile Page." YouTube. 27 Nov. 2008. Web. 28 Nov. 2008.

---. "Wasabi Boy–No Engrish." YouTube. 5 Mar. 2008. Web. 28 Nov. 2008.

Using Footnotes and Endnotes

Although MLA style relies primarily on in-text citations and a final bibliography—unlike Chicago style, which uses primarily footnotes or endnotes—there are two specific cases when you will want to include a note. First, if you want to include extra explanatory information (definitions of key terms, background material, alternative perspectives, or historical data) but don't want to break the flow of your argument, you can provide that information in a **content note**, whether as an endnote, which appears at the end of your paper, before the bibliography, or as a footnote, which appears at the bottom or *foot* of the page. Each would be anchored to your main argument through use of a superscript numeral that links the note to that particular point in your essay.

A second use of notes offers you the chance to point readers to additional information without the need for an explanatory narrative. In this case, you would create a **bibliographic note**, simply listing additional sources in that note that relate to a specific point. This strategy not only directs your reader to supporting materials but also builds your *ethos* as a writer and researcher who is situating her work in terms of the larger conversation about your topic.

7.3 How do I produce a Works Cited list in MLA style?

PRODUCING A WORKS CITED LIST IN MLA STYLE

You've seen how documentation works as a cross-referencing system, in which the in-text citation within parentheses points the reader directly to the source in the bibliography. In MLA style, the bibliography is called a **Works Cited** list because it refers explicitly to the works (or sources) you have cited (or quoted) in your paper. Sometimes a Works Cited list is accompanied by another section called a **Works Consulted** list, which names all the other sources you may have read and studied but did not actually quote from in your final revision. You can also combine the two by creating a **Works Cited and Consulted List**.

Realize that this list of sources provides a moment of *ethos* building as well: by listing both works *cited* and works *consulted*, you demonstrate your research process and new knowledge. You also invite your readers to explore the topic in depth with you.

LOGIC OF MLA STYLE

AUTHOR'S NAME	TITLE	PUBLICATION INFORMATION
List the author's name first, by last name. If there are multiple authors, include them all, following the order listed in the publication. If there is no author, use the publishing organization (if available) or just move on to the title.	The title comes next. For books and films, italicize the title. For shorter pieces (such as articles, TV shows, songs, etc.), put the title in quotation marks, with the larger publication (the collection of essays, TV series, or album) italicized.	Last comes publication information: place, publisher or company, date, and medium of publication. For shorter pieces, include the complete range of page numbers, followed by a period. For online articles, list the medium of publication (Web) followed by a period and conclude with a date of access.

PRINT EXAMPLE:

Satrapi, Marjane. *Persepolis: The Story of a Childhood.* New York: Pantheon, 2004. Print.

ONLINE EXAMPLE

Yagoda, Ben. "You Need to Read This: How Need to Vanquished Have to, Must, and Should." *Slate*. Washington Post Newsweek Interactive, 17 July 2006. Web. 20 July 2006.

Documentation for Print and Online Text-Based Sources

Below, you'll find example citations for print and online text-based sources that apply the logic of MLA style. Use them as a reference to guide your own citation practices:

- Single-Author Book
- Multiple-Author Book
- Electronic Books (e-books)
- Anthology or Edited Collection of Essays
- Introduction, Preface, Foreword, or Afterword in a Book
- Two or More Books by the Same Author
- Article in a Collection of Essays
- Article from a Print Journal
- Article from a Journal Published Only Online
- Article from a Popular Magazine Published Monthly (print and online)
- Article from a Newspaper or News Website
- Article Found through a Database (including Google Books)
- Website (entire)
- Page from a Website
- Definition
- Letter to the Editor
- News Op-Ed
- Letter or Memo

- Dissertation (unpublished)
- Government Publication
- Interview
- Survey
- Email
- Blog Post
- Facebook Post
- Tweet
- Reddit Post
- Text Message, Chat Room Discussion, or Real-Time Communication

Single-Author Book

Satrapi, Marjane. *Persepolis: The Story of a Childhood*. New York: Pantheon, 2004. Print.

Multiple-Author Book

Heath, Joseph, and Andrew Potter. *Nation of Rebels: Why Counterculture Became Consumer Culture*. New York: Harper, 2004. Print.

Booth, Wayne C., Gregory G. Colomb, and Joseph M. Williams. *The Craft of Research*. 3rd ed. Chicago: U of Chicago P, 2008. Print.

For an e-book, list the type of medium at the end of the citation (e.g., Nook file, Kindle file, iBooks file, Google Books file). When in doubt, use the term "Digital file" at the end instead.

Electronic Books (e-books)

Brooks, Max. *World War Z: An Oral History of the Zombie War*. N.p.: Crown, 2006. iBook file.

Davis, Mike. *City of Quartz*. N.p.: Verso, 2006. Nook file.

Anthology or Edited Collection of Essays

Waggoner, Zach, ed. *Terms of Play: Essays on Words That Matter in Videogame Theory*. Jefferson: McFarland, 2013. Print.

Andrews, Maggie, and Mary M. Talbot, eds. *All the World and Her Husband: Women in Twentieth-Century Consumer Culture*. London: Cassell, 2000. Print.

Introduction, Preface, Foreword, or Afterword in a Book

Gerbner, George. Foreword. *Cultural Diversity and the U.S. Media*. Ed. Yahya R. Kamalipour and Theresa Carillia. New York: State U of New York P, 1998. xv-xvi. Print.

Cohen, Mitchell, and Dennis Hale. Introduction. *The New Student Left.* Ed. Cohen and Hale. Boston: Beacon Press, 1967. xvii-xxxiii. Print.

Two or More Books by the Same Author

When you have two or more texts by the same author in your works cited, use dashes in the place of the author's last name for the second book. Alphabetize by the title of the book or article.

Palmer, William J. *Dickens and New Historicism.* New York: St. Martin's, 1997. Print.

---. *The Films of the Eighties: A Social History.* Carbondale: Southern Illinois UP, 1993. Print.

Article in a Collection of Essays

Boichel, Bill. "Batman: Commodity as Myth." *The Many Lives of the Batman*. Ed. Roberta Pearson and William Uricchio. New York: BFI, 1991. 4-17. Print.

Article from a Print Journal

Roberts, Garyn G. "Understanding the Sequential Art of Comic Strips and Comic Books and Their Descendants in the Early Years of the New Millennium." *Journal of American Culture* 27.2 (2004): 210-17. Print.

Article from a Journal Published Only Online

Note that for online sources, the most the most recent MLA Handbook states, "You should include a URL as supplementary information only when the reader probably cannot locate the source without it or when your instructor requires it" (182).

Martin, Paul. "The Pastoral and the Sublime in *Elder Scrolls IV: Oblivion*." *Game Studies* 11.3 (2011): n. pag. Web. 8 Nov. 2012.

Parish, Rachel. "Sappho and Socrates: The Nature of Rhetoric." *Kairos* 17.1 (2012): n. pag. Web. 12 Dec. 2012.

Article from a Popular Magazine Published Monthly (print and online)

Maney, Kevin. "The New Face of IBM." *Wired* July 2005. Web. 18 Aug. 2005.

Sontag, Susan. "Looking at War." *New Yorker* 9 Dec. 2002: 43-48. Print.

Article from a Newspaper or News Website

Haughney, Christine. "Women Unafraid of Condo Commitment." *New York Times* 10 Dec. 2006, sec. 11: 1. Print.

Cowell, Alan. "Book Buried in Irish Bog Is Called a Major Find." *New York Times*. New York Times, 27 July 2006. Web. 31 July 2006.

Quade, Alex. "Elite Team Rescues Troops Behind Enemy Lines." CNN.com. Cable News Network, 19 Mar. 2007. Web. 19 Mar. 2007.

If you use a database (such as ProQuest, LexisNexis, or EBSCO) to locate an article, you include that information in your citation. The MLA Handbook includes Google Books under this category.

Article Found through a Database (including Google Books)

Chun, Alex. "Comic Strip's Plight Isn't Funny." *Los Angeles Times* 27 Apr. 2006, Home ed.: E6. *LexisNexis*. Web. 4 May 2006.

Gottesman, Jane. *Game Face: What Does a Female Athlete Look Like?* New York: Random, 2001. *Google Book Search*. Web. 15 July 2004.

Rosette, Ashleigh Shelby and Robert W. Livingston. "Failure is Not an Option for Black Women: Effects of Organizational Performance on Leaders with Single versus Dual-Subordinate Identities." *Journal of Experimental Psychology* 48.5 (2012): 1162-1167. *Academic Search Premier*. Web. 5 Jan. 2013.

Website (entire)

Wounded Warrior Project. N.p. 2015. Web. 12 Feb. 2015.

Library of Congress. N.p. N.d. Web. 1 Jan. 2014.

Page from a Website

"Marie Curie—Facts." *NobelPrize.org*. N.d. Web. 14 June 2015.

"Calamity Jane—Rowdy Woman of the West." *Legends of America*. N.d. Web. 3 Feb. 2013.

Definition

"Diversity." *American Heritage Dictionary of the English Language*. 4th ed. Houghton, 2000. Print.

"Greek Mythology." *Wikipedia*. Wikimedia Foundation, 16 Apr. 2010. Web. 5 May, 2010.

Letter to the Editor

Tucker, Rich Thompson. "High Cost of Cheap Coal." Letter. *National Geographic* July 2006: 6-7. Print.

News Op-Ed

Woodlief, Wayne. "Time Heals Biden's Self-Inflicted Wound." *Boston Herald* 26 Jan. 2007: 19. Print.

Letter or Memo

Greer, Michael. Letter to the authors. 30 July 2006. Print.

Dissertation (unpublished)

Li, Zhan. "The Potential of America's Army: The Video Game as Civilian-Military Public Sphere." Diss. Massachusetts Institute of Technology, 2004. Print.

Government Publication

United States. Census Bureau. Housing and Household Economics Statistics Division. *Poverty Thresholds 2005*. US Census Bureau, 1 Feb. 2006. Web. 20 May 2006.

Interview

Tullman, Geoffrey. Personal interview. 21 May 2006.

Cho, Ana. Telephone interview. 4 June 2005.

When writing a citation for an interview, include the mode of interview (e.g., telephone interview, Skype interview).

Survey

Meyer-Teurel, Fiona. "Hacking and Modding in Video Games." Survey. 23 May 2013.

For a survey you conduct yourself, list yourself as the author, then the name of the survey (or the word survey), and the date you conducted it.

Email

Tisbury, Martha. "Re: Information Overload." Message to Max Anderson. 27 Mar. 2008. Email.

Blog Post

Gardner, Traci (Tengrrl). "Oh Internet, You Pandora's Box!" *Pedablogical*. Pedablogical, 13 Apr. 2009. Web. 14 June 2013.

When citing an online posting (from a blog, Twitter, Reddit, etc.), use the author's real name if you know it, followed by the username in parenthesis. If the real name is unknown, simply list the username.

When writing a citation for a Tweet, include the entire tweet as the title.

Facebook Post

Pond, Amelia. "Time travel is possible . . ." Facebook.com. 24 Apr. 2010. Web. 25 Apr. 2010.

The White House. "Spurring Innovation, Creating Jobs." Facebook.com. 5 Aug. 2009. Web. 13 Feb. 2010.

Tweet

Booker, Cory (CoryBooker). "I'd rather have my ship sunk at sea than rot in the harbor. To exceed our limits we must test them; to fly we must risk falling." 11 June 2013, 6:51 a.m. Tweet.

Reddit Post

Examples of Good. "My Mom Made Me Lunch." Reddit.com. Fri. 23 Apr. 2013.

Text Message, Chat Room Discussion, or Real-Time Communication

Zhang, Zhihao. "Revision Suggestions." *Cross-Cultural Rhetoric Chat Room*. Stanford U. 25 May 2006. Web. 5 June 2008.

Documentation for Visual, Audio, and Multimedia Sources

MLA documentation style was devised principally with text-based images in mind. However, since some of the materials for your research project might be visual or multimodal texts, you need to consider ways to adapt the principles of MLA citation style to these different forms.

This may seem daunting at first, but if you remember the logic of MLA style, you'll find you can apply the basic principles of this format to any medium. In a humorous but informative YouTube video, "How to Cite a Cereal Box in MLA 2009," Martine Courant Rife makes exactly this point by taking her viewer through the steps for citing a cereal box (because, as she says, "if you can cite a cereal box, you can cite anything"). The key is to examine and evaluate your source closely—for a cereal box, looking at each side of the box, even inside—and then consider how the information provided there helps you fill out the categories of *author*, *title*, and various *publication* information that we discussed above.

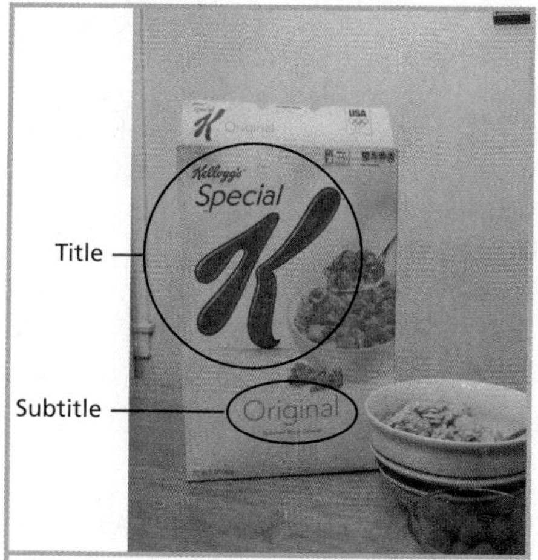

FIGURE 7.2 Examining the front of the cereal box provides us with the title for our citation.

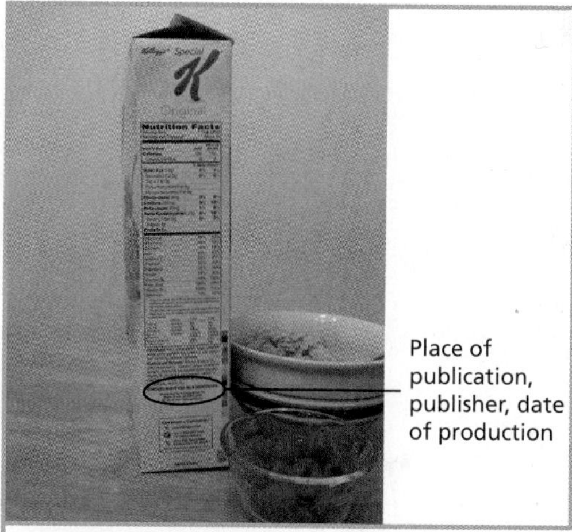

FIGURE 7.3 Close analysis of the side shows us the place of publication, publisher, and the date of production.

Consider how we might cite this Special K box. As Figure 7.2 shows, while there is no clear author, we can identify the title as "Kellogg's Special K: Original." Publication data can be found on the side: as seen in Figure 7.3, we can find place of publication (Battle Creek, MI), publisher or corporate sponsor (Kellogg Sales Co.), and date of production or publication (2013) in the fine print. The medium itself is clear: It's a cereal box. Our citation, then, following the model of a citation for a print text, might look something like this:

"Kellogg's Special K: Original." Battle Creek: Kellogg, 2013.
  Cereal Box.

While there may be no official way to confirm the accuracy of this particular citation, the principles we used to create it follow the rationale of MLA form. Below, you'll find example citations for many types of media texts you might use in your research paper. However, if the type of source you are using does not appear in the list below, simply follow the logical steps for citing print and online sources (as we did with Special K).

- Cartoon or Comic
- Photograph
- Painting
- Screenshot
- Advertisement
- Cover (Magazine, Book, DVD, etc.)
- Map
- TV Program
- Film
- Online Video
- Website
- Website Homepage
- Videogame
- Radio Essay
- Lecture
- Presentation or Speech
- Performance

Editorial Cartoon or Comic Strip

Grondal, Cal. "Reasonable Search." Cartoon. *Cagle.com* 11 June 2013. Web. 12 June 2013.

Pastis, Stephen. "Pearls before Swine." Comic strip. *Comics.com* 18 Apr. 2006. Web. 16 May 2006.

Wilkinson, Signe. Cartoon. *San Francisco Chronicle* 1 June 2010: A13. Print.

Photograph

When writing a citation for a photograph you took yourself, list yourself as the photographer, then the title or location of the photo, the year you took it, and then the file type.

Alfano, Christine. "Golden Gate Bridge, San Francisco." 2004. JPEG file.

Goldin, Nan. *Jimmy Paulette & Misty in a Taxi, NYC*. 1991. Photograph. San Francisco Museum of Modern Art, San Francisco.

Liss, Steve. "Trailer-Park Picnic in Utah, 1997." *Great Images of the 20th Century*. Ed. Kelly Knauer. New York: Time Books, 1999. 41-42. Print.

Sherman, Cindy. *Untitled Film Still*. 1978. Museum of Modern Art. *The Complete Untitled Film Stills of Cindy Sherman*. Web. 7 July 2006.

Painting

Warhol, Andy. *Self Portrait*. 1986. Andy Warhol Museum, Pittsburgh. *The Warhol: Collections*. Web. 3 Aug. 2006.

Screenshot

Fielding, Geri. "Happy Doggie." *Instagram*, 24 Feb. 2010. Web. 26 Feb. 2010.

"Star Wars Galaxies." Sony Online Entertainment, n.d. Web. 5 Feb. 2005.

Advertisement

Diet Coke. Advertisement. *Wired* Oct. 2012: 78. Print.

Doritos. Advertisement. ESPN. 7 June 2013. Television.

Nike. "We Are All Witnesses." Advertisement. *Nikebasketball*. 3 Jan. 2006. Web. 15 June 2006.

Palmolive Soap. "Would Your Husband Marry You Again?" *Harper's Bazaar*. 1921. *Ad*Access*. Web. 25 Feb. 2013.

Cover (Magazine, Book, DVD, etc.)

Adams, Neil. "Deadman." *Comics* VF.com. Comics VF, 1978. Web. 23 Oct. 2005.

Cover. *Gameinformer*. May 2013. Print.

Map

Hong Kong Disneyland Guide. Map. Disney, 2006. Print.

"Providence, Rhode Island." Map. *Google Maps*. Google, 11 Mar. 2012. Web. 1 Mar. 2012.

TV Program

"The Diet Wars." *Frontline*. PBS, 2004. Web. 16 Aug. 2006.

"Farmer Guy." Prod. Seth McFarlane, et al. *Family Guy*. Fox, 12 May 2013. *hulu*. Web. 15 May 2013.

Film

Beyond Killing Us Softly: The Impact of Media Images on Women and Girls. Dir. Margaret Lazarus and Renner Wunderlich. Prod. Cambridge Documentary Films, 2000. Film.

"A Brief History of America." *Bowling for Columbine*. Dir. Michael Moore. United Artists, 2002. *Bowling for Columbine*, n.d. Web. 13 June 2006.

Online Video

Ingham, Ben. "An African Race." Vimeo. 7 June 2013. Web. 13 June 2013.

Wesch, Michael. "A Vision of Students Today." YouTube. 12 Oct. 2007. Web. 31 Mar. 2010.

Website

Cartoonists Index. MSNBC, n.d. Web. 4 Nov. 2005.

Website Homepage

Corrigan, Edna. Home page. *Ednarules*. N.p., n.d. Web. 24 Oct. 2005.

Videogame

Infinity Ward. *Modern Warfare 2*. Activision. 2009. Playstation 3.

Rovio Entertainment. *Angry Birds Space*. Apple App Store. 2012. iPhone.

Second Life. Your World. Linden Labs, n.d. Web. 7 May 2006.

Radio Essay

Ydstie, John. "Book Marketing Goes to the Movies." *Morning Edition.* Natl. Public Radio. 18 July 2006. Radio.

Lecture

Connors, Fiona. "Visual Literacy in Perspective." English 210B. Boston U. 24 Oct. 2004. Lecture.

Delagrange, Susan, and Ben McCorkle. "What Is a Public Service Announcement (PSA)?" Writing II: Rhetorical Composing. Coursera. May 2013. Lecture.

Presentation or Speech

Bu, Lisa. "How Books Can Open Your Mind." TED Conference Feb. 2013. Lecture. *TED: Ideas Worth Spreading*. TED, May 2013. Web. 23 May 2013.

Jobs, Steve. Commencement Address. Stanford U., Palo Alto, 12 June 2005. *iTunes U*. Apple. Web. 27 July 2006.

Reagan, Ronald. "The Space Shuttle *Challenger* Tragedy Address." 28 Jan. 1986. *American Rhetoric.* Web. 5 Mar. 2006.

Rheingold, Howard. "Technologies of Cooperation." Annenberg Center for Communication. U of Southern California, Los Angeles. 3 Apr. 2006. Speech.

Performance

Phedre. By Jean Racine. Dir. Ileana Drinovan. Pigott Theater, Memorial Hall, Stanford, 10-13 May 2006. Performance.

Student Paper in MLA Style

To see how texts you might encounter in your research process today will range across varied formats and media, let's consult a student paper by Stephanie Parker, who focused on how digital communities, such as Soompi (a Korean pop culture Website), have transformed ideas of racial identity. Stephanie incorporated an impressive array of both print and electronic sources in her project, including books, book chapters, and journal articles; e-books, online newspaper articles, and telephone and online interviews; YouTube videos, Websites, screenshots, blog posts, and more.

Parker 1

Stephanie Parker
Dr. Christine Alfano
PWR 2 Cultural Interfaces
7 December 2008

Soompi and the "Honorary Asian": Shifting Identities in the Digital Age

Every morning at 7:00 am, Norwegian James Algaard turns on his computer and joins Soompi IRC: a chatroom for members of a Korean Pop Culture discussion forum. James' daily entrance into the chatroom is enthusiastically greeted by online acquaintances who know him as <SeungHo>, a connoisseur of Korean

Stephanie heads her paper in proper MLA form, with her name, her instructor's name, the class title, and the date, all flush to the left margin.

Parker 2

Hip Hop and a collector of limited edition sneakers. Seungho Lee was born in South Korea, but was adopted by a Norwegian family; websites like Soompi are his only connection to Korean culture. Thousands of miles away in Los Angeles, it is 10:00 pm when I, an American with a strong interest in Asia, join the same chatroom to spend time with Seungho and thirty other "Soompiers," people from around the world who have come together to form a strong and tight-knit online community. The chatroom itself [...] is visually mundane—a window that gradually fills with text as different users type, but Soompi IRC is an organic and multicultural part of cyberspace where people communicate in English, Korean, Mandarin, Cantonese, Spanish, Norwegian, Swedish, Vietnamese, Japanese, Tagalog, and French about every topic imaginable, 24 hours a day.

Stephanie lists both the author and page number in her citation. Notice that she is citing this source even though she is only paraphrasing his ideas.

We Soompiers are representatives of "Generation I"—we have grown up with the Internet and are using it to define ourselves in a more globalized society (Gates 98). A decade ago, cultural identity for people like Seungho and me was limited by factors like geography, language, and ethnicity; with the emergence of new technology and online communities, we have access to an ever-growing variety of choices for personal expression. Soompi and other cyber communities are at the forefront of a larger movement towards redefining how we culturally relate to one another. This movement will extend past the reach of the Internet and act as a catalyst for cross-cultural interaction and understanding on a level never seen before.

Stephanie closes her introduction with a two-sentence thesis that outlines the claim that she will support through her textual and cultural analysis in the rest of the paper.

* * *

Parker 9

"This Site is My Life": Soompi Addicts and the Asian Fix

For the past decade, most academic research on cyber culture has focused on the type of social interaction that takes place within the digital medium. Scholars Howard Rheingold, Elisabeth Reid, Amy Jo Kim, and Lisa Nakamura have all helped to build the foundations for the study of online group behavior. But there is also another important part of Internet life that is only beginning to develop with the current generation of web users—how membership in an online group affects a person's self-perception in relation to others in real life. Nessim Watson is a Professor of Communication at Westfield State College, and has devoted years to the study of American mass media and cultural representations. After spending two years participating in and studying an online fan club, he concluded that, "those youth formed a community which created not only individual benefits for participants but also a group strength" (102). It is those "individual benefits" that should provide the next source of material for research. The strong allegiance to a web-based group is not something that an Internet user logs in and out of—they take this allegiance with them and it influences their decisions and behavior in the real world: their mode of personal expression, their opinions about other groups, and especially their cultural identity.

Soompi is one of the best venues to observe the brand new phenomenon of people gaining a real sense of culture from an online source. According to Quantcast, a free internet ratings site, Soompi.com has 26 million page views per month, with a full 66% accomplished by "Addicts," or users who log on more than once every day ("Traffic Stats"). For them, Soompi is the most convenient place to get their fix of Asian culture. This makes sense, and is in line with a report published in 2001 by the Pew Internet & American Life Project, "Asian-Americans and the Internet: The Young and Connected." According to the study, English-speaking Asian-Americans "are the Net's most active users... and have made the Internet an integral part of their daily lives" (Spooner 2). For hundreds of thousands of people in this demographic, Soompi has definitely become an important force in their personal lives and decisions, and in some cases, is the only website visited besides

Stephanie's page numbers skip to 9 here since we've abridged her paper.

In this section, midway through her paper, Stephanie synthesizes a variety of different types of sources to make her point.

Stephanie cites the page number for the print source from which she took this direct quote. Notice that because she used the author's name earlier in the sentence, she does not need to include it again in her parenthetical citation.

She cites the source for the statistics she uses. Since her source had no author, she refers to it here with an abbreviation of its title, which she places in quotation marks since it is the title of the article. In the Works Cited, she lists this source by its title as well, so it is easy for the reader to cross-reference.

Even though Stephanie reads this as an electronic file, Spooner's study was in PDF form and therefore has page numbers that she could refer to in her citations.

This source is a discussion thread from the Website that Stephanie is discussing, but for the purposes of citation, she refers to it by its title, just as she would for an article that had no author listed.

Since Stephanie is working with two different texts written by Nakamura, here she specifies which she is referring to by including the title as well as the author and page number in the citation.

The second time that Stephanie references Nakamura's book, she does not need to include the author or title in the citation since they are exactly the same as in the previous citation.

Since this quotation is from an interview, there is no page number to cite. However, since Stephanie lists more than one source from Shim in her Works Cited, here she includes a citation that makes it clear that this quote was taken from her online interview with him.

Parker 10

social utilities like Facebook ("What Would You"). They can use Soompi to build their knowledge of Asian culture, and to form new connections with other people they can relate to around the world. In September of 2008, a discussion topic was posted on the Forums: "What Would You Do Without Soompi?" Certain self-proclaimed "addicts" left replies such as, "I probably wouldn't be so into Asian stuff," and "I would be a lot less knowledgeable about the world" ("What Would You"). For thousands of Soompiers, the Forums are where they learn Asian-specific modes of fashion, style, speech patterns, and other cultural behaviors of expression.

This part of personal development is extremely important in the case of Asian-Americans living in predominantly non-Asian areas, without an "Asian group" of friends to participate in cultural activities with. Prominent scholars in Asian-American studies constantly emphasize the unique relationship between the Asian-American community and New Media, and its power to change traditional ideas about identity, culture, and the potential fluidity of both (Nakamura, *Digitizing Race* 184). Lisa Nakamura recognizes in *Digitizing Race: Visual Cultures of the Internet* that "[i]nteractive media like the Web can question identity while building discursive community in ways that other static media cannot" (184). It allows anyone who wishes to contribute to the evolution of Asian-American culture to effectively "log in" and express their approval, resistance, or creativity in the largest Forum on the planet, all while strengthening the bonds of a real community. Daniel Shim relates his own experience: "I was born in Canada in white communities & I grew up to be like them. Soompi has given me knowledge about Asian culture that I would not get from my school or family" (Online interview). To follow that point further, in her book, Nakamura argues that the Internet provides a Forum for "questioning a rigid and essentialized notion of Asian American 'authenticity'" (185). This is extremely important—the idea of culture being inextricably linked to ethnicity, language, and geographic location becomes irrelevant in the face of rising online communities, the organic and global nature of which forces the issue of what makes a person "Asian," or "American."

Parker 11

Since Daniel joined Soompi and began to use the Internet as a tool for personal expression, his popularity online has grown enormously: his YouTube videoblog, in which he comments on events in his daily life and makes fun of Asian stereotypes, has almost 30,000 subscribers and is the 4th most popular comedy blog in all of Canada (Shim, "Shimmycocopuffsss's"). Without having grown up around many Asian young people, Daniel has been extremely successful in navigating the cultural landscape with the help of his online community, even producing his own ideas about Asian-American identity as a New Media celebrity (see Figure 6). For young people like Daniel in Toronto and Seungho in Norway, Susan Kang says that "online is pretty much the only place they feel like they can connect to other Asians." Soompi makes it not only possible, but easy for Asians who live in a non-Asian place to immerse themselves in Asian culture and comment on it—an unprecedented step in the separation of culture and a static location.

FIGURE 6 Daniel Shim's parody video, "Wasabi Boy–NoEngrish" confronts Asian stereotypes with comedy and has been viewed almost 200,000 times. Author screenshot.

Stephanie once again takes a direct quote from an interview she conducted and so does not cite a page number or author here. The curious reader would look up "Kang" on the Works Cited and discover that the quote came from a personal interview.

This Works Cited represents an abridged version of the much longer Works Cited that Stephanie included with her full paper.

All the sources in the Works Cited listed in alphabetical order by author's last name, or, in the cases where there is no identified author, by title.

Stephanie lists a variety of sources here, from academic journal articles, to books, newspaper articles, advertisements, and even online sources such as Webpages, YouTube videos, and discussion list postings.

Notice the formatting of the entries: the first line of each entry is flush left, with a hanging indent in the wrapped lines so readers can skim the Works Cited easily.

When there is no author, the title is listed first.

Parker 20

Works Cited

Bell, David. *An Introduction to Cyberculture*s. London: Routledge, 2001. Print.

Chen, Louie Haoru. Online interview. 16 Nov. 2008.

"Crazy Sale for Korean Fashion." Advertisement. *Yesstyle.* 10 Nov. 2008. Web. 10 Nov. 2008.

Dator, Jim, and Yongseok Seo. "Korea as the Wave of a Future: The Emerging Dream Society of Icons and Aesthetic Experience." *Journal of Futures Studies* 9:1 (2004): 31-44. Print.

Gates, Bill. "Enter 'Generation I.'" *Instructor* Mar. 2000: 98. Print.

Gulia, Milena, and Barry Wellman. "Virtual Communities as Communities: Net Surfers Don't Ride Alone." *Communities in Cyberspace.* Ed. Mark A. Smith and Peter Kollock. New York: Routledge, 1999. 167-194. Print.

Herring, Susan C. "Questioning the Generational Divide: Technological Exoticism and Adult Constructions of Online Youth Identity." *Youth, Identity, and Digital Media*. Ed. David Buckingham. Cambridge: MIT Press, 2000. 72-95. Print.

Jones, Steven G. *Virtual Culture: Identity and Communication in Cybersociety*. London: Sage, 1997. Print.

Kang, Susan. Online interview. 25 Oct. 2008.

Kim, Amy Jo. *Community Building on the Web*. Peachpit Press, 6 Apr. 2000. Web. 24 Oct. 2008.

Ko, Shu-ling. "GIO Looking to Take Foreign Soap Operas off Prime Time TV." *Taipei Times* 11 Jan. 2006. *AsiaMedia.* 11 Jan. 2006. Web. 20 Nov. 2008.

"Korea Wave Hits Middle East." *Dae Jang Geum* 13 Dec. 2005. Web. 1 Nov. 2008.

Lee, Hyuk Min. Telephone interview. 15 Oct. 2008.

Nakamura, Lisa. *Cybertypes.* New York: Routledge, 2002. Print.

---. *Digitizing Race: Visual Cultures of the Internet*. Minneapolis: U of Minnesota P, 2008. Print.

Parker 21

Reid, Elisabeth."Electropolis: Communications and Community on Internet Relay Chat."Honors Thesis. U of Melbourne, 1991. Print.

Rheingold, Howard. *The Virtual Community: Homesteading on the Electronic Frontier*. Addison-Wesley, 1993. Print.

Shim, Daniel. Online interview. 12 Nov. 2008.

---."Shimmycocopuffsss's Profile Page" YouTube. 27 Nov. 2008. Web. 28 Nov. 2008.

---."Wasabi Boy–No Engrish." YouTube. 5 Mar. 2008. Web. 28 Nov. 2008.

Spooner, Tom."Asian-Americans and the Internet: The Young and Connected."*Pew Internet and American Life Project.* 12 Dec. 2001. PDF file.

"Traffic Stats for soompi.com."Quantcast.com. 1 Nov. 2008. Web. 1 Nov. 2008.

"Wannabe Asians/Wasians"1721 Posts. *Soompi.* Started 28 July 2006. Web. 1 Oct. 2008.

Watson, Nessim."Why We Argue about Virtual Community: A Case Study of the Phish.net Fan Community."Jones 102-110. Print.

"What Would You Do without Soompi? How Would Your Life Be Different?"95 posts. *Soompi.* Started 1 Sept. 2008. Web. 1 Oct. 2008.

Yang, Jeff."On Top of YouTube: Happy Slip, Choi, KevJumba." *San Francisco Chronicle* 6 June 2008. Web. 20 Oct. 2008.

When an author's name appears more than once, three hyphens (—) stand in for the name in the second and subsequent entries, and the entries by the same author are alphabetized by title.

Notice here how in the Watson entry, Stephanie cross-references with the Jones citation above so as not to be redundant.

THE WRITER'S PROCESS

In this chapter you've learned about the importance of source attribution, the concept of intellectual property, the dangers of plagiarism—whether accidental or not—the rhetorical purpose for documentation styles, the cross-referencing system of in-text citations, and the logic behind constructing entries for your MLA Works Cited and Consulted list. Now it's time for you to implement these practices in your own writing.

Take a look at your own research sources as they appear in your written draft. Have you acknowledged all your sources in full? Are the names of authors "hidden" in parentheses or in notes listing a range of sources? Should you instead name the authors in the prose of your essay and include just the page numbers in parentheses? In that way, you make your conversation with these authors move overt, and your source attribution of their work is more respectful.

Now take a look at all your online, visual, and multimedia sources. Did you include proper and concise parenthetical attributions for each one in the paper? Does your Works Cited list provide an alphabetized account of all your research, even the materials that may be so new that we haven't invented ways to cite them yet? Realize that you, as an emerging writer, can use the lessons from this chapter in order to think through the logic of documentation, include the newest sources in your essay, and develop your contribution to an ongoing research conversation.

WRITING ASSIGNMENTS

MyWritingLab

1. **Documentation Log:** Develop your own system of note taking and ethical citation of sources to avoid unintentional plagiarism. Create citations for your works cited using MLA form. Follow the order in the checklist below in formatting your citation; keep in mind, depending your source, not all of these categories may apply:

   - ❑ Author or authors
   - ❑ Title of book or article
   - ❑ If an article, title of journal or book within which it was published
   - ❑ Place of publication
   - ❑ Publisher
   - ❑ Date of publication
   - ❑ If a printed or PDF article, page span
   - ❑ If online article from a database, the database or search engine
   - ❑ Medium of publication
   - ❑ The URL for a Website, inserted in brackets, if your instructor requires it or if the site would be difficult to find without it

2. **Citations Peer Review:** Share your draft paper with your peers and have them check to see which sources need citation. Does your paper contain knowledge you must have obtained from a source? If so, you need to acknowledge the source of that knowledge. Do certain passages seem to be common knowledge? If so, you don't need to cite them. What paragraphs could go into notes? What aspects of your paper need more explanation and could use a note?

3. **Writing with Technology:** You might find it helpful to turn to one of the scholarly tools for producing a Work Cited list. These include *Easybib*, *Ref Works*, *End Note*, *Citelighter*, and *Zotero*. Many researchers and scholars depend on these tools, keeping notes right in the program, inserting all identifying information for a source, and then selecting the documentation format needed for their papers. The technology then produces a list in the chosen documentation style. However, you will definitely need to double-check the list for accuracy, using what you learned in this chapter.

MyWritingLab Visit Ch. 7 Documenting Sources and Avoiding Plagiarism in MyWritingLab to complete the Writer's Practices, Spotlighted Analyses, and Writing Assignments, and to test your understanding of the chapter objectives.

CHAPTER 8

Designing Arguments

Chapter Preview Questions

8.1 What is decorum and how does this rhetorical principle govern document design?

8.2 What are the conventions for academic writing?

8.3 What techniques can I learn to integrate images effectively into my writing?

8.4 How can I compose an abstract about my essay, a "bio" about myself as a writer, or a writing portfolio?

8.5 How do audience and purpose affect my document design?

8.6 How can I create multimodal arguments, such as op-ads, photo essays, and Websites?

FIGURE 8.1 This opinion advertisement by DCVote.org relies on a carefully designed visual argument.

We've used the word "writing" so far in *Envision* to refer predominantly to written text, printed letters and words. However, as you probably know from your own experience, today's definition of "writing" incorporates many different forms of communication, and, as we've seen through the numerous examples that we've examined in the last seven chapters, the idea of argument itself is not bound to just words on page: it can assume any one of a number of forms, from a traditional academic article, to a political cartoon, advertisement, photo essay, propaganda poster, website, film trailer, or even a mash-up of different texts. This is the reason rhetoric itself is such a powerful lens through which to understand how to be persuasive communicators: it is flexible and adaptive, focusing on *strategies of persuasion* rather than a particular type of text. Rhetoric allows us to be versatile communicators, choosing the type of argument best suited to our audience, purpose, occasion, and context.

The protean nature of modern argument is evident all around us. Consider, for instance, the way the advocacy group DC Vote mobilized its message about the need to give the District of Columbia local budget control and equitable representation in Congress through a variety of platforms: press releases, a website, YouTube videos, and even an op-ad campaign featuring posters such as the one seen in Figure 8.1. Notice the way in which that visual argument enacts many of the same strategies as you might find in a written argument: it structures itself conceptually and visually as a comparison/contrast argument; it relies on *logos*, or a logical line of reasoning, to argue its position; it uses strategic arrangement of elements (the mirrored figures, the hierarchical structure of information, from broad claim to increased detail); it employs culturally resonant language ("taxation without representation") to connect with its audience. As an argument, it is as carefully designed as a written text – but is perhaps better suited than that form to an audience who might be riding the Metro or waiting for a bus or train. DC Vote recognized that they needed to adapt their arguments to suit different rhetorical situations, a strategy essential for effective communicators in today's society.

In this chapter, you'll learn how to deliver your own arguments in a variety of modes. As you read the pages that follow, we invite you to consider how you can communicate your ideas, research, and writing in various formats—including the conventional academic paper but also expanding out to include creative cover pages, multimedia representations in word and image, and even texts that combine voice, moving images, and animation. But whether your project is conventional or creative, you need to learn the principles of **document design**—the guidelines that determine the best medium and method of communicating your idea in a specific format. We'll provide specific guidelines for academic essays, including line-spacing, margin size, page numbering, and other considerations. You'll learn how to write an academic abstract to provide an overview of your argument, a short biography to build your credibility as the author, and a portfolio of your work, as well as how to insert images correctly into your written essay. Then, in the second half of the chapter, we'll examine ways you can compose effective arguments in less traditionally "academic formats," such as op-ads, photo essays, newsletters, brochures, Websites, online videos, and other multimodal projects. In doing so, you'll receive an overview of the many modes of persuasion available to you as a twenty-first century writer.

8.1 What is decorum, and how does this rhetorical principle govern document design?

UNDERSTANDING DOCUMENT DESIGN AND DECORUM

First, in order to grasp the concept of document design more fully, let's return to Alex, our hypothetical student from Chapter 1. For one of her classes, she has completed a research paper on "greenwashing," that is, the corporate practice of promoting a "green" public image in order to deflect attention from environmentally questionable business practices. She now needs to format her paper to submit it to her teacher, and she also is considering submitting it for publication in her college's undergraduate research journal. Moreover, her teacher wants her to convert her paper into a visual argument to appear in a class exhibit. She therefore has an important task in front of her: to learn appropriate design strategies for both academic essays and visual arguments. In each case, she has four key decisions to make: Alex must identify her *argument* (her main point); her *audience* (whom she intends to reach); her *medium* (printed article, abstract, advertisement, photo essay, or multimedia montage); and the specific *form* (the layout and design aspects) for her composition. What governs her choices is a matter of document design strategy, or the choices writers make in formatting their work.

To use terms from classical rhetoric, the decisions you face for document design have to do with **decorum**—a word defined as "appropriateness." In everyday language, someone who exhibits decorum in speaking knows the right kinds of words and content to use given the circumstances and audience. For example, you might swear or shout with joy at a baseball game, but not at a job interview when talking about how your team won the game. But decorum as a rhetorical principle extends beyond choosing the right words and phrases for the occasion.

Seeing Connections
Chapter 3 offers additional discussion of style in relation to argumentative writing.

In the Roman rhetorical tradition, Cicero separated decorum into three levels of style that he assigned to different argumentative purposes. Cicero defined the *grand style* as the most formal mode of discourse, employing sophisticated language, imagery, and rhetorical devices; its goal is often to move the audience. He considered *middle style* less formal than grand style but not completely colloquial; although it uses some verbal ornamentation, it develops its argument more slowly in an attempt to persuade the audience by pleasing them. The final level, *plain style,* mimics conversation in its speech and rhythms, aiming to instruct or inform the audience in a clear and straightforward way. By adding decorum to our rhetorical toolkit, we can make decisions about how to design documents. As demonstrated in the Levels of Decorum table, we can attend to argument, audience, medium, and form by understanding the *level of style* for a particular occasion. Like our classical counterparts, we must understand our rhetorical situation and use a style that best suits the circumstance.

LEVELS OF DECORUM

LEVEL	CHARACTERISTICS	EXAMPLE: WRITTEN ARGUMENT	EXAMPLE: VISUAL ARGUMENT
Grand or high style	Ornate language, formal structures, many rhetorical devices	Academic paper to be published in a scholarly journal	An information graphic in a scholarly journal
Middle style	Some ornamentation, less formal language, argument is developed at a leisurely pace	Feature article or editorial column	A photo essay for a school exhibit
Plain or low style	The least formal style; closest to spoken language; emphasis on clarity, simplicity, and directness	A blog post or contribution to an online forum	A series of Tumblr posts, showcasing personal perspective or experience

For the rest of this chapter, we'll look at various models for document design, examining the way in which we need to adjust our choice of style according to the formal and rhetorical demands of each situation.

UNDERSTANDING ACADEMIC WRITING CONVENTIONS

8.2 What are the conventions for academic writing?

The format of a page matters to an audience: from the paragraph indents to the margins and double-spaced lines, to the rhetorical placement of images—all these design decisions are ways of conveying your level of decorum and your purpose to your specific audience. When we say "first impressions," we often mean how well a writer meets the conventions anticipated by the audience. From the perspective of *decorum*, the conventional academic essay falls under either grand or middle style, depending on the preferences of your audience. Characteristics of academic writing include:

- Using language more sophisticated than ordinary speech
- Using formal structures to organize your paper, including the following elements:
  - ❑ An informative and catchy title that comes under your identifying information
  - ❑ A complete introduction containing your *thesis statement*
  - ❑ Clear subsections for each part of your argument, often using rhetorical subheads
  - ❑ A substantial conclusion in its own paragraph
- Accurately and ethically acknowledging your sources and providing a Works Cited list

Seeing Connections
See Chapter 6 for guidance on writing rhetorical subheads.

Adhering to these characteristics in the document design of your writing signals your membership in a scholarly community, since you demonstrate knowledge of the format conventions for academic papers. It's similar to using table manners in a particular community or waiting in line to pay at a store; the conventions reflect consensus concerning shared expectations or practices that in turn to promote unity, consistency, and familiarity.

These guidelines are very pragmatic in nature, driven by a deeper purpose than simply following rules. Most have to do with the rhetorical relationship between yourself, your text, and your readers. By double-spacing your document and providing 1-inch margins on all sides, you leave ample room for reviewers to comment on lines or paragraphs. You include page numbers and your name on the corner of your essay to enable readers to keep track of whose paper they are reading and to easily refer to your writing by page number

AT A GLANCE

Key Elements of Academic Document Design

- Double-space all pages.
- Provide 1-inch margins on all sides.
- Use a professional but easily readable font, such as Times New Roman or Arial.
- Number pages at the top right; include your last name before the page number.
- Use subheads to separate sections.
- Use citations to acknowledge research sources.
- Use endnotes or footnotes for additional information.
- Include a list of references at the end, preferably a Works Cited and Consulted List.
- Staple, clip, or bind the paper together.

when commenting on a specific point. By using subheads, you help structure what might be a complicated argument to make it more accessible to your audience. Finally, when you include citations, footnotes, and references, you demonstrate your *ethos* as a writer and researcher by giving credit to your sources.

It might seem like an overstatement to argue that a detail as basic as the spacing and alignment of words on a title page can contribute to your *ethos*. However, consider the different rhetorical force of the three cover pages reproduced in Figures 8.2, 8.3, and 8.4. The first contains all the relevant information: the title, the author's name, the date, and the class for which the essay was written, yet it makes a less powerful impression than the other examples. Why is that? In Figure 8.3, Alex took into account very simple design principles when formatting the page. She changed to a more accessible font, to increase *readability*. She used *contrast* to differentiate the title, with its large, bold font, from the rest of the words on the page. She experimented with *proximity*, grouping related items together to help her reader conceptualize levels of importance. In Figure 8.4, she took the process one step further. She used the principle of *alignment,* moving elements into visual connection with one another on the page so as to give a sense of rhetorical purposefulness behind the layout; finally, she decided to reformat

Seeing Connections
See Chapter 3 for a discussion of crafting a rhetorically effective title.

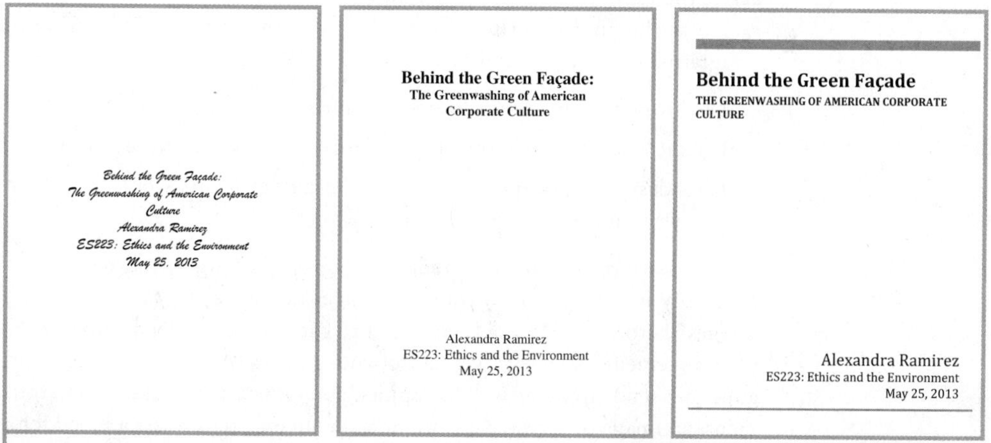

Behind the Green Façade:
The Greenwashing of American Corporate
Culture
Alexandra Ramirez
ES223: Ethics and the Environment
May 25, 2013

Behind the Green Façade:
The Greenwashing of American
Corporate Culture

Alexandra Ramirez
ES223: Ethics and the Environment
May 25, 2013

Behind the Green Façade
THE GREENWASHING OF AMERICAN CORPORATE CULTURE

Alexandra Ramirez
ES223: Ethics and the Environment
May 25, 2013

FIGURE 8.2–8.4 Alex experimented with several different formats in designing her cover page for her research project.

her subtitle in small capitals, a technique she would use for her subheads in the rest of the essay, to give the entire document a sense of coherence through strategic *repetition*. She could even have integrated a relevant cover image or quotation to set the mood for her essay.

As these examples indicate, format is not something simply imposed on you and your writing. It involves a set of *rhetorical acts* that influence the way that your readers encounter, experience, and are persuaded by your argument.

8.3 What techniques can I learn to integrate images effectively into my writing?

INTEGRATING IMAGES IN ACADEMIC WRITING

Just as there are proper academic conventions for designing the writing and layout of your essay, there exist specific guidelines for how best to integrate images into your writing. But first, consider the rhetorical purpose of your images. If they are just for decoration, then they are not essential to your argument. By contrast, if your essay focuses on a visual topic, such as the analysis of ads or films, then you probably want to include images or screen shots as *primary sources* or *exhibits* to analyze in the essay itself. Moreover, if your argument relies on images—such as political campaigns from billboards or Websites—as supporting *evidence* for your thesis, then you also want to allow your readers to consult that material alongside your prose about the text. When considering how to include an image in your essay, return to the guiding principles we discussed in Chapter 6 in relation to integrating quotations; ask yourself:

Does it provide **evidence** for my argument?

Does it lend ***ethos*** by representing a primary source for my argument?

Is its design or **composition** so unique that elements would be lost in written description?

Even once you decide to include an image in your argument, realize that randomly inserting it into your paper does not serve the *purpose* of using images rhetorically. Instead, you need to carefully consider your strategy of arrangement and the placement of your images. An image placed in an appendix tends to be viewed as supplementary, not as integral to an argument; an image on a title page might act as an epigraph to set a mood for a paper, but it is less effective as a specific visual example. If you want to use your images as *argumentative evidence*, you need to show them to your readers as you analyze them; therefore, what would be most successful would be inserting them next to the part of your argument that they support. Each decision is both a stylistic and rhetorical choice.

AT A GLANCE

Including Visuals in a Paper

- Decide whether it's appropriate to include an image based on assessing its function in terms of evidence, *ethos*, and composition.
- Position it strategically and describe its relevance in your main text so that your readers don't skim over it.
- Include a figure number and caption or brief description that explains how the image contributes to your argument.
- Refer to the figure number or image title when writing the prose of your essay (e.g., "See Figure 1").
- List the complete image source information in your bibliography.

Once you have determined the placement that best serves your rhetorical purpose, you need to insert the image in a way that maximizes its impact on your argument. Like a quotation, an image cannot be dropped into a text without comment; it needs to be **signposted**, or connected to your argument through deliberate textual markers. You can accomplish this by making explicit **textual references** to the image—for example, "shown in the image at the right" or "(see Figure 3)"—and by taking the time to explain the rhetoric of the image for readers. In addition, just like words quoted from a book or an interview that you might use as evidence, visual material needs *your interpretation* for readers to view it the way you do. Your analysis of its meaning will advance your argument by persuading readers to see the image as you do, and in the process, readers will pause to consider the evidence rather than skip over it.

It is also crucial to draft a **caption** for the image that reiterates the relationship between the point you are making in the paper and the visual evidence you include. This dialogue between image and ideas will help remind you to use your images rhetorically and analytically, as evidence, rather than just as decoration. Remember, however, that what is most important is the analysis of the image you include in the body of your paper; don't hide the meaning of the image in the caption. Captions should be concise; they should not do the work of the written argument.

Design of Academic Papers

A page from student Kim Felser's essay on the addictive properties of sugar provides an example of both effective academic writing conventions and the strategic placement and captioning of visuals (see Figure 8.5). In Chapter 5,

Sugar addiction, of course, satisfies all of these categories, just as fully as do more widely recognized drugs of abuse like cocaine, hydrocodone, and alcohol.

Consuming the highly concentrated sugars that abound in our current food market not only triggers the feelings of pleasure associated with agreeable flavors, as is suggested by our evolutionary development, but also releases opiate chemicals – substances just a few bonds away from heroin and morphine.[1] Consumption of such substances is quickly followed by a the priming of endorphins and dopamine in the region of the brain known as the nucleus accumbens, often called the "hedonic hot spot" by researchers in the field (see Figure 3 to the right).[2] The impact is immediate: the opiates moderately anesthetize pain,[3] while the abundance of endorphins and dopamine encourages a sugar "high" of chemically synthesized happiness.[4] Alcohol, too, acts upon the same chemical pathways in the brain by priming the release of dopamine in the nucleus accumbens, and encouraging a similar state of artificial bliss.[5] These "euphoric neural effects"[6] of both sugar and alcohol, as Dr. Jeffery L. Fortuna puts it, prove highly addicting, for in both cases a severe inability to inhibit additional consumption of the substance follows.[7] Despite the fact that the high is not as intense as that of cocaine or alcohol, users still find themselves returning to the drugs again and again in an unconscious endeavor to recreate such a pleasurable mental state, especially as "highs" grow less intense with further use – just as with other drugs of dependence. In short, willpower proves ineffectual, and repeated use of the drug only serves to worsen the addiction as tolerance to the substance at hand increases.

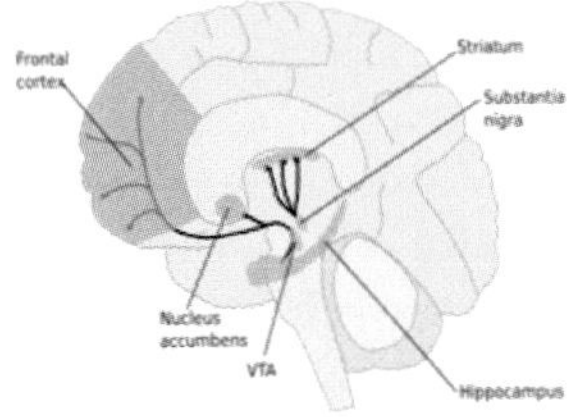

Figure 3: Diagram illustrating the central location of the nucleus accumbens (the "hedonistic hot spot") in the brain. *Source: Wikimedia Commons*

FIGURE 8.5 This excerpt from Kim's essay, "Sugar: The Hidden Drug," provides an example of polished academic design.

we looked at an excerpt from Kim's Dialogue of Sources on this topic; here we can see how in this final draft, she has spotlighted her argument and integrated her source materials to support her points. In addition, we can see her strategic use of visual evidence to help her reader visualize the different areas of the brain affected by sugar consumption. Rather than relegate this image to an appendix, Kim positioned it in the paper with the text wrapped around it, making the visuals an integral part of her argument that resonated with the surrounding text. She then emphasized the importance of the image by giving it a meaningful, rhetorical caption that paraphrased his central point.

Kim's careful attention to academic conventions—from her last name and page number at the top, to the readable typeface, clear structure, and purposeful integration of an image as evidence for her central claim—adds *ethos* to an already articulate and well-researched argument.

TOOLS OF DESIGN FOR ACADEMIC AUDIENCES

8.4 How can I compose an abstract about my essay, a "bio" about myself as a writer, or a writing portfolio?

In addition to attending to the format of the research paper itself and integrating visuals as evidence correctly, you may also need to write supplemental materials that provide readers with a preview of your argument and information about yourself as the author. The materials are commonly known as the academic abstract and author bio. In some cases, you also may be asked to collect a sample of your writing into a writing *portfolio*, prefaced by a reflective cover memo. These are all standard components of conventional academic writing; by learning their formal design properties, you can confidently add them to your toolkit of writing strategies.

Writing an Abstract

The **research abstract** is a professional academic genre designed to present the research topic and to lay out the argument. Abstracts differ depending on the disciplinary audience and the purpose of the writing. When applying to academic conferences in the humanities, for example, scholars often must write abstracts that predict the paper's argument, research contribution, and significance, while writers in the sciences or social sciences typically write abstracts *after* the paper has been completed to serve as a short summary of the article. You will encounter abstracts when you begin searching for research articles; they often precede a published paper or accompany

Seeing Connections
Chapter 5 discusses how you might evaluate published abstracts during your research.

bibliographic citations in online databases. Abstracts can range from a few sentences to a page in length, but they are usually no longer than two paragraphs. The key in writing an abstract is to explain your argument in one brief, coherent unit. While some characterize an abstract as simply a summary, others suggest it can have a more complex structure. In their seminal work, *The Craft of Research*, Wayne Booth, Gregory Colomb, and Joseph Williams propose the following model for abstracts: Context + Problem + Main Point or Launching Point. According to their interpretation, an abstract clarifies not only the topic, but a tension in that topic and the way that the written piece addresses that tension. As you read the abstract below, consider the ways in which the author adheres to this structure.

In the first sentence, the authors establish the context for their research.

The second and third sentences convey the tension or problem that their particular project addresses.

In the final sentences of the abstract, the authors suggest both their main point and some of their methodology, providing the reader with a clear overview of what to expect when reading the whole paper and their contribution to the conversation on this topic.

Serious games have received much positive attention; correspondingly, many researchers have taken up the challenge of establishing how to best design them. However, the current literature often focuses on best practice design strategies and frameworks. Fine-grained details, contextual descriptions, and organisational factors that are invaluable in helping us to learn from and reflect on project experiences are often overlooked. In this paper, we present five distinct and sometimes competing perspectives that are critical in understanding factors that influence serious game projects: *project organisation*, *technology*, *domain knowledge*, *user research*, and *game design*. We explain these perspectives by providing insights from the design and development process of an EU-funded serious game about conflict resolution developed by an interdisciplinary consortium of researchers and industry-based developers. We also point out a set of underlying forces that become evident from viewing the process from different perspectives, to underscore that problems exist in serious game projects and that we should open the conversation about them.

AT A GLANCE

Design for Composing an Abstract

- What level of decorum do you wish to use?
- How will the style predict the tone of your essay and establish your persona as a researcher?
- If you use "I" in the prose, can it be *ethos*-based in terms of your research or experience?
- How much specificity should you include from the essay?
    - Do you want to identify key examples you analyze in your writing?
    - Do you want to give an overview of your argument?
    - Should you name any important sources you use in making your argument?
    - What is your major research contribution?
    - What is the larger significance of your essay?

In composing your abstract, you will need to make several rhetorical decisions, outlined in the questions in the "At a Glance" box.

Constructing Your Bio

While the abstract offers a concise statement of the argument, the **bio**, short for biography, is a brief paragraph that conveys aspects of the author's experiences or credentials to the intended audience. In this way, the bio functions as a short written account of your *persona.* Its purpose is to persuade readers of your depth of knowledge about or research into your topic. Moreover, a successful bio usually connects aspects of the research topic to the writer's experiences, interests, and motivations for engaging in research work. Eric Wiebacher's bio for his essay, "India's National Solar Program: A Case Study in Developing Clean Energy Infrastructures," follows this model, resembling the polished "About the Author" paragraph that you might find at the back of a book or in the headnote of an academic article:

> Eric Wiebacher is a junior pursuing a double major in Public Policy and Environmental studies. He has taken several environmental policy courses focused on natural resource policy, climate change and alternate energy, and international policy and management. While spending a semester abroad in India,

Eric names specific qualifications and experiences he has had that make him an authority in this area.

he had the opportunity to visit the village of Dharnai, the first village in India to be powered exclusively by solar energy. He has used this research project to help him deepen his understanding of India's microgrid project and to formulate ways to share his ideas with a broader audience. For his major capstone project, he plans to build on this research by expanding to consider the intersection between policy and implementation of alternate energy programs in other countries as well, such as China, Kenya, and Turkey.

He ends the bio with his future plans in this area of research that suggest his pursuit of a "research line" or academic path of scholarly inquiry.

When formatting your own bio, you might decide to include a photograph of yourself. Select your picture carefully, with attention to its rhetorical impact in conveying your *persona*. Many students who choose to write a traditional bio like Eric's opt for a formal school portrait; other students might choose a more humorous picture to complement the tone of their bios. One student, when writing about online gaming communities, even used Photoshop to create a portrait of herself standing next to her onscreen avatar identity to represent the two perspectives she was bringing to her research. As you can tell, the picture works with the bio not only to construct a *persona* for the writer but also to suggest that writer's rhetorical stance.

Creating a Portfolio

In some cases, you might need to take a step back from focusing in individual essays and assignments and create a *writer's portfolio*, a collection or sampling of your work. You might be asked to produce a portfolio for one of any number of contexts: as the culmination of your work in a writing class, as a representation of your work in your major, as a requirement for graduation, or even as part of an application for graduate school or a job. Each of these situations implies a slightly different purpose and audience, both of which will influence the shape of your portfolio.

The first step in assembling an effective portfolio is to determine its goals. In general terms, a portfolio can serve one of two functions:

- to showcase excellence
- to demonstrate improvement or development over time

The first instance might be the most intuitive: you would select those pieces of writing (or other types of work, depending on the portfolio requirements) that best represent your proficiency and, more to the point, your mastery of a form, convention, discipline, or practice.

However, you might find the second scenario more challenging. Your goal would be to include process-related documents, some of which might not always show off your work to its best advantage. In this case, however, remember that your portfolio is operating as a *narrative*; you are essentially telling the story of your growth as an author (or researcher, or disciplinary specialist, etc.) to your readers. For this reason, the steps along the way are an integral part of that journey. In such a portfolio, you might choose to include the following:

- draft and revised versions of the same paper
- process-related materials, such as freewrites, graphic brainstorms, or outlines
- peer review comments on your drafts
- feedback from your instructor that guided your revision
- reflective letters or cover memos related to the different pieces of writing

In both cases, the key is to be *selective* in the materials you choose to include. As with any argument, it's more important to be focused and specific rather than to be expansive and dilute the force of your message. Likewise, you'll also need to attend to organization and the canon of arrangement in creating your portfolio. Think about the best order for your materials, the one that puts them in dialogue with one another in a productive way. This might be most straightforward for the "development" portfolio; its change-over-time approach lends itself directly to a predominantly chronological mode of arrangement. For the "excellence" portfolio, however, you might need to be more mindful about how to use arrangement persuasively. You will need to identify key characteristics of the different samples (do they exemplify a particular strategy? a particular disciplinary approach? a different genre?) and order them in a way that allows them to dialogue productively with one another and make a cogent argument about you and your work.

However, perhaps equal in importance to the material that comprises your portfolio is the text that pulls it all together: the reflective statement or cover memo. This letter offers you the opportunity for meta-commentary, so you can direct the reader's understanding of your portfolio and present an argument about the significance of the work you included. The criteria and content for your reflective letter will vary depending on your assignment and the type of portfolio you're creating, but the chart below provides an overview of some common goals.

"Excellence" portfolio reflection	**"Development" portfolio reflection**
• Identify and define the qualities of excellence (related to your writing, your research, or your work in your discipline) that you've designed your portfolio to present • Describe the reason you selected the materials: how do they represent excellence? • Clarify the rationale behind the way you arranged the texts; suggest the "arc" of your materials • Explain how each text demonstrates one or more of the qualities of excellence, providing context and dialogue between the different examples • Reflect on your achievement—and the process it took to accomplish it—rather than just summarizing the examples • Share any additional information that might be relevant to your reader's understanding of how the texts demonstrate excellence	• Identify the goal (as a writer, as a researcher, as a member of your discipline) that you're trying to achieve • Describe the reason you selected the materials: how do they contribute to understanding your development? • Clarify the rationale behind the way you arranged the texts; suggest the "arc" of your materials (often, for this type of portfolio, you might arrange materials chronologically) • Explain your writing process, the rhetorical choices you made as a writer, the changes you made during revision, and any particular challenges you faced • Assess your final written products and how close they come to fulfilling your objective, what you have learned, and what you'd still like to accomplish • Reflect on your overall development as a writer • Share any additional information that might be relevant to your reader's understanding of how the texts demonstrate your development

In general, you should approach your reflection letter as you would any other argumentative text: make sure you have a thesis or central claim (what is the main point you want your reader to understand about your portfolio based on reading the letter?) and point to specific examples from your materials to support your claims, prioritizing critical thinking and analysis over summary. Additionally, keep in mind the importance of the letter as a rhetorical text; since it provides the framework through which your reader understands your portfolio, take care to develop an effective persona through attention to style and your own rhetorical choices.

WRITER'S PRACTICE MyWritingLab

To prepare for writing a reflective letter about your own portfolio, freewrite answers to the following questions:

- What is the rhetorical situation of your portfolio? Consider purpose, audience, genre, and exigence.
- What's the story you want your portfolio to tell to your reader? What argument would you like to make about your persona as a writer/scholar? What supporting materials would you point to in order to support that claim?
- How do these materials reflect your writing process and your growth as a writer/scholar? Alternately, how do these materials reflect your strengths as a writer/scholar?
- What work have you done that you're most proud of and/or what work shows your greatest development as a writer?
- Which do you consider the weakest piece in your portfolio? Why? How could it have been improved?
- How do the materials interconnect with one another? How does the arrangement of materials reinforce this?
- What else would you want your reader to know about you or your writing that's not necessarily reflected in the materials you included?
- What opportunities or constraints were presented by the medium of your portfolio (binder; online folder; website)?

FORMATTING WRITING FOR AUDIENCE AND PURPOSE

8.5 How do audience and purpose affect my document design?

The types of texts we've discussed so far in this chapter – the essay, the abstract, bio, and even portfolio reflection – all tend to follow the format of academic writing, aligning with the reader's expectations of traditional written discourse. When your argumentative purpose and your audience allow you to move an exclusive focus on written text, you have the opportunity to produce a **multimodal composition**—literally a composition that operates in more than one mode, such as visual, aural, or written. A feature article for a magazine, a newsletter aimed at a community audience, or an online

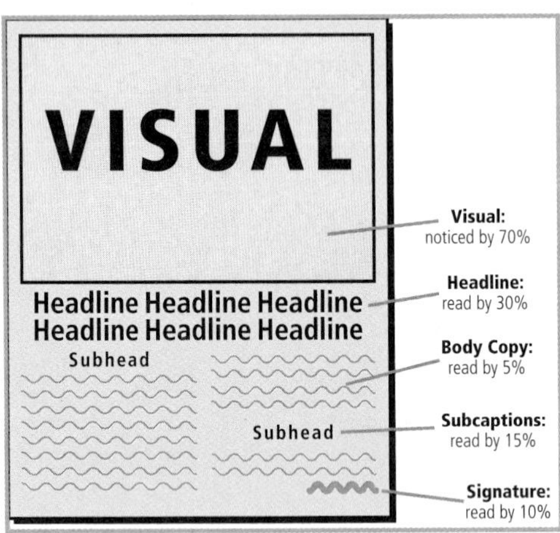

FIGURE 8.6 A graphic representation of what readers notice most on a page: visuals grab attention most.

article for diverse readers: each of these texts has the potential to operate through multimodality. An important factor to keep in mind in designing such texts is that research conducted by Adbusters, an organization devoted to cultural criticism and analysis, has shown that readers notice the *visual part* of any page significantly more than any text on the same page (see Figure 8.6). Adbusters uses this finding to provide advice for creating ads, but we can apply the insight to all rhetorical compositions—whether academic or popular—that combine multiple elements.

Let's look at how this attention to design informs a style of writing that is increasingly common in today's society: the online article. In the following reading, originally published online, the author employs many conventional elements of document design, including a title, subheads, references, and a list of sources at the end. But notice how it adapts some of these elements to meet the viewing needs of online readers. The author also includes hyperlinks, ALL CAPS for some titles, and sections of varying lengths. Finally, is not just the format that sets this article apart from traditional academic discourse: the writing style itself has been changed to meet the expectations of the online writing audience.

The title is in plain style and all capital letters, with the subtitle in lowercase. This font decision makes it appealing to online readers.

WHAT'S WRONG WITH THE BODY SHOP?

—a criticism of 'green' consumerism—

REFERENCED VERSION—all the facts and opinions in THE London Greenpeace A5 'Body Shop' leaflet validated. Note: most references are given just by way of example.

The Body Shop have successfully manufactured an image of being a caring company that is helping to protect the environment

[1] and indigenous peoples [2], and preventing the suffering of animals [3]—whilst selling 'natural' products [4]. But behind the green and cuddly image lies the reality—the Body Shop's operations, like those of all multinationals, have a detrimental effect on the environment [5] and the world's poor [6]. They do not help the plight of animals [7] or indigenous peoples [8] (and may be having a harmful effect), and their products are far from what they're cracked up to be [9]. They have put themselves on a pedestal in order to exploit people's idealism [10]—so this leaflet has been written as a necessary response.

Companies like the Body Shop continually hype their products through advertising and marketing, often creating a demand for something where a real need for it does not exist [11]. The message pushed is that the route to happiness is through buying more and more of their products. The increasing domination of multinationals and their standardised products is leading to global cultural conformity [12]. The world's problems will only be tackled by curbing such consumerism—one of the fundamental causes of world poverty, environmental destruction and social alienation [13].

FUELLING CONSUMPTION AT THE EARTH'S EXPENSE

The Body Shop have over 1,500 stores in 47 countries [14], and aggressive expansion plans [15]. Their main purpose (like all multinationals) is making lots of money for their rich shareholders [16]. In other words, they are driven by power and greed. But the Body Shop try to conceal this reality by continually pushing the message that by shopping at their stores, rather than elsewhere, people will help solve some of the world's problems [17]. The truth is that nobody can make the world a better place by shopping.

20% of the world's population consume 80% of its resources [18]. A high standard of living for some people means gross social inequalities and poverty around the world [19]. Also, the mass production, packaging and transportation of huge quantities of goods is using up the world's resources faster than they can be

The numbers correspond to notes and sources at the end. These notes are hyperlinked, so readers can jump there easily while reading on the web.

Here, the writing itself verges on *low style* with the contraction and the slang work "cracked"—this serves to entice online audiences to keep reading.

The article employs British spelling for many words, such as standardised, colours, criticised, and organise, since the authors are located in Britain. Moreover, as this line indicates, the article against the Body Shop is one in a series of pieces that critique multinational corporate practices.

The article uses argumentative subheads, as might an academic paper. They convey points of argument being made in the article. Moreover, they keep readers interested.

Notice how the article uses all CAPS to draw the online reader's attention and even begins a new section with a two-word question.

renewed and filling the land, sea and air with dangerous pollution and waste [20]. Those who advocate an ever-increasing level of consumption, and equate such consumption with personal well-being, economic progress and social fulfillment, are creating a recipe for ecological disaster [21].

Rejecting consumerism does not mean also rejecting our basic needs, our stylishness, our real choices or our quality of life. It is about creating a just, stable and sustainable world, where resources are under the control of local communities and are distributed equally and sparingly—it's about improving everyone's quality of life. Consuming ever more things is an unsatisfying and harmful way to try to be happy and fulfilled. Human happiness is not related to what people buy, but to who we are and how we relate to each other. LET'S CONSUME LESS AND LIVE MORE!

MISLEADING THE PUBLIC

Natural products? The Body Shop give the impression that their products are made from mostly natural ingredients [22]. In fact like all big cosmetic companies they make wide use of non-renewable petrochemicals, synthetic colours, fragrances and preservatives [23], and in many of their products they use only tiny amounts of botanical-based ingredients [24]. Some experts have warned about the potential adverse effects on the skin of some of the synthetic ingredients [25]. The Body Shop also regularly irradiate certain products to try to kill microbes—radiation is generated from dangerous non-renewable uranium which cannot be disposed of safely [26].

Some sections are very short, a common feature in online writing, where information is "chunked" into accessible segments.

CENSORSHIP

As the Body Shop rely so heavily on their 'green', 'caring' image, they have threatened or brought legal action against some of those who have criticised them, trying to stifle legitimate public discussion [46]. It's vital to stand up to intimidation and to defend free speech.

WHAT YOU CAN DO

Together we can fight back against the institutions and the people in power who dominate our lives and our planet. Workers can and do organise together to fight for their rights and dignity. People are increasingly aware of the need to think seriously about the products we use, and to consume less. People in poor countries are organising themselves to stand up to multinationals and banks which dominate the world's economy. Environmental and animal rights protests and campaigns are growing everywhere. Why not join in the struggle for a better world? London Greenpeace calls on people to create an anarchist society—a society without oppression, exploitation and hierarchy, based on strong and free communities, the sharing of precious resources and respect for all life. Talk to friends and family, neighbours and workmates about these issues. Please copy and circulate this leaflet as widely as you can.

The article uses direct address, the pronoun you, to engage readers. This design strategy again indicates the use of the plain style.

The conclusion's turn to ask a rhetorical question and then end with a strong call to action also reflect a writing style more common to online writing than to conventional essays, which are often more subdued in tone.

REFERENCES

1. See "Fuelling Consumption" paragraphs in the leaflet and associated references.
2. See "Exploiting Indigenous Peoples" paragraphs in the leaflet and associated references.
3. See "Helping Animals?" paragraph in the leaflet and associated references.
4. See "Natural products?" paragraph in the leaflet and associated references.

[...]

10. [Numerous publications, statements, advertisements, etc. by the Body Shop.] For example, the company's Mission Statement (1998) says that they are dedicating their business "to the pursuit of social and environmental change" and are trying to ensure that their business "is ecologically sustainable, meeting the needs of the present without compromising the

Since these notes are positioned far down on the page, they can go into more detail because they assume that only very interested readers will be accessing this part of the composition.

future."“For us, animal protection, human rights, fair trade and environmentalism, are not just fads or marketing gimmicks but fundamental components in our holistic approach to life of which work and business are a part" [Gordon Roddick (Chairman) quoted in 1996 *Body Shop* publication "Our Agenda".] "I'd rather promote human rights, environmental concerns, indigenous rights, whatever, than promote a bubble bath" said Anita Roddick (the *Body Shop* founder and Chief Executive) [speech at 'Academy of Management', Vancouver (Aug 95).]

Back to 'Beyond McDonald's—Retail' Section

London Greenpeace Press Release

WWW Body Shop FAQ

London Greenpeace reply to Body Shop statement

A5 Version of 'What's Wrong with the Body Shop'

From a design perspective, the final series of links for future reading signifies one of the great benefits of writing in a digital environment.

As you can tell from this article, the same strategies of design that shape academic research papers also apply to other modes: what is most important in each is a consideration of *purpose*, *audience*, and *argument*. Think about how readers will interact with your writing—whether as a print copy handed in for comments (in which case you double-space and follow academic guidelines); as a newsletter (in which case you might open with a powerful image, lay out the writing in columns or boxes, and use an interesting page size); or as a piece to be read on the web (in which case you include hyperlinks, single-space, create shorter chunks, and use font strategically).

In your own writing, you likewise will have the opportunity to present your arguments in multiple modes. In the pages that follow, we'll walk through some of the most common forms you might encounter and consider how to apply the design strategies we have discussed so far to a diverse range of texts.

DESIGNING ARGUMENTS IN POPULAR FORMATS

8.6 How can I create multimodal arguments, such as op-ads, photo essays, and Websites?

While it is important to understand the conventions of academic writing, increasingly teachers are inviting students to experiment with alternative forms of making arguments, often modeled on popular or nonacademic texts. Many of these—such as op-ads, photo essays, Websites, or short films—are visual or multimodal in nature, yet still rely on the same foundations of rhetoric that govern persuasion as a whole. When you construct an argument in a more popular format, you should still apply strategies for inventing, arranging, and producing the design, just as you would for a conventional essay. The goal is the same: to design a powerful text to persuade your audience to agree with your message.

Keep in mind, however, that each medium structures information in a distinct way. A photo essay is set up differently than a Webpage, just as a Webpage is set up differently than an online video. Therefore, part of creating a powerful multimodal argument lies in identifying your chosen medium's conventions of structure and style and adjusting the form of your argument—its layout, design, style, and organization of information—to be the most appropriate choice for your project.

In order to transform your research into a more popular format, you should follow a process of *selection, organization,* and *translation.* First, **select** the subset of research you intend to share with your audience. To facilitate this process, ask yourself:

- What matters most about this project?
- What is my purpose in sharing my argument?
- What do I want my audience to walk away thinking when I'm done?

You may find invention strategies such as we discussed in Chapter 3 and Chapter 4 useful for refocusing your argument in this way.

Once you've decided upon the material you wish to include, you now face the task of **organization**. Approach it like you would the task of organizing information for a written argument, using outlining strategies (from post-its, to storyboards, graphic flowcharts, to formal outlines) such as those discussed in Chapter 6. You might ask yourself the following questions:

- How can I hook my audience?
- How will I convey my thesis claim?

- What strategies and structures can I use to organize my content?
- What opportunities and constraints of the mode I'm using?

The final step in developing your multimodal argument is to **translate** your argument into more popular discourse. Some modes rely predominantly on the visual to convey information; others represent a collaboration between both verbal and visual rhetoric. Assess the balance you need to achieve between these elements and the level of decorum most appropriate to your mode, audience, and purpose.

In the pages that follow, we explore more specific guidelines for developing many of the different multimodal genres that you might consider while designing your argument.

Crafting an Op-Ad

The **op-ad**, or **opinion advertisement**, is one of the most concise forms of visual argument and one favored by many nonprofit organizations, special interest groups, and political parties as a way of reaching their target audiences. Like all ads, the op-ad is a compact persuasive text, one that uses rhetorical appeals to convey its message. However, what makes it different from traditional ads is that what it advertises is not a commercial product, but an opinion or strong stand on an issue.

The op-ad in Figure 8.7, for instance, makes a strong argument in favor of a national ban on assault weapons. The organization, Moms Demand Action, crafted a striking argument that communicates its message through a collaboration between visual and verbal elements. The centerpiece and primary focal point is the pair of young girls – a clear *pathos* appeal – that sets up an implicit comparison/contrast strategy: we notice that one girl holds a copy of *Little Red Riding Hood* and the other an assault rifle, an odd juxtaposition for a setting that looks like an elementary school library. The book, the backdrop, and the American flag in the corner put us in mind of school shootings, making the weapon seem even more out of place and alarming. Our eye next moves to the header above the girls' heads: "One child is holding something that's been banner in America to protect them. Guess which one." Based on our initial interpretation of the photo, this riddle seems like an easy one to solve.

However, our final move – to the fine print – confounds our understanding of what the image means. By revealing that it is *Red Riding* Hood that is banned, not the assault rifle, the op-ad invites us to reexamine our own assumptions. It is through such strategic rhetorical crafting of the op-ad –

Seeing Connections
See Chapter 2 for strategies for analyzing op-ads rhetorically.

creating an incongruity of the messaging and the image as well as a seemingly flawed logical circuit between question and answer — that Moms Demand Action succeeds in delivering its powerful message. In this way, the op-ad makes its audience think twice about its assumptions about gun control and what's banned – and what's not banned – to "protect" children in America.

FIGURE 8.7 This powerful op-ad draws attention to logical incongruities in how we "protect" American children.

To understand how to compose your own op-ad, let's look at the process by which one student, Angie Sorentino, constructed her visual argument. After writing an effective research paper that presented the dangers of texting while driving, Angie decided to reformulate her argument as an op-ad to reach a larger audience. Her initial considerations were her visual format and her headline—two elements of her ad that underwent some revision. In her project reflection letter, she explained:

> I originally thought I wanted to lay it out as a text message, using text lingo (LOL, OMG, and the like) because I thought it would appeal to my audience, who I assumed would be teenagers. However, then I realized that I wanted to use a different appeal instead. I wanted the people who looked at my op-ad to have a really powerful emotional reaction to the argument. Also, I started to think that maybe my idea of my audience was too narrow. So, while I tried to avoid blood and graphic imagery (I thought that might be too much like a scare tactic fallacy), I wanted to shock them. I decided on the shattered phone and car wreck because they seemed like symbols that could convey the seriousness of the issue.

FIGURE 8.8 Angie Sorentino's op-ad uses foreground and background images in combination with a powerful statistic to make its argument against texting while driving.

As shown in her completed op-ad (see Figure 8.8), Angie paired those powerful images with strong language ("It's not worth it") and a striking statistic. It's in the collaboration between word and image that we find the main work of argumentation in

AT A GLANCE

Guidelines for Designing an Op-Ad

- Decide on your purpose (to inform, to persuade, to move to action).
- Identify your audience.
- Know your argument.
- Determine which appeals to use (*pathos*, *logos*, *ethos*).
- Select key images for your ad.
- Write your print text; decide how it will function in relation to your image(s).
- Draft a gripping headline to complement your image.
- Experiment with layout—arrangement, image size, organization of text—to arrive at the most effective design.

her op-ad. She used the visual to grab the attention and hook her audience, but then amplified the effect with a strong headline, statistic, and the implicit direct address to her audience ("Don't become a statistic"). It's also worth noting that she chose public domain images and cited the source for her statistic, both in the op-ad itself and separately in a works cited. Through such careful (and ethical) practices, she created a powerful rhetorical argument designed to speak to a teen audience.

Creating a Photo Essay

Although an op-ad offers a concise, forceful argument, you may wish to develop your points more thoroughly than one page allows or use visual space to show the range of material with which you've been working. If so, consider the **photo essay**—a text in which photographs, rather than print text, convey the central argument. In a word-based essay, the verbal text takes priority, and images often appear as isolated points of evidence. In a photo essay, by contrast, the visual either collaborates with the verbal or becomes the *primary mode* of argumentation and persuasion.

As a genre, the photo essay first emerged in 1936 with the launching of *Life* magazine, whose mission statement was "to see life; to see the world." Over the 63 years it remained in print, *Life* hosted many of America's most famous photo essays, covering a range of topics from the space race to the Vietnam War, the civil rights movement, and rock and roll. But the photo essay can assume many different forms and use diverse media: it could be a series of documentary photographs and articles about southern sharecroppers published together in book form, such as Walker Evans's and James Agee's *Let Us Now Praise Famous Men* (1941); it could be a book-length photo essay that juxtaposes images with first-person narratives, such as Lauren Greenfield's *Girl Culture* (2002); it could be a striking 27-page color spread in a magazine, such as William Albert Allard's "Solace at Surprise Creek" in the June 2006 issue of *National Geographic*; or it could even be an online arrangement of captioned photos, such as *A Rescue Worker's Chronicle*, created by paramedic Matthew Levy. In each case, the photographs and written text work together, or the images themselves carry the primary weight of the argument.

Today electronic photo essays are essential conveyers of important events, a result of Internet news sources like CNN.com, Time.com, and MSNBC.com, which routinely publish photo essays as "picture stories" on their Websites. Such texts are composed of a series of images and words that work together to convey an argument about a person, event, or story. Each electronic photo essay typically contains (1) a photo, (2) an accompanying caption, (3) an audio option, and (4) a table of contents toolbar that allows readers to navigate through the images. The result is an electronic text that maintains many structural similarities to print text: it offers readers a clear sense of progression from beginning to end while investing its argument with the rhetorical force of multiple media (word, image, sound).

Let's now consider how Conor Henriksen created a photo essay to fulfill an assignment about outdoor art on campus. Figures 8.9 and 8.10 represent two different pages from the longer piece, in which the author complemented photographs he took himself of sculpture and fountains around campus with brief captions, descriptions, and relevant quotations from secondary sources. The photographs themselves clearly appeal to the reader most directly through their vibrant color, strategic arrangement, and visual composition. Despite the surface similarities in layout, we can see that there are different strategies at work: in Figure 8.9, Conor paired a wide shot of the sculpture with a close-up of one figure to give a dual perspective on the installation; in Figure 8.10, he provides a variety of vantages on the fountain, each designed to focus on a different way of understanding it in context. The text he includes works in conjunction with the images it accompanies, but does not dominate. While it provides a

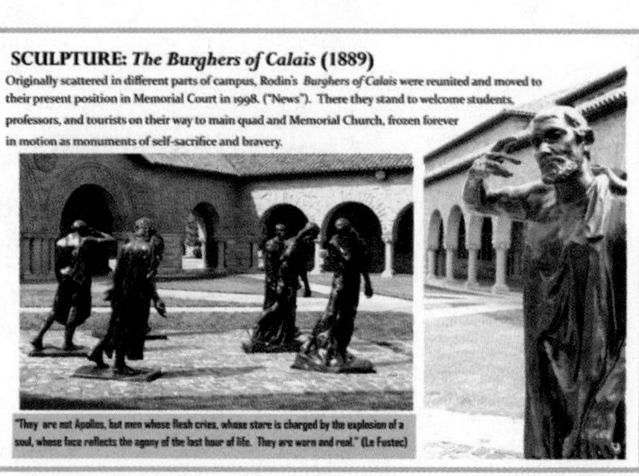

FIGURE 8.9 Through this photo essay, the author makes a visual argument about art on campus.

FOUNTAINS: *The Claw* (1964)
"When you hear the splash of the water drops that fall in the stone bowl, You will feel that all the dust of your mind is washed away"
- Zen Tea Master (qtd in Herda 94)

FIGURE 8.10 A second page from Conor's photo essay.

AT A GLANCE

Guidelines for Designing a Photo Essay

1. Decide on the argument for your project.
2. Arrange your images so they support this argument.
3. Draft written text to accompany or preview each image or set of images.
4. Determine your layout by experimenting with ways of formatting the words and images.

conceptual frame, the photographs themselves provide the most forceful argument about the beauty and significance of outdoor art on campus.

The photo essay works best if you have a topic that can be effectively argued through an accumulation of visual evidence presented as a sequence of images. Keep in mind that designing a photo essay is like drafting a research paper: you may take pages of notes, but the task of crafting the argument involves sifting through information, deciding between relevant and irrelevant materials, and arranging the most powerful evidence in your finished product. In addition, while images have priority in a photo essay, keep in mind the importance of strategically selected and deployed text to accompany your visual argument. Overall, remember to shape your photo essay around your argument through carefully made rhetorical choices about purpose, audience, and medium.

Composing in Newsletter or Magazine Format

Another familiar multimodal format is the newsletter or magazine article. Even with the explosion of online texts, publishers have gone to great lengths to devise ways for articles to retain this popular format even when they appear on the screens of Nooks, Kindles, and iPads. The advice from Adbusters is particularly resonant when we consider the design principles of this form of writing. As Figure 8.6 suggests, a much higher percentage of readers notice visuals than any other component, with the headline being second in significance. We can see the truth in this assertion every time we open an issue of *Time, Wired,* or *Vogue.* An engaging image captures our eye; a provocative headline draws us in; only then do we settle in to dive into the main body of the article.

Taking this into account, consider the importance of visuals as you approach designing your own articles of this sort. Choose images with rhetorical impact to hook your reader and position supporting images strategically in the main body to complement your main points. As for your headline, follow a suggestion from Adbusters: "The most important thing to remember here is that your headline must be short, snappy, and must touch the people that read it. Your headline must affect the readers emotionally, either by making them laugh, making them angry, making them curious, or making them think." Clearly, headlines work through rhetorical appeals: you need to think carefully about which appeal—*pathos, ethos,* or *logos*—would provide the most effective way to engage your audience.

Let's look at the design decisions Miranda Smith made in formatting her writing project on the topic of famine relief in Africa. The assignment invited her to experiment with a popular publication format, so Miranda decided to create her own feature article from a news magazine, taking *Time Magazine* as her model. In designing her text, she not only took into account her argument but also, as Figure 8.11 makes clear, deliberately designed

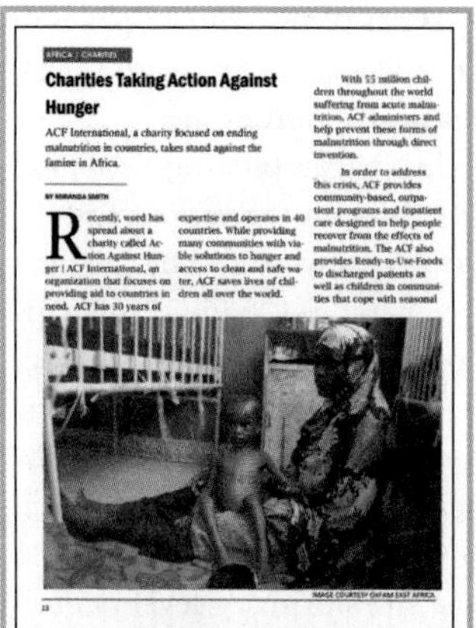

AFRICA | CHARITIES

Charities Taking Action Against Hunger

ACF International, a charity focused on ending malnutrition in countries, takes stand against the famine in Africa.

BY MIRANDA SMITH

Recently, word has spread about a charity called Action Against Hunger | ACF International, an organization that focuses on providing aid to countries in need. ACF has 30 years of expertise and operates in 40 countries. While providing many communities with viable solutions to hunger and access to clean and safe water, ACF saves lives of children all over the world.

With 55 million children throughout the world suffering from acute malnutrition, ACF administers and help prevent these forms of malnutrition through direct invention.

In order to address this crisis, ACF provides community-based, outpatient programs and inpatient care designed to help people recover from the effects of malnutrition. The ACF also provides Ready-to-Use-Foods to discharged patients as well as children in communities that cope with seasonal

500,000 **215 TONS** **10,000**

There are many diseases linked to malnutrition, including diarrhea, dysentery, and cholera. Unfortunately, many of the diseases are obtained through unhygienic living conditions and unclean water.

ACF helps communities at risk by teaching the people healthy practices and constructing water filters using basic materials. In addition, in order to make living conditions more hygienic, ACF groups build hand washing stations and latrines, along with distributing hygiene kits.

ACF also recognizes the need to deal with unclean water in communities. To address this problem, they drill and decontaminate wells where the water is either unsafe or lacking. As far as protecting existing clean water, they try hard to protect all natural springs. During droughts and water shortages, ACF installs emergency storage tanks and reservoirs full of water into the affected areas.

ACF focuses much of its efforts on Africa. Some of the African countries they are helping include Burkina Faso, the DRC, Ethiopia, Kenya, Niger, and Somalia.

"We strive to deliver effective humanitarian assistance wherever it's most needed."

Burkina Faso is currently experiencing a shortage of natural resources (from crops, to water), which is a significant problem due to the fact that they are dependent on an agricultural economy. The ACF is currently sending supplies their way.

In the Democratic Republic of Congo, they are enduring many outbreaks of very bad malnutrition. In response, Action Against Hunger is focusing on improving the health care system. In 2010, they supplied 476 treatment centers and trained 4,000 public health workers. From this action, 42,000 malnourished people received care that saved their lives.

In Ethiopia, it is expected that Action Against Hunger will aid over 285,000 people by the end of 2011. Already 150,000 have been aided. The Ethiopians need assistance because approximately 5 million people are at risk to drought-related health problems.

In addition, the ACF is intensifying the emergency nutrition programs in Kenya as the

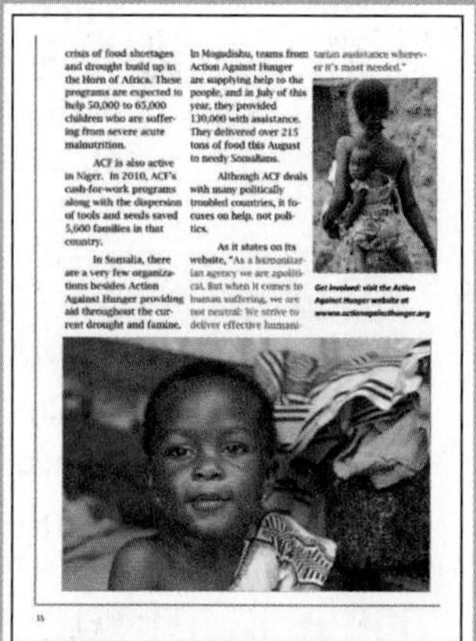

crisis of food shortages and drought build up in the Horn of Africa. These programs are expected to help 50,000 to 65,000 children who are suffering from severe acute malnutrition.

ACF is also active in Niger. In 2010, ACF's cash-for-work programs along with the dispersion of tools and seeds saved 5,600 families in that country.

In Somalia, there are a very few organizations besides Action Against Hunger providing aid throughout the current drought and famine. In Mogadishu, teams from Action Against Hunger are supplying help to the people, and in July of this year, they provided 130,000 with assistance. They delivered over 215 tons of food this August to needy Somalians.

Although ACF deals with many politically troubled countries, it focuses on help, not politics.

As it states on its website, "As a humanitarian agency we are apolitical. But when it comes to human suffering, we are not neutral: We strive to deliver effective humanitarian assistance wherever it's most needed."

Get involved: visit the Action Against Hunger website at www.actionagainsthunger.org

FIGURE 8.11 Miranda Smith's research project on famine relief in Africa, presented in the form of a feature article.

AT A GLANCE

Guidelines for Designing a Newsletter or Magazine Article

1. Decide on the thesis for your project.
2. Categorize your images, arranging them within thematic groups.
3. Organize them into different configurations: by chronology, concept, and subject.
4. Draft written text in the form of headings, captions, and paragraphs.
5. Determine your layout by experimenting with formatting the words and images.

the layout, placement of images, font size, color, and overall look of the piece with painstaking care. Her rhetorical choices establish a hierarchy of information: she strategically uses a header and subheader; she pulls out a key quote on her second page to accentuate an important point; she uses the *logos* of statistics to frame and define the information in the second half of the article; and finally, she selects several images to complement her written argument. Her article ends powerfully with a *pathos*-based appeal, namely, a small child looking directly at the reader as if inviting her to "get involved," a visual echo of the call to action positioned above his head. We can see here how the visual and verbal operate in tandem as powerful persuasive tools for this multimodal composition.

Composing a Website

If you decide to move your project online and produce a Website, your readers will then encounter your visual argument as a series of interlinked pages (or *hypertext*). Web authors construct a framework for an argument through the **homepage** (the site's introduction), the **navigation scheme** (the site's organizational structure), and the contents of individual pages, offering both internal and external links designed to guide readers through the various levels of argument and evidence. In effect, a *hypertext argument* is produced by the interactive collaboration between the author's direction and the readers' participation, so that the audience plays an active role in the construction of meaning.

This dynamic determines the argumentative structure for Causes.com's homepage (see Figure 8.12). The site's target audience is one that is probably already predisposed to participate in social activism or community service, therefore much of the page is designed to provide readers with examples of opportunities and prompt them to action. The site's primary level of decorum is plain style: through simple language, clean, uncluttered design, and engaging visuals, the Website seeks to persuade viewers that they too can make a difference in the world.

FIGURE 8.12 The homepage for Causes.org is organized to provide structure while encouraging exploration.

Part of the power of this multimodal argument lies in its engaging opening hook—similar to the hook you would find in the introductory paragraph of an academic essay—which centers the audience's attention on an example of a person who took action for social good. The *homepage* cycles through a series of such examples, such as Paul who protected the rainforests, Kellie who is protecting pets, Jo who speaks out against animal cruelty, and Eric who fought cancer (see Figure 8.12). Looking closely at Eric in Figure 8.12, we can see the effective design decisions at work: the header is punchy and succinct, putting us on a first-name basis with the character and clearly identifying his accomplishment; the realistic cartoon, with Eric dressed in business casual attire, making eye contact with the audience, relies on *pathos*; the more detailed explanation below the header creates *ethos* by mentioning Eric's full name and also draws the readers even deeper into the site with the lure, "read the whole story." Taken together, these elements effectively personalize the Causes.org experience to appeal to its audience.

Even more significant than the example itself is the way it operates in tandem with the Website frame. Text above and below the central example deliberately encourages audience participation. The top menu offers the principal navigational menu for the site, organized thematically around particular issues. The intent is not linearity, but that exploration of the site will be guided by the visitor's interests; the prominence of the search field in the upper left attests to this as well. Similarly, in the upper right, the audience is prompted to "Start a Campaign," a call to action that is articulated even more forcefully beneath the image. In the footer beneath Eric, in large font, the visitor is asked to put himself in Eric's (or Jo's, or Kellie's, or Paul's) shoes: "How will you use Causes to make a difference?" The shift to second person, coupled with the green "Get Started" imperative that follows, makes clear the argument of this site: its entire design is geared toward providing

Seeing Connections
See Chapter 3 for instructions and advice on writing a hook for the introduction of your essay.

visitors with possibilities and inspiration that will prompt them to start their own activist campaign.

Clearly, while the Causes.org Website on the surface seems simplistic and minimalist, its design was informed by strategic rhetorical decisions that took into account audience and purpose. Based on this example, the process of authoring your own Website may seem daunting at first. However, in many ways drafting text for the web resembles drafting the complex argument of a long research paper: in both cases, you need to identify the necessary elements of your composition, and then you need to follow a process of careful planning and organization.

In designing your Website, you will need to account for three levels of information: a *homepage* at the **primary level** (which will serve as the introduction to your site and draws your audience further into your site); a *series of topic pages* at the **secondary level** (which will contain both content and, sometimes, links to further, more specialized subtopic pages); and the *subtopic pages* at the **deep level** (which will contain content and perhaps even more links). There is no limit on the number of topic and content pages you can include; you should determine the scope of your project and number of pages based on your assessment of how to make your argument most effectively.

WRITER'S PRACTICE MyWritingLab

In terms of design, composing a Website resembles the process of outlining a research paper. Yet there are important differences between digital writing and writing for print readers. For a Website:

- *Chunk* your information—or divide it into manageable parts.
- *Strive for consistency* of theme, font, and/or color throughout your site; avoid visual clutter and ineffectual use of images.
- *Consider creating a template,* or visual precedent, that establishes the key elements for the rest of the site, much as an introduction in a written paper often sets the style and conventions for the rest of the argument to follow.
- *Use subheads* to structure your argument and help readers navigate your text.

Let's now look at a student's web project on the visual rhetoric surrounding the 1963 March on Washington. In designing the site, Hailey Larkin intended to encourage readers to engage with the primary texts within the framework of a researched argument.

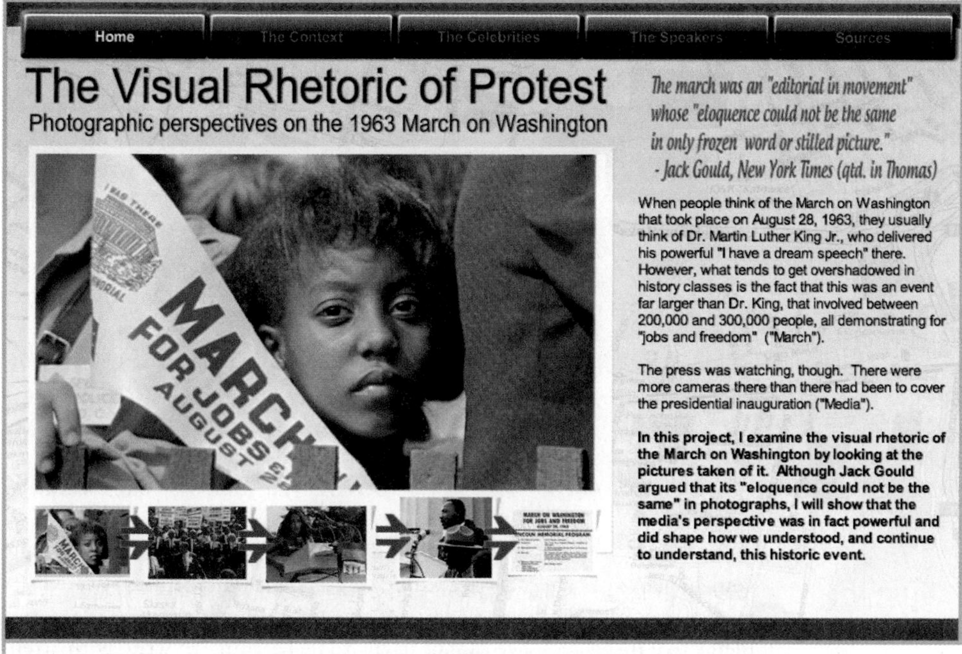

FIGURE 8.13 This project on the 1963 March on Washington uses a carefully designed Website as its medium.

The homepage for this site (see Figure 8.13) models the composition of the entire project. The most striking element is the photograph, used here to underscore the author's argument. Notice the way the homepage:

- pairs image with text
- uses a quote (in blue) as an epigraph
- explicitly states its argument in bold
- meticulously cites its sources (with parenthetical, hyperlinked references to the Sources page)
- shows careful attention to copyright issues by using public domain images

On the subpages, Hailey supports her researched argument through reference to secondary sources and analysis of the primary texts. For

AT A GLANCE

Guidelines for Designing a Website

- Decide on your audience and purpose.
- Draft a header; include an image in it.
- Map a logical organization for your site to help readers find information easily and understand your purpose and argument.
- Be consistent in imagery and font; avoid jarring color combinations or visual clutter.
- Be strategic in your use and placement of images; be clear in your word choice.
- Link to subpages and external sites.
- Provide a feedback link for comments, and include a "last updated" notice.
- Test your site for usability—both in terms of its general user friendliness and its accessibility to users with disabilities.

instance, on the "Celebrities" page, she analyzes photographs of Joan Baez, Bob Dylan, Harry Belafonte, Sammy Davis, Jr., and Charlton Heston. The homepage also demonstrates the site's attention to organization. The tabbed menu at the top is duplicated by the visual menu below, where each subpage is assigned a representative image. Color is used strategically in both instances (white font; yellow border) to help the viewers locate themselves in relation to the larger structure of the argument.

As you compose your own Website as a visual argument, be sure to consider **usability**—how user friendly your hypertext is and how accessible to users with disabilities. Even a site with professional design and a state-of-the-art graphic interface is ultimately ineffective if the audience cannot navigate it. Learning to write with attention to diverse readers will make you a more rhetorically savvy and effective communicator.

Creating a Podcast

If given the opportunity to choose a popular format for your argument, you might consider the podcast—a short audio essay such as those broadcast as part of WNYC's *Radiolab* or NPR's *This American Life.* While a podcast can be comprised of a scripted argument or essay read by a narrator, it is very well-suited to research projects that rely on interviews as a primary sources. By integrating interviews into your script, you have the unique opportunity to bring your sources' voices literally into your argument. In this way, your project comes closer to the model of *conversation* that we explored in Chapter 5 as a way of understanding the process of research.

While in many places in *Envision* we've talked about using visual rhetoric as a strategy of persuasion, with podcasts you can explore the potential for *sound* to function as a persuasive tool. Podcasts can use sound in many ways as a strategy of development:

- To tie the audio essay together by using the same musical tracks to accompany the introduction and conclusion, and sometimes even the transitions between segments
- To set the tone through voice intonation, music, and style
- To signal transitions between segments or parts of your argument
- To accent or enrich points through integrating sounds that suggest setting, background, or an ambient awareness of context
- To give added power to direct ("live") quotations from sources

AT A GLANCE

Guidelines for Creating a Podcast

- Decide on the format you want to use (completely scripted, interview based, combination model).
- Use colloquial language in plain or middle style.
- Lead with a two- to three-sentence introduction that previews the topic and focus of the podcast.
- Include a "hook" in the first segment of your podcast to engage your audience.
- Develop your ideas in additional segments.
- Include a conclusion that sums up the main point and argument.
- Use music to tie the podcast together, especially the introduction and conclusion.

As with any persuasive text, however, be sure to start by analyzing your rhetorical situation when creating a podcast. What is your argument? Who is your audience? What is the purpose of your podcast? What is your rhetorical stance? What persona do you want to project? Finally, consider how this medium affects the delivery of your argument: How does the audio format influence the way in which you'll craft your argument? What extra opportunities does the rhetoric of sound afford you? What limitations will you face as you move from printed to spoken word?

WRITER'S PRACTICE MyWritingLab

Listen to two different podcasts, one from *RadioLab* and one from *This American Life*. Pay particular attention to the following:

- What is the purpose of the podcast? The audience? How do you know?
- How is music used rhetorically in the podcast? How are other sounds used rhetorically?
- What level of decorum does the narrator use? How does she or he establish that style? How does she or he establish tone, mood, and persona?
- How are sources integrated?
- What is the structure of the podcast? Where is the argument most clearly articulated?

Use these questions as the foundation for brainstorming your own list of best practices for creating an audio essay or podcast as a way of sharing a research-based argument.

Producing an Online Video

Another popular format you might consider is one that you encounter everyday on the channels of Vimeo, YouTube, and the like: the online video. Whether you watch weekly videoblogs, technology product reviews, make-up or fashion tips, celebrity gossip reports, or even gaming walk-throughs, chances are you are quite familiar with one of the genres of homegrown video currently available on the Internet. And with camera hardware and editing software coming hardwired with increased frequency on smartphones, laptops, and tablets these days, more and more people find themselves with the opportunity to be their own cameraman, director, producer, and film star.

Consider the Internet sensation *danisnotonfire*. British-born Dan Howell rose quickly to fame in 2010–2011 for his vlog and, as of November 2015, his YouTube channel boasted over five million subscribers. His video blogs often center on personal narrative; in typical YouTube style, he directly addresses the audience, looking into the camera as if to make eye contact; his pieces incorporate occasional cuts between takes to enhance continuity, create a story structure, and emphasize certain ideas. He also at times superimposes text onto the screen to accentuate a point. While clearly gravitating toward a plain or low style, he creates an engaging text defined by his own persona and through a perspective that keeps his viewers coming back for more.

You may notice similar strategies enacted on other Internet celebrity's channels. PewDiePie; Tyler Oakley; Jenna Marbles; Joey Graceffa: all these vloggers trade on similar rhetorical principles for success: they rely on plain style; they use camera techniques to simulate direct interaction and conversation with their followers; they develop engaging personas through the visual and verbal style of their videos; and they assume an effective (if not amusing) rhetorical stance in relation to their audience and topic.

Seeing Connections
See Chapter 3 for a discussion of persona and rhetorical stance

If creating a video, take into account how best to use the particular features of this genre to connect with or persuade your audience. While you might narrate or appear in the video, you might also use footage of events, interviews, locales, or even animation to drive your argument. Consider the ways some students have utilized the short video format to convey a powerful message:

- For a collaborative project on the impact of the Nintendo 64, one group of students constructed its video around a series of interviews they conducted, creating an argumentative structure in which they presented the interview question in type on the screen, following each with "answers" in the form of footage from the interviews. The *ethos* of the interviewees and the careful selection of sound bytes drove home their argument.

- Another student designed a short video argument about current war protests, showing an escalating sequence of images—news photographs of the war-torn landscape, of protest demonstrations, and politicians speaking about the military campaign—set against the soundtrack of the song "Wake Me Up" by Evanescence. The rapid succession of images paired with stirring music provoked an emotional reaction in the audience, without the need for verbal commentary. Since this project included copyrighted materials, the students did not publish it online but instead simply showed it at a class exhibit.
- Yet another group, designing a video argument on *locavorism* (the movement to eat foods grown locally rather than those shipped from around the world), filmed footage inside two markets: the local Albertsons (a big chain supermarket) and their nearby Whole Foods (a natural food market). Using a news reporting style, they examined fruits and vegetable in the produce section in both locales, comparing price, availability, and quality so as to make their argument about the feasibility of adhering to a locavore diet.

In your own film project, use *invention*—perhaps drafting your ideas on a storyboard, as discussed in Chapter 6. Consider levels of style—plain, middle, or grand—and how to best convey these through tone, choice of images, types of camera shots, and persona or voice. Work with the canon of arrangement, as discussed in Chapter 3, to consider how edits, order of scenes, and transitions can contribute to the persuasiveness of your argument.

AT A GLANCE

Guidelines for Producing an Online Video

1. Decide on how you might approach video as a medium to best engage your audience.
2. Use storyboarding to brainstorm or *invent* your ideas.
3. Create a script and build on your storyboard to develop a visual outline.
4. Practice your drafted scenes; if you film the drafts, do a self-assessment or peer review to help you revise.
5. Film your revised scenes, labeling each "draft" as a take for future analysis.
6. Use the strategies you learned in Chapter 6 for revision as you edit your film.
7. When you feel the text is complete, prescreen it with a test audience and receive feedback.
8. Finally, submit it to your audience and then write up a reflection on your work.

Designing a Poster

In some cases, you might be asked to provide a summary of your research in the form of a research poster. This presentation style is used most frequently in the sciences, where **poster sessions** are common at conferences and large conventions. Visitors walk through exhibit halls where hundreds of posters are on display, stopping to read those that interest them and often requesting copies of the complete research paper. If you plan on pursuing a science major, you might want to ask your instructor if a poster presentation would be an acceptable form to use for reporting your research findings.

One of the challenges of creating a poster lies in deciding what information to include. The argument presented by a poster is limited by both space (the physical dimensions of a poster constrain the amount of information that realistically can be included) and time (most readers rarely spend more than 5 minutes perusing a poster). For this reason, it's important to be *selective* in the material you use, *clear* in the way you convey it, and *strategic* in your persuasive design. A poster is a glimpse or summary of your work; a longer research essay or article would be the place to more fully represent your findings and argument.

Another consideration is the logistics of the *delivery* of the information. At times, researchers create "stand-alone" posters, which are designed to be self-contained and present the information without any accompanying oral component. That is, the researcher does not physically stay with the poster to explain it; it "stands alone" in presenting the research. In an alternative model, however, authors stand with their posters in the exhibition hall, symposium, or poster session, using the poster as a way to direct or focus a discussion of their research (see Figure 8.14). Therefore, in determining what information to include, you likewise should consider whether you're developing a stand-alone poster or one that will serve as a visual/

FIGURE 8.14 Poster session.

verbal complement to your oral presentation of research. That decision will influence how much information you include and how you communicate it.

Once you determine what type of poster is most appropriate, you can turn to questions of design. Effective poster design balances two priorities: audience engagement and clear organization. Your design must both draw the audience in—through effective display of visual information and concise and clear writing—and lead them clearly through your information.

Many posters facilitate this process by relying on a column-based mode of organization, where information is distributed in almost a newspaper column format, so that readers are encouraged to follow the flow of information from top left, through columns, until they arrive at the bottom right. Alternately, sometimes more innovative poster designs use a key, central image as an anchor and then organize the information so it radiates out from there. What's most important is that your viewer can follow the progression of your ideas and that you adhere to the requirements of your poster session. Both types of posters can benefit from implementing strategic tactics to signpost for their viewers information and its degree of relevance: clear headers to guide readers, often linked to recognizable components of the research process (i.e., Methods, Results, Discussion); visual hierarchies, so the most important words and images are larger than the less important; and strategic repetition in design to help pull the poster as a whole together.

Let's look at how these elements work together in an award-winning poster from an undergraduate research symposium (Figure 8.15). The poster demonstrates certain key features:

- A hybrid form that organizes information in columns, but around a central image
- Bold headings that are easy to read from a distance

AT A GLANCE

Guidelines for a Designing a Poster

- Be selective in the information you include; integrate key points related to background, method, data, and your analysis or argument.
- Put the poster's title, authors, and academic affiliation at the top.
- Avoid visual clutter; consider using white space to offset various elements, including tables, figures, and written texts.
- Arrange materials in columns or around a central visual anchor.
- Avoid long passages of texts.
  - Include images, charts, and graphs as modes of visual persuasion.
  - Make sure your poster is readable from a distance; size your fonts accordingly.
- Always check with the conference organizers for their specific guidelines.

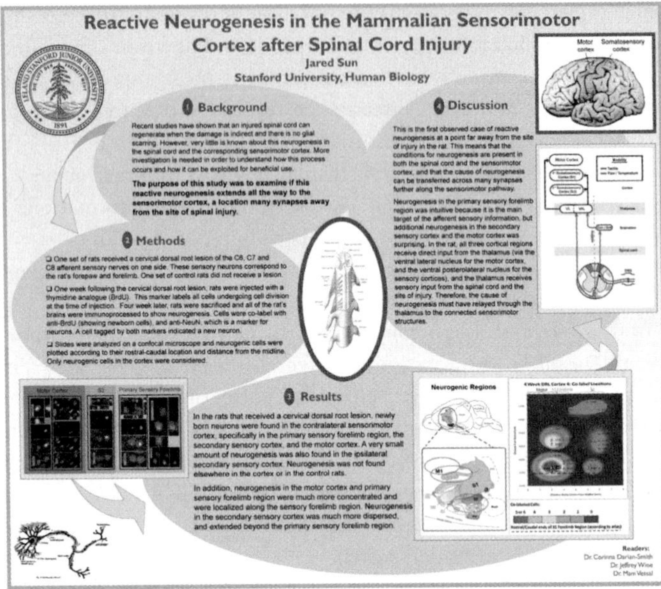

FIGURE 8.15 This poster by Jared Sun combines engaging information graphics with a concise overview of his project.

- Clear hierarchies of information
- Concise written content paired with compelling images
- Signposting involving both numbered sections and arrows
- Concise but specific discussion of research

When you create your own poster, keep in mind the fundamental elements for poster design described in the At a Glance box on p. 333. By following these guidelines, you can create effective public displays of argument that are consistent in format and easily understood by audience members.

Developing a Multimedia Presentation

In today's increasingly tech-mediated environment, multimedia presentations have become very popular in both academic and professional contexts. As with the other types of arguments we've discussed so far, consideration of the rhetorical situation (such as the concepts of audience, purpose, and persona) can help focus the task. If you think of all the different presentations you've encountered in school or everyday life, from an engaging TED talk, to a professor's lecture, or even a guest speaker at a school event, it becomes clear that each adapted their presentation to suit their particular rhetorical situation. Steve Jobs, for instance, perfected a particularly powerful and unique presentation style for his MacWorld presentations (see Figure 8.16). With his trademark black turtleneck and jeans, his emphatic hand gestures, his direct, plain style of discourse, and his skilled use of multimedia support, he was recognized as one of the most persuasive public speakers of the early twenty-first century. You, too, can carefully construct your presentation to be a powerful visual and verbal argument.

FIGURE 8.16 Steve Jobs, co-founder and former Apple CEO, presenting a new product at MacWorld 2008.

Your first step involves assessing the rhetorical situation. Ask yourself:

1. What format will my presentation take?
2. Who is my audience?
3. What is my purpose?
4. What persona do I want to convey?
5. What supporting materials do I plan to use?

Once you've completed this preliminary brainstorming, you can attend to the three components of a presentation: oral argument, multimedia support, and delivery.

AT A GLANCE

Key Steps in Transforming Your Research Argument into a Presentation

- ***Scope.*** How do I convert 10, 15, or even 20 pages of written argument into a 5-, 10-, or 15-minute oral presentation? Answer: Selection.
- ***Content.*** How do I reframe the content so that it makes sense to my audience? Answer: Organization.
- ***Style.*** How do I change the written word to a spoken, visual, and digital medium? Answer: Translation.

Oral Argument At the heart of any presentation lies the oral argument that supports it. In order to transform your research argument into one that you can present orally, you need to follow a process of *selection, organization,* and *translation* outline earlier in this chapter.

Selection: In most cases, you'll need to cut down the sheer amount of material you can convey; for instance, if you have 15 pages of written argument, it would probably take 40 minutes or more to read your words out loud. In fact, most of us speak for longer than we realize, so always plan for a shorter presentation time than what you actually have allotted. This means making hard choices about which subset of your research or argument you'll share with your audience.

Organization: As you transform your research into an oral presentation, you have an opportunity to reorganize your written argument to meet the expectations of a listening audience. You might for instance, begin with your conclusion and then convey the narrative of your research. Or you might want to show your visual evidence fist, ask questions, and then provide your thesis at the end. In other words, your presentation doesn't need to be a miniature version of your written argument. Be innovative, and think about what structure would be most effective for your audience.

Translation: You might find the most challenging step to be translation; for many rhetoricians, it can be difficult to **translate** your writing from text meant to be read to text meant to be heard. To do so, examine your language, assessing the length of your sentences and the complexity of your diction. Make sure to avoid jargon and to define any terms with which your audience might not be familiar. Lastly, add clear signposting (words and phrases like *first*, *second*, *third*, *for example*, *in conclusion*) to clearly indicate your structure to your audience. Listeners also respond to humor, direct address, familiar examples, and even questions. Attending to how to transform your argument in this way – for a listening audience – is key to laying a solid foundation for your presentation as a whole. Be sure to draft a formal script for your translated argument; even if you end up using it merely as notes, the process of writing out your argument completely will ensure that you give careful attention to the structure and style of your oral argument.

Seeing Connections
For an example of translation between oral and written forms, see excerpts from Nicholas Christakis's academic journal article and TED presentation in Chapter 3.

Multimedia Support Once you've drafted your script, you can consider what types of multimedia would best support your argument. We use the word "support" deliberately. Any time you consider incorporating multimedia into a presentation, be sure to keep in mind the following: these multimedia components are *secondary* to your argument. It's the argument itself, not the technology, that should drive the presentation.

There are a range of options available to today's presenter: PowerPoint, Keynote, Prezi, or Google slides; film or audio clips; screencasts; projection of digital images; even, in some cases, live Web browsing or video conferencing with guest speakers. Many factors will influence your choice of multimedia, including your access to technology, the capabilities of the room in which you are presenting, the requirements of your presentation assignment, and your own technological expertise. However, you might also consider the choice of multimedia as a rhetorical one:

A **slidedeck** has been the standard mode of information display for many years. It is designed to showcase your material in a linear format, allowing you to clearly organize your ideas and to distill your points into "power-points" designed to persuade.

A **prezi** presents a creative alternative to the traditional slide deck, allowing for increased customization and a linked or non-linear structure.

A **whiteboard**, though often considered as "old school," can provide a versatility missing from slides or prezis in that it allows you to showcase process by creating notes on the spot to underscore points as you present.

There is no one set of rules for developing effective multimedia support, although, in general, you may find it helpful to remember that your slides or accompanying visuals should be designed to aid the audience's understanding of your argument, not to provide you with notes for your presentation. You may find it helpful to keep these suggestions in mind:

- Use purposeful visuals, not clip art
- Plan to spend time discussing the images you use as visual evidence
- When using a film or audio clip, be selective in how much to show so it doesn't overwhelm your presentation
- Don't put too much text on each slide or frame or rely too heavily on bullet lists
- Use animation to stagger the amount of information you present to your audience at any one time
- Keep fonts consistent in style, size, and color, to avoid distracting the audience
- Break complicated ideas into multiple slides or frames
- Use clear, interesting headers to help visually structure your argument
- Tie your slides together with a visual theme or template that, if possible, reflects the content of your topic
- Include sound effects and animation rhetorically and sparingly
- Give a handout with full quotations or infographics as necessary

The most important thing to remember as you develop your multimedia support is that it should function not as a *script* for you to use, but rather as a *rhetorical act of persuasion* that should engage your audience.

Delivery The last component of a multimedia presentation that you should attend to are components of the live delivery. Indeed, delivery is so important that, when asked which three of the five canons of rhetoric he considered the most valuable to successful public speaking, the Greek orator Demosthenes replied, "delivery, delivery, delivery." When considering delivery for contemporary multimedia presentations, we point to many of the same elements that classical rhetoricians focused on as well.

- **Voice**: pitch, tone, loudness, softness, and enunciation
- **Embodied rhetoric**: use of the body, posture, dress or outfit, appearance, mannerisms
- **Gesture**: use of hands to communicate or punctuate information
- **Pacing**: speed of words, visuals and argument; use of strategic pauses
- **Visuals**: interaction with visual support
- **Style**: inclusion of elements such as repetition, allusion, metaphor, stories, personal narrative, and jokes

As you can see, many aspects of delivery resonate with our previous discussions of oral argument and multimedia support: delivery itself is the performative element of the presentation, the way in which you draw together the different components of your argument and *deliver* them to your audience.

As you craft your own presentation, remember the old adage, "Practice makes perfect." Peer review and revision are as important to your presentation as collaboration on drafts and revisions are to your written work. They enable you to anticipate problems and harness your creativity as you shape your ideas into a memorable, moving, and persuasive form of rhetorical communication.

THE WRITER'S PROCESS

In this chapter, you've learned how to design and produce your texts in ways that meet your purpose and match the expectations of your audience. Often this means knowing, understanding, and adhering to conventions set forth by a community of scholars, readers, or writers. This is the case for the document design of your research essay, cover page, abstract, and bio. At other times, this means exploring innovative approaches to design in multimedia contexts. All modes of design depend on your rhetorical expertise in choosing a level of decorum, in knowing what strategies best work for your situation, in deciding on your medium and your format, and then in having these choices support your purpose in designing your work. By examining academic essays and a variety of multimodal arguments, you have seen that the rhetorical principles of audience, argument, form, and purpose carry across diverse media. With the ever-changing features of modern media, you have an increasing number of choices for designing arguments with purpose, power, and creativity. It's time now for you to make your contribution. Start brainstorming your ideas, and begin to design your own argument.

WRITING ASSIGNMENTS

MyWritingLab

1. **Write an Analysis of a Multimodal Argument.** Select an argument (a YouTube video blog, a work of graffiti art from a community center, a parody poster from a campus organization, for instance) and using the strategies developed in this chapter, analyze how it uses style and design elements to construct its argument. Use the checklist below to help you with this process.

   - **Argument:** What is the text's topic? What is its argument? What evidence is used to support the argument? What is the rhetorical stance and point of view on the topic? What role does verbal, visual, or multimedia play in persuasion in this text? Are words and images complementary or does the argument work primarily through one means?
   - **Audience:** Whom is the argument intended to reach? What response seems to be anticipated from the audience? Sympathetic? Hostile? Concerned?
   - **Medium:** Is the medium used appropriate for the argument and its target audience? What type of interaction does the medium create with its audience?
   - **Form:** What are the specific characteristics of the medium? Consider layout, images, style, and font. How are these elements organized?
   - **Purpose:** What is the purpose in presenting the argument to the audience in this design? To move them to action? Inform them? Teach them? What type of decorum or style (grand, middle, or plain) is used to realize this purpose?

2. **Design Elements to Accompany Your Final Essay Revision:** Write an abstract and bio for your research paper. Adhere academic document design. Post all your documents online as a showcase of your work as a writer and researcher.

3. **Visual Argument:** Create a photo essay based on the argument from your research paper or as part of an independent project. The images you use in your photo essay may be from your paper, or you can use a completely new set, particularly if you did not use images in your original essay. Your argument may mirror that found in your research paper, or you may focus on a smaller portion of your overall argument. The style, arrangement, medium, and rhetorical strategies of your photo essay should match your audience and your purpose. Include written text in your photo essay strategically. Once you have finished, write a one-page reflection on the strategies you used in this project.

4. **Multimodal Argument:** Transform your written essay into one of the creative formats you've learned in this chapter: try creating an op-ed, a Website, an online film, a visual collage, or text combining multiple modes, such one that uses words or audio strategically as part of the text's persuasive power. If using audio, match your images to a recorded argument. Alternatively, combine visual images with a soundtrack, and post your work on a Website that you design; pick your music carefully, and time each image to match a particular mood or moment in the music. If you are transforming your essay into a short online film, modify your organization, arrangement, text selection, and even order of images to accommodate this shift in medium. Once you have finished, write a one-page reflection on your work.

MyWritingLab Visit Ch. 8 Designing Arguments in MyWritingLab to complete the Writer's Practices, Spotlighted Analyses, and Writing Assignments, and to test your understanding of the chapter objectives.

Part IV

READINGS

CHAPTER 9

You Are What You Eat

We take as the title for this chapter the phrase "You Are What You Eat" because never before has this simple idiom held such complex meanings. The dinner table has long been a site of negotiation between children and parents, but the conflicts have moved from whether to eat your vegetables and finish what's on your plate to a much larger arena. Food studies as a field have become a battleground between epicureans and nutritionists, ranchers and activists, and local growers and big business. Thinking about food and its impact on the individual, the environment, and the future has become a new obsession.

Let's consider the ways that our discussions about food have moved out of the kitchen. Walk into any bookstore and you'll not only find glossy-covered gourmet magazines and fully illustrated cookbooks, but you'll probably also encounter a display adorned with copies of Maria Rodale's *Organic Manifesto*, Bryant Terry's *Vegan Soul Kitchen*, Peter Singer's *The Ethics of What We Eat*, and numerous copies of Michael Pollan's best-selling books: *Cooked*, *In Defense of Food*, and *Food Rules*. Feel like watching a film? You can select from a variety of movies that celebrate food, relationships, and community: from *Julie and Julia* to *Chocolat*, *Tampopo*, *Eat Drink Man Woman*, *Babette's Feast*, *Jiro Dreams of Sushi*, and even *Willy Wonka & the Chocolate Factory*. Perhaps you simply decide to browse online. You're likely to come across a recipe site aggregating family recipes, a food blogger photo-documenting her every meal on Instagram, or a food activist providing commentary on the latest incursion against processed foods, GMOs, and fast food chains. The chains themselves have entered the fray: Chipotle, one of the fastest-growing "fast casual" chains in the U.S., announced in 2015 that it was "G-M-Over It" and committed to using only non-GMO (genetically modified) ingredients in all its food. Even a stroll down the street will bring food culture into sharp focus, from the rampant spread of Noodles & Company, Starbucks, and Chipotle into the empty nooks and crannies of our consumer spaces to the rise of specialty markets like Trader Joe's and Whole Foods. Food provides more than just sustenance; it increasingly has come to shape and mediate our understanding of ourselves and our culture.

Perhaps because of the omnipresence of food culture, we are also witnessing a growing critique of it. To see this, we need look no further than our local movie theater and the release of several documentary films over the past ten years that have challenged us to reevaluate the role of food in our lives. While *Fast Food Nation* and *Super Size Me* began the trend in the mid-2000s by targeting the fast food industry and its deleterious effects on American health, these two ground-breaking films were followed by a series of similarly food-focused documentaries. One standout example is the 2009 film *Food, Inc.*, which shifted attention from individual eating habits to corporate farming and industrialized agriculture. The theatrical release poster, shown in Figure 9.1, succinctly epitomizes this critique. What we notice first in the poster is the stereotypical scene of bucolic America, a cow standing in a green field under a vivid blue sky, with an iconic red barn in the background. However, one detail disrupts this idealistic vision: the large barcode branded broadly across the cow's side. This film's goal, the poster argues, is to challenge our romantic notions of food culture, to expose the inner workings of this big business industry, and to problematize our understanding of our relationship to our food.

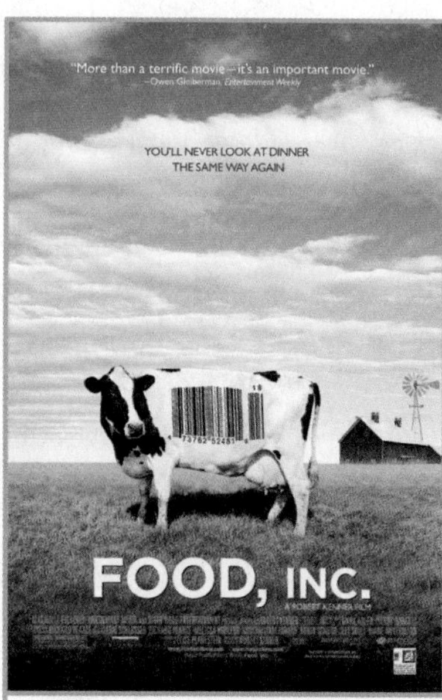

FIGURE 9.1 This poster for *Food, Inc.* challenges the romantic ideal of the food industry.

In the readings that follow, you'll be introduced to the range of commentaries on food culture today, from the food bloggers who memorialize each meal with a smart-phone photo and pithy commentary to activists who draw a link between processed foods, a sedentary lifestyle, and the rise of obesity among American children. We'll look carefully at the government nutritional information graphic and also consider ways that locavorism and "eating local" have become a topic of conversation and debate. Finally, we'll delve into the controversy surrounding genetically engineered crops, looking at their viability as a solution to world hunger. As you read through these selections, we invite you to contemplate your own eating habits and ask yourself: How are food and culture linked? How does what we eat, how we eat, where we eat, and who we eat with shape our ideas of ourselves and our community?

REFLECT & WRITE MyWritingLab

- ❑ Notice the subtitle to *Food, Inc.* at the top of Figure 9.1. How does it complement and complicate the argument of the poster's central image and main title?
- ❑ Considering that this film exposes some of the more controversial practices in the food industry, why do you think the poster designers chose this image rather than one that would have more shock value?
- ❑ **Write.** Compose a rhetorical analysis of this image that uses a strong thesis statement and specific references to the visual composition of the poster. Argue about the significance of this image in relation to the film's title and main idea.

■ *In this blog post, freelance food and culture writer* **Jamie Schler** *explores the ethics of food blogging and asks whether writers like herself should model and promote healthy eating in a culture of excess. Schler's blog is called* Life's a Feast, *where she also writes about the hotel she and her husband run in Chinon, France. "You Are What You Eat" originally appeared on the* Huffington Post *in 2012.*

You Are What You Eat: A Food Blogger's Dilemma

Jamie Schler

Information spreads, food cultures merge, and awareness grows. America has embraced the green, the local and the seasonal, organic is all the rage and farmer's markets are the latest trend. Culinary discoveries surround us, new cuisines and exotic ingredients now a simple shopping trip or Internet connection away. There has been a return to home cooking in leaps and bounds by both men and women alike. Whether we grew up with the boxed and the frozen or with a mother who created stunning meals straight from the pages of *Mastering the Art of French Cooking*, we are discovering the joys of measuring, chopping, stirring, simmering and kneading, of putting a comforting, healthy home-cooked meal on the table for friends and family.

Or so I hear. I have been rather stunned, confused and dismayed by the deluge of junk food posing as the homebaked and homecooked on so many American food blogs, and I am not alone. Beautifully photographed recipes, which I tend to consider not so much recipes as arts & crafts' instructions, are rampant: meals made from cans and prepackaged sauces, desserts based on boxed cake and brownie mixes, canned frosting, jars of marshmallow fluff and then stuffed or topped with industrial marshmallows and chopped candy bars. Layers of gaudy, day-glo snacks and desserts on more than one high-trafficked, well-known blog feature Twinkies or Oreos as the main ingredient, seemingly now a widespread trend. Call me a food snob, if you will, but I don't get it. Haven't we moved on? Don't we in the food blogging world have the desire and the goal to achieve something healthier, tastier, slightly more elevated than what my own parents made 40 years ago when all of this boxed and packaged stuff was new and exciting? We have knowledge and information at our fingertips, we have time and all the necessary technology so why not use it all towards something a tad more noble?

Food blogging, for many of us, began as a way to record and share favorite recipes and connect with other like-minded souls, maybe even learning something about new ingredients, cuisines or technique along the way. Today, it seems that food blogging has simply become big business; branding, traffic, stats, monetizing, advertising, SEOs and cookbook deals are the driving forces and defining factors for many. Shock value and visual appeal seem to be more important than quality content and healthful, creative recipes, the former apparently drawing a much bigger audience. And who can deny that a gorgeous photo doesn't distract the visitor from the actual ingredients? For each of these confections filled with artificial ingredients, sugar and chemicals, overloaded with butter and fat, dazzling with packaged marshmallows, candies and cookies, hundreds of comments from thousands of readers ooze adoration and exclaim a ravenous desire to succumb to sin and partake. A culture of decadence, a culture of excess, junk food has now become retro classic.

Sadly, it seems that food like this, or rather what passes for food, has become the bread and butter for many food bloggers. Don't get me wrong, I have eaten my fair share of sugary cereals, boxed cookies and cakes made from mixes and I have always been an avowed addict of industrial bagged marshmallows. But that was the 1960's and 70's when the frozen, boxed, prepackaged and the mass produced were all part of a thoroughly modern food revolution, created for a new generation of busy working parents; it was all born out of post-war abundance and Space Age progress, a time of convenience when our hours could be better spent playing, working or studying. And who knew any better? Who spoke of chemicals, high fructose corn syrup, preservatives or artificial colorings and flavorings? We simply gloried in the modernization of preparing and eating family meals and snacks.

5 There are a multitude of excellent food blogs featuring creative recipes, healthy and delicious, from-scratch dishes and desserts, as well as food blogs introducing us to certain ethnic and traditional cuisines, so why are so many food blogs that offer, well, trash, getting such high traffic and so many cookbook deals? A friend's fiery

article on the *Huffington Post* called many of today's television cooking shows little more than entertainment, creating and selling a brand; in other words, a moneymaking machine. Should we be questioning the motives of food blogs as well? Indeed, blogs are personal and to each his or her own, yet once we have a reading public who may actually look up to us, emulate us, cook the recipes we offer, do we have a responsibility to move beyond the junk, the chemical and the overly fatty? Have food blogs become just another form of entertainment, mere moneymaking machines? One must, in fact, wonder if these bloggers actually feed what appears on their blogs to their families; many of those who post one unhealthy treat made of processed and artificial ingredients after another, day in and day out, are parents of young children claiming to be devoted to offering their families healthy things to eat. If they are, in reality, not baking these snacks for their families, at whom are these concoctions aimed and what exactly are they trying to promote? Instead of promoting this kind of trash food, maybe we food bloggers should somehow aspire to something better, to inform or educate, to encourage and inspire our readers to bake and cook from scratch, no matter how simple, using something other than the bagged, the boxed and the industrial. Is it our responsibility to create content and recipes with integrity and thoughtfulness and not simply out of the desire to draw more traffic to our blog?

We are living in a society of excess and consumerism and one in which obesity, heart disease, diabetes and other illnesses are raging out of control. Are these food blogs that seem to elevate junk food to some glorified culinary height and give it value contributing to our national health problems, feeding into and reinforcing the accepted food culture of unhealthy eating? Whether or not we indulge in the occasional Rice Krispie Treat and Oreo-stuffed brownie in the privacy of our own home, do they have a place on a food blog? And even if I make it in my home is it truly homemade, are these recipes really recipes? Some say there is room in the blogosphere for both the truly homemade and these semi-homemade, purely indulgent convenience foods, but what message is this sending out to our readers? Where do consumerism, moneymaking and entertainment end and responsibility and smart kick in? I would like to see more food bloggers ask themselves these questions. Or maybe I am simply a wide-eyed idealist.

REFLECT & WRITE

MyWritingLab

- ❑ What strategy does Schler use to hook her readers into the article?
- ❑ Schler's second paragraph begins with a short sentence fragment: "Or so I hear." How does she use this device to indicate a shift in her argument? How would you describe that shift?

- ❑ How does Schler use rhetorical questions to present and develop her argument?
- ❑ What evidence does Schler use to support her general claims? To what extent are you convinced that the problem she addresses in this post is important? Why?
- ❑ In the last paragraph, Schler makes a distinction between private indulgence and public promotion. Does she implicitly argue that food blogs, as a form of public discourse, have an additional responsibility to promote healthy lifestyles? Do you agree with this? What is your assessment of how the rhetorical situation of food blogging (the relationship between audience, argument, and author) should influence the types of arguments that food bloggers make?
- ❑ **Write.** Schler argues that some food blogs "elevate junk food to some culinary height." Do some research to identify a selection of food blogs that you find visually and rhetorically interesting. Write a response in the form of a blog post in which you use these blogs as evidence to confirm or challenge Schler's general claims about the celebration of junk and processed foods.

WRITING COLLABORATIVELY

MyWritingLab

How is eaters' relationship to food influenced by the way in which that food is offered to them? This is the question you'll answer for the collaborative writing project in which you and a group will visit three types of restaurants: a fast food restaurant, a family style chain restaurant, and an upscale gourmet restaurant. For each one, perform a rhetorical analysis of the menu. How, when, and where is the menu presented to the eater? How is it designed in terms of color, layout, and even the materials used? What is contained on the menu? Price? Ingredients? Calories? Which information is presented as the most important to the eater? How can you tell? If you have permission from the establishment, take photographs of the menu to use as visual evidence. Having performed your analysis, write a summary of your findings as a team and develop a claim about how the rhetoric of menus mediates or influences the customer's encounter with the restaurant's food. Present your analysis (with the photographic examples, if you have them) to the class.

Circulated through social networks like Flickr and Instagram, photographs such as these not only document food but also are composed in deliberate ways to make a specific argument about that food.

Food Photographs

FIGURE 9.2 Laura Thal first shared her image of "happy-go-latte" on Facebook.

FIGURE 9.3 Stella HaYoung Shin originally shared this photo with her Facebook friends, captioning it with the name of the restaurant that made the meal.

FIGURE 9.4 Originally saved on Facebook by Caroline Grant, co-editor of *The Cassoulet Saved Our Marriage*, this photograph of homemade mint stracciatella ice cream was tagged #happysummer.

REFLECT & WRITE

MyWritingLab

- ❑ Consider the title of Laura Thal's photograph in Figure 9.2: "happy-go-latte." How does the composition of the photo work together with the title? What argument about culture is the photograph making?
- ❑ Look at the perspective of Stella's photograph (see Figure 9.3). What impression do the layout, the framing, and the angle make on the audience? What is the photo's argument?
- ❑ What argument is Caroline making about her ice cream in Figure 9.4? What distinguishes this photo from other food blog photographs that you have seen? What is it about the photograph that makes that argument persuasive?
- ❑ **Write.** Visit the "I Ate This" pool on Flickr.com. Select three images that work in dialogue to make a specific argument about food or food consumption: draft a thesis statement that presents your

interpretation. Now, working with the canon of arrangement, order the images strategically in a slideshow to make that claim. Present the slideshow to your classmates and ask them to identify your argument. At the end of your discussion, share your thesis statement with them and discuss to what extent the audience's experiences of the argument were the same as your authorial purpose.

Seeing Connections
See Chapter 3 for a further discussion of the canon of arrangement.

■ *According to the official White House press release, the "Let's Move!" campaign is designed to "combat the epidemic of childhood obesity through a comprehensive approach that builds on effective strategies, and mobilizes public and private sector resources." Spearheaded by First Lady* **Michelle Obama**, *the mission of "Let's Move!" is to marshal government, educational, and medical resources to support parents in creating healthier eating and lifestyle habits among children, with the goal of solving the problem of childhood obesity within a generation. What follows are the remarks prepared for the First Lady to deliver at the launch in Washington, DC, on February 9, 2010.*

Remarks of First Lady Michelle Obama as Prepared for Delivery Let's Move Launch

Washington, DC

February 9, 2010

Hello everyone, thank you so much. It is such a pleasure to be here with all of you today.

Tammy, thank you for that wonderful introduction and for your outstanding work in the White House garden.

I want to recognize the extraordinary Cabinet members with us today—Secretaries Vilsack, Sebelius, Duncan, Salazar, Donovan and Solis—as well as Surgeon General Benjamin. Thanks to all of you for your excellent work.

Thanks also to Senators Harkin and Gillibrand, and Representatives DeLauro, Christensen and Fudge for their leadership and for being here today.

5 And I want to thank Tiki Barber, Dr. Judith Palfrey, Will Allen, and Mayors Johnson and Curtatone for braving the weather to join us, and for their outstanding work every day to help our kids lead active, healthy lives.

And I hear that congratulations are in order for the Watkins Hornets, who just won the Pee Wee National Football Championship. Let's give them a hand to show them how proud we are.

We're here today because we care deeply about the health and well-being of these kids and kids like them all across the country. And we're determined to finally take on one of the most serious threats to their future: the epidemic of childhood obesity in America today—an issue that's of great concern to me not just as a First Lady, but as a mom.

Often, when we talk about this issue, we begin by citing sobering statistics like the ones you've heard today—that over the past three decades, childhood obesity rates in America have tripled; that nearly one third of children in America are now overweight or obese—one in three.

But these numbers don't paint the full picture. These words—"overweight" and "obese"—they don't tell the full story. This isn't just about inches and pounds or how our kids look. It's about how our kids feel, and how they feel about themselves. It's about the impact we're seeing on every aspect of their lives.

Pediatricians like Dr. Palfrey are seeing kids with high blood pressure and high cholesterol—even Type II diabetes, which they used to see only in adults. Teachers see the teasing and bullying; school counselors see the depression and low-self-esteem; and coaches see kids struggling to keep up, or stuck on the sidelines.

Military leaders report that obesity is now one of the most common disqualifiers for military service. Economic experts tell us that we're spending outrageous amounts of money treating obesity-related conditions like diabetes, heart disease and cancer. And public health experts tell us that the current generation could actually be on track to have a shorter lifespan than their parents.

None of us wants this kind of future for our kids—or for our country. So instead of just talking about this problem, instead of just worrying and wringing our hands about it, let's do something about it. Let's act … let's move.

Let's move to help families and communities make healthier decisions for their kids. Let's move to bring together governors and mayors, doctors and nurses, businesses, community groups, educators, athletes, Moms and Dads to tackle this challenge once and for all. And that's why we're here today—to launch "Let's Move"—a campaign that will rally our nation to achieve a single, ambitious goal: solving the problem of childhood obesity in a generation, so that children born today will reach adulthood at a healthy weight.

But to get where we want to go, we need to first understand how we got here. So let me ask the adults here today to close your eyes and think back for a moment … think back to a time when we were growing up.

Like many of you, when I was young, we walked to school every day, rain or shine—and in Chicago, we did it in wind, sleet, hail and snow too. Remember how, at school, we had recess twice a day and gym class twice a week, and we spent hours running around outside when school got out. You didn't go inside until dinner was ready—and when it was, we would gather around the table for dinner as a family. And there was one simple rule: you ate what Mom fixed—good, bad, or ugly. Kids had absolutely no say in what they felt like eating. If you didn't like it, you were welcome to go to bed hungry. Back then, fast food was a treat, and dessert was mainly a Sunday affair.

In my home, we weren't rich. The foods we ate weren't fancy. But there was always a vegetable on the plate. And we managed to lead a pretty healthy life.

Many kids today aren't so fortunate. Urban sprawl and fears about safety often mean the only walking they do is out their front door to a bus or a car. Cuts in recess and gym mean a lot less running around during the school day, and lunchtime may mean a school lunch heavy on calories and fat. For many kids, those afternoons spent riding bikes and playing ball until dusk have been replaced by afternoons inside with TV, the Internet, and video games.

And these days, with parents working longer hours, working two jobs, they don't have time for those family dinners. Or with the price of fresh fruits and vegetables rising 50 percent higher than overall food costs these past two decades, they don't have the money. Or they don't have a supermarket in their community, so their best option for dinner is something from the shelf of the local convenience store or gas station.

So many parents desperately want to do the right thing, but they feel like the deck is stacked against them. They know their kids' health is their responsibility—but they feel like it's out of their control. They're being bombarded by contradictory information at every turn, and they don't know who or what to believe. The result is a lot of guilt and anxiety—and a sense that no matter what they do, it won't be right, and it won't be enough.

20 I know what that feels like. I've been there. While today I'm blessed with more help and support than I ever dreamed of, I didn't always live in the White House.

It wasn't that long ago that I was a working Mom, struggling to balance meetings and deadlines with soccer and ballet. And there were some nights when everyone was tired and hungry, and we just went to the drive-thru because it was quick and cheap, or went with one of the less healthy microwave options, because it was easy. And one day, my pediatrician pulled me aside and told me, "You might want to think about doing things a little bit differently."

That was a moment of truth for me. It was a wakeup call that I was the one in charge, even if it didn't always feel that way.

And today, it's time for a moment of truth for our country; it's time we all had a wakeup call. It's time for us to be honest with ourselves about how we got here. Our kids didn't do this to themselves. Our kids don't decide what's served to them at school or whether there's time for gym class or recess. Our kids don't choose to make food products with tons of sugar and sodium in super-sized portions, and then to have those products marketed to them everywhere they turn. And no matter how much they beg for pizza, fries and candy, ultimately, they are not, and should not, be the ones calling the shots at dinnertime. We're in charge. We make these decisions.

But that's actually the good news here. If we're the ones who make the decisions, then we can decide to solve this problem. And when I say "we," I'm not just talking about folks here in Washington. This isn't about politics. There's nothing Democratic or Republican, liberal or conservative, about doing what's best for our kids. And I've spoken with many experts about this issue, and not a single one has said that the solution is to have government tell people what to do. Instead, I'm talking about what we can do. I'm talking about commonsense steps we can take in our families and communities to help our kids lead active, healthy lives.

This isn't about trying to turn the clock back to when we were kids, or preparing five course meals from scratch every night. No one has time for that. And it's not about being 100 percent perfect 100 percent of the time. Lord knows I'm not. There's a place for cookies and ice cream, burgers and fries—that's part of the fun of childhood.

Often, it's just about balance. It's about small changes that add up—like walking to school, replacing soda with water or skim milk, trimming those portion sizes a little—things like this can mean the difference between being healthy and fit or not.

There's no one-size-fits-all solution here. Instead, it's about families making manageable changes that fit with their schedules, their budgets, and their needs and tastes.

And it's about communities working to support these efforts. Mayors like Mayors Johnson and Curtatone, who are building sidewalks, parks and community gardens. Athletes and role models like Tiki Barber, who are building playgrounds to help kids stay active. Community leaders like Will Allen who are bringing farmers markets to underserved areas. Companies like the food industry leaders who came together last fall and acknowledged their responsibility to be part of the solution. But there's so much more to do.

And that's the mission of Let's Move—to create a wave of efforts across this country that get us to our goal of solving childhood obesity in a generation.

30 We kicked off this initiative this morning when my husband signed a presidential memorandum establishing the first ever government-wide Task Force on Childhood Obesity. The task force is composed of representatives from key agencies—including many who are here today. Over the next 90 days, these folks will review every program and policy relating to child nutrition and physical activity. And they'll develop an action plan marshalling these resources to meet our goal. And to ensure we're continuously on track to do so, the Task Force will set concrete benchmarks to measure our progress.

But we can't wait 90 days to get going here. So let's move right now, starting today, on a series of initiatives to help achieve our goal.

First, let's move to offer parents the tools and information they need—and that they've been asking for—to make healthy choices for their kids. We've been working with the FDA and several manufacturers and retailers to make our food labels more customer-friendly, so people don't have to spend hours squinting at words they can't pronounce to figure out whether the food they're buying is healthy or not. In fact, just today, the nation's largest beverage companies announced that they'll be taking steps to provide clearly visible information about calories on the front of their products—as well as on vending machines and soda fountains. This is exactly the kind of vital information parents need to make good choices for their kids.

We're also working with the American Academy of Pediatrics, supporting their groundbreaking efforts to ensure that doctors not only regularly measure children's BMI, but actually write out a prescription detailing steps parents can take to keep their kids healthy and fit.

In addition, we're working with the Walt Disney Company, NBC Universal, and Viacom to launch a nationwide public awareness campaign educating parents and children about how to fight childhood obesity.

35 And we're creating a one-stop shopping Website—LetsMove.gov—so with the click of a mouse, parents can find helpful tips and step-by-step strategies, including healthy recipes, exercise plans, and charts they can use to track their family's progress.

But let's remember: 31 million American children participate in federal school meal programs—and many of these kids consume as many as half their daily calories at school. And what we don't want is a situation where parents are taking all the right steps at home—and then their kids undo all that work with salty, fatty food in the school cafeteria.

So let's move to get healthier food into our nation's schools. That's the second part of this initiative. We'll start by updating and strengthening the Child Nutrition Act—the law that sets nutrition standards for what our kids eat at school. And we've proposed an historic investment of an additional $10 billion over ten years to fund that legislation.

With this new investment, we'll knock down barriers that keep families from participating in school meal programs and serve an additional one million students in the first five years alone. And we'll dramatically improve the quality of the food we offer in schools—including in school vending machines. We'll take away some of the empty calories, and add more fresh fruits and vegetables and other nutritious options.

We also plan to double the number of schools in the Healthier US School Challenge—an innovative program that recognizes schools doing the very best work to keep kids healthy—from providing healthy school meals to requiring physical education classes each week. To help us meet that goal, I'm thrilled to announce that for the very first time, several major school food suppliers have come together and committed to decrease sugar, fat and salt; increase whole grains; and double the fresh produce in the school meals they serve. And also for the first time, food service workers—along with principals, superintendents and school board members across America—are coming together to support these efforts. With these commitments, we'll reach just about every school child in this country with better information and more nutritious meals to put them on track to a healthier life.

These are major steps forward. But let's not forget about the rest of the calories kids consume—the ones they eat outside of school, often at home, in their neighborhoods. And when 23.5 million Americans, including 6.5 million American children, live in "food deserts"—communities without a supermarket—those calories are too often empty ones. You can see these areas in dark purple in the new USDA Food Environment Atlas we're unveiling today. This Atlas maps out everything from diabetes and obesity rates across the country to the food deserts you see on this screen.

So let's move to ensure that all our families have access to healthy, affordable food in their communities. That's the third part of this initiative. Today, for the very first time, we're making a commitment to eliminate food deserts in America—and we plan to do so within seven years. Now, we know this is ambitious. And it will take a serious commitment from both government and the private sector. That's why we plan to invest $400 million a year in a Healthy Food Financing initiative that will bring grocery stores to underserved areas and help places like convenience stores carry healthier food options. And this initiative won't just help families eat better, it will help create jobs and revitalize neighborhoods across America.

But we know that eating right is only part of the battle. Experts recommend that children get 60 minutes of active play each day. If this sounds like a lot, consider this: kids today spend an average of seven and a half hours a day watching TV, and playing with cell phones, computers, and video games. And only a third of high school students get the recommended levels of physical activity.

So let's move. And I mean that literally. Let's find new ways for kids to be physically active, both in and out of school. That's the fourth, and final, part of this initiative.

We'll increase participation in the President's Physical Fitness Challenge. And we'll modernize the challenge, so it's not just about how athletic kids are—how many sit-ups or push-ups they can do—but how active they are. We'll double the number of kids who earn a Presidential Active Lifestyle Award in the next school year, recognizing those who engage in physical activity five days a week, for six weeks. We've also recruited professional athletes from a dozen different leagues—including the NFL, Major League Baseball, and the WNBA—to promote these efforts through sports clinics, public service announcements and more.

So that's some of what we're doing to achieve our goal. And we know we won't get there this year, or this Administration. We know it'll take a nationwide movement that continues long after we're gone. That's why today, I'm pleased to announce that a new, independent foundation has been created to rally and coordinate businesses, non-profits, and state and local governments to keep working until we reach our goal—and to measure our progress along the way. It's called the Partnership for a Healthier America, and it's bringing together some of the leading experts on childhood obesity, like The Robert Wood Johnson Foundation, The California Endowment, The Kellogg Foundation, the Brookings Institution, and the Alliance for a Healthier Generation, which is a partnership between the American Heart Association and the Clinton Foundation. And we expect others to join in the coming months.

So this is a pretty serious effort. And I know that in these challenging times for our country, there are those who will wonder whether this should really be a priority. They might view things like healthy school lunches and physical fitness challenges as "extras"—as things we spring for once we've taken care of the necessities. They might ask, "How can we spend money on fruits and vegetables in our school cafeterias when many of our schools don't have enough textbooks or teachers?" Or they might ask, "How can we afford to build parks and sidewalks when we can't even afford our health care costs?"

But when you step back and think about it, you realize—these are false choices. If kids aren't getting adequate nutrition, even the best textbooks and teachers in the world won't help them learn. If they don't have safe places to run and play, and they wind up with obesity-related conditions, then those health care costs will just keep rising.

So yes, we have to do it all … we'll need to make some modest, but critical, investments in the short-run … but we know that they'll pay for themselves—likely many times over—in the long-run. Because we won't just be keeping our kids healthy when they're young. We'll be teaching them habits to keep them healthy their entire lives.

We saw this firsthand here at the White House when we planted our garden with students like Tammy last Spring. One of Tammy's classmates wrote in an essay that her time in the garden, and I quote, "… has made me think about the choices I have with what I put in my mouth …"

Other wrote with great excitement that he'd learned that tomatoes are both a fruit and a vegetable and contain vitamins that fight diseases. Armed with that knowledge, he declared, "So the tomato is a fruit and is now my best friend."

Think about the ripple effect when children use this knowledge to make healthy decisions for the rest of their lives. Think about the effect it will have on every aspect of their lives. Whether they can keep up with their classmates on the playground and stay focused in the classroom. Whether they have the self-confidence to pursue careers of their dreams, and the stamina to succeed in those careers. Whether they'll have the energy and strength to teach their own kids how to throw a ball or ride a bike, and whether they'll live long enough to see their grandkids grow up—maybe even their great grandkids too.

In the end, we know that solving our obesity challenge won't be easy—and it certainly won't be quick. But make no mistake about it, this problem can be solved.

This isn't like a disease where we're still waiting for the cure to be discovered—we know the cure for this. This isn't like putting a man on the moon or inventing the Internet—it doesn't take some stroke of genius or feat of technology. We have everything we need, right now, to help our kids lead healthy lives. Rarely in the history of this country have we encountered a problem of such magnitude and consequence that is so eminently solvable. So let's move to solve it.

I don't want our kids to live diminished lives because we failed to step up today. I don't want them looking back decades from now and asking us, why didn't you help us when you had a chance? Why didn't you put us first when it mattered most?

55 So much of what we all want for our kids isn't within our control. We want them to succeed in everything they do. We want to protect them from every hardship and spare them from every mistake. But we know we can't do all of that. What we can do ... what is fully within our control ... is to give them the very best start in their journeys. What we can do is give them advantages early in life that will stay with them long after we're gone. As President Franklin Roosevelt once put it: "We cannot always build the future for our youth, but we can build our youth for the future."

That is our obligation, not just as parents who love our kids, but as citizens who love this country. So let's move. Let's get this done. Let's give our kids what they need to have the future they deserve.

Thank you so much.

REFLECT & WRITE

MyWritingLab

- ❑ Look at the first six paragraphs of the speech. To what extent do they serve a rhetorical purpose in relation to the rest of the speech or in terms of the First Lady's assessment of the audience and rhetorical situation?
- ❑ How does the First Lady establish *ethos* in her speech? What types of authority does she invoke? Find specific phrases or passages where she establishes her credibility. Why does she construct *ethos* in this way? How does it contribute to the persuasiveness of her speech?
- ❑ Where does the call to action begin in the speech? How does she build up to it? Is it an appropriate place in the speech to shift to a call to action? Would you have done it earlier? Later? Why?
- ❑ Analyze the movement in this speech from the focus on the individual, to the community, to the government. How effective is this structure for her argument?
- ❑ Consider the rhetorical repetition of the phrase "let's move." What multiple meanings does it hold?
- ❑ Look carefully at the language and word choice Michelle Obama uses in the conclusion of her speech. What deliberate rhetorical choices did she make to bring her speech to a powerful close?
- ❑ **Write.** Clearly this argument was written to be delivered orally. Condense this speech into a 1½–2 page memo between a local representative of "Let's Move!" and a community's Parent Teacher Organization. What changes in content, development, style, and format do you need to institute to accommodate the shift in rhetorical situation and genre?

■ *Since World War II, the* **United States Department of Agriculture (USDA)** *has used information graphics to represent the recommended daily intake of different food categories. The following images represent diagrams released over a span of 70 years.*

USDA Nutritional Information Graphics

FIGURE 9.5 The USDA first published "The Basic Seven" diagram in 1943 as a way of helping to maintain attention to nutrition despite World War II food rationing.

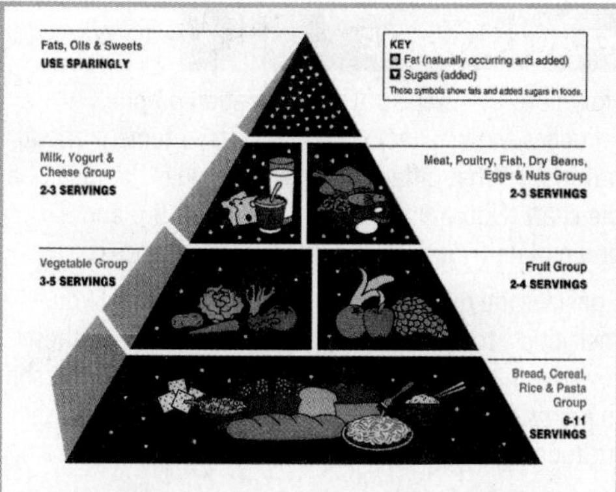

FIGURE 9.6 The original food pyramid was the first released by the USDA in 1992 and was based on a similar model published in Denmark in 1978. Many food packages still feature this pyramid.

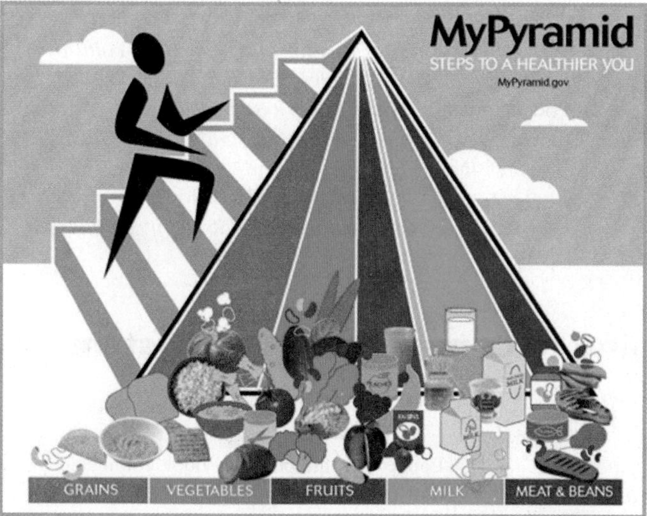

FIGURE 9.7 Released in 2005, the MyPyramid graphic revised the pyramid design to reflect shifts in the American approach to "a healthier you."

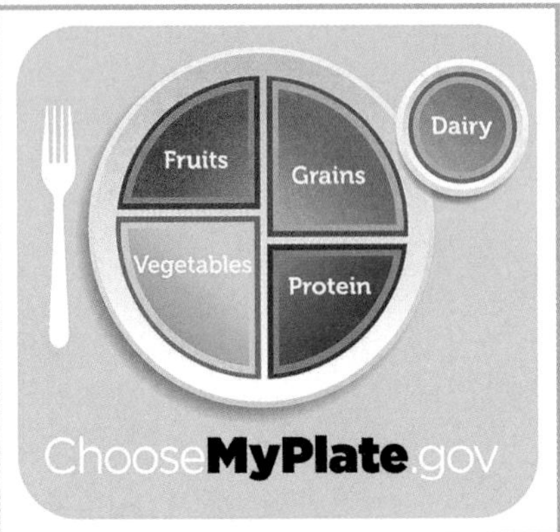

FIGURE 9.8 In 2011, USDA moved away from the pyramid model, instituting instead a plate-based framework to structure its nutritional recommendations.

REFLECT & WRITE MyWritingLab

- ❑ How does the shape of the information graphics influence the way that each makes its argument about nutrition? What different impressions does the idea of a pie chart (Figure 9.5), a pyramid (Figures 9.6 and 9.7), and a plate (Figure 9.8) make on the audience?
- ❑ Consider the differences between the graphics, from their titles, to layout, style, and content. How do these revisions alter the USDA's argument? How does the shift in *kairos* reflect a similar shift in cultural approaches and attitudes (*doxa*) with regard to eating and health?
- ❑ **Write.** Take the information from the MyPlate chart, and rework it into two different types of information graphics (for instance, a bar graph and a pie chart). How does the change in the delivery of the argument transform the argument itself?

■ *In recent years,* **Michael Pollan** *has become one of America's leading writers on food culture. Some of his most notable works include* Cooked *(2013);* Food Rules: An Eater's Manual *(2009), a guide to sensible eating;* In Defense of Food: An Eater's Manifesto *(2008), which won the James Beard Award; and* The Omnivore's Dilemma *(2006), which has won numerous awards and was named one of the ten best books of 2006 by both the* Washington Post *and the* New York Times. *In the following piece, originally published in the October 3, 2011, issue of the* Nation, *Pollan exposes the rift between the food movement's power to change public sentiment and its ability to affect federal legislation.*

How Change Is Going to Come in the Food System

Michael Pollan

In the forty years since the publication of Frances Moore Lappé's *Diet for a Small Planet*, a movement dedicated to the reform of the food system has taken root in America. Lappé's groundbreaking book connected the dots between something as ordinary and all-American as a hamburger and the environmental crisis, as well as world hunger. Along with

Wendell Berry and Barry Commoner, Lappé taught us how to think ecologically about the implications of our everyday food choices. You can now find that way of thinking, so radical at the time, just about everywhere—from the pages of *Time* magazine to the menu at any number of local restaurants.

To date, however, the food movement can claim more success in changing popular consciousness than in shifting, in any fundamental way, the political and economic forces shaping the food system or, for that matter, in changing the "standard American diet"—which has only gotten worse since the 1970s. Recently there have been some political accomplishments: food movement activists played a role in shaping the FDA Food Safety Modernization Act and the Child Nutrition Reauthorization Act, both passed in the last Congress, and the last couple of farm bills have thrown some significant crumbs in the direction of sustainable agriculture and healthy food. But the food movement cannot yet point to legislative achievements on the order of the Clean Air Act or the Clean Water Act or the establishment of the Environmental Protection Administration. Its greatest victories have come in the media, which could scarcely be friendlier to it, and in the food marketplace, rather than in the halls of Congress, where the power of agribusiness has scarcely been disturbed.

The marked split between the movement's gains in the soft power of cultural influence and its comparative weakness in conventional political terms is faithfully mirrored in the White House. While Michelle Obama has had notable success raising awareness of the child obesity problem and linking it to the food system (as well as in pushing the industry to change some of its most egregious practices), her husband, after raising expectations on the campaign trail, has done comparatively little to push a reform agenda. Promising anti-trust initiatives to counter food industry concentration, which puts farmers and ranchers at the mercy of a small handful of processors, appear to be languishing. Efforts to reform crop subsidies during the last farm bill debate were half-hearted and got nowhere. And a USDA plan to place new restrictions on genetically modified crops (in order to protect organic farms from contamination) was reportedly overruled by the White House.

There are two ways to interpret the very different approaches of the president and the first lady to the food issue. A cynical interpretation would be that the administration has decided to deploy the first lady to pay lip service to reform while continuing business as usual. But a more charitable interpretation would be that President Obama has determined there is not yet enough political support to take on the hard work of food system reform, and the best thing to do in the meantime is for the first lady to build a broad constituency for change by speaking out about the importance of food.

5 If this is the president's reading of the situation, it may well be right. So far, at least, the food movement has only a small handful of allies in Congress: Tom Harkin, Jon Tester and Kirsten Gillibrand in the Senate; Earl Blumenauer and Jim McGovern in the House. The Congressional committees in charge of agricultural policies remain dominated by farm-state legislators openly hostile to reform, and until big-state and urban legislators decide it is worth their while to serve on those committees, little of value is likely to

emerge from them. Whatever its cost to public health and the environment, cheap food has become a pillar of the modern economy that few in government dare to question. And many of the reforms we need—such as improving conditions in the meat industry and cleaning up feedlot agriculture—stand to make meat more expensive. That might be a good thing for public health, but it will never be popular.

So what is to be done? The food movement has discovered that persuading the media, and even the president, that you are right on the merits does not necessarily translate into change, not when the forces arrayed against change are so strong. If change comes, it will come from other places: from the grassroots and, paradoxically, from powerful interests that stand to gain from it.

The most promising food activism is taking place at the grassroots: local policy initiatives are popping up in municipalities across the country, alongside urban agriculture ventures in underserved areas and farm-to-school programs. Changing the way America feeds itself has become the galvanizing issue for a generation now coming of age. (A new FoodCorps, launched in August as part of AmeriCorps, received nearly 1,300 applications for fifty slots.) Out of these local efforts will come local leaders who will recognize the power of food politics. Some of these leaders will run for office on these issues, and some of them will win.

It's worth remembering that it took decades before the campaign against the tobacco industry could point to any concrete accomplishments. By the 1930s, the scientific case against smoking had been made, yet it wasn't until 1964 that the surgeon general was willing to declare smoking a threat to health, and another two decades after that before the industry's seemingly unshakable hold on Congress finally crumbled. By this standard, the food movement is making swift progress.

But there is a second lesson the food movement can take away from the antismoking campaign. When change depends on overcoming the influence of an entrenched power, it helps to have another powerful interest in your corner—an interest that stands to gain from reform. In the case of the tobacco industry, that turned out to be the states, which found themselves on the hook (largely because of Medicaid) for the soaring costs of smoking-related illnesses. So, under economic duress, states and territories joined to file suit against the tobacco companies to recover some of those costs, and eventually they prevailed.

10 The food movement will find such allies, especially now that Obama's Patient Protection and Affordable Care Act has put the government on the hook for the soaring costs of treating chronic illnesses—most of which are preventable and linked to diet. No longer allowed to cherry-pick the patients they're willing to cover, or to toss overboard people with chronic diseases, the insurance industry will soon find itself on the hook for the cost of the American diet too. It's no accident that support for measures such as taxing soda is strongest in places like Massachusetts, where the solvency of the state and its insurance industry depends

on figuring out how to reduce the rates of Type 2 diabetes and obesity.

The food movement is about to gain a powerful new partner, an industry that is beginning to recognize that it, too, has a compelling interest in issues like taxing soda, school lunch reform and even the farm bill. Indeed, as soon as the healthcare industry begins to focus on the fact that the government is subsidizing precisely the sort of meal for which the industry (and the government) will have to pick up the long-term tab, eloquent advocates of food system reform will suddenly appear in the unlikeliest places—like the agriculture committees of Congress.

None of this should surprise us. For the past forty years, food reform activists like Frances Moore Lappé have been saying that the American way of growing and eating food is "unsustainable." That objection is not rooted in mere preference or aesthetics, but rather in the inescapable realities of biology. Continuing to eat in a way that undermines health, soil, energy resources and social justice cannot be sustained without eventually leading to a breakdown. Back in the 1970s it was impossible to say exactly where that breakdown would first be felt. Would it be the environment or the healthcare system that would buckle first? Now we know. We simply can't afford the healthcare costs incurred by the current system of cheap food—which is why, sooner or later, we will find the political will to change it.

REFLECT & WRITE

MyWritingLab

- ❑ How does Pollan use Lappé to frame his argument? How does the Lappé reference operate in his introduction? Why do you think he chose to return to him again in his conclusion?
- ❑ Look carefully at that first time that Pollan refers to President Obama. What is the impact of his referring to him in this way? How does he follow up on this initial strategy in the way he refers to the president later in his article?
- ❑ How does Pollan use the analogy to the tobacco industry and the antismoking campaign to shore up his argument? Is this an effective rhetorical technique?
- ❑ **Write.** Right now, Pollan's piece follows the form of an op-ed (or opinion editorial) in that it offers an informed and persuasive opinion on a current issue. Revise it into more of a call to action, either one that is intended to be print-based or that follows more of the op-ad model discussed in Chapter 8. Use at least two to three facts or points from Pollan's piece to inform your call-to-action.

Originally published in August 2011 on the Mother Nature Network website, this information graphic provides an overview to define the different between a "locavore" and "globavore" approach to food consumption.

Information Graphic: Locavorism vs. Globavorism

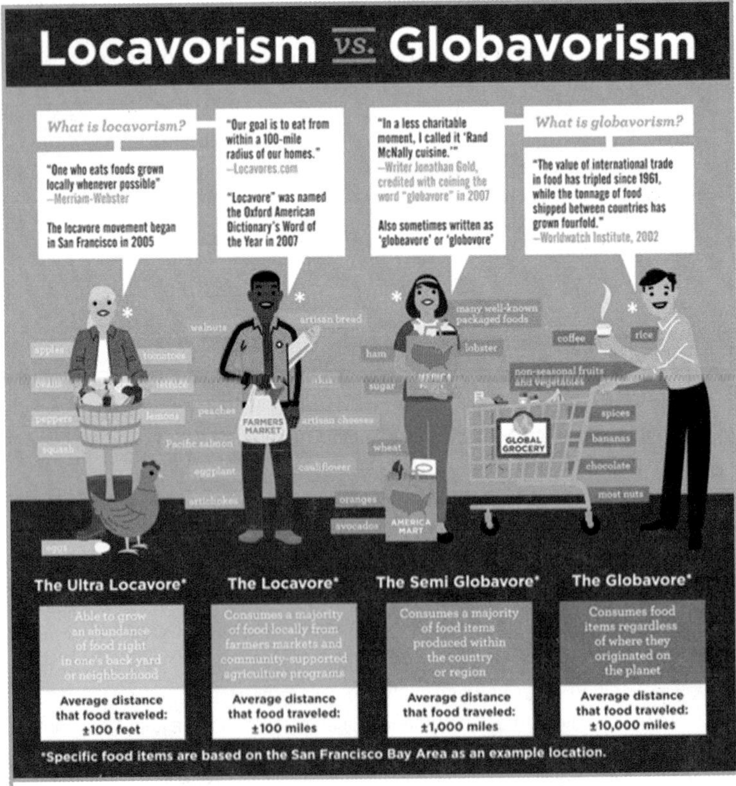

FIGURE 9.9 This information graphic from the Mother Nature Network explicates the differences between the locavore and globavore lifestyles.

REFLECT & WRITE

MyWritingLab

- ❑ The MNN editors called this image a "beginner's guide to what being a 'locavore' or 'globavore' really means." How is this infographic composed to appeal to "beginners"? Consider content, style, and design in your analysis.
- ❑ How does the infographic utilize *ethos, pathos*, and *logos* in developing its definitions? What strategies of argumentation do you see at work?
- ❑ This infographic suggests that it is simply informative, providing definitions, but it implicitly makes an argument. What is the claim it makes about locavorism vs. globavorism? How does it suggest this position on the issue?
- ❑ **Write.** Focus on one individual identity ("The Ultra Locavore"; "The Locavore"; "The Semi Globavore"; "The Globavore") as represented in this image, looking carefully at the various ways in which the artist defined each particular stance. Write a paragraph organized around the strategy of *definition* in which you synthesize the different points made about that character type into a single, unified, and cohesive paragraph.

Seeing Connections
Refer to Chapter 2 for more on rhetorical appeals and strategies of argumentation.

■ *The ideal of eating local, "locavorism," has inspired many writers to explore the benefits to individual and environmental health provided by a diet high in locally cultivated foods.* **Steve Sexton**, *a contributor to a blog called* Freakonomics: The Hidden Side of Everything, *takes a broad, analytical view based on economic data, to explore how eating local may be an inefficient solution to global hunger and climate change.*

The Inefficiency of Local Food

Steve Sexton

Two members of Congress earlier this month introduced legislation advancing a food reform movement promising to help resolve the great environmental and nutritional problems of the early 21st century. The intent is to remake the agricultural landscape to look more like it did decades ago. But unless the most basic laws of economics cease to hold, the smallholder farming future envisioned by the local farming movement could jeopardize natural habitat and climate change mitigation efforts, while also endangering a tenuous and temporary victory in the battle against human hunger.

The "Local Farms, Food and Jobs Act" sponsored by Senator Sherrod Brown of Ohio and Representative Chellie Pingree of Maine, throws about $200 million to local farm programs. That's a rounding error in the $3.7 trillion federal budget. But the bill follows on a federal rule that gives preference to local farms in contract bidding for school lunches. It also builds on high-profile advocacy by Michelle Obama, who has become a leader of the food reform movement, joining the likes of Michael Pollan, the author of *The Omnivore's Dilemma*, and famed-chef Alice Waters. The bill's introduction came as the world population hit 7 billion, a milestone that provides a stark reminder of the challenge agriculture faces to feed a world population expected to grow to 9 billion by 2050. Experts estimate that in the next 50 years, the global food system likely needs to produce as much food as it did in the previous 10,000 years combined.

Amid heightened concern about global climate change, it has become almost conventional wisdom that we must return to our agricultural roots in order to contain the carbon footprint of our food by shortening the distance it travels from farm to fork, and by reducing the quantity of carbon-intensive chemicals applied to our mono-cropped fields.

But implicit in the argument that local farming is better for the environment than industrial agriculture is an assumption that a "relocalized" food system can be just as efficient as today's modern farming. That assumption is simply wrong. Today's high crop yields and low costs reflect gains from specialization and trade, as well as scale and scope economies that would be forsaken under the food system that locavores endorse.

Specialization and Trade

5 Economists have long recognized the welfare gains from specialization and trade. The case for specialization is perhaps nowhere stronger than in agriculture, where the costs of production depend on natural resource endowments, such as temperature, rainfall, and sunlight, as well as soil quality, pest infestations, and land costs. Different crops demand different conditions and vary in their resilience to shocks. So California, with mild winters, warm summers, and fertile soils produces all U.S.-grown almonds and 80 percent of U.S. strawberries and grapes. Idaho, on the other hand, produces 30 percent of the country's russet potatoes because warm days and cool nights during the season, combined with rich volcanic soils, make for ideal growing conditions.

In 2008, according to the USDA, Idaho averaged 383 hundredweight of potatoes per acre. Alabama, in contrast, averaged only 170 hundredweight per acre. Is it any wonder Idaho planted more acres of potatoes than Alabama?

Forsaking comparative advantage in agriculture by localizing means it will take more inputs to grow a given quantity of food, including more land and more chemicals—all of which come at a cost of carbon emissions.

It is difficult to estimate the impact of a truly locavore farming system because crop production data don't exist for crops that have not historically been grown in various regions. However, we can imagine what a "pseudo-locavore" farming system would look like—one in which each state that presently produces a crop commercially must grow a share proportional to its population relative to all producers of the crop. I have estimated the costs of such a system in terms of land and chemical demand.

My conservative estimates are that under the pseudo-locavore system, corn acreage increases 27 percent or 22 million acres, and soybean acres increase 18 percent or 14 million acres. Fertilizer use would increase at least 35 percent for corn, and 54 percent for soybeans, while fuel use would climb 23 percent and 34 percent, for corn and soybeans, respectively. Chemical demand would grow 23 percent and 20 percent for the two crops, respectively.

10 In order to maintain current output levels for 40 major field crops and vegetables, a locavore-like production system would require an additional 60 million acres of cropland, 2.7 million tons more fertilizer, and 50 million pounds more chemicals. The land-use changes and increases in demand for carbon-intensive inputs would have profound impacts on the carbon footprint of our food, destroy habitat and worsen environmental pollution.

It's not even clear local production reduces carbon emissions from *transportation*. The Harvard economist Ed Glaeser estimates that carbon emissions from transportation don't decline in a locavore future because local farms reduce population density as potential homes are displaced by community gardens. Less-dense cities mean more driving and more carbon emissions. Transportation only accounts for 11 percent of the carbon embodied in food anyway, according to a 2008 study by researchers at Carnegie Mellon; 83 percent comes from production.

Economies of Scale

A local food production system would largely upend long-term trends of growing farm size and increasing concentration in food processing and marketing. Local "food sheds" couldn't support the scale of farming and food processing operations that exist today—and that's kind of the point. Large, monocrop farms are more dependent on synthetic fertilizers and tilling operations than small polycrop farms, and they face greater pest pressure and waste disposal problems that can lead to environmental damage.

But large operations are also more efficient at converting inputs into outputs. Agricultural economists at UC Davis, for instance, analyzed farm-level surveys from 1996–2000 and concluded that there are "significant" scale economies in modern agriculture and that small farms are "high cost" operations. Absent the efficiencies of large farms, the use of polluting inputs would rise, as would food production costs, which would lead to more expensive food.

Health Implications

A local food system would raise the cost of food by constraining the efficient allocation of resources. The monetary costs of increased input demands from forsaken gains from trade and scale economies will directly bear on consumer welfare by increasing the costs of food. And, as we try to tackle obesity, locavorism is likely to raise the cost of precisely the *wrong* foods. Grains can be grown cheaply across much of the country, but the costs of growing produce outside specific, limited regions increase quickly. Thus, nutrient-dense calories like fruits and vegetables become more expensive, while high fructose corn syrup becomes relatively cheaper.

Finally, higher costs on certain foods may be a solution to the big health challenge in the developed world. But higher prices on any food are precisely the wrong prescription for the great health problems in the developing world, where millions remain undernourished. As the food crisis of 2007–08 revealed, winning the war on human hunger requires a constant commitment to getting more food out of less land, water, and other inputs.

From roughly 1940–1990, the world's farmers doubled their output to accommodate a doubling of the world population. And they did it on a shrinking base of cropland. Agricultural productivity can continue to grow, but not by turning back the clock. Local foods may have a place in the market. But they should stand on their own, and local food consumers should understand that they aren't necessarily buying something that helps the planet, and it may hurt the poor.

REFLECT & WRITE

MyWritingLab

- ❑ What level of decorum (high style, middle style, plain style) does Sexton use to make his argument? What elements of his writing style contribute to the level of decorum he chose?
- ❑ Thinking back to our discussion of Toulmin logic in Chapter 3, some might argue that at one point in this piece, Sexton questions the "warrant" of the argument that local farming is better for the environment. What warrant is he challenging? Do you find this part of his argument persuasive?
- ❑ Sexton's article is written in part as a response to a particular piece of proposed legislation. What is Sexton's argument about that legislation? How does he use the occasion to develop broader claims? What are his primary claims?
- ❑ **Write.** To better understand Sexton's argument and how he supports it, create a reverse outline of this essay. Be sure to include notations for both his main points and a brief note of the different evidence he uses to support them.

Seeing Connections
See p. 102 in Chapter 3 for a discussion of the Toulmin method of argumentation.

Like Sexton, **Maisie Ganzler**, *offers a pointed perspective on what has become a wide-ranging discussion about the economics and the ethics of local food. Ganzler, who has contributed to several local food initiatives, writes in the* Huffington Post *that the personal and cultural benefits of local food outweigh any potential inefficiencies.*

The Non-Controversy Surrounding Local Food

Maisie Ganzler

A recent glut of books, studies and news articles aim to perpetuate the argument that local food is actually less environmentally friendly than its industrially raised counterpart. Claims range from "factory farms are better for the environment because they are more centralized" to "local farmers are not sophisticated enough to provide adequate food safety precautions."

The contentions that local food's opponents are putting forth are actually founded largely on credible data, and this is in part why the "controversy" surrounding local food persists. However, examining why locavorism does or does not make sense in 21st Century America via only one or two specific data points is leading people to the wrong conclusions.

While authors, the media and the entities paying for some of these studies all have vested interest in stirring the pot—either selling books and magazines or maintaining their hold on our food system—I think the American public is smart enough to see through these one-dimensional arguments, to hold more than one idea in our mind when it comes to local food.

Most local food advocates now know that the notion of food miles (the distance food travels from farm to table) isn't a proxy for sustainability, that is, short distances don't always equal less energy. And yes, transportation only accounts for a small percentage of the environmental impact of food production. That does not mean, however, that food grown on small-scale farms is not planet-friendly.

5 In fact, when you add in the issues that climate change is creating, local food's practicality and environmental importance becomes even clearer. With this summer's drought and the devastating hurricane Sandy nearly unanimously attributed in part to climate change, the need for localized food systems is increasing. They provide insurance against natural disasters happening thousands of miles away disrupting the food supply system where we live. Predictions of increased flooding, wildfire, drought and powerful storm systems signal increasing risk to the infrastructure that allows tomatoes to travel routinely from Florida to Ohio. Locally grown food provides a safety net in this increasingly unpredictable situation.

Another benefit local food provides in this age of climate change: early warning. In Santa Cruz, where I grew up, a put-down among local farmers regarding other farmers was that they should "go to Chualar"—an area where nothing would grow. Now, Chualar is a burgeoning growing region for grapes, lettuce and strawberries. In the space of 20 years, a region once generally considered inhospitable to these crops is now producing them in abundance. These are the realities of climate change, and local farmers are on the frontlines. Especially in rural areas, where formal studies on the local impact of climate change may be few and far between, the anecdotal evidence that local farmers can provide—the same sort of knowledge that was passed around and led to "go to Chualar" becoming sage advice versus an insult—is essential to understanding what is happening around us.

Local food impacts our quality of life beyond its positive environmental effects. When urban land use is agricultural, the amount of open space in a geographical area is increased. This type of open space provides not only economic benefits in the form of increased property values in these urban and semi-urban areas, but aesthetic and ecological benefits as well.

And then there is community. Farmers' markets have figuratively replaced the town square, something we have lost over the last decades due to sprawl and urbanization. In many communities around the country, farmers' markets are where we chat with neighbors, make new connections and find out about the issues at play in our communities. According to the United States Department of Agriculture, there are 7864 farmers' markets operating today—a 348% increase since 1994. Clearly they are providing value to the American public.

The pace of modern American life is such that we want—maybe even need—to boil complex issues down to essential truths. Yet isolating a few specific factors and extrapolating solely from these to proclaim that local food is not eco-friendly, or not a viable solution, is irresponsible. This is not to say that measuring a single issue like carbon emissions as it relates to food production and transportation is not important; it is vitally important.

10 But, there are many more factors at play—some very tangible, some less so—in evaluating the importance of local food. We are literally losing ground in this country, and the role that local food plays in ensuring we are preserving and protecting that ground—and the communities built on it, the lives lived on it—should no longer be up for debate.

REFLECT & WRITE

MyWritingLab

- ❑ Why does Ganzler use the word "non-controversy" in her title? Does her essay support the view that local food is a "non-controversy"? How?
- ❑ How would you describe the voice and style of Ganzler's article? How does it compare to the style Sexton uses? Why might Ganzler have chosen to use the style she does?

- ❑ Consider Ganzler's conclusion. Why do you think she chose to end her essay in this way? To what extent does it reinforce—or perhaps even undermine—her argument?
- ❑ **Write.** Sexton and Ganzler, taken together, offer an interesting cross section of recent writing around the topic of local food. As is often the case, defining the terms of the argument is often as important as presenting evidence to support claims. Can you identify any common ground on which Sexton and Ganzler might agree? Write a "dialogue of sources" essay in which you offer a summary and synthesis of these two essays.

Seeing Connections
See Chapter 5 for more information about how to create a dialogue of sources with two or more readings.

In 2005, photojournalist **Peter Menzel** *and his wife, writer* **Faith d'Aluisio**, *published* Hungry Planet, *an extensive look at eating habits around the world through photographs and essays. This work received numerous awards, including the 2006 James Beard Foundation award for Book of the Year and the 2006 Harry Chapin World Book of the Year award from the World Hunger Media Foundation. A selection of the images from* Hungry Planet *was published by* Time *magazine as a photo essay called "What the World Eats," with the subtitle "What's on family dinner tables around the globe?" The images and captions that follow are taken from that photo essay.*

Photographs from *Hungry Planet*

FIGURE 9.10 Mexico: The Casales family of Cuernavaca
Food expenditure for one week: 1862.78 Mexican Pesos or $189.09
Favorite foods: pizza, crab, pasta, chicken

FIGURE 9.11 Chad: The Aboubakar family of Breidjing Camp
Food expenditure for one week: 685 CFA Francs or $1.23
Favorite foods: soup with fresh sheep meat

REFLECT & WRITE

MyWritingLab

- ❑ Look carefully at the captions, reproduced as they originally appeared in the *Time* photo essay. What information is included? Judging by this information, what types of comparisons does the photo essay encourage the readers to make between the different families?
- ❑ Consider the staging of the food and the use of space. How do these elements contribute to each photograph's argument?
- ❑ Which photograph surprised you the most? Why? Did either of them seem to reinforce common stereotypes? Did any of them resist those stereotypes?
- ❑ **Write.** First, choose one of the pictures and write a rhetorical analysis of its argument, referring to specific elements in the photo and caption as evidence. Then, find a copy of *Hungry Planet* in your local library or bookstore. Look through the book to find the photo you selected and examine it within this different context, reading through the text that accompanies it in *Hungry Planet* as well. Now, as an addendum to your initial analysis, write a reflection on how your understanding of the argument of the photograph changes with the different rhetorical situations. Be sure to take into account the issue of audience, purpose, and medium (book versus online photo essay) in your writing.

Few developments have more dramatically impacted our eating habits than the rise of genetically modified food. Genetically modified organisms (GMO) are a subject of intense debate, and many consumers have decided to limit or avoid eating GMO foods entirely. Identifying foods that have or have not been genetically modified proves to be a challenge, as **James McWilliams** *argues in this essay, originally published in 2014 by* Pacific Standard. *McWilliams is an associate professor of history at Texas State University, and the author of* Just Food: Where Locavores Get It Wrong and How We Can Truly Eat Responsibly *(2010).*

Label Me Confused

James McWilliams

We want labels on our food products and we should. Labels are ostensibly intended to clarify and, in an age when food companies are doing strange things to their products, it has never been more important to have a steady stream of clarification. Some critics even go so far as to say we have a basic human right to know—explicitly stated on a label—what's in our food. It generally seems safe to say that the more accurate information we have about our food, the better.

This idea currently works—up to a point. I'm sitting here looking at a bag of Basmati rice. The ingredient list is simple enough: "Basmati rice." The nutritional information is straightforward: lots of carbs, protein, iron, and fiber, and no fat or cholesterol. The front of the bag tells me the rice is "Carolina Basmati." Geography matters, so it's nice to know that the rice came from somewhere on the East Coast between Georgia and Virginia. The package also notes that the rice is "naturally fragrant," a telling addition aiming to assure jaded consumers that the unique aroma of Basmati is, as another word on the label offers, "authentic," rather than the result of yet another industry trick. In addition to the fact that the bag weighs two pounds and that a cup of dry rice yields four servings, this is the extent of the "easy-to-digest" information that comes with my bag. At this point, I'm a well-informed cook.

But if I wanted to become confused all I'd have to do is continue reading. A little stamp on the back of the bag says "origin Pakistan," leading me to wonder what happened in Carolina and what happened in Pakistan. Does "Carolina Basmati" mean that Carolina is importing my rice while Pakistan is growing it? And if so, what about food miles? What's the distance from Pakistan to Carolina and by what mode of transport did the rice travel (by boat or airplane)? What does it mean, as the bag further explains, that the rice was "packed for: Riviana," a distributor of specialty rice products based out of Houston, Texas? Did the rice skip Carolina and go directly from Jinnah International Airport to George Bush Intercontinental?

And now that we're on the topic of Pakistan, what kind of growing methods do they use there? Are farmers using their own seed or are they beholden to a rapacious international seed company? What kinds of chemicals—natural or otherwise—are permitted in Pakistani agriculture? What's the water situation like? This Basmati rice—with which I made a fluffy pilaf last night—is some of the finest I've used. But the bag it came in, for all of the immediate information it provides, leaves me with more questions than answers.

5 Even the seemingly most basic labels that carry the most weight with consumers—organic and local—can sow considerable confusion. A recent study published in the *International Food and Agribusiness Management Review* confirms a wide range of perceptions and misperceptions over what these terms mean for concerned consumers. Almost a quarter of all consumers surveyed erroneously conflated local and organic, thinking them to be more or less the same thing. Roughly one out of five consumers thought "local" meant non-GMO, lower greenhouse gas emissions, and having a longer shelf life. Closer to 30 percent believed the local label meant the food was healthier, and 44 percent believed the food tasted better. Of course, it is true in some cases that local means all of these things. But it's just as likely untrue. The local label itself makes no absolute claims about any of these factors. The only thing local means—the only honest point made by the label—is that there were "decreased miles to transport product." Somehow, 33 percent of consumers weren't aware of this.

The organic label, despite established and readily available USDA standards, is equally confusing to many consumers. Twenty-five percent of those surveyed believed that no natural pesticides are used to grow organic food. Forty percent associated the organic label with more nutritious food, and nearly as many thought organic implied better-tasting produce. Nearly 40 percent did not know that natural fertilizer can be used in organic agriculture.

Again, these answers reflect considerable confusion vis-à-vis the reality of organic—not to mention agriculture in general. And none of it is new. Back in 2005, another study on consumer perceptions found that 40 percent of those surveyed linked the organic label with "chemical free," an association that is flatly incorrect. What does become clear in reading these studies is that the organic label, much like the local label, is less a marker of concrete information than a term upon which consumers are quick to project a set of desired images.

Food labels, even in an honest attempt to clarify, are necessarily complicated because food, despite our wish otherwise, is necessarily complicated. The terminology upon which we now depend is, for reasons only hinted at here, inadequate. Organic can mean a million things just as local can mean a million miles. It would be nice if we could just go in the opposite direction and insist that the more information we have the better. But if that were true for my Basmati label, it could have noted that the reason my kitchen smelled so lovely when I was cooking my pilaf was because of a chemical in the rice called 2-actyl-1-pyrroline, the inclusion of which might scare away the chemically illiterate—which is most of us. (Plus, as Michael Pollan says, "if you can't say it, don't eat it.")

What we need in terms of labeling is something that rarely happens in the food world: a compromise. What I would like to know about any whole food that I buy is this: What country was it grown in? Were workers paid a living wage? What pesticides were applied and how often? What was the rate of fertilizer run-off? How far was the farm from a petrochemical or coal-fired power plant? What was the yield per acre? And how biologically diverse was the farm? I'd forgo any other labels for this kind of data. But I'm not holding my breath.

REFLECT & WRITE

MyWritingLab

- ❑ McWilliams focuses his essay on a single bag of rice. What does this narrow focus enable him to show readers? Do you find the strategy effective?
- ❑ What would McWilliams like to see on the label on the bag of rice he describes in this essay? Why?
- ❑ McWilliams uses many different rhetorical techniques in his argument, for instance: deliberate repetition, *logos*, *ethos*, definition, and example. Pinpoint places in the essay where he uses these techniques and consider how they contribute to the development of his argument.
- ❑ In his conclusion, McWilliams calls for "a compromise." What is the nature of the compromise that McWilliams would like to see? How can you tell? Why does McWilliams say that he is "not holding my breath" to wait for such a compromise?
- ❑ **Write.** McWilliams provides a brief overview of the items he would like to see added to a label on a bag of rice. Based on his essay, and your own experiences buying and preparing foods, develop a list of things you think should appear on food labels. Write a proposal to redefine the required information that should be provided on food packaging. You may want to include a proposed design for an improved food label as part of your proposal.

■ **Tamar Haspel** *is an oyster farmer on Cape Cod who also writes about food and science. Her essay, "The GMO Debate: Five Things to Stop Arguing," was published by the* Washington Post *in October 2014 and offers us another perspective on the GMO debate.*

The GMO Debate: 5 Things to Stop Arguing

Tamar Haspel

BREAK OUT the party hats! Unearthed is one year old—and it has been one interesting, gratifying year. To celebrate, I'm revisiting the issue that kicked off this column a year ago: genetically modified organisms (GMOs). You might not think much of my idea of celebration, but I'm guessing you'd agree that the public debate about GMOs isn't playing out in a constructive way. Both sides have dug trenches, and they're lobbing grenades over the wall while nothing much changes. It's the World War I of food issues, and something's gotta give.

I'm going to suggest five somethings. Each is an argument, from one side or the other, that I think should be retired. If we all agreed to stop lobbing these particular grenades, we could move on to more substantive issues and perhaps generate a little goodwill in the bargain.

1. GMOs are dangerous to eat.

It's impossible to be certain that a GM food, or anything else, is safe. But all uncertainty is not created equal, and the chance that the genetically modified crops in our food supply pose a danger to human health is extraordinarily small. There have been thousands of studies on these foods, many of them long-term and independently funded, and virtually every mainstream science organization has come down on the side of safety.

One of the most compelling studies came out just last month, and it had billions of subjects that eat GMOs almost exclusively: livestock. Researchers from the University of California at Davis looked at health data on more than 100 billion animals and found no ill effects—in fact, no effects at all—attributable to a switch from non-GMO feed to GMO.

5 There is a consensus on the safety of GM crops. Consensus doesn't mean every last person on the planet; there are people who still say GMOs are dangerous, and some of those people have advanced degrees. But siding with those people, in the face of the consensus, just makes it easier for others to dismiss you as an anti-science (more on that later) zealot. Arguing that GMOs pose a significant human health risk is unreasonable.

2. Labeling is unnecessary because GMOs are safe.

This argument misses the point. If GMOs were dangerous, the FDA wouldn't label them, it would ban them. The items on our food labels run the gamut and include substances that pose a risk to some people (peanuts), substances that public health authorities recommend we should all limit (salt) and lots of ingredients with no health implications at all. There are indications of how a product is made (orange juice from concentrate) and where it comes from (country of origin). Some vitamins and nutrients are listed, others aren't. There is no grand unifying theory of what goes on a label. It's all case-by-case.

The argument for labeling is simply that consumers want to know, but that's not a particularly strong argument. Anyone can come up with a "want to know" list that includes both the ridiculous (farmworkers' race) and the reasonable (farmworkers' wage). Is wanting to know about GMOs reasonable?

Sometimes it's not (see Argument 1), but let's take a GMO skeptic who says herbicide-tolerant crops concern her because they might foster herbicide-intensive agriculture, with negative environmental consequences, and that we need to start building more transparency into our agricultural system so consumers can vote with their wallets for the kind of system they want to see. You might disagree with her, but I don't think she's unreasonable.

A constructive debate has to address reasonable concerns. The safety argument doesn't.

3. Only Big Ag benefits from GMOs.

10 It's unfortunate that Americans' first exposure to genetically engineered crops was to herbicide-tolerant corn and soy. Because the benefits of those most widely planted GMOs *do* accrue chiefly (not exclusively, but I won't quibble) to commodity farmers and agribusiness, all other genetically modified foods have been tarred with the same brush. The ringspot-resistant papaya is rarely part of the discussion and, no matter how often I flog my favorite, the yeast that produces healthful long-chain omega-3 fats, it just doesn't make a dent in the association that GMOs have with Big Ag.

The list of GMOs with benefits to the rest of us is long. There's the mosquito that helps control dengue fever by mating with disease-carrying mosquitos and passing on a gene that kills the offspring. A cow resistant to the organism responsible for sleeping sickness (a trypanosome) can no longer pass the disease to humans via a tsetse fly. How about the orange tree resistant to citrus greening? Or crops with more vitamins, or more healthful oils? And don't forget my omega-3 yeast.

Don't let your distrust of herbicide-tolerant crops extend to GMOs in general.

4. We've been genetically modifying crops for thousands of years.

What GMO supporters mean, of course, is that we've been cross-breeding for thousands of years. Which is true but irrelevant, because the people who are concerned about GMOs are concerned precisely because the technology is very different from cross-breeding. In making this argument, supporters completely ignore the basis of opponents' skepticism, and that's condescending and counterproductive.

It also undermines what may be one of the most interesting and compelling arguments in favor of GMOs: That the techniques used to insert individual genes enable changes in the organisms that are much more predictable, and therefore less likely to be harmful, than the wholesale changes that come from cross-breeding. That argument works only if you admit from the get-go that transgenic breeding is materially different from what we've been doing for thousands of years.

5. GMO supporters are Monsanto shills, and opponents are anti-science.

15 The shill part is pretty obvious. Please just stop.

The anti-science part is more complicated. The people who study how we make decisions about issues of science and policy tell us that our positions on those issues tend to determine our perception of the science, not the other way around. Most GMO opponents aren't anti-science; they're anti-GMO, and therefore see the large body of science that contradicts their ideas as tainted by association with industry, flawed methodologically, done by biased scientists or otherwise dismissible. They are, in fact, pro-science—toward science that confirms their beliefs. (GMO supporters, and humans in general, are just as susceptible to this kind of confirmation bias.)

Yale Law School professor Dan Kahan, whose Cultural Cognition Project investigates how values and group affiliations influence beliefs, says that "conflict entrepreneurs who are trying to turn GM food risks into a polarizing issue" may deserve the anti-science charge, but that the charge itself, deployed more widely, is also polarizing. "In general, the anti-science trope is noxious," he says, both because "it's not an empirically supported account of the sorts of positions it is usually invoked to explain, and because it tends to pollute the science communication environment." Most of the public doesn't give a fig about GMOs, but the more we throw around the anti-science charge, the higher the risk that this issue becomes entrenched as an emblem of cultural identity. Think climate change.

Entrenchment is what we're trying to avoid here. Stop making these arguments, at least for a while, and see if it doesn't help. While you're at it, reach out to someone you respect who disagrees with you, and listen. If you're a scientist, academic, activist, journalist or any other type who gets invited to speak on panels, insist that the panel represent both sides fairly; choir-preaching doesn't help. We need to come to some kind of reasonable consensus on this issue. Give peace a chance.

REFLECT & WRITE

MyWritingLab

- ❑ How does Haspel rely on *ethos* to bolster her argument? To what end? Find at least two points in her piece where she does so.
- ❑ Does Haspel take sides in the debate? Why or why not? Where would you expect her to locate herself in the GMO discussion? Why?
- ❑ **Write.** Haspel describes the debate surrounding GMO foods as "the World War I of food issues." Do some additional research to locate a few sources on the GMO foods debate. Write a synthesis of these sources in which you confirm or challenge Haspel's description of the debate as "entrenched."

ANALYZING PERSPECTIVES ON THE ISSUE

MyWritingLab

1. Search for food blogs online and look at examples of posts and photos, developing a sense of the format of this particular genre of writing. Now, keep your own food blog for a week, incorporating both written texts and your own photos. After a week, share your blog posts with the class and write a brief reflection about the process of food blogging and what you learned about yourself and your relationship to food from this experience.
2. Watch the video of Michelle Obama delivering her announcement of the "Let's Move!" project, available on the Let's Move Website and on YouTube. As you watch, take notes, comparing it to the content and composition of the "Let's Move!" launch speech you read in this chapter. How is the rhetorical situation of the two pieces different? How did Obama modify her script for the online version? What did she emphasize more or less in her revision? Think also about her delivery and the staging of the video. What images were chosen, how were they arranged, and how do they complement oral delivery? Use these notes to produce a comparative analysis essay of the two texts.

Seeing Connections
For further discussion about translating between written and oral texts, see Chapter 8.

3. Search the Chipotle "Scarecrow" and "Back to the Start" commercials online and watch each one. How do they use the conversation about healthy foods as a starting point to persuade the viewer to visit their restaurants? Look carefully at the extent to which they use the different rhetorical appeals in their advertising and at how they use elements such as music, animation, pacing, comparison-contrast, narrative, and other rhetorical strategies to make their point. Write a brief rhetorical analysis of one these texts. See the Spotlighted Analysis on p. 86 of Chapter 2 for some brainstorming questions to help you begin your analysis.

FROM READING TO RESEARCH ASSIGNMENTS

MyWritingLab

1. Many doctors and scholars have looked at how American children suffer from a culture of poor eating practices. Raj Patel, among many others, has written about the marketing practices of fast food companies and their contributions to the overeating epidemic. Find and read his April 9, 2010 post, "Down on the Clown," on his Website. Then write a response to his post that links your assessment of his call to action with the material contained in the Obama reading from this chapter as well as statistics and data gathered from your own independent research on this topic: be sure to use reputable sources in gathering your information. See Chapter 5 for strategies for effectively evaluating online sources.
2. Working in small groups, create your own contribution to the "What the World Eats" series by taking a "What the American College Student Eats" photograph. Consider the following: Who should be in the photo? What location or setting should you use? What foods should you represent? How should you arrange and stage them? After taking your photograph, write a caption similar to the ones found in Figures 9.10 and 9.11. Print out your photo and mount it and the caption on foam board for a class exhibit. Tour the exhibit with your class and then compare your different interpretations of the typical college diet. Discuss the results of your field research with the class.
3. Do your own primary research about American food culture by considering the visual rhetoric of food advertisements. Collect a set of ads and, using the checklist found in the Spotlighted Analysis feature in Chapter 2, analyze the way in which they produce an argument about food consumption. Your ads should have a clear relationship to one another, for instance: ads for a single brand or type of food spanning several decades; contemporary food ads aimed at children (fast food, cereal, even vitamins); ads from a single food industry, such as dairy farmers or the meat industry; or even ads for a nutritional supplement or weight-loss program. Write an analysis in which you make a strong claim about how these ads use specific rhetorical strategies to make an argument to the consumers about the food they eat. To find ads, use online advertising archives, search the Library of Congress Website, or look through books and collections at your university library.
4. Since at least 2009, the issue of genetically modified organisms (GMOs) and genetically modified foods has often been in the spotlight. Research a key player or event in this debate: the agricultural biotechnology company, Monsanto; the Greenpeace anti-GMO protests; the California Prop 37 initiative (2012); Barack Obama's so-called Monsanto Protection Act (2013); or Colorado's Proposition 105, Right to Know GMO, which failed in 2014. Use primary and secondary sources to create an argument about the GMO controversy; include quotations from the opinions shared by McWilliams or Haspel, as appropriate. Be sure to use MLA form for citations.

Seeing Connections
For guidance on how to integrate direct quotes correctly, see Chapter 6. See Chapter 7 for more on MLA documentation form.

MyWritingLab Visit Ch. 9 You Are What You Eat in MyWritingLab to complete the *Anayzing Perspectives on the Issue* and *From Reading to Research Assignments*.

CHAPTER 10

Life Online

Is life online eclipsing life offline? Economist Edward Castronova describes an ongoing "exodus to the virtual world." Everywhere you look, people are hunched over their mobile devices, posting photos, tweets, and Facebook updates to friends and family who are somewhere else. How much time do you spend online? Do you ever worry that your real life is just a performance enacted for the sake of your online friends? Does an experience somehow become more real for you once you post it online?

Digital interfaces mediate our lived experiences at every turn. We spend our leisure time in immersive environments and alternate worlds, or gaming with systems that enable multiplayer campaigns or that track our physical movements and translate them to the screen. We watch our media on tablets, smartphones, 4K TVs, and in the theater in 3D with digital surround sound. We catch our television shows on Hulu and Netflix, and we follow both friends and celebrities on Tumblr, Twitter, YouTube, Facebook, and Pinterest, maybe even becoming minor Internet celebrities ourselves. We create and recreate multiple online identities and profiles, and we connect with our friends through pithy 140-character updates, textspeak-laden instant messages, opinionated blog posts, and videochat. We constantly share images with our friends: selfies and group shots on Facebook, filtered and edited photos on Instagram, pinned favorites on Pinterest, and sometimes overly candid pictures on Snapchat. In many ways, our lives have become so integrated with and mediated by online culture that we can't even imagine life without it.

We can find a prime example of this movement toward integrating lived and virtual experience in Figure 10.1, a photograph of a group of models wearing the Oculus Rift Virtual Reality headset. In March 2014, Facebook bought the company that makes the Oculus Rift VR headset for $2 billion. Announcing the deal, Facebook founder Mark Zuckerberg wrote, "This is really a new communication platform. By feeling truly present, you can share unbounded spaces and experiences with the people in your life. Imagine sharing not just moments with your friends online, but entire experiences

FIGURE 10.1 The Oculus Rift Virtual Reality headset being used in March 2015 as part of an immersive fashion "experience" in London.

and adventures." Immersive gaming is the first step for the Oculus headset, which is expected to go on sale to consumers in 2016 for about $400. Virtual reality once existed only in the pages of futuristic science fiction. How will the ability to share "entire experiences" change the way we live, communicate, and interact? Not everyone shares Facebook's utopian vision for a VR-enhanced future. What happens to privacy when people around you might be recording at any time? What happens to equal access when those with visual impairments find themselves unable to take advantage of the technology? What happens to our ability to focus when we wear our distraction on our head? What happens when we are always connected, never alone?

Clearly the shift to living life online is hardly unproblematic. Scholars from many disciplines are just starting to make sense of how such online interactions are changing our lived experience. In this section, we'll explore different views on the effects of our technological dependence and will challenge you to take a careful look at the way you interface with your own experience. In doing so, we'll ask you to complicate your own relationship with technology to better comprehend how it is encoding your understanding of who you are, of how you experience the world, and of what *life* and *culture* even mean in this hyperconnected world.

REFLECT & WRITE MyWritingLab

- ❑ What story does this photograph tell about the Oculus Rift VR headsets? What argument is it making?
- ❑ Consider the choice of models, perspective, and setting. How might a different story about Oculus Rift be told by changing some of these elements in the photograph?
- ❑ **Write.** Visit the Oculus Website. Look specifically at the Rift pages, and analyze the way in which the entire site functions as an advertisement for this product and defines how it can augment our lives. Write a paragraph-long rhetorical analysis; make sure you refer to particular elements of the site, use of appeals, and strategies of development to support your claim.

In this cartoon from the March 15, 2010, issue of the New Yorker, *editorial artist* **Mick Stevens** *makes a pointed statement about the ubiquity of social media in modern life.*

Editorial Cartoon

FIGURE 10.2 In this cartoon, Mick Stevens provides a visual argument conveying the idea: "I text; therefore, I am."

REFLECT & WRITE

MyWritingLab

- ❑ A common scene in hospitals today would be the new parent texting about a baby's birth. What is the significance of having the texter be the infant himself? What does this add to the cultural critique at work here?
- ❑ Why do you think Stevens only shows the baby's hands? How would showing the baby's head, face, or body have changed the emphasis of the image?
- ❑ Why include the nurse in the frame? What does she contribute to the cartoon?
- ❑ **Write.** This cartoon makes an argument about one generation's interaction with technology and social media. Sketch either a single-panel or multiple-panel cartoon that provides an argument about an older generation's relationship to technology.

■ **Peggy Drexler, Ph.D**. *is a research psychologist and assistant professor of psychology at Cornell University. She is author of two books about modern families and the children they produce. In this article, originally published as a blog post* on Psychology Today *in September 2013, Drexler reflects on why we take selfies and what they say about us.*

What Your Selfies Say About You

Peggy Drexler

EARLIER THIS WEEK, a Texas mother of four, Kimberly Hall, made national headlines with her online manifesto to teenage girls prone to taking and posting self-portraits on social media. "Who are you trying to reach?" the mom asked. "What are you trying to say?" Girls who keep this sort of thing up, the mom went on to write, will be blocked in her household, because "Did you know that once a male sees you in a state of undress, he can't ever un-see it? You don't want the Hall boys to only think of you in this sexual way, do you? Neither do we."

Though her post is rife with sexism—the post runs beneath a photograph of her own three boys shirtless on the beach and includes no mention of the responsibility of the viewer, or her sons, in how he/they respond to such images—Hall makes a valid point. Ever since smartphones came equipped with cameras that face not just outward but also backward at the user, the self-portrait—dubbed the "selfie"—has taken over social media, particularly Instagram. (It's popular on dating sites, as well.) Because of the selfie's close-up nature, it's far more intimate than, say, the portrait your sister took of you standing in front of the Grand Canyon. Many selfies carry sexual undertones, especially since the majority of selfies are, obviously, user-approved, and designed to leave a positive impression or elicit a positive response. But it's not just technology that has driven the selfie—and it's not only teenage girls and singles using it to take control of how they present themselves to the world.

Sarabeth, a 40-year-old, married chief operating officer of a digital media company, routinely wove magazine-worthy photographs of herself lounging seductively on the beach, laughing by candlelight, and snuggling with her kids into her Instagram feed. They weren't all posed, though all were flawless, and served to project a certain image, that of money, power, and love of what, by all visual accounts, was her amazingly fun-filled life. "I don't put much thought into what I post other than if it's a nice photograph of a meaningful moment, I like to share it," she told me. "But no, if I look godawful, that's not a photo that will see the light of day."

On the surface, the trend is sort of affirming, if undeniably self-absorbed: Women, whether rich and powerful like Sarabeth or otherwise, increasingly have a healthy image of themselves. That's a good thing. *Girls* creator Lena Dunham is a big fan of the selfie, both on social media and through her show—which shares with selfies a confessional quality. On TV, Dunham's character often appears naked or in various states of undress; in real life, her Instagram selfies aren't necessarily flattering by typical standards. They challenge the "Hollywood ideal" and that, too, is a good thing, especially when size 0 celebrities dominate so much of the modern day visual barrage. The more we see a range of body types, the better.

5 And yet selfies are also a manifestation of society's obsession with looks and its ever-narcissistic embrace. There's a sense that selfie subjects feel as though they're starring in their own reality shows, with an inflated sense of self that allows them to believe their friends or followers are interested in seeing them lying in bed, lips pursed, in a real world headshot. It's like looking in the mirror all day long, and letting others see you do it. And that can have real and serious implications. Excessive narcissism, studies have found, can have adverse effects on marriage and relationships, parenting, and the workplace. One study found a link between excessive narcissism and violence.

What's more, a recent study out of the U.K. found that the selfie phenomenon may be damaging to real world relationships, concluding that both excessive photo sharing and sharing photos of a certain type—including self-portraits—makes people less likeable. The same study found that increased frequency of sharing self-portraits is related to a decrease in intimacy with others. For one thing, putting so much emphasis on your own looks can make others feel self-conscious about theirs in your presence. The pressure to be "camera-ready" can also heighten self-esteem issues and increase feelings of competition among friends.

The trick with selfies may be to look at why you're taking them—and what they do for you. Posting affirming selfies can be empowering. They can help readjust the industry standard of the beauty ideal. But they can also help reinforce the idea that what matters most in this world is how things, and people, look. For Sarabeth, the problem she noticed first, before she even noticed her increasing fixation with her own appearance and that of her family, was the fact that she was so busy controlling her image that she'd often miss the moment in real life. Capturing something on camera took priority over reacting to something in person. "Documenting the experience took precedence over living it," she said. "And finally I realized, well, how can I expect others to pay attention to what's happening in my life when I can't even say the same for myself?"

REFLECT & WRITE

MyWritingLab

- ❑ Many would consider "selfies" to be a frivolous or shallow topic for an essay. How does Drexler give it merit and traction as a persuasive argument? How does she establish her own authority, and what other authorities does she evoke to make her points convincing?
- ❑ How does Drexler draw in the reader? Find at least two particular strategies that she uses in the article that are designed specifically to engage her audience.
- ❑ Drexler's article focuses on one selfie-taker in particular, Sarabeth. Why do you think Drexler chooses Sarabeth as a focal point for her analysis? What does Sarabeth represent? What arguments about selfies does Sarabeth support, if she is considered a type of evidence or case study?
- ❑ **Write**. Drexler concludes by stressing the importance of considering why you are taking selfies and what they do for you. How would you answer her question for yourself? Do you think your experiences with selfies are typical? Imagine that you are posting a comment to respond to Drexler's original post. How would you respond? Which parts of her argument do you agree with? Why? What other perspectives would you share on the topic of selfies and self-image? Write a one- or two-paragraph response in the style you would use in an online comment thread for a public audience.

■ *The selfies on the next page, submitted by student readers of* Envision, *are representative of the "selfie phenomenon" written about by Drexler and others and resemble many of the types of photos that appear everyday on social media platforms. Each one offers a moment of self-representation and identity construction, carefully composed to make a particular argument about the person represented.*

REFLECT & WRITE

MyWritingLab

- ❑ What "argument" do you think the photographers are making about their identity through the selfie? What elements of the composition of the image lead you to that conclusion?
- ❑ Taken together, how do these selfies suggest a counterargument to Drexler's piece? Do you find your interpretation of them to be influenced by her argument?
- ❑ Some might argue that selfies are a generational phenomenon, linked to the "Millenials" (the generation of people born between the late 1980s and the early 2000s). Do you think this is the case? Visit a social media site and look at selfies from a different generation. What similarities and differences do you notice?
- ❑ **Write.** Look carefully at the selfies to the left as well as others—your own and those from your friends—on the social media platforms you frequent. Formulate a taxonomy of selfies; what are the different types of selfies that you observe? Write a list of four to six different categories or types of selfies, giving each one an identifying name (i.e., "The Serious Selfie") and following it with a one to two sentence description that makes a claim about persona for each one. For added challenge, take selfies of yourself that mirror each of the types you identify and insert them as examples into your document. Compare your taxonomy with a partner's to see how your arguments about the types of selfies differ.

■ *"Love Online," originally published in* the MIT Technology Review *in 2002, describes the first face-to-face meeting between the author's then 15-year-old son and his girlfriend. The essay is a sensitive portrait of young love, online and off.* **Henry Jenkins** *describes himself as an "aca-fan," an academic who is also a fan of digital pop culture. Jenkins has written numerous books, the most recent of which is* Spreadable Media: Creating Value and Meaning in a Networked Culture *(2013). Jenkins teaches communication and film at USC.*

Love Online

Henry Jenkins

When my son Henry was fifteen, we made a trip from Cambridge to Omaha so that he could meet his girlfriend face to face for the first time. Though they met online, this is not the story of a virtual relationship; their feelings were no less real to them than the first love of any other teenager, past or present.

When I was suffering the first pangs of unrequited adolescent longing, there weren't a lot of girls in my immediate vicinity who would risk the stigma involved in going out with me. One summer I met a few girls at a camp for honors students but our relationships withered once we returned to our own schools and neighborhoods. My son, finding slim pickings at school, cast a wider net, seeking kindred spirits wherever they dwelt in a neighborhood as big as cyberspace itself. Online, he had what it took—good communication skills.

He met Sarah in an online discussion group; they talked through private e-mail; after getting to know her a little he finally got the courage to phone her. They dated in chat rooms. They sent each other virtual candy, flowers, and cards downloaded off various Websites. They spoke of "going out," even though they sat thousands of miles apart.

Sarah's father often screened her telephone calls and didn't want her to talk with boys. He didn't pay the same degree of attention to what she did online. He quickly ran up against the difference between his expectations of appropriate courtship and the realities of online love. He felt strongly that boys should not talk to his daughter on the telephone or ask them out on dates unless they were personally known to him. Henry had to go through the ritual of meeting him on the telephone and asking his permission to see her before we could make the trip.

5 Long-distance communication between lovers is hardly new. The exchange of love letters was central to the courtship of my grandparents (who were separated by the First World War) and of my parents (who were separated by my father's service after the Second World War). By the time that my wife and I were courting, we handed our love letters back and forth in person and read them aloud to each other. Our courtship was conducted face to face or through late-night telephone conversation. The love letter was a residual form-though we still have a box of yellowing letters we periodically reread with misty-eyed nostalgia.

Sarah and Henry's romantic communications might seem, at first, more transient, bytes passing from computer to computer. Yet, he backlogged all of their chats and surprised Sarah with a printout. In this fashion, he preserved not only the carefully crafted love letters but the process of an evolving relationship. It was as if my wife and I had tape-recorded our first strolls in the park together.

Henry and Sarah would not have met outside the virtual communities the Internet facilitates. But they were both emphatic that purely digital communication could not have sustained their relationship. The first time Sarah confirmed that she shared my son's affections, she spoke her words of love on a chat room without realizing that he had been accidentally disconnected. By the time he was able to get back online, she had left in frustration. Wooing must be difficult if you can't even be sure the other party is there.

The medium's inadequacies are, no doubt, resulting in significant shifts in the vocabulary of love. In cyberspace, there is no room for the ambiguous gestures that characterized another generation's fumbling first courtships. In a multi-user domain, one doesn't type, "Henry smiles. He moves his hand subtly towards her in a gesture that might be averted at the last moment if she seems not to notice or to be shocked." The language of courtly love emerged under similar circumstances: distant lovers putting into writing what they could not say aloud.

They may have met online but they communicated through every available channel. Their initial exchange of photographs produced enormous anxiety as they struggled to decide what frozen image or images should anchor their more fluid online identities. In choosing, my son attempted to negotiate between what he thought would be desirable to another 15-year-old and what wouldn't alienate her conservative parents.

10 The photographs were followed by other tangible objects, shipped between Nebraska and Massachusetts. These objects were cherished because they had achieved the physical intimacy still denied the geographically isolated teens. Henry sent her, for example, the imprint of his lips, stained in red wine on stationery. In some cases, they individually staged rituals they could not perform together. Henry preserved a red rose he purchased for himself the day she first agreed to go steady. Even in an age of instant communication, they still sent

handwritten notes. These two teens longed for the concrete, for being together in the same space, for things materially passed from person to person.

Barring that, they cherished their weekly telephone calls. Talking on the telephone helped make Sarah real for Henry. When his friends at school challenged his inability to "produce" his girlfriend for inspection and asked how he knew she wasn't a guy, he cited their telephone conversations. Even for these teens, the fluidity of electronic identities posed threats. Once, early in their relationship, Henry jokingly told Sarah that they went to the same school, never imagining that she would believe him. The results were both farcical and tragic as she searched in vain for her mystery date.

After a while, they started to fear that they might break up without ever having seen each other in the flesh and they didn't want it to end that way. After some pleading, I agreed to accompany Henry on the trip.

Henry and Sarah first "met" in an airport. He almost didn't recognize her since she was so different from the single photograph she had sent. From the start, their interaction was intensely physical. Henry said that what had given him the most pleasure was being able to play with her hair, and Sarah punched him in the arm so many times he was black and blue. Sarah's mother and I watched two slouching teens shuffle through the terminal, learning to walk in rhythm.

As would-be dramatists, they wondered what they should say at that first meeting. Sarah solved the problem by shouting "Sony PlayStation" across the crowded airport. The two of them had a running debate about the relative merits of different game systems. Their first date was to an arcade where Sarah made good her long-standing boasts and beat him at Street Fighter II before Henry got his revenge on NFL GameDay. Sarah made the state finals in a video game competition, so it was no surprise this proved central to the time they spent together. Sarah's mother purchased some new games and—ever the chaperone—brought the game system down to the parlor from Sarah's room so they could play together.

If we are going to talk, from Cambridge to Omaha, with people we've never met before, we need something to talk about. For Henry and Sarah, that common culture consisted not only of different games and game systems, but also a shared enthusiasm for professional wrestling. They met on rec.sport.pro-wrestling, brought together by a shared interest in the Undertaker, a star of the World Wrestling Federation. They both were participants in an electronic pro wrestling role-playing game. Henry brought a cardboard sign with him to a televised wrestling event, pushed his way through the crowd, and got on camera so he could send Sarah a broadcast message.

Popular culture also helped to bridge the awkward silences in my exchanges with Sarah's parents. I had wondered what a media scholar from "the People's Republic of Cambridge" would say to two retired Air Force officers from Nebraska. As Sarah's mother and I sat in the arcade, trying to dodge religion and politics, we found common ground discussing Star Trek, the original Saturday Night Live cast, and of course, Mutual of Omaha's Wild Kingdom.

Henry and Sarah broke up sometime after that trip-not because they had met online or because the real life experience hadn't lived up to their expectations but because they were fifteen, their interests shifted, and they never really overcame her father's opposition. Henry's next relationship was also online-with a girl from Melbourne, Australia, and that experience broadened his perspective on the world, at the price of much sleep as they negotiated time differences. Now 21, he has gone through his normal share of other romantic entanglements, some online, more face to face (with many of the latter conducted, at least in part, online to endure the summer vacation separation).

We've read more than a decade of press coverage about online relationships-much of it written since my son and I made this trip together.

Journalists love to talk about the aberrant qualities of virtual sex. Yet, many of us embraced the Internet because it has fit into the most personal and banal spaces of our lives. Focusing on the revolutionary aspects of online courtship blinds us to the continuities in courtship rituals across generations and across media. Indeed, the power of physical artifacts (the imprint of lips on paper, the faded petals of a rose), of photographs, of the voice on the telephone gain new poignancy in the context of these new relationships. Moreover, focusing on the online aspects of these relationships blinds us to the agility with which teens move back and forth across media. Their daily lives require constant decisions about what to say on the phone, what to write by hand, what to communicate in chat rooms, what to send by e-mail. They juggle multiple identities-the fictional personas of electronic wrestling, the constructed ideals of romantic love, and the realities of real bodies and real emotions.

REFLECT & WRITE

MyWritingLab

- ❑ How does Jenkins use his own experiences with dating and romance to compare with his son's experiences? What argument is Jenkins making about how dating has changed with the advent of online communication?
- ❑ How would you describe the *ethos* or persona Jenkins creates and uses in this essay? How does he connect to readers and to his subject matter? Does Jenkins represent himself as a scholar in this article? Why or why not?
- ❑ How do you think Jenkins's story might have been different if the young couple was same-sex? To what extent are the "dating rituals" described in "Love Online" specific to heterosexual couples?
- ❑ What broader claims does Jenkins make about online communication and human behavior? How does he use his son's story as an example of some more general narrative? Is this strategy convincing? Why or why not?
- ❑ **Write.** In his conclusion, Jenkins writes, "[M]any of us embraced the Internet because it has fit into the most personal and banal spaces of our lives." He describes the "multiple identities" that daily life requires us to juggle. What are some of your own identities? Compose a visual–verbal profile of yourself, such as you might post on an online dating site. Choose two photographs of yourself, one a head shot and one another image to represent your interests, and add to them a short verbal description. What style and genre conventions would you use to represent yourself? Why?

The **Pew Internet & American Life Project** *conducts studies examining the impact of the Internet on twenty-first-century culture, including families, education, and civic life. The project, which sent out its first survey in 2000, is one of seven projects that comprise the Pew Research Center, an organization focused on investigating the social forces and trends that shape contemporary American life. What follows is a section from its report "Teens, Kindness and Cruelty on Social Network Sites," which was published in November 2011. The lead author of the report is Amanda Lenhart, the director of the project's research on teens and their families; its findings were based primarily on a survey of 799 teens (aged 12–17) between April and July 2011.*

Excerpt from "Teens, Kindness and Cruelty on Social Network Sites"

Amanda Lenhart, Mary Madden, Aaron Smith, Kristen Purcell, Kathryn Zickuhr, and Lee Rainie

Part 2: Social Media and Digital Citizenship: What teens experience and how they behave on social network sites

Section 1: The majority of teens have positive online experiences, but some are caught in an online feedback loop of meanness and negative experiences.

The majority of social media-using teens say their experience is that their peers are mostly kind to one another on social network sites, but their views are less positive when compared with similar assessments from online adults.

We asked teens the following question about what they see in social network spaces: "Overall, in your experience, are people your age mostly *kind* or mostly *unkind* to one another on social network sites?" Most of the 77% of all teens who use social media say their experience is that people their age are mostly kind to one another on social network sites. Overall, 69% of social media-using teens say their experience is that peers are mostly kind to each other in social network spaces. Another 20% say their peers are mostly unkind, while 11% volunteered that "it depends." However, in a similar question asked of adults 18 and older, 85% of social media–using adults reported that their experience was that people are mostly kind to one another on social network sites, while just 5% reported that they see people behaving in mostly unkind ways.

Overall, in your experience, are people your age mostly kind or mostly unkind to one another on social network sites?

% of teens and adults who use social media

	teens 12-17 (n=623)	adults 18+ (n=1047)
People are mostly kind	69%	85%*
People are mostly unkind	20%*	5%
Depends	11%*	5%
Don't know	1%	4%
Refused	0%	1%

Note: The question wording for adults was "Overall, in your experience, are people mostly kind or mostly unkind to one another on social networking sites?" * indicates a statistically significant difference between bars.

Source: The Pew Research Center's Internet & American Life Teen-Parent survey, April 19-July 14, 2011. N=799 for teens and parents, including oversample of minority families. Interviews were conducted in English and Spanish. Data for adults is from Pew Internet's August Tracking survey, July 25-August 26, 2011. Nationally representative, n=2260 adults 18+, includes cell phone & Spanish language interviews.

Girls ages 12–13 have the most negative assessment of social network spaces.

While teens across all demographic groups generally have positive experiences watching how their peers treat each other on social network sites, younger teenage girls (ages 12–13) stand out as considerably more likely to say their experience is that people are mostly unkind. One in three (33%) younger teen girls who uses social media says that people her age are mostly unkind to one another on social network sites, compared with 9% of social media–using boys 12–13 and 18% of boys 14–17. One in five older girls (20%) who uses social media says that in her experience people her age are mostly unkind to one another on these sites.

How peers treat one another on social media
% of teens who use social media

	Mostly Kind	Mostly Unkind	Depends	Don't Know
Race/ethnicity				
White	72%*	20%*	9%	0%
Black	56%	31%*	9%	4%
Hispanic	78%*	9%	13%	0%
Location				
Urban	68%	23%*	8%	0%
Suburban	73%	14%+	13%	0%
Rural	57%	28%	12%	3%
Household income				
Less than $30K	61%	22%	16%	2%
$30–49K	67%	25%	9%	0%
$50–75K	78%	15%	7%	0%
$75,000 or more	72%	18%	10%	0%
Age				
Teens ages 12–13	70%	22%	8%	0%
Teens ages 14–17	68%	19%	12%	1%
Sex				
Girls	66%	23%	10%	0%
Boys	71%	16%	12%	1%
Age + sex				
Girls 12–13	65%	33%*	3%	0%
Boys 12–13	77%	9%+	14%	0%
Girls 14–17	67%	20%	13%	0%
Boys 14–17	69%	18%+	12%	1%

Note: * indicates statistically significant difference between rows within each column and section. In sections with +, the data point with the * is only statistically significantly different than the data points with + symbol.

Source: The Pew Research Center's Internet & American Life Teen-Parent survey, April 19-July 14, 2011. N=799 for teens and parents, including oversample of minority families. Interviews were conducted in English and Spanish.

Black teens are less likely to say their experience is that people their age are kind to one another on social network sites.

Black social media users are less likely than white and Latino users to report that people their age are mostly kind online. While 72% of whites and 78% of Latino youth say that their experience is that people are usually kind on social network sites, just over half (56%) of blacks say the same.

Teens tend towards negative words when describing how people act online.

5 As a part of this project, we conducted seven focus groups with teens ages 12 to 19 to ask teens more in-depth questions about their experiences interacting with others on social network sites. In the groups, we asked the teen participants questions about how people usually acted online. In some cases, we asked students to tell us about their observations of online behavior and then tell us how they thought people *should* act in online spaces. In one exercise, we asked the participants to write down words or phrases that they felt captured these concepts. As the word clouds[1] 20 created from the words they shared suggest, teens overwhelmingly chose negative adjectives to describe how people act online. Words that appeared frequently included "rude," "mean," "fake," "crude," "over-dramatic," and "disrespectful."

[1]Word clouds were created with wordle.net. The size of the word increases the more frequently it is found in the set of words included in the cloud. So, the most frequently occurring words are the largest.

Some teens did use positive words like the frequently mentioned "funny" and the less common "honest," "clever," "friendly," "entertaining," and "sweet," but overall the frequency of positive words was substantially lower. Other terms shared by participants could be interpreted differently depending on the context of use—these include the popular term "different"

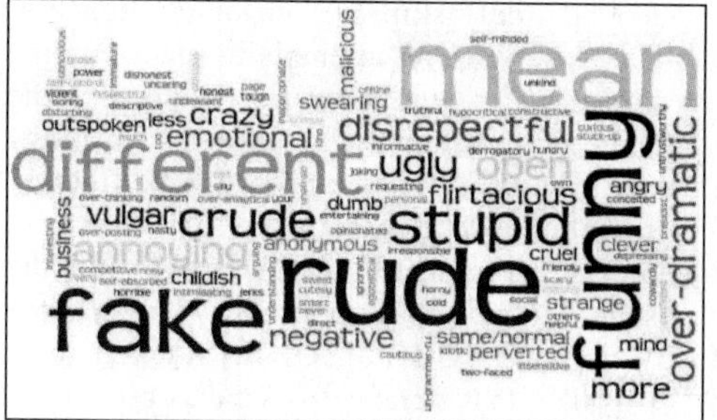

and others like "emotional," "cautious," "outspoken," "strange," and "open."

Of the teens who were asked about how they thought people should act online, the responses were substantially more positive and included words like "respectful," "nice," "friendly," "mature," "peaceful," and phrases

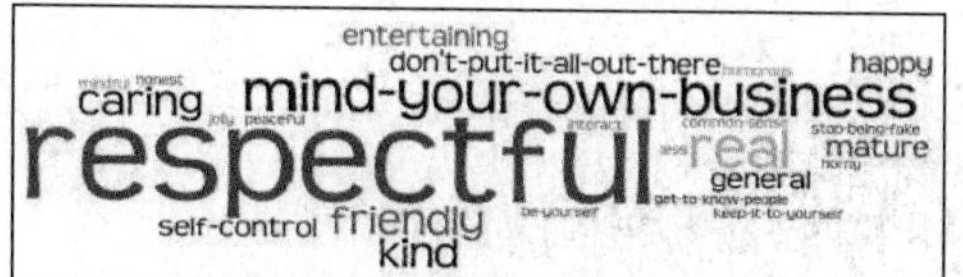

like "mind your own business" and "don't put it all out there."

After the exercise, we asked the focus group participants follow-up questions to plumb the discrepancies between the way they had witnessed people acting on social media and how they thought people should act on the sites.

Many teens told us that they just felt like different people on these sites and thought that people they see online often act very differently on social media from how they act in person and at school.

- *MIDDLE SCHOOL GIRL: That's what a lot of people do. Like, they won't say it to your face, but they will write it online ...*
- *MIDDLE SCHOOL BOY: I know people who, in person, like refuse to swear. And online, it's every other word.*
- *MIDDLE SCHOOL GIRL: I think people get—like when they get on Facebook, they get ruthless, stuff like that.... They act different in school and stuff like that, but when they get online, they like a totally different person. You get a lot of confidence.*
- *HIGH SCHOOL BOY: [There's] this real quiet girl who go to my school, right, but when she's on Facebook she talks like some wild—like, be rapping and talking about who she knew and some more stuff and you would, like, never think that's her. You would think that's somebody else ...*

Teens also identified specific online social spaces—open comment spaces and question and answer sites—that feel particularly unwelcoming:

- *HIGH SCHOOL BOY: YouTube comments are pretty bad. They're, like, oh my God.*
- *HIGH SCHOOL BOY: I have a friend who came out and he had a Formspring[2] and,*

[2]Formspring is an anonymous question and answer Website.

like, a bunch of people from this school, like, attacked his Formspring and, like, wrote really, really homophobic things on it.

10 Often teens felt bolder, ruder, or more empowered because they did not fear physical violence in the online space. One middle school girl told us that she thought people were ruder online "because you can't hurt anybody online. You can't punch nobody through the screen."

- *MIDDLE SCHOOL GIRL 1. I think I act ruder to online people.*
- *MODERATOR. You act ruder? How come?*
- *MIDDLE SCHOOL GIRL 2. Because she doesn't have to see them, so they can't beat her up.*

For some teens we spoke with—particularly middle school girls—fights and drama on social media flowed back and forth between school, the street, and Facebook, often resulting in physical fights during the in-person portions of the conflict.

- *MIDDLE SCHOOL GIRL: I read what they were talking about online, then I go offline and confront the person who was saying something to her.*
- *MIDDLE SCHOOL GIRL:...Like that's how most people start fighting because that's how most of the fights in my school happen—because of some Facebook stuff, because of something you post, or like because somebody didn't like your pictures.*

One middle school girl detailed the circular flow of conflict between her social network site and her in-person life, and the ways that she, at her mother's behest, tries to break the cycle.

"...the other day, Monday, I was not cool with somebody and so they tried to put on their status something about me. But I didn't reply to that because my mother told me not to say nothing back because she didn't want anything more to happen."

She further explains a physical fight she was supposed to have and the ways in which others taunted her offline and online about her allegedly skipping out on the conflict. She describes her attempts to ignore online comments made about her "ducking" the fight, until the taunting escalated to insulting her friend. "...I was supposed to be fighting somebody Monday, but the security guard picked me up and brung me back inside the school. Yeah, they were like, 'oh my man, [MIDDLE SCHOOL GIRL] ducked it.' I was like, that's crazy, but I didn't reply back and then she said something about my best friend..."

15 For other teens, the fact that they can act differently on social media translates into more real, positive experiences. Instead of seeing social media as a place that fomented conflict or bad behavior, some teens felt as though it increased a sense of closeness and allowed people to be authentic or more real than they could be offline:

- *HIGH SCHOOL GIRL: I think people act different on Facebook because that's like their—I mean, I think the self that they show you on Facebook could be their true self, like who they actually want to be.*
- *MIDDLE SCHOOL GIRL: Yeah, I act the same how I act in school. Like online I'm still goofy and stuff like that.*

Several teens told us that they find friends and romantic interests easier to talk to and more open in these online social spaces.

- *HIGH SCHOOL GIRL: But I feel like, since it's on Facebook, I guess it's easier to talk to people, or like, admit things and, like, you just have, like, open conversations because they're not, like face-to-face, so it's not as, like—they're not, like, embarrassed or nervous or something.*
- *HIGH SCHOOL BOY: [O]n Facebook definitely people…can be more open in some ways than in real life. Like, they'll say more than they will because it's not, like, face-to-face, so. Like, some things that might be awkward in real life won't be that awkward in a conversation on Facebook.*

At least one teen with whom we spoke attributed the ease of conversation in social media with a sense of privacy in social chat spaces:

- *MIDDLE SCHOOL BOY: I don't know, it just feels like in person, it can be awkward and weird if you're trying to tell something, like, personal and secret because you're looking at them…But like on a Facebook chat, it is very—it's like there's no one unless it's like a hacker or something. But that's rare. You can talk where you can actually tell them lots of things, or send them a private message, not, like, public.*

And others do not find friends changed when they talk to them online:

- *HIGH SCHOOL GIRL: I don't really have a like, kind of, issue, I guess. I mean, when I talk to someone online—like…my best friend since sixth grade—she doesn't change when she's online or when I see her in person. I don't really get to see her that often because she goes to a different school, but no, she doesn't ever change.*

Other teens spoke of the challenges of managing disparate friend groups in the same public space visible to all of them:

- *HIGH SCHOOL GIRL: Well, I think—I still—I think people still make personas in real life too. It's just, like, like if I'm with a different group of friends I'll be more one way than I am with another group of friends just because that's how—it's more comfortable for them and it makes it fun for the group.*

REFLECT & WRITE

MyWritingLab

- ❑ Which is the most surprising statistic contained in this section of the report. Why?
- ❑ How do the report's assertions about the relationship between race, gender, age, and online behavior resonate with your own observations?
- ❑ Which was the most persuasive part of this section? Why?
- ❑ This section contains both traditional information graphics as well as word art. What different purposes do these serve as visual rhetoric? Is one more effective than the other? Why or why not?

❑ **Write.** In one section of the article, the researchers discuss how they "asked the participants to write down words or phrases" that they felt summarized their observations about online behavior, which they used to generate a word cloud. Conduct a similar experiment with at least 20 of your friends; use the online program Wordle or the software of your choice to generate a similar word cloud about online behavior and then write a one-page reflection on the results you observed from your survey.

■ *The authors of the following piece are two of the most prominent researchers of teens and social media in the United States today.* **danah boyd** *is a fellow at Harvard University's Berkman Center for Internet and Society and a social media researcher at Microsoft Research New England. Her most recent book is titled,* It's Complicated: The Social Lives of Networked Teens. **Alice Marwick** *is an assistant professor of communication and media studies at Fordham University and also works with boyd as a researcher at the Berkman Center. Like boyd, Marwick focuses her research principally on youth and social media, a topic about which they both have presented and written frequently. The following is an excerpt from their essay "Social Privacy in Networked Publics: Teens' Attitudes, Practices, and Strategies," which they originally prepared as a presentation for a 2011 Symposium on the Dynamics of the Internet and Society.*

Excerpt from "Social Privacy in Networked Publics: Teens' Attitudes, Practices, and Strategies"

Danah Boyd and Alice Marwick

Waffles, 17, NC:[3] Every teenager wants privacy. Every single last one of them, whether they tell you or not, wants privacy. Just because an adult thinks they know the person doesn't mean they know the person. And just because teenagers use internet sites to connect to other people doesn't mean they don't care about their privacy. We don't tell everybody every single thing about our lives. We tell them general information—names, places, what we like to do—but that's general knowledge. That's not something you like to keep private—"Oh, I play games. I better not tell anybody about that." I mean—that's not something that we do. So to go ahead and say that teenagers don't like privacy is pretty ignorant and inconsiderate honestly, I believe, on the adult's part.

There's a widespread myth that American teenagers don't care about privacy. The logic is simple: Why else would teenagers share so much on Facebook and Twitter and YouTube?[4] There

[3]The names used in this article are pseudonyms. Some were chosen by the participants themselves; others were chosen by the authors to reflect similar gender and ethnic roots as are embedded in the participants' given names. All identifying information in teens' quotes has been altered to maintain confidentiality.

is little doubt that many—but not all—American teens have embraced many popular social media services.[5] And there is little doubt that those who have are posting photos, sharing links, updating status messages, and commenting on each other's posts.[6] Yet, as Waffles explains above, participation in such networked publics does not imply that today's teens have rejected privacy as a value. All teens have a sense of privacy, although their definitions of privacy vary widely. Their practices in networked publics are shaped by their interpretation of the social situation, their attitudes towards privacy and publicity, and their ability to navigate the technological and social environment. As such, they develop intricate strategies to achieve privacy goals. Their practices demonstrate privacy as a social norm that is achieved through a wide array of social practices configured by structural conditions. How teens approach privacy challenges the ways in which privacy is currently conceptualized, discussed, and regulated.

[4]A 2008 Harris Interactive/CTIA survey about teens' relationship to their mobile was publicized as indicating that kids don't care about privacy because only 41% indicated that they were concerned about privacy and security issues when using their mobile: http://files.ctia.org/pdf/HI_TeenMobileStudy_ResearchReport.pdf. In 2010, Chris Jay Hoofnagle, Jennifer King, Su Li, and Joseph Turow found that young people's attitudes about privacy parallel adults' attitudes, but their skills in managing privacy online are often lacking.

[5]As of September 2009, the Pew Internet and American Life Project found that 73% of American teens ages 12–17 use a social network site; only 8% of teens in their sample used Twitter. See Lenhart et al. 2010.

[6]Of teens who are on social network sites, Pew found that 86% comment on friends' posts. They also found that 38% of teens ages 12–17 shared content online; 14% keep a blog. See Lenhart et al. 2010.

What Is Privacy?

Privacy is a fraught concept, with no clear agreed-upon definition. Philosophers and legal scholars have worked diligently to conceptually locate privacy and offer a framework for considering how and when it has been violated.[7] Yet, fundamentally, privacy is a social construct that reflects the values and norms of everyday people. How people conceptualize privacy and locate it in their life varies wildly, highlighting that a universal notion of privacy remains enigmatic.[8] When we asked teens to define privacy for us, their cacophonous responses reveal the diverse approaches that can be taken to understand privacy.[9]

[7]The definitions of privacy are numerous. Helen Nissenbaum (2010) relates multiple definitions of privacy and groups them based on whether they are normative or descriptive; emphasize access vs. control; or emphasize promoting other values vs. protecting a private realm. These include definitions from Ruth Gavison ("a measure of the access others have to you through information, attention, and physical proximity") (68); Jeffrey Reiman ("the condition under which other people are deprived of access to either some information about you or some experience of you") (1976, 30); Westin's "the claim of individuals, groups, or institutions to determine for themselves when, how, and to what extent information about them is communicated to others (Westin 1967, 7), and Anita Allen (who defines three types of privacy: physical privacy, informational privacy, and proprietary privacy, 71). See Nissenbaum 2010 for a full discussion.

[8]Anthropologists have found wild variations in how different communities understand and prioritize privacy. John L. Locke's *Eavesdropping: An Intimate History* (2010) weaves together many of these different accounts.

[9]Teens are not alone in having diverse views about what constitutes privacy. Diverse adult perspectives are well documented in Christena Nippert-Eng's *Islands of Privacy* (2010).

While these discussions do not help to determine a precise definition of privacy, how teens attempt to explain privacy demonstrates its importance to them.

When trying to locate privacy, young people circle around the tropes that adults use to discuss privacy. They speak of secrets and trust, and highlight particular spaces as more or less private. Throughout these conversations, teens consistently come back to the importance of control and personal agency. They believe that privacy has to do with their ability to control a social situation, how information flows, and when and where they can be observed by others. Unfortunately, teens often struggle to assert control over situations, particularly when technology usurps their control or when their agency is undermined. More often than not, teens acknowledge this lack of control when people who hold power over them—e.g. their parents—insist on violating boundaries that teens create or social norms that they declare. Therein lies the key hypocrisy surrounding teens and privacy. Alongside adults' complaints that teens don't care about privacy when it comes to online activities is an ongoing belief that teens do not have the right to privacy when it comes to their physical spaces—or, in many cases, their online activities.[10] Parents often use the accessibility of teens' online vocalizations as justification for violating teens' privacy.

5 In 2006, 17-year-old Bly Lauritano-Werner from Maine created a Youth Radio episode to highlight this hypocrisy. In it, she argued *"My mom always uses the excuse about the internet being 'public' when she defends herself. It's not like I do anything to be ashamed of, but a girl needs her privacy. I do online journals so I can communicate with my friends. Not so my mother could catch up on the latest gossip of my life."*[11] In doing so, Bly is arguing an age-old refrain; she wants the right to be let alone[12] even—and perhaps especially—when she's socializing with friends.

Teens like Bly lack the agency to be able to assert social norms and adults regularly violate teens' understandings of social decorum. Consider what happened in Old Saybrook, Connecticut when local law enforcement and teachers put together an assembly for students on privacy.[13] To make a point about privacy, the educators put together a slide show of images grabbed from students' Facebook profiles and displayed these images to the student body. Students were furious. One student told a reporter that this stunt is "a violation of privacy." Most adults find this incredulous given that the content was broadly accessible—and that the students in the school had already most likely seen many of these images because they certainly had access to them. Yet, by taking the images

[10]Marwick, A., Murgia-Diaz, D., & Palfrey, J. (2010). *Youth, privacy and reputation (literature review)* (Berkman Center Research Publication No. 2010-5). Boston: Berkman Center for Internet and Society at Harvard University. Retrieved from http://papers.ssrn.com/sol3/papers.cfm?abstract_id=1588163

[11]Youth Radio broadcast "Reading My LiveJournal" by Bly Lauritano-Werner: http://www.youthradio.org/oldsite/society/npr060628_onlinejournal.shtml

[12]Warren, S.D. & Brandeis, L.D. (1890). Right to Privacy. Harvard Law Review, 4, 193.

[13]Misur, S. (2011, April 11). Old Saybrook High School makes privacy point; some perturbed when real students shown in social-media slide show. *Shoreline Times*. New Haven, CT. Retrieved from http://www.shorelinetimes.com/articles/2011/04/11/news/doc4da2f3cb5caae518276953.txt

out of context, the educators had violated students' social norms and, thus, their sense of dignity, fairness, and respect. As one student explained to a reporter, "I kind of thought, it's like if you put it online, anyone can see it, but then at the same time, it's like kind of not fair for the police officers to put that on display without their permission and without them knowing." This incident does not reveal that teens don't understand privacy, but rather, that they lack the agency to assert social norms and expect that others will respect them. Those who have power over them—their parents and the police—can use their power to violate teens' norms, using accessibility as their justification. In this way, adults further marginalize young people, reinforcing the notion that they do not have the social status necessary to deserve rights associated with privacy.

In an era of social media where information is often easily accessible, it's all too easy to conflate accessibility with publicity. Yet, just because teens are socializing in a public setting doesn't mean that they want to be public figures nor does it mean that they want to be the object of just anyone's gaze. What's at stake concerns not just the right to be invisible, but who has the right to look, for what purposes, and to what ends. Finding a way to manage boundaries is just one of the challenges that teens face in navigating networked publics because privacy isn't simply about control over the social situation; it also requires enough agency to affect these situations.

As they enter into networked publics, teens are grappling with the tensions that surround privacy and publicity. They are trying to find ways to have agency and assert control in settings where both the architecture and their social position make it very difficult for them to control the flow of information. Yet, in exploring strategies for maintaining social privacy in networked publics, they reveal how social norms are enacted. Privacy is both a social norm and a process; it is not something that is had so much as something that is negotiated. And the practices which teens engage in while attempting to negotiate privacy show that this social construct is not disappearing simply because technology introduces new hurdles.

Variations in Privacy Norms and Practices

Even though all the teens we interviewed expressed an appreciation for privacy at some level, they did not share a uniform set of values about privacy and publicity. Just as some teenagers are extroverted and some introverted, some teens are more exhibitionist and some are more secretive. Variations among individuals are shaped by local social norms; sharing is viewed differently in different friend groups, schools, and communities. There's also a gendered component to it, with teens having different ideas of what is appropriate to share that map to stereotypical understandings of male and female emotional behavior. When 17-year-old Manu emphasizes that he's "not that kind of person," he's also enacting fairly widespread norms of masculinity:

danah: When you broke up with your girlfriend, did you write anything about it on Facebook?

Manu, 17, NC: No. I'm like—I'm not that kind of person—I find it really weird to have my emotions or anything on Facebook or Twitter, and it's just—I don't do stuff—I know other people do, but I feel like I'll get judged or just—I'm not that kind of person to let stuff out like that. I don't do statuses, actually, either.

10 Privacy must be contextualized. Teen understandings of privacy and how they carry

these out varies by individual, by community, by situation, by role, and by interaction. In other words, privacy—and the norms surrounding privacy—cannot be divorced from context.[14]

When teens share information about themselves, thereby increasing their exposure, they do so because they gain something from being visible. There is always a trade-off, as teens account for what they might gain and what they might lose and how such cost-benefit analyses fit into their own mental models of risk and reward. Thus, when teens are negotiating privacy, they aren't simply thinking about a "loss"; they're considering what they might gain from revealing themselves.

Consider the words of Meixing, a bubbly 17-year-old from Tennessee who shares extensively on Facebook:

Meixing, 17, TN: Most of the time I'm a pretty extroverted person so I share a lot of things with people anyways...

danah: That means you don't care about privacy?

Meixing: I mean I do care about privacy, but if I found someone that I could trust then my first instinct would be to share stuff with that person. For example, I think, like my last boyfriend and I we were really close and then we had each other's passwords to Facebook and to emails and stuff. And so if I would get something that I didn't know about then he would notify me and look over my stuff... It made me feel safer just because someone was there to help me out and stuff. It made me feel more connected and less lonely. Because I feel like Facebook sometimes is kind of like a lonely sport, I feel, because you're kind of sitting there and you're looking at people by yourself. But if someone else knows your password and stuff it just feels better.

Meixing is highlighting the trade-offs that she faces when she's thinking about privacy. On one hand, she cares about privacy, but she's willing to expose herself in intimate situations because it makes her feel more connected. Her barriers to sharing are rooted in her sense of trust. She's not willing to expose herself to just anyone; she shares both because and as a signal that she trusts someone.

Trust is a very significant issue for teenagers and it regularly emerges in discussions about privacy. Many teens aren't confident that they can trust those around them, even their closest friends. All too often, teens use the information that they gather about others to "start drama," performing gossip and social conflict for a wide audience on social media.[15] This makes some teens very nervous about sharing, even with their closest friends. Taylor, a 15-year-old in Massachusetts, questions the motivations behind her friends' decisions to invade her privacy.

Taylor, 15, MA: So I usually give people the light version because I don't want them in my business and I really don't think that they have any right to be in my business.

danah: Why do they think they have a right?

Taylor: Because they're my friends, so they put themselves in my business sometimes, so they think that they should be there to help me and protect me with things but I can deal with it myself.

15 Taylor doesn't want her friends "in her business" because she's worried that she'll lose

[14]Nissenbaum 2010.

[15]Marwick, Alice and boyd, danah. (2011). "The Drama! Teens, Gossip and Celebrity." *Popular Culture Association/American Culture Association Annual Meeting*, San Antonio, TX, April 20–24.

control, so she purposely avoids sharing anything that is personal or intimate. But this doesn't stop her from sharing altogether. A photographer, she regularly uploads her work to Facebook precisely because she wants feedback and public validation.

Taylor, 15, MA: [A comment] gives me input and it makes me feel good....Even if it's negative I'd probably like it as a comment. It's just like a message is more personal, which I appreciate, but when people can see that they like my work, I like it when people can see that other people like it because I don't know, I just like getting lots of comments on one picture and seeing people read them.

In choosing to share her photographs but not her personal thoughts, Taylor is trying to assert control, thereby enacting privacy by selecting what should and should not be shared. She is not alone in this approach. Many teens who seemingly share a lot online are actually consciously limiting what is available. Consider Abigail's perspective:

Abigail, 17, NC: I actually know everybody I'm friends with [on Facebook]...But I'm not good friends with everybody on Facebook. The people that I go to school with I know I know what they're doing. That's why I'm friends with them on Facebook but they don't need to know what I'm exactly doing today. I'm eating breakfast, then I'm going to swim practice, then I'm doing my history homework, then I'm going to do this. They don't need to know all that. I can just put an overview like "Practice, homework, then Allie's," or something. I don't need to say exactly everything I'm doing at times and stuff.

The affordances of networked publics that make widespread sharing possible also motivate teens to use more private channels of communication—like text messaging or Facebook chat—to discuss things that are embarrassing or upsetting, intimate or self-exposing. Although most teens are quite conscious about what they choose to share, they don't always have complete control over what others share about them. Facebook, Flickr and other social media sites let users tag pictures of other users, while Twitter creates affiliations between users through @replies. In North Carolina, 17-year-old Jacquelyn finds it "weird" and embarrassing that her mother regularly posts pictures of her on Facebook. While she's uncomfortable with her mother sharing photos of her, she also understands the impulse. *"I guess as a parent, it's different than being a teenager because we're her kids so she wants to show all her college friends and high school friends what we're up to because obviously, we're not going to friend her high school friends because we don't know them. It makes sense, I guess. I don't know."*

20 In trying to navigate privacy, teens must not only contend with what they choose to share, but what others choose to share about them. While networked privacy is not unique to networked publics, the affordances of networked publics magnify this issue, reifying the public-by-default nature of such environments. Those who are more inclined to share often expect those who don't want information shared to speak up. Abigail, for example, posts all photos from her camera to Facebook because it's easier for her than filtering. She goes through her photo albums and tags the photos with her friends' names, deleting any photos that are blurry. Most of the pictures she puts up have multiple people in them, so she's not inclined to delete them, but understands if her friends untag themselves. If a friend is "really bothered" by a photo and complain to her directly, she'll delete it. The assumption in Abigail's friend group is that content is public-by-default. Such a setting forces teens to make a conscious choice about what to obscure, rather than what to publicize.

The public-by-default nature of networked publics is especially acute on Facebook and Twitter because of the role that social streams play in those environments. Facebook's news feed broadcasts both implicit actions (e.g., a broken heart when two people stop being "in a relationship") and shared content (e.g., newly uploaded photographs). The news feed and Twitter's stream are central to those sites and the first thing that most participants see when they login. While Facebook's news feed was controversial when it first launched,[16] it's now a fundamental part of Facebook's architecture. Teens share updates to be seen by their friends, but they also recognize that not everything shared through this mechanism is actually seen by their friends. While some teens expect their friends to read every update and picture that they post, others see the public-by-default dynamic as an opportunity to reduce expectations. Consider why Vicki, a 15-year-old from Georgia, posts status updates in lieu of sending private messages:

Vicki, 15, GA: Because a status update, everybody can read. Like, everybody who wants to read it can read it, but they're not obligated to read it. Like, when you send a message, it's, "Oh my gosh, this person sent me a message. Now I have to read this." But, when it's an update, it's, like, if I don't want to read your status, I'm not going to read yours. But I'm going to read the next person's, like, if I want to read theirs. You don't have to look at it if you don't want to.

Content that is publicly accessible is not necessarily universally consumed. Likewise, information that is publicly accessible is not necessarily intended to be consumed by just anyone. While teens may be negotiating privacy in a public-by-default environment, social norms also serve a critical role in how teens do boundary work.

[16]boyd, danah. 2008. "Facebook's Privacy Trainwreck: Exposure, invasion, and social convergence." *Convergence: The International Journal of Research into New Media Technologies* 14 (1): 13–20.

References

Allen, A. L. (1999). Coercing Privacy. William and Mary Law Review 40 (3): 723–724.

boyd, danah. (2008a). Facebook's Privacy Trainwreck: Exposure, invasion, and social convergence. Convergence: The International Journal of Research into New Media Technologies 14 (1): 13–20.

Gavison, Ruth. (1980). Privacy and the limits of the law. Yale Law Journal 89: 421–471.

Hoofnagle, Chris Jay, Jennifer King, Su Li, and Joseph Turow. (2010, April 14). "How Different are Young Adults from Older Adults When it Comes to Information Privacy Attitudes and Policies?" Working paper available at: http://papers.ssrn.com/sol3/papers.cfm?abstract_id=1589864

Lenhart, Amanda, K. Purcell, A. Smith, and K. Zickuhr. (2010). Social media and young adults. Washington, DC: Pew Internet & American Life Project, February 3. http://pewinternet.org/Reports/2010/Social-Media-and-Young-Adults.aspx.

Locke, John L. (2010). Eavesdropping: An Intimate History. New York: Oxford University Press, USA.

Marwick, Alice, Murgia-Diaz, D., & Palfrey, John. (2010). Youth, privacy and reputation (literature review) (Berkman Center Research Publication No. 2010-5). Boston: Berkman Center for Internet and Society at Harvard University. Retrieved from http://papers.ssrn.com/sol3/papers.cfm?abstract_id=1588163.

Marwick, Alice and danah boyd. (2011b). "The Drama! Teens, Gossip and Celebrity." Popular Culture Association/American Culture Association Annual Meeting, San Antonio, TX, April 20–24.

Misur, S. (2011, April 11). Old Saybrook High School makes privacy point; Some perturbed when real students shown in social-media slide show. Shoreline Times. New Haven, CT. Retrieved from http://www.shorelinetimes.com/articles/2011/04/11/news/doc4da2f3cb5caae518276953.txt

Nippert-Eng, Christena E. (2010). Islands of Privacy. Chicago: University of Chicago Press.

Nissenbaum, Helen. (2010). Privacy in Context: Technology, Policy, and the Integrity of Social Life. Palo Alto, CA: Stanford University Press.

Reiman, J. (1976). Privacy, intimacy and personhood. Philosophy and Public Affairs 6(1): 26–44.

Warren, S. D. & Brandeis, L. D., (1890). Right to Privacy. Harvard Law Review, 4, 193.

Westin, A. (1967). Privacy and Freedom. New York: Atheneum.

REFLECT & WRITE

MyWritingLab

- ❑ Perform a quick rhetorical analysis of this selection from boyd and Marwick's essay. Where do they rely on *logos*? *ethos*? *pathos*? How is each of the appeals used strategically in the essay?
- ❑ How do the authors use quotations, paraphrase, and summary in this piece? Which are from primary sources? Which are from secondary sources? How do their choices about working with her sources affect the persuasiveness of their argument?

Seeing Connections
Refer to Chapter 6 for a more detailed discussion of choosing between summary, paraphrase, and direct quotation in your own writing.

- ❑ How might boyd and Marwick have used visual evidence to support their points? How might inserting photographs of teenagers produce a different impact than integrating screenshots from Facebook? Which types of visual rhetoric do you think would most strongly underscore their argument?
- ❑ **Write.** Draft a response to boyd and Marwick in the form of a blog comment in which you confirm, refute, or qualify their assessment of how teens understand the concept of privacy in their online interactions. Refer to specific passages from their article in your response as well as evidence drawn from your own experience.

■ *A writer for* The New York Times Magazine, **Clive Thompson** *specializes in writing about technology and society. He is also a columnist for* Wired *magazine and contributes articles to* Fast Company. *In addition, Thompson also posts his insights on* Collision Detection, *his blog about science, technology and culture. The reading below is an excerpt from his book,* Smarter Than You Think *(2013), in which Thompson argues that technology is changing our minds for the better. "Ambient awareness" is a term Thompson uses to describe the effect of repeated connections with people over long periods of time on social media.*

Ambient Awareness

Clive Thompson

Who cares what you ate for breakfast?

That question has become a cliché of Internet criticism, the go-to response to social networking sites like Facebook and Twitter. And there is, it's true, something off-putting about the world's newest literary form, the bit-size "status statement," at least at first glance. There's the 140-character tweet about a celebrity or the Facebook link to a gushy news story you just read or a picture of your cat filtered to look like an acid flashback. Then there's the "like"—a single flip of a social bit. When you consider the oceanic volume of stuff, you might well conclude that it's further proof that the Internet has shriveled our attention spans and strip-mined human intimacy. Why do we post so many teensy utterances? And why do we so eagerly devour them?

Ben Haley, a technical support specialist in Seattle, pondered this puzzle when, at the urging of a friend, he first signed up for Twitter in 2007. Like many, he couldn't figure out why anyone would care about such brief messages. One friend tweeted about how she was becoming sick. Another posted links to random stories he was reading. Yet another—straight out of that playbook for vapid updates—would describe her lunch, every single day. Each tweet was so brief as to be virtually meaningless.

But as the months went by, something changed. By following his friends' updates, Haley began to sense the rhythms of their lives. He developed a mental map of what they were doing and even thinking. He could tell when his friend was recovering from her illness. He could track his friend's obsessions by seeing (and sometimes reading) articles he was linking to. Even the litany of sandwiches became spellbinding, a glimpse into the cadence of his friend's life, wryly humorous and even poignant in their detail.

5 The flow began to seem like "a type of ESP," Haley told me, an invisible dimension of information floating above everyday life. "It's like I can distantly read everyone's mind," he added. "I love that. I feel like I'm getting to something raw about my friends. It's like I've got this heads-up display for them." It also led to more real-life contact: When one member of Haley's group broadcasted his plans to go to a bar, the others would see it, and some would drop by—a type of ad hoc self-organizing that has become common in young people's lives. And Haley also noticed that when he did socialize face-to-face, the conversation was subtly altered. He and his friends didn't need to ask, "So what have you been up to?" because they already knew. Instead, they'd begin discussing something one of the friends posted that afternoon, as if picking up a conversation in the middle.

Social scientists have a phrase for this type of ESP: "ambient awareness." Ambient awareness is, they say, almost like being in the same room as someone and picking up on his mood and thoughts by the stray signals he gives off. You create a picture of someone else's internal state gradually, almost unconsciously, by assembling many small observations.

Mizuko Ito, a cultural anthropologist, first noticed this effect more than ten years ago while studying text messaging in Japan. Ito talked to young Japanese couples, all of whom lived in separate apartments (and in one case, separate cities). She found that the couples would trade short text messages all day and night to establish a sense of connection. They'd ping each other with tidbits like "I guess I'll take a bath now," "Just bought a pair of shoes," or "The episode today sucked today, didn't it?" One young businessman jokingly described his text messages to his girlfriend as "mutterings" and the responses he got as "mutterings in reply."

The result, Ito discovered, was that they felt uncannily proximal to each other. Their sense of co-presence, Ito writes, was "similar to the kind of awareness of another one would have when physically co-located...a way of entering somebody's virtual peripheral vision or as she explains it to me," It's like you're in the room and you just sort of share a sign or a facial expression."

This is the paradox of status updates. Each little update—each individual bit of social information—is, on its own, pretty insignificant, even mundane. But taken together over time the snippets coalesce into a surprisingly sophisticated portrait of your friends' inner lives, like dots forming into a pointillist painting. "It's an aggregate phenomenon," Marc Davis, a partner architect at Microsoft, tells me. "No message is the single-most-important message."

10 Before modern technology, this type of awareness wasn't possible. No friend would bother to call you up daily and detail the sandwiches she was eating, the articles she'd read, or the miles she'd walked today; indeed, if she did you'd have have found it annoying and intrusive. But ambient tools weave this knowledge into a tapestry you can glance at, which makes the picture both more complete and more inviting. Unlike a series of phone calls, it's optional—so, as Davis points out, it invites

your attention, rather than demanding it. (Or, as he adds, it's like the difference between a friend in the 1970s forcing you to sit through their agonizingly long vacation slide show and the friend posting the photos online so you can riffle through whichever and whenever you'd like.)

Right now, if you concentrate for a few seconds, you can probably conjure up a recent map of the doings—even the *thinkings*—of the people you follow. I physically talk with my college friend Bret only once a year, when I visit Toronto at Christmas. But I nonetheless know what he's up to right now, including: After reading *The Intuitionist*, a novel about elevator repair, he became obsessed with hunting down vintage-elevator videos on YouTube; that he's doing a lot of weird cooking experiments, including make high-end processed cheese; that he recently rediscovered posters of his university band and started playing music again; and that watching the Mars *Curiosity* rover landing restoked his Canadian appreciation for collective government action. There are professional colleagues I follow who "thoughtcast" their work—like the sociologist Tricia Wang, who spent seventeen months traveling through the impoverished provinces of China and posting pictures on Instagram (trains jammed with migrant workers, hungry school-children receiving their first free school lunch). And like many people, I follow interesting strangers—great curators, provocative thinkers, or simply famous folks whose posts intrigue me.

Of course, it's my personal interest in my friends (and these strangers) that makes their feeds meaningful. If *you* were to glance at the people I follow, you'd just see disjointed info. You wouldn't have developed the big picture that makes each small utterance interesting. Vice versa is also true: If I look at yours, I just see noise. This is precisely why critics of social media can so easily point to any individual status update and proclaim that it's a snippet of meaningless tripe. Without context, it can certainly look that way.

But ambient awareness is all about slowly amassing an enormous, detailed context. Follow someone's ambient signals for a day and it seems like trivia. In a week it seems like a short story. In six months, a novel.

This isn't just idle interest in others' doings, though. Ambient awareness also endows us with new, sometimes startling abilities. When groups of people "think aloud" in this lightweight fashion, they can perform astonishing acts of collaborative cognition. Scientists have known about this for years because they've seen it happen offline, in the physical world.

15 Back in the early 1990s, for example, the British social scientists Christian Heath and Paul Luff began studying the coordination of staff in the control rooms of the complex London underground system. If one train becomes delayed or the drivers aren't available, the controllers have to quickly "reform" the system, deciding which trains need to be taken out of service, which should be rescheduled, and which drivers should be assigned to which trains. "Reforming" is a challenge because different staff members need to be on the same page and aware of each other's actions—but they don't always have enough time to confer about who's doing what.

To solve this problem, the control staff developed a clever technique: They would talk aloud. Each time they altered the system, they'd enunciate what they were doing. They weren't talk *to* anyone in particular. They were doing ambient broadcasting—speaking into the air, for anyone to hear. This sort of "self talk," Heath and Luff noted, helped the group very rapidly establish a common awareness of what was going on. It could even establish the thinking that was going on: By talking out loud, the controller "renders visible to his colleagues the course of reasoning involved in making particular changes," Heath and Luff wrote. With this level of group awareness, the staffers could perform clever feats of collective problem solving. In a sense, they were doing status updates before status updates existed. And subway-control workers aren't the only ones who use this technique, either: Huff and other academics have documented the talking-aloud-to-the-room strategy in surgical teams, newsrooms, airport luggage-control rooms, and financial-industry teams.

Today, this sort of group awareness happens constantly online. I think of it as a form of proprioception, our body's awareness of where its limbs are. That subliminal sense of orientation is crucial for coordination: It keeps us from accidentally bumping into objects and makes possible extraordinary feats of balance and dexterity. When you're able to pass a baseball from your left hand to your right hand behind your back, that's proprioception. When groups of people—friends, family, workmates—keep in lightweight online contact, it gives us *social* proprioception: a group's sense of itself.

Social life is now filled, in a manner at once banal and remarkable, with just this type of self-organization. When my wife went on a work trip to Los Angeles, she originally didn't plan to do any socializing. But when she wrote a Facebook status statement about watching a Demi Moore movie in her hotel room, she began getting pinged by old friends whom she had forgotten lived in the city. (She wound up with invitations to dinner and a concert.) At professional conferences, attendees use everything from tweets to pictures and check-ins to develop a communal sense of what's going on and what interesting presentations each person might have missed, providing fodder for conversations when they all meet up face-to-face at dinner.

These are simple, quotidian examples, but serious ones abound, too. Among political activists, ambient contact has proved particularly powerful in moments of crisis. In November 2011, the Egyptian American journalist Mona Eltahawy was arrested by the Egyptian security forces during a protest and fired off the single tweet: "Beaten arrested in interior ministry." Friends and followers worldwide, accustomed to glancing at Eltahawy's utterances online, instantly learned of the arrest and began talking about it. One was Zeynep Tufekci, an assistant professor who studies technology and society at the University of North Carolina at Chapel Hill; she contacted NPR's Andy Carvin, a friend who tweets about the Middle East, and the two set up a hashtag—#FreeMona—to coordinate how to help Eltahawy. A mere twenty minutes later, so many supporters were discussing how to help that #FreeMona became a worldwide trending topic. Hundreds more sprang into action: Sara Badr, a designer, called the U.S. embassy and tweeted her conversation alerting them; Anne-Marie Slaughter, a former director of policy planning at the U.S. State Department, contacted her former employer; and Egyptians began dialing Egyptian media and al-Jazeera to encourage them to cover Eltahawy's case. It's not easy to pressure the Egyptian military, but the coordinated burst of activity worked. The next day, the military released Eltahawy, whose left arm and right hand had been broken during her ordeal.

20 Ambient awareness on a global scale is strange and new. But it works so well because it taps into older social skills, including our ability to "read" other people. Indeed, when you're

in regular enough digital contact, even *silence* becomes a readable signal—much as you can sense someone' mood shift at a dinner table if she clams up. For example, Lisa Hickey, a journalist I know, one day began to subconsciously sense the "something was up" with an old friend. "When I finally contacted her, it turned out that she'd suddenly gone into the hospital for a life-threatening emergency," Hickey says. At that point Hickey realized, post hoc, where her intuition had come from: Her friend, normally fairly chatty on Facebook, hadn't posted anything for several days and also hadn't posted any explanation for why she'd gone dark. It was the sudden quiet that had alerted Hickey. "And I realized, Oh, this is the invisible ESP."

Indeed, our online and offline people-reading skills appear to be quite closely linked. The personality psychologist Sam Gosling has conducted clever experiments that illustrate how our real-life, physical possessions reveal our personalities. In one, subjects gave Gosling permission to bring strangers into their houses while they were away. After only a few minutes examining their bedrooms, the strangers could produce eerily accurate descriptions of the subjects' personalities. Gosling wondered whether Facebook pages would be equally revealing, so he repeated the experiment online, arranging to have strangers inspect the Facebook pages of experimental subjects. Sure enough, they were able to accurately describe those personalities, too. The ambient signals given off by status updates and streams of photos can be as powerful as those from real-life objects.

Indeed, they're sometimes *more* revelatory. One of the hilarities of ambient life is discovering how much weirder people are than you thought, even those you believed you knew well. Jack Dorsey, the creator of Twitter, once told me that when his parents began using the service, their updates revealed sides he'd never known. "They like to party. They're big fans of going out and drinking!" he said. "And they like to *cuss*. And I learned some of their eating habits, and just a lot of stuff I didn't consider. Text is very freeing especially short bits of text. It allows you to abstract yourself and reflect in a different way. So my mom just ... writes in a way I never heard her speak."

REFLECT & WRITE

MyWritingLab

- ❑ What strategy does Thompson use to start his article? To what extent is it successful in drawing the reader in and setting up background for the rest of the essay?
- ❑ Thompson poses a series of questions in his introduction, one of which is "[W]hy do we so eagerly devour them?", with "them" meaning the "teensy utterances" we post about our daily lives. How does this excerpt answer that question? Does Thompson conclude that social media has "shriveled our attention spans and strip-mined human intimacy"? Why or why not?
- ❑ How does Thompson use historical context and social science to bolster his commentary? How do these choices influence the persuasiveness of his claims?
- ❑ What kinds of evidence does Thompson use to illustrate and support his claims? How convincing are his choices? How does he use individual stories and anecdotes to illustrate a broader theme or trend?

- ❑ **Write.** Thompson suggests that "ambient awareness is all about slowly amassing an enormous, detailed context." Think of some online friends you may have with whom you have that kind of accrued context. Think of friends that may have an "ambient awareness" of you. How would you represent them in a composition? Thompson says, "right now, if you concentrate for a few seconds, you can probably conjure up a recent map of the doings—even the *thinkings*—of the people you follow." Compose a visual text in which you try to represent that map. Then write a short description to explain the process you used to design and develop the visual map of your awareness of your friend.

WRITING COLLABORATIVELY

MyWritingLab

Pull up a random profile page on Facebook (note: if you are going to work with the profile page of one of your Facebook friends, ask his/her permission before sharing it with the group). Analyze the visual rhetoric of the page, paying special attention to the layout, use of color, content, design, and organization. How do these elements combine to create an impression about the persona of the page's author? What "argument" is the author making about him or herself on the profile page? Now, perform the same analysis, but this time on a random Tumblr page or, if you have access, a LinkedIn page. As a group, compare your findings, and develop a claim about the different ways in which Tumblr, Facebook, and LinkedIn help their users construct an online identity.

■ **Evgeny Morozov** *is best known for his work as a contributing editor to* Foreign Policy *and for running* "Net Effect," *the magazine's blog about global politics and the Internet age. Currently a Yahoo! Fellow at Georgetown University's Institute for the Study of Diplomacy, Morozov has published broadly in many venues, including in the* Economist, *the* Wall Street Journal, Newsweek, *the* Times Literary Supplement, *and the* San Francisco Chronicle. *The following article was first posted on September 5, 2009, to the* "Net Effect" *blog.*

From Slacktivism to Activism

Evgeny Morozov

Below is the text of a talk about "slacktivism"—a subject that has received considerable attention on this blog and elsewhere—that I delivered at Festival Ars Electronica this morning (the session was dedicated to "cloud intelligence").

As someone who studies how the Internet affects global politics, I've grown increasingly skeptical of numerous digital activism campaigns that attempt to change the world through Facebook and Twitter. To explain why, let me first tell you a story about a campaign that has gone wrong.

If you have been to Copenhagen, you probably have seen the Stork Fountain, the city's famous landmark. A few months ago, a Danish psychologist Anders Colding-Jørgensen, who studies how ideas spread online, used Facebook to conduct a little experiment using the Stork Fountain as his main subject. He started a Facebook group, which implied—but never stated so explicitly—that the city authorities were planning to dismantle the fountain, which of course was NEVER the case. He seeded the group to 125 friends who joined in a matter of hours; then it started spreading virally. In the first few days, it immediately went to a 1000 members and then it started growing more aggressively. After 3 days, it began to grow with over 2 new members each minute in the day time. When the group reached 27,500 members, Jørgensen decided to end the experiment. So there you have it: almost 28,000 people joined a cause that didn't really exist! As far as "clouds" go, that one was probably an empty one.

This broaches an interesting question: why do people join Facebook groups in the first place? In an interview with the Washington Post, Jørgensen said that "just like we need stuff to furnish our homes to show who we are, on Facebook we need cultural objects that put together a version of me that I would like to present to the public." Other researchers agree: studies by Sherri Grasmuck, a sociologist at Temple University, reveals that Facebook users shape their online identity implicitly rather than explicitly: that is, the kind of campaigns and groups they join reveals more about who they are than their dull "about me" page.

5 This shopping binge in an online identity supermarket has led to the proliferation of what I call "slacktivism," where our digital effort make us feel very useful and important but have zero social impact. When the marginal cost of joining yet another Facebook group are low, we click "yes" without even blinking, but the truth is that it may distract us from helping the same cause in more productive ways. Paradoxically, it often means that the very act of joining a Facebook group is often the end—rather than the beginning—of our engagement with a cause, which undermines much of digital activism.

Take a popular Facebook group "saving the children of Africa." It looks very impressive—over 1.2 million members—until you discover that these compassionate souls have raised about $6,000 (or half a penny per person). In a perfect world, this shouldn't even be considered a problem: better donate a penny than not to donate at all. The problem, however, is that the granularity of contemporary digital activism provides too many easy way-outs: too many people decide to donate a penny where they may otherwise want to donate a dollar.

So, what exactly plagues most "slacktivist" campaigns? Above all, it's their unrealistic assumption that, given enough awareness, all problems are solvable; or, in the language of computer geeks, given enough eyeballs all bugs are shallow. This is precisely what propels many of these campaigns into gathering signatures, adding new members to their Facebook pages, and asking everyone involved to link to the campaign on blogs and Twitter. This works for some issues—especially local ones. But global bugs—like climate change—are bugs of a different nature. Thus, for most global problems, whether it's genocide in Darfur or climate change, there are diminishing returns to awareness-raising. At some point one simply needs to learn how to convert awareness into action—and this is where tools like Twitter and Facebook prove much less useful.

This is not to deny that many of the latest digital activism initiatives, following the success of the Obama electoral juggernaut, have managed to convert their gigantic membership lists into successful money-raising operations. The advent of micro-donations—whereby one can donate any sum from a few cents to a few dollars—has enabled to raise funds that could then be used—at least, in theory—to further advance the goals of the campaign. The problem is that most of these campaigns do not have clear goals or agenda items beyond awareness-raising.

Besides, not every problem can be solved with an injection of funds, which, in a way, creates the same problem as awareness-raising: whether it's financial capital or media capital, spending it in a way that would enable social change could be very tough. Asking for money could also undermine one's efforts to engage groups members in more meaningful real-life activities: the fact that they have already donated some money, no matter how little, makes them feel as if they have already done their bit and should be left alone.

10 Some grassroots campaigns are beginning to realize it: for example, the website of "Free Monem", a 2007 pan-Arab initiative to free an Egyptian blogger from jail carried a sign that said "DON'T DONATE; Take action" and had logos of Visa and MasterCard in a crossed red circle in the background. According to Sami Ben Gharbia, a Tunisian Internet activist and one of the organizers of the campaign, this was a way to show that their campaign needed more than money as well as to shame numerous local and international NGOs that like to raise money to "release bloggers from jail", without having any meaningful impact on the situation on the ground.

That said, the meager fund-raising results of the Save the Children of Africa campaign still look quite puzzling. Surely, even a dozen people working together would be able to raise more money. Could it be that the Facebook environment is putting too many restraints on how they might otherwise have decided to cooperate?

Psychologists offer an interesting explanation as to why a million people working together may be less effective than one person working alone. They call this phenomenon "social loafing." It was discovered by the French scientist Max Ringelmann in

1913, when he asked a group of men to pull on a rope. It turned out they each pulled less hard than when they had to pull alone; this was basically the opposite of synergy. Experiments prove that we usually put much less effort into a task when other people are also doing it with us (think about the last time you had to sing a Happy Birthday song). The key lesson here is that when everyone in the group performs the same mundane tasks, it's impossible to evaluate individual contributions; thus, people inevitably begin slacking off. Increasing the number of other persons diminishes the relative social pressure on each person. That's, in short, what Ringelmann called "social loafing."

Reading about Ringelmann's experiments, I realized that the same problem plagues much of today's "Facebook" activism: once we join a group, we move at the group's own pace, even though we could have been much more effective on our own. As you might have heard from Ethan Zuckerman, Facebook and Twitter were not set up for activists by activists; they were set up for the purposes of entertainment and often attracted activists not because they offered unique services but because they were hard to block. Thus, we shouldn't take it for granted that Facebook activism is the ultimate limit of what's possible in the digital space; it is just the first layer of what's possible if you work on a budget and do not have much time to plan your campaign.

So far, the most successful "slacktivist" initiatives have been those that have set realistic expectations and have taken advantage of "slacktivist" inclinations of Internet users rather than deny their existence. For example, FreeRice, a website affiliated with the UN Food Program, which contains numerous education games, the most popular of which are those helping you to learn English. While you are doing so, it exposes you to online ads, the proceeds of which go towards purchasing and distributing rice in the poor countries (by FreeRice's estimates, enough rice is being distributed to feed 7,000 people daily).

15 This is a brilliant approach: millions of people rely on the Internet to study English anyway and most of them wouldn't mind being exposed to online advertising in exchange for a useful service. Both sides benefit, with no high words exchanged. Those who participate in the effort are not driven by helping the world and have a very selfish motivation; yet, they probably generate more good than thousands of people who are "fighting" hunger via Facebook. While this model may not be applicable to every situation, it's by finding practical hybrid models like FreeRice's that we could convert immense and undeniable collective energy of Internet users into tangible social change.

So, given all this, how do we avoid "slacktivism" when designing an online campaign? First, make it hard for your supporters to become a slacktivist: don't give people their identity trophies until they have proved their worth. The merit badge should come as a result of their successful and effective contributions to your campaign rather than precede it.

Second, create diverse, distinctive, and non-trivial tasks; your supporters can do more than just click "send to all" button" all day. Since most digital activism campaigns are bound to suffer from the problem of diffusion of responsibility, make it impossible for your supporters to fade into the crowd and "free ride" on the work of other people. Don't give up easily: the giant identity supermarket that Facebook has created could actually be a boon for those organizing a campaign; they just need to figure out a way in which to capitalize on identity aspiration of "slacktivists" by giving them interesting and meaningful tasks that could then be evaluated.

Third, do not overdose yourself on the Wikipedia model. It works for some tasks but for most—it doesn't. While inserting a comma into yet another trivia article on Wikipedia does help, being yet another invisible "slacktivist" doesn't. Finding the lowest common denominator between a million users may ultimately yield lower results than raising the barrier and forcing the activists to put up more rather than less effort into what they are doing. Anyone who tells you otherwise is insane. Or, worse, a slacker! Thank you.

REFLECT & WRITE

MyWritingLab

- ❑ Think carefully about Morozov's choice for an opening example. How would starting the essay with a positive example of online activism have changed his reader's understanding of the topic?
- ❑ What is "social loafing," and why is it an important concept for Morozov's definition of online activism?
- ❑ Toward the end of the article, Morozov moves from an article focused on example and analysis to one that operates as a call to action. Why did he make that transition? How would the article have been different if he hadn't?
- ❑ **Write.** Early in his article, Morozov suggests that "Facebook users shape their online identity implicitly rather than explicitly: that is, the kind of campaigns and groups they join reveal more about who they are than on their dull 'about me' page." However, some readers have contended that a factor missing from Morozov's analysis is the role of peer pressure, namely, that many times users join a group, "like" a cause, or share an activist-oriented image because of the influence of their friends, not because they are deliberately trying to craft an online persona. Using examples from your own Facebook experience or that of friends, write a one-page position paper that assesses Morozov's claim in terms of this idea of social pressure.

Jane McGonigal *is a designer of alternate-reality games—"games designed to improve real lives and solve real problems," as she describes on her blog. McGonigal designed a game called* SuperBetter *to help players overcome issues like depression and brain trauma. Her book,* Reality Is Broken: Why Games Make Us Better and How They Can Change the World *(2011) was a bestseller, and continues to influence conversations about game design and its applications in education, health care, and personal growth. The excerpt printed here is from Chapter 7, "The Benefits of Alternate Realities," in* Reality Is Broken.

Quest to Learn—and Why Our Schools Should Work More Like a Game

Jane McGonigal

Today's "born-digital" kids—the first generation to grow up with the Internet, born 1990 and later—crave gameplay in a way that older generations don't.

Most of them have had easy access to sophisticated games and virtual worlds their entire lives, and so they take high-intensity engagement and active participation for granted. They know what extreme, positive activation feels like, and when they're not feeling it, they're bored and frustrated.[17] They have good reason to feel that way: it's a lot harder to function in low-motivation, low-feedback, and low-challenge environments when you've grown up playing sophisticated games. And that's why today's born-digital kids are suffering more in traditional classrooms than any previous generation. School today for the most part is just one long series of *necessary* obstacles that produce negative stress. The work is mandatory and standardized, and failure goes on your permanent record. As a result, there's a growing disconnect between virtual environments and the classroom.

Marc Prensky, author of *Teaching Digital Natives*, describes the current educational crisis:

> "Engage me or enrage me," today's students demand. And believe me, they're enraged. All the students we teach have something in their lives that's really engaging—something that they do and that they are good at, something that has an engaging, creative component to it .... Video games are the epitome of this kind of total creative engagement. By comparison, school is so boring that kids, used to this other life, can't stand it. And unlike previous generations of students, who grew up without games, they know what real engagement feels like. They know exactly what they're missing.[18]

To try to close this gap, educators have spent the past decade bringing more and more

[17]Ito, Mizuko, Heather A. Horst, Matteo Bittanti, Danah Boyd, Becky Herr-Stephenson, Patricia G. Lange, C.J. Pascoe, and Laura Robinson, et al. "Living and Learning with New Media: Summary of Findings from the Digital Youth Project." White paper, The John D. and Catherine T. MacArthur Foundation Reports on Digital Media and Learning, November 2008. http://digitalyouth.ischool.berkeley.edu/report

[18]Prensky, Marc. "Engage Me or Enrage Me: What Today's Learners Demand." *Educause Review*, September/October 2005, 40(5): 60. http://net.educause.edu/ir/library/pdf/erm0553.pdf.

games into our schools. Educational games are a huge and growing industry, and they're being developed to help teach pretty much any topic or skill you could imagine, from history to math to science to foreign languages. When these games work—when they marry good game design with strong educational content—they provide a welcome relief to students who otherwise feel under-engaged in their daily school lives. But even then, these educational games are at best a temporary solution. The engagement gap is getting too wide for a handful of educational games to make a significant and lasting difference over the course of a student's thirteen-year public education.

5 What *would* make the difference? Increasingly, some education innovators, including Prensky, are calling or a more dramatic kind of game-based reform. Their ideal school doesn't *use* games to teach students. Their ideal school *is* a game, from start to finish: every course, every activity, every assignment, every moment of instruction and assessment would be designed by borrowing key mechanics and participation strategies from the most engaging multi-player games. And it's not just an idea—the game-reform movement is well under way. And there's already one new public school entirely dedicated to offering an alternate reality to students who want to game their way through to graduation.

Quest to Learn is a public charter school in New York City for students in grades six through twelve. It's the first game-based school in the world—but its founders hope it will serve as a model for schools worldwide.

Quest opened its doors in the fall of 2009 after two years of curriculum design and strategic planning directed by a joint team of educators and professional game developers, and made possible by funding from the MacArthur Foundation and the Bill and Melinda Gates Foundation. It's run by principal Aaron B. Schwartz, a graduate of Yale University and a ten-year veteran teacher and administrator in the New York City Department of Education. Meanwhile, the development of the school's curriculum and schedule has been led by Katie Salen, a ten-year veteran of the game industry and a leading researcher of how kids learn by playing games.

In many ways, the college-preparatory curriculum is like any other school's—the students learn math, science, geography, English, history, foreign languages, computers, and arts in different blocks throughout the day. But it's how they learn that's different: students are engaged in gameful activities from the moment they wake up in the morning to the moment they finish up their final homework assignment at night. The schedule of a sixth-grader named Rai can help us better understand a day in the life of a Quest student.

7:15 a.m. Rai is "questing" before she even gets to school. She's working on a secret mission, a math assignment that yesterday she discovered hidden in one of the books in the school library. She exchanges text messages with her friends Joe and Celia as soon as she gets up in order to make plans to meet at school early. Their goal: break the mathematical code before any of the other students discover it.

10 This isn't a mandatory assignment—it's a secret assignment, an opt-in learning quest. Not only do they not have to complete it, they actually have to *earn the right* to complete it, by discovering its secret location.

Having a secret mission means you're not learning and practicing fractions because you have to do it. You're working toward a self-chosen goal, and an exciting one at that: decoding a secret message before anyone else. Obviously not all schoolwork can be special, secret missions. But when every book could contain a secret code, every room a clue, every handout a puzzle, who wouldn't show up to school more likely to fully participate, in the hopes of being the first to find the secret challenges?

9:00 a.m. In English class, Rai isn't trying to earn a good grade today. Instead, she's trying to level up. She's working her way through a storytelling unit, and she already has five points. That makes her just seven points shy of a "master" storyteller status. She's hoping to add another point to her total today by completing a creative writing mission. She might not be the first student in her class to become a storytelling master, but she doesn't have to worry about missing her opportunity. As long as she's willing to tackle more quests, she can work her way up to the top level and earn her equivalent of an A grade.

Leveling up is a much more egalitarian model of success than a traditional letter grading system based on the bell curve. Everyone can level up, as long as they keep working hard. Leveling up can replace or complement traditional letter grades that students have just one shot at earning. And if you fail a quest, there's no permanent damage done to your report card. You just have to try more quests to earn enough points to get the score you want. This system of "grading" replaces negative stress with positive stress, helping students focus more on learning and less on performing.

11:45 a.m. Rai logs on to a school computer to update her profile in the "expertise exchange," where all the students advertise their learning superpowers. She's going to declare herself a master at mapmaking. She didn't even realize mapmaking could count as an area of expertise. She does it for fun, outside of school, making maps of her favorite 3D virtual worlds to help other players navigate them better. Her geography teacher, Mr. Smiley, saw one of her maps and told her that eighth-graders were just about to start a group quest to locate "hidden histories" of Africa: they would look for clues about the past in everyday objects like trade beads, tapestries, and pots. They would need a good digital mapmaker to help them plot the stories about the objects according to where they were found, and to design a map that would be fun for other students to explore.

The expertise exchange works just like video game social network profiles that advertise what games you're good at and like to play, as well as the online matchmaking systems that help players find new teammates. These systems are designed to encourage and facilitate collaboration. By identifying your strengths and interest publicly, you increase the chances that you'll be called on to do work that you're good at. In the classroom, this means students are more likely to find ways to contribute successfully to team projects. And the chance to do something you're good at as part of a larger project helps students build real esteem among their peers—not empty self-esteem based on nothing other than wanting to feel good about yourself, but actual respect and high regard based on contributions you've made.

2:15 p.m. On Fridays, the school always has a guest speaker, or "secret ally." Today, the secret ally is a musician named Jason, who uses computer programs to make music. After giving a live demonstration with his laptop, he announces that he'll be back in a few weeks to help the students as a coach on their upcoming "boss level." For the boss level, students will form teams and compose their own music. Every team will have a different part to play—and rumor has it that several mathematical specialists will be needed to work on the computer code. Rai really wants to qualify for one of those spots, so she plans to spend extra time over the next two weeks working harder on her match assignments.

As the Quest website explains, boss levels are "two-week 'intensive' [units] where students apply knowledge and skills to date to propose solutions to complex problems." "Boss level" is a term taken directly from video games. In a boss level, you face a boss monster (or some equivalent thereof)—a monster so intimidating it requires you to draw on everything you've learned and mastered in the game so far. It's the equivalent of a midterm or final exam. Boss levels are notoriously hard but immensely satisfying to beat. Quest schedules boss levels at various points in the school year, in order to fire students up about putting their lessons into action. Students get to tackle an epic challenge—and there's no shame in failing. It's a boss level, and so, just like any good game, it's meant to whet your appetite to try harder and practice more.

Like collaborative quests, the boss levels are tackled in teams, and each student must qualify to play a particular role—"mathematical specialist," for example. Just as in a big *World of Warcraft* raid, each participant is expected to play to his or her strengths. This is one of Quest's key strategies for giving students better hopes of success. Beyond the basic core curriculum, students spend most of their time getting better at subjects and activities—ones they have a natural talent for or already know how to do well. This strategy means every student is set up to truly excel at something, and to focus attention on the areas in which he or she is most likely to one day become extraordinary.

6:00 p.m. Rai is at home, interacting with a virtual character named Betty. Rai's goal is to teach Betty how to divide mixed umbers. Betty is what Quest calls a "teachable agent": "an assessment tool where kids teach a digital character how to solve a particular problem." In other words, Betty is a software program designed to know *less* than Rai. And it's Rai's job to "teach" the program, by demonstrating solutions and working patiently with Betty until she gets it.

20 At Quest, these teachable agents replace quizzes, easing the anxiety associated with having to perform under pressure. With a teachable agent, you're not being tested to see if you're really learned something. Instead, you're mentoring someone because you really have learned something, and this is your chance to show it. There's a powerful element of naches—vicarious pride—involved here: the more a student learns, the more he or she can pass it on. This is a core dynamic of how learning works in good video games, and at Quest it's perfectly translated into a scalable assessment system.

Secret missions, boss levels, expertise exchanges, special agents, points, and levels instead of letter grades—there's no doubt that Quest to Learn is a different kind of learning environment, about as radically different a mission as any charter school has set out in recent memory. It's an unprecedented infusion of gamefulness into the public school system. And the result is a learning environment where students get to share secret knowledge, turn their intellectual strengths into superpowers, tackle epic challenges, and fail without fear.

Quest to Learn started with a sixth-grade class in the fall of 2009, and it plans to add a new sixth-grade class each year as the previous year graduates upward. The first senior class will graduate from Quest to Learn in 2016, and potentially from college by 2020. I'm willing to bet that that graduating class will be full of creative problem solvers, strong collaborators, and innovative thinkers ready to wholeheartedly tackle formidable challenges in the real world.

REFLECT & WRITE

MyWritingLab

- ❑ What is the argument made by this excerpt? How does *Quest to Learn* illustrate the potential benefits of designing a school to work like a game?
- ❑ Do you identify yourself as a "born digital" student, like those McGonigal describes? To what extent does her argument apply to you and to the way you like to learn? How would you use McGonigal's perspective to critique your own educational experiences?
- ❑ **Write.** Write a proposal to redesign one of your current courses as a game. Using the terms and concepts McGonigal describes in this excerpt, consider how the idea of making schools work like a game might be applied to college courses in subjects like, say, first-year composition. What would a "game-like" writing course look like? Imagine that you are teaching the course, and design a course description and syllabus that you could propose to a department chair to gain support for a game-like learning experience.

■ *The following screenshots are taken from games linked through the Website for* **Games for Change**, *an organization devoted to using persuasive games to produce "real world impact." These are "serious games," or games with an agenda, which, by definition, means that they are designed to argue a specific position about issues as varied as the environment, human rights, and world hunger.*

Screenshots: Games for Change

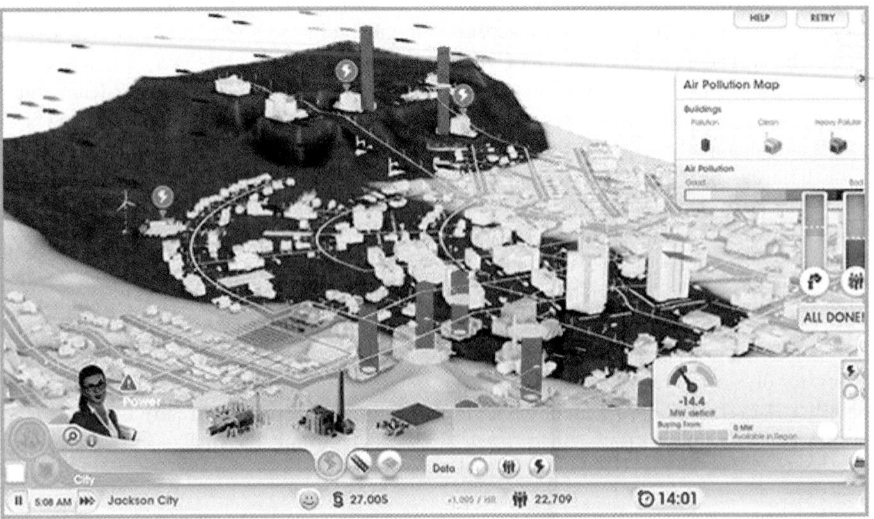

FIGURE 10.3 This screenshot from *SimCityEDU Pollution Challenge!* shows how the game invites players to solve complex problems and interpret complex data about the environment and city planning.

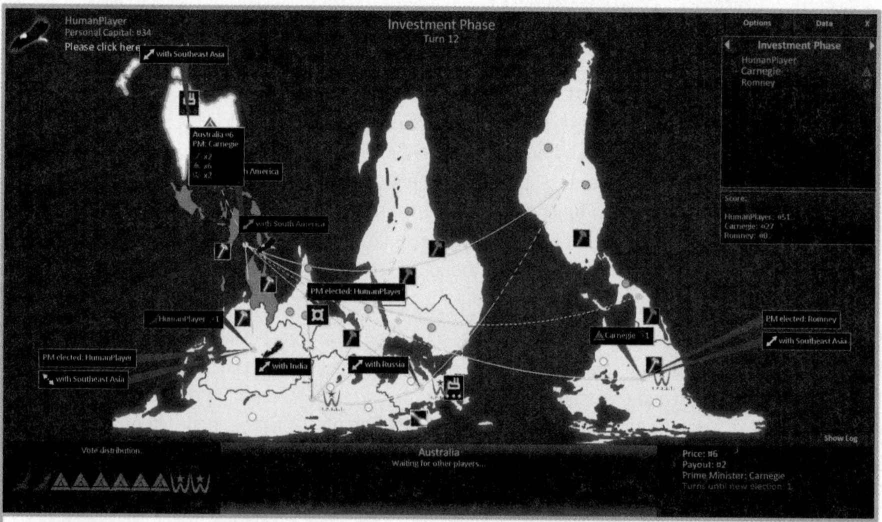

FIGURE 10.4 *Neocolonialism* is a global strategy and resource-allocation game that simulates geopolitical negotiation and economic planning.

REFLECT & WRITE

MyWritingLab

- ❑ Examine the interface provided by each game. Is the player invited in through a "God view" (looking down from above)? Does the player seem to be given a more direct, first-person perspective? How might that perspective affect game play?
- ❑ How does the color palette of the game set the mood for the game play?
- ❑ Are the graphics realistic? Cartoonish? How might that affect the message of the game? How would changing the graphics to be more realistic or more cartoonish alter that message? Why do you think the designers made that choice?
- ❑ **Write.** Visit the Games for Change Website, and play one of the games linked there. Write an analysis of the game that answers the following questions: Who is the intended audience? How can you tell? What type of game is it (i.e., shooter game, role-playing game, strategy game, simulation game)? How does this design choice determine the argument the game makes? What is that argument? To what extent is the game driven by *pathos*? By *ethos*? By *logos*? Can a game like this actually effect social change? Why or why not?

ANALYZING PERSPECTIVES ON THE ISSUE

MyWritingLab

1. In their current edited form for this edition of *Envision*, both the Clive Thompson and Jane McGonigal excerpts end rather abruptly. Review criteria for effective conclusions in Chapter 3 and draft an alternative closing paragraph for either article that pulls together key points from the essay, yet which also moves beyond simple summary to function as an interesting and provocative closing paragraph on its own merits. Consider using example, quotation, key terms, voice or tone, visual evidence, stylistic resonance with the introduction, or other strategies of development to give your concluding paragraph additional power.

Seeing Connections
For further discussion of crafting a powerful conclusion, see Chapter 3.

2. Several of the texts in this chapter make arguments about the power of social media: Drexler, Jenkins, and Thompson all directly comment on the power of social media and online communication to shape human identity and communication. Imagine that you are moderating a debate among these authors. What questions would you ask them? Why? Compose a list of about ten questions you would use to prompt an engaging debate among them. Write a sentence or two about each question to explain what you are trying to learn by asking it.
3. As boyd and Marwick's article indicates, privacy remains a hot topic in relation to any discussion of social media. How do you feel about the privacy controls currently in place on Facebook or the other social networks that you participate in? What are the dangers of lax privacy restrictions? What are the benefits of more public access to information? Draft a short satiric piece in which you convey your stance on the Facebook privacy controversy; you can create a written satire (like Jonathan Swift's *Modest Proposal* or an article from *The Onion*), a comic-based satire (like an editorial cartoon or Web comic), or even a video satire (like a segment from *The Daily Show*, a YouTube short, or even a clip modeled on *South Park*-styled animation).
4. Many scholars, including Morozov, are skeptical about the effectiveness of Twitter as an agent of social action. Drawing from information in the Morozov article, create an editorial cartoon in which you argue for—or against—the effectiveness of Twitter as a political medium.

FROM READING TO RESEARCH ASSIGNMENTS

MyWritingLab

1. Read the full report on "Teens, Social Media, and Privacy" on the Pew Research Center Website. Using statistics and information from this report, storyboard a short five-minute film on this topic intended to be shown to high school and college students. Change up the title, include visual examples, strategically organize your information, select some direct quotes, and most importantly, identify and develop a claim that you want to make about social media usage. For added challenge, produce your film and share it with your class.

2. Randomly select at least five of your Facebook or Twitter friends and research their status updates or tweets for the last month. For each friend, cut and paste their updates or feeds into a Word document in chronological order, then read through them sequentially, looking for trends in the way they use the microblogging function. Do they use it to narrate their lives? For self-promotion? To advertise causes? To share links? To experiment in poetry? To quote their favorite lyrics or lines from movies? Based on your research, define at least three different categories or "types" of updates and write an analysis that describes each one and then makes a claim for how each one represents a different way of managing online identity and relationships through social media.
3. In "From Slacktivism to Activism," Morozov argues that social activism on social network sites like Facebook has little real impact for social change. Research a recent social media activist campaign, such as the Ice Bucket Challenge, #bringbackourgirls, #BlackLivesMatter, or another example of your choice. Drawing on both primary and secondary sources, make an argument for the efficacy of social media to produce opportunities for real activism.
4. Working in groups, research an important issue and develop a stance. Your topic might be campus-based (workers' rights, alcohol on campus, student fees), local (tax increases, community-recycling, school redistricting), or national (human rights violations, global poverty, global conflict). Conduct field research about this issue by interviewing members of the community. Draft a storyboard for an online game designed to persuade viewers to your point of view. Prepare a pitch for a fictional governing board in which you argue for the effectiveness of your game in effecting positive social change. Be sure in your pitch to include the following: whom the game will reach; how players will access the game; what the rhetorical features of the game are in terms of design and content; and why this form of interactive media would be an effective persuasive tool.

MyWritingLab Visit Ch. 10 Life Online in MyWritingLab to complete the *Analyzing Perspectives on the Issue* and *From Reading to Research Assignments*.

CHAPTER 11

Playing Against Stereotypes

Sports figures play many different roles in contemporary culture. These roles range from models of physical perfection to embodiments of national pride; they span from representations of local identity to symbols of global community. For many viewers and readers, these figures become much larger than life.

How is the media complicit in this process? Scholar Paul Mark Pederson has suggested, "Sport and mass media are inextricably linked together in a symbiotic relationship. These two institutions rely on each other—the mass media sell sport and sport sells the mass media." In this chapter, we'll explore the way that the media constantly projects images of athletes to the consumer public, whether from the glossy covers of magazines, in flashy TV ad campaigns, or even on giant posters plastered on the sides of buses, billboards, or in the corridors of malls. Too often, images of sports celebrity remain flat and two-dimensional, even if scaled to poster size or projected in surround sound on a high-definition TV. That is, we tend to see not complex, fully developed individuals, but instead figures that feed into and perpetuate certain cultural stereotypes. So a key question emerges: how do sports—and in particular the media coverage of sports—both reinforce and dismantle such stereotypes?

FIGURE 11.1 Ikram Moukhlis, member of the Moroccan team, at the 2012 Homeless World Cup in Mexico City. Moukhlis lives in a shelter for Muslim women in Tangier, Morocco.

We can see the complicated relationship between stereotype and media at work in the series of soccer images below. In the first (Figure 11.1), a young Moroccan woman, Ikram Moukhlis, balances a soccer ball on her head during a practice for the 2012 Homeless World Cup in Mexico City. Her headscarf (hijab) marks her difference from stereotyped images of soccer players; her status as homeless, while not immediately visible, is another element of her identity as an athletic competitor. The second image (Figure 11.2) features the Guerreros Aztecas, Mexico City's first amputee soccer team. The Guerreros and other teams in the amputee league have done much to showcase athletic talent in a nation often characterized by discrimination against people with disabilities. Hope Solo (Figure 11.3) is one of the most recognizable players on the U.S. Women's Soccer Team; since 2014, she has also been one of its most controversial. Her arrest in June 2014 on domestic violence charges (later dropped) led to calls for her suspension or removal from the team. She was compared to other high-profile athletes accused of assault and domestic violence, like Ray Rice of the NFL, who was suspended after video of him punching his fiancée in an elevator was publicized. By juxtaposing these images, we'd like you to consider: what does a soccer player look like? Or, more broadly, what does an athlete look like? What are their responsibilities as role models? As athletes? Do not make assumptions about athleticism based on stereotype, these images caution: great athletes come in all shapes and forms.

In the readings that follow, we'll look carefully at the complex media messages about sports and uncover how sports figures become subject to gender and race stereotyping by reading articles that examine sports coverage, advertising, and photojournalism in depth. You'll learn to turn a critical eye on all future media coverage of the sports you may love—and those that may be quite new to you. In the process, you'll have a chance to contribute your own responses to this ongoing debate about sports and media.

FIGURE 11.2 Guerreros Aztecas ("Aztec Warriors") play against Los Dragones in Mexico City in 2014. Guerreros Aztecas is Mexico City's first amputee soccer team.

FIGURE 11.3 U.S. goalkeeper Hope Solo in a 2015 match against Mexico. Arguably the best goalkeeper in women's soccer, Solo has been trailed by controversy. Some members of the media called for Solo's suspension following her 2014 arrest for domestic violence. The charges were dismissed on procedural grounds, and Solo played in the 2015 Women's World Cup.

REFLECT & WRITE MyWritingLab

- ❑ How do the three images (Figures 11.1, 11.2, and 11.3) compare to other images of soccer players from the mainstream media? How does each challenge stereotypes? Do any of the images reinforce stereotypes?
- ❑ Think about your own relationship to soccer. Do you play? Are you a fan? How does your personal experience and history with the sport affect the way you respond to these images?
- ❑ Figures 11.1 and 11.2 suggest that sport can play a role in helping people overcome challenges, including financial hardship and physical impairments. How do you respond to these images? What emotions do the photos evoke for you? Why?
- ❑ **Write.** Visit the U.S. Soccer Website and watch the video about Hope Solo in the "23 Stories" feature. How is Solo presented in that video? How does her portrayal in the video compare with other stories about her? How is "Hope Solo" in some ways a product of these visual narratives? Write a short profile of Hope Solo in which you reflect on the different ways stereotypes of her—as a soccer player, woman, and person—have circulated in media culture.

These photographs capture images of athletes who defy stereotypes about "ableness," pushing beyond physical limitations to embody examples of athletic excellence. As photojournalist Carlos Serrao has stated, "In the future, disabled athletes will be 'limited' only by how fast, high and far their man-made limbs can take them. For some … the future is already here."

Defying Stereotypes of Ability

FIGURE 11.4 High-jumper Jeff Skiba, pictured here cresting the bar in his event, won a gold medal during the 2008 Summer Paralympics and was the first amputee in history to clear the 7 foot mark in the high jump—a distinction he earned at the 2008 Asuza Pacific Invitational in Los Angeles.

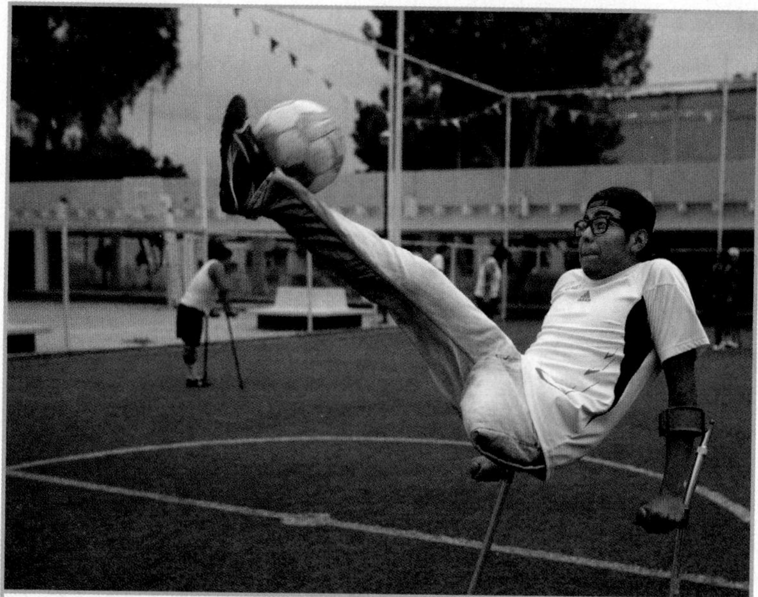

FIGURE 11.5 Baruch Ramirez, 18, captain of the Guerreros Aztecas amputee soccer team, performs an overhead volley in Mexico City, June 2014.

REFLECT & WRITE

MyWritingLab

- ❑ How do these images play to stereotypes of athletes? How do they defy them? Consider the composition of the photos in your analysis, including perspective, layout, focus, and framing.
- ❑ To what extent do these images become images of ability instead of disability? How do their messages differ from that which might be found in a photo focusing, for instance, on Jeff Skiba stretching to prepare for his event or Baruch Ramirez outside a café, posing for the camera?
- ❑ What differences do you see in the way the photographers chose to portray these athletes? Which photograph do you find more inspiring? Why?
- ❑ **Write.** Visit the PBS Website and locate the photo essay called "Paralypmic Athletes Go for Gold in 'Medal Quest.'" Look at that photo essay online. Suggest an alternate arrangement for the eight photos featured in it, and write a short preface to your revised photo essay about athletes, stereotypes, and differing abilities.

Seeing Connections
Review the section on Arrangement in Argument in Chapter 3.

In the following excerpt, researchers Carolyn Hodges, Daniel Jackson, Richard Scullion, Shelley Thompson, *and* Mike Molesworth *explore relationships between experiences of disability and disability sport, focusing on the occasion of the 2012 London Paralympic Games. The complete study was published in September 2014. The first section here provides an overview of recent scholarly work on media representations of disability sport, and the second focuses on a profile of "Magdala," one of five participants in the research study.*

Media Representations of Disability Sport

Carolyn Hodges, Daniel Jackson, Richard Scullion, Shelley Thompson, and Mike Molesworth

It has long been understood that the media has the power to shape the representation of social issues and to influence the understanding that publics have of the world (Howe 2008a: 35; Ellis 2008). DePauw (1997: 424) offers a useful three-tiered typology to help explain the low profile of disability within sport, stating that disabled people might have (a) been largely invisible or excluded from sport (invisibility of disability in sport), (b) become visible in sport as disabled athletes (visibility of disability in sport) and, (c) increasingly become visible in sport as athletes (the '(in)Visibility of disAbility in sport'). DePauw (1997: 425) defines the '(in)Visibility of disAbility' in sport as a situation whereby disabled athletes are "visible in sport as athletes or a time when an athlete's disability is no longer visible." As Purdue and Howe (2012: 193) suggest, the resultant invisibility of disability might, at first, seem positive but, to do so, they advocate, could result in a barrier developing between disabled athletes deemed "worthy" of the name "elite athlete" and other disabled people who do not regularly engage in physical exercise. Furthermore, the Paralympic community could itself become fractured, the authors go on to argue, as a divide emerges between those with less severe disability who might gain acceptance as examples of "elite athletic performance", and others who would not fit the model.

As we suggested earlier in this report, the Paralympics is often regarded as inferior to the Olympics (Fitzgerald 2012; Thomas & Smith 2003; Gilbert & Schantz; Ellis 2008), as sport has historically been a place where physicality is admired (DePauw 1997: 423; Fitzgerald 2012: 249) and the symbolic representation of the "strong, well-formed, non-disabled, masculine body" continues to dominate as the perceived epitome of elite sporting prowess (Hughes 2009: 400). This has led the media to typically frame the performances of elite disabled athletes in ways that may reinforce certain stereotypes of disability. In particular, the emphasis placed upon the therapeutic qualities of Paralympic sports by journalists during the 2004 Paralympic Games in Athens, suggestive of a belief that the Paralympics was less serious than the Olympics (Howe 2008a) or, alternatively, representations of Paralympic athletes as possessing extraordinary and heroic qualities; the so-called "inspirational supercrip" athlete, identified in the sports sociology literature, which serves to glorify "special achievements" (Gold & Gold 2007; Hardin & Hardin 2004; Darcy 2003). Such portrayals are regarded by many as "patronising" (for example, Brittain 2009; 2010), due to their inspirational stories of overcoming the odds through courage, dedication and hard work which, it is claimed, foster unrealistic expectations about what disabled people can or should be able to achieve (Duncan 2001; Hockenberry 1995; Shapiro 1993; Wendell 1996).

According to critics, the supercrip mystique encourages the public to adopt "self-made wo/man" and "blaming-the-victim" ideologies (Ryan 1971) that work against progressive social change (Smart 2001). However, research with disabled people has found mixed support for the supercrip critique. Qualitative research with wheelchair athletes has illustrated an awareness of the supercrip in media coverage, but varied acceptance of the assumptions embedded within the term (Berger 2008). Other research found that some disabled people identified with Olympians and Paralympians in whom they saw achievement and social connectedness personified (Gaskina, Andersen & Morris 2010). It is important to note again here that whilst debates surrounding disability sports continue, many elite athletes are not necessarily preoccupied with their place in the disability movement (Huang & Brittain 2006; Thomas & Smith 2003). Their identities may not be substantially invested in positioning themselves in the vanguard of disability rights, and in their day-to-day lives they may not think much about oppositional disability consciousness (Berger 2008; Deal 2003; Galvin 2003; Watson 2002).

The complexities of the Paralympics classification system is not often discussed in the media reports of the Games, leaving audiences with little meaningful understanding of Paralympic sport (Howe 2008b). There can also be a tendency to downplay disability and difference. Instead, we might find the media embracing of a "hierarchy of acceptability", placing emphasis upon those representations of disability considered to be most 'normal' or least 'different' or 'unpalatable'; focusing on wheelchair users and individuals who have acquired disability following an accident or illness, rather than on athletes with cerebral palsy, for example (Hodges, Jackson & Scullion 2014a; Bush, Silk, Porter & Howe 2013; Ellis 2008; Thomas & Smith 2003; Schell & Duncan 1999). Furthermore, whilst news stories focused on nondisabled elite sport might highlight both positive and negative attributes associated with sports and the sporting personalities who practice them, Howe (2008a) suggests that Paralympic sports are "not yet ready to embrace the old adage that 'any publicity is good publicity'." As such, Howe proposes, greater control is placed upon journalists "to present positive coverage within the limited Paralympic spotlight" (p. 148). As Howe (2008a: 139) maintains, by allegedly leveraging a certain amount of control over how coverage of the Paralympic Games is presented, the International Paralympic Committee (the IPC) might not be able to "provide the public with an understanding of the distinctive culture of the sport that is closely tied to the process of classification. This means that the public gain little knowledge about the relationship between impairment and the practice of sport."

Summarising Howe's (2008a) argument, the media has framed Paralympic sport as a (sub) culture, with established boundaries, but seldom does coverage explore what makes it culturally distinctive. There is some evidence to suggest that in the UK, Paralympic events can be reported in ways that are broadly consistent with sports reporting more generally (Thomas & Smith 2003). In the process of emphasising what is perceived as the sporting achievements of elite disabled athletes, however, such events can often be juxtaposed with those of nondisabled athletes, which may inadvertently reinforce "what might be considered as a stereotypical perception of disability and a preoccupation with ablebodiedness" (Thomas & Smith 2003: 180). In other words, disability sports still struggle to gain acceptance in their own right. There exists a palpable tension for broadcasters in terms of balancing their framing of disability, and disability sports, in particular. The social appraisal of a disabled individual and that of an elite athlete within the same body at the same time is regarded as contradictory and incompatible (Purdue & Howe 2012). Purdue and Howe (Ibid.) attempted to explain this by way of the concept of the Paralympic paradox i.e. the fundamental need for non-disabled audiences to be able to identify a Paralympian as possessing some form of disability to perceive of them as a credible and justified member of a disability sport competition, whilst, consequently, the more a Paralympian's disability is de-emphasised (the desired reception of a non-disabled audience), the more disabled audiences may become further alienated from, and fail to identify with, disability sport. Purdue and Howe (Op Cit: 199—drawing on Bourdieu 1977, 1984) argue that it is possible for the same Paralympic Games to be perceived to possess different purposes at the same time, as individuals who have different "habitus", occupy different vantage points from which they interpret and make sense of the Paralympic Games and society more broadly. If the media attention is focussed upon disability, then it may be patronising Paralympians as well as disabled audiences. If the focus is placed on athletes, then it may be difficult for some audiences to follow, thus leaving prejudice, at least overtly, unchallenged.

'Magdala': Opening Her Eyes to a Broader Perspective on what 'Disability' Means

When we first met her, Magdala was a trainee teacher in her early twenties living in North London with her mother and one of her three brothers. She was bubbly and articulate, with a keen interest in the world around her. Her weekend routine typically comprised meeting friends for coffee or dinner or going clubbing. She used to be a member of a gym but quit as she found it 'depressing'; she now had her basic fitness equipment (cross-trainer etc.) at home. Magdala confessed that she was not a fan of sport as she didn't like the competitive element to it. She found it 'quite stressful'. This stemmed from her youth when her elder brothers made everyw game a sport and took the fun out of it. Her real passion was travelling and, when we first met her, she was learning Spanish. Magdala planned to spend a couple of months in Spain improving her Spanish before travelling to South America to experience a 'complete change of culture'. Magdala was not a fan of backpacking, however, as she didn't like the 'instability'. Instead, she would prefer to live in another country, like Colombia, for a year.

TV habits

Magdala watched some TV but was not overly interested in it—probably because she had so many other things going on in her life. When she did tune in, it was usually to watch 'trashy TV' such as, "The Hills", "Glee", "Gossip Girl", "Geordie Shore" and soap operas. Magdala referred to this as 'feel good TV' that was entertaining and helped her to switch off. She might also watch some documentary programmes because of their value to her teaching activities. She always tried to watch lifestyle programmes such as "Embarrassing Bodies" and "Supersize Vs Superskinny" but watched these mostly online in her room either on her own or with her boyfriend. In the living room she sometimes watched films with her Mum.

Limited experiences of disability

During her teacher training, Magdala worked in a variety of challenging school environments, which she described as being more like 'social work' than teaching. One of the schools was in a deprived area of London. Several of the children had behavioural issues, and a few of the children were disabled. In another school, she had a student in her class with cerebral palsy. Magdala's early engagement with the Paralympics and interest in disability, therefore, was what one might expect from a teacher—she regarded both as issues that formed a significant part of the learning experience of young children, and she could see the value and importance of her pupils engaging with such issues. Despite communicating an enthusiasm for events such as the World Cup and Olympics because of the sense of occasion they brought, Magdala did not appear initially to engage personally with the Paralympics. In early interviews, she seemed unaware of what the Paralympics consisted of, enquiring what 'types' of disability were included in the Games.

Learning about disability and disability sport

The second time we met Magdala she had recently been affected by temporary disability herself following an injury—a piece of glass cut through one of the tendons in her arm. The accident left her unable to use her arm for three months and this meant she could not complete her teaching training placement. Magdala explained how she learned to do things differently and just 'got on with it'. In later interviews, unashamed of the scar on her wrist, she remembered that the injury, and her experiences of a lack of mobility, in part influenced her perceptions of disability. Magdala tended to associate disability primarily with injury and war, with the missing limbs of athletes a common theme during our discussions of the Paralympics.

A year later in June 2012, there had been some changes in Magdala's circumstances. She no longer enjoyed teaching as much as she had anticipated and she didn't believe she was passionate enough to continue. Instead, she wanted to do a Master's degree. She planned to visit Morocco the following week and to go inter-railing around Europe during the summer. Magdala would, therefore, miss the Olympics; however given the 'hell' she thought there would be in London, she was quite glad she would be missing it. By this stage, Magdala had not seen any of the Paralympics-related programmes on Channel 4, but she was looking forward to the Games because they would be more interesting to watch than the Olympics. Her interest in the Paralympics was more a 'fascination', almost a learning experience, finding out about the people, their disabilities and 'how the fake limbs are attached'; 'is it painful when they run?'

Following the Paralympics, Magdala commented that the opening ceremony was both shocking and emotional, with people from around the world 'no matter what state they are in [...] grouped together because they are athletes, but mainly because they are disabled.' Although she had always empathised with disabled people, summer 2012 was important in raising Magdala's 'awareness' of disability. The Paralympics and the time she spent travelling with her friend who worked with children with learning disabilities, had taught her more about it. Talking with her friend about disabilities and seeing 'profoundly disabled people' when out in nightclubs in Budapest, made her more aware and made disability seem more 'normal'. Magdela also felt that the Paralympics had led to disabled people being seen as less vulnerable and weak.

Magdala and a friend had been to watch some of the Paralympic events at the Olympic Park, which she found fun and inspiring. Both had injuries at the time, which they considered to be temporary disabilities (Magdala's severed tendon and her friend's broken leg). The realisation of seeing disabled people carry out such impressive feats made her think that maybe she should try more, saying 'we can do anything really.' Magdala described it as a very surreal experience, commenting that often it was hard to 'work out why people are in the Paralympics.' She suggested that, in many cases, the prosthetics were hardly visible and it led her to think about how they organised athletes into competitive categories.

Magdala watched the athletics at the stadium, but didn't watch much of the Games on TV. She was more interested in the documentaries before the event, to find out: 'Who are these people?' and why are they in the Paralympics? She was not particularly interested in the sport, but the competitors amazed her. Disability in sport was like an 'emotional rollercoaster', she said, as it was both 'quite sad' yet also 'quite uplifting' and it was the emotion that made the Paralympics 'much more touching' than just watching someone compete in the Olympics. The Paralympics, for Magdala, was 'less of a competition and more of a statement to raise awareness.' She said that she 'knows she should call it a competition but she sees it as more of an opportunity.' She found it hard to consider the Olympics and Paralympics as the same thing because they had been divided into two events reflected in the coverage and timings.

Magdala talked about her thoughts regarding cultural perceptions of disability. She commented that she found it 'amazing' to see people from third world countries in the Paralympics. Whilst the UK and US were much more 'politically correct', other countries such as India and China were less sensitive of disabilities and may even consider those with disabilities to be 'evil and not worthy.' She 'learnt' about this through reading and meeting different people from different cultures. She said she thought it was more of an achievement for the less supporting countries athletes to be there, against the odds. Magdala found the Paralympics more interesting than the Olympics as it was not just about winning, the event was more about showcasing success: 'look at me I'm alive, look what I've done. I can still move and compete in a competition with millions of people watching me.' For Magdala, the Paralympics were inspirational to everyone, regardless of disability: 'Reminding you to never give up, you can do what you like.' The key message she took from the summer of sport was 'how clever the human body is, and that you are always able to increase your fitness. And you are always able to try hard … You can do anything … Don't write off disabled people.'

That said, Magdala commented that, whilst she would watch the Paralympics again, she wouldn't go out of her way to keep up with the news.

Summary

Over the course of the 2 years, Magdala's engagement with the Paralympics changed from being largely apathetic (she didn't appear to engage personally with the Paralympics or sport more generally) to empathy and an attempt to 'bridge' experiences after having direct, albeit temporary, experience of disability herself when she severed a tendon in her arm. That injury, and the time she spent with limited mobility; in part, influenced her perceptions of disability, which she tended to associate (at a distance) primarily with injury and war. Her engagement with the Paralympic Games became more personal when she attended some of the events together with a friend. Magdala described this as something of an 'emotional rollercoaster' and reflected a narrative of 'admiration for achievement against the odds.

References

Brittain, I. (2010) 'British media perceptions of the Paralympics', in Schantz, O. J. & Gilbert, K. (eds.) *Heroes or zero's: The media portrayal of Paralympic sport*, Champaign, Il.: Commonground Publishing.

Brittain, I. (2009) *The Paralympic Games explained*, London: Routledge.

Darcy, S. (2003) 'The politics of disability and access: the Sydney 2000 Games experience', *Disability and Society, 18(6)*, pp.737–757.

DePauw, K. P. (1997) 'The (in)visibility of disability: Cultural contexts and "sporting bodies"', *Quest, 49,* pp. 416–430. DOI: 10.1080/00336297.1997.10484258

Ellis, K. (2008) 'Beyond the Aww Factor: Human interest Profiles of Paralympians and the media navigation of physical difference and social stigma', *Asia Pacific Media Educator, 19,* pp. 23–35.

Fitzgerald, H. (2012) 'Paralympic Athletes and "Knowing Disability"', *International Journal of Disability, Development and Education, 59(3),* pp. 243–255.

Gilbert, K. & Schantz, O. (eds.) (2008) *The Paralympic Games: Empowerment or side show?* New York: Meyer & Meyer.

Gold, J. R. & Gold, M. M. (2007) *Olympic Cities: City Agendas, Planning and the World's Games, 1896–2012*, London: Routledge.

Hardin, M. M. & Hardin, B. (2004) 'The "supercrip" in sport media: Wheelchair athletes discuss hegemony's disabled hero', *Sociology of Sport Online, 7(1),* Online, Available http://physed.otago.ac.nz/sosol/v7i1/v7i1_1.html (accessed 17/02/2014).

Howe, P. D. (2008a) 'From Inside the Newsroom: Paralympic Media and the 'Production' of Elite Disability', *International Review for the Sociology of Sport, 43,* p. 135, DOI: 10.1177/1012690208095376

Purdue, D. E. J. & Howe, P. D. (2012) 'See the sport, not the disability: exploring the Paralympic paradox', *Qualitative Research in Sport, Exercise and Health, 4(2),* pp. 189–205, DOI: 10.1080/2159676X.2012.685102

Thomas, N. & Smith, A. (2003) 'Pre-occupied with able-bodiedness? An analysis of the British media coverage of the 2000 Paralympic games', *Adapted Physical Activity Quarterly, 20,* pp. 166–181.

REFLECT & WRITE MyWritingLab

- ❑ The first section of the report discusses what the authors refer to as the "inspirational supercrip" stereotype. What do they mean by this term? How would you summarize the authors' critique of this "supercrip" narrative?

- ❑ The second excerpt focuses on one woman, "Magdala," whose personal experiences contributed to a change in her views of disability sport. What purpose does Magdala's story serve in the broader argument the authors are making in their study? Why do you think they chose to focus on Magdala in particular?
- ❑ Hodges et al. provide insight into the power of media and events like the Paralympic Games to change viewers' perceptions of disability sports and athletes. What is their overarching claim or argument? How does this argument compare to your own experiences as a viewer? In what ways have the Paralympics and other disability sports events shaped the way we watch, talk about, and participate in disability sports?
- ❑ **Write.** Locate the complete report online. Focus especially on the executive summary, and then choose a second case study to explore in detail. Draft a one-page response to the report, analyzing one case study in detail to support your general responses. What advice or insight would you offer to future sports broadcasters and media representatives, based on the report?

■ Ta-Nehisi Coates *writes about race and culture for* The Atlantic. *Born in Baltimore in 1975, Coates is author of a memoir called* The Beautiful Struggle, *and is also author of* Between the World and Me *(2015), a mix of personal narrative and history. Coates is one of the most influential writers on the subject of race and racism in the United States. In this short essay from* The Atlantic, *originally published in September 2014, Coates argues that the conversation about Hope Solo's domestic violence arrest "erases the historical truth about domestic violence."*

No, Hope Solo Is Not "Like" Ray Rice

Ta-Nehisi Coates

To say the female soccer star accused of assault is the same as the football player who pummeled his fiancé erases the historical truth about domestic violence.

Soccer star Hope Solo is alleged to have assaulted her sister and 17-year old nephew in June of this year. Unlike Ray Rice, Solo is still plying her trade as a goalkeeper for the national team. This led several people to claim that Solo is the beneficiary of a double standard. In *The New York Times* Juliet Macur makes the argument:

One can argue the differences between an N.F.L. player punching his soon-to-be wife and a soccer star brawling with her family, but it is indisputable that both qualify as domestic violence. The glaring contrast in Solo's case is that while several football players recently accused of assaults have been removed from the field, she has been held up for praise by the national team.

On Thursday she was even given the honor of wearing the captain's armband in celebration of her setting the team's career

> record for shutouts in its previous game. The question is why.
>
> 5 Celebrating Solo's achievement right now is like allowing running back Adrian Peterson, who has been accused of child abuse, to continue to play for the Minnesota Vikings—and then awarding him the game ball for his next 100-yard game.

This analysis strikes me as incorrect, as it does for Slate's Amanda Hess. It also exists outside the bounds of human history. Ray Rice did not so much "brawl with his family" as he pummeled his fiancé into unconsciousness. Contrary to the flimsy notion that Real Men don't hit women, Real Men have been pummeling women for much of human history.

It is now becoming fashionable to ignore human history and dump all manner of insupportable violence committed by athletes into the same bucket. The label on that bucket reads "Something Bad, Which We Should Punish." It is true that what Ray Rice did was violent and wrong. It is also true that what Adrian Peterson did was violent and wrong. And it also true that what Hope Solo is alleged to have done is violent and wrong. But they are not the same specimen of violent and wrong.

In our society we recognize different kinds of violence. We understand, for instance, that lynching enjoys a particular place in American history. We generally grant that Emmett Till was not merely murdered, but that he was murdered in a fashion that places his death in a specifically heinous tradition in our history. And thus we understand that what happened to Till, or what James Byrd, or what happened to Sam Hose is not the same thing as what happened to Tupac Shakur or Sam Cooke. This does not mean that what happened to Shakur or Cooke was good. It means that it wasn't a lynching.

In the history of humanity, spouse-beating is a particularly odious tradition—one often employed by men looking to exert power over women. Just as lynching in America is not a phenomenon wholly confined to black people, spouse-beatings are not wholly confined to women. But in our actual history, women have largely been on the receiving end of spouse-beating. We have generally recognized this in our saner moments. There is a reason why we call it the "Violence Against Women Act" and not the "Brawling With Families Act." That is because we recognize that violence against women is an insidious, and sometimes lethal, tradition that deserves a special place in our customs and laws.

10 There is a reason why we have a "Violence Against Women Act," not a "Brawling With Families Act."

This is the tradition with which Ray Rice will be permanently affiliated. Hope Solo is affiliated with a different tradition—misdemeanor assault. If she is guilty she should be punished. And perhaps we do need to have a conversation about punishing athletes for assaulting people. But we don't need Ray Rice to make that case. And we should not pretend that if Ray Rice were accused of assaulting his younger brother and his 17-year old nephew, we would be having this conversation.

Hope Solo only becomes Ray Rice through the annihilation of inconvenient history—through some forgery that implies that there is no tradition of men controlling women through violence. We are familiar with other such forgeries. It is how a conversation about the racism of Richie Incognito becomes a conversation about banning black people from using the word "nigger." Or how the destruction of Mike Brown's body becomes a debate about "black-on-black crime." Or how Ray Rice knocking his wife unconscious morphs into, "Yes, but women do it too." Indeed they do—but neither with the consistency, nor urgency, nor lethality of men.

REFLECT & WRITE MyWritingLab

- ❑ What does Coates mean when he writes that "Hope Solo only becomes Ray Rice through the annihilation of inconvenient history"? Do you agree? Why or why not?
- ❑ What is the primary thesis of Coates's argument? Why is it important for him to make a key distinction between Hope Solo and Ray Rice? What larger argument about gender (and race) is Coates making?
- ❑ Coates quotes another writer, Juliet Macur, from the *New York Times*, as an example of how much of the media has written about Solo. What is Coates's criticism of Macur? How does that criticism support his argument?
- ❑ Coates refers to a number of historical precedents (Emmett Till, James Byrd, and others). Do some research to learn more about one of these figures. Why does Coates refer to them in this story? What point is he making?
- ❑ **Write.** Coates makes an argument in this essay that media accounts of violence by athletes now tend to be written in a similar way ("dumped into the same bucket"). To what extent is that true? Locate some stories about Hope Solo, and analyze them in terms of the framework provided by Coates. Draft a response to Coates in which you use your analysis to confirm, challenge, or complicate his argument.

■ *In 2012, ESPN surveyed 82 pro athletes, including members of the NBA, WNBA, NFL, NHL, MLB, and MMA, about their perceptions of race issues in sports. The following selections are from the anonymous survey responses. The results were originally published in the December 28, 2012 issue of* ESPN The Magazine.

From "Black Athlete Confidential"

Who are the three most important African-American athletes ever?

Totals (Please note that because this question asked for three responses, the totals add up to more than 100 percent):

1. **Jackie Robinson:** 74 percent
2. **Muhammad Ali:** 60.5 percent
3. **Michael Jordan:** 48.1 percent
4. **Magic Johnson:** 16 percent
5. **Jesse Owens:** 14.8 percent
6. **Arthur Ashe:** 13.6 percent

7. **Wilma Rudolph, Tiger Woods:** 7.4 percent
8. **Jim Brown:** 6.2 percent
9. **Tommie Smith:** 4.9 percent

Female Olympian: "Jackie Robinson, because in a sport that, at the time, was not played by African-Americans at the major league level, he broke through. At a time when there was segregation and black people were looking for a presence to be known as people, he was a way through athletics. He became a voice for this. He was a voice for America, which was just starting to unite. He was a gateway for African-Americans to get into sports and becoming public figures."

NBA player: "Muhammad Ali stood up for everything he believed in. He was a confident African-American athlete at a time when it was hard to be confident. Imagine if we had a draft today, and a guy like LeBron refused to go to war. Ali persevered through that. Incredible."

NBA player: "I'd say Jackie Robinson, Muhammad Ali and Michael Jordan. I'm sure MJ will be picked a lot, but I always think about how he was such an innovator. He took the barriers that Jackie Robinson, Ali, Arthur Ashe, etc. broke through and added to it. Before, the idea of a black athlete being a superstar on the court and an endorsement superstar seemed impossible."

WNBA player: "Arthur Ashe. I remember my mom always talking about Arthur Ashe and the impact he had on breaking the color barriers in the world of tennis."

WNBA player: "Without Jackie Robinson, there would be no Cam Newton or Magic Johnson."

MLB player: "Magic Johnson. I define important by how many people you've helped. Magic Johnson has helped a lot of people."

Olympic athlete: "Michael Jordan. He's probably the first athlete that people didn't even think about what color his skin was."

MMA fighter: "If I had to pick one, it would be Ali, hands down. He was the most influential athlete in sports history. No one stood for more."

Female Olympian: "Michael Jordan. During the London Olympic games, there was a documentary on the Dream Team. Originally in the interviews, he said he wasn't interested in being on the Dream Team. He thought it was a fake political statement and too much drama. Then he started talking to other players and saw this was more than just being an NBA star playing on the Olympic team. It was representing your nation and being a voice for the American people and competing on the world stage. Then you look at how he created another gateway door opening for African-Americans in sports through sponsorship deals. He really, really allowed sports to evolve in this area."

What is the image of the black athlete?

Totals:
Very positive: 8.8 percent
Somewhat positive: 42.5 percent
Neither positive nor negative: 25 percent
Somewhat negative: 17.5 percent
Extremely negative: 6.2 percent

Female Olympian: "C. I have to go in the middle. Somewhat positive, because the African-American youth look up to African-American athletes. A lot of African-American athletes in the limelight right now come from nothing to something. They're really trying to be proactive in the community and show through their story that you can make something of yourself if you're determined enough. But I also think there is a negative connotation that all we have is sports because we're not educated, and all we have is natural talent, and all we want is to make the money and not do anything to get there. So I think there is a little bit of back and forth between positive and negative."

NFL player: "Extremely negative. Everybody thinks that we spend all our money on cars, rims, etc., and that we are outspoken and not really hard workers. None of that is true."

WNBA player: "It's sad. I hate talking about it, really. The image is terrible, and to be honest, I think people and the media in general just look at the negative too much. There are a lot of strong, hard-working black athletes who do great things. But that's lost in the news."

Boxer: "Somewhat negative. Look at Floyd Mayweather. He's one of the best boxers ever. But when he was Pretty Boy, he was not a big name. Now that he's Money Mayweather, with a flashy persona, that's what people get behind. With blacks like him, probably most of white America wants to see him lose."

MMA fighter: "It's D, somewhat negative. But over the last decade, it has gotten better. Our image still suffers with some of the preconceived ideas of selfishness, overextravagance, unfaithfulness."

How does the image of the black athlete compare with reality?

Totals:
Image is the same as reality: 28.8 percent
Image is better than reality: 25 percent
Image is worse than reality: 46.2 percent

Female Olympian: "C, worse than the reality. I think if a black athlete does something that is particularly negative or shocking, the media grabs onto it right away. If it were an athlete from another race, that may not be the case."

NBA player: "C, worse than reality. White people think we're not smart. Not true. I know a lot of smart black athletes like Andre Iguodala, who's one of the smartest guys I know. People expect us just to be athletes. All throughout college and high school, I was a good athlete, and people looked at me as being a dumb athlete, a dumb jock."

NBA player: "B, image is better than reality. For black athletes, a lot of things are publicized and look really glamorous, and they are. It's amazing the things that we're able to accomplish and be blessed with. But there are also things that aren't so glamorous. Our bodies are put on the line—look at football guys who get concussions and it affects them down the line. So it's not as good as what everybody thinks it is."

Boxer: "C. Guys like Floyd Mayweather put on a bad-guy, tough-guy act. He's got bravado, all this money, people look at that and decide they can do without the antics. It's imitation Ali, it's out of control, and that gives us a black eye, it stops us from being loved. The average person can't get down with that."

On a scale of 1 to 10 (1 being absolutely not; 10 being absolutely yes), are black athletes expected to be role models for the black community?

Average answer: 8.7

Female Olympian: "10, absolutely yes. It's an unwritten rule and part of your duty. If you make it out of misfortune and hardships, then it's almost an obligation to be a role model to others who have similar situations."

Male Olympian: "Nine. Coming from a black community, there aren't a lot of people who come out of them and are able to go back and show this is what I learned, that I've been where you've been, and this is what it takes to be successful. It is a responsibility to go and show these African-American kids that their dreams can come true through a lot of work and having a team around you who believes in the same thing you want to believe in, and stay away from a lot of the negativity. Because it's out there."

NFL player: "Seven. You have people that look up to you. Now, do I agree with it? No. Don't think that just because I'm on TV, I'm a role model. I've made so many mistakes in my life, a lot of which you don't even know about. Trust me: I'm no role model. Don't look up to me."

WNBA player: "10. It's a responsibility that comes with being a professional athlete. Kids love athletes, and it's our job to give them someone to look up to outside the home."

Boxer: "Eight. It's important. But at the same time, those athletes who are role models have an obligation to use that to make sure kids know their real role models should be moms, dads, teachers, etc."

MMA fighter: "10. The kids in those communities look up to the wrong type of people—the people who make money now and deal with the consequences later. That was my existence in the inner city. I would be working out, running on the streets, and they had cars, girls, etc. It was hard to do right when you see that other guy living the extravagant lifestyle. For those fortunate enough to have had people help them see through that and get out, it's on us now to be part of the community, to be role models."

Woman Olympian: "10. We do have that obligation. But it's funny, because I bet if you asked star athletes who they most admired and who were their role models growing up, you would get some mentions of Muhammad Ali, Willie Mays, Tommie Smith, Wilma Rudolph. But you'd get more votes for moms and dads and teachers and youth coaches. I want to be a role model for my community, but I also think you got problems if young people are only looking up to athletes. That's not how most of us have achieved what we've achieved."

True or false: TV announcers use terms like "smart" and "cerebral" to describe white athletes more than black athletes.

Totals:
True: 54.4 percent
False: 45.6 percent

NFL player: "True. When you hear them talking about black athletes, you hear 'Oh, the guy is fast, he's athletic. He's got all the natural ability.' Most of the linebackers and white quarterbacks, it's 'He's smart.' But they're just as athletic as the black players, and the black players are just as smart. We all made it to the NFL, but it's just the way they describe them that is different."

NFL player: "True. I'm always hearing 'smart' and 'cerebral,' and here's another one: 'high-motor.' I'm always hearing how white players are high-motor. What does that even mean? What, they play hard? Don't black players play hard? Oh, I forgot, we rely on our talent only. Right?"

WNBA player: "True. White athletes are smart and gutsy. Black athletes are just athletic."

Male Olympian: "True. I've seen it and heard it. Or take Andrew Luck and RG III. They say Luck is smart, consistent, knows the playbook. But RG III is a great athlete, fast, strong and can throw far. People that are African-American are assumed to be naturally gifted as opposed to white players who have to work."

NBA player: "True. Put on an NBA game sometime when there is a good white player on the court and just listen to all the code words that get used. If you hear, 'scrappy,' 'tough' or 'hard-nosed,' look up and the white player probably made a steal. I don't even know what hard-nosed means. I mean, my nose seems pretty hard."

When thinking of the image of black athletes from the past, what three words come to mind?

Totals *(most named words, by number of mentions):*
Strong: 26
Perseverance: 21
Tough: 15
Pioneers, inspirational: 10 each
Courageous, disciplined, talented: eight each
Resilient: six

Female Olympian: "Resilient. We've come so far, and it's because those athletes were resilient enough to fight for their dreams and keep going despite how many times they were hammered down and told they can't. They said, 'No, I can,' and they pushed through."

NBA player: "Disciplined, because, I mean, if you and me walked through the hallway and people are throwing drinks and stuff at us and cussing us out and punching us and doing whatever they can to hurt us, I think me and you would have a problem with that and would react to it. But those guys went through that every game night in and night out."

MLB player: "I'd say strong. Those athletes went through more in one year than we'll ever have to deal with in our whole athletic careers. It's actually hard to get your mind around, some of the hurdles they overcame."

WNBA player: "Perseverance. You hear and read stuff about black athletes these days, and that's just crap you get on Twitter or on the Internet. Our predecessors had to persevere through that stuff in every game, in every stadium."

REFLECT & WRITE

MyWritingLab

- ❑ Reflect on the responses to the survey questions. What do they say about the stereotype of black athletes today?
- ❑ In sharing the results of their survey, the authors had to carefully sift through the responses to decide which quotations were worth including in the article. Which quotations seem particularly powerful to you? Why? Which quotations seem less impactful?
- ❑ Consider the canon of arrangement. Why do you think the authors chose to list the comments and questions in this particular order? Select a particular example of a quotation or question and analyze how its placement was rhetorically strategic.
- ❑ Why do you think the survey writers included a question about the relationship of the athlete to the larger community? Why is a question like this important when considering stereotype?
- ❑ Consider a revision of the final question of the series: When thinking of the image of black athletes, what three words come to mind? Answer that question, using tangible examples as evidence to support your claim.
- ❑ **Write.** Conduct your own similar survey, sampling at least 20 sports fans (rather than athletes) and asking the same questions listed in the preceding paragraphs. Compare their responses to the ones given by the professional athletes. Write up a short report in which you evaluate the similarities and differences between their responses, taking into account the difference in demographics (athlete versus fan) between the original survey respondents and your own.

■ Rob Ruck *teaches history at the University of Pittsburgh and writes about the history of sport, especially baseball, for a number of academic publications. He is author of* Raceball: How the Major Leagues Colonized the Black and Latin Game *(2011). The essay reprinted here originally appeared in 2011 in* Americas Quarterly, *a policy journal focused on economic and social issues in the Western Hemisphere.*

Baseball's Recruitment Abuses

Rob Ruck

Baseball may no longer be the national pastime in the United States, but it remains a pan-Caribbean passion. No other region celebrates the game with such panache or sends so many stellar players to the major leagues. If you visit any ballfield in the Caribbean, it will be hard to miss the talent scouts lurking on the sidelines, systematically picking off young boys who show flashes of athletic promise. But Caribbean baseball's success has a dark side. The promise of multi-million-dollar payoffs in the north has triggered unscrupulous tactics by a growing industry seeking to profit from the region's juvenile talent.

The high-stakes game for recruits and prospects has given rise to a feeding frenzy involving a wide range of players, from local talent-spotters and foreign investors to nongovernmental organizations and representatives of Major League Baseball (MLB) teams. The lives of boys and the game's honor—at least what's left of it—hang in the balance.

So does baseball's potential to serve as a way to strengthen local communities and economies in the region.

Since Jackie Robinson opened Major League Baseball to darker-skinned players in 1947, the trickle of Latin Americans to the majors has become a torrent. They now comprise more than a quarter of all major leaguers, about half of all minor leaguers, and they dominate the ranks of the game's best players. Latinos won half the Silver Slugger Awards—given to the best offensive players at each position in the National and American Leagues—last season and represent a staggering 40 percent of the players nominated for the 2011 All-Star game.

5 The Dominican Republic, a country of only 9.3 million, accounts for more than a tenth of all major leaguers, with 86 players on opening-day rosters this year. Players from Venezuela, Puerto Rico, Mexico, Cuba, Nicaragua, Panama, and Colombia represent another 17 percent of major league players. And rosters are also sprinkled with dozens of Hispanic Americans who grew up in the United States.

These players have turned baseball into a multi-billion dollar Caribbean industry, especially in the Dominican Republic, the game's regional epicenter. In addition to about $1 billion in salaries paid annually to professionals from Latin America and the Caribbean, teams spend approximately $100 million per season operating some 40 year-round baseball academies in the Dominican Republic and Venezuela. They also pay several hundred million dollars in signing bonuses each year to boys who then enter the Dominican Summer League, the cornerstone of MLB's player development system.

This bonanza has spawned a profitable market in young talent and made the procurement of Latino players akin to the trafficking of children. Most of these boys are poor and lack good counsel, but they benefit from MLB policies that exempt them from the draft and prevent them from signing contracts until the year they turn 17. This minimum age was instituted after the Toronto Blue Jays were derided for signing a 13-year-old Dominican boy, Jimy Kelly, in 1984.

The rule, though, has also created an opening for self-styled agents known as *buscones* (from the word *buscar*, to search) who lure boys as young as 13 to their own training facilities—with the promise of developing their baseball talent—until they are old enough to be peddled to major league teams as free agents.

The exemption from the annual draft (restricted to boys from the U.S., Canada and Puerto Rico who have reached the age at which their high school class would graduate) means that Latin American players can begin their careers as free agents. As Latinos have become more sophisticated about the workings of the baseball industry, that loophole has led to increasingly lucrative signing bonuses for top prospects, further fueling the *buscón* industry. For their part, teams abhor paying these sums, and view the inflation in signing bonuses with trepidation.

Exploitation and Deceit

10 In 1990, major league clubs signed about 300 Dominican boys to contracts for a total of $750,000. Most received bonuses of between $2,000 and $5,000. Fifteen years later, the average signing bonus for the 407 young players who signed in 2005 had risen to about $33,000. And then the full impact of the *buscones* began to hit. In the first four months of 2011, the 188 boys signed by major league organizations received bonuses averaging almost $131,000.

The bonus spiral has upped the rewards and spurred competition among *buscones*. In the Dominican Republic, more than a thousand *buscones* search for boys they hope to turn into saleable commodities. In return for investing in a young player, the *buscón* takes as much as a third of the bonus and salary if a prospect signs professionally. Several *buscones* run their own academies, sometimes backed by U.S. investors and agents who see these kids as a futures market.

But no laws govern the *buscón*–boy relationship. Parents, who are most often poorly educated and know little about the business of baseball, rarely serve as a check on less-than-ethical *buscones*.

The higher-end facilities, like one operated by former U.S. ambassador to the Dominican Republic Hans Hertell and former Yankees Chairman Steve Swindal, offer comfortable quarters and competent instruction. Perhaps a dozen *buscones* aspire to fill this niche. But most run ramshackle accommodations filled with vulnerable boys.

For some of the aspiring players, a *buscón*'s intervention is the best thing that ever happened. The *buscón* will facilitate player development, create a market for their talents and drive up bonuses. Few *buscones*, though, see to it that their young charges remain in school; many are more like hustlers than surrogate fathers. They might steal from a boy, enmesh him in career-damaging fraud (several boys have been suspended or had contracts revoked after being caught lying about their age) and even administer performance-enhancing drugs (PEDs) in the guise of B-12 shots to add pop to a player's bat or speed to his fastball.

15 Scores of Dominican minor leaguers have been suspended for the use of illegal PEDs, with players in the Dominican Summer League having the highest rate of positive drug tests for PEDs in professional baseball. The deception doesn't play well on the receiving end. Major league clubs do not enjoy being made the fool when a steroid-enhanced prospect's towering shots turn into lazy fly balls or his fastballs lose 10 miles per hour after he stops juicing.

Other *buscones* falsify birth certificates to lower a boy's age, knowing that ballclubs pay more for younger prospects who might have higher upsides. The Washington Nationals were caught flatfooted when they paid $1.4 million to 17-year-old Esmailyn 'Smiley' González in 2006, only to find out he was neither 17 nor Esmailyn González. Instead, he was 21-year-old Carlos Álvarez Lugo posing as a relative, a boy with disabilities who rarely left his home in a small rural town. Those who knew of the deception were either bought off or gladly cooperated to benefit the families involved.

These issues led MLB owners to send Sandy Alderson, a former executive with the Oakland Athletics and San Diego Padres, to the Dominican Republic in 2010 with a mandate to reassert control over the player development system and restore their profitable control over the talent it produces. Alderson spoke of creating MLB-run youth leagues for Dominicans under age 17 to displace the *buscones*, and called for drug-testing and fingerprinting prospects as young as age 15 to create a database to verify age and identity.

But he ran into criticism for his plans as well as his demeanor. Alderson "came into the Dominican Republic with an air of imperiousness and a swagger that can only be likened to the U.S. Marines invading a Caribbean nation," said anthropologist Alan Klein. *Buscones* feared that Alderson's agenda would weaken their grip on talent and that MLB intended to undercut free agency by extending the draft to the Caribbean, thus driving down signing bonuses. In response, the *buscones*, along with the boys they train, demonstrated against Alderson outside the hotel where he was meeting with MLB scouts during his visit to Santo Domingo.

But Dominican concerns were allayed, at least for the time being, when Alderson resigned his position after the 2010 baseball season to become the New York Mets' general manager. Further expansion of the draft awaits the next collective bargaining agreement (December 2011), and it would require the Major League Baseball Players Association's approval. While Latin American ballplayers will oppose extending the draft, the Players Association might be willing to allow it in exchange for other concessions from owners.

20 These aborted and timid efforts by MLB to address the exploitation of young baseball talent in the Dominican Republic underscore the responsibility of Latin Americans themselves. The delay in action by MLB gives the region a chance to clean up player recruitment and limit the damage *buscones* and foreign investors can do to its baseball patrimony, before MLB seizes greater jurisdiction.

Baseball's Caribbean Roots

And it is their patrimony. In the Caribbean, baseball is as much a part of the cultural heritage as it is in the United States. And in the former, it remains vital, as the U.S. game loses ground to football, soccer, basketball, and other sports.

The Caribbean began to embrace baseball in the 1860s after expatriate Cubans, including students, brought the U.S. game back to the island. What they took home was not simply sport. Baseball, historian Louis A. Pérez Jr. has written, was soon perceived as "a paradigm of progress." It did not take long before Cubans made baseball their own game.

By the late nineteenth century, in the eyes of those struggling to end Spanish colonialism and welcome the twentieth century, Cuban baseball had become a symbol of modernity and democracy. Bullfighting was linked in Cuban minds to Spain's brutal colonial rule, while baseball was idealized as a sport in which distinctions of class, race and gender could be set aside, an arena where mobility and freedom prevailed.

While baseball's image as a sport free of racial constraints could scarcely have been imagined in the U.S., it rang true in Havana in the early 1900s. Segregation in the U.S. confined African Americans to their own teams and leagues, but the Cuban game was multiracial. Its ballfields reflected the racial diversity of the Cuban people. Each winter they played host to the best North Americans, white and black. Cuba, of course, was not immune to racial prejudice, but for decades, the *Liga Cubana* was the only place in the world where the best ballplayers of all nations and colors competed with and against one another.

25 And it was the Cubans who brought baseball—their multiracial version of the game—to the Dominican Republic, Venezuela, Puerto Rico, and Mexico's Yucatán Peninsula.

By the early 1900s, North American clubs were visiting the island. As much of the Spanish-speaking Caribbean adopted baseball as its sport, these U.S. teams began to see the region as an ancillary source of revenue. Major league teams barnstormed there during the winter off-season, playing local squads or each other with a share of the gate receipts and bragging rights as their rewards.

In addition, individual Major and Negro Leaguers picked up paychecks by joining island clubs during the winter season. They joined Latin Americans of various hues on teams that paid minimal attention to racial issues.

The better Latin American players, meanwhile, journeyed northward each summer. Although these men might have been teammates in Cuba and elsewhere in the Caribbean, in the U.S., the lighter-skinned players joined a major league club or one of its minor league affiliates, while their darker counterparts competed in the Negro Leagues.

For a quarter of a century, professional baseball in the U.S. and the Caribbean peacefully co-existed. Then, in 1937, Caribbean baseball posed its first challenge to U.S. professional baseball. That season, emissaries of Dominican strongman Rafael Trujillo raided the Negro League's Pittsburgh Crawfords for players who could bolster his club, Los Leones de Ciudad Trujillo, as it contested the Dominican title. The Leones won their championship, but the Crawfords—black baseball's leading club—never recovered from the defections of nine of their players, including future Hall of Famers Satchel Paige, Cool Papa Bell and Josh Gibson.

Mexican entrepreneur Jorge Pasquel soon posed a far more serious threat. After reorganizing the Mexican League in 1940, he signed scores of the best Negro Leaguers and Cubans to play in it during World War II. Afterwards, in 1946, Pasquel not only continued to seek top Negro League and Cuban players, but pursued major leaguers, too. He paid top dollar, treating players with the kind of personal touch they had never received from major league moguls, and offered African-American and Afro-Caribbean players a progressive atmosphere where race hardly mattered.

Already concerned about its own future—racial integration and player unionization were on the horizon—Major League Baseball attacked the Mexican League. It blacklisted North American players who jumped to Mexico, warned Cuban teams and players not to cooperate with Pasquel, and even made concessions to major league players to stave off Pasquel's effort to create a league that would rival the U.S. major leagues.

If the Cuban league had joined with Pasquel to create a combined summer and winter league operation, he might have pulled off his audacious plan. But when Cuba fell into line with MLB, and after sustaining huge financial losses, Pasquel ended his challenge to the major leagues.

Soon, winter leagues in Cuba and elsewhere in the region accepted Major League Baseball's authority. MLB determined under what conditions their players, including Latin Americans, could play in these leagues. Within a few years, only the Mexico league retained a summer schedule. The rest shifted almost exclusively to winter play.

Mexican baseball went its own way, and MLB agreed that Mexican players who signed first with a Mexican team could not be signed by a major league organization. Mexican teams, for their part, stopped raiding major league clubs.

This would favor MLB for years to come. Cuba, meanwhile, left MLB's orbit after the Cuban Revolution. Still, Cubans continue to play baseball at the highest level, but mostly as a noncommercial game that has become an instrument of statecraft and internal cohesion. Since the collapse of the Soviet Union disrupted the Cuban economy in the 1990s, though, the lure of major league contracts has seduced many players to defect and sign with U.S. clubs.

While MLB salivates over the prospect of Cuban talent once the island normalizes relations with Washington, the Dominican Republic, Venezuela and the rest of the region have more than made up for the absence of Cuban players.

Fixing the System

MLB has long benefited from the supply of talented players coming from the Caribbean, profiting immensely by signing players for tiny bonuses and discarding all but the few who make it professionally. In 1957, Hall of Famer Juan Marichal received $500 when he signed to play for the New York Giants. Thirty years later, the Los Angeles Dodgers paid Pedro Martínez $6,500, while the Texas Rangers signed Sammy Sosa for $3,500. Their signing bonuses seem laughable by current standards. *Buscones*, by forcing teams to bid for their clients, have pushed bonuses skyward, sometimes topping $3 million or even $4 million.

But too many boys aspiring to become multi-millionaire *peloteros* become casualties instead. In recent years, often aided by *buscones*, many players have been shamed by steroid use, and lies about age and identity have ensnared others. Latin American players, particularly Dominicans, have become complicit in the game's ethical decline. It is up to them to institute the reforms that will restore ethics to Caribbean baseball and preserve its rich cultural legacy.

So far, reforms have been slow in coming. Dominicans—including President Leonel Fernández, ballplayers Felipe Alou and Juan Marichal, and ex-major leaguers like Winston Llenas and Junior Noboa—must be bolder in reclaiming the island's baseball infrastructure. A few, notably Noboa, have built and rented academies to major league clubs, but there is still more to be done.

40 Several former players and NGOs have begun building baseball academies that compete with the *buscones*. They include the Dominican Republic Sports and Education Academy, the Puerto Rico Baseball Academy and High School, and the International Baseball Academy of Central America in Nicaragua. Some are profit-oriented; others emphasize education and building the fabric of society via baseball; still others emphasize instruction in religion alongside baseball. Nicaraguan Hall of Famer Dennis Martínez has opened an academy on his country's Pacific coast; Pedro Martínez and his wife, Carolina Cruz, are developing one in conjunction with a school in Manoguayabo, his home town.

Taking ownership of the game also means spearheading the effort to stop abuses in player procurement and development, and holding MLB to much higher standards than in the past. Priority must be placed on reclaiming the job of player development from the *buscones*.

This will not be easy, given the stranglehold *buscones* have over the system. MLB teams feel they have little choice but to deal with *buscones*, even though the league has committed itself, at least rhetorically, to implementing higher standards of scrutiny regarding age, identity and drug use. As the driving economic force in the business, MLB will need to be part of the solution to the problems plaguing Latin baseball.

But who will hold MLB accountable? Left to themselves, major league teams will enact measures that drive down player development costs and minimize the embarrassment of any scandals. Instead, MLB needs to invest more in young players' education so that viable options exist if professional baseball careers do not work out. Attorney Adam Wasch has called for MLB to adopt a corporate code of conduct on child labor modeled on the codes adopted by several multinationals after troubling scandals in their plants in developing countries. But some entity will need to police such a code. The bottom line is that given how much profit MLB has derived from Caribbean baseball talent, the league should invest more in the social fabric of the region.

Nor should the MLB Players Association be left off the hook. For once, this notoriously self-interested guild needs to think about the needs and rights of those who are not its members. They should oppose the extension of the draft to the region, barring major reforms that protect the rights and interests of its youth.

45 Without greater initiative by Latin Americans to force action, there will be irreparable damage to the sport. If Caribbean baseball becomes little more than a predatory business, it will not only be young people who suffer—but fans in stadiums from Santo Domingo to New York.

REFLECT & WRITE

MyWritingLab

- ❑ How does Ruck engage his audience in his topic from the beginning of the essay? Look at both the language he uses and the strategy of development. How might he have started the essay differently? How would that have changed the way that he constructed his argument?
- ❑ How does Ruck use *logos* in his essay? How does he use direct quotation? Where does he bring in these elements and to what effect?
- ❑ How does Ruck use historical context and narrative to explain the importance of baseball in the Caribbean? How is this background important to his argument?
- ❑ Look at the structure of Ruck's argument. How does he create a frame? How do his introduction and conclusion work together? What is the effect of that cooperation?
- ❑ **Write.** Take Ruck's argument and transform it into a 2–3 minute oral presentation designed to open up this question of responsibility to a very specific audience: Rob Manfred, Commissioner of Baseball. How would you persuade him of the importance of this issue? Consider issues of arrangement, style, example, embodied rhetoric, and multimedia support in planning your presentation. Script your presentation in middle- to high-style.

■ *During the 2009 World Championships, South African Caster Semenya won a gold medal in the women's 800 meter race with a record time of 1.55.45. Shortly afterward, the International Association of Athletics Federations (IAAF) insisted that Semenya go through a process of gender verification to prove that she was, in fact, genetically female, a request that was widely criticized. In 2010, the IAAF cleared her return to international competition. She has since won silver metals in the 2011 World Championships and the 2012 Summer Olympics. Award-winning cartoonist* Jonathan Shapiro *("Zapiro"), also from South Africa, published the following cartoon in August 2009, at the height of the controversy.*

Jealousy of Caster Semenya

FIGURE 11.6 Zapiro's cartoon about South African runner Caster Semenya appeared in August 2009, during the height of the controversy over her gender.

REFLECT & WRITE

MyWritingLab

- ❑ What claim is the cartoon making in relation to the controversy over Caster Semenya?
- ❑ How does the cartoon play with the audience's assumptions? Looking quickly at the image, what did you think it was about? How did that change when you looked at it more carefully? Why would Zapiro play with your assumptions in this way?
- ❑ Examine how the eyes are drawn on the different characters in the cartoon. What do you notice? Why might Zapiro have drawn them this way?

- ❑ How does Zapiro portray Semenya herself? Compare her portrayal to news photographs of her that you find online. How might Zapiro have altered his depiction to create a different argument?
- ❑ **Write.** Create a revision of this cartoon (free-hand or using Photoshop) that takes a different stance about Caster Semenya. Focus less on the artistic polish of your cartoon than on the way you will change the different elements of the argument to represent this alternate position.

■ *As a public record of American sporting history,* Sports Illustrated *has charted the rise of female athletes on its covers, featuring sports figures from Mary Lou Retton to Candace Parker. Its treatment of these "cover girls" reflects the conflicted attitude toward women in sports, as demonstrated in the following examples.*

Sports Illustrated Covers

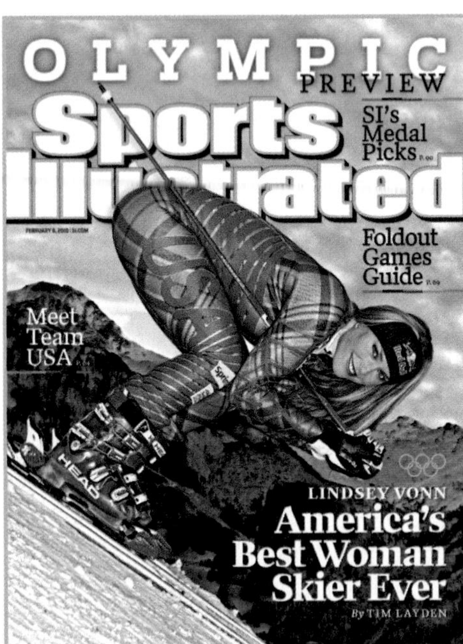

FIGURE 11.7 The Olympic Preview issue of the *Sports Illustrated* from February 8, 2010, featured World Cup alpine ski racer Lindsey Vonn.

FIGURE 11.8 *Sports Illustrated* spotlighted the fans' love-hate relationship with tennis star Serena Williams on the cover of the magazine's July 12, 2010, issue.

REFLECT & WRITE

MyWritingLab

- ❑ Compare the way the different female athletes are portrayed in each of their cover shots; observe their facial expressions, the staging, the background, and their postures. To what extent does the accompanying text resonate with these choices?
- ❑ If these covers are about female agency—showing strong, dominant women—how do the images show this dominance in different ways?
- ❑ To what extent does an idea of gender or the female athlete influence the design of the cover? How does each one define what it means to be a woman in sports?
- ❑ **Write.** Compose a letter to the editor of *Sports Illustrated* and present your perspective on the covers, suggesting a layout, design, and caption for a cover featuring your own favorite female athlete.

■ *Title IX of the 1972 Education Amendments Act states, "No person in the United States shall, on the basis of sex, be excluded from participation in, be denied the benefits of, or be subjected to discrimination under any education program or activity receiving Federal Assistance." When this amendment was passed, the influence of Title IX was felt immediately in athletics programs, where it translated into an impetus to provide girls equal opportunities to participate in school sports. In this article, originally published in the June 22, 2012 issue of* Mother Jones, **Maya Dusenbery** *and* **Jaeah Lee** *reflect on the impact of this legislation four decades after its original passage. Dusenbery is a contributor at Feministing.com; Lee is a blogger for* Mother Jones.

The State of Women's Athletics, 40 Years After Title IX

How the landmark gender-equity law has—and hasn't—evened the playing field.

Maya Dusenbery and Jaeah Lee

When Title IX, the landmark legislation that bans sex discrimination in any educational program receiving federal funding, was signed into law by President Richard Nixon 40 years ago this weekend, gender equality in sports wasn't the point. Supporters of the law had no idea this single sentence—slipped without much fanfare into an education bill—would be a game-changer for women's athletics:

"No person in the United States shall, on the basis of sex, be excluded from participation in, be denied the benefits of, or be subjected to discrimination under any educational program or activity receiving Federal financial assistance."

Bernice Sandler, who helped draft the legislation back in 1972, recently told ESPN, "The only thought I gave to sports when the bill was passed was, 'Oh, maybe now when a school holds

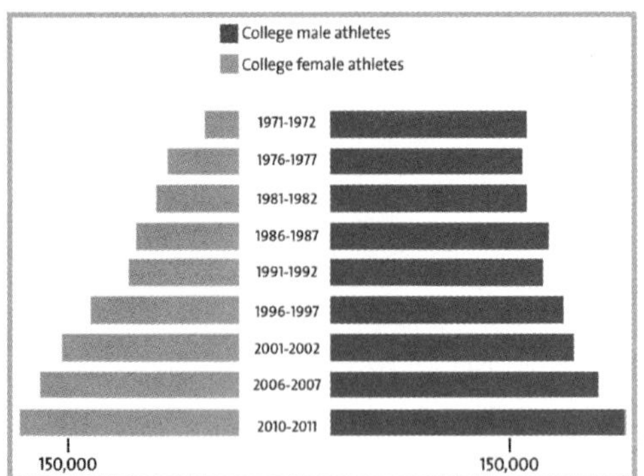

its field day, there will be more activities for the girls.'" During the Senate hearings on the bill—aside from one Senator's crack about coed football which drew hearty guffaws—sports weren't mentioned at all.

My, how things change. Forty years later, despite the important impact it's had in other areas, from math and science education to the rights of pregnant students, Title IX is best known for transforming women's athletics. In 1972, just 1 in 27 girls participated in high school sports; today, about two in five do, according to the Women's Sports Foundation. The number of women playing at the college level has skyrocketed by more than 600 percent. (Incidentally, these days coed football teams aren't a joke either.)

5 Yet progress towards gender equity in sports has been uneven and incomplete. Here are five charts showing what's changed—and what hasn't—since Title IX's passage in 1972.

Between 1972 and 2011, the number of girls competing in high school sports jumped from under 295,000 to nearly 3.2 million, according to data from the National Federation of State High School Associations. But girls' opportunities still haven't reached the level that boys were at back when Title IX was passed, and high schools today provide 1.3 million fewer chances for girls to play sports.

There are more women playing collegiate sports—about 200,000—than ever before. The number of female athletes at NCAA schools has increased from less than 30,000 to over 193,000 since 1972, but women still have over 60,000 fewer participation opportunities than their male counterparts.

Women now make up more than half of all college undergraduates, but they still don't get an equal portion of athletic opportunities—and schools spend proportionally less money on them. For example, in 2010 at NCAA Division I schools, women composed almost 53 percent of the aggregate student body but were under 46 percent of the schools' student athletes. Women's teams received just 41.4 percent of the money spent on head coach salaries, just 36.4 percent of the recruiting dollars, and just 39.6 percent of overall athletic expenses—a figure that's remained virtually unchanged for several years. (Most of the spending gaps can be explained by the schools' money-hogging and revenue-generating men's football programs.)

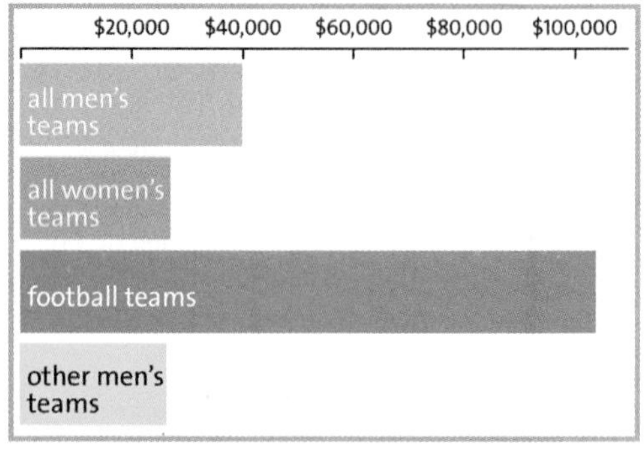

(Note: FBS institutions have football teams eligible for post-season bowl games.)

Median Spending Per Athlete, NCAA Division I FBS Schools

Speaking of coaching, the spike in female athletes hasn't led to a corresponding rise in women coaches—quite the opposite, actually. While women coached more than 90 percent of women's teams in 1972, today that number has dropped to about 43 percent, according to the most recent survey of NCAA schools by Brooklyn College researchers. The percentage of men's teams coached by women has continued to hover around a negligible 3 percent.

10 And despite the fact that millions of women and girls are competing, they're unlikely to see athletic role models of their own gender in the media. A 20-year study of sports coverage by University of California and Purdue researchers shows the short shrift women's sports receives compared to men's on network news and ESPN Sportscenter: In 2009, women's sports got only 1.6 percent of the airtime, down from 6.3 percent in 2004.

Network Air Time Breakdown for Men's and Women's Sports Teams

Most importantly, Title IX hasn't managed to extend the enormous social and health benefits of sports to all girls equally. In 2008, a national survey of third- through 12th-graders by the Women's Sports Foundation found that 75 percent of white girls play sports, compared to less than two-thirds of African-American and Hispanic girls, and about half of Asian girls. And while boys from immigrant families are well-represented in youth sports, less than half of girls from those families are playing. The gender gap is also worse in urban schools and among kids from low-income families.

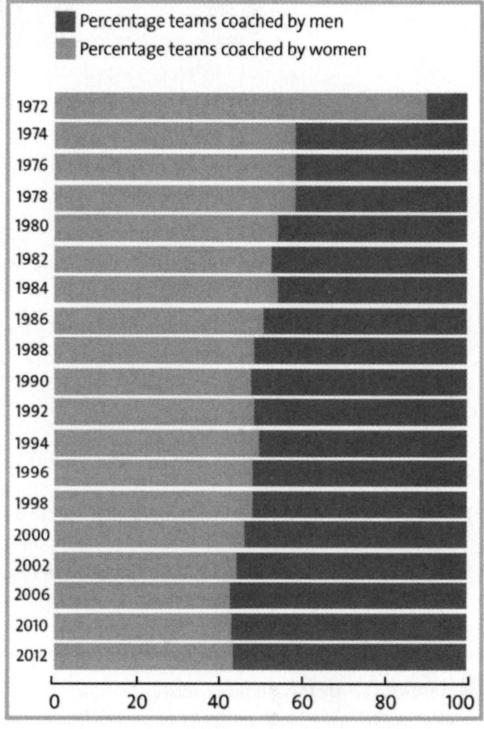

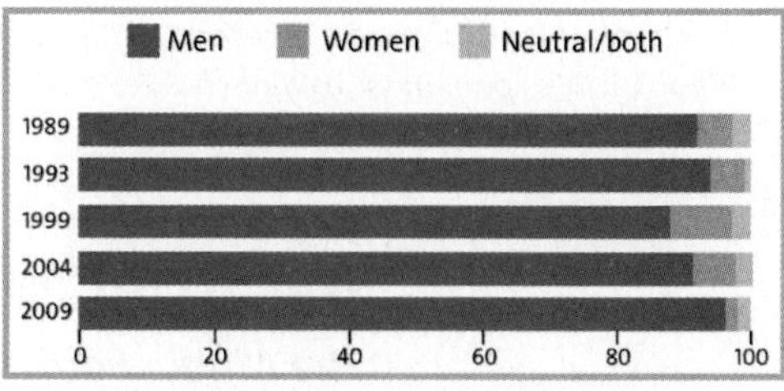

These disparities in youth sports persist at the collegiate level. African-American women are underrepresented in all sports except Division I basketball and track and field, and Latinas make up just 4 percent of female athletes in the NCAA. As Benita Fitzgerald Mosley, an Olympic gold medalist in track and field, recently explained to the *New York Times*, "[I]n the grand scheme of things, Caucasian girls have benefited disproportionately well, especially suburban girls and wealthy Caucasian girls."

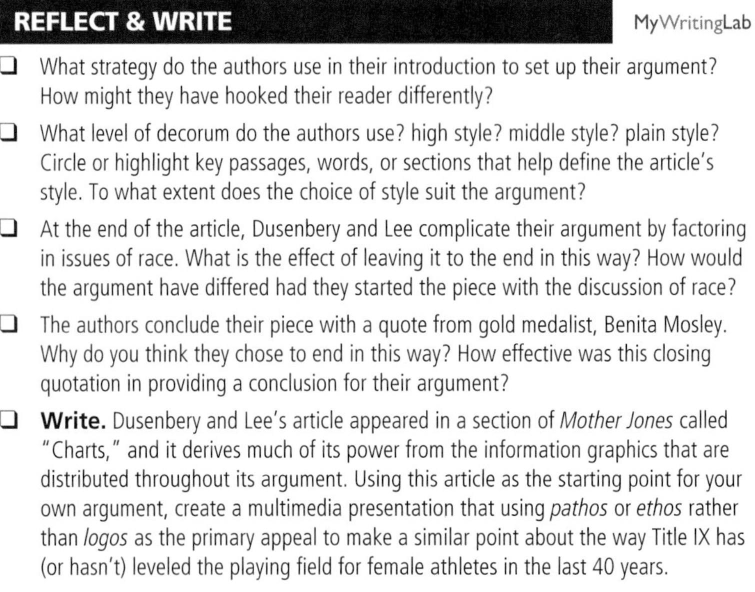

REFLECT & WRITE MyWritingLab

- ❑ What strategy do the authors use in their introduction to set up their argument? How might they have hooked their reader differently?
- ❑ What level of decorum do the authors use? high style? middle style? plain style? Circle or highlight key passages, words, or sections that help define the article's style. To what extent does the choice of style suit the argument?
- ❑ At the end of the article, Dusenbery and Lee complicate their argument by factoring in issues of race. What is the effect of leaving it to the end in this way? How would the argument have differed had they started the piece with the discussion of race?
- ❑ The authors conclude their piece with a quote from gold medalist, Benita Mosley. Why do you think they chose to end in this way? How effective was this closing quotation in providing a conclusion for their argument?
- ❑ **Write.** Dusenbery and Lee's article appeared in a section of *Mother Jones* called "Charts," and it derives much of its power from the information graphics that are distributed throughout its argument. Using this article as the starting point for your own argument, create a multimedia presentation that using *pathos* or *ethos* rather than *logos* as the primary appeal to make a similar point about the way Title IX has (or hasn't) leveled the playing field for female athletes in the last 40 years.

■ *Produced by the* Media Education Foundation, *a nonprofit organization specializing in providing educational resources designed to encourage media literacy,* Playing Unfair *(2003) is a short film designed to provide analysis of the role of gender in sports 30 years after Title IX legislation mandated equal privileges for female athletes. The film integrates short clips from media footage with commentary by three prominent media scholars: Mary Jo Kane from the University of Minnesota, Pat Griffin from the University of Massachusetts, and Michael Messner from the University of Southern California.*

Transcript: Playing Unfair

The Media Education Foundation

Introduction—The Best of Times and The Worst of Times

[***News voice-over***] *Is the American public ready to embrace professional women's teams and the image of a tough, physical, female athlete?*

MARY JO KANE: As we enter a new century, we are in what I call the Best of Times and the Worst of Times with respect to media representations of female athletes.

There has been both widespread acceptance and movement of women in sport that was unheard of thirty years ago, and at the same time there's been an increasing backlash about their success and their presence.

MICHAEL MESSNER: I think not too long ago, it was very easy to equate athleticism, strength, physical power, with men, and by contrast to think about women as weak, as supportive for men, purely as sexual objects. Now that landscape has changed somewhat with the tremendous growth of girls, and women's sports.

[*Sports commentator*] *There's Rebecca Lobo with a jumper!*

MICHAEL MESSNER: Everybody has the opportunity to see strong, powerful, physically competent, competitive women and I think that really challenges that simple gender dichotomy that we used to take so much for granted.

5 PAT GRIFFIN: Sport is not just a trivial activity for fun. It has real, deep cultural meaning in this society. And I think that to challenge that meaning in terms of what it means to be a man in this culture, by inviting women in and acknowledging that women are also athletic and muscular and strong, is a real challenge to that cultural norm that we live in.

MARY JO KANE: There is a cultural assumption that I think persists even to this day, that because of the definition of masculinity and sport, part of the birthright of being male in this culture is owning sport. You own sport. As women move into this once exclusive domain of male power and privilege and identity, there's been a tremendous backlash, and a desire to push back, and either to push women out of sport altogether or certainly to contain their power within in and keep them on the margins.

Out of Uniform—The Media Backlash Against Female Athletes

MICHAEL MESSNER: If you just watch the sports news, and you just watched ESPN, and if you just picked up *Sports Illustrated Magazine* for your main print source of information about what's going on in the sports world, it would be easy to continue to conclude that there is no women's sports happening.

MARY JO KANE: Women are significantly underrepresented with respect to amount of coverage, even though women represent 40% of participants nationwide in terms of sport and physical activity. What all the studies indicate is they represent about 3–5% of all the coverage. So we give viewers a very false impression if you just rely on the media, that women simply aren't participating in sports in the numbers that they are.

MICHAEL MESSNER: Over the course of a decade that we were doing research on the coverage of women's and men's sports, our dominant finding was how much the coverage of women's sports had not changed. About 5% of the airtime was given to women's sports. In our most recent study, ten years later that had gone up to about 8%, which is still miniscule. I mean it's really a tiny increase in over a ten year period in coverage of women.

[*NBC News*] *They are very excited. The NBA playoffs have arrived and while the Knicks are dominating …*

MICHAEL MESSNER: You set the tone and make a statement about what's most important and what the key happenings of the day were with your lead story.

[*NBC News*] *a big night coming up in sports as the Islanders …*

MICHAEL MESSNER: What we found is almost always the lead stories were about men's sports. They put a lot more production value into the men's coverage. There's tape, there's graphics, there's interviews and so forth.

[*ESPN promo*] *June heats up on ESPN.*

MICHAEL MESSNER: When women do kind of peak into the frame, though, it's usually in ways that are mostly dismissive or disrespectful.

[*ABC News Channel 7*] *Finally, a hearty erin go braugh to my countrymen and women out there, and in your honor we have a little Erin Go Bra-less.*

MICHAEL MESSNER: In our study, one of the longest stories that was done on the sports news for instance was on a female nude bungee jumper on St. Patrick's Day who had painted her body green and jumped off of a bridge and they did a very long story on this—on the sports—meanwhile ignoring all the sports women had been playing that day: a major golf tournament and so forth.

[*ABC News Channel 7*]

— *That's wonderful; do we have to slow that down?*

— *That was amazing, I'll remember it forever.*

— *… And so will we.*

MICHAEL MESSNER: Well we all know that news isn't totally objective, but it's supposed to be a picture of what happened today in the world.

MARY JO KANE: What we know in terms of the data is that women athletes are significantly more likely than male athletes to be portrayed off the court, out of uniform, and in these hyper feminized roles. The thing that we infrequently see is images of women athletes as athletes. I think we need to talk about why that is and who benefits from *not* seeing women athletes as athletes.

PAT GRIFFIN: Who's controlling the images that we see in the media, and I think particularly if you look at sports media, by and large, the decisions about what images are portrayed, what images are used, who gets coverage, are still made by men. They're part of a culture that sees women in a particular way. And so I think they prefer to see women athletes portrayed in a more feminine way, it's more comfortable.

MICHAEL MESSNER: When television does cover women's sports, they're most likely going to cover women's tennis, and during certain seasons and certainly during the Olympics, women's figure skating. There's a traditional equation of femininity with tennis and figure skating that makes some sports commentators more comfortable with covering them—they fit more in their own ideological frame about what women are supposed to look like and how they're supposed to act. There's still a tendency, we found, in the play-by-play coverage of tennis to call women athletes more often by their first names, as though there's some sort of familiarity that the commentator has with them.

[*Tennis commentator*] *... to counter Jennifer's return.*

[*Tennis commentator*] *... you just never know which Amelie's going to show up.*

[*Tennis commentator*] *... Monica, trying to hang on, but Serena's serve ...*

MICHAEL MESSNER: And to call men athletes by their last name or by their last and first name.

[*Tennis commentator*] *... and Ruzesky takes the game ...*

[*Tennis commentator*] *... Agassi, through to the semis, and coming off his French Open win.*

MICHAEL MESSNER: People who work in an office, the boss will call the secretary by her—or his, if it's a male secretary—first name, and the referent the other way is always "Mr." or "Mrs." or some title.

PAT GRIFFIN: I think what's going on is we still have a lot of cultural anxiety about strong women and what that means about them as women. And until we can sort of move much further, as a culture in opening up the boundaries for what we consider to be OK for girls and women in sport, we're always going to have that ambivalence there.

MARY JO KANE: As we went into the women's World Cup soccer, nobody knew who Brandi Chastain was. We knew who Mia Hamm was, but we didn't know who Brandi Chastain was. We know who she is now.

[*Newscaster*] World Cup hero Brandi Chastain, throws the first pitch—tank top, no sports bra.

[*ABC News Channel 7*] And uh, Brandi did keep her shirt on, but did take a sweater off, during warm-ups.

[***ABC News Channel 7***] It was announced Nike will exploit Brandi Chastain's strip tease by attaching her to a line of sports bras.

35 MARY JO KANE: It immediately got turned into "Brandi Chastain took her shirt off," rather than "what fabulous athletes these women are!"

MICHAEL MESSNER: How many times did we see images of Jenny Thompson actually swimming in *Sports Illustrated*? But when she posed for *Sports Illustrated* in that way, we saw her and now we know who she is.

MARY JO KANE: What got taken up in the press and the public discourse wasn't who Jenny Thompson was and what she'd accomplished as a great swimmer, an Olympic swimmer, but what did it mean to have Jenny Thompson take her shirt off?

[***Montage of images of female athletes and non-athlete models***]

MARY JO KANE: And the images that you see of women being physically powerful and strong and contrast that to the images of women athletes as little sex kittens, it's an enormous difference. And it is such a powerful contrast that I would argue that is exactly why those images are suppressed. Because sport is all about physical, emotional, and mental empowerment. And so what do you do with all these women who are becoming great athletes and learning the lessons of empowerment and self respect and pride that you get from participating in sport? How are you going to keep that force at bay? And one way that you do that is to do a very time honored and tested mechanism of keeping women's power at bay and that is to sexualize them, trivialize them, and marginalize them.

40 There are more and more images of women athletes that bear alarming resemblances to soft pornography. What you see is an emphasis, not on their athleticism and their athletic achievements, or their mental courage and toughness, but on their sexuality, their femininity, and their heterosexuality. So what better way to reinforce all of the social stereotypes about femininity and masculinity than to pick up *Sports Illustrated* or *Rolling Stone* or *Maxim* or *Gear* and see an image of a female athlete, not as strong and powerful but as somebody that you can sexualize and feel power over. I don't think that there's a more overt example of that these days than in the world of professional tennis in the image of Anna Kournikova. She has the most corporate sponsorship of any professional female athlete and it is not because of her athletic competence because she is as of this date, still has never won any singles tournament, let alone a Major.

PAT GRIFFIN: What it says to me is that an athlete's sexual appeal quotient is much more important than her athletic ability quotient and her athletic accomplishment quotient. And it's very difficult to imagine the same kind of thing happening in men's tennis—a player who has never won a major tournament getting the kind of attention—media attention and endorsement in terms of money that Anna Kournikova gets. And I think that as long as that's possible, it really gives us a pretty good gauge of what are the important things in women's sports.

MICHAEL MESSNER: One of the new things over the last several years is there definitely is more media sexualization of men and men athletes in particular. Men are being viewed as sexy, mostly because of what they do. Of course they have to look good, but they're viewed as sexy primarily for what they're doing on the court or on the field, how good an athlete they are, how powerful they are, how they move when they play. Women are being viewed as sexy not for what they're doing on the court or for what they're doing on the field, but for how they look and what they wear off the field and how they pose off the field, and that's the key difference.

[***ESPN: World's Sexiest Athlete***] *The world's sexiest athlete? Anna Kournikova, hands down. Have you seen the billboard of it? That explains enough.*

Kournikova: *All athletes are entertainers. As long as people like what they're seeing, they're going to keep coming back, so I think that's good.*

Playing Along—Empowerment or Exploitation?

45 MARY JO KANE: It's not just how the media portray women athletes. It's how they are promoted and how they portray themselves. They simply feed into and keep the engine going of the way in which the media portray women athletes.

[***Entertainment Tonight!: Brandi Chastain interview***] *It was something that I'm glad I did and if it got attention for soccer, then good.*

MICHAEL MESSNER: Those are paradoxical images that both suggest empowerment for women and suggest that this media is still trying to frame women in conventionally sexualized ways. And I think that plays into very easily the idea that I, as an individual, need to feel empowered or do feel empowered by taking off my clothes and posing and getting myself into a major national magazine and maybe getting some endorsements.

PAT GRIFFIN: There are other women that I've talked to—young women—who see this in a real different way. They don't really see that as compromising or an expression of concern about how people see them. They just see that as—"that's just my individual way of expressing myself." And I think that certainly could be true for a certain number of them. But what I always want to say to them is it's important to look at the larger picture of pressures, that it's not just about individual choice. That if you look at how women athletes portray themselves, and how they're portrayed in the media, it's a part of a much larger cultural expectation. Is this the kind of image that we want young girls who are interested in sport to aspire to? Do we want them to think that in order to be respected as an athlete, they have to strip?

MARY JO KANE: And a very common retort is "what's wrong with being portrayed as feminine?" and "we want to be portrayed as well-rounded" and "there's nothing wrong with showing off our bodies. We're *proud* of our bodies." And on the surface, I think that all of those are very legitimate arguments. The problem that I have is that for women to show that they have strong and powerful bodies, it does not require them to take their clothes off. The way that those images get taken off is basically in terms of locker room titillation. It has absolutely nothing to do with men sitting around, saying, "Boy, I really respect them as fabulous athletes." It's about consuming their bodies for men's sexual pleasure. So that in no way empowers them or is done as an empowering image.

MICHAEL MESSNER: I don't think you'd have near the amount of controversy or debate if a woman occasionally decides to pose half-clothed in front of a camera for *Sports Illustrated* or something. But it's the dearth of coverage of women and the dearth of respectful coverage of women's athletics in those major media that makes those images stand out so much and be so controversial.

The Glass Closet—Homophobia in Sport and Sports Media

MARY JO KANE: Homophobia is in the bone marrow of women's athletics, you simply cannot get around it.

[*ABC News*] *Billie Jean King, the undisputed Queen of Tennis. Last Friday, facing what is certainly the most serious crisis of her career, thirty-seven year old Billie Jean admitted she had had a homosexual affair with her former secretary Marilyn Barnett.*

[*NBC News*] *Billie Jean King's contract to make television ads for ER Squibb Company is not being renewed. The* New York Daily News *quotes a company official as saying she was too strong a personality, that she was overpowering the product. He denied that the company's decision had anything to do with Mrs. King's disclosure of a lesbian relationship. The* News *says Avon Products is reviewing its connection with Mrs. King cautiously.*

MARY JO KANE: I think it's pretty clear that if you're a female athlete and you want corporate sponsorship, you'd better project a wholesome image. And part of that wholesomeness is the assumption that you are not lesbian, that you are heterosexual. So you'll have a disproportionate number of images of women athletes with children, with boyfriends, with husbands, to clearly mark themselves as heterosexual.

55 PAT GRIFFIN: Sometimes I refer to that as sort of the protective camouflage of feminine drag that women athletes and coaches feel sort of compelled to monitor in themselves and in others. Certainly it's this need to reassure people—I'm an athlete, I may be a great athlete, but don't worry, I'm still a normal woman.

MARY JO KANE: The acronym for the professional golf tour is the LPGA, as in the Ladies Professional Golf Association and I think it has been widely known or feared for many years that the "L" stands for "lesbian." The LPGA and the women who've played in the Tour have taken great pains to distance themselves from that lesbian image and to again, very overtly and explicitly identify themselves as heterosexual.

[*TV ad*] *Hey Laura Baugh, UltraBrite toothpaste would like to proposition you.*

Laura: *Right here? On national television?*

MARY JO KANE: Jan Stephenson who was a well-known professional golfer was part of an LPGA calendar—"we're professional golfers by day but we're really sexy gals by night." A disproportionate amount of the coverage given to Nancy Lopez who's one of the greatest golfers ever on the Tour was about her marriage to Ray Knight who's a professional baseball player with the Mets, and her role as a mother. There were lots of pictures of Laura Baugh when she was pregnant and playing on the Tour. The LPGA rarely gets any media coverage and yet there was a lot of media coverage around "is she going to be able to get through the round and the tournament and not go into labor?" The media or the corporate sponsors or the women athletes themselves specifically identify themselves with the role of wife and mother, which clearly marks them as heterosexual.

60 **[*ABC News*]** *For Chris Evert this will be her nineteenth and last US Open.*

MARY JO KANE: In the late 1980s, one of the greatest professional tennis players this country has ever produced, Chris Evert, announced her retirement. *Sports Illustrated* chose to put her on the cover: "Now I'm going to be a full time wife." They chose to portray her as somebody who was giving up her career to become a full-time wife. On the inside, with the profile, they had a pictorial chronology of Evert's "career" in sport. This isn't in "Bride Magazine" or in "Heterosexual Magazine"—it's in *Sports Illustrated,* talking about her retirement as being a professional tennis player, and yet the focus, certainly in terms of the visual images you were given, was of Chris Evert as a heterosexual wife and mother.

PAT GRIFFIN: The more we focus on women athletes as heterosexual and sexy and feminine, the more lesbians in sport become invisible. It's difficult enough in many cases to be a lesbian in sport, but to be held up against that standard that is not about me—that sense of being made to feel as if I must be invisible for the sake of women's sports, for the sake of not creating controversy—it's a huge pressure, and it keeps us from really dealing with some of the key issues in women's sports which have to do with heterosexism and homophobia.

[***ABC News***] *It has added to the torment she has long suffered, from the public acknowledgement of her homosexuality.*

Martina: *It's much easier being heterosexual, believe me. It's much easier pretending.*

65 PAT GRIFFIN: There are heterosexual women in sport who are very much threatened by the idea that someone might think that they're a lesbian, or would call them a lesbian. And lesbians in sport are very much concerned—and rightly so—about being discriminated against, if they're identified in sport. And you put that together and it really drives a wedge between women in sport. And that wedge serves a larger social function of keeping women from forming alliances to really further women's sport as a whole.

[***Tennis commentator***] ... *I mean she came out and openly declared her sexuality and in team sports of course that would be suicidal—I don't mean that literally, but I mean it would be a very, very hard thing.*

PAT GRIFFIN: I think it's amazing to me that in the WNBA, there is not one publicly out basketball player. And yet we know that there are many lesbians in basketball as there are in any sport. But none of them have felt personally safe enough, or I think another factor is feeling like the league itself, the women's basketball professional league, is safe enough to withstand the potential media scrutiny of acknowledging that there are lesbian players. You know, the weird thing is everyone knows there are lesbian players. So we have this strange sort of paradox of lesbians feeling that they need to hide, yet everyone knows that they're there—I often call it the "glass closet."

MARY JO KANE: The WNBA is very much aware that a large part of their fan base is lesbian. They're a new league, they are struggling to survive. So they certainly don't want to alienate any section of their fan base, especially one that's so prominent and loyal. On the other hand, they take great pains to market themselves as a family-friendly entertainment venue. And so because of homophobia and cultural stereotypes, we see that there's this contradiction on the one hand wanting to market yourself as family values entertainment, and on the other hand, what do you do with the fact that you have these lesbians in the stands?

MICHAEL MESSNER: There are stars that were put forward to promote the league, were positioned as the "girl next door," like Rebecca Lobo, a mother—Cheryl Swoops, or a fashion model—Lisa Leslie. And in doing that what they did was they pushed certain women forward as representing the league, who could exemplify what they saw as pretty conventional, heterosexual roles for women.

70 MARY JO KANE: I think the struggle is, how do you show athletic competence, athletic strength, athletic power—beating up and beating down your opponent—in ways that don't trigger cultural stereotypes about women athletes being too butch, being too manly, being too aggressive?

[*Basketball Coach Pat Summit*] *Get tough! Get tough!*

MARY JO KANE: In order for women athletes to be taken seriously as athletes, they have to be portrayed as competent, which in sports like basketball, by definition means being big, strong, tough, fast, powerful. You can't have one without the other, and yet to equate them means to challenge every stereotype and construction of femininity and masculinity we have in the culture.

Fair Play—Women Athletes in Action

PAT GRIFFIN: Masculinity and femininity are not natural things. You know, boys don't pop out of the womb with a football in their arm, and girls don't pop out with a doll. We have to be *taught* very carefully how we're supposed to act to conform to those artificial expectations of masculinity and femininity. And to the extent that sport is very gendered in this culture—it's one of the ways that masculinity and femininity are taught.

MICHAEL MESSNER: One of the things that people haven't really talked about that much though is that having more images of powerful women, respectful coverage of women's sports, is also potentially very good for boys. Boys are growing up in a world where they're going to have women co-workers, women bosses—the foundations for their views of women are being laid during their childhood. If what they're seeing is a sea of imagery that still suggests to them that athleticism is to be equated entirely with men and masculinity and that women are there simply as support objects or as objects of ridicule or as sexual objects, that is helping to shape the images that boys have of women. I don't believe that there's a conspiracy in the media to say "let's not cover women's sports" or "lets make fun of women athletes," but I think that especially sports desks and sports news people have not caught on to the fact yet that the culture has changed.

75 PAT GRIFFIN: Well, I don't think any social change happens in a nice, smooth sort of step-by-step path, onward and upward. If you look at any social change movement, whether we're talking about the black civil rights movement, the women's movement in general, the gay, lesbian, bisexual, transgender movement—when there are

changes, there's always a pushback. And so change sort of happens in that way, and I think that's what we're seeing here.

MARY JO KANE: All I'm asking is, turn the camera on, and let us see what it looks like when women participate in sports. And what we'll see is that they are terrific athletes who are enormously gifted and enormously committed to something that many people in this country love, and that's sport.

REFLECT & WRITE

MyWritingLab

- ❑ What issues concerning sexuality and the female body are raised by this film transcript?
- ❑ How do the speakers raise concrete points of evidence concerning the media's unfair depiction of women in sports? Discuss the use of names, the framing, the tapes, the particular sports shown, and the focus on clothes and on sexual preference. Which of these media infractions do you think has the greatest consequences? Why?
- ❑ Do you agree with the contention that the media representation of several female athletes verges on "soft porn"? Argue for both sides of this debate.
- ❑ **Write.** Draft a letter to the *Sports Illustrated* from the perspective of Chris Evert, Rebecca Lobo, and Anna Kournikova. How would each woman respond to the arguments made by this film? Quote from passages in the transcript in your letter.

WRITING COLLABORATIVELY

MyWritingLab

Get into groups of three for this activity. Using at least three different examples of a single type of sports coverage (for instance, three news reports, three newspaper articles, or three articles in a sports-oriented magazine), explore how the amount and tone of coverage of women athletes reveal the relationship between gender stereotype and sports media. Pick two recent and concrete examples to prove your assertions. Present your findings to the class as either a slide-based presentation or a poster presentation.

In this article, journalist **Maggie Mertens** *contrasts her experiences attending the men's and women's World Cup soccer tournaments in 2014 and 2015. The article first appeared in* The Atlantic *in June, 2015.*

Women's Soccer Is a Feminist Issue

Maggie Mertens

When I told my friends and family I'd be going to Brazil for the World Cup last year, they looked at me like I'd just won the lottery. In a sense, I had; I'd entered a lottery just to be able to purchase tickets. In Recife, I attended games at a brand-new stadium with a bright-green grass pitch, along with 40,000 other soccer fans from around the world. For months leading up to the event I saw news coverage on TV, in newspapers, and in magazines hyping Team USA, even though they had a virtually nonexistent chance of victory. By the time I left for Brazil, friends who I never knew to be soccer fans were telling me who their favorite players were, jealous that I would see "our boys" play against the tournament favorites, Germany.

This year, I'm going to the World Cup again. There was no lottery, and tickets were half the cost of the ones I bought last year, including a ticket to the final. (Which, last year, would have been nearly impossible to come by, not to mention afford.) The games I'll attend this month will be played at a 32-year-old stadium with an artificial-turf field. Some of the games in the tournament will be played at a stadium with 10,000 seats, while the smallest stadium in Brazil seated 37,634. Even though this year Team USA are favorites to win, there's been little preview coverage of the tournament. When I tell people I'm going, most of them say, "There's a World Cup this year?" There is, only it's being played by women, not men.

Starting this month, millions of viewers will watch women's soccer on television, and even start to recognize players by their first names. Some might wonder why audiences only see these world-class players, like Abby Wambach, who holds the international goal-scoring record—for women and men—for a few weeks every two years at the World Cup or the Olympics. But most, even those who care about equality for women, won't consider how different these athletes' careers are compared to those of men who do the exact same thing for a living.

Today, the gap between men's and women's wages, the tiny fraction of female CEOs at Fortune 500 companies, and the lack of respect for Hollywood actresses and directors receive regular and impassioned coverage in both the mainstream and feminist media. The gender inequities in sports are just as vast as those faced by women in corporate offices and on movie sets, but for some reason they fail to incite the same level of outrage.

5 In 1978, in the midst of the second-wave feminist movement, Hollis Elkins, a professor of women's studies at the University of New Mexico, Albuquerque, published a paper that asked why the women's movement hadn't ever concerned itself with equality in sports. (This was six years after the passage of Title IX, which prohibited sex discrimination in federally funded schools, including in athletic departments.) Elkins died in 2013, but if she were alive today, she'd likely still be asking the same question.

Elkins laid out four main reasons why the women's movement was wary about involving itself in sports. One: Female athletes were perceived as either unconcerned with or hostile toward the women's movement. Two: Feminists didn't want to be "doubly damned" by "the suspicion of lesbianism" that both feminists and female athletes faced. Three: Sports was seen as a realm where men proved their manliness, negatively predisposing many feminists toward sports in general. And four: Sports was considered "frivolous." It wasn't seen as being as important as issues like the right to work, abortion, and equal pay.

In October of last year, the biggest names in women's soccer did something unprecedented: They sued the world soccer governing body. A group of top international players including Wambach, Brazil's Marta, and Germany's Nadine Angerer filed a gender-discrimination lawsuit against the Canadian Soccer Association and FIFA citing the fact that this year's World Cup in Canada would be played on artificial turf instead of natural grass. All six prior women's World Cups, and all 20 men's, have been played on grass fields, because it's considered a superior playing surface. Simply by pointing to gender discrimination, the lawsuit did something female athletes don't usually do.

"There's a major fear of the explicit use of the term feminism to sell women's soccer," says Rachel Allison, a professor of sociology at Mississippi State University who has studied women's professional soccer. "The one major event that's broken that trend is the FIFA turf lawsuit."

When this explicitly feminist issue arose, it went unmentioned on websites such as *Jezebel*, *Everyday Feminism*, and *The Feminist Wire*. *Ms. Magazine*'s blog wrote one post on the issue with no follow-up, and *Feministing.com* posted one link to an outside story on the topic in a news roundup-type post.

10 This isn't the first time feminist issues in sports have gone relatively unnoticed by sites that focus on women's issues. In 2012, *Jezebel* and *Feministing* both lamented the folding of the Women's Professional Soccer league, though neither site had covered the league in any prior stories. And neither *Jezebel, Feministing*, *Everyday Feminism,* nor *The Feminist Wire* have ever run a story on the current women's league, the National Women's Soccer League. *Ms.* has published one blog post about an NWSL team, written by a fan.

"It's not like we never thought about sports stories," says Dodai Stewart, the former deputy editor of *Jezebel*. "If there were notable newsy things happening in the world of women's sports we would cover that. But it wasn't like we were existing for sports coverage. In the atmosphere we were in, it just didn't feel like, 'oh, this thing is lacking,' even though it was."

The problem is, sports media isn't covering women's sports either. In 2014, ESPN's *SportsCenter* dedicated 2 percent of its on-air time to covering women's sports, according to a study published this week in the journal *Communication & Sport*. The study found that three local Los Angeles news networks did slightly better, devoting 3.2 percent of their sports coverage to women athletes.

Cheryl Cooky, one of the study's co-authors and a professor of women's studies at Purdue, says these numbers are actually lower than they were when this study began 25 years ago. But even this clearly unequal treatment is difficult for people to understand as sexist.

"There's still this cultural investment in the idea that sport is this space wherein talent and hard work is what matters, and things like race, gender and sexual orientation don't," Cooky says. The thinking goes that if women's sports were worthy of more coverage, they would receive it. But as Cooky points out, a lot of our perceptions of how interesting women's sports are come from the media itself. "Men's sports are going to seem more exciting," she says. "They have higher production values, higher-quality coverage, and higher-quality commentary ... When you watch women's sports, and there are fewer camera angles, fewer cuts to shot, fewer instant replays, yeah, it's going to seem to be a slower game, [and] it's going to seem to be less exciting."

15 In Seattle, where I live, the men's professional soccer team, the Sounders, draws 44,000 fans on average to every home game. The women's professional soccer team, the Reign, draws 3,500. This disparity exists in a place where, while I was growing up, the majority of boys and girls I knew played on a soccer team, at a time when Brandi Chastain's game-winning penalty kick to win the 1999 women's World Cup was the most memorable sports moment any of us had been alive to see.

The Reign isn't lacking star power. U.S. national-team superstars Hope Solo and Megan Rapinoe are on its roster. To be fair, the Reign is only in its third season of existence. But the Seattle Sounders are only in their eighth year in the MLS, and by their third year, they were averaging 36,000 fans per game at CenturyLink Field, where the Seattle Seahawks play.

Kiana Coleman, co-founder of the Royal Guard, the main supporter group for the Seattle Reign, points to the dearth of media coverage.

"Most people, even soccer fans around here, don't even know the team exists," she says. "How would they? Women's soccer isn't on ESPN except for the World Cup. I've sent messages to [local news station] KING 5 ... The Mariners could be in a deep, dark hole and they still don't cover the Reign. Last year, we [almost] never lost, and still nothing."

This disparity in coverage is gender inequality at work, says Cooky. "The media plays a huge role in building and sustaining audiences for sport and they do it very well for men's sports and they do it horribly for women's sports." The World Cup, when more Americans watch and get excited about women's soccer, proves her point.

20 It's a chicken and an egg problem, says Allison, the Mississippi State professor. "This huge media platform doesn't exist for the national league. So media often tells the women's league, you don't have the level of interest we need to make this successful. But that narrative falls apart when we see how they are able to do just that with the World Cup."

"When people find out you're a professional soccer player, they think it's awesome," says Jazmine Reeves, Rookie of the Year for the NWSL's Boston Breakers in 2014. "But they think it's awesome because there are certain assumptions that go along with the life of being a professional athlete. And they don't realize that for us [women], it's kind of like the exact opposite."

Last year *The New York Times* ran an article on the tight financial circumstances many male professional soccer players face in the still-fledgling MLS. "Many in MLS Playing Largely for Love of the Game," read the headline. The minimum salary? $36,500.

Reeves made $11,000 last season, more than the 2014 NWSL league minimum of $6,000, but less than a third of what her male peers were making. The team tried to offset her expenses, as it does with many players, by placing Reeves with a host family in Boston during the season so she wouldn't have to pay rent. "My host family was great, but at the same time, as an adult, you want to be able to pay for your own apartment," she says.

This season, the NWSL minimum went up to $6,842. The MLS minimum jumped to $60,000 thanks to a contract renegotiation. Still peanuts compared to male professional athletes in the MLB, NBA, or NFL, but at least it's a salary, not a four-figure joke.

25 "I never really thought about it until I was playing professionally," Reeves says. "Then I realized, wow, there's a team down the street from us playing in Gillette Stadium and we can't even get a consistent training field half the time ... You can't deny the fact that there's a pattern."

Reeves does see hope in the way one city embraced its female players. "I did not feel like a professional athlete until we went to Portland," she says. She likely won't be on the field to see NWSL's future, however. At the end of the season, at age 22, she retired from professional soccer to take a job with Amazon.

What Reeves felt during that game against the Portland Thorns was the effect of 14,383 fans dressed in Thorns red packing the same stadium where the MLS' Portland Timbers play. At their home games a rowdy crowd waves flags, sings songs and performs cheers led by Capos, fans who stand with their backs to the field the entire game simply to fire up the crowd. In other words, Reeves played in an environment very similar to the one most men's professional soccer teams experience.

In some ways Portland, where soccer scarves—often representing both the Timbers and the Thorns—hang from the walls and ceilings of bars across the city, is uniquely set up to support a women's soccer team. The Portland MLS and NWSL teams have the same ownership, a distinction shared by just one other of the nine NWSL teams in the league. And it helps that the Timbers are incredibly popular. The waiting list for Timbers season tickets is reportedly more than 10,000 strong. Providence Park, where the teams play, holds 22,000. Marketing the Thorns to these soccer-hungry fans is a no-brainer.

"When the [Thorns] team was announced people stepped up immediately and said we want to make sure the support for them is equal to that for the Timbers," says Kristen Gehrke, one of the leaders of the Rose City Riveters, the main Thorns supporter group.

30 But without a built-in MLS infrastructure that promises media, advertising, and audience support, the NWSL fan base in most cities has struggled. Not counting Portland, the average attendance in 2014 was a little less than 3,000, with many of those being families or youth-soccer players.

The Thorns prove that a deeper and more diverse fan base exists for women's soccer when male and female teams are treated more equally. Hours before the kickoff of a Thorns game against the Washington Spirit in Portland in May, Thorns jerseys could be spotted on the streets of the city. And though the stadium filled with many young soccer players and families early on, groups of 20- and 30-somethings of both genders filled many of the seats before the first whistle, as well as the bars near the stadium before and after the game.

So why, in 2015, is sports, a multi-billion dollar industry that so many take so seriously, still seen as a "frivolous" issue by many feminists, as Elkins suggested in 1978? There are a few small groups advocating for more women coaches and better treatment for women athletes. But according to Allison, "even in the academy, studying sports is often considered a less serious pursuit than studying the economy, or politics."

And that, says Cooky, is wrong. Feminists need to focus on sports because it's an institution of massive cultural significance and an area rife with "serious" issues, such as sexual violence, pay inequality, and a lack of women in leadership positions. "Who wouldn't want to do what they love and say that's their job?" says Reeves. "I'm not saying I would never play again, but I can't live off of what they gave me. I can't."

REFLECT & WRITE

MyWritingLab

- ❑ How does Mertens use a narrative to draw readers into the essay and establish her primary argument?
- ❑ Why, according to Mertens, have feminist writers and critics historically avoided or ignored talking about women in sport? What has changed to make the conversation possible today?
- ❑ How might visual rhetoric be used to complement the written argument? Consider how different types of images would affect the way the readers understood Mertens's points.
- ❑ **Write.** Take on the persona of a feminist sports critic and write a brief response to this article that discusses the U.S. Soccer team's marketing strategy in terms of gender politics.

Photograph: Brandi Chastain's 1999 FIFA victory

■ *When soccer great Brandi Chastain made her game-winning penalty kick in the 1999 FIF Women's World Cup, she celebrated by whipping off her team jersey, falling to her knees, and shouting in victory. The image was captured by many photographers, from many angles (such as the one shown here), and versions of it were featured on the covers of newspapers and magazines worldwide. Some commentators call it the most memorably victory photo – of a man or woman – ever taken.*

FIGURE 11.9 Brandi Chastain's 1999 FIFA victory.

REFLECT & WRITE

MyWritingLab

- ❑ Why do you think that this image so powerfully captured the public imagination? Consider its contextual significance as well as the details of the shot itself. How does it participate in or defy ideas about athleticism, femininity, and success?
- ❑ Sports sociologist Mary Jo Kane critiqued the widespread publication of the photo as shifting the focus from sports to sports bras. Consider the merits of her critique. What are the dangers of this shift? Why does it matter?

❑ **Write.** Find a copy of Mary Jo Kane's book, *Game Face: What Does a Female Athlete Look Like?* in your library or browse it on Google Books. Look over the different images and descriptions that she includes in her work to understand how she uses the canons of invention, style, arrangement, and delivery to make a powerful argument about female athleticism. Now create your own "Game Face" text, featuring at least 4 female athletes, either from the news or from your local college teams, strategically drawing on both visual and verbal rhetoric to make your claim

ANALYZING PERSPECTIVES ON THE ISSUE

MyWritingLab

1. Consider the media portrayal of athletes of different races—for instance, Giancarlo Stanton, David Beckham, Kobe Bryant, LeBron James, Peyton Manning, Serena Williams, Maria Sharapova, Johnny Manziel, Tiger Woods, David Ortiz, Albert Pujols, or Brittney Griner. How does each portrayal support or dismantle racial stereotypes? gender stereotypes?
2. Read through the different points of view represented in "Black Athlete Confidential." Write an essay in which you make a claim about the culture of the black athletes, synthesizing the diverse points of view represented in the survey. Be sure to include direct quotes from the survey, using strategies from Chapter 6 to help you with integrating source material.
3. Compare the portrayal of Lindsey Vonn and Serena Williams on the *Sports Illustrated* covers with the way women athletes are featured in the *Playing Unfair* transcript. Alternately, compare the cover in Figure 11.8 to the 2015 Sports Illustrated cover that features Serena Williams as the 2015 Sportsperson of the Year. Write an essay in which you use these diverse representations as evidence for discussing the stereotypes and challenges facing women and girls in sports coverage today.

FROM READING TO RESEARCH ASSIGNMENTS

MyWritingLab

1. Visit *Sports Illustrated*'s cover archive online, and look at the covers from a few years. Consider different ways that one particular type of athlete has been represented. Write an essay in which you analyze the stereotypes of femininity, masculinity, heterosexuality, ethnic identity, and/or race at work in these covers. Center your argument on how far the media has—or hasn't—come in its representations of athletes.
2. Choose an advertisement or series of advertisements for an athletic product, team, or event. Drawing on the readings in this chapter on the role of media in sports stereotype, develop a claim about how these ads construct or rely upon a specific stereotype about sports identity. Perform a rhetorical analysis of the advertisement(s), taking into consideration the readings on how race, gender, and sexual orientation factor into sports stereotype. Use quotations from the articles

in this chapter as secondary sources, as relevant, to support your claim. You may also bring in additional primary and secondary source materials by consulting your library. See Chapter 5 for various kinds of research you might consult and Chapter 6 for strategies on incorporating sources in your writing.

3. Both "Black Athlete Confidential" and *Playing Unfair* make claims about how the news media portray athletes in terms of their race. Conduct your own study on media responses. Either identify a particular sports show (such as ESPN's *Sports Center*) and watch three to four episodes or a particular type of sporting event (a set of Sunday afternoon NFL games) and consider whether race plays a factor in the media coverage. Consider word choice in the commentary, the arguments being made, the amount of minutes of coverage, types of players and the types of plays featured, etc. Based on this evidence, write an essay in which you make a claim about race, sports, and media coverage; integrate quotations and evidence from the articles in this chapter as appropriate.

4. Explore the importance of Title IX in the history of women's participation in sports and the consequent representations of gendered athletes. Conduct research on the topic and formulate your perspective into a research argument. You might want to interview coaches as well as athletic women from diverse generations to get a range of viewpoints on this issue. Construct a list of questions based on the issues raised by the film *Playing Unfair*. For added challenge, transform your research report into a script for a film, with your interviewees as the key players in your movie.

MyWritingLab Visit Ch. 11 Playing Against Stereotypes in MyWritingLab to complete the *Analyzing Perspectives on the Issue* and *From Reading to Research Assignments.*

CHAPTER 12

Crisis and Resilience

With the ubiquity of news coverage and global media today, we get our understanding of both local and world events from powerful images. From Hurricane Sandy to the Boston Marathon bombing, we get a glimpse into the suffering of others through vivid photos, news films, blog posts, and videos from those on the ground.

Consider the photograph in Figure 12.1, taken in the wake of devastating floods in Boulder County and along Colorado's Front Range. The image captures a spot where the road has completely washed away from the floods.

FIGURE 12.1 In September 2013, raging floodwaters in Colorado washed away roads, cutting off entire towns and communities.

In another context, this might seem to be an environmentalist's photo of how abandoned roads can crumble and the land can return to nature. But what effect do the other photographic elements have in constructing the meaning of the text as one of crisis?

Notice how the double yellow lines just stop, leaving an eerie gap before the creek waters spill out into a cluster of rocks, tree branches, and floating debris. The shred of pink clothing on the left side of the photo is a compositional element that evokes emotion in the viewer and reminds us of the suffering of people who experienced this natural disaster. In these ways, the photo makes a power visual argument about severity of the destruction wreaked by five days of solid rainfall and extensive flooding which destroyed thousands of homes, damaged dams and sewer plans, and forced the evacuation of towns across three counties.

Analyze the written caption accompanying the photograph. How does the phrase "cutting off entire towns and communities" shape our interpretation of the visual text? How do words and image combine to place our emotional sympathy with the people experiencing this crisis? At the same time, consider the possible *motive* of the photographer. How does the rhetorical strategy of depicting the exact spot where the road ends focus our attention on the severity of the damage?

Now compare the photo in Figure 12.1 with the photo in Figure 12.2, which shows two houses crashed into one another and even collapsed into the creek. How does the inclusion of former homes serve to humanize this environmental disaster? Observe the details: a family's possessions still visible through a mud-splattered widow, the satellite dish that brought in entertainment now perched precariously on the roof, the overlapping layers of asphalt, sidewalk, creek barrier, and rocks making passage impossible. What is the *pathos* effect of such signs of crisis in this image? How does a photo make an argument that competes with statistics for its power?

And yet, the photo could also be interpreted as an image of resilience. Despite the ravages of nature, two houses did survive somewhat intact. The truck parked in the distance suggests the massive rebuilding that began almost immediately. Even the wet side of the house, which shows that the waters have receded, offers a glimpse of hope. The visual rhetoric of the photograph thus bridges experiences of ruin and recovery, crisis and resilience.

As we see from these examples, photography offers a powerful interpretive lens on our world. By seizing a moment and turning it into a static

FIGURE 12.2 Two houses, swept from their foundations, collide in the creek in Boulder, CO.

text, the photographer (or *author*) makes an argument about the lives, experiences, emotions, and reactions of people (his *subjects*) to all kinds of events. How we read and analyze such images as *rhetorical texts* will be the focus of this chapter. In looking at images, captions, and arguments that such texts make, we'll come to a deeper understanding of how invention and selection work with regard to images we see in the media, and how the arrangement of these texts influences our understanding of events both at home and abroad, both occurring right now and recorded in history as merely one version of what happened.

In this way, we'll discover how images literally shape what is possible for us to know about a crisis on a personal, national, or even global scale. But can images also help us develop resiliency and work through difficult events? In this chapter, we'll consider all kinds of events—including flooding and fires, bomb attacks and war. Approaching visual images about these events as rhetorical texts, we'll question how the selection of certain photos persuades us to view the event through a particular perspective—not only to understand the destruction that occurred but also for insight as to how people involved might go about the work of *recovery* from such incidents.

We'll also ask challenging questions about the ethics of representing the suffering of others. What does it mean to freeze identity in time and place, as many images do? On the one hand, photographs of conflict and war can serve as *testimony*, as a form of "witness," to use the words of the famous photographer James Nachtwey. But according to others, images of people in faraway places struggling through crisis can often result in sensationalism and even exploitation of that suffering in order to sell news. This chapter will engage you in this debate: between considering visual rhetoric as witness or as sensationalism, as representing a series of events and people's road to recovery, or as locking history in one single—perhaps inaccurate—instant through publication in print and online.

In addition, we'll consider how the very mechanics of creating visual texts has changed with technological advances and political perspectives on who can "author" a text or create an "authoritative" version of an event through media. Indeed, since the American Civil War, photojournalism has evolved with changing technologies to include color images and film footage, political stances on how much the public can see, and ethical concerns over the consequences of war. We'll trace this process by examining the significance of photos taken by Charles Porter, an onlooker at the Oklahoma City bombing. We'll learn how people snapping cell phone shots in the London Underground can be regarded through Mark Glaser's term as "citizen paparazzi." We'll see how two photos capturing New York City's experience of Hurricane Sandy provide almost opposite perspectives on the event.

Today, just as the line between amateur and professional "author" has shifted with modern technology, the line between "objective reporter" and "expert-by-experience" has slipped too. Analyzing celebrated photos taken in the context of what the military and the media call "embedded journalism"—the practice of assigning photographers to a troop unit during war—we'll ask, with David Leeson, how the position of the photographer shapes the argument. Finally, we'll end the chapter by asking how images can mobilize social change, as demonstrated by visual artists who have both documented and participated in the Occupy movement that protested Wall Street greed and corporate politics across the United States.

REFLECT & WRITE

MyWritingLab

- ❑ Analyze and compare the rhetorical properties of the photos in Figures 12.1 and 12.2. Consider the cropping, angle, color, and compositional elements for each one. How does each aspect contribute to the argument as a whole?
- ❑ What is the effect of there being no people in the photos? Recall photos from other disasters—or locate some of the Colorado floods online—that do show people caught in the crisis or engaged in rebuilding. How does the human figure change a photo's emotional appeal? its logical argument? its impact on your memory as a viewer?
- ❑ **Write.** Conduct historical research by looking at old newspapers from your town or community. How do photographs of past disasters—or even moments of celebration such as paving the main street, opening a church, or holding a fair—shape the story of your town's identity? What can you learn about the struggles and resilience of people from those photographs? Pick the most compelling photos from your town's historical archives and write a short rhetorical analysis essay about them.

Published on September 17, 2013, in Salon.com, *this piece by* **Drea Knufken** *explores America's growing indifference to situations of crisis. As a freelance writer, ghostwriter, and editor, Knufken maintains a blog and has co-authored the book* The Backroads and Byways of Colorado. *She has written for BOCA Communications, Google, Blogger, and the Website* Discover Los Angeles. *She lives in Colorado and, since the publication of this piece, has added a list of disaster resources to her blog.*

Help, We're Drowning!: Please Pay Attention to Our Disaster

Drea Knufken

Here in the horrible Colorado flood, people are dead and homes destroyed. But the scary part is everyone's reaction.

As I write this, Colorado's Front Range is in the middle of its worst natural disaster in about 100 years. For people like me, who live here, it is a flood of tragic proportions. To the world, it is just another disaster. When many of my out-of-town friends, family and colleagues reacted to the flood with a torrent of indifference, I realized something. As a society, we've acquired an immunity to crisis. We scan through headlines without understanding how stories impact people, even those we love. Junk news melds with actual emergencies, to the point that we can't gauge danger anymore.

Even in Boulder, at the beginning of the flood, everyone welcomed the deluge. College kids rode their bikes through the knee-deep water that had settled over the bike path. Families trundled into newly formed lakes with their inner tubes. Children splashed with delight in the muddy, opaque water, the same water that would soon become a burial ground.

Night fell, and so did rain, in sheets. Families put their kids to bed; everyone attempted life as usual. Wesley Quinlan and Wiyanna Nelson, a 19-year-old couple, were driving home from a party with two friends. When their car got stuck in the torrent of water that had submerged Linden Street in North Boulder, Quinlan, Nelson and their friend Nathan Jennings climbed out of the car to swim to safety. Jennings and the other friend survived. Quinlan and Nelson drowned, their bodies concealed for hours by the muddy waters of the flood.

5 In nearby Lefthand Canyon, a firefighter was examining the damage when he saw a wall of water approaching. He climbed a nearby tree just before the water hit. Trapped above the rapids, he remained in the branches all night, the first of many captives of the flood.

It was hard to understand the full extent of the flooding that first night, though the evacuation sirens along Boulder Creek offered hints. The next morning, when images showed the mountain towns of Jamestown and Lyons transformed into islands without drinking water or electricity, when it became clear that newly formed rogue rivers were collapsing bridges and uprooting homes by their foundations, we Coloradans finally began to realize that life wasn't going to be the same for a while.

Nobody ever anticipated a FEMA-level disaster. And when it became clear to us that things were bad, the rest of the world still lacked comprehension. Perhaps disasters have become clichéd. In the same breath that we view images of destruction on the news, we text friends and read about Kardashians. We don't see our own vulnerability until we're standing knee-deep in mud in our basements.

In a matter of hours, the dry, sunny town that I call home was transformed into a delta of rubble and debris, a generic Disaster Zone.

I wanted to help, but the rain wouldn't stop. All I could do, all any of us could do was watch and wait, watch and wait.

So far, we've watched and waited for five days. Emergency management officials are saying that nearly 18,000 homes were damaged and about 1,500 destroyed. Eleven thousand, seven hundred people have been evacuated. Six are dead. No, seven. I just read it in the news.

10 Boulder is my backyard, my home. To me, the floods are urgent; they are an emergency. To others, our floods are another face in the crowd of headlines. Today alone, I read in the news that 260,000 people had to evacuate Kyoto due to a typhoon. In Washington's Navy Yard, someone murdered 13 people with a gun. There's the new episode of "Breaking Bad" and the threat of war in Syria. Every headline screams to be first in line. Everything is a crisis. And let's face it, in media language, Colorado is a small mountain state that likes to ski and smoke pot. Decimation here doesn't echo as loudly as it does in New York, Washington, D.C., or Los Angeles.

I wasn't that surprised when only one of my out-of-town friends called to check on me that first morning of the flood. People are busy. They're stoned on headlines and tweets, emails and texts. But on the second and third days of the flood, I still only had two friends contact me. When I sent my immediate family an email stating our Colorado situation in no uncertain terms, they responded with surprise. They knew about the floods, they said. But they didn't realize that I was affected.

I'd like to think that in our networked world, it's easy to comprehend how the things we read about in the news or on social media might be impacting friends and loved ones. It seems, however, that we're so drowned in data that we've become comfortably numb. Even our reactions have become passive, disconnected. Hitting "like" on Facebook or leaving a sympathetic tweet doesn't come close to the human power of a phone call, especially for someone facing the loss of their home, their health, their life. We're too disengaged to connect the dots between disaster and its human impact. And that scares me.

REFLECT & WRITE

MyWritingLab

- ❑ Compare the *pathos* appeal of the title to the calm first line of the piece. What is the effect of this sudden switch? Now trace the emotional response produced by each subsequent paragraph. How does the writer's style work as a persuasive tool to make you as a reader identify with her plight, then experience humor, and then feel alarm or even outrage? What is your overall sentiment at the end of reading the piece? What do you learn about using emotion in writing?
- ❑ Notice the mention of specific people in the article. How does that writing technique build the writer's *ethos* or credibility? What other elements in the piece also establish her authority as a witness and commentator on the crisis?
- ❑ The author makes a strong argument at the end of her first paragraph: "Junk news melds with actual emergencies, to the point that we can't gauge danger anymore." Scholars have termed this state "compassion fatigue." How common is

"compassion fatigue" in your life? Bring to mind instances where friends or family have not taken a crisis seriously. What do you think is the writer's larger message about this situation? Locate the sentences as evidence for your answer.

- ❑ **Write.** Throughout the article, Knufken points to social media as well as news media as part of the problem. What is her argument about communication in today's networked world? Create a digital position paper in response to her argument. You can write a blog post, draft a series of tweets, or set up a photo album with captions on Facebook. Whatever medium you choose, be sure to quote some of Knufken's lines and then compose your own position as a reply.

■ *On April 15, 2013, two bombs exploded near the finish line during the Boston Marathon. Three people were killed in the explosion and over 250 more were injured. In response to the tragedy and the media frenzy that followed,* **Tom Hawking** *published the following article on the Flavorwire Website on the morning after the bombing. Hawking is deputy editor at Flavorwire, and he writes frequently about music and sports. In this essay, Hawking poses important questions about the ethics of publishing and circulating graphic images of events like the Boston bombing.*

The Ethics of Disaster Photography in the Age of Social Media

Tom Hawking

Like everyone else in America, we were appalled and saddened by the bombings in Boston yesterday. We're an entertainment publication, and we don't presume to provide any sort of coverage of yesterday's tragic events. But from a purely photography-related point of view, we have followed the debate about publishing graphic images of the event, and pondered what it means for photojournalism and for the role of the mainstream media in the 21st century, when the ubiquity of camera phones, social media, and always-on Internet connections means that images—often graphic and disturbing ones—spread with terrifying speed.

The debate over the publication of graphic images is as old as photography itself. Susan Sontag discussed it extensively in *On Photography*, and the subject has been key to the question of the ethics of photojournalism as a profession. The question of balancing the right to privacy and dignity of people injured in events like yesterday's bombing with the public interest of reporting those events … it's ultimately a subjective one, and it's perhaps one that no one's managed to answer definitively.

In the past, when control over the distribution of images was limited to news agencies and whoever published their photos, some sort of editorial control was possible. Certain events are defined as much by the absence of imagery as its presence—but then, try to think of one. It's hard. Photos define our memory. Other events are defined by a single image—the picture of Phan Thi Kim Phúc fleeing a napalm attack, or the picture of Jack Ruby shooting Lee Harvey Oswald as the guy in the white suit and hat looks on with an expression that remains forever frozen between fear, shock, and simple amazement.

As in many areas, it was September 11 that represented a real change on this front: it took place in an era before YouTube and Twitter, but still, it corresponded with the growing ubiquity of digital photography and widespread Internet connections. The result, as an essay by *Vanity Fair* creative director David Friend argues, is that it was "the most photographed breaking news event in human history, witnessed on television and the Internet that day by an estimated two billion people—a third of the human race."

Even so, there was a huge debate at the time over whether to publish images like [a famous photograph by Richard Drew] which captured an office worker jumping from one of the stricken World Trade Center towers. That isn't a luxury that anyone has these days, because in the 21st century, it's largely a redundant debate, because graphic images *will* proliferate whether they're published in the newspaper or not. Within literally seconds of the bombing yesterday, images and footage started appearing online—a photo here, a terrifying Vine there. Once those things are online, they're online for good, and in the age of Facebook and Twitter, they spread with exponential rapidity.

This raises many questions, not least of which is what effect seeing a constant stream of awful images has on the viewer. Sontag discussed this to an extent later in her life [...] arguing that "photographs of human suffering no longer move the public ... repeated exposure to photographed atrocities habituates us to horror, leading us to view even the most graphic images as 'just pictures.'"

Not everyone agrees. *The Atlantic Wire*, for instance, ran an article today about the possible role of social media in catalyzing post-traumatic stress disorder: "Monday's horrific events at the Boston Marathon produced horrific images which in the age of social media news means an inescapable constant, unsolicited bombardment of the gruesome aftermath of a gruesome event. While Twitter offered the fastest, most up-to-date, and accurate information, it also served as an unfiltered chronicle of the most distressing imagery, which can have lasting mental and physical effects."

In any case, apart from the effect of yesterday's deluge of imagery on the public, there's also the question of what it means for the mainstream media. As Hoax-Slayer's Brett Christensen points out, "An unfortunate aspect of social media is that idle speculation and wacky conspiracy theories can spread as rapidly—if not even faster than—genuine news reports about such attacks." You could argue that this makes genuine news reports largely redundant, but I'd argue the opposite. It means the media's role has changed somewhat: instead of merely reporting events like this, the responsibility of online, newspaper, and TV journalists alike is to act as a filter, sorting the facts from the noise, the real story from the huge amount of material that appears as soon as something drastic happens. And this makes their role all the more important.

This is particularly apposite given that, people being what they are, the volume of imagery that arises after a tragedy means—counter-intuitively, perhaps—that the distinction between what's real and what isn't is more slippery than ever. "The camera always lies" and "the camera never lies" are equally ancient fallacies, but now we live in an age when anyone with a bit of skill and a pirated copy of Photoshop can knock up a convincing fake in no time. Photos have long been doctored for propaganda purposes (viz. people who fell out of favor with Stalin magically disappearing from photos), but it's never been so easy for people to exploit tragedy for their own ends.

So it went yesterday, sadly. There was an eight-year-old killed in the blast—but despite what 40,000 retweets would have you believe, this [photo] isn't her. (In fact, it was an eight-year-old boy who was killed.) There was also the awful photo, purporting to show a runner who had his legs blown off—it circulated quickly on Facebook, and a [large number] of comments ensued, going back and forth over whether it was faked. Sadly, it turned out to be all too real—the victim has been identified as Jeff Bauman Jr., and he has had both legs amputated.

Quite how to deal with images like this is, again, a question that no one's answered. *The Atlantic* ran the picture uncropped, but with Bauman's face blurred "out of respect for his privacy," although sadly his privacy was gone the minute the image hit the web. Other outlets have chosen to crop out Bauman's grievously injured legs, or cover them with a black bar. We chose to crop it.

But the unedited image is pretty much everywhere, though it would almost certainly never have been published in the past. And for all that it must be indescribably distressing to the poor man's family, it's hard to argue that it should have been suppressed, even if it could have been. It's not the role of our media and our journalists to shield us from truth; it's their job to confront us with it. In this respect, the plurality of imagery is both a blessing and a curse, because in the sort of panic that follows an event like yesterday's bombing, *anything* could be real. But equally, it's also the volume of images and coverage—graphic and otherwise—that help us get a clearer picture of reality than we ever did in the days when our opinion was shaped by one journalist and a few photographs.

And ultimately, it's this plurality that gets us closer to the truth. (Quite literally, in the case of the ongoing investigation.) Again, 9/11 was the turning point here, and its lessons are instructive: as Friend argues in his essay, "If this abundance of imagery offered any sort of certainty, it was this: that in this camera-laden age, history's revisionists would find it nearly impossible to erase the event from civilization's conscience. We had the goods; we had the pictures. Photographs provided a baseline that would make it much more difficult for the public record to be challenged in years to come ... due to the multiplicity of subjective visual perspectives on the event, can be reconstructed in the aggregate in a manner approaching objectivity." And all those perspectives are important, even those that make for stomach-churning viewing.

REFLECT & WRITE

MyWritingLab

- ❑ What are the most common arguments made for why graphic images should be published, according to Hawking? What are the arguments against publishing such photos?
- ❑ If you were in a position to decide whether or not to publish a graphic photo, what criteria would you apply? How does Hawking help to define a process for making such a decision?
- ❑ What is your position on the ethics of publishing graphic and emotional photos? What more recent events can you recall that faced similar controversy in the media's choice of specific visual rhetoric?
- ❑ **Write.** Draft your own captions for contemporary examples of ethically troubling photographs that you find for a recent conflict in the world today. Then compose a letter as if you were the editor of a journal defending their publication on the front page.

Photographs: After the Boston Marathon Bombings

Within hours after the Boston Marathon bombings, friends, families, and residents of the Boston area created makeshift memorials to honor the victims, transforming the area around Boylston Street – where the bombs went off – into a site of remembrance and even hope. This same sentiment fueled the emergence of a new tagline – "Boston Strong" – which helped unify and inspire the community during a time of such tragedy.

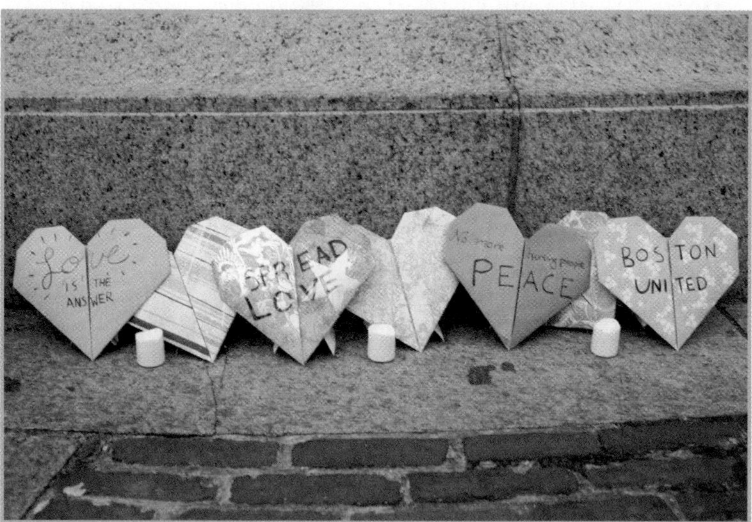

FIGURE 12.3 M. Scott Brauer's photograph focuses on a series of origami hearts left as a memorial in Boston Common on the day after the bombing.

FIGURE 12.4 Photographer Michael Reynolds captures the image of a mother and her two-year-old son placing a poster at one of the memorials sites near the finish line, several days after the bombing.

REFLECT & WRITE: MyWritingLab

- ❑ How do the two photographs above provide examples of resilience? To what extent do the images balance sorrow and strength?
- ❑ How does each of the images create a different impression on the viewer? Consider the differences in setting, staging, and subjects. Does one photograph seem more powerful than the other? Use the Spotlighted Analysis questions on p. 131 in Chapter 3 to help guide your analysis.
- ❑ **Write.** While the photographs above capture a glimpse of the ways that the victims were memorialized, another prominent set of images in the months that followed were triumphant or celebratory shots of survivors – many of whom were runners who had lost limbs to the explosion. Find a few of these images and write a rhetoric analysis comparing these two types of photographed resilience – memorials vs. survivors – and the role of such photos in helping communities recover from tragedy.

■ **Charles Porter** *is a bank clerk and an amateur photographer; he captured the defining images of the Oklahoma City bombing in April 1995, for which he won a Pulitzer Prize. The selection here is a transcription of his account of taking the photographs as told to BBC News, which published the article and images on its Website on May 9, 2005.*

Tragedy in Oklahoma

Charles Porter

I am talking about two photographs that I took on 19 April 1995 from the Oklahoma City bombing.

One being of a policeman handing an infant to a fireman and the other of a fireman gently cradling this lifeless infant.

I have these images in front of me here, looking at them now, and there are things that strike me.

One is that the fireman has taken the time to remove his gloves before receiving this infant from the policeman.

5 Anyone who knows anything about firefighters know that their gloves are very rough and abrasive and to remove these is like saying I want to make sure that I am as gentle and as compassionate as I can be with this infant that I don't know is dead or alive.

And the second image is of this fireman just cradling this infant with the utmost compassion and caring.

He is looking down at her with this longing, almost to say with his eyes: "It's going to be OK, if there's anything I can do I want to try to help you."

He doesn't know that she has already passed away.

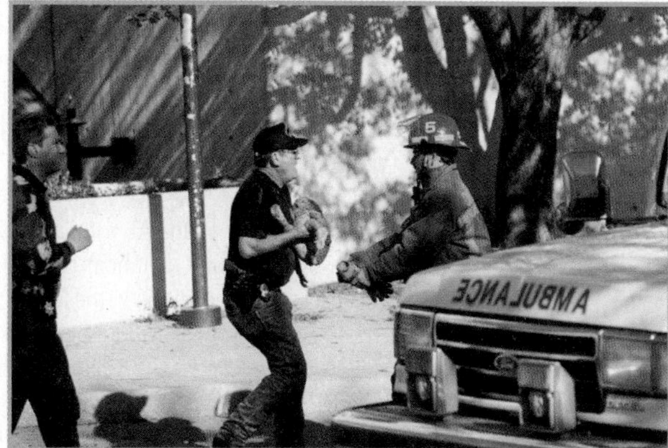

Spring Morning

And these images are in such contrast with the day.

It was such a beautiful, crisp, bright spring morning. And at 0902 it was just amazing.

Our building shook and I looked out the window and saw this huge brown cloud of dust and debris and papers just flying in the air, and as I ran across towards the debris cloud, I turned this corner at the building and the street was covered with glass.

There were people on the street that were injured and bleeding, and there was a gentleman that was walking towards me who had taken his dress shirt off from the office building that he was in and had it to his head, and blood was dripping from that.

I just took my camera out and instinctively started taking pictures.

I ran to the front of the building and took some images of that, and as I ran back down the side, I noticed this ambulance where these fire-fighters were working on these people that were wounded and mortally wounded, and I noticed something out of the corner of my eye that was running across my field of vision.

I didn't know what it was, but I trained my camera on it and it was this police officer.

And as this policeman handed this infant to the fireman, I took one frame and then as the fireman is cradling this infant I took the second frame and that is exactly how these images came to be on 19 April 1995.

After I left I got my film developed and called a friend who was the head of photography at a local university.

I called him, and he said: "If you have images that have just happened, you need to go to somebody that wants to see them, like the Associated Press or some-body like that."

I looked the address up in the phone book, I got in my car. I drove over there. I knocked on the door and I went in and said: "Hi, I've got some images of what you're seeing on TV and wanted to know if you would like to look at them?"

Speechless

20 "Chills go over me just to think about the magnitude and the enormity of where that picture went."

Wendel Hudson, who was the AP photo editor at Oklahoma City at the time, picked them out immediately and said: "We'd like to use these." And I thought: "Wow!"

It went out on the AP wire, and not knowing exactly what the AP wire is, I go home and I honestly went home and told my wife: "You know what, I just took some images and they might be in the *Daily Oklahoma* tomorrow."

I go home about 1300. About 1320 I get this phone call from this lady and she says: "Hi, I am so-and-so from the *London Times* and I want to know if you are Charles Porter."

I said: "Yes I am, but how do *you* know who I am?"

25 She said: "Well I just received your image over the AP wire …"

And she proceeded to explain to me what the Associated Press wire was.

I said that I didn't know how to respond and she said, "Well sir, can I ask you one question?" And this is where it hit home: "Could I get your reaction and response to what your feelings are going to be, knowing that your image is going to be over every newspaper and every magazine in the entire world tomorrow?"

I was silent and speechless, and chills go over me just to think about the magnitude and the enormity of where that picture went and the impact that picture had at that time. It was beyond my scope of comprehension and understanding, way beyond.

■ **Joe Strupp** *is an investigative reporter and senior editor at* Media Matters for America. *Previously, he was an associate editor at* Editor & Publisher, *where this article appeared one month after the Oklahoma City bombing. Strupp has been an invited media commentator on* The O'Reilly Factor, The Fox Report, *Air America Radio, National Public Radio, Wisconsin Public Radio, Voice of America, and WPIX TV News in New York City. He has won two Jesse H. Neal Business Journalism Awards, the "Pulitzer Prize" of business journalism, and also contributes to* Salon.com.

The Photo Felt Around the World

Joe Strupp

Seeing Connections
Compare this professional abstract to the student samples in Chapter 8 as you learn to write your own abstract.

Abstract: Bank clerk Charles H. Porter took a picture of a firefighter cradling a burned infant in his arms right after the Oklahoma City bombing, in OK, in April 1995. The photograph was sold to an AP state photo editor who sent it over the wires. Different newspapers discussed how they should use such an emotionally-charged picture, and, after its publication, many readers called to ask what happened to the baby. Other readers called to protest the picture's publication. However, most newspaper officials believed that it captured the tragedy of the situation in a wordless moment. The baby died the day after the picture was taken.

It sparked heated debate in several newsrooms, caused one veteran newspaper editor to cry, and, for most photo editors, became the focal front-page shot of the tragic April 19 bombing in Oklahoma City.

"It was the photo that was felt around the world," said Tommy Almon, the baby's grandfather.

President Bill Clinton even mentioned it in a televised address.

Ironically, however, the dramatic photo of firefighter Chris Fields cradling the badly burned body of infant Baylee Almon in his arms—which landed on numerous front pages the next day—was shot by a local amateur, developed at a one-hour photo shop, and nearly missed being distributed by the Associated Press.

5 Charles H. Porter IV, a 25-year-old Oklahoma City bank clerk, shot the picture of Fields holding the child, just moments after the bomb blast occurred.

He then sold the photo to AP state photo editor David Longstreath, who sent it over the wires.

"It was everything that was indicative of the bombing," said Longstreath. "It was one of those rare shots that gives the entire story, but in a way that words cannot."

Once Porter took the picture, and developed it with other bomb-blast photos, he still had nowhere to publish it. He initially took the shot to Dan Smith, a photographer at the University of Central Oklahoma, who knew Longstreath.

Longstreath said Smith called him and sent the photo over to AP to be considered. But, in the chaos that followed the explosion, Longstreath almost ignored the shot.

10 "My initial reaction when he sent it was that I was too busy," said Longstreath. "I looked at the roll he shot and took that frame. He took the rest of the roll and left that afternoon."

The infant, who had turned one-year-old the day before the explosion, was pronounced dead at the scene. The baby also was the subject of another widely distributed photo, which showed the infant being handed from police Sgt. John

Avera to firefighter Fields, just moments before the Porter picture was taken.

Once it reached the AP nationwide photo wire, the shot of Fields holding the young baby became the subject of debate for several major newspapers, and the main front-page photo for many others.

The *Philadelphia Inquirer*, which played the picture on Page One the following day, made it the solo front-page art, except for a small, inside tease photo along the left column.

"That photo showed what happened better than anything I've seen," said Ashley Halsey, the *Inquirer's* national editor. "There wasn't a photo that better captured what happened there, so we decided to use it."

15 Halsey, a 27-year newspaper veteran, said he briefly discussed the decision to play up the shot with fellow editors, but believed the tragic elements were important to the story.

"When you have an event that is this absolutely horrible, you will have this kind of photo," Halsey said. "It was deeply disturbing, but it best captured the tragedy."

Halsey said the photo sparked about a dozen phone calls from concerned readers the next day, including several who opposed its publication. But, he said, most agreed it was proper.

"It touched me very deeply because I have a child that same age," Halsey said. "After we put the paper to bed, I walked out to the parking lot and cried. I have never done that before."

Other editors, such as Morton Saltzman of the *Sacramento Bee*, chose not to print the photo, deciding it was inappropriate.

"We had a rather lengthy discussion about which photo to use on the front page, and we decided not to use it because we believed the baby was dead," said Saltzman, the Bee's assistant managing editor for news. "We viewed it as a picture of a corpse, even though there was no information about the baby's condition. It was the most dramatic photo and very compelling, but we chose to go with a photo of a live child rather than a dead one."

For other newspapers, the decision to use the Porter photo or various others involving bloody victims also included lengthy discussions and compromises.

The *San Francisco Chronicle*, for example, published the firefighter photo, but did not use it as its main art. The *Chronicle* also took the unusual step of printing a short message to readers, warning them of the brutal pictures.

"There was a lot of discussion over that baby and firefighter photo, and everyone agreed that it had to be used because there were so many children who died," said Lance Iverson, the *Chronicle*'s picture editor. "But, at the same time, we didn't want to shock or offend anyone. We just wanted to tell the story and give a visual impression; that is why we ran it."

The response from readers about the baby's condition was so great, the *Chronicle* published a short story the next day explaining how the child had died.

"We got close to 100 phone calls asking what happened to the baby, and we had to report it was deceased," said Iverson. "We rarely get phone calls on photos; I can't recall the last time."

At the *New York Daily News*, where the shot of Avera handing the baby to firefighter Fields made Page One, executive editor Debby Krenek said the emotion of the shot made the decision easy.

"We thought it showed the gripping feeling of the situation," said Krenek. "We didn't think it was too harsh; there were a lot of other ones that we used inside that had blood running down shirts and on faces, but this was Page One."

Still, can a newspaper go too far in portraying such a tragic, bloody event as the Oklahoma City bombing? And did the dramatic firefighter/baby photo cross that line?

For Professor Tom Goldstein, dean of graduate journalism studies at the University of California at Berkeley, the answer is no.

"Newspapers are supposed to reflect the world, and that's what they did," Goldstein said. "There seems to be absolutely no doubt in my mind that those riveting photos should have been used, no doubt. It's not something that you necessarily want to look at during breakfast, but they are riveting."

REFLECT & WRITE

MyWritingLab

- ❑ Both Porter's and Strupp's articles cover the same event and raise the ethical question of whether or not to publish a disturbing photo of a baby who later died as a result of the Oklahoma City bombing. What is the argument of each one? How does the first-person testimony by Porter convey a different perspective than Strupp's more journalistic coverage? What rhetorical strategies are at work in each one?
- ❑ Porter's account ends with the offer of publication and Strupp's article takes up the debate among editors and officials about whether to publish. How does each one address a different audience? What is the *kairos* shaping each stance and the argument of each?
- ❑ Compare the styles of the two articles, noting rhetorical appeals, language, and even formality. How do these choices influence you as a reader?
- ❑ **Write.** Strupp's article mentions hundreds of calls and protests. Imagine that you are against the publication of this photo for ethical reasons. Consult a recent Prezi presentation created by three students who take this stance; see http://prezi.com/ddkhyxcmu35p/the-photo-felt-around-the-world/ and then compose a storyboard for your own Prezi presentation in which you include more photos and quotations from callers and writers in protest of the photo. Design your presentation to make your argument clear and sound.

■ **Mark Glaser** *is executive editor of PBS MediaShift and Idea Lab and an expert on online media. Formerly a freelance journalist, he wrote a weekly column for* Online Journalism Review, *where this article appeared on July 13, 2005, five days after the London bombings. Glaser has also written essays for Harvard's* Nieman Reports *and the* Yale Center for the Study of Globalization, *as well as for the* Los Angeles Times, CNET, HotWired, The New York Times, Conde Nast Traveler, Entertainment Weekly, *and the* San Jose Mercury News. *He was the lead writer for the Industry Standard's award-winning Media Grok daily email newsletter, named a finalist for 2004 Online Journalism Awards, and he won the 2010 Innovation Journalism Award. He received a Bachelor of Journalism from the University of Missouri at Columbia and lives in San Francisco.*

Did London Bombings Turn Citizen Journalists into Citizen Paparazzi?

Mark Glaser

July 7, 2005, was one of the darkest days for London, as terrorists blew up three underground trains and a double-decker bus, killing scores and injuring hundreds. But out of that darkness came an unusual light, the flickering light from survivors such as Adam Stacey and Ellis Leeper as they shot the scene underground using cameraphones and videophones.

Like the tsunami disaster in Southeast Asia, the first reports came from people at the scene who had videocameras. In this case, the cameras were smaller and built into phones. But despite the day being a major breakthrough for citizen media—from Wikipedia's collective entry to group blogs such as Londonist's hour-by-hour rundown—it also brought out the worst in some bystanders.

A London blogger who identifies himself only as Justin and blogs at Pfff.co.uk, told his story of surviving the bombing on the train that exploded near Edgware Road.

His harrowing account includes this scene as he finally comes out of the underground tunnel and into the fresh air: "The victims were being triaged at the station entrance by Tube staff and as I could see little more I could do so I got out of the way and left," he wrote. "As I stepped out people with cameraphones vied to try and take pictures of the worst victims. In crisis some people are cruel."

The next day, Justin reflected a bit more on the people outside who were trying to photograph the victims.

"These people were passers-by trying to look into the station," Justin wrote. "They had no access, but could have done well to clear the area rather than clog it. The people on the train weren't all trying to take pictures, we were shocked, dirty and helping each other. People were stunned, but okay. The majority of the train was okay as I walked from my carriage (the last intact one) down through the train I saw no injuries or damage to the remaining four or so carriages. Just people dirty and in shock. The other direction wasn't so pretty, but you don't need an account of this and what I saw, watching TV is enough."

While citizen media efforts became another big story, quickly picked up by the *Los Angeles Times* and *Wall Street Journal*, among many others, Justin was not so quick to exploit his story. In fact, his first impulse was not to watch any news accounts and not to give interviews to media outlets that wanted to glorify his situation.

I left a comment for him on his blog, asking him if he realized that all the people with cameraphones that day were helping to tell the story to the world. Was there a way they could tell that story in a more sensitive way?

"The news does hold a role and it's important for people to understand, comprehend and learn," Justin replied to me in another blog comment. "To ensure they're safe, systems and procedures change, that the world ultimately gets better. I don't even hold contempt really for the cameraphone people, but you must appreciate something else—were those people taking photos helping or were those people shocking the world? I've alluded to seeing [gruesome] things in the tunnel and carriage, but I've not documented them in any detail. I feel it is inappropriate and does not contribute to fact and information."

So far, gruesome images from the attacks haven't been widely distributed online or given a prominent place in Western media. That contrasts sharply with the response in the Spanish media after the Madrid train bombings on March 11, 2004, when bloody photos were on TV and in newspapers, according to a Reuters story.

The Best and Worst in All of Us

In fact, online news sources were at the top of their game on July 7 and beyond. The BBC Website experienced its most trafficked day ever on July 7 and was inundated with eyewitness accounts from readers—20,000 emails, 1,000 photos and 20 videos in 24 hours, according to editor and acting head of BBC News Interactive Pete Clifton.

"It certainly did feel like a step-change [on July 7]," Clifton told me via email. "We often get pictures from our readers, but never as many as this, and the quality was very high. And because people were on the scenes, they were obviously better than anything news agencies could offer. A picture of the bus, for example, was the main picture on our front page for much of the day."

The BBC and *Guardian* both had reporters' blogs that were updated as events unfolded, and group blogs such as *BoingBoing* and *Londonist* became instant aggregators of online information.

More surprising was the importance of alternative news sources such as Wikipedia and its useful entry created by volunteer hordes and the inundation of images on Flickr. Even across the pond, MSNBC.com experienced double its usual weekday traffic on July 7, with 10.2 million unique users, and set a record with 4.4 million users of streaming video that day.

Interestingly, both the BBC and MSNBC.com gave particular citizen journalists who survived a bit more room to tell their story on instant diaries set up for the occasion. The diarist on the BBC, a woman who would only identify herself as Rachel (previously just "R"), was not totally thrilled about becoming a media sensation herself.

15 "More journos phoned yesterday," Rachel wrote in one post. "I must have given my mobile to the stringer who was asking questions when I was wandering outside the hospital getting fresh air after being stitched still in shock. The Mail on Sunday and Metro wanted to send a photographer round! I said no way. I said I felt it was important to get witness statements out at the time as I was there and felt relatively untraumatized so I'd rather they spoke to me than shoved their mikes and cameras in the faces of those who were shell-shocked or more injured. Having done that I really do not want any more fuss... . I was incredibly lucky but I have no desire to become a 'Blast Survivor Girlie' one week on."

That naked impulse to tell a disaster story, glaring kleig lights and all, was once the province of mainstream and tabloid news organizations. But no longer. Now, for better and worse, our fellow citizens stand by, cameraphones in pockets, ready to photograph us in our direst times. Xeni Jardin, a freelance technology journalist and co-editor of BoingBoing, was aghast at the behavior of the citizen paparazzi at the scene described by Justin.

"It's like the behavior when you see with a car wreck on the highway," Jardin told me. "People stop and gawk. There's a sense that this is some sort of animal behavior that's not entirely compassionate or responsible. The difference here is that people are gawking with this intermediary device. I'm not sure if the people who did this were saying 'I've got to blog this and get it to the BBC!' But when everyone is carrying around these devices and we get used to this intuitive response of just snapping what we see that's of interest—as surreal and grotesque as that scenario sounds, I imagine we will see a lot more of that."

Jardin compared the behavior to the paparazzi that chased Princess Diana before her fatal car crash and noted that the ethical issues raised then are now applicable beyond just professional photographers.

"These are ethical issues that we once thought only applied to a certain class of people who had adopted the role of news as a profession," Jardin said. "Now that more of us have the ability to capture and disseminate evidence or documentation of history as a matter of course, as a matter of our daily lives—as a casual gesture that takes very little time, no money, not a lot of skill—those ethical issues become considerations for all of us."

Society Under Surveillance

Citizen paparazzi is not really a new concept, and the proliferation of cameras has continued unabated since the first point-and-shoot 35mm cameras took off right through cheap digital cameras. But while a few amateur photos might have made it into print magazines in the past, now the Internet is awash in photos and video taken by amateurs. As the term citizen journalist becomes part of mainstream thought—spurred on by Big Media outlets and startups—what role do these outlets play in spurring or reining in paparazzi behavior?

Dan Gillmor, founder of citizen media site Bayosphere, wrote in his landmark book We the Media about the proliferation of cameras in public spaces. "We are a society of voyeurs and exhibitionists," he wrote. "We can argue whether this is repugnant, but when secrets become far more difficult to keep, something fundamental will have changed. Imagine Rodney King and Abu Ghraib times a million… . Everyone who works, or moves around, in a public place should consider whether they like the idea of all their movements being recorded by nosy neighbors."

When I talked to Gillmor about the citizen paparazzi at the London bombing sites, he said he hoped that societies will eventually develop a zone of privacy for people in public places—but realistically didn't think it would happen.

"The line between an obviously important public event like what happened last week and public voyeurism is unclear," Gillmor said. "It's probable that there are pictures from last week floating around that are far too gruesome for any news organization to ever go near it… . In the end, we're going to have to develop new cultural norms, and I hope at some level that the more we wipe out the notion of privacy in a public space, the more I hope we end up with a kind of unwritten Golden Rule about privacy in public spaces and give people some space. I doubt it, but I hope people start to think about it."

Counterbalancing that was Gillmor's journalistic instinct, which said that news is news and is fair game for citizen journalists. "In a catastrophe, that's news, and I'm not going to tell people not to take photos of historic events," he said.

Jeff Jarvis, outspoken blogger at Buzzmachine and former president of Advance.net, trusts that normal folks using cameras will be more polite than paparazzi.

"The more I think about it, the more I do believe that most people will be more polite than paparazzi because they aren't motivated to get the picture no one else has to make a buck," Jarvis said via e-mail. "More reporters is merely more of what we have now. And believing in the value of news and reporting openness I think we need to see this as good. Are citizen journalists rude? Are professional journalists? Same question. Same answer."

Citizen journalism efforts are slowly coming out of beta, though there's room for more maturation in the relationship between contributors and media outlets. Andrew Locke, director of product strategy at MSNBC.com, said that his site made every effort to contact citizen journalists and pulled down contributions that didn't sit right with the editorial team.

"Jeanne Rothermich, who leads our small CJ team, has put a great deal of emphasis on fostering dialogue and partnership with individual citizen reporters," Locke told me. "We not only get more accurate information, but richer, more detailed accounts that we can share with the larger audience."

The advantage of the media sites over unmediated sources such as Flickr is that they can use the wisdom of photo and editorial staff to vet contributions and filter out insensitive or invalid material. But Locke says the next step for citizen media is more than just mentoring contributors.

"Over time, we want to turn those passing relationships into lasting bonds [with citizen journalists]," Locke said. "Once you have a real, ongoing relationship, then you can start sharing information and wisdom back and forth. You can develop a code of conduct that means something and can stick. It's not simply about us mentoring citizen journalists like cub reporters, it's about the community itself developing norms and standards of propriety. Yes, we'll always act as a gatekeeper, but once you're in the gate as a citizen journalist, you should be an empowered member of the storytelling community. We still have a long way to go, but for citizen journalism to grow to its full potential we have to get there."

REFLECT & WRITE

MyWritingLab

- ❑ What might be Mark Glaser's purpose as a writer in linking this story to the 2004 tsunami in Southeast Asia? How does this strategy broaden the scope of his argument's significance?
- ❑ How do the integrated quotations work to increase the force of this argument? Consider the quotes by London blogger Justin and the email response from BBC News Interactive's Pete Clifton. Why might the writer want to include such different sources? What can you learn about the power of field research as evidence in your writing from these examples?
- ❑ What larger questions of privacy and decency are coming to light with the advent of new technologies? How is our visual world transforming? Answer by building on key passages from Glaser's article. How would you respond to Glaser?
- ❑ **Write.** Glaser raises a key issue about the ethics of everyday people—not just of photojournalists. Do you think there should be an ethical code of conduct for cell phone camera users and citizen journalists so that they don't become citizen paparazzi? Draft what such a code might look like. Use examples of infamous photo-taking during tragic incidents such as in December 2012 when a man named Ki-Suck Han was pushed into the New York Subway and photographing observers did not step in to help.

■ *Taken during the height of Hurricane Sandy, which ravaged seven countries in the Caribbean and the entire length of the eastern United States in October of 2012, two photos capture distinctly different representations of the crisis and people's response to it.*

Pictures of Hurricane Sandy

FIGURE 12.5 In this moment of crisis, water from Manhattan's East River floods East 20th Street near the FDR Drive just a few hours before the next high tide.

FIGURE 12.6 Deliverymen in NYC still working during the hurricane demonstrate resilience in spite of the havoc wreaked on New York by Hurricane Sandy.

REFLECT & WRITE

MyWritingLab

- ❑ How do the compositional elements of Figure 12.5 suggest the surreal nature of the crisis, during which the storm surge flooded streets, subways, and tunnels across Manhattan? What emotional response does the author of the photo seek to produce in the audience?
- ❑ Now compare Figure 12.5 to Figure 12.6, with its caption suggesting the resilience of New Yorkers in the face of "Superstorm Sandy." How does *pathos* operate in this image through the careful selection and arrangement of visual elements?
- ❑ **Write.** Returning to what you learned in Chapter 1 on composing a thesis, generate an argument about images of crisis and resilience that reveals your interpretation of the purpose and power of these photos in combination. If you like, include in your argument a position on climate change and how the photos can serve as evidence for your stance on this issue.

Seeing Connections
Follow the guidelines on crafting a thesis statement in Chapter 1.

WRITING COLLABORATIVELY

MyWritingLab

Call to mind—or search online and share with the class—other photos that have been taken by "Citizen Journalists" in times of crisis, including the Boston Marathon bombings, the crash landing of Asiana Airlines Flight 214 in San Francisco, the 2015 Paris terrorist attacks, or events in your own community. What ethical issues are involved in the taking of such photos at the scene of the conflict and in the publication of these images on the Internet? What about images of sexual activity and assaults at parties, such as those circulated via social media from Steubenville, Ohio, or those from Saratoga, California, concerning Audrie Pott, or those from Nova Scotia, Canada, with regard to Rehtaeh Parsons? Together, develop a research-based argument about the ethical implications of such photo-documentation and digital dissemination. What print and visual campaigns might your group create to persuade viewer of your position? What might you write in an op-ed to your local or school paper about these issues?

Photographer **David Leeson** *is well known for his impressive fieldwork and powerful photography. A staff photographer for the* Dallas Morning News *since 1984, Leeson has covered stories in 60 countries across the globe: from homelessness in Texas, to death row inmates across the United States, the apartheid in South Africa, Colombia's drug wars, and the civil war in Sudan. While on assignment in 2003, he was embedded with the Third Infantry Division in Iraq, a unit that saw a record 23 days of sustained army conflict. Leeson, along with his colleague Cheryl Diaz -Meyers, was awarded a Pulitzer Prize for his work in Iraq. He has also won two Robert F. Kennedy Journalism Awards for outstanding coverage of the problems of the disadvantaged, as well as a national Edward R. Murrow award, National Headliners award, and a regional Emmy for his videos and documentaries. The text on these pages represents Leeson's own descriptive captions for the four photos he took in Iraq.*

Photographs and Stories

David Leeson

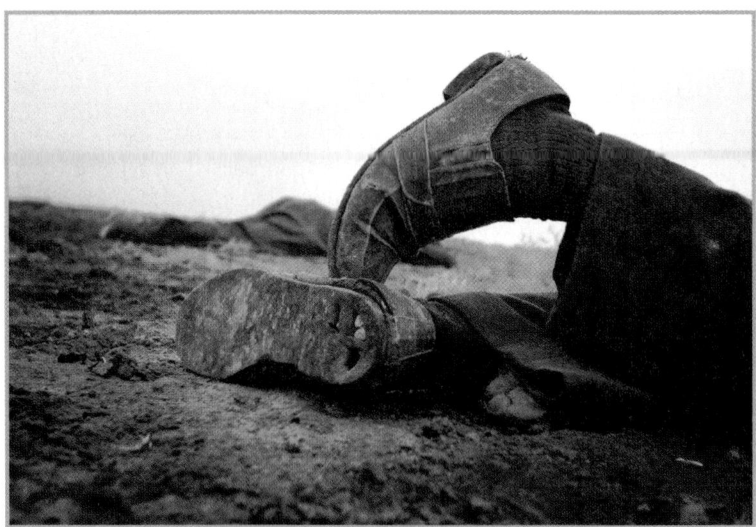

FIGURE 12.7 David Leeson's photo of a dead man's shoes from Iraq carries the haunting title "Body and Sole."

Body and Sole, Iraq

The shoes on the body of an Iraqi soldier killed as Army troops advanced north to Baghdad tell a story about a poorly equipped army. Almost all of the Iraqi dead—more than eight in this location—were wearing worn-out civilian-style shoes. Young soldiers came to view the bodies. A sergeant reminded them that 'this could 'be one of us' and that, for these war dead, 'their families will never know … they will just never come back home.'

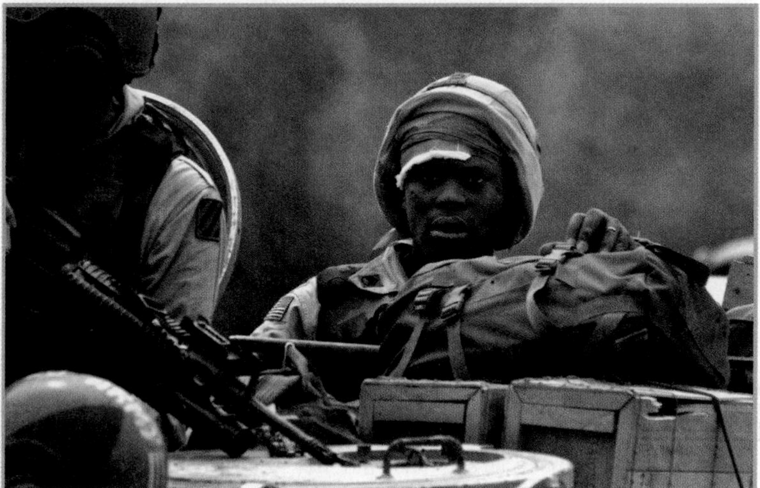

FIGURE 12.8 In this photograph by Leeson, a soldier's blank stare shows the ravages of war, yet his steady body shows him carrying on with his duty in the tank.

Blank Stare

There was a tremendous firefight. Three soldiers died. I saw the blank stare of this wounded soldier as he passed by. I have no idea who he is. I never noticed his bandage until he filled the frame with my 200mm lens. It was his eyes I saw that day and remember.

FIGURE 12.9 Leeson's photo of an American military unit arresting an Iraqi civilian appeared on the front page of 43 newspapers. Leeson titled the photo "Search Party."

Search Party

3rd Infantry Division soldiers from Fort Benning, Georgia, disembark from a Bradley Fighting Vehicle to surround a man who was stopped for suspicious activity somewhere in Iraq. An AK-47 automatic rifle and ammunition were found in the man's vehicle in which he traveled with another person.

This was my first "action" photo from Iraq. My video camera was still operational and I had to make a quick decision on which camera to grab first—my still camera or the video camera. I had made a commitment to place still photos above video in every reasonable circumstance so I made the photos as quickly as possible. As soon as I was satisfied that the still image was secured I switched to video and made very similar frames. The video from this scene became part of my documentary about the invasion.

The next day I learned that this image appeared on the front page of 43 newspapers nationwide and a video I had made the day before was aired on World News Tonight. My video camera succumbed to the dust not long after I made these final frames.

FIGURE 12.10 In "Taking the Plunge," Leeson captures a moment when soldiers relax through a swim in an irrigation pond in Iraq.

Taking the Plunge

(L to R) Spc. George Gillette and Spc. Robert Boucher with Task Force 2–69 Armor, 3rd Brigade Combat Team, 3rd Infantry Division from Fort Benning, Georgia, jump into an irrigation pond somewhere in Iraq. I had a goal to shoot at least one good photo each day—if possible. This image, part of the Pulitzer portfolio, was made near sunset on the drive to Baghdad. I had not made a single image all day. I was about to give up the idea that I would see anything worth shooting when I heard that soldiers were headed to some "pond" in the desert. The truth is I was very tired and was almost disappointed that I was going to have to grab my camera and follow. But, duty called and I went. Both of these soldiers stood on the side of the irrigation pond and discussed if they would get in trouble if they jumped.

I kept my mouth shut and watched. I knew if they jumped it would make a great photo but also knew that journalistic integrity meant that I could not enter into their decision-making process on whether to jump or not. Of course, they finally decided it was worth the risk and made the plunge. After making the photo—I jumped too. The water was very cold but after weeks without a bath it was a wonderful respite from the reality of war.

REFLECT & WRITE

MyWritingLab

- ❑ How does each photographic text—as a visual reading—offer a specific perspective on the battle in Iraq and on war more generally? What rhetorical aspects shape the composition of the text? How does Leeson's position as an embedded journalist make his photos different from those we have studied so far?
- ❑ Look closely at Figure 12.7, "Body and Sole." How might you analyze the various visual elements, including what kind of shoe you see? How do visual signs such as shoes provide readers with *context* about persona, nationality, economic status, and history? What kind of argument would a different set of shoes make on this Iraqi—expensive combat boots, religious slippers, or bare feet? How do the words of the photo's title shape your interpretation of the argument made by the photo?
- ❑ In the text for Figure 12.8, "Blank Stare," Leeson asserts that he "never noticed his bandage until [the soldier] filled the frame with my 200mm lens." How might the camera enable the photographer to see more details in times of war? How is the camera as a tool of photojournalism a vehicle for helping us see? for helping viewers develop compassion?
- ❑ Consider how Leeson's stories operate in conjunction with his images to produce a particular perspective on the war. How do his comments reshape your interpretation of the images? How do the images suggest different meanings without his stories about the images? How does the last image suggest Leeson's construction of a soldier's journey from crisis to resilience, or what he calls "a wonderful respite from the reality of war"?
- ❑ **Write.** Analyze all the images from the perspective of a soldier. What is the argument about the reality of war from this angle of vision? What kind of writing would a soldier produce to explain what these photos mean? Write out that perspective in words. Consider locating additional images and creating a photo essay.

■ **Michael Cavna** *is a writer and cartoonist who covers visual and comic arts for several publications. The article here originally appeared in the* Washington Post *in November 2011. The Occupy Movement began in the fall of 2011 as participants camped out in temporary housing in Zuccotti Park near the New York Stock Exchange. The Occupy campsites grew to encompass many cities in the United States and globally in the fall of 2011. The movement protests economic inequality and has popularized the slogan "We are the 99%."*

Occupy Comics: Cartoon Movement Journalists Sketch a Multi-City Composite

Michael Cavna

In the thick of the Occupy Movement, Matt Bors sees an opening for comics journalists.

"News outlets are beginning to realize that comics journalism is a serious form of reporting," Bors tells Comic Riffs, "and it's particularly helpful with a movement like Occupy."

As a syndicated editorial cartoonist, Bors has been on the scene at Occupy Portland, recording and occasionally tweeting the city's protest play-by-play. And as the comics journalism editor at the site Cartoon Movement, he has been coordinating the cartoon contributions of such visual journalists as Stephanie McMillan (DC and elsewhere), Shannon Wheeler (New York), Sharon Rosenzweig (Chicago) and Susie Cagle (Oakland)—who have drawn from the encampments amid skirmishes and, sometimes, official evictions.

Today, their collected effort—"Occupy Sketchbook"—has been posted.

Part of the reason Bors views this as a golden opportunity, he says, is because it's easier to earn a protestor's trust with a sketch pad than a news camera.

"Corporate media is met with skepticism by protesters—and with good reason," Bors tells 'Riffs. "I've found that sitting and talking to people with a sketchbook is a far better way to gain insight than shoving a network camera in their face. That only yields sound bites.

"Susie Cagle's approach of essentially being an embedded journalist with the movement," Bors continues, "will no doubt result in great comics and the kind of insight you aren't going to find on television."

As a comics reporter, Bors has told Comic Riffs he's a fan of such veterans as Joe Sacco, David Axe (with whom he created the book "War Is Boring") and Ted Rall (with whom he traveled to Afghanistan in 2010). But unlike traveling to war zones, the Occupy movement offers a less perilous way for artists to be near a front line.

"The artists for this project [Occupy Sketchbook] were pulled from our group of contributors around the globe,. as well other cartoonists I found who were attending events to sketch," says Bors, who also notes: "Occupy has become bigger than I think anyone imagined at first."

In contrast to comic journalists, McMillan attended twin protests in Washington as a participant.

"When I heard about 'Stop the Machine,' it seemed to have more potential than traditional protests, because they declared that they weren't going to leave until their demands were met," McMillan tells Comic Riffs of one of the D.C. protests. "It promised a higher level of determination and militancy than the usual actions—so I really wanted to go and be a part of it.

"Meanwhile, during the period before 'Stop the Machine' was due to begin, Occupy Wall Street emerged, and many other encampments in its wake," McMillan continues. "It seemed that the American people were waking up and deciding that they were no longer prepared to silently tolerate the many injustices that those in power have been perpetrating on the people and the planet."

"I wanted to include, through dialogue and description, the major currents, trends and struggles within the [protests], like the debate around nonviolence, the demand for demands, and the desire for everyone to be heard balanced with the challenges of the consensus model of decision-making."

McMillan says part of the challenge was condensing so much reporting into relatively few pages.

"I had to leave out a lot of things I would have liked to include or dig into more deeply," McMillan tells 'Riffs. "The [Cartoon Movement] pieces are a synthesis and distillation of what I heard and saw.

"I tried to be representative of the various viewpoints to give as complete a picture as possible within the framework provided."

These following selections from the Occupy Sketchbook *present examples of the way in which different editorial cartoonists (what Cavna calls "visual journalists") used visual rhetoric to capture and comment on the Occupy Movement. The sketchbook was published online in November 2011 by the Cartoon Movement, a publishing platform for comics journalism.*

Sketches from the Occupy Sketchbook

FIGURE 12.11 A selection from *Occupy Sketchbook* by Sharon Rosenzweig, drawn at Occupy Chicago in October 2011.

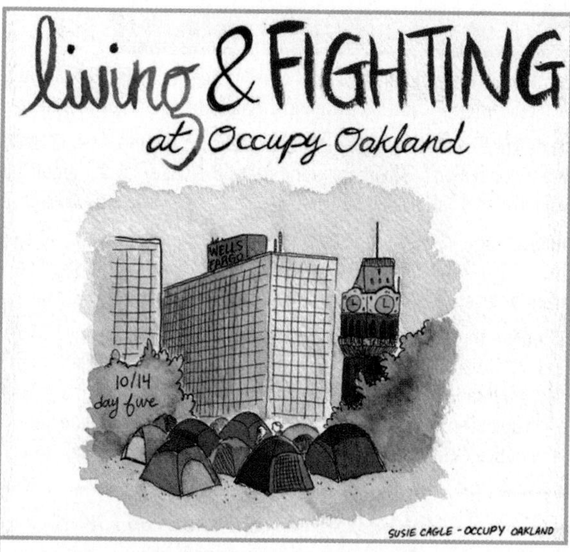

FIGURE 12.12 A selection from *Occupy Sketchbook* by Susie Cagle, drawn at Occupy Oakland, October 4, 2011.

FIGURE 12.13 A selection from *Occupy Sketchbook* by Shannon Wheeler, drawn at Occupy Wall Street, October 2011. The sign on the left reads "I am not a protestor, I am an agent of change." The caption beneath the police officer on the right reads, "No opinion one way or another."

REFLECT & WRITE

MyWritingLab

- ❑ According to Cavna, how are cartoon artists and other "visual journalists" different from traditional news media when it comes to covering events like the Occupy movement?
- ❑ How does Cavna describe the cartoonists' relationship to the Occupy movement? How does this compare to the notion of "journalistic objectivity"? What is Cavna's argument for the importance of the kind of visual journalism represented by the *Occupy Sketchbook*?
- ❑ How would you describe the different visual styles of the three selections from the *Occupy Sketchbook* (Figures 12.11–12.13)? How does each example use visual rhetoric to capture an event?
- ❑ **Write.** Browse online through some news photographs from the Occupy Movement. Write a comparative response to the Occupy comics and 2–3 photographs that you find. How does a hand-drawn visual style present a different view of a social movement like Occupy than that captured by a camera lens? What other events or issues might be effectively covered by a cartoon artist instead of a photographer?

Matthew Christopher *started photographing abandoned spaces while researching the decline of the state hospital system. He holds an MFA in Fine Art Photography and his work has been featured in gallery shows as well as in* Photographer's Forum, *the* International Journal of Arts and Humanities, *and the* United Nations Chronicle. *The website showcasing his work, abandonedamerica.us, has gained international attention. Christopher also works as a site preservation consultant.*

Abandoned America

FIGURE 12.14 Matthew Christopher's photo of an undisclosed church in a state of "elegant decay" demonstrates a crisis of faith and economics in America.

FIGURE 12.15 Christopher captures a hotel room in ruins, with only the plastic television set resisting the ravages of time and neglect.

REFLECT & WRITE

MyWritingLab

- ❑ How might Figures 12.14 and 12.15 function both as documentation of the "crisis" in America—economic and social decay, lowered church attendance, de-institutionalization of mental health patients—and as a tribute to the endurance of such structures?
- ❑ One viewer of Figure 12.14 posted a comment that the piano seems to be making a "last stand trying to defend the church." What argument could you make about the light fixtures in Figure 12.15? the mirror? the TV? Consider *kairos* and make an environmental argument. Consider *doxa* and generate a claim about social values.
- ❑ **Write.** Consider the author's *motive* for the statement: "It is my hope to reach out to those who might originally have seen an abandoned site as an eyesore and encourage them to rethink their estimations and strive to foster civic pride and partnership in these vestiges of bygone eras—thus looking forward to a future where we can build on our past rather than erasing it." Create a publicity campaign, using either Figures 12.14 and 12.15 or your own choice of images from Christopher's website, to construct an op-ed that argues for the preservation of such spaces.

ANALYZING PERSPECTIVES ON THE ISSUE

MyWritingLab

1. The situations covered in this chapter range from natural disasters to acts of military force. In each case, within hours, photographs of the crisis swept across streaming media, satellite news feeds, and newspapers worldwide. What purpose does such extensive coverage serve? Is visual rhetoric the best method for garnering support for people in crisis?
2. In his article, Tom Hawking questions what it means to raise awareness about disaster through provocative visuals. Drea Knufken points out the problem of media overload and viewer indifference to suffering and tragedy, while Matthew Christopher suggests that people actually have a fascination with images of ruin and decay. Given these competing arguments, consider your responses to the articles and images in this chapter. What is your perspective as a contributor to this conversation?
3. Reflecting on the images taken with camera phones after the 2005 London bombings, Mark Glaser raises crucial concerns about privacy and human nature. Keeping his claims in mind, think about how the question of privacy is in fact a key issue in each of the articles in this chapter, even if the writers do not overtly mention it. Pick three articles to revisit in formulating your stance on this issue. Draft your own position paper on privacy in our age of technological innovation and ease of digital publication.
4. While discussing "Search Party," Leeson explores the different kinds of photographs possible with different technological tools—the still shot from a camera and the video. How might a series of photos or a video shape a reader's opinion differently? What is the relationship between the photographer as visual writer of moments in crisis and the visual text as one of many possible drafts? How do the words of the photographers shape our own understanding of these texts as persuasive images? How can you evaluate a photographic text to determine whether it represents crisis or resilience? Consider this question with regard to the abandoned sites of Matthew Christopher's photography as well.

FROM READING TO RESEARCH ASSIGNMENTS

MyWritingLab

1. Read Professor Paul Lester's book, *Photojournalism: An Ethical Approach*, and famous critic Susan Sontag's article, "Regarding the Torture of Others." What arguments are shared between the writers? How might each one contribute to your understanding of the issues involved in photo ethics, both nationally and internationally? Using these sources as a starting point, compose a research-based argument in which you provide your own perspective on these questions. You might format your argument as a feature article modeled after Tom Hawking's piece. Refer to Chapter 1 for strategies on developing a thesis and to Chapter 3 for guidance on incorporating multiple perspectives.

2. With regard to *embedded journalism*, do photographers remain "objective" reporters or do they somehow become part of the military mission? What happens when photographers stand aside in the face of danger—when they refuse to save a life, pick up a gun, or help those who have been protecting them? Conversely, what happens when photographers do become combatants? Locate the NPR story "War, Live," to consult various viewpoints on this question. Then develop an argument about how representations of photojournalism in wartime reflect our changing attitudes about viewing—and experiencing—images of crisis, draft out your research argument.

3. Based on your reading of the articles in this chapter, how might you argue that photojournalism has changed over the years through developments in writing and communication technologies? How do new technologies—such as blogs, video footage, multimedia reports, photo essays, email, Twitter, Vine, Instagram, Vimeo, Periscope, and more—transform our understanding of the issues involved in covering events? Conduct research on this topic and compose a photo essay or Prezi to post online. Include a script for a voice-over of your argument to function as a stand-alone multimedia presentation.

4. Research and collect additional images that showcase resilience. Look, for instance, at Lalage Snow's collection "We Are the Not Dead," which features photographs and words of soldiers before, during, and after their time served in Afghanistan. How does this multimedia exhibit give returning soldiers a voice and inspire others toward resiliency? Additionally, explore Liora K's photography gallery, "Feminism," where seminaked bodies with words written on them challenge hateful social norms. How does writing on the body and photographing those posed messages function as both "an artistic response" and a "great catalyst for change"? Draft a storyboard for your own exhibition on "resilience."

MyWritingLab Visit Ch. 12 Crisis and Resilience in MyWritingLab to complete the *Analyzing Perspectives on the Issue* and *From Reading to Research Assignments*.

CHAPTER 13

Claiming Citizenship

Surveying the social and political landscape today, it is clear that America is a place where many cultures combine and cross over one another. And yet even as we have grown accustomed to this reality, the fact of our ever-increasing diversity remains the subject of ongoing, often intense, debate. In the wake of continued demographic changes, key questions arise. In the face of competing interests, whose needs are recognized, and whose viewpoints are overlooked? What does it mean to "claim citizenship" in this country—but also in a larger global community? Questions such as these carry real power, in part because they require us to negotiate representations of identity, ideals about belonging, and structures that often decide for us the parameters within which we live. How can we preserve the democratic principles of equality and opportunity, while confronting at the same time the many boundaries—of race and ethnicity, gender and sexuality, class and national origin—that seem to divide us? And how are these boundaries both reflected in and maintained by aspects of visual culture all around us?

FIGURE 13.1 A road sign near the U.S.-Mexico border, titled "Caution," is caught in this Flickr photo by Penny Green.

To get started thinking about these questions, examine the photo in Figure 13.1, of a sign found on the freeway near San Diego. What do you make of the characters' shapes on the sign? Does the stance and lines of their bodies look like they are running? What might be suggested through the choice of hairstyle on the woman and the girl? How does this highway sign, located just inside the American border, speak to the tension and the trauma surrounding the borderlands of America and Mexico?

Now consider the image in Figure 13.2. How does this image challenge what we might have in our minds about who or what defines "an American"? This map, from the Library of Congress, reveals the shifting history of our country's demographics through visual rhetoric. Examine the words beneath or above the images of people who were all once considered "immigrants," crossing from one culture to another, shaping what we now consider to be "American identity" and claiming American citizenship. Both Figures 13.1 and 13.2 present a visual argument about belonging, about who has the right to live, work, be educated, and participate in America.

FIGURE 13.2 A dynamic map reveals the history of immigration through a combination of words and images.

Throughout this chapter, you'll encounter many arguments that build on the points raised by these two images, and you'll have a chance to explore vital issues such as the fight for equal rights, the struggle for access to land and jobs, and the movement of American culture outward, across the globe, even as new populations seek to enter and become part of this country's citizenry. In making your way through theses texts, you'll have the opportunity to reflect in critical ways on what it means to claim citizenship in a country—and a world—as diverse and in flux as our own.

REFLECT & WRITE MyWritingLab

- ❑ Analyze Figures 13.1 and 13.2 to determine how each one uses *pathos* or *logos* to make an argument about belonging to America's citizenry? Does either image rely on stereotypes? How do the texts confirm or refute your understanding of America's overall *ethos* as a nation?
- ❑ Revise Figure 13.2 to reflect "the changing face" of your own community. What community members are left out? What story will your images tell?
- ❑ **Write.** Compose new captions for these images that reveal your current thinking about America, citizenship, and civil rights. After working through this chapter, return to your captions and see what you would revise or keep.

■ *The Center for American Progress, based in Washington, D.C., is an independent nonpartisan educational institute dedicated to developing policy ideas and promoting those ideas through media coverage and national debate. The following infographic maps data from the 2010 Census and offers projections about future changes in the USA.*

Infographic: The New Demographics

The Center for American Progress

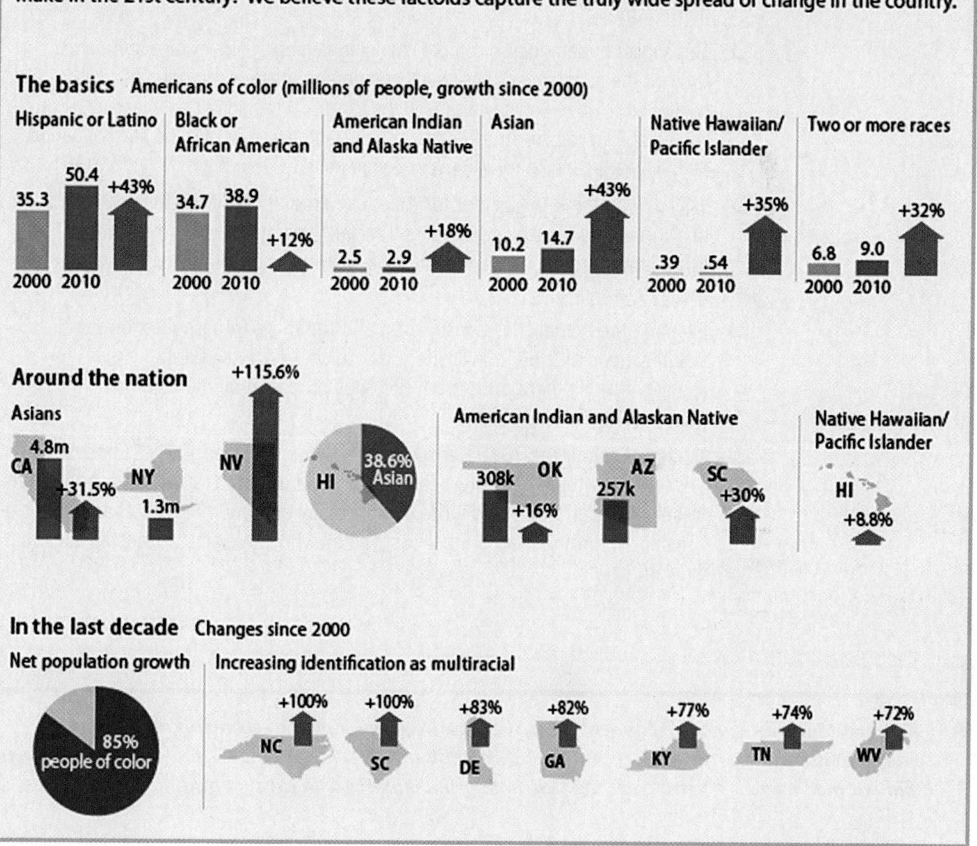
The New Demographics
Since 2000, U.S. communities have grown exponentially and trended toward greater ethnic and racial diversity nationwide. The release of 2010 Census data has only further illustrated a definitive decade of change in the American landscape. Progress 2050 has selected some existing facts and exciting projections from the newly released data to highlight the numerical gains communities of color have and will make in the 21st century. We believe these factoids capture the truly wide spread of change in the country.
The basics Americans of color (millions of people, growth since 2000)
Hispanic or Latino
35.3
50.4
+43%
2000 2010
Black or African American
34.7
38.9
+12%
2000 2010
American Indian and Alaska Native
2.5
2.9
+18%
2000 2010
Asian
10.2
14.7
+43%
2000 2010
Native Hawaiian/ Pacific Islander
.39
.54
+35%
2000 2010
Two or more races
6.8
9.0
+32%
2000 2010
Around the nation
Asians
CA
4.8m
+31.5%
NY
1.3m
NV
+115.6%
HI
38.6% Asian
American Indian and Alaskan Native
OK
308k
+16%
AZ
257k
SC
+30%
Native Hawaiian/ Pacific Islander
HI
+8.8%
In the last decade Changes since 2000
Net population growth
85% people of color
Increasing identification as multiracial
NC +100%
SC +100%
DE +83%
GA +82%
KY +77%
TN +74%
WV +72%

FIGURE 13.3 Focusing on racial data from the U.S. Census, these charts demonstrate the changing face of America.

REFLECT & WRITE

MyWritingLab

- ❑ How do the visuals in Figure 13.3 shape the findings of the 2010 U.S. census—the most extensive survey that collects data about the residential patterns, racial and ethnic backgrounds, education levels, and work experiences of all people in the country—into arguments about the key changes (social, cultural, demographic) in the country?
- ❑ This subset of data focuses on the changing demographics of race in America. How do the numbers and the charts compare to the demographics of your community? How would you modify the charts? What additional measures would you add? Can you construct charts to represent identity along the lines of gender, sexuality, age, and so forth for your community?
- ❑ Why do you think the Center for American Progress (CAP) includes a section on "Increasing identification as multiracial"? What might be their *motive*? What larger argument are they making with the rhetorical choice to visualize these data?
- ❑ Examine the actual U.S. Census data and the many infographics or data visualizations of it on its website. How do the charts and data representations there differ from the ones produced by the CAP as a progressive organization?
- ❑ **Write.** Explore the 2010 Census data for your state, or pick a "Census Report" on a topic of interest to you. Conduct a rhetorical analysis of that data visualization or report and write a short essay on how it reveals changes in citizenship within the United States as well as who can claim citizenship for your chosen focus.

■ **Richard Mertens** *is a correspondent for the* Christian Science Monitor, *where this article was originally published in March 2015. As its title suggests, this article presents a case study of one small town that has made strides toward blending new immigrant cultures with existing traditions and values.*

How One Small Midwest Town Has Turned Immigration into Positive Change

Richard Mertens

West Liberty, Iowa—It's Thursday morning, and in one classroom fifth-graders cluster in small groups, studying mathematics. Only today it's *matematicas*, and everyone is speaking Spanish.

Ten-year-old Joshua Perez stares at a whiteboard, confronting the mysteries of place value. One classmate, a girl with long brown hair and a stern gaze, points to a row of numbers and empty boxes.

"*Donde pone los centenas*?" she asks, her precise Spanish betraying a strong Iowa accent. "Where do the hundreds go?"

Joshua hesitates, then reaches up and scrawls a blue C in the hundreds box. "*Si*," the girl says. "*Muy bien*."

5 Here at West Liberty Elementary School, mathematics is about more than numbers and shapes. It's a blending of two languages, two cultures, and two very different groups of people that have come to inhabit this small town in rural Iowa. Like scores of rural communities across the Midwest and Great Plains, West Liberty has been transformed in the past several decades by an influx of newcomers, most of them Latinos who came to work in the big turkey processing plant that sits just beyond the downtown.

In Willmar, Minnesota, a multicultural business center has been helping local immigrants start businesses by offering microloans and advice on how to file taxes or figure a payroll. Local leaders in Storm Lake, Iowa, started a bilingual health center to help poor and underserved residents—often immigrants. And officials in Monmouth, Ill., worked with a political class at the local college to study best practices in 34 towns across the Midwest that had meatpacking plants and large immigrant populations.

But West Liberty has gone further than most towns toward turning an influx of immigrants—that most American of phenomena—from a potential problem to a source of possibility. There have been challenges. Some people simply left town as Spanish became an unofficial second language, and differences persist. But today, interest in the city schools' dual-language program is so high—among both Anglos and Latinos—that there is a waiting list. Indeed, for many, becoming the first majority-Hispanic town in Iowa is looking more like cultural addition than subtraction.

Making Spanish equal to English in the schools is just one of the ways that West Liberty (pop. 3,736) has accommodated its Hispanic residents. Similar efforts can be found at City Hall, in the police department, and at a range of businesses and civic institutions. At the annual Muscatine County Fair parade, the biggest event of the year in West Liberty, taco and egg roll concessions join the Rotary Club's popular turkey leg stand, while the horses of Mexican cowboys, the vaqueros, close out the show.

"It's been a good change over the years," says Mike Duytschaver, a 37-year resident and president of the local school board.

10 Anglo residents have a strong incentive to welcome immigrants. Many residents say immigrants have helped the town avoid the fate of many rural communities, with their dwindling populations and dying downtowns.

West Liberty's Remarkable Resolve

But what makes West Liberty remarkable is that its efforts have taken place in a state that has been profoundly ambivalent about immigrants. In the 1970s, Iowa took in many refugees from Southeast Asia. But unlike some neighboring states, including Minnesota, Nebraska, and Illinois, Iowa has refused to adopt policies to make life easier for the many immigrants here illegally, such as allowing them to pay in-state tuition at state universities or get a driver's license.

In West Liberty, "it's not perfect, but most people are committed to working together to be inclusive and to improve the quality of life for Latinos and other immigrant groups," says Sal Valadez, a union organizer who lives here. "I think we're doing a lot better job than other places."

The dual-language program starts in kindergarten, with students learning half their subjects, including math and language arts, in both English and Spanish. The program, which is voluntary, has attracted more and more students each year and is now more popular than the regular English-only classes.

It wasn't always this way. It took three referendums before the measure finally passed. Afterward, some families left. "They didn't want their kids speaking Spanish," says Conrad Gregg, a longtime resident and member of the West Liberty Heritage Foundation.

15 That was 17 years ago. Today, families move to West Liberty to enroll their kids in the program. Anglo parents like it because they want their kids to learn a second language. Hispanic parents like it because they don't want their kids to forget where they came from. When school officials raise questions about the program—it's expensive, and some worry that it draws resources away from the rest of the curriculum—parents pack school board meetings to defend it.

'Are you real police?'

The overall integration effort, meanwhile, remains a work in progress. When Lawrence McNaul became police chief in 2013, he discovered that none of West Liberty's six officers lived in town, and only one spoke Spanish. This is typical of towns with large Hispanic populations. There was a "trust gap," says Mr. McNaul, who recently became city manager.

So McNaul asked his officers to recruit some local people. "I was told, 'Good luck,' " he says. "I wouldn't find any."

He found four—part-time officers who will likely be first in line when a full-time job opens. Three are Hispanic; two are women. One is Pamela Romero, who came from Mexico when she was 9. She spoke no English. Today, at 36, she works as a secretary at the elementary school while she finishes her year-long police training course, mostly on weekends.

Some of her fellow Latinos are surprised when they see her in uniform.

20 "Most of them know me," she says. "They say, 'Oh, are you real police?' "

She is. Recently she was able to interpret when she and an English-speaking officer responded to the report of a domestic dispute and found that the woman spoke only Spanish. "I want to help the community," she says. "I want them to really know that the police department is trying its best to understand them, to speak their own language."

McNaul is trying to make similar changes in other departments. He wants to post notices in Spanish and hire more bilingual employees. The idea seems to be working, he says. People are minding their dogs better now that the town has hired a Hispanic animal-control officer, he says. And for the first time, visitors to the water department can discuss a leaky pipe in Spanish.

Meanwhile, Anglo-owned businesses are learning how to do business with Hispanic customers. Larry Miller, a co-owner of Fred's Feed and Supply, says he studied Spanish in high school but "not enough for it to stick." Still, he finds ways to communicate with customers who don't speak English, at times resorting to pantomime. Sometimes, he concedes, "you hear disparaging remarks" about local Latinos. But mostly people get along.

"The Spanish have sort of assimilated to us, and we've assimilated to them," says Mr. Miller, who likes to lunch on ham and jalapeño sandwiches from the Mexican bakery up the street.

25 Few businesses have adapted to the town's immigrant community as well as Jeff's Market, an independent grocery at the edge of the downtown. The store was struggling when Aaron Thoma bought it in 2006, and Mr. Thoma resolved to cater more to Latinos. He hired Latino workers and began stocking food that Latino families wanted, including jalapeños, cactus, several varieties of green onions, and "tons of cilantro."

He had a lot to learn, he says. But he was willing to do it. New Hispanic hires were indispensable; they not only brought new customers, they taught Thoma new ways of doing business.

"It's not an easy change to make," he says. "It took me a while to gain the trust of the population in town to feel that this is an OK place for Latinos to shop." Some businesses are doing this better than others, he says.

From Dropouts to Pre-med

In the schools, language hasn't been the only issue. When Mike Gunn took over as soccer coach at the high school eight years ago, there was a high dropout rate among Latino boys. Mr. Gunn, who is also a high school science teacher, began asking eighth-grade teachers which boys were most at risk of dropping out. He started the West Liberty Soccer Club and made sure that these boys joined. Today, the West Liberty Soccer Club has 250 players from elementary school age to high-schoolers. Some of Gunn's former players are at universities in engineering and pre-med programs. Most go to college. Everyone graduates.

"Soccer provided an incentive to achieve in school that was just enough to make the difference f or many young men," he says.

30 One sign of change in West Liberty is the rise of one of its newest town councilors, Jose Zacarias. Mr. Zacarias is a short, stocky, outgoing man who arrived in West Liberty 31 years ago from Mexico. He had a law degree but no visa. Like many immigrants in the country illegally, he found a job cutting up turkeys at the processing plant, slicing one to a pile of bones in less than a minute.

Zacarias eventually married an American. (They have since divorced.) He bought property, including an old farmhouse on the edge of town. He joined the school board. Two years ago, he became the third Hispanic ever elected to the town council here.

"The problem with Hispanics is how to get them enthusiastic about political and community things," Zacarias says. "In our culture, we don't have anything like volunteering. When I try to explain to my friends that you are doing this city council thing for nothing, they can't believe it."

Zacarias, at least, seems at home here. Whether fist-bumping fifth-graders at the elementary school—"I know their families," he says—or just strolling through the downtown, he seems to know just about everyone, and everyone seems to know him.

"With a lot of limitations," he says, "I think you can call this a success."

REFLECT & WRITE

MyWritingLab

- ❑ What cultural stereotypes about "small town" America does the writer evoke with vivid descriptions and quotations from his field research? How does the tone of the writing and the arrangement of evidence indicate the author's stance on these stereotypes?
- ❑ Analyze the visual aspects of the language that describe the challenges confronting many rural small towns. Where does the author use visual description to help readers see how immigration has changed the look of the town?

- ❑ One centerpiece of the article is its focus on the blending of languages in the schools. How does the author use language as an element of the argument? What larger point does the article make about the importance of language?
- ❑ **Write.** Look up the images that originally accompanied the article. How do the visual texts support or complicate the portrait of small town life presented here? What larger point about racial diversity and life on America's rural communities can you glean from the images? Select the most powerful images and construct a photo essay in response to the article. Include captions and an introduction to show your stance on these social trends.

■ **Alex Webb** *is an award-winning photographer and the author of seven photography books. A graduate of Harvard, Webb also studied at the Carpenter Center for the Visual Arts. He joined Magnum Photos in 1976, around the same time he began photographing Mexico, the Caribbean, and the American South. His work has been exhibited across America and Europe. He writes of his art: "What does a street photographer do but walk and watch and wait and talk, and then watch and wait some more, trying to remain confident that the unexpected, the unknown, or the secret heart of the known awaits just around the corner." The photos here appeared as part of a* Time *Special Report on "The New Frontier/La Nueva Frontera."*

Life on the Border

Alex Webb

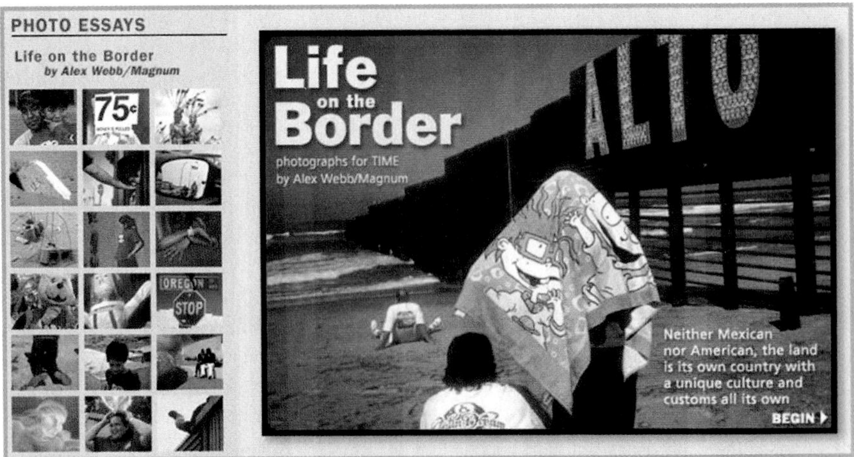

FIGURE 13.4 On the beach beside the border, a wall stretching out in the ocean, people take shelter from the heat under towels bearing the visual rhetoric of American cartoons.

FIGURE 13.5 Webb captures the man caught between two cultures, literally standing between two visual signs of American commercialism, Pepsi and Aquafina.

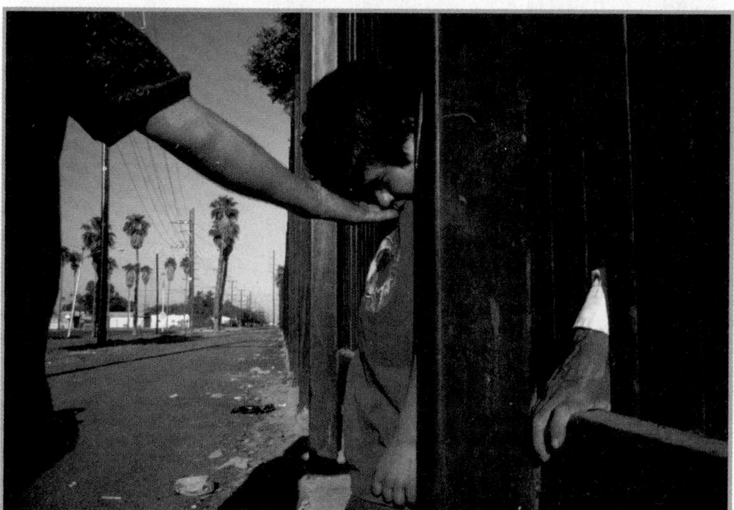

FIGURE 13.6 Families separated by the border reveal the deep emotional impact of immigration.

FIGURE 13.7 The visual signs of life on the borderlands reveal themselves in this photo of people kneeling for a make-shift Catholic mass.

REFLECT & WRITE

MyWritingLab

- ❑ How do the photos provide an argument about what life is like for immigrants and their families on both sides of the border?
- ❑ What appeals tell the story most powerfully? the emotions or *pathos* of the boy by the fence? the logical comparison of Pepsi and water vending machines? or the *ethos* or character of people practicing their faith by kneeling in the dirt? What other rhetorical elements do you notice?
- ❑ Discuss in small groups how you might develop your own photo essay about cultures in your community. What images would you include? What captions would you write to tell this story?
- ❑ **Write.** Compose your own captions for these images that show what you have learned about citizenship by studying these texts. Then, write an imaginary email to the photographer, Alex Webb, sending him your new captions and explaining to the photographer what you learned from his work.

Teaching Tolerance *is a project of the Southern Poverty Law Center, which describes its mission as "reducing prejudice, improving intergroup relations, and supporting equitable school experiences for our nation's children." The educator's guide reprinted here was originally published in 2014.*

An Educator's Guide to the Immigration Debate

Teaching Tolerance

"With driver cards, illegal immigrants will take Oregon jobs."—Op Ed, Oregonlive.com, January 2014

"Local protestors fast and pray for immigration reform."—CW39 News, KIAH-TV, Houston, Texas, February 2014

"Illegal immigrants deserve deportation."—Letter, The Baltimore Sun, February 2014

For at least a decade, headlines like these have shaped the way students and their families think about immigration. They have opinions; many have first-person experience. That range of opinion and experience makes teaching about current immigration policy a daunting task, one that some teachers choose to avoid.

Everyone—across the political spectrum—agrees that our current immigration system is broken. Although it's by no means certain that Congress will pass comprehensive immigration reform this year, the issues are too important not to discuss in class. And, the issues are perennial. We face many of the same questions policymakers have faced since the 1790s.

Immigration policy concerns us all, and students deserve to be part of the debate surrounding it. If anything, the fact that the topic is controversial makes it even more urgent that we help students untangle emotions from facts and see how complex policy can emerge from the democratic process.

Facilitating those discussions is easier with some background knowledge about the legacy of immigration in the United States and the current state of U.S. immigration policy.

Who's Invited?

5 It's a question barely asked for the first 85 years of the country's history. Even as the states voted to ratify the Constitution, the doors to immigrants—at least to Western European immigrants—were wide open. The nation needed settlers to fill up the newly-organized territories that extended to the Mississippi and, except for some worries about immigrants entangling the country in foreign intrigue, most immigrants were welcomed without question and with little red tape.

The process of immigration was virtually unregulated. There was no national office to oversee the admission of immigrants. If a person could afford to pay for passage, he was almost guaranteed entry into the United States. Only those with terrible diseases (such as yellow fever or smallpox) were kept out, and they were simply quarantined until they were no longer contagious.

In the mid-1840s, when the first great wave of poverty-stricken Irish immigrants arrived, new factories and a growing web of railroads absorbed the unskilled labor. Even though Irish labor was welcome, the Irish themselves weren't—groups like the nativist Know-Nothing Party saw these immigrants' Catholicism, poverty and lack of education as a cultural threat.

The need for labor, coupled with a seemingly endless expanse of open country, kept immigration wide open until the 1880s. That decade brought the first restriction in the form of the Chinese Exclusion Act, passed only after the West Coast railroads were built and the low-cost labor the Chinese supplied was no longer needed. This decade also ushered in federal control, most notably in the establishment of immigrant intake stations, such as Ellis Island.

Racial and ethnic fears, as well as a decreasing need for foreign labor, shaped a rising tide of anxiety about immigrants over the next 40 years as new groups—this time from Eastern and Southern Europe—arrived. Like the Irish, these new immigrants were often poor and uneducated. Unlike the Irish, they arrived speaking no English; many of them were Jews.

By the 1920s, the assembly line and increasing automation meant that business no longer needed an endless supply of unskilled labor. The gates could close, and close they did with the passage of the National Origins Act, a law that set quotas for entry based on ethnicity. Congress made it clear: British, German, Scandinavian and Irish immigrants were fine, but everyone else was more or less undesirable.

The Act set up a "line" to get in; it set quotas and, for the first time, required immigrants to obtain visas before leaving their country of origin. With the arrival of the Great Depression, the doors closed even tighter; many Jews trying to escape from Germany and Eastern Europe were denied access because of the quota system. With the beginning of the Cold War in the 1950s, the United States opened the doors a crack for refugees from Communism, but people from Africa, Asia and most of Latin America were still out of luck.

In 1965, President Lyndon B. Johnson threw out the racist quota system when he signed sweeping immigration reform. Sitting at the feet of the Statue of Liberty, Johnson said that U.S. immigration policy "has been twisted and has been distorted by the harsh injustice of the national origins quota system." The old law, he added, was "un-American," and he promised "that it will never again shadow the gate … with the twin barriers of prejudice and privilege."

The new law dramatically changed whom the United States welcomed. It opened, for the first time, large-scale immigration from the Americas. Numerical limits still applied, but this law gave preference based on skills and residential status of family rather than nationality.

More recently, reforms in the 1980s and 1990s tinkered with these numerical limits and introduced greater border security (nonexistent for most of U.S. history). The system of limits and preferences meant that, for some people, there was no way to enter the country, so the laws also attempted to deal with the problem of illegal immigration.

Warm Welcome or Cold Shoulder

The country's gates may have been open wide during much of the 19th century, but American arms were not. As early as the 1750s, Benjamin Franklin famously complained about the Germans settling in Pennsylvania. "Not being used to liberty," he grumbled, "they know not how to make a modest use of it." He worried that they were clannish and refused to learn English.

That complaint would be echoed in one form or another, against different targets, for the next 250 years. In the 1790s, Americans feared French immigrants would bring revolution; in the 1840s, some claimed the Irish were a separate race that took away American jobs; and, in the 1890s, Jews from Eastern Europe were accused of being too different and bringing anarchist thinking. The Ku Klux Klan in the 1920s was as much anti-immigrant as it was anti-black, and early 21st-century rhetoric about Mexican immigrants follows this old pattern.

Can I See Your Papers?

Before the 1880s, there were no illegal immigrants, because there were no limits on immigration. With restrictions—of Chinese, then Japanese, then the quota systems—came illegal immigration, and deportation.

It wasn't until the 1940s, though, that noncitizens needed "paperwork" to live in the United States. As war began in Europe, Congress passed the Alien Registration Act, which established for the first time two categories of noncitizens: legal residents and those who weren't. It was the beginning of what we now call the green card.

Today, we've multiplied those categories, complicating the paperwork. People who have permanent residency status (the green card) may become citizens if they want. Others, however, only have permission to be in the country for the time being. Their visas spell out the conditions under which they are here: as students, visitors or guest workers.

The Bracero program, created in 1942 as a wartime measure, ushered the first guest workers (mainly Mexican) into the country to harvest crops. That program ended after two decades, but not before being replaced by another guest-worker program that was also mainly for agricultural workers. Under immigration reform passed in 1986, the guest-worker program grew larger. Today, many guest workers toil in agriculture, but even highly-educated immigrants, such as teachers, can become trapped with no path to permanent residency or citizenship.

Guest workers have no path to citizenship; their visas typically allow them to stay in the country only for a year. They are often tied to an employer who has paid to bring them here, and they are easily exploited. With temporary residency, guest workers have few legal protections or rights.

I Will Support and Defend

The history of naturalization—the process by which a person becomes a citizen—stands in stark contrast to that of immigration. While immigration started out wide open and gradually came under federal control and grew more restrictive, the rules for naturalization have been firmly under federal control from the beginning. Two hundred years ago, the process of becoming a citizen was relatively easy—but few people qualified.

The Naturalization Act of 1795 set up a path to citizenship, but only free white persons were eligible. For others, like Asians and free persons of color, there was no path. Their children were not citizens either. That didn't improve with ratification of the 14th Amendment and birthright citizenship; it took 30 years of court cases for natural-born children of people of color to be guaranteed citizenship. Until passage of the 19th Amendment, a woman shared the citizenship status of her father or husband.

For a freeborn white man, the process was simple. He had to live in the country for five years, swear allegiance to the United States, renounce other loyalties and convince his local court that he believed in the principles of the Constitution, was of sound character and was a productive member of society. Virtually all of this could be done in a simple two-step process: Go to the county court to declare the intention to seek citizenship, and then appear before the judge again three years later to petition for it.

Today, eligibility is broader, but the process has become more difficult and expensive. Two requirements endure: a residency period and belief in American ideals and values as represented in the Declaration of Independence and Constitution. Under the Alien and Sedition Acts of 1798, the residency period grew to 14 years, but it was rolled back to five years in 1802. In the 1850s, the American

Party (the Know-Nothings) fought unsuccessfully to have it lengthened to 21 years.

Since then, other requirements have been added. The ability to speak English was added in 1906. Today, you need to be a permanent resident (have a green card), take a civics and language test and appear in federal court. The application is complicated and many prospective citizens employ lawyers.

Today's Debate

Students should know that the United States has a checkered history when it comes to immigration, residency and naturalization. Our need for immigrant labor has offset (but not neutralized) the fear of those who are different. At times, we've celebrated the great salad bowl, and, at other times, we've worried about assimilation and threats to our ways of life. Immigrants have been allowed in or turned away based on the needs of powerful economic interests, and those who are allowed in have often been met with xenophobic and nativist reactions.

It's important for students to look at today's immigration debate in light of past policy debates. How were previous policies made? How were economic, racist or other factors at play? What is different today, and, more importantly, what is the same?

REFLECT & WRITE

MyWritingLab

- ❑ The educator's guide ends with the claim that "it's important for students to look at today's immigration debate in light of past policy debates." What evidence does the article provide to support this claim? How does teaching the history of immigration change the way it might be taught today?
- ❑ Who is the intended audience of this article? How can you tell? What rhetorical strategies does the article use to connect with its audience? To what extent does the article succeed in engaging its audience?
- ❑ Find the original online version of this article and take note of the photographs used to accompany the teacher's guide. How might these images be used to construct a visual history of immigration in the United States? How would a teacher use a visual history to teach some of these topics?
- ❑ The guide concludes with the point that "the United States has a checkered history when it comes to immigration, residency, and naturalization." Why, according to this article, is it important to acknowledge this "checkered history"? What would be the risk of erasing this, or telling a different story about the past?
- ❑ **Write.** Based on the information and strategies presented in the educator's guide, construct a lesson plan and visual storyboard for a class lesson on immigration in America. Choose a specific age group of students, and explain how your visual images and design choices appeal to that specific audience.

■ **Lesli A. Maxwell** *is an editor and writer at* Education Week. *She writes on topics including English language learners, bilingual education, and school district leadership. The selection below was published in 2013 as part of a larger feature on "Education in Indian Country."*

Betting on a School

Lesli A. Maxwell

Ninety miles east of downtown Los Angeles in the San Bernardino Mountains, a school for Native American children peers down onto its main benefactor, a glittering, Las Vegas-style casino and hotel owned and operated by the Morongo Band of Mission Indians.

Millions of dollars spent in the casino by gamblers playing the slots, shooting craps, and wagering on poker hands are flowing into the Morongo School and fueling what could be the tribe's most important enterprise yet: taking control over the education of its own children.

The Morongo School—which opened in 2010 on this 35,000-acre reservation tucked into a narrow pass between the San Bernardino and San Jacinto mountains—is the Morongo tribe's biggest bet at the moment. After nearly 20 years of stunning economic development and the virtual elimination of poverty for its 1,000 members, the tribe is investing millions of dollars in education in the hope of reversing decades of low academic achievement, high dropout rates, and low rates of college attendance and graduation for its children.

State-of-the-Art School

On a drizzly October morning on the reservation, school bus No. 5 rolls up in front of the beige portable buildings that house the Morongo School's lower grades. Principal Mason Patterson and faculty members greet the stream of children and lead them through an open courtyard with expansive views of the mountains, covered with red oak, creosote bushes, and pinyon pine. The entire student body is 140 children, ranging from preschool through 9th grade. Older students now either attend public high schools nearby or use an independent-study program to earn their diplomas. The Morongo School will graduate its first class in 2017.

5 No class has more than 15 students, and every teacher in the lower grades has an aide. The school has adopted the Common Core State Standards, and its classrooms are outfitted with up-to-date educational technology, including iPads and Apple TVs. Completely funded by the tribe and available at no cost to children with a parent who is an enrolled member, the school operates mostly free of state and federal requirements around academic standards and accountability.

"We didn't want any government money," Mr. Martin says. "We didn't want the curriculum controlled by anyone else, and we know we are fortunate to be in that position."

"I think our small class sizes are so important," says 4th grade teacher Christina Alaniz, who grew up on the reservation and went to public schools. "We really know our students, and they really know each other well, too."

Twice a week, tribal elders spend the day with Morongo students, teaching them the nearly extinct Cahuilla (ka-wee-yah) and Serrano languages and cultural traditions unique to the Cahuilla people, a broader group of Native Americans that includes the Morongo tribe.

Most of the language instruction comes through the teaching of traditional "bird songs," which tell stories, often from the perspectives of birds, of journeys that the Cahuilla people would take from their desert and mountain homes and about the creation of the natural world.

Bridging cultural distances between the students and their heritage—which grew as tribal members' married outside the community and moved from the reservation—was another driving force behind the tribe's push to create its own school, says Mr. Martin, the tribal-council chairman.

California is home to more Native Americans than any other state, and most tribal children are enrolled in public schools scattered across cities, suburbs, and rural areas—often with few other Native peers. In Riverside County, where the Morongo reservation is located, American Indian students make up less than 1 percent of public school enrollment, even though there are 12 federally recognized tribes in the county.

For Morongo children, most of whom attended the public schools in nearby Banning before the Morongo School opened, that disconnection from their heritage contributed to feelings of isolation and low self-esteem, Mr. Martin says. Tribal leaders believed that young people were not getting enough meaningful exposure to the history and experience of California tribes, which was affecting their achievement. And those youths were increasingly facing a new stereotype: the rich Indian.

"I saw it happen with my own daughter," Mr. Martin says. "She wanted to quit school in the 9th grade because of negative comments she heard a teacher make about Indians. We had to enroll her in independent study so she could finish."

Sharing the Wealth

As Indian gaming has expanded rapidly across the U.S. over the past 25 years, some tribes like Morongo have been sinking their newfound resources into education programs and taking advantage of their sovereign status to build schools, hire teachers, and create a curriculum that they believe best serves their children.

For the Morongo tribe—with a sophisticated business portfolio that now includes a bottled-water operation, skilled-nursing facilities, and agriculture—raising a new generation of entrepreneurs and well-trained leaders is critical to sustaining its enterprises.

"We'd known for years that the public schools weren't equipped to teach most of our children, because our kids were failing," says Robert Martin, the longtime chairman of Morongo's tribal council.

"We wanted to take control of how to educate our young people," he says.

The Morongo tribe is among the wealthiest and most influential in both California and the nation. It was the tribe's 1987 U.S. Supreme Court case, Cabazon v. California, that produced a ruling that state and local authorities could not shut down bingo operations and other gaming ventures on reservations. That led to federal legislation that threw open the doors to the gaming industry for tribes across the country.

More than 230 tribes operate about 400 casinos now, says Steven Andrew Light, a co-director of the Institute for the Study of Tribal Gaming Law and Policy at the University of North Dakota in Grand Forks.

"If you look at gaming as an economic-development tool, nothing has impacted tribal communities more," Mr. Light says. "And tribes across the United States have made their own decisions on how to allocate their revenue, but the key pillars for investment have been housing; public services such as roads, police, and fire protections; and education programs."

Having started with a modest bingo parlor in 1983, the Morongo tribe opened a $250 million casino and hotel in 2004 and now employs roughly 3,000 people in the region. Its business enterprises—primarily the Morongo Casino, Resort, and Spa—are estimated to generate $3 billion in economic activity annually, according to an economic impact study commissioned by the tribe.

Enrolled members of the tribe receive regular "per capita" payments—Morongo leaders will not disclose how much—that provide most families with a comfortable living. Since 1996, the tribe has required members who turn 18 to earn a high school diploma or a GED credential before they can receive the payments.

On the reservation, though, many people are loath to forget the hardships that dominated the tribe's existence for generations. Families have built new, multilevel homes right next to the dilapidated houses and rundown trailers that sheltered them in more difficult times.

Yet economic success did little to move the needle on academic achievement for most of the tribe's young people, even though they were growing up in far more privileged circumstances than their parents and grandparents enjoyed.

Tribal leaders know only anecdotally that graduation rates were low and that too few young people were enrolling in college and earning degrees, even though the tribe covers all college and living costs for its students who enroll. (The tribe also fully pays for other post-secondary options, such as trade schools.)

Building on Foundations

The tribe had already been running a preschool for 3- and 4-year-olds, right on the reservation. And it had created and expanded a successful tutoring program in the late 1990s.

Working closely with the Banning school district, tutors hired by the tribe went into the schools with Morongo children to offer them supports, both in the classroom and outside of school, says Mr. Patterson, the Morongo School's principal, who began his career with the tribe as one of those tutors.

Tutors came to know students and their teachers, and provided a link between reservation families and the local schools. Graduation rates for Morongo students started to rise.

So when the tribe began serious discussions about starting a school, the community immediately bought into the idea, Mr. Patterson says.

"There was a lot of trust already that the tribe itself was in the best position to educate its own children," he says.

In 2012, the school received a three-year accreditation from the Western Association of Schools and Colleges, the regional accreditation agency.

Growth in mathematics and reading performance has been strong, according to the school's own data. At the end of 2011, the school's first year, only around 30 percent of students—at the time, there were 23 students in grades K-6—were reading and doing math on grade level as measured by their performance on the Stanford Achievement Test. Two years later, 61 percent of students were performing at grade level in math; 51 percent were doing so in reading.

For tribe member Norman Toro the school offers the promise of radically changing his family's education trajectory in one generation.

Forty years ago, Mr. Toro was an 8-year-old boy living in a crowded, ramshackle house on the reservation with his extended family. He was a high school dropout before he turned 16.

"I spent a lot of time up in the canyons hunting with my uncles," Mr. Toro says, "but when it came to my education, I didn't spend too much time thinking about it."

Now his 8-year-old daughter, Vanessa, is a 3rd grader at the Morongo School. Mr. Toro marvels at how much she loves school and how quickly she is absorbing the Cahuilla bird songs and language that he never learned.

"If I had had this school," he says, "I think I would have had a shot at graduating."

REFLECT & WRITE

MyWritingLab

- ❑ Maxwell chooses to focus on one specific location and school to illustrate her discussion about educational opportunities for Native American children. How does this case study approach help her to develop her argument? Why did she choose this particular focus?
- ❑ Locate the original feature story, "Education in Indian Country," online. How do the photographs and other graphic elements (line graphs and charts) contribute to the argument developed in the written text? What additional information and context do they provide to help understand the importance of the case study?
- ❑ What are the challenges faced by Native American children in reservation schools today, according to Maxwell? How is the Morongo school used as an example to show how these challenges can be addressed?
- ❑ **Write.** Compose a commentary in response to Maxwell, addressing the points made in the Teaching Tolerance educator's guide, and including your own view on immigration. Decide on your own tone and choice of metaphors. When you are done, set up a class debate to share perspectives and open up even more views on this issue.

Lexington *is a regular columnist for the* Economist. *He also keeps a blog, called* Lexington's Notebook, *posting opinions about "America's political fray."*

The Hub Nation

Lexington

Immigration places America at the centre of a web of global networks. So why not make it easier?

Immigrants benefit America because they study and work hard. That is the standard argument in favour of immigration, and it is correct. Leaving your homeland is a big deal. By definition, it takes get-up-and-go to get up and go, which is why immigrants are abnormally entrepreneurial. But there is another, less obvious benefit of immigration. Because they maintain links with the places they came from, immigrants help America plug into a vast web of global networks.

Many people have observed how the networks of overseas Chinese and Indians benefit their respective motherlands. Diasporas speed the flow of information: an ethnic Chinese trader in Indonesia who spots a commercial opportunity will quickly alert his cousin who runs a factory in Guangdong. And ties of kin, clan or dialect ensure a high level of trust. This allows decisions to be made swiftly: multimillion-dollar deals can sometimes be sealed with a single phone call. America is linked to the world in a different way. It does not have much of a diaspora, since native-born Americans seldom emigrate permanently. But it has by far the world's largest stock of immigrants, including significant numbers from just about every country on earth. Most assimilate quickly, but few sever all ties with their former homelands.

Consider Andres Ruzo, an entrepreneur who describes himself as "Peruvian by birth; Texan by choice". He moved to America when he was 19. After studying engineering, he founded a telecoms firm near Dallas. It prospered, and before long he was looking to expand into Latin America. He needed a partner. He stumbled on one through a priest, who introduced him to another devout IT entrepreneur, Vladimir Vargas Esquivel, who was based in Costa Rica and looking to expand northward. It was a perfect fit. And because of the way they were introduced—by a priest they both respected—they felt they could trust each other. Their firm now operates in ten countries and generates tens of millions of dollars in annual sales. Mr Ruzo wants the firm, which is called ITS Infocom, to go global. So although he and Mr Vargas Esquivel natter to each other in Spanish, they insist that the firm's official language must be English.

Trust matters. Modern technology allows instant, cheap communication. Yet although anyone can place a long-distance call, not everyone knows whom to call, or whom to trust. Ethnic networks can address this problem. For example, Sanjaya Kumar, an Indian doctor, arrived in America in 1992. He developed an interest in software that helps to prevent medical errors. This is not a small problem. Perhaps 100,000 Americans die each year because of preventable medical mistakes, according to the Institute of Medicine.

FIGURE 13.8 This illustration, which originally accompanied Lexington's article, makes a visual argument about our changing world community.

Dr Kumar needed cash and business advice to commercialise his ideas, so he turned to a network of ethnic Indian entrepreneurs called Tie. He met, and was backed by, an Indian-American venture capitalist, Vish Mishra. His firm, Quantros, now sells its services to 2,300 American hospitals. And it is starting to expand into India, having linked up with a software firm there which is run by an old school chum of one of Dr Kumar's Indian-American executives.

5 Ethnic networks have drawbacks. If they are a means of excluding outsiders, they can be stultifying. But they accelerate the flow of information. Nicaraguan-Americans put buyers in Miami in touch with sellers in Managua. Indian-American employees help American consulting firms scout for talent in Bangalore. The benefits are hard to measure, but William Kerr of the Harvard Business School has found some suggestive evidence. He looked at the names on patent records, reasoning that an inventor called Wang was probably of Chinese origin, while some called Martinez was probably Hispanic. He found that foreign researchers cite

American-based researchers of their own ethnicity 30-50% more often than you would expect if ethnic ties made no difference. It is not just that a Chinese boffin in Beijing reads papers written by Chinese boffins in America. A Chinese boffin in America may alert his old classmate in Beijing to cool research being done at the lab across the road.

Network effects

In Silicon Valley more than half of Chinese and Indian immigrant scientists and engineers report sharing information about technology or business opportunities with people in their home countries, according to AnnaLee Saxenian of the University of California, Berkeley. Some Americans fret that China and India are using American know-how to out-compete America. But knowledge flows both ways. As people in emerging markets innovate—which they are already doing at a prodigious clip—America will find it ever more useful to have so many citizens who can tap into the latest brainwaves from Mumbai and Shanghai. Immigrants can also help their American employers do business in their homelands. Firms that employ many ethnic Chinese scientists, for example, are more likely to invest in China and more likely to do so through a wholly owned subsidiary, rather than seeking the crutch of a joint venture, finds Mr Kerr. In other words, local knowledge reduces the cost of doing business.

Immigration provides America with legions of unofficial ambassadors, deal-brokers, recruiters and boosters. Immigrants not only bring the best ideas from around the world to American shores; they are also a conduit for spreading American ideas and ideals back to their homelands, thus increasing their adoptive country's soft power.

All of which makes the task of fixing America's cumbersome immigration rules rather urgent. Alas, Barack Obama has done little to fulfil his campaign pledge to do so. With unemployment still at nearly 10%, few politicians are brave enough to be seen encouraging foreigners to compete for American jobs.

REFLECT & WRITE

MyWritingLab

- ❑ How does the illustration in Figure 13.8 reflect and even extend the argument of the article? Can it be seen as a visual abstract for the writer's main point about immigrants as a "conduit for spreading American ideas and ideals back to their homelands"?
- ❑ Although there is only one subhead in this piece, how does it unite the two parts of the argument and propel the writer's thesis forward? What additional subheads might you compose if asked to do so? How would these new subheads influence readers?
- ❑ Assess the tone and stance by looking at word choice, sentence length, and specific examples. What passages work best for you as a reader? How would you characterize the writer's style?
- ❑ What do you make of the author's argument that "America will find it ever more useful to have so many citizens who can tap into the latest brainwaves from Mumbai and Shanghai"? Do you see America looking outward or not?

- ☐ **Write.** Draft a mock column for publication in *The Economist* describing "networks" in your own community, or observations you have had of immigration conduits. Include drawings or photos as visual rhetoric.

WRITING COLLABORATIVELY MyWritingLab

Together with two or three peers, explore additional legal, political, economic, or even social issues concerning "citizenship"—whether that refers to native or naturalized membership in a state or nation, or more metaphorically, as a "citizen" member of a certain community or group. You might decide to focus on a legal issue, such as the controversial overturn of the Voting Rights Act of 1965, or the disputes over the "Stand Your Ground" law to protect American citizens. Alternatively, you could look into issues of national security and how government surveillance by the NSA compromises or defends the rights and privileges of citizens. Develop your project by writing a research proposal (see Chapter 4 for guidelines), and then develop a multimedia presentation (based on the lessons from Chapter 8) to present your proposed research project to the class.

Jeffrey N. Wasserstrom *is a historian and director of the East Asian Studies Center at Indiana University. In this essay, originally published in* Yale Global Online *in 2003, Wasserstrom argues that standardized American products like Big Macs or Starbucks coffee hold different meanings in different cultures and contexts.*

A Mickey Mouse Approach to Globalization

Jeffrey N. Wasserstrom

From Buenos Aires to Berlin, people around the world are looking more and more American. They're wearing Levis, watching CNN, buying coffee at interchangeable Starbucks outlets, and generally experiencing life in 'very American' ways. Looking only at the surface of this phenomenon, one might erroneously conclude that

US cultural products are creating a homogenized global community of consumers. But the cultural aspects of the globalization story are far more complex than might be assumed from looking at just consumer behavior. Even when the same shirt, song, soda, or store is found on all five continents, it tends to mean different things depending on who is doing the wearing, singing, drinking, or shopping. The 'strange' fate of global products in China illustrates these points.

Consider, first of all, the Chinese meaning of Big Macs. In *The Lexus and the Olive Tree*, Thomas Friedman says he has eaten McDonald's burgers in more countries than he can count and is well qualified to state that they "really do all taste the same." What he actually means, though, is they all taste the same to him. Nearly identical Big Macs may be sold in Boston and Beijing, but as anthropologist Yan Yunxiang has convincingly argued, the experiences of eating them and even the meaning of going to McDonalds in these two locales was very different in the 1990s. In Beijing, but not in Boston, a Big Mac was classified as a snack, not a meal, and university students thought of McDonald's as a good place to go for a romantic night out. To bite into a Big Mac thinking that you are about to do something pleasantly familiar or shamefully plebian—two common American experiences—is one thing. To bite into one imagining you are on the brink of discovering what modernity tastes like—a common Chinese experience—is another thing altogether.

Or take the curious arrival of Mickey Mouse in China, which I witnessed first-hand. While living in Shanghai in the mid-1980s, two things I remember seeing are sweatshirts for sale on the streets emblazoned with the face of Disney's most famous creation, and a wall poster showing a stake being driven through Mickey's heart. Were these signs that a big American corporation was extracting profits from a new market and that local people were angered by cultural imperialism? Hardly. Yes, Disney was trying to make money, offering Chinese state television free cartoons to show in the hope that viewers would rush out and buy authorized products. But the plan went astray: the sweatshirts I saw were all knock-offs. The only people making money from them were Chinese entrepreneurs. And the wall poster was, of all things, part of a Communist Party health campaign. A call had just gone out for all citizens to work hard to rid their cities of rats, which are called "laoshu," the same term used for mice. It wasn't long before enterprising local residents put up posters showing various forms of violence being directed at "Mi Laoshu," as Mickey is known in Chinese, not because they hated America but simply because he was the most famous rodent in China.

Flash forward to the year 2000, when Starbucks first opened in both the American town I live in (Bloomington, Indiana) and the Chinese city I study (Shanghai), and we see further evidence of the divergent local meanings of globally familiar icons. In Bloomington, Starbucks triggered mixed reactions. Some locals welcomed its arrival. Others staged non-violent protests or smashed its windows, complaining that the chain's record on environmental and labor issues was abysmal and that Starbucks would drive local coffee shops out of business. In Shanghai, by contrast, there were no demonstrations. The chain's arrival was seen as contributing to, rather than putting a check upon, the proliferation of new independently run coffeehouses.

5 The local meanings of Shanghai Starbucks do not stop there. For example, when outlets open in Europe, they are typically seen, for understandable reasons, as symbols of creeping—or steam-rolling—Americanization. In Shanghai, though, guidebooks sometimes classify Starbucks as a "European-style" (as opposed to "Japanese-style") foreign coffee house. To further complicate things, the management company that operates the dozens of Shanghai Starbucks outlets is based not in Seattle but in Taiwan.

These examples of American products taking on distinctly new cultural meanings when moved from the US to China are useful in undermining superficial assertions equating globalization with 'Americanization'. But it is important not to stop there. The same thing has happened—and continues to happen—with the global meanings of Asian icons in America. Here, again, a Chinese illustration seems apt; that of a Middle Kingdom figure, Chairman Mao, whose face nearly rivals Mickey Mouse's in terms of global recognition.

One indication of the fame and varied meanings of Mao's visage is that in 2002 news stories appeared that told of the simultaneous appearance of the Chairman's image in three totally different national contexts. Representations of Mao showed up in the huts of Nepalese guerrillas; on posters carried by protesting laid-off workers in Northeast China; and in a London art exhibit. In Nepal, Mao was invoked because he endorsed peasant revolt. In Northeast China, his link to the days when Chinese workers had iron rice bowls for life was what mattered. And in London, it was his status as a favorite subject of a pop art pioneer that counted: the exhibit was a Warhol retrospective.

There is, in sum, more to keep in mind about globalization than Friedman's divide between the worlds of mass-produced Lexus cars and individuated olive trees. One reason is simply that a Lexus can mean myriad things, depending on where it is. Whether one first encounters it in the showroom or working the assembly line matters. And it makes a difference whether the people who watch it are seeing it whiz by as they walk the streets of Toledo or seeing it crawl as they sit on a Tokyo-bound Bullet Train. It is not just in physics, after all, but also in cultural analysis, that the complex workings of relativity need to be kept in mind.

REFLECT & WRITE

MyWritingLab

- ❑ How does Wasserstrom describe the differences between eating a Big Mac in Boston or in Beijing? Why is this difference important? How does Wasserstrom use descriptive, sensory language to make a broader point about cultural location and difference?
- ❑ Wasserstrom wants to distinguish his argument about globalization from that of Thomas Friedman. In what ways does Wasserstrom seek to define the experience of globalization differently from Friedman? Why?
- ❑ How does Wasserstrom define globalization and Americanization? Are these two terms equivalent? Why or why not?
- ❑ **Write.** Compose a *personal narrative* about how elements of diverse cultures intersect in the community around you. Include visual evidence and explore how each text shapes how you might think of yourself as participating in a "world community." Integrate your images strategically in your personal essay, and then share your work with others.

■ *The two pieces that follow appeared in Rutgers University's newspaper, the* Daily Targum, *in October 2002. The* Targum *ran the first piece, written by 2001 Rutgers graduate* **Joseph Davicsin**, *in its October 16 edition; "Globalization or McDonaldization?" appeared in response the following day. Its author,* Jeremy Sklarsky, *was a first-year student at Rutgers at the time.*

The Daily Targum: Two Opinions on McDonaldization

Corporations Leave Small Business Behind

Joseph Davicsin

Three months ago, a coffee shop opened on Church Street—where the used CD store "Tunes" was—called Basic Elements. This shop offered homemade beverages and food

Globalization or McDonaldization?

Jeremy Sklarsky

I am writing in response to Joseph Davicsin's commentary about international corporations conquering the world and eliminating "mom and pop" establishments. Davicsin's comments exemplify some of the most commonly at prices comparable to similar chain stores. I say "offered" because, as of recently, the place has flown the coop like so many boiler room scams. I later saw the proprietors at Starbucks doing espresso shots and mumbling Wicca chants at the Cranium board game. Basic Elements deserved a hell of a lot more than it was given—a crappy side street with little visibility, despite being right near the Court Tavern (which I know for a fact that you frequent because I can never get a square foot of space to stand on when I'm in there), irregular hours—which is understandable in a quality place run by two people (you can't expect Walmart)—and most of all, our apathy.

Our apathy is linked largely to globalization, which is trying to unite the planet in blanket sameness so that you can experience a thrill at the notion of shopping at a Gap in Prague and eating at a McDonalds in India. Now, something in your mind should tell you there's something wrong with going to a McDonalds in India. The idea of going abroad is to experience new things outside your microcosm. But alas, the success of these businesses in pandering their crack all over the world has gotten people comfortable with this sameness. We stick to the chains because they're familiar, convenient and plowed into our faces on a regular basis. When you get that taste of mocha, you're hooked and nothing else seems to matter.

Of course, if it were simply laziness and chemical brainwashing causing the underdogs to fail, it would be easier to rectify, but life is never that simple. There's also the notion of capital to think of. Corporations like Starbucks have enough money to keep their prices relatively the same no matter where you go, so there's not only uniformed coverage, but held misperceptions about globalization and corporations.

Globalization is not an enemy. It is an international, socioeconomic-political system. Due to advances in information technology, the rise of a postindustrial economy and the collapse of the bipolar Cold War world, a system has arisen in which the interests of individuals and governments around the world are intertwined. The overlap of people's interests has led to increased global cooperation. It can even be argued that the motivation for acts of international terrorism like Sept. 11 is actually a categorical rejection of the globalization system. The young men who crashed airplanes into the World Trade Center were born and raised in some of the countries that are the least globalized.

Globalization is not trying to "unite the planet in blanket sameness." Actually, quite the contrary is true. Take McDonald's, a notorious symbol of globalization, for example. McDonald's was not introduced into foreign countries in order to push American cultural hegemony over the rest of the world. McDonald's was mostly imported into foreign countries by nationals of those countries that wanted to make some profit—not as a part of a master plan to make everyone American. McDonald's is just a company that wants to make money. It isn't part of a "conspiracy of American corporations to take over the world."

Furthermore, a quick trip to the McDonald's Web site will put to rest anyone's fears that Ronald and friends are trying to undermine the culture of a local population. In Italy, McDonald's serves Mediterranean salads. Japanese customers can get teriyaki burgers. In Israel there are several kosher McDonald's restaurants, and in Mexico burritos are served. These are just a few examples of when McDonald's has actually changed itself to fit into the local culture. In also uniformed prices. The same cannot be said of the localized stores because they have less coverage and really need the extra money to stay alive, forcing them to increase their prices to compete. This delegates them to the "fine arts" category in which only the wealthy can indulge, resulting in an even split between cheap and prevalent and expensive and exclusive, with the midways—i.e., the moderately priced Basic Elements—getting squished in the ever-shrinking gap. Our culture becomes the following: Either you go to McSystem for victuals or spend exorbitant amounts of cash on the trendier French fry.

Then, of course, there's the small matter of demand, and that's when convenience takes precedence. Anyone who still reads out there will have little hope of finding a Recto & Verso when the majority only cares about getting textbooks and spirit clothing. The alternative is Barnes and Noble. If you want a real alternative you have to walk the world over to Pyramid Books in Highland Park, which, judging by the abundance of romance novels infesting their shelves, leads me to believe that they too are trying desperately to stay afloat.

5 Countless fables tell of local pizza places rejecting the system, but are they really? Or are they just biding their time before Burger King offers pizza for breakfast? They too seem to be getting increasingly gimmicky (check out King's Pizza and the ultimate tax write-off that is their wide-screen TV) and streamlined (toppings ranging from tortellini to ecstasy). There are still a few locales, like Noodle Gourmet, that do solid business on their own two legs, but it's not enough. What we need to do is

India, the country that Davicsin used in his column as an example, consumers can get McDonald's sandwiches made with mutton and chicken instead of beef, as McDonald's recognizes the importance of the dietary laws in Indian religions and cultures. McDonald's has also initiated many community service programs. In Saudi Arabia, it was the first chain restaurant to sponsor a campaign to increase seatbelt awareness.

5 A McDonald's in every country? Sounds good to me. Thomas Friedman, columnist for The New York Times, recently put forth a theory—which has been proven—that states that no two countries with a McDonald's has gone to war with each other since McDonald's arrived in their countries. In Friedman's own words, people in countries that have developed an economy at the level needed for McDonald's to be successful would rather "wait in line for burgers instead of in line for gas masks."

Davicsin refers to corporations as though they are some supernatural enemy imposed upon us by some external forces. Where did they get all of their money? And why are they so successful? A chain like McDonald's or Starbucks Coffee has had so much success for one simple reason: They are just better than the "corner shop." But chances are, if a local store can make a lower-priced product of higher quality, it will thrive. Take another corporation—Pizza Hut. Pizza Hut just isn't that good. Result? There are hundreds of individually owned pizza parlors around America. We shouldn't, however, support every local pizza place just for the sake of fighting corporations—that's just silly.

I'm not suggesting globalization or corporations are perfect—they are far from it. Many alternate our habits a little. Back to coffee—like Café 52? I know you do because I see you bastards flood it every Monday night for the free music, then try West End on alternate nights. Spread out! Balance the pros and cons of each place and try to find a niche in one when the other doesn't meet your needs. But above all, give newer places your undivided attention because they may not be around long enough without you. Show the smaller places that there's a need for them and that quality need not mean pricey. And don't let companies know where you're going, lest they turn that into a trend as well. Be as random as a chaos pendulum.

Third World countries would probably be better off if the World Bank or IMF behaved better. And corporations could probably afford to pollute a little less and pay their workers a little bit more. But that's really not the issue. The point is that globalization is not a choice. The real question is how everyone is going to act in order to benefit from its existence. If local coffee shops wish to thrive in the globalization system, they'd better be damned good, otherwise Starbucks will run them out of business—and for good reason. Consumers deserve to consume good products. If the only reason to go to a local burger joint is to prevent the domination of McDonald's, then I'll have another Big Mac.

REFLECT & WRITE

MyWritingLab

- ❑ Notice how each writer relies on a different understanding of "globalization" and what it means to be a member of such a radically changing society. Based on this, map out the points of each argument. How does each writer use concrete examples and structure his perspective through carefully chosen rhetorical appeals?
- ❑ Davicsin emphasizes the necessity of what he calls "visibility" and small establishments. How does his language create a favorable image for local stores in contrast to his disparagement of "blanket sameness" across the globe?
- ❑ How does Sklarsky structure his rebuttal? What points does he choose to refute and do you follow the logic of his conclusion? Which piece is more persuasive to you, and why?
- ❑ **Write.** Draft a response to both pieces, advancing beyond the debate between Davicsin and Sklarsky. Be certain to quote passages from both in your own article and offer your own argument about where we stand with regard to our participation or place in a global economy. Finally, where might you publish your composition?

The three photos below represent possible images of globalization. In each case, a recognizable American brand icon appears in a new, international context.

Images of Globalization

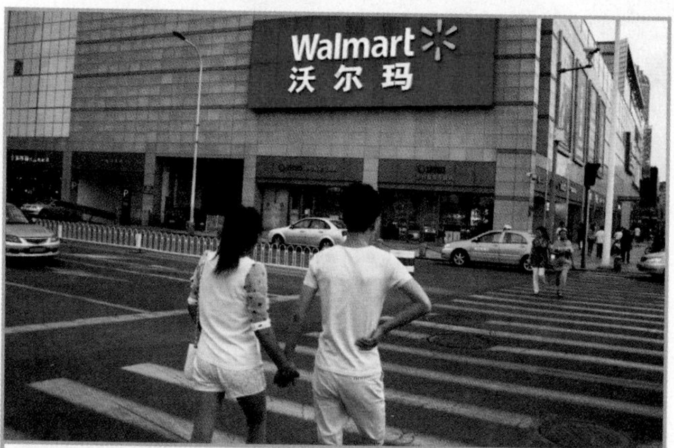

FIGURE 13.9 Walmart in China. Photo by Zhang Peng.

FIGURE 13.10 Starbucks in India. People gather outside the first Starbucks in Mumbai, in October 2012. Photo by Punit Paranjpe.

FIGURE 13.11 McDonald's in Brazil. A Big Mac in Sao Paulo, October 2008. Photo by Paulo Fridman.

REFLECT & WRITE

MyWritingLab

- ❑ How do these three images combine to make a visual argument about globalization and the spread of American brands? How would writers like Wasserstrom, Davicsin, or Sklarsky respond to these images?
- ❑ What role do visual stereotypes play in this piece? How does each image represent an international culture in a specific way?
- ❑ What visual examples might be found in your own community to show how your environment is becoming more globalized? more Americanized? more homogenous? Do you find more global brands in your visual environment?
- ❑ Can you find any counterexamples in your own visual culture? Are there examples of international brands or iconic images from outside of the United States that you encounter? What are some examples of these?
- ❑ **Write.** Compose your own blog post about encountering McDonald's or another similar American brand—either in your community or on a recent trip away from home. Be sure to include subtitles that indicate your argument. Include images and structure your writing around a series of scenes. Use your blog title to indicate your argument about citizens in the kingdom of McDonald's.

Colleen Walsh *is a staff writer for the* Harvard Gazette, *where the following article appeared in May 2013. The piece profiles the efforts of one now-famous entrepreneur, Salman Khan, who harnesses open source technologies of the Web to make college-level classroom instruction available to anyone around the globe, free of charge, through his nonprofit enterprise, the Khan Academy.*

Education Without Limits

Colleen Walsh

When he was filling out the forms to establish his new nonprofit in 2008, Salman Khan paused at the mission statement section.

The Massachusetts Institute of Technology grad, a math and computer whiz with an M.B.A. from Harvard Business School, thought for a moment, and

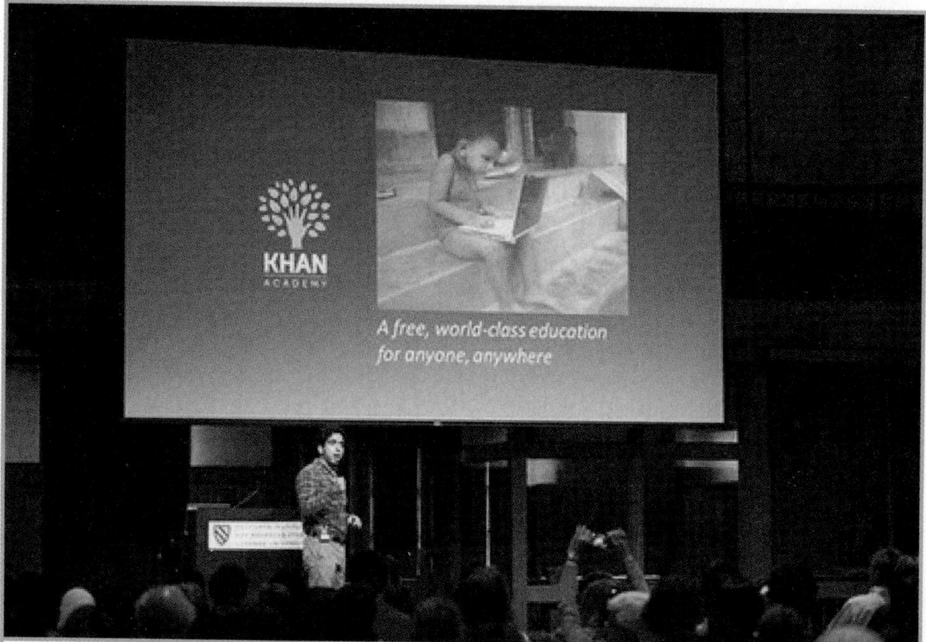

FIGURE 13.12 In his multimedia presentation, Salman Khan shares his vision for a world with education available to all.

then jotted down a powerful response: "A free world-class education for anyone anywhere."

With the academy, Khan told a crowded Radcliffe Gymnasium on Wednesday during an Askwith Forum sponsored by the Harvard Graduate School of Education, he hopes to advance a vision of education as "a fundamental human right."

He is well on his way. Khan Academy offers, at no cost, entertaining and informative videos, online lessons, and interactive software tools its founder hopes will help transform teaching and learning.

5 With Khan's digital tools, teachers can closely track student performance through a color-coded spreadsheet, identifying learners who are excelling and those who need help. Khan said his videos and tutorials also enable each learner to master introductory concepts at his or her own pace before moving on to harder topics.

"In a traditional academic model we group kids together usually by age ... and then we move them all together at a set pace." Khan described the familiar process: a series of lectures and homework assignments, and then an exam to test students' knowledge and understanding.

Not all students do well on the test. Nonetheless, the entire class moves to a harder subject.

"Imagine if we applied that process to other parts of our life, say building a house," he said. If a contractor with limited time did the best job he or she could on a foundation and an inspector rated it 85 percent complete, he went on, no one would say: "Great, let's build a first floor!"

If that home topples, the first person held responsible is the contractor, much like the teacher in a classroom with struggling students. And while some teachers (and contractors) deserve the blame, more often it's the process that's at fault, said Khan. "You are artificially constraining how long someone had to work on something. And then when you inspected it and identified weaknesses, you just ignored them and moved on to the next thing, often with something that is going to build on the weaknesses that you just identified."

10 In Khan's model, struggling students receive the help they need, sometimes from peers who have mastered the material.

Early results are promising. Khan said his system is being used in a number of schools and charter networks in California. The data show students considered below average often "go on to become the best or second-best student in the class," he said.

In addition to the classroom benefits, the academy is also an effective "research tool in and of itself," Khan said.

With roughly 3 million exercises done on the site every day, Khan and his team of 40 researchers experiment with questions, adding comments, explanations, and sometimes even just an inspiring quote about the importance of flexing one's brain, in an effort to track what encourages learning.

Khan said his work also has implications for the developing world. While the nonprofit has traditionally more focused on English-speaking countries, it now has 7,000 videos in other languages, including Mandarin, Farsi, Bengali, and Portuguese, with plans to develop many more.

During a question-and-answer session, one listener asked Khan for his thoughts on the growing interest in online education, including Harvard's involvement with edX, a partnership with MIT that promotes Web-based, interactive study and learning.

"EdX we are very close to. Anant Agarwal [the edX president] is actually one of my former professors. So we want to coordinate with them as much as possible," he said.

The onetime financier walked the crowd through his organization's humble beginnings. In 2004 Khan was an analyst at a Boston hedge fund when he began helping his young niece with math via Internet and phone.

Word quickly spread that he was offering free tutoring. Soon he was working with a group of about 15 cousins and friends of the family. Khan started recording math tutorials in a closet in his home and posting them to YouTube.

Then his students told him they preferred the YouTube Khan to the real thing.

A little surprised, Khan realized their comments made perfect sense. "The first time you are learning a concept the last thing you need is someone standing right there saying 'It's easy, right?'"

Khan kept making videos, viewership spiked, and the positive reviews piled up.

"One woman wrote, 'My entire family prays for your entire family every night.' You have to put things into perspective. I was an analyst at a hedge fund. There was not a lot of prayer going on. Well, at least in that way," joked Khan.

Khan quit his job in 2009 and devoted his time to fundraising for the new project. His finances and prospects looked dire several months in, until an enthusiastic donor gave him $10,000. They met, he described his vision, and 10 minutes after they parted she wired him another $100,000.

"So that's a good day."

25 Other good days followed, including a meeting with Microsoft's Bill Gates, who became a major backer, as did Google. Today Khan's nonprofit reaches millions of students a day and is used in 30,000 classrooms around the world.

The morning assembly was also something of a recruiting session. Following the talk, Khan, who'd encouraged those interested in careers at his academy to stick around, drew a crowd.

REFLECT & WRITE

MyWritingLab

- ❑ Take a close look at Figure 13.12, the visual that accompanies this article. What does it suggest about the rhetorical strategies Salman Khan uses to make the argument that education is "a fundamental human right"? How does the solo image of the nearly naked child evoke *pathos*? How does *logos* enter through the words on the bottom of the slide? Why might Khan choose this image to go beside his company icon and how does it build his *ethos*?
- ❑ In making the case for "education without limits," Khan compares the role of the teacher to that of a contractor tasked with building a house: "If that home topples, the first person held responsible is the contractor, much like the teacher in a classroom with struggling students." In your view, does this analogy accurately reflect what the role of a teacher actually involves?
- ❑ "The Khan Academy," Walsh notes, "offers, at no cost, entertaining and informative videos, online lessons, and interactive software tools its founder hopes will help transform teaching and learning." How might this new vision of education open doors for people with less access to such resources to become members of an educated community? What can you imagine would be the benefits of such globally expansive and technologically based educational communities? What might be the downsides?
- ❑ **Write.** For generations, the promise of the American Dream—that anyone can be successful through education and hard work—has been compromised by real economic obstacles restricting those who can't afford higher education. But with new digital tools such as those used by the Khan Academy, as well as the emergence of MOOCs (massive online open courses), these boundaries might just be falling away. Compose two position papers in which you argue for and against the expansion of education to include all interested global citizens. Then find common ground between these two sides using Rogerian argument and develop a concluding position that marshalls empathy to offer a final view on this issue of "education without limits."

Seeing Connections
For guidelines on Rogerian argument, see Chapter 3.

ANALYZING PERSPECTIVES ON THE ISSUE

MyWritingLab

1. Compare how the Center for American Progress infographics (Figure 13.3) and Mertens's profile of immigration and small town life make use of research. While the format of each—image versus feature article—is quite different, in many ways their arguments are complementary. What points of convergence can you discover? How does the strategic reliance on research evidence help each text make its points persuasively? Which format appeals to you most?
2. Consider the views of Teaching Tolerance and Richard Mertens on immigration's benefit to the American economy. Which writing strategies do you admire more? How convincing is each argument? Can you read the Lexington piece as a third perspective on this issue? Now, write your own article as a fourth response to this issue. Be sure to quote from all the previous pieces and also to use evidence or case studies from your own life or community.
3. Which texts in this chapter seem to be in direct conversation with each other? What do you think Lesli A. Maxwell would say in response to the piece by Jeffrey N. Wasserstrom? How does the feature on Salman Khan broaden out the very notion of "citizenship" to a more global context and how could you see his slide (Figure 13.12) as a visual response to the stereotypical image that opened the chapter with the word, "Caution" (Figure 13.1)? What can you learn from these various strategies of argument and how they work as a collection?
4. Examine the visuals throughout this chapter. How do road signs, data visualizations, documentary photographs, and slideshows reveal or extend the controversies covered by the articles? What additional images would you add to this chapter to capture and convey issues of civil rights, citizenship, expanding opportunities, and changing communities?

FROM READING TO RESEARCH ASSIGNMENTS

MyWritingLab

1. Select one of the subtopics within this chapter on "Claiming Citizenship." It could be the battle concerning immigration, local attitudes concerning English-only or second-language signage, globalization and its effects on the American economy and American identity, or the new technology wave in education. Conduct research by looking up the subtopic through the search strategies you learned in Chapter 5. Once you have five to six additional sources on the topic, read them and take notes. Develop a thesis for your own stance, and compose a research-based argument that includes the sources you have located but emphasizes your own contribution to the conversation.
2. Review the photos by Alex Webb on immigration (Figures 13.4–13.7). Then, make a storyboard that will help you create your own visual argument about immigration. Conduct field research by interviewing members of your community. After arranging and editing your materials, create a video montage that reveals, in moving photos, your stance. You might also forge a

"Director's Cut" that includes your voice-over, explaining the rationale for your images, interviews, and scenes, as well as your indebtedness to Webb's work.

3. In what ways is America expanding beyond its borders? Consider the views on globalization and the new developments in education. How might the two intersect? What will the future of the world look like in terms of who works with whom and what hubs of connection bring people into shared spaces? Compose an op-ed targeted for publication in your school newspaper. Illustrate your thesis about this broader notion of "citizenship" with an accompanying drawing.

MyWritingLab Visit Ch. 13 Crisis and Resilience in MyWritingLab to complete the *Analyzing Perspectives on the Issue* and *From Reading to Research Assignments*.

CREDITS

Images

Chapter 1

p. 1: Thomson Reuters.
p. 3, Figure 1.1: Mike Luckovichy, Editorial Cartoon used with the permission of MIke Luckovich and Creators Syndicate. All rights reserved.
p. 5, Figure 1.2: K. Clare Conrotto
p. 5, Figure 1.3: Christine Alfano
p. 6: Figure 1.4: Fernando Veludo/epa/Corbis
p. 7: Lunsford, Andrea.
p. 8, Figure 1.6: phdcomics.com
p. 9: Bitzer, Lloyd
p. 10, Figure 1.8: Cagle Cartoons, Inc.
p. 11: Lucas, George, Star Wars Episode IV, Disney.
p. 13: McCloud, Scott, "Understanding Comics".
p. 15, Figure 1.10: Bramhall, Bill, "I Can't Breathe", December 4, 2014 © Daily News, L.P. (New York). Used with permission.
p. 18, Figure 1.12: Clay Bennett Editorial Cartoon used with the permission of Clay Bennett, the Washington Post Writers Group and the Cartoonist Group. All rights reserved.
p. 19: McCloud, Scott, "Understanding Comics".
p. 27, Figure 1.14: Markstein, Gary, "Domestic Violence", September 12, 2014. Reprinted with permission by Creators.
p. 29, Figure 1.15: Cagle Cartoons, Inc.

Chapter 2

p. 43, Figure 2.1: JEWEL SAMAD/Getty Images
p. 45, Figure 2.2: Anheuser-Busch/Splash News/Corbis
p. 46, Figure 2.3, LEGO Juris A/S
p. 48, Figure 2.4: Bank of America
p. 56, UF2-A: Library of Congress, Prints & Photographs Division, [LC-USZC4-4440]
p. 58, Figure 2.6:Juan Carlos/Bloomberg/Getty Images
p. 66, Figure 2.7: Hugo Ortuño Suárez/Demotix/Corbis
p. 67, Figure 2.8: Natan Dvir/Polaris/Newscom
p. 75, Figure 2.9: Advertising Archives
p. 75, Figure 2.9: The Coca-Cola Company. Advertisement for Coca-Cola entitled "Coca-Cola goes along" and accompanying marks of The Coca-Cola Company. Used with permission.
p. 77, Figure 2.10: Richard Levine/Demotix/Corbis
p. 77, Figure 2.10: Cindy Ord/Getty Images

Chapter 3

p. 89, Figure 3.1: Eric Gay/AP Images
p. 92: Cicero
p. 93, Figure 3.3: Margaret Bourke-White/Masters/Time Life Pictures/Getty Images
p. 94, Figure 3.4: Library of Congress, Prints & Photographs Division, [3b06165r]
p. 94, Figure 3.5: Library of Congress Prints and Photographs Division[LC-USZ62-95653]
p. 97, Figure 3.6: Todd Heisler/Polaris Images
p. 98, Figure 3.7: Library of Congress Prints and Photographs Division
p. 98, Figure 3.8: Library of Congress Prints and Photographs Division
p. 99, Figure 3.9: Library of Congress Prints and Photographs Division
p. 99, Figure 3.10: Library of Congress Prints and Photographs Division
p. 114, Figure 3.14: Susan Walsh/AP Images
p. 119, Figure 3.16: The Columbian, September 2, 2005.
p. 119, Figure 3.15: From Anchorage Daily News, September 2 © 2005 McClatchy. All rights reserved. Used by permission and protected by the Copyright Laws of the United States. The printing, copying, redistribution, or retransmission of this Content without express written permission is prohibited.
p. 122, Figure 3.17: Library of Congress, Prints & Photographs Division, [0007q]

Chapter 4

p. 136, Figure 4.1: Alexandra Fischer
p. 138, Figure 4.2: Hoover Institution Archives
p. 140, Figure 4.3: Library of Congress, Prints and Photographs Division, LC-USZC4-5603
p. 145, UnFigure_4a: Palczewski, Catherine H. Postcard Archive. University of Northern Iowa. Cedar Falls, IA.
p. 145: Palczewski Suffrage Postcard Archive. Courtesy of University of Northern Iowa.
p. 149, Figure 4.6a: National Archives and Records Administration
p. 149, Figure 4.6b: Archive Images/Alamy
p. 149, Figure 4.6c: Library of Congress, Prints and Photographs Division
p. 149, Figure 4.6d: Gianni Dagli Orti/The Art Archive at Art Resource, NY
p. 149, Figure 4.6e: Library of Congress, Prints and Photographs Division
p. 151, Figure 4.7: Alexandra Fischer
p. 151, Figure 4.8; Alexandra Fischer
p. 151, Figure 4.9: Lalo Alcaraz

Chapter 5

p. 166, Figure 5.1: Nevada Wier/Corbis
p. 167, Figure 5.2a: Nigel Cattlin/Alamy
p. 167, Figure 5.2b: Paul Abbitt/Alamyp.
p. 167, Figure 5.2c: Danita Delimont/Alamy
p. 167, Figure 5.2d: Tom Wood/Alamy
p. 169, Figure 5.3: Steve Bronstein/Stone/Getty Images
p. 177, Figure 5.5: US Army, Getty Images

p. 183, Figure 5.7: National Institutes of Health
p. 185, Figure. 5.7: Copyright EBSCO Publishing, Inc. 1999. All rights reserved.
p. 195, Figure 5.8: Vincent Chen
p. 197, Figure. 5.9a: Ryan O'Rourke
p. 197, Figure. 5.9b: Ryan O'Rourke

Chapter 6

p. 211: Zoe Saldana/Everett Collection
p. 212, Figure 6.1: AF archive/Alamy
p. 219, Figure 6.4a: Everett Collection
p. 219, Figure 6.4c: Everett Collection
p. 219, Figure 6.4b: Zoe Saldana/Everett Collection

Chapter 7

p. 265, Figure 7.1: Justin Cone
p. 283, Figure 7.2: Christine Alfano
p. 283, Figure 7.3: Christine Alfano
p. 291, UnFigure_07a: Daniel Shim. "Wasabi-Boy No Engrish" video screen shot. Used by permission.

Chapter 8

p. 296, Figure 8.1: DC Vote
p. 315: Body Shop Mission Statement
p. 316: Roddick, Gordon quoted in Body Shop publication "Our Agenda", 1996.
p. 316: Roddick, Anita speech at Academy of Management, Vancouver, August 1995.
p. 319, Figure 8.7: The Advertising Archives
p. 319, Figure 8.7: **Moms Demand Action**
p. 320, Figure 8.8b: Christina Alfano
p. 320, Figure 8.8: Konstantinos Moraiti/Fotolia
p. 321, Figure 8.9: Chris O'Brien
p. 322, Figure 8.10a: Chris O'Brien
p. 322, Figure 8.10b: Chris O'Brien
p. 322, Figure 8.10c: Chris O'Brien
p. 323, Figure 8.11a: AP Photo/Farah Abdi Warsameh
p. 323, Figure 8.11b: Ulrich Doering/Alamy
p. 323, Figure 8.11c: Richard Lord/Alamy
p. 325, Figure 8.12: Screencapture, Eric fought against cancer, www.causes.com. Reprinted with permission.
p. 327, Figure 8.13: Screencapture, Visual Rhetoric of Protest, http://mirandarose.wix.com/march-on-washington.
p. 332, Figure 8.15: Dennis Schroeder/NREL/U.S. Department of Energy
p. 334, Figure 8.16: Jared Sun
p. 335, Figure 8.17: Paul Sakuma/AP Image

Chapter 9

p. 341: Eugene Hoshiko/AP Photo
p. 343, Figure 9.1: Magnolia Pictures/Everett Collection
p. 348, Figure 9.2: Laura Thal
p. 348, Figure 9.3: HaYoung Shin
p. 348, Figure 9.4: Photo by Caroline M. Grant
p. 358, Figure 9.5: United States Department of Agriculture
p. 359, Figure 9.6: United States Department of Agriculture
p. 359, Figure 9.7: United States Department of Agriculture
p. 360, Figure 9.8: United States Department of Agriculture
p. 364, Figure 9.9: Courtesy of Mother Nature Network (www.mnn.com).
p. 371, Figure 9.10: © Peter Menzel/menzelphoto.com
p. 372, Figure 9.11: © Peter Menzel/menzelphoto.com.

Chapter 10

p. 381, Figure 10.1: Tim P. Whitby/Getty Images
p. 382, Figure 10.2: Mick Stevens/The New Yorker Collection/www.cartoonbank.com
p. 386, UF10-A: Trevor Rex
p. 386, UF10-B: Samantha Kargilis
p. 386, UF10-C: Miranda Alfano-Smith
p. 386, UF10-E: Michael Vela
p. 386, UF10-D: Emmanuel Omari Omvenga
p. 386, UF10-F1: Tucker Burnett
p. 386, UF10-F2: Claire Shu
p. 386, UF10-F3: William Hang
p. 386, UF10-F4: Lucas Lin
p. 418, Figure 10.4: Sim City EDU: Pollution Challenge, Games For Change, GlassLab Inc. Reprinted with permission.
p. 419, Figure 10.5: Subaltern Games, LLC. Screenshot of "Neocolonialism." Used by permission. http://www.gamesforchange.org/g4cwp/wp-content/uploads/2013/11/neocolonialism_0_10_4.png

Chapter 11

p. 422, Figure 11-1: Keith Dannemiller/Corbis/AP Images
p. 423, Figure 11-2: Bénédicte Desrus/AP Images
p. 423, Figure 11.3: Ringo H.W. Chiu/AP Images
p. 425, Figure 11-5: Benedicte Desrus/AP Images
p. 447, Figure 11.6: Jonathan Shapiro, www.zapiro.com/BERG + BACH B.V.
p. 448, Figure 11.7: Bob Martin/Sports Illustrated/Getty Images
p. 448, Figure 11.8: Mike Powell/Sports Illustrated/Getty Images
p. 467, Figure 11.9: Roberto Schmidt/AFP/Getty Images

Chapter 12

p. 470, Figure 12.1: Chris O'Brien
p. 472, Figure 12.2: Chris O'Brien
p. 481, Figure 12.3: Michael Reynolds/epa/Corbis
p. 481, Figure 12.3b: M. Scott Brauer/Demotix/Corbis
p. 483, Figure 12.4: Samuel Rigelhaupt/Sipa USA/AP Images
p. 492, Figure 12.5: Navid Baraty
p. 492, Figure 12.6: David Leeson/Dallas Morning News
p. 494, Figure 12.7: David Leeson/Dallas Morning News
p. 495, Figure 12.8: David Leeson/Dallas Morning News
p. 496, Figure 12.9: David Leeson/Dallas Morning News
p. 497, Figure 12.10: Cartoon Movement
p. 500, Figure 12.11: Cartoon Movement

p. 501, Figure 12.12: Charles Porter/ ZUMA Press

p. 501, Figure 12.13: Cartoon Movement

p. 502, Figure 12.14: Matthew Christopher Photography

p. 503, Figure 12.15: Matthew Christopher Photography

Chapter 13

p. 506, Figure 13.1: James Steidl/ Shutterstock

p. 507, Figure 13.2: Library of Congress, Prints & Photographs Division.

p. 509, Figure 13.3: This material was created by the Center for American Progress (www.americanprogress.org).

p. 514, Figure 13.4: Alex Webb/ Magnum Photos

p. 515, Figure 13.5: Alex Webb/ Magnum Photos

p. 515, Figure 13.6: Alex Webb/ Magnum Photos

p. 516, Figure 13.7: Alex Webb/ Magnum Photos

p. 526, Figure 13.8: Kevin Kal Kallaugher, The Economist, kaltoons.com

p. 535, Figure 13.9: Zhang Peng/LightRocket/Getty Images

p. 535, Figure 13.10: Punit Paranjpe/ AFP/Getty Images

p. 536, Figure 13.11: Paulo Fridman/ Bloomberg/Getty Images

p. 537, Figure 13.12: Stephanie Mitchell/ Harvard Gazette

Text

Adbusters, "Create your own print ad", https://www.adbusters.org/spoofads/printad.

An Educator's Guide to the Immigration Debate". Teaching Tolerance, Number 47: Summer 2014. Reprinted with permission of Teaching Tolerance, a project of the Southern Poverty Law Center. www.tolerance.org.

Baker, Chris,"Is Darth Disney Destroying Star Wars' Expanded Universe?" Wired, June 12, 2014. Copyright Conde Nast. Used with permission.

Barry, Doug. Excerpt from "Refreshing Tide Commercial Manages Not to Rely on Goon-Dad Caricature for a Change" by Doug Barry. March 15, 2013. Copyright © 2013. http://jezebel.com/5990826/refreshing-tide-commercial-manages-not-to-rely-on-goon-dad-caricature-for-a-change. Used with permission of Gawker Media.

Batouli, Ali. Reprinted with permission.

Bitzer, Lloyd, This paper was presented as a public lecture at Cornell University in November 1966 and at the University of Washington.

Black athlete confidential", December 28, 2012. © 2013, ESPN. Reprinted with permission by ESPN.

Bogost, Ian, Persuasive Games: The Expressive Power of Videogames, excerpt: 334 words, © 2007 Massachusetts Institute of Technology, by permission of The MIT Press.

Boyd, danah and Alice Marwick, "Social Privacy in Networked Publics: Teens' Attitudes, Practices, and Strategies" from Paper for 2011 Symposium on the Dynamics of the Internet and Society. Reprinted with permission.

Canva, Michael, "Occupy Comics: Cartoon Movement Journalists Sketch A Multi-City Composite". From The Washington Post, October 27 © 2014 Washington Post Company. All rights reserved. Used by permission and protected by the Copyright Laws of the United States. The printing, copying, redistribution, or retransmission of this Content without express written permission is prohibited.

Christakis, Nicholas A. M.D., Ph.D., M.P.H., and James H. Fowler, Ph.D, "The Spread of Obesity in a Large Social Network over 32 Years", New England Journal of Medicine, July 26, 2007.

Christakis, Nicholas. "The hidden influence of social networks." TED talks, May 2010. Copyright © 2010 TED Conferences, LLC. Used by permission of TED.

Christakis, Nicholas. "The hidden influence of social networks." TED talks, May 2010. Copyright © 2010 TED Conferences, LLC. Used by permission of TED.

Coates, Ta-Nehisi. "No, Hope Solo Is Not" Like "Ray Rice." © 2014 The Atlantic Media Co., as first published in The Atlantic Magazine. All rights reserved. Distributed by Tribune Content Agency, LLC. Reprinted with permission.

Conrotto, Clare, "Dialogue of Sources."

Conrotto, K. Clare, "I'll Have the Lies on the Side, Please". Reprinted with permission.

Conrotto, K. Clare, "Salvador Allende's government in Chile in the 1970s". Reprinted with permission.

Conrotto, Kim Clare, "Sugar: The Hidden Drug."

Curtis, James C., "Dorothea Lange, Migrant Mother, and the Culture of the Great Depression", Winterthur Portfolio, Vol. 21, No. 1 (Spring, 1986), pp. 1-20, The University of Chicago Press.

Diamond, Matthew, From No Laughing Matter: Post-September 11 Political Cartoons in Arab/Muslim Newspapers.

Drexler, Peggy, "What Your Selfies Say About You," from Psychology Today, September 16, 2013. Reprinted with permission.

Dunn, Geoffrey, "Photographic License", © San Luis Obispo New Times, January 17, 2002. Reprinted with permission.

Dusenbery, Maya and Jason Lee, "The State of Women's Athletics, 40 Years After Title IX" ©2012, Foundation for National Progress. This material was originally published in Mother Jones and has been reprinted courtesy of Mother Jones. To view the articles as they originally appeared, please visit MotherJones.com.

Fehr, Molly, "Inspiring Nazi Germany". Reprinted with permission.

Ganzler, Maisie, "The Non-Controversy Surrounding Local Food," The Huffington Post, November 26, 2012. Reprinted with permission.

Gerrig, Richard J. and Zimbardo, Philip G. PSYCHOLOGY AND LIFE, 2012. Pearson Education.

Giménez, Andrés de Rojas, "May the Force be with…Mickey Mouse?" Used with permission of the author.

Glaser, Mark, "Did London Bombings Turn Citizen Journalists into Citizen Paparazzi?" from Online Journalism Review, July 13, 2005 Edition. Used with permission by the author and the publisher.

Haspel, Tamar, "The GMO Debate: 5 Things To Stop Arguing," From The Washington Post,October, 27 © 2014 Washington Post Company. All rights reserved. Used by permission and protected by the Copyright Laws of the United States. The printing, copying, redistribution, or retransmission of this Content without express written permission is prohibited.

Hawking, Tom, "The Ethics of Disaster Photography in the Age of Social Media," Flavorwire, April 16, 2013. Reprinted with permission.

Hodges, Dr. Caroline E. M, Dr. Daniel Jackson, Dr. Richard Scullion, Dr. Shelley Thompson and Dr. Mike Molesworth, "Tracking changes in everyday experiences of disability and disability sport within the context of the 2012 London Paralympics," CMC Publishing, Bournemouth University, September, 2014. Reprinted with permission.

Horsey, David. "Obnoxious Freedom", LA Times, January 9, 2015. © Tribune Content Agency, LLC. All Rights Reserved. Reprinted with permission.

Jenkins, Henry: "Love Online" by Henry Jenkins. Originally published October 4, 2002 in MIT Technology Review. Reprinted by permission of Wright's Media. Copyrighted 2015. Technology Review. 119114:0915AM

Kemp, Raymond, via Twitter, October 30, 2012. Reprinted with permission.

Knufken, Crea, "Help, We're Drowning! Please Pay Attention to Our Disaster", Salon.com, Septemer 17, 2013. This article first appeared in Salon.com, at http://www.Salon.com An online version remains in the Salon archives. Reprinted with permission.

Leeson, David, "Visual and Verbal Reading" from Photographs and Stories, March 2005 Edition. Reprinted with permission.

Lenhart, Amanda, et al., "Teens, Kindness and Cruelty on Social Network Sites; Part 2, Section 1," Pew Internet, 11/9/2011

Lenhart, Amanda, et al., Figure: How peers treat one another, from "Teens, Kindness and Cruelty on Social Network Sites; Part 2, Section 1," November 9, 2011. Reprinted with permission.

Lenhart, Amanda, et al., Figure: How peers treat one another, from "Teens, Kindness and Cruelty on Social Network Sites; Part 2, Section 1," November 9, 2011. Reprinted with permission.

Lenhart, Amanda, et al., Figure: Mostly kind, from "Teens, Kindness and Cruelty on Social Network Sites; Part 2, Section 1," Pew Internet, November 9, 2011. Reprinted with permission.

Lenhart, Amanda, et al., Figure: Mostly kind, from "Teens, Kindness and Cruelty on Social Network Sites; Part 2, Section 1," Pew Internet, November 9, 2011. Reprinted with permission.

Lenhart, Amanda, et al.,Word cloud how people behave, from Teens, Kindness and Cruelty on Social Network Sites; Part 2, Section 1. November 9, 2011. Reprinted with permission.

Lenhart, Amanda, et al.,Word cloud how people behave, from Teens, Kindness and Cruelty on Social Network Sites; Part 2, Section 1. November 9, 2011. Reprinted with permission.

Lexington, "The Hub Nation," The Economist Newspaper Limited, London © 2010. Reprinted with permission.

Light, Jennifer S. "When Computers Were Women." Technology and Culture 40:3 (1999), 455-483. © 1999 by the Society for the History of Technology. Reprinted with permission of Johns Hopkins University Press.

Martel, William C., "Ban on Photography Military Coffins Protected Grieving Families from Media", U.S. News and World Report. Used by permission of Wright's Media.

Maxwell, Lesli A., "Betting on a School". As first appeared in Education Week, December 4, 2013. Reprinted with permission from the author.

McGonigal, Jane, "The Benefits of Alternate Realities", from REALITY IS BROKEN: WHY GAMES MAKE US BETTER AND HOW THEY CAN CHANGE THE WORLD by Jane McGonigal, copyright (c) 2011 by Jane McGonigal. Used by permission of Penguin Press, an imprint of Penguin Publishing Group, a division of Penguin Random House LLC.

McWilliams, James, "Label Me Confused" © 2015 The Miller-McCune Center for Research, Media and Public Policy. Reprinted with permission.

Mertens, Maggie. "Women's Soccer Is a Feminist Issue…" (c) 2014 The Atlantic Media Co., as first published in The Atlantic Magazine. All rights reserved. Distributed by Tribune Content Agency, LLC. Reprinted with permission.

Mertens, Richard, "How one small Midwest town has turned immigration into positive change," Christian Science Monitor, March 14, 2015. Reprinted with permission.

Morozov, Evgeny, "From Slactivism to Activism", Net Effect Blog,

September 5, 2009. Reprinted with permission.

Morrill, Barbara, "Violent Rhetoric and the Attempted Assassination of Gabrielle Giffords", Daily Kos, Kos Media, LLC.

Morrill, Barbara, "Violent Rhetoric and the Attempted Assassination of Gabrielle Giffords", Daily Kos, Kos Media, LLC.

Obama, Michelle, Remarks of First Lady Michelle Obama As Prepared for Delivery Let's Move Launch, Washington, DC February 9, 2010.

Parker, Stephanie, "Soompi and the "Honorary Asian": Shifting Identities in the Digital Age". Reprinted with permission.

Pederson, Paul Mark, "Examining Equity in Newspaper Photographs: A Content Analysis of the Print Media Photographic Coverage of Interscholastic Athletics." International Review for the Sociology of Sport December 2002 vol. 37 no. 3-4 303-318.

Playing Unafir, 2003. Media Education Foundation (MEF) www.mediaed.org. Reprinted with permission.

Pollan, Michael, "How Change Is Going to Come in the Food System." From The Nation, November 14, 2005. © 2005 The Nation Company, LLC. All rights reserved. Used by permission and protected by the Copyright Laws of the United States. The printing, copying, redistribution, or retransmission of this Content without express written permission is prohibited.

Pollitt, Kate,"The Hunger Games' Feral Feminism." THE NATION. April 03, 2012.

Porter, Charles, "Picture Power: Tragedy in Oklahoma" from BBC News Online, May 9, 2005. Reprinted with permission.

Prensky, Marc, "Engage me or Enrage me: What today's learners demand." First published in Educause Review, Sept/Oct 2005. Reprinted with permission.

Ruck, Rob, "Baseball's Recruitment Abuses". This article was originally published in the Summer 2011 issue of Americas Quarterly (www.americasquarterly.org)

Schler, Jamie, "You are What You Eat: a Food Blogger's Dilemma," The Huffington Post, March 15, 2012. Jamie Schler is a freelance food and culture writer living in Chinon, France. She writes the blogs Life's a Feast and Plated Stories. www.jamieschler.com. Reprinted with permission.

Schmid, J., Bowen, L. (1997). "Minority Presence and Portrayal in Mainstream Magazine Advertising: An Update," Journalism & Mass Communication Quarterly Vol. 74(1) pp. 134-146. Coopyright 1997 by Association for Education in Journalism and Mass Communication. Reprinted by permission of SAGE Publications, Inc.

Sexton, Steve, "The Inefficiency of Local Food," in Freakonomics Blog © 201. Reprinted with permission.

Sklarsky, Jeremy, "Globalization or McDonaldization?" The Daily Targum, October 16, 2002. Reprinted with permission.

Steinem, Glorida, "Sex, Lies, and Advertising," Ms. Magazine, July 1990. Reprinted with permission.

Strupp, Joe, "The Photo Felt Around the World," Editor & Publisher, May 13, 1995. Reprinted with permission.

Thompson, Clive, From SMARTER THAN YOU THINK: HOW TECHNOLOGY IS CHANGING OUR MINDS FOR THE BETTER by Clive Thompson, copyright (c) 2013 by Clive Thompson. Used by permission of Penguin Press, an imprint of Penguin Publishing Group, a division of Penguin Random House LLC.

Thompson, Derek. "Turning Customers into Cultists." (c) 2014 The Atlantic Media Co., as first published in The Atlantic Magazine. All rights reserved. Distributed by Tribune Content Agency, LLC. Reprinted with permission.

Throckmorton, Ada, "Obnoxious Freedom: A Cartoonist's Defense of the Freedom to be Crass".

Throckmorton, Ada, "Balancing the Soft and the Passionate Rhetorician". Reprinted with permission.

Throckmorton, Ada, "Environmental Leadership Working Draft and Outline". Reprinted with permission.

Throckmorton, Ada, "Obnoxious Freedom: A Cartoonist's Defense of the Freedom to Be Crass". Reprinted with permission.

Understanding Comics by Scott McCloud, copyright 1993, 1994 by Scott McCloud. Reprinted by permission of HarperCollins Publishers.

Walsh, Colleen, "Education Without Limits," Harvard Gazette, May 9, 2013. Reprinted with permission.

Wasserstrom, Jeffrey, "A Mickey Mouse Approach to Globalization", June 16, 2003. © 2003 Yale Center for the Study of Globalization. Reprinted with permission.

"What's Wrong with the Body Shop?," McSpotlight, http://www.mcspotlight.org/beyond/companies/bodyshop.html

Wolff, Alexander, "The Hoop Life", Sports Illustrated, 2009.

Zeligs, Michael, Student Essay. Reprinted with permission.

Zyglis, Adam, "How We Color Our Conversation on Race", The Buffalo News, December 6, 2014. Reprinted with permission.

Zyglis, Adam, "Digital Privacy", The Buffalo News, September 7, 2014. Reprinted with permission.

INDEX

A

B

C

D

J

K

L

M

N

Q

S

Y

Z